Que for the Soul

An Introduction to Philosophy

Fourth Edition

Keith W. Krasemann

Copley Publishing Group
Acton, Massachusetts 01720

Copyright © 2003 by Keith W. Krasemann. All rights reserved
Printed in the United States of America

ISBN 1-58152-236-3

No part of this book may be reproduced in any manner without written permission from the publisher.

Acknowledgments:

pp. 3–9: "Reading Philosophy at Night" by Charles Simic, from *The Shape of this Century*, edited by Ridger and Waugh. Copyright © by Harcourt Brace & Company, Inc. Reprinted by permission.

pp. 10–11: From *The Aims of Education* by Alfred North Whitehead. Copyright © 1929 by Macmillan Publishing Company; copyright renewed © 1957 by Evelyn Whitehead. Reprinted by permission of Scribner, and imprint of Simon & Schuster Adult Publishing Group.

pp. 12–18: From *Three Ways of Thought in Ancient China* by Arthur Waley. Copyright © 1956 by Arthur Waley. Reprinted by permission of The Arthur Waley Estate.

pp. 19–25: From *On History* by Immanuel Kant, translated by Lewis White Beck. Copyright © 1963 by the Macmillan Publishing Company, renewed 1991 by Pearson Education, Inc. Reprinted by permission.

pp. 58–66: From *Feminist Perspectives in Philosophy* by Morwenna Griffiths, edited by Margaret Whitford. Copyright © 1988 by Morwenna Griffiths. Reprinted by permission of Indiana University Press.

pp. 67–76: From *Pulse of Wisdom*, 1st edition by Michael C. Brannigan. Copyright © 1995 by M. Brannigan. Reprinted by permission of Wadsworth, a division of Thomson Learning. Fax 800-730-2215.

pp. 77–85: From *African Philosophy: The Essential Readings* by Innocent Onyewuenyi. Copyright © 1991. Published by Heldref Publications.

pp. 95–102: From *Siddhartha* by Hermann Hesse. Copyright © 1951 by New Directions Publishing Corporation. Reprinted by permission of New Directions Publishing Corporation.

pp. 108–119: "Pre-Socratic Philosophers," translated by George Weick for Kentucky State University. Appeared in *Foundations of Cultures*, second edition. Reproduced by permission of George Weick and the Institute for Liberal Studies, Kentucky State University.

pp. 131–144: From *Crest-Jewel of Discrimination with a Garland of Questions and Answers* by Shankara, translated by Prabhavananda and Isherwood. Copyright © 1970, 1946. Published by Vedanta Press. Reprinted by permission.

pp. 181–193: From *The Philosophical Works of Descartes* by René Descartes, translated by Elizabeth Haldane and G. R. T. Ross. Copyright © 1931 by Cambridge University Press. Reprinted by permission of Cambridge University Press.

pp. 194–199: An excerpt from René Descartes, *Discourse on Method*, 2nd edition, translated by Donald Cress. Copyright © 1980 by Hackett Publishing Company Inc., reprinted by permission of Hackett Publishing Co. All rights reserved.

pp. 235–241: From *What Can She Know? Feminist Theory and the Construction of Knowledge* by Lorraine Code. Copyright © 1991 by Blackwell Publishers.

pp. 281–291: From *Philosophical Fragments* by Søren Kierkegaard, edited and translated by Howard V. Hong. Copyright © 1985 by Howard V. Hong and Postscipt, Inc. Reprinted by permission of Princeton University Press.

pp. 292–311: From the book *Existence and Being* translated by R. F. C. Hull and Alan Crick. Copyright © 1949 by Henry Regnery Publishing. All rights reserved. Reprinted by special permission of Regenery Publishing, Inc. Washington, DC.

pp. 312–319: From *Liberation and Ethics: Essays in Religious and Social Ethics in Honor of Gibson Winter* edited by Charles Amjad-Ali and W. Alvin. Copyright © 1985 by the Society for the Scientific Study of Religion. Reprinted by permission on the publisher via the Copyright Clearance Center.

pp. 325–327: From *Candide, Zadig, and Selected Stories. by Voltaire* by Franciose Voltaire, translated by Donald M. Frame. Copyright © 1961 by Donald M. Frame. Reprinted by permission of Dutton Signet, a division of Penguin Putnam.

pp. 328–336: From *Bhagvad Gita*, translated by Sarvepalli Radhakrishnan. Copyright © 1948 by Allen & Unwin Pty. Ltd, Sydney, Australia.

pp. 349–350: From *World Philosophy: A Text with Readings* edited by Robert Solomon and Kathleen Higgs, translated by Eric Ormsby. Copyright © 1995. Published by McGraw-Hill, Inc.

pp. 351–355: From *A Source Book in Chinese Philosophy*, edited by W. Chan. Copyright © 1963, renewed 1991. Reprinted by permission of Princeton University Press.

pp. 390–400: From *A Companion to Ethics* edited by Peter Singer. Copyright © 1992 by Peter Singer. Reprinted by permission of Blackwell Publishers, Ltd.

pp. 401–404: From *Life Ahead* by J. Krishnamurti, edited by D. Rajago. Copyright © by the Krishnamurti Foundation, Ojai, CA. Reprinted with permission.

pp. 405–412: From "Anthropology and the Abnormal" by Ruth Benedict, in *The Journal of General Psychology*. Copyright © 1934. Reprinted with permission of the Helen Dwight Reid Educational Foundation. Published by Heldref Publications, 1319 Eighteenth St. N.W., Washington, DC 20036–1802.

pp. 416–417: From *Letters to a Young Poet* by Ranier Maria Rilke, translated by Stephen Mitchell. Copyright © 1984 by Stephen Mitchell. Reprinted by permission of Random House, Inc.

pp. 418–426: From *The Collected Dialogues of Plato*, edited by Edith Hamilton and Huntington Cairns. Copyright © 1961 by Princeton University Press. Reprinted by permission of the publisher.

pp. 427–430: From *Twilight of the Idols: The Portable Nietzsche*, edited and translated by Walter Kauffman. Copyright © 1968 by Walter Kauffman, renewed by Penguin Books, Ltd. Reprinted by permission of the publisher via the Copyright Clearance Center.

pp. 431–434: From *The Birth of a Tragedy* by Friedrich Nietzsche, translated by Walter Kaufmann. Copyright © 1967 by Walter Kaufmann. Reprinted by permission of Random House, Inc.

pp. 435–438: From *What Is Art?* by Leo Tolstoy, translated by Maude. Copyright © 1960 by Prentice-Hall, Inc.

pp. 439–444: From *Illuminations: Essays and Reflections* by Walter Benjamin. Copyright © 1955 by Suhrkamp Verlag, Frankfurt A. M., English translation by Harry Zohn Copyright © 1968 and renewed 1996 by Harcourt, Inc. Reprinted by permission of Harcourt, Inc.

pp. 445–453: "On Elegance in Japan" by Barbara Sandrisser, from *Aesthetics in Perspective*, edited by Kathleen Higgins and Robert Solomon. Copyright © 1966 by Harcourt Brace & Company.

pp. 454–457: From *Understanding the Chinese Mind*, edited by Robert E. Allinson. Copyright © 1989 by Oxford University Press, Hong Kong. Reprinted with permission.

pp. 462–466: Abridged and reprinted with the permission of the Free Press, a division of Simon & Schuster Adult Publishing Group, from *Medieval Philosophy: From St. Augustine to Nicholas of Cusa*, edited by John F. Wippel and Allan B. Wolter. Copyright © 1969 by the Free Press.

pp. 471–473: From *The Basic Writings of St. Thomas Aquinas*, edited by Anton C. Pegis. Copyright © 1945 by Anton C. Pegis, renewed by the Estate of Anton C. Pegis. Reprinted by permission.

pp. 474–479: From *Pensées* by Blaise Pascal, translated by A. J. Krailsheimer. Copyright © 1966 by Penguin Books, Ltd. Reprinted by permission of the publisher via the Copyright Clearance Center.

pp. 480–488: From *Philosophical Fragments* by Søren Kierkegaard, edited and translated by Howard V. Hong. Copyright © 1985 by Howard V. Hong and Postscipt, Inc. Reprinted by permission of Princeton University Press.

pp. 500–507: From *Philosophy of Religion* by John Hick. Copyright © 1963 by Prentice-Hall, Inc. Reprinted by permission of the publisher.

pp. 512–520: From *Metaphysics*, third edition by Richard Taylor. Copyright © 1983 by Prentice-Hall, Inc. Reprinted by permission of the publisher.

pp. 521–525: From *Freedom: Its History, Nature, and Varieties*, edited by R. Dewey and J. Gould. Copyright © 1970 by Macmillan College. Reprinted by permission of Prentice-Hall, Inc.

pp. 526–530: Excerpt from *An Idealist View of Life*, by Sarvepalli Radhakrishnan. Copyright © 1932 by George Allen & Unwin, a division of Unwin Hyman, Ltd., London. Copyright renewed by HarperCollins Publishers, Ltd. Reprinted by permission.

pp. 531–547: From *Being and Nothingness* by Jean Paul Sartre, translated by Hazel E. Barnes. Copyright © 1966 by Philosophical Library. Reprinted by permission.

pp. 564–569: "Freedom and the Control of Men" by B. F. Skinner appeared in *American Scholar*, volume 25, number 1, Winter, 1956. Copyright © 1955 by B. F. Skinner, renewed by the Estate of B. F. Skinner. Reprinted by permission.

pp. 570–578: From *Man's Search for Meaning: An Introduction to Logotherapy* by Viktor E. Frankl. Copyright © 1959, 1962, 1984, 1992 by Viktor E. Frankl. Reprinted by permission of Beacon Press, Boston.

pp. 579–587: From *Man's Search for Himself* by Rollo May. Copyright © 1953 by W. W. Norton & Company, Inc., renewed © 1981 by Rollo May. Used by permission of W. W. Norton & Company, Inc.

pp. 592–597: "The Wine Is in the Glass" by Daniel Kolak. Copyright © 1989 by Daniel Kolak. Reprinted by permission.

pp. 598–608: From *Religions of Asia in Practice* edited by Donald Lopez Jr. Copyright © 2002 by Princeton University Press. Reprinted by permission of the publisher.

pp. 609–611: "A Treatise on Death" by Wang Chong is from *A Source Book in Chinese Philosophy*, edited and translated by Wing-Tsit Chan. Copyright © 1963 by Princeton University Press. Reprinted by permission of the publisher.

pp. 612–614: From *Introductions to Philosophical Analysis*, third edition by John Hospers. Copyright © 1988 by Prentice-Hall, Inc. Reprinted by permission of the publisher.

pp. 618–621: From *The Extant Remains*, translated by Cyril Bailey. Copyright © 1926. Reprinted by permission of Oxford University Press.

pp. 622–625: From *Buddhist Scriptures* edited and translated by Edward Conze. Copyright © 1959 by Edward Conze. Reprinted by permission of Penguin Books Ltd.

pp. 633–640: "Night-Sea Journey," copyright © 1966 by John Barth (first published in Esquire magazine). From *Lost in the Funhouse* by John Barth. Used by permission of Doubleday, a division of Random House, Inc.

pp. 641–643: From *The Poetry of T'ao Ch'ien* edited by James Robert Hightower. Copyright © 1970 by Oxford University Press, Ltd. Reprinted by permission of the publisher via the Copyright Clearance Center.

pp. 665–675: From *The Myth of Sisyphus and Other Essays* by Albert Camus, translated by Justin O'Brien. Copyright © 1955 by Alfred A. Knopf, a division of Random House, Inc. Reprinted by permission of the publisher.

pp. 676–681: From *The Way of Response* edited by Nahum N. Glatzer. Copyright © 1966 by Nahum N. Glatzer.

p. 682: From *Why I Am Not a Christian* by Bertrand Russell. Copyright © 1957 by The Bertrand Russell Peace Foundation, Ltd. Reprinted by permission of the publisher via the Copyright Clearance Center.

pp. 684–686: From *Introduction to Logic* by Irving M. Copi. Copyright © 1953 by Macmillan Publishing Company. Reprinted by permission of Prentice-Hall, Inc.

pp. 687–688: From *The Student's Guide to Philosophy* by Peter A. Facoine. Copyright © 1988 by the Mayfield Publishing Company. Reprinted by permission of the publisher.

In memory of my father, Howard C. Krasemann

Contents

Preface	xvii

Chapter I: Philosophy's Value: Wisdom and Insight — 1

Reading Philosophy at Night *Charles Simic*	3
Wisdom *Alfred North Whitehead*	10
Stories of Chuang Tzu and Hui Tzu *Arthur Waley*	12
What Is Enlightenment? *Immanuel Kant*	19
The Apology *Plato*	26
Life in the Woods *Henry David Thoreau*	49
Feminism, Feelings, and Philosophy *Morwenna Griffiths*	58
Philosophical Thinking in India, China, and Japan *Michael C. Brannigan*	67
Is There an African Philosophy? *Innocent Onyewuenyi*	77
The Value of Philosophy *Bertrand Russell*	86

Chapter II: Being — 93

from Siddhartha *Hermann Hesse*	95
Tao-Te Ching *Lao Tzu*	103

The Pre-Socratic Philosophers   108
  Thales
  Anaximander
  Anaximenes
  Heraclitus
  Parmenides
  Zeno
  Empedocles
  Anaxagoras
  Democritus
  Pythagoras

Two Tables   120
  Sir Arthur Eddington

Reality Consists of Ideas   124
  George Berkeley

The Crest-Jewel of Discrimination   131
  Shankara

Chapter III: Knowledge   145

Knowledge Is Recollection   148
  Plato

The Divided Line   161
  Plato

The Allegory of the Cave   175
  Plato

from Meditations on First Philosophy   181
  René Descartes

What Is Indubitable?   194
  René Descartes

Scepticism   200
  David Hume

An Empiricist Theory of Knowledge   206
  John Locke

The Problem of Induction   220
  David Hume

x

Is the Sex of the Knower Epistemologically Significant?   235
Lorraine Code

Practice and Contradiction   242
Mao Tse-Tung

Chapter IV: Truth   253

Truth as Correspondence   255
Bertrand Russell

Truth Is Established by Coherence   262
Francis H. Bradley

Pragmatism's Conception of Truth   269
William James

The Subjective Truth   281
Søren Kierkegaard

On the Essence of Truth   292
Martin Heidegger

from Cultural Gaps: Why Do We Misunderstand?   312
Isamu Nagami

Chapter V: Goodness   321

Story of a Good Brahman   325
Voltaire

Work, Nonattachment, and Wisdom   328
from *Bhagavad Gita*

from The Analects of Confucius   337

On Cultivation of Character   349
Yahyā ibn ʿAdī

Human Nature Is Evil   351
Xunzi

Virtue and Happiness   356
Aristotle

Friendship   367
Aristotle

A Good Will   373
   Immanuel Kant

from Utilitarianism   379
   John Stuart Mill

The Idea of a Female Ethic   390
   Jean Grimshaw

Ambition   401
   J. Krishnamurti

Ethics Are Relative   405
   Ruth Benedict

Chapter VI: Beauty   413

Letters to a Young Poet   416
   Rainer Maria Rilke

The Form of Beauty   418
   Plato

On Beauty and Ugliness   427
   Friedrich Nietzsche

Apollo and Dionysus   431
   Friedrich Nietzsche

What Is Art?   435
   Leo Tolstoy

The Work of Art in the Age of Mechanical Reproduction   439
   Walter Benjamin

On Elegance in Japan   445
   Barbara Sandrisser

Chinese Aesthetics   454
   Kuang-Ming Wu

Chapter VII: God   459

The Ontological Argument   462
   Saint Anselm and *Gaunilon*

The Teleological Argument   467
   William Paley

The Five Ways 471
   Saint Thomas Aquinas

The Wager 474
   Blaise Pascal

The Leap of Faith 480
   Søren Kierkegaard

The Will to Believe 489
   William James

Agnosticism 497
   T. H. Huxley

The Problem of Evil 500
   John Hick

Chapter VIII: Freedom 509

Fate 512
   Richard Taylor

Determinism 521
   Baron d'Holbach

Karma and Freedom 526
   Sarvepalli Radhakrishnan

Absolute Freedom 531
   Jean Paul Sartre

The Legend of the Grand Inquisitor 548
   Feodor Dostoyevsky

Freedom and the Control of Men 564
   B. F. Skinner

Choice and Human Dignity 570
   Viktor Frankl

Freedom and Inner Strength 579
   Rollo May

Chapter IX: Immortality 589

The Wine Is in the Glass 592
   Daniel Kolak

The Law of the Spirits *Valerie Hansen*	598
A Treatise on Death *Wang Chong*	609
Is the Notion of Disembodied Existence Intelligible? *John Hospers*	612
Phaedo *Plato*	615
Letter to Menoeceus *Epicurus*	618
from Scripture of the Pure Land	622
Death Is Swallowed Up in Victory *I Corinthians 15*	626
The Dead in Christ Shall Rise First *I Thessalonians 4*	629

Chapter X: Meaning — 631

Night-Sea Journey *John Barth*	633
Substance, Shadow, and Spirit *T'ao Ch'ien*	641
My Confession *Leo Tolstoy*	644
The Death of Ivan Ilych *Leo Tolstoy*	654
The Myth of Sisyphus *Albert Camus*	665
Response *Martin Buber*	676
Three Passions *Bertrand Russell*	682

Appendix 683

Truth and Validity 684
Irving M. Copi

Common Fallacies and Errors of Reasoning 687
Peter A. Facoine

Index of Philosophers' Quotations 689

Preface

In November, 1995 I attended a humanities conference in Washington, DC at which I gave a presentation on Chinese philosophy. On Saturday morning I had the good fortune to have breakfast with Pulitzer Prize winning author and former Librarian of Congress, Daniel Boorstin. For several years I had wanted to write a book on philosophy and the breakfast meeting rekindled my desire to write and the conversation with Boorstin provided the inspiration to follow my dream.

Later that day I met Lucy Miskin from Copley Publishing and we discussed my conception for a new book on philosophy. She was receptive to the notions I presented and encouraged me to develop my ideas. We continued our conversation and, within the space of one hour, I agreed to write the book and Copley agreed to publish the work.

In the evening, through the efforts of Christopher Walker, I was given a private tour of the White House. I spent two hours in the quiet halls of the White House. I experienced a deepening of my sense of history. I reflected on the power inherent in great ideas. I thought about the ways in which great ideas possess the capacity to transform individual lives and to shape the destiny of peoples.

It was snowing when I left the White House. I walked through the empty Washington streets to the Mayflower Hotel. I had a late-night dinner and two glasses of wine. I read Boorstin's essays. I borrowed a pen from the waiter and wrote on a napkin—*Questions for the Soul: An Introduction to Philosophy*. On the napkin I also sketched out the main structure of the book exactly as it appears in final form.

This book presents philosophy as questions for the soul. The activity of philosophy consists in sustained reflection on these questions in the context of concrete life experiences within a particular world. In addition, this book attempts to expand the possible answers to life's fundamental questions by locating the questions within the scope of world philosophies. As such, this book is a break with standard approaches of presenting philosophy solely based on western foundations and traditions.

Furthermore, this book revives the concept of soul that has fallen out of favor in much of recent philosophy largely due to the dominance of a legitimate, though narrow, use of the term. Many philosophers have refused to use this term because of conceptual baggage the term carries. The term is often laden with theological assumptions and religious presuppositions. This dominant position views the soul exclusively as a metaphysical entity. In contrast, others have attempted to replace the concept with terms such as "consciousness," "mind," "mental states," etc. The dominant position is too narrow but the alternatives fail to capture the fullness and richness of all the term soul embodies when properly understood. However, this term is arguably one of the central concepts in the entire history of world philosophy. One cannot understand the history of philosophy or its problems without an accurate conception of "soul." The concept of soul is critical to the study of philosophy and, in the brief comments below, I attempt to reorient the reader to a more accurate and expansive sense of the term and thereby free it from its current narrow usage. In doing so, it is hoped that the reader's mind will also be liberated from the constraints imposed by the terms current usage and that individuals may more fully appreciate the many references to this term that have been employed in the history of human thought.

By "soul" I do not necessarily imply a metaphysical entity. I am using the concept in a way that is consistent with the Hebrew *nephesh*, the Classical Greek *psyche*, the Koine *psuch-*, and the Latin *anima* to mean, no more and no less than, the life of an individual. This notion includes both physical life and consciousness (especially self-consciousness and the totality of the human inner life). It is the seat of personal identity. Soul is the life of a man or woman in the world with all of its possibilities. Whether this life continues after the death of the body is part of the question of immortality.

Questions for the soul are those questions that most profoundly and deeply concern the life of a human being. They are questions that are properly philosophical in nature and questions which admit to no final answer. These questions issue forth from the depths of the human soul and from the human condition. These questions arise in the process of authentically engaging life in the world. Questions for the soul must be asked because we are human. Some would claim that we are human because we ask these questions.

Questions for the soul are those questions that seek an understanding of great ideas. By "great ideas" I mean two things: First, great ideas are ideas which are intrinsically worth contemplating. Examples would be God, truth, goodness, beauty, freedom and justice. And, second, great ideas are so rich that no human mind (or cumulative human thought) can fully exhaust their content. That is to say, when thinking is done—there is always more.

Questions for the soul are the questions that call forth thinking in its most basic and important sense. These questions ask us to think deeply and to reflectively consider, in an ongoing manner, self, world, and God. They ask what it means to be and they ask us to ponder the essence of truth. Questions for the soul beckon us to think about what is most important in life. Questions for the soul ask us to think about things that matter.

Since questions for the soul admit of no final answers they are precisely the questions that can sustain us, nourish us, and guide us throughout an entire lifetime. Questions for the soul allow us the possibility to continually expand our understanding and to enrich and ennoble our lives. As we personally and authentically take up these questions our lives are transformed. We think and understand, as well as choose and act freely, from an enlarged and more informed perspective. Questions for the soul call forth our very lives.

This book is intended as an introduction to philosophy. It is hoped that the reader appropriate to, and for, himself or herself, not so much the thinking of others concerning life's most fundamental questions, but, rather, the questions themselves.

What Is Philosophy?

In the Spring of 1997, while attending a tea and reception, I had a most interesting conversation with a member of the Chinese diplomatic corps and a Japanese colleague. We discussed several items but when the topic of philosophy was introduced the conversation took on a new mood and shifted to a higher level. The formal conversation ceased—because it ceased to be important. A sense of childlike wonder replaced the official mood. Instantly a twinkle appeared in the eyes of the Chinese Vice-Consul. "Philosophy," he thought aloud, "is the soul of everything." "Yes," remarked my Japanese colleague, "philosophy is the [mind's] farthest grasp."

Time stopped. In that brief space, the reception and the business (and "busy-ness") of life disappeared. We talked of deep and fantastic things.

What is philosophy? The insights of my two associates point the way to the heart of what the question asks. Philosophy is both "the soul of everything" and "the [mind's] farthest grasp." Philosophy is a reflective and rational process that seeks to understand self, world, and God. It is the thinking and understanding that goes before and stands behind culture, science, and all institutions. Philosophical thinking moves inward to attempt to grasp the most basic structures of reality and it stretches outward to the very limits of the world.

The word philosophy is of Greek origin. It means, literally, "the love of wisdom" (from: *philos* = love and *sophia* = wisdom). This meaning is at once the simplest and, perhaps, the best definition of the term.

The ancients taught that philosophy was born of wonder. Plato said that, "Wonder is the feeling of a philosopher" and "all philosophy begins in wonder." Aristotle wrote: "It is owing to [because of] wonder, that men at first began and continue to philosophize."

The sense of wonder is a sense of "awe" or "amazement." When lived experience transcends the mind's ability to make sense of the experience—human beings wonder. From this sense of wonder the individual formulates and asks questions. Questions call forth thinking. Questions ask. Questions beckon the individual to respond. Certain questions, those questions I have called *questions for the soul*, are the questions about which men and women philosophize. They call forth our thinking in basic and original ways. They ask us to think about those things that are most important in life.

Traditionally, philosophy has grouped questions into five branches or areas of study: Logic, Metaphysics, Epistemology, Ethics and Aesthetics. Logic is a normative discipline. It deals with the rules and principles of correct thinking. Metaphysics investigates the question of being and related questions concerning that which is ultimately real. Epistemology is that branch of philosophy that engages problems associated with the nature of human knowledge and theories of truth. Ethics attempts to understand the moral dimension of human existence and is also concerned with the practical business of living well. Aesthetics is that branch of philosophy that is primarily involved with the nature of beauty and the study of values with respect to works of art. The essays in this volume include topics from the entire field of philosophy.

The approach to philosophy taken in this book is thematic. I look first at philosophy's value and then consider, in order, the basic questions of being, knowledge, truth, goodness, beauty, God, freedom, immortality, and meaning. I have included in this volume many classic philosophical texts. I have included recent philosophical essays that I felt were both interesting and relevant. I have included non-philosophical writings from inspired texts or literature insofar as their content has bearing on philosophical questions. And finally, I have included non-Western writings in order to expand the possibilities of thinking about human questions.

About the Book

The fourth edition of *Questions for the Soul* contains four new selections. These selections expand the non-Western and intercultural aspects of the book by including works on Arabic, Chinese and Japanese philosophy. This edition also contains Martin Buber's "Response."

Furthermore critical questions, key ideas, and important quotations within each selection have been set in boldface type. It is hoped that this feature will help the reader more easily identify central philosophical problems, grasp the main point(s) of the various essays, and quickly be able to locate some of the most significant and oft quoted passages in the history of human thought.

An index of the philosophers in this text along with selected quotations has also been included.

Acknowledgments

I am grateful to my teachers and my students for all they have done to help me think and re-think life's great questions. I want to thank Ed Kies, Duane Ross, and Ed Storke for giving me the opportunities and freedom to teach an atypically wide and varying range of courses. This has contributed immeasurably to my ability to integrate ideas and to see life holistically. Special thanks to Nicoleta Apostle, Thomas Elkins, Scott Jonsson, Jack Judson, Werner Kriegelstein, Mandy Lobraico, Robert Lorek, Bill McCarthy, John Modschiedler, Amy Olberding, Donna Rocha, Isabel Sabau, Anjli Sandhir, Shingo Satsutani, Misty Sheehan, and Herman Stark.

Lucy Miskin's contributions to this work are manifold. This book would not have been finished without her diligence. I want to thank her for her continued friendship, encouragement, advice, and support.

Special thanks to Haojie Qin for her help in the revision of this manuscript.

KWK

Sycamore, Illinois
November 11, 2002

Chapter I: Philosophy's Value: Wisdom and Insight

In this section the philosophers speak for themselves concerning philosophy's value. "Whoever reads philosophy," said Charles Simic, "reads himself as much as he reads the philosopher." In reading philosophy individuals enter into a dialogue with certain decisive events in their lives as much as with the ideas on the page. Sometimes the text is difficult and that which one is trying to grasp is often elusive. At other times the reader's mind wanders. But, according to Simic, there are those moments when "it all comes together" and one sees—"in the sense of being able to picture and feel the human weight of another's solitude." For Whitehead the aim of philosophy is wisdom, the "active mastery" of knowledge and, for Kant it is enlightenment—to learn "how to think" and "to think for yourselves, inquire for yourselves, stand on your own two feet."

The selection between the essays by Whitehead and Kant is Arthur Waley's translation of "Stories of Chuang Tzu and Hui Tzu." Hui Tzu complains to Chuang Tzu, "Your teachings are of no practical use." Many people today believe that there are no practical benefits to be derived from the study of philosophy. But, the Taoist philosopher replies, "Only those who already know the value of the useless can be talked to about useful."

Plato's *Apology* gives an account of the trial of Socrates. At his trial Socrates declared that "the unexamined life is not worth living." He held that the practice of philosophy is a great benefit to humankind because it makes possible the proper care of the soul. Socrates was a critic of his society and its traditions and stood for the freedom to think, to inquire, and to independently pursue truth.

Henry David Thoreau stated: "The mass of men lead lives of quiet desperation. However," he added that ". . . it is a characteristic of wisdom not to do desperate things." For Thoreau, philosophy will enable individuals to "live with the license of a higher order of beings." Philosophy provides that intuitive insight that allows people to confidently pursue their dreams.

In her article "Feminism, Feelings, and Philosophy," Morwenna Griffiths claims that feminist views about human feelings "constitute a significant criticism of much mainstream Western philosophy. . . ." However, the positive result of this type of critique is that men and women come to reach a better understanding of themselves and of one another.

Michael Brannigan introduces the reader to basic philosophical thinking in India, China, and Japan. In his essay he tells us that philosophy provides people with a way to deal with ultimate questions that inevitably arise in the mortal condition of suffering. Philosophy often originates from dissatisfaction with life and the condition of human suffering. The chief of philosophical concern in India is essentially self-deliverance. The act of philosophical questioning "transforms the questioner." The main goal of pursuing philosophy in China is to achieve harmony. Particularly, the goal is to strike a balance between reason and feelings. By means of self-cultivation and moral development, philosophy helps the individual learn how to become truly human. Japanese philosophical thinking promotes simple and direct encounters with reality, personal expression, and a sense of connectedness because it stresses the importance of immediacy, sensitivity, and relationality.

Innocent Onyewuenyi asks, "Is there an African philosophy?" His answer is that while every culture has its own worldview, nevertheless, "philosophizing is a universal experience." Furthermore, he contends that the themes and questions are the same in all cultures and that the value of philosophy is to establish order among things and events so as to produce an intelligible world.

Finally, for Bertrand Russell the value of philosophy lies in the questions themselves:

> . . . because these questions enlarge our conception of what is possible, enrich our intellectual imagination, and diminish the dogmatic assurance which closes the mind against speculation; but above all because, through the greatness of the universe which philosophy contemplates, the mind also is rendered great, and becomes capable of that union with the universe which constitutes its highest good.

The challenge now set before the reader is to consider the questions for himself or herself and thus, through the practice of philosophy, experientially understand philosophy's value.

Reading Philosophy at Night

Charles Simic

It is night again around me; I feel as though there had been lightning—for a brief span of time I was *entirely* in my element and in my light.

Nietzsche

The mind loves the unknown. It loves images whose meaning is unknown, since the meaning of the mind itself is unknown.

Magritte

I wore Buster Keaton's expression of exaggerated calm. I could have been sitting on the edge of a cliff with my back to the abyss trying to look normal.

Now I read philosophy in the morning. When I was younger and lived in the city it was always at night "That's how you ruined your eyes," my mother keeps saying. I sat and read late into the night. The quieter it got, the more clearheaded I became—or so it seemed to me. In the sparsely furnished room above the Italian grocery, I would be struggling with some intricate epistemological argument which promised a magnificent insight at its conclusion. I could smell it, so to speak. I couldn't put the book away, and it was getting very late. I had to be at work in the morning. Even had I tried to sleep my head would have been full of Immanuel Kant. So, I wouldn't sleep. I remember well such moments of decision: the great city that had suddenly turned quiet, the open book, and my face reflected dimly in the darkened windowpane.

At such hours I thought I understood everything. The first time it happened I was twenty. It was six o'clock in the morning. It was winter. It was dark and very cold. I was in Chicago riding the El to work seated between two heavily bundled-up old women. The train was overheated, but each time the door opened at one of the elevated platforms, a blast of cold air would send shivers through us. The lights, too, kept flickering. As the train changed tracks, the lights would go out and I would stop reading the history of philosophy I had borrowed the previous day from the library. "Why is there something rather than nothing?" the book asked, quoting Parmenides. It was as if my eyes were opened. I could not stop looking, at my fellow passengers. How incredible, I thought, being here, existing.

I have a recurring dream about the street where I was born. It is always night. I'm walking past vaguely familiar buildings trying to find our house, but somehow it is not there. I retrace my steps on that short block of only a few buildings, all of which are there except the one I want. The effort leaves me exhausted and saddened.

In another version of this same dream, I catch a glimpse of our house. There it is, at last, but for some reason I'm unable to get any closer to it. No lights are on. I look for our window, but it is even darker there on the third floor. The whole building seems abandoned. "It's not possible," I tell myself.

Once in one of these dreams, many years ago, I saw someone at my window, hunched over, watching the street intently. That's how my grandmother would wait late into the night for us to come home, except this was a stranger. Even without being able to make out his face, I was sure of that.

Most of the time, however, there's no one in sight during the dream. The façades of buildings still retain the pockmarks and other signs of the war. The streetlights are out and there's no moon in the sky so it's not clear to me how I am able to see all that in complete darkness.

Whoever reads philosophy reads himself as much as he reads the philosopher. I am in a dialogue with certain decisive events in my life as much as I am with the ideas on the page. Meaning is the matter of my existence. My effort to understand is a perpetual circling around a few obsessive images.

Like everyone else, I have my hunches. All my experiences make a kind of untaught ontology which precedes all my readings. What I am trying to conceptualize with the help of the philosopher is that which I have already intuited.

That's one way of looking at it.

> The Meditation of yesterday filled my mind with so many doubts that it is no longer in my power to forget them. And yet, I do not see in what man-

ner I can resolve them; and, just as if I had all of a sudden fallen into very deep water, I am so disconcerted that I can neither make certain of setting my feet on the bottom, nor can I swim and so support myself on the surface. I shall nevertheless make an effort and follow anew the same path as that on which I yesterday entered, i.e., I shall proceed by setting aside all that in which the least doubt could be supposed to exist, just as if I had discovered that it was absolutely false; and I shall ever follow in this road until I have met with something which is certain, or at least, if I can do nothing else, until I have learned for certain that there's nothing in the world that is certain. Archimedes, in order that he might draw the terrestrial globe out of its place, and transport it elsewhere, demanded only that one point should be fixed and immovable; in the same way I shall have the right to conceive high hopes if I am happy enough to discover one thing only which is certain and indubitable.

I love this passage of Descartes; his beginning again, his not wanting to be fooled. It describes the ambition of philosophy in all its nobility and desperation. I prefer this doubting Descartes to his famous later conclusions. Here everything is still unsettled. The poetry of the moment still casts its spell. Of course, he's greedy for the absolute, but so is his reader.

There's an Eastern European folk song which tells of a girl who tossed an apple higher and higher in the air until she tossed it as high as the clouds. To her surprise the apple didn't come down. The cloud got it. She waited with arms outstretched, but the apple stayed up there. All she could do is plead with the cloud to return her apple, but that's another story. I like the first part when the impossible happens.

I remember lying in a ditch and looking at some pebbles while German bombers were flying over our heads. That was long ago. I don't remember the face of my mother nor the faces of the people who were there with us, but I still see those perfectly ordinary pebbles.

"It is not *how* things are in the world that is mystical, but that it exists," says Wittgenstein. I had a feeling of great clarity. Time had stopped. I was watching myself watching the pebbles and trembling with fear. Then time moved on.

The pebbles stayed in their otherness, stayed forever as far as I am concerned. I'm talking about the experience of heightened consciousness. Can language do it justice? Speech is always less. When it comes to consciousness, one approximates, one speaks poorly. Competing phenomenologies are impoverishments, splendid poverties.

Wittgenstein puts it this way: "What finds its reflection in language, language cannot represent. What expresses *itself* in language, we cannot express by means of language." We are not, most certainly, thinking about the same thing, nor were he and his followers subsequently very happy with this early statement of his, but this has been my experience on a number of occasions.

I knew someone who once tried to persuade me otherwise. He considered himself a logical positivist. There are people who tell you, for example, that you can speak of a pencil's dimension, location, appearance, state of motion or rest but not of its intelligence and love of music. The moment I hear that the poet in me rebels and I want to write a poem about an intelligent pencil in love with music. In other words, what they regard as nonsense, I suspect to be full of unknown imaginative possibilities.

There's a wonderful story told about Wittgenstein and his Cambridge colleague, the Italian economist Piero Sraffa. Apparently they often discussed philosophy. "One day," as Justus Hartnack has it, "when Wittgenstein was defending his view that a proposition has the same logical form as the fact it depicts, Sraffa made a gesture used by Neapolitans to express contempt and asked Wittgenstein what the logical form of that was. According to Wittgenstein's own recollection, it was this question which made him realize that his belief that a fact could have a logical form was untenable."

As for my logical friend, we argued all night: "What cannot be said, cannot be thought." And then again, after I blurted out something about silence being the language of consciousness, "you're silent because you have nothing to say." It got to the point where we were calling each other "you dumb shit." We were drinking large quantities of red wine, misunderstanding each other liberally, and only stopped bickering when his disheveled wife came to the bedroom door and told us to shut up.

Then I told him a story.

One day in Yugoslavia, just after the war, we made a class trip to the town War Museum. At the entrance we found a battered German tank which delighted us. Inside the museum one could look at a few rifles, hand grenades and uniforms, but not much else. Most of the space was taken up by photographs. These we were urged to examine. One saw people hanged and people about to be hanged; people on tips of their toes. The executioners stood around smoking. There were piles of corpses everywhere. Some were naked. Men and women with their genitals showing. That made some kid laugh.

Then we saw a man having his throat cut. The killer sat on the man's chest with a knife in his hand. He seemed pleased to be photographed. The victim's eyes I don't remember. A few men stood around gawking. There were clouds in the sky.

There were always clouds, as well as blades of grass, tree stumps, bushes and rocks no one was paying any attention to. At times the earth was covered with snow. A miserable, teeth-chattering January morning and someone making someone's life even more miserable. Or the rain would be falling. A small hard rain that would wash the blood off the hands immediately, that would make one of the killers catch a bad cold. I imagined him sitting that same night with his feet in a bucket of hot water and sipping tea.

That occurred to me much later. Now that we had seen all there was to see, we were made to sit on the lawn outside the museum and eat our lunch. It was poor fare. Most of us had plum jam spread on slices of bread. A few had lard sprinkled with paprika. One kid had nothing but bread and scallions. Everybody thought that was funny. Someone threw his thick slice of black bread in the air and got it caught in a tree. The poor fellow tried to get it down by throwing pebbles at it. He kept missing. Then, he wanted to climb the tree. He kept sliding back. Even our teacher who came over to look thought it was hilarious.

As for the grass, there was plenty of it, each blade distinct and carefully sharpened, as it were. There were also clouds in the sky and many large flies of the kind one encounters at slaughterhouses that kept interrupting our thoughts and our laughter.

And here's what went through my head just the other night as I lay awake in the dark:

The story had nothing to do with what you were talking about.

The story had everything to do with what we were talking about.

I can think of a hundred objections.

Only idiots want something neat, something categorical . . . and I never talk unless I know!

Aha! You're mixing poetry and philosophy. Bertrand Russell wouldn't give you the time of day . . .

"Everything looks very busy to me," says Jasper Johns, and that's the problem. I remember a strange cat, exceedingly emaciated, that scratched on my door the day I was scratching my head over Hegel's phenomenology.

Who said, "Whatever can be thought must be fictitious"?

You got me there! Error is my first love. I'm shouting her name from the rooftops.

Still and all! And nevertheless! And above all! Let's not forget "above all."

"The Only Humane Way to Catch a Metaphysical Mouse" is the name of the book I work on between three and four in the morning.

Here's what Nietzsche said to the ceiling: "The rank of the philosopher is determined by the rank of his laughter." But he couldn't really laugh. No matter how hard he tried he couldn't laugh.

I know because I'm a connoisseur of chaos. All the good-looking oxymorons come to visit me in my bed . . .

Wallace Stevens has several beautiful poems about solitary readers. "The House Was Quiet and the World Was Calm" is one. It speaks of a "truth in a calm world." It happens! The world and the mind being so calm that truth becomes visible.

It must be late night—"where shines the light that lets be the things that are"—which might be a good description of insomnia. The solitude of the reader and the solitude of the philosopher drawing together. The impression that one is on the verge of anticipating another man's next turn of thought. My own solitude doubled, tripled, as if I were the only one awake on the earth.

Understanding depends upon the relation of what I am to what I have been. The being of the moment, in other words. Consciousness waking up conscience—waking up history. Consciousness as clarity and history as the dark night of the soul.

The pleasures of philosophy are the pleasures of reduction—the epiphanies of saying in a few words what seems to be the gist of the matter. It pleases me, for instance, to think of both philosophy and poetry as concerned with Being. What is a lyric poem, one might say, but an acknowledgment of the Being of beings. The philosopher thinks Being; the poet in the lyric poem re-creates the experience of Being.

History, on the other hand, is antireductive. Nothing tidy about it. Chaos! Bedlam! Hopeless tangle! My history and the History of this century like a child and his blind mother on the street—and the blind mother leading the way! You'd think the sole purpose of history is to stand truth happily upon its head.

Poor poetry! For some reason I can't get Buster Keaton out of my mind. Poetry as imperturbable Keaton alone with the woman he loves on an ocean liner set adrift on the stormy sea. Or, poetry as that kid throwing stones at a tree to bring down his lunch. Wise enough to play the fool, perhaps?

And always the dialectic: I have Don Quixote and his windmills in my head and Sancho Panza and his mule in my heart.

That's a figure of speech—one figure among many other figures of speech. Who could live without them? Do they tell the truth? Do they conceal it? I don't know. That's why I keep going back to philosophy.

It is morning. It is night. The book is open. The text is difficult, the text is momentarily opaque. My mind is wandering. My mind is struggling to grasp the always elusive . . . the always hinting . . . What do you call it?

It, it, I keep calling it. An infinity of *it* without a single antecedent—like a hum in my ear.

Just then, about to give up, I find the following on a page of Heidegger:

> No thinker has ever entered into another thinker's solitude. Yet it is only from its solitude that all thinking, in a hidden mode, speaks to the thinking that comes after or that went before.

And it all comes together: poetry, philosophy, history. I see—in the sense of being able to picture and feel the human weight of another's solitude. So many of them. Seated with a book. Day breaking. Thought becoming image. Image becoming thought.

Wisdom

Alfred North Whitehead

The fading of ideals is sad evidence of the defeat of human endeavor. In the schools of antiquity philosophers aspired to impart wisdom, in modern colleges our humbler aim is to teach subjects. The drop from the divine wisdom, which was the goal of the ancients, to text-book knowledge of subjects, which is achieved by the moderns, marks an educational failure, sustained through the ages. I am not maintaining that in the practice of education the ancients were more successful than ourselves. You have only to read Lucian, and to note his satiric dramatizations of the pretentious claims of philosophers, to see that in this respect the ancients can boast over us no superiority. My point is that, at the dawn of our European civilisation, men started with the full ideals which should inspire education, and that gradually our ideals have sunk to square with our practice.

But when ideals have sunk to the level of practice, the result is stagnation. In particular, so long as we conceive intellectual education as merely consisting in the acquirement of mechanical mental aptitudes, and of formulated statements of useful truths, there can be no progress; though there will be much activity, amid aimless re-arrangement of syllabuses, in the fruitless endeavour to dodge the inevitable lack of time. We must take it as an unavoidable fact, that God has so made the world that there are more topics desirable for knowledge than any one person can possibly acquire. It is hopeless to approach the problem by the way of the enumeration of subjects which every one ought to have mastered. There are too many of them, all with excellent title-deeds. Perhaps, after all, this plethora of material is fortunate; for the world is made interesting by a delightful ignorance of important truths. . . . Though knowledge is one chief aim of intellectual education, there is another ingredient, vaguer but greater, and more dominating in its importance. The ancients called it "wisdom." You cannot be wise without some basis of knowledge; but you may easily acquire knowledge and remain bare of wisdom.

Now wisdom is the way in which knowledge is held. It concerns the handling of knowledge, its selection for the determination of relevant issues, its employment to add value to our immediate experience. This mastery of knowledge, which is wisdom, is the most intimate freedom obtainable. The ancients saw clearly—more clearly than we do—the necessity for dominating knowledge by wisdom. But, in the pursuit of wisdom in the region of practical education, they erred sadly. To put the matter simply, their popular practice assumed that wisdom could be imparted to the young by procuring philosophers to spout at them. Hence the crop of shady philosophers in the schools of the ancient world. The only avenue towards wisdom is by freedom in the presence of knowledge. But the only avenue towards knowledge is by discipline in the acquirement of ordered fact. . . .

The importance of knowledge lies in its use, in our active mastery of it—that is to say, it lies in wisdom. It is a convention to speak of mere knowledge, apart from wisdom, as of itself imparting a peculiar dignity to its possessor. I do not share in this reverence for knowledge as such. It all depends on who has the knowledge and what he does with it. That knowledge which adds greatness to character is knowledge so handled as to transform every phase of immediate experience. It is in respect to the activity of knowledge that an over-vigorous discipline in education is so harmful. The habit of active thought, with freshness, can only be generated by adequate freedom. Undiscriminating discipline defeats its own objects by dulling the mind. If you have much to do with the young as they emerge from school and from the university, you soon note the dulled minds of those whose education has consisted in the acquirement of inert knowledge. . . . Furthermore, this overhaste to impart mere knowledge defeats itself. The human mind rejects knowledge imparted in this way. The craving for expansion, for activity, inherent in youth is disgusted by a dry imposition of disciplined knowledge. The discipline, when it comes, should satisfy a natural craving for the wisdom which adds value to bare experience. . . .

In my own work at universities I have been much struck by the paralysis of thought induced in pupils by the aimless accumulation of precise knowledge, inert and unutilised. **It should be the chief aim of a university professor to exhibit himself in his own true character—that is, as an ignorant man thinking, actively utilising this small share of knowledge.** In a sense, knowledge shrinks as wisdom grows: for details are swallowed up in principles. The details of knowledge which are important will be picked up *ad hoc* in each avocation of life, but the habit of the active utilisation of well-understood principles is the final possession of wisdom. . . .

Stories of Chuang Tzu and Hui Tzu

Arthur Waley

Hui Tzu said to Chuang Tzu, "Your teachings are of no practical use." Chuang Tzu said, "Only those who already know the value of the useless can be talked to about the useful. This earth we walk upon is of vast extent, yet in order to walk a man uses no more of it than the soles of his two feet will cover. But suppose one cut away the ground round his feet till one reached the Yellow Springs,[1] would his patches of ground still be of any use to him for walking?" Hui Tzu said, "They would be of no use." Chuang Tzu said, "So then the usefulness of the useless is evident."

Hui Tzu recited to Chuang Tzu the rhyme:

*I have got a big tree
That men call the* chü.
*Its trunk is knotted and gnarled,
And cannot be fitted to plumb-line and ink;
Its branches are bent and twisted,
And cannot be fitted to compass or square.
It stands by the road-side,
And no carpenter will look at it.*

"Your doctrines" said Hui Tzu, "are grandoise, but useless, and that is why no one accepts them." Chuang Tzu said, "Can it be that you have never seen the pole-cat, how it crouches waiting for the mouse, ready at any moment to leap this way or that, high or low, till one day it lands plump on the spring of a trap and dies in the snare? Again there is the yak, 'huge as a cloud that covers the sky.' It can maintain this great bulk and yet would be quite incapable of catching a mouse. . . . As for you and the big tree which you are at a loss how to use, why do you not plant it in the realm of Nothing Whatever, in the wilds of the Unpastured Desert, and aimlessly tread the path of Inaction by its side, or vacantly lie dreaming beneath it?

*What does not invite the axe
No creature will harm.
What cannot be used
No troubles will befall.*

Hui Tzu said to Chuang Tzu, "The king of Wei gave me the seed of one of his huge gourds. I planted it, and it bore a gourd so enormous that if I had filled it with water or broth it would have taken several men to lift it, while if I had split it into halves and made ladles out of it they would have been so flat that no liquid would have lain in them. No one could deny that it was magnificently large; but I was unable to find any use for it, and in the end I smashed it up and threw it away." Chuang Tzu said, "I have noticed before that you are not very clever at turning large things to account. There was once a family in Sung that possessed a secret drug which had enabled its members for generations past to steep silk floss without getting chapped hands. A stranger hearing of it offered to buy the recipe for a hundred pieces of gold. The head of the family pointed out to his kinsmen that if all the money that the family had made in successive generations through the use of the drug were added together it would not come to more than one or two pieces of gold, and that a hundred pieces would amply repay them for parting with their secret. The stranger carried off the recipe and spoke of it to the king of Wu, whose country was being harried by the battleships of Yüeh. The stranger was put in command of the Wu fleet, and so efficacious was the remedy that despite the bitter cold (for it was a winter's day) the fingers of the Wu sailors never once grew chapped or numbed, and the fleet of Yüeh was entirely destroyed. The land of Yüeh was divided and the stranger rewarded with a fief.

"The sole property of the drug was that it prevented hands from getting chapped. Yet so much depends on the user that, if it had stayed with the man of Sung, it would never have done more than help him to steep floss; while no sooner had it passed into the stranger's possession than it gained him a fief. As for you and your large gourd, why did you not tie it as a buoy at your waist, and, borne up by it on the waters, float to your heart's content amid the streams and inland seas? Instead, you grumble about its gigantic dimensions and say that ladles made from it would hold nothing; the reason being, I fear, that your own thoughts have not learnt to run beyond the commonplace."

• • •

Hui Tzu said to Chuang Tzu, "Can a man really become passionless?" Chuang Tzu said, "He can." Hui Tzu said, "A man without passions cannot be called a man." Chaung Tzu said, "'Tao gave him substance,

Heaven gave him form;' how is it possible not to call him a man?" Hui Tzu said, "I would rather say, Granted that he is still a man, how is it possible for him to be passionless?" Chuang Tzu said, "You do not understand what I mean when I say 'passionless.'[2] When I say 'passionless' I mean that a man does not let love or hate do damage within, that he falls in with the way in which things happen of themselves, and does not exploit life." Hui Tzu said, "If he does not exploit life, what is the use of his having a body?" Chuang Tzu said:

Tao gave him substance,
Heaven gave him form;
Let him not by love or hate
Bring this gift to harm.

Yet here are you,

Neglecting your soul,
Wearying your spirit,
Propped against a pile of books you drone,
Leaning against your zithern you doze.
Heaven made you sound and whole;
Yet all your song is hard *and* white.[3]

When Chuang Tzu's wife died, Hui Tzu came to the house to join in the rites of mourning. To his surprise he found Chuang Tzu sitting with an inverted bowl on his knees, drumming upon it and singing a song.[4] "After all" said Hui Tzu, "she lived with you, brought up your children, grew old along with you. That you should not mourn for her is bad enough; but to let your friends find you drumming and singing—that is going too far!" "You misjudge me" said Chuang Tzu. "When she died, I was in despair, as any man well might be. But soon, pondering on what had happened, I told myself that in death no strange new fate befalls us. In the beginning we lack not life only, but form. Not form only but spirit. We are blended in the one great featureless indistinguishable mass. Then a time came when the mass evolved spirit, spirit evolved form, form evolved life. And now life in its turn has evolved death. For not nature only but man's being has it, seasons, its sequence of spring and autumn, summer and winter. If some one is tired and has gone to lie down, we do not pursue him with shouting and bawling. She whom I have lost has lain down to sleep for a while in the Great Inner Room. To break in upon her rest with the noise of lamentation would but show that I knew nothing of nature's Sovereign Law. That is why I ceased to mourn."

Chuang Tzu and Hui Tzu were strolling one day on the bridge over the river Hao. Chuang Tzu said, "Look how the minnows dart hither and thither where they will. Such is the pleasure that fish enjoy." Hui Tzu said, "You are not a fish. How do you know what gives pleasure to fish?" Chuang Tzu said, "You are not I. How do you know that I do not know what gives pleasure to fish?" Hui Tzu said, "If because I am not you, I cannot know whether you know, then equally because you are not a fish, you cannot know what gives pleasure to fish. My argument still holds." Chuang Tzu said, "Let us go back to where we started. You asked me how I knew what gives pleasure to fish. But you already knew how I knew it when you asked me. You knew that I knew it by standing here on the bridge at Hao."

When Hui Tzu was minister in Liang, Chuang Tzu decided to pay him a visit. Someone said to Hui Tzu, "Chuang Tzu is coming and hopes to be made Minister in your place." This alarmed Hui Tzu and he searched everywhere in Liang for three days and three nights to discover where Chuang Tzu was. Chuang Tzu, however, arrived on his own accord and said, "In the South there is a bird. It is called *yüan-ch'u*.[5] Have you heard of it? This *yüan-ch'u* starts from the southern ocean and flies to the northern ocean. During its whole journey it perches on no tree save the sacred *wu-t'ung*,[6] eats no fruit save that of the *lien*,[7] drinks only at the Magic Well. It happened that an owl that had got hold of the rotting carcass of a rat looked up as this bird flew by, and terrified lest the *yüan-ch'u* should stop and snatch at the succulent morsel, it screamed, 'Shoo! Shoo!' And now I am told that you are trying to 'Shoo' me off from this precious Ministry of yours."

• • •

Once when Chuang Tzu was walking in a funeral procession, he came upon Hui Tzu's tomb, and turning to those who were with him he said, "There was once a wall-plasterer who when any plaster fell upon his nose, even a speck no thicker than a fly's wing, used to get the mason who worked with him to slice it off. The mason brandished his adze with such force that there was a sound of rushing wind; but he sliced the plaster clean off, leaving the plasterer's nose completely intact; the plasterer, on his side, standing stock still, without the least change of expression.

"Yüan, prince of Sung, heard of this and sent for the mason, saying to him, 'I should very much like to see you attempt this performance.' The mason said, 'It is true that I used to do it. But I need the right stuff to work upon, and the partner who supplied such material died long ago.'

"Since Hui Tzu died I, too, have had no proper stuff to work upon, have had no one with whom I can really talk."

• • •

It was not always by dialogue that Chuang Tzu warred with the logicians. Another of his weapons was parody. A favourite method of the argumentative school of philosophy was to take an imaginary case: "take the case of a man who . . . ," they constantly say to illustrate their argument.

• • •

"Take the case of some words," Chuang Tzu says, parodying the logicians, "I do not know which of them are in any way connected with reality or which are not at all connected with reality. If some that are so connected and some that are not so connected are connected with one another, then as regards truth or falsehood the former cease to be in any way different from the latter. However, just as an experiment, I will now say them: 'If there was a beginning, there must have been a time before the beginning began, and if there was a time before the beginning began, there must have been a time before the time before the beginning began. If there is being, there must also be not-being. If there was a time before there began to be any not-being, there must also have been a time before the time before there began to be any not-being. But here am I, talking about being and not-being and still do not know whether it is being that exists and not-being that does not exist, or being that does not exist and not-being that really exists! I have spoken, and do not know whether I have said something that means anything or said nothing that has any meaning at all.

'Nothing under Heaven is larger than a strand of gossamer, nothing smaller than Mt. T'ai. No one lives longer than the child that dies in its swaddling-clothes, no one dies sooner than P'êng Tsu.[8] Heaven and earth were born when I was born; the ten thousand things and I among them are but one thing.' All this the sophists have proved. But if there were indeed only one thing, there would be no language with which to say so. And in order that anyone should state this, there must be more language in which it can be stated. Thus their one thing together with their talk about the one thing makes two things. And their one thing together with their talk and my statement about it makes three things. And so it goes on, to a point where the cleverest mathematician could no longer keep count, much less an ordinary man. Starting with not-being and going on to being, one soon gets to three. What then would happen if one started with being and went on to being?"

• • •

Tzu-lai fell ill. He was already at the last gasp; his wife and children stood weeping and wailing round his bed. "Pst" said Tzu-li, who had come to call, "stand back! A great Change is at work; let us not disturb it." Then, leaning against the door, he said to Tzu-lai, "Mighty are the works of the Changer! What is he about to make of you, to what use will he put you? Perhaps a rat's liver, perhaps a beetle's claw!" "A child" said Tzu-lai, "at its parents' bidding must go north and south, east or west; how much the more when those parents of all Nature, the great powers Yin and Yang command him, must he needs go where they will. They have asked me to die, and if I do not obey them, shall I not rank as an unmanageable child? I can make no complaint against them. These great forces housed me in my bodily frame, spent me in youth's toil, gave me repose when I was old, will give me rest at my death. Why should the powers that have done so much for me in life, do less for me in death?

"If the bronze in the founder's crucible were suddenly to jump up and say, 'I don't want to be a tripod, a plough-share or a bell. I must be the sword *Without Flaw*,' the caster would think it was indeed unmannerly metal that had got into his stock.

"In this life I have had the luck to be fashioned in human form. But were I now to say to the Great Transformer, 'I refuse to let anything be made out of me but a man,' he would think that it was indeed an unmannerly being who had come into his hands."

• • •

How do I know that wanting to be alive is not a great mistake? How do I know that hating to die is not like thinking one has lost one's way, when all the time one is on the path that leads to home? Li Chi was the daughter of the frontier guardsman at Ai. When first she was captured and carried away to Chin, she wept till her dress was soaked with tears. But when she came to the king's palace, sat with him on his couch and shared with him the dainties of the royal board, she began to wonder why she had wept. How do I know that the dead do not wonder why they should ever have prayed for long life? It is said that those who dream of drinking wine will weep when day comes; and that those who dream of weeping will next day go hunting. But while a man is dreaming, he does not know that he is dreaming; nor can he interpret a dream till the dream is done. It is only when he wakes, that he knows it was a dream. Not till the Great Wakening can he know that all this was one Great Dream. . . .

Once Chuang Chou[9] dreamt that he was a butterfly. He did not know that he had ever been anything but a butterfly and was content to hover from flower to flower. Suddenly he woke and found to his astonishment that he was Chuang Chou. But it was hard to be sure whether he really was Chou and had only dreamt that he was a butterfly, or was really a butterfly, and was only dreaming that he was Chou.

Notes

[1] The world of the dead.
[2] The "—less" has dropped out of the original.
[3] That is to say, is concerned with the problem of logic, such as the question whether hardness and whiteness exist separately from an object that is hard and white.
[4] Both his attitude and his occupation were the reverse of what the rites of mourning demand.
[5] Identified nowadays with the Argus pheasant, but used by Chuang Tzu in a mythological sense.
[6] The kola-nut tree.
[7] Identified nowadays with the Persian Lilac.
[8] The Chinese Methusaleh.
[9] I.e., Chuang Tzu.

What Is Enlightenment?

Immanuel Kant

Enlightenment is man's release from his self-incurred tutelage. Tutelage is man's inability to make use of his understanding without direction from another. Self-incurred is this tutelage when its cause lies not in lack of reason but in lack of resolution and courage to use it without direction from another. *Sapere aude!*[1] "Have courage to use your own reason!"—that is the motto of enlightenment.

Laziness and cowardice are the reasons why so great a portion of mankind, after nature has long since discharged them from external direction (*naturaliter maiorennes*), nevertheless remains under lifelong tutelage, and why it is so easy for others to set themselves up as their guardians. It is so easy not to be of age. If I have a book which understands for me, a pastor who has a conscience for me, a physician who decides my diet, and so forth, I need not trouble myself. I need not think, if I can only pay—others will readily undertake the irksome work for me.

That the step to competence is held to be very dangerous by the far greater portion of [humankind]—quite apart from its being arduous—is seen to by those guardians who have so kindly assumed superintendence over them. After the guardians have first made their domestic cattle dumb and have made sure that these placid creatures will not dare take a single step without the harness of the cart to which they are tethered, the guardians then show them the danger which threatens if they try to go alone. Actually, however, this danger is not so great, for by falling a few times they would finally learn to walk alone. But an example of this failure makes them timid and ordinarily frightens them away from all further trials.

For any single individual to work himself out of the life under tutelage which has become almost his nature is very difficult. He has come to be fond of this state, and he is for the present really incapable of making use of his reason, for no one has ever let him try it out. Statutes and formulas, those mechanical tools of the rational employment or rather misemployment of his natural gifts, are the fetters of an everlasting tutelage. Whoever throws them off makes only an uncertain leap over the narrowist ditch because he is not accustomed to that kind of free motion. Therefore, there are few who have succeeded by their own exercise of mind both in freeing themselves from incompetence and in achieving a steady pace.

But that the public should enlighten itself is more possible: indeed, if only freedom is granted, enlightenment is almost sure to follow. For there will always be some independent thinkers, even among the established guardians of the great masses, who, after throwing off the yoke of tutelage from their own shoulders, will disseminate the spirit of the rational appreciation of both their own worth and every man's vocation for thinking for himself. But be it noted that the public, which has first been brought under this yoke by their guardians, forces the guardians themselves to remain bound when it is incited to do so by some of the guardians who are themselves capable of some enlightenment—so harmful is it to implant prejudices, for they later take vengeance on their cultivators or on their descendants. Thus the public can only slowly attain enlightenment. Perhaps a fall of personal despotism or of avaricious or tyrannical oppression may be accomplished by revolution, but never a true reform in ways of thinking. Rather, new prejudices will serve as well as old ones to harness the great unthinking masses.

For this enlightenment, however, nothing is required but freedom, and indeed the most harmless among all the things to which this term can properly be applied. It is the freedom to make public use of one's reason at every point.[2] But I hear on all sides, "Do not argue!" The officer says: "Do not argue but drill!" The tax collector: "Do not argue but pay!" The cleric: "Do not argue but believe!" Only one prince in the world says, "Argue as much as you will, and about what you will, but obey!" Everywhere there is restriction on freedom.

Which restriction is an obstacle to enlightenment, and which is not an obstacle but a promoter of it? I answer: The public use of one's reason must always be free, and it alone can bring about enlightenment among men. The private use of reason, on the other hand, may often be very narrowly restricted without particularly hindering the progress of enlightenment. By the public use of one's reason I understand the use which a person makes of it as a scholar before the reading public. Private use I call that which one may make of it in a particular civil post or office which is entrusted to him. Many affairs which are conducted in the interest of the community require a certain mechanism through which some members of the community must passively conduct themselves with an artificial unanimity, so that the government may direct them to public ends, or at least prevent them from destroying those ends. Here argument is certainly not allowed—one must obey. But so far as a part of the mechanism regards himself at the same time as a member of the whole community or of a society of world citizens, and thus in the role of a scholar who addresses the public (in the proper sense of the word) through his writings, he certainly can argue without hurting the affairs for which he is in part responsible as a passive member. Thus it would be ruinous for an officer in service to debate about the suitability or utility of a command given to him by his superior; he must obey. But the right to make remarks on errors in the military service and to lay them before the public for judgment cannot equitably be refused him as a scholar. The citizen cannot refuse to pay the taxes imposed on him; indeed, an impudent complaint at those levied on him can be punished as a scandal (as it could occasion general refractoriness). But the same person nevertheless does not act contrary to his duty as a citizen when, as a scholar, he publicly expresses his thoughts on the inappropriateness or even the injustice of these levies. Similarly a clergyman is obligated to make his sermon to his pupils in catechism and his congregation conform to the symbol of the church which he serves, for he has been accepted on his condition. But as a scholar he has complete freedom, even the calling, to communicate to the public all his carefully tested and well-meaning thoughts on that which is erroneous in the symbol and to make suggestions for the better organization of the religious body and church. In doing this there is nothing that could be laid as a burden on his conscience. For what he teaches as a consequence of his office as a representative of the church, this he considers something about which he has no freedom to teach according to his own lights; it is something which he is appointed to propound at the dictation of and in the name of another. He will say, "Our church teaches this or that; those are the proofs which it adduces." He thus extracts all practical uses for his congregation from statutes to which he himself would not subscribe with full conviction but to the enunciation of which he can very well pledge himself because it is not impossible that truth lies hidden in them, and, in any case, there is at least nothing in them contradictory to inner religion. For if he believed he had found such in them, he could not conscientiously discharge the duties of his office; he would have to give it up. The use, therefore, which an appointed teacher makes of his reason before his congregation is merely private, because this congregation is only a domestic one (even if it be a large gathering); with respect to it, as a priest, he is not free, nor can he be free, because he carries out the orders of another. But as a scholar, whose writings speak to his public, the world, the clergyman in the public use of his reason enjoys an unlimited freedom to use his own reason and to speak in his own person. That the guardians of the people (in spiritual things) should themselves be incompetent is an absurdity which amounts to the eternalization of absurdities.

But would not a society of clergymen, perhaps a church conference or a venerable classis (as they call themselves among the Dutch), be justified in obligating itself by oath to a certain unchangeable symbol in order to enjoy an unceasing guardianship over each of its members and thereby over the people as a whole, and even to make it eternal? I answer that this is altogether impossible. Such a contract, made to shut off all further enlightenment from the human race, is absolutely null and void even if confirmed by the supreme power, by parliaments, and by the most ceremonious of peace treaties. **An age cannot bind itself and ordain to put the succeeding one into such a condition that it cannot extend its (at best very occasional) knowledge, purify itself of errors, and progress in general enlightenment. That would be a crime against human nature,** the proper destination of which lies precisely in this progress; and the descendants would be fully justified in rejecting those decrees as having been made in an unwarranted and malicious manner.

The touchstone of everything that can be concluded as a law for a people lies in the question whether the people could have imposed such a law on itself. Now such a religious compact might be possible for a short and definitely limited time, as it were, in expectation of a better. One night let every citizen, and especially the clergyman, in the role of scholar, make his comments freely and publicly, i.e., through writing, on the erroneous aspects of the present institution. The newly introduced order might last until insight into the nature of these things had become so general and widely approved that through uniting their voices (even if not unanimously) they could bring a proposal to the throne to take those congregations under protection which had united into a changed religious organization according to their better ideas, without, however, hindering others who wish to remain in the order. But to unite in a permanent religious institution which is not to be subject to doubt before the public even in the lifetime of one man, and thereby to make a period of time fruitless in the progress of mankind toward improvement, thus working to the disadvantage of posterity—that is absolutely forbidden. For himself (and only for a short time) a man may postpone enlightenment in what he ought to know, but to renounce it for himself and even more to renounce it for posterity is to injure and trample on the rights of mankind.

And what a people may not decree for itself can even less be decreed for them by a monarch, for his law-giving authority rests on his uniting the general public will in his own. If he only sees to it that all true or alleged improvement stands together with civil order, he can leave it to his subjects to do what they find necessary for their spiritual welfare. This is not his concern, though it is incumbent on him to prevent one of them from violently hindering another in determining and promoting this welfare to the best of his ability. To meddle in these matters lowers his own majesty, since by the writings in which his subjects seek to present their views he may evaluate his own governance. He can do this when, with deepest understanding, he lays upon himself the reproach, "Caesar non est supra grammaticos."[3] Far more does he injure his own majesty when he degrades his supreme power by supporting the ecclesiastical despotism of some tyrants in his state over his other subjects.

If we are asked, "Do we now live in an *enlightened age?*" the answer is, "No," but we do live in an *age of enlightenment*.[4] As things now stand, much is lacking which prevents men from being, or easily becoming, capable of correctly using their own reason in religious matters with assurance and free from outside direction. But, on the other hand, we have clear indications that the field has now been opened wherein men may freely deal with these things and that the obstacles to general enlightenment or the release from self-imposed tutelage are gradually being reduced. In this respect, this is the age of enlightenment, or the century of Frederick.

A prince who does not find it unworthy of himself to say that he holds it to be his duty to prescribe nothing to men in religious matters but to give them complete freedom while renouncing the haughty name of *tolerance*, is himself enlightened and deserves to be esteemed by the grateful world and posterity as the first, at least from the side of government, who divested the human race of its tutelage and left each man free to make use of his reason in matters of conscience. Under him venerable ecclesiastics are allowed, in the role of scholars, and without infringing on their official duties, freely to submit for public testing their judgments and views which here and there diverge from the established symbol. And an even greater freedom is enjoyed by those who are restricted by no offcial duties. This spirit of freedom spreads beyond this land, even to those in which it must struggle with external obstacles erected by a government which misunderstands its own interest. For an example gives evidence to such a government that in freedom there is not the least cause for concern about public peace and the stability of the community. Men work themselves gradually out of barbarity if only intentional artifices are not made to hold them in it.

I have placed the main point of enlightenment—the escape of men from their self-incurred tutelage—chiefly in matters of religion because our rulers have no interest in playing the guardian with respect to the arts and sciences and also because religious incompetence is not only the most harmful but also the most degrading of all. But the manner of thinking of the head of a state who favors religious enlightenment goes further, and he sees that there is no danger to his law-giving in allowing his subjects to make public use of their reason and to publish their thoughts on a better formulation of his legislation and even their open-minded criticisms of the laws already made. Of this we have a shining example wherein no monarch is superior to him whom we honor.

But only one who is himself enlightened is not afraid of shadows, and who has a numerous and well-disciplined army to assure public peace, can say: "Argue as much as you will, and about what you will, only obey!" A republic could not dare say such a thing. Here is shown a strange and unexpected trend in human affairs in which almost everything, looked at in the large, is paradoxical. A greater degree of civil freedom appears advantageous to the freedom of mind of the people, and yet it places inescapable limitations upon it; a lower degree of civil freedom, on the contrary, provides the mind with room for each man to extend himself to his full capacity. As nature has uncovered from under this hard shelf the seed for which she most tenderly cares—the propensity and vocation to free thinking—this gradually works back upon the character of the people, who thereby gradually become capable of managing freedom; finally, it affects the principles of government, which finds it to its advantage to treat men, who are now more than machines, in accordance with their dignity.[5]

Notes

[1] ["Dare to know!" (Horace, *Ars poetica*). This was the motto adopted in 1736 by the Society of the Friends of Truth, an important circle in the German Enlightenment.]

[2] [It is this freedom Kant claimed later in his conflict with the censor, deferring to the censor in the "private" use of reason, i.e., in his lectures.]

³ ["The emperor is not above the grammarians." Perhaps, an allusion to a response to Voltaire said to have been made by Frederick the Great: "Caesar est supra grammaticam." But the sentiment was not original with Frederick, and has been attributed to the Emperor Sigismund at the Council of Constance (1414): "Ego sum rex Romanus et supra grammaticam."]

⁴ ["Our age is, in especial degree, the age of criticism, and to criticism everything must submit" (*Critique of Pure Reason*, Preface to first edn., Smith trans.]

⁵ Today I read in the *Büschingsche Wöchentliche Nachrichten* for September 13 an announcement of the *Berlinische Monatsschrift* for this month, which cites the answer to the same question by Mr. Mendelssohn.* But this issue has not yet come to me: if it had, I would have held back the present essay, which is now put forth only in order to see how much agreement in thought can be brought about by chance.

> * [Mendelssohn's answer was that enlightenment lay in intellectual cultivation, which he distinguished from the practical. Kant, quite in line with his later essay on theory and practice, refuses to make this distinction fundamental.]

The Apology

Plato

In 399 B.C. Socrates was brought to trial before a court composed of 501 Athenian citizens. In his defense he spoke as follows:

How you, O Athenians, have been affected by my accusers, I cannot tell; but I know that they almost made me forget who I was—so persuasively did they speak; and yet they have hardly uttered a word of truth. But of the many falsehoods told by them, there was one which quite amazed me;—I mean when they said that you should be upon your guard and not allow yourselves to be deceived by the force of my eloquence. To say this, when they were certain to be detected as soon as I opened my lips and proved myself to be anything but a great speaker, did indeed appear to me most shameless—unless by the force of eloquence they mean the force of truth; for if such is their meaning, I admit that I am eloquent. But in how different a way from theirs! Well, as I was saying, they have scarcely spoken the truth at all; but from me you shall hear the whole truth: not, however, delivered after their manner in a set oration duly ornamented with words and phrases. No, by heaven! but I shall use the words and arguments which occur to me at the moment; for I am confident in the justice of my cause: at my time of life I ought not to be appearing before you, O men of Athens, in the character of a juvenile orator—let no one expect it of me. And I must beg of you to grant me a favor:—If I defend myself in my accustomed manner, and you hear me using the words which I have been in the habit of using in the agora, at the tables of the money-changers, or anywhere else, I would ask you not to be surprised, and not to interrupt me on this account. For I am more than seventy years of age, and appearing now for the first time in a court of law, I am quite a stranger to the language of the place; and therefore I would have you regard me as if I were really a stranger, whom you would excuse if he spoke in his native tongue, and after the fashion of his country:—Am I making an unfair request of you? Never mind the manner, which may or may not be good; but think only of the truth of my words, and give heed to that: let the speaker speak truly and the judge decide justly.

And first, I have to reply to the older charges and to my first accusers, and then I will go on to the later ones. For of old I have had many accusers, who have accused me falsely to you during many years; and I am more afraid of them than of Anytus and his associates, who are dangerous, too, in their own way. But far more dangerous are the others, who began when you were children, and took possession of your minds with their falsehoods, telling of one Socrates, a wise man, who speculated about the heaven above, and searched into the earth beneath, and made the worse appear the better cause. The disseminators of this tale are the accusers whom I dread; for their hearers are apt to fancy that such enquirers do not believe in the existence of the gods. And they are many, and their charges against me are of ancient date, and they were made by them in the days when you were more impressible than you are now—in childhood, or it may have been in youth—and the cause when heard went by default, for there was none to answer. And hardest of all, I do not know and cannot tell the names of my accusers; unless in the chance case of a comic poet. All who from envy and malice have persuaded you—some of them having first convinced themselves—all this class of men are most difficult to deal with; for I cannot have them up here, and cross-examine them, and therefore I must simply fight with shadows in my own defence, and argue when there is no one who answers. I will ask you then to assume with me, as I was saying, that my opponents are of two kinds; one recent, the other ancient: and I hope that you will see the propriety of my answering the latter first, for these accusations you heard long before the others, and much oftener.

Well, then, I must make my defence, and endeavour to clear away in a short time, a slander which has lasted a long time. May I succeed, if to succeed be for my good and yours, or likely to avail me in my cause! The task is not an easy one; I quite understand the nature of it. And so leaving the event with God, in obedience to the law I will now make my defence.

I will begin at the beginning, and ask what is the accusation which has given rise to the slander of me, and in fact has encouraged Meletus to prefer this charge against me. Well, what do the slanderers say? They shall be my prosecutors, and I will sum up their words in an affidavit: "Socrates is an evildoer, and a curious person, who searches into things under the earth and in heaven, and he makes the worse appear the better cause; and he teaches the aforesaid doctrines to others." Such is the nature of the accusation: it is just what you have yourselves seen in the comedy of Aristophanes, who has introduced a man whom he calls Socrates, going about and saying that he walks in air, and talking a deal of nonsense concerning matters of which I do not pretend to know either much or little—not that I mean to speak disparagingly of any one who is a student of natural philosophy. I should be very sorry if Meletus could bring so grave a charge against me. But the simple truth is, O Athenians, that I have nothing to do with physical speculations. Very many of those here present are witnesses to the truth of this, and to them I appeal. Speak then, you who have heard me, and tell your neighbours whether any of you have ever known me hold forth in few words or in many upon such matters.... You hear their answer. And from what they say of this part of the charge you will be able to judge of the truth of the rest.

As little foundation is there for the report that I am a teacher, and take money; this accusation has no more truth in it than the other. Although, if a man were really able to instruct mankind, to receive money for giving instruction would, in my opinion, be an honour to him. There is Gorgias of Leontium, and Prodicus of Ceos, and Hippias of Elis, who go the round of the cities, and are able to persuade the young men to leave their own citizens by whom they might be taught for nothing, and come to them whom they not only pay, but are thankful if they may be allowed to pay them. There is at this time a Parian philosopher residing in Athens, of whom I have heard; and I came to hear of him in this way:—I came across a man who has spent a world of money on the Sophists, Callias, the son of Hipponicus, and knowing that he had sons, I asked him: "Callias," I said, "if your two sons were foals or calves, there would be no difficulty in finding some one to put over them; we should hire a trainer of horses, or a farmer, probably, who would improve and perfect them in their own proper virtue and excellence; but as they are human beings, whom are you thinking of placing over them? Is there any one who understands human and political virtue? You must have thought about the matter, for you have sons; is there any one?" "There is," he said. "Who is he?" said I; "and of what country? and what does he charge?" "Evenus the Parian," he replied; "he is the man, and his charge is five minae." Happy is Evenus, I said to myself, if he really has this wisdom, and teaches at such a moderate charge. Had I the same, I should have been very proud and conceited; but the truth is that I have no knowledge of the kind.

I dare say, Athenians, that some one among you will reply, "Yes, Socrates, but what is the origin of these accusations which are brought against you; there must have been something strange which you have been doing? All these rumours and this talk about you would never have arisen if you had been like other men: tell us, then, what is the cause of them, for we should be sorry to judge hastily of you." Now, I regard this as a fair challenge, and I will endeavour to explain to you the reason why I am called wise and have such an evil fame. Please to attend then. And although some of you may think that I am joking, I declare that I will tell you the entire truth. Men of Athens, this reputation of mine has come of a certain sort of wisdom which I possess. If you ask me what kind of wisdom, I reply, wisdom such as may perhaps be attained by man, for to that extent I am inclined to believe that I am wise; whereas the persons of whom I was speaking have a superhuman wisdom, which I may fail to describe, because I have it not myself; and he who says that I have, speaks falsely, and is taking away my character. And here, O men of Athens, I must beg you not to interrupt me, even if I seem to say something extravagant. For the word which I will speak is not mine. I will refer you to a witness who is worthy of credit; that witness shall be the god of Delphi—he will tell you about my wisdom, if I have any, and of what sort it is. You must have known Chaerephon; he was early a friend of mine, and also a friend of yours, for he shared in the recent exile of the people, and returned with you. Well, Chaerephon, as you know, was very impetuous in all his doings, and he went to Delphi and boldly asked the oracle to tell him whether—as I was saying, I must beg you not to interrupt—he asked the oracle to tell him whether any one was wiser than I was, and the Pythian prophetess answered, that there was no man wiser. Chaerephon is dead himself; but his brother, who is in court, will confirm the truth of what I am saying.

Why do I mention this? Because I am going to explain to you why I have such an evil name. When I heard the answer, I said to myself, What can the god mean? and what is the interpretation of his riddle? for I know I have no wisdom, small or great. What then can he mean when he says that I am the wisest of men? And yet he is a god, and cannot lie; that would be against his nature. After long consideration, I thought of a method of trying the question. I reflected that if I could only find a man wiser than myself, then I might go to the god with a refutation in my hand. I should say to him, "Here is a man who is wiser than I am; but you said that I was the wisest." Accordingly I went to one who had the reputation of wisdom, and observed him—his name I need not mention; he was a politician whom I selected for examination—and the result was as follows: When I began to talk with him, I could not help thinking that he was not really wise, although he was thought wise by many, and still wiser by himself; and thereupon I tried to explain to him that he thought himself wise, but was not really wise; and the consequence was that he hated me, and his enmity was shared by several who were present and heard me. So I left him, saying to myself, as I went away: Well, although I do not suppose that either of us knows anything really beautiful and good, I am better off than he is,—for he knows nothing, and thinks that he knows; I neither know nor think that I know. In this latter particular, then, I seem to have slightly the advantage of him. Then I went to another who had still higher pretensions to wisdom, and my conclusion was exactly the same. Whereupon I made another enemy of him, and many others besides him.

Then I went to one man after another, being not unconscious of the enmity which I provoked, and I lamented and feared this: but necessity was laid upon me,—the word of God, I thought, ought to be considered first. And I said to myself, Go I must to all who appear to know, and find out the meaning of the oracle. And I swear to you, Athenians, by the dog I swear!—for I must tell you the truth—the result of my mission was just this: I found that the men most in repute were all but the most foolish; and that others less esteemed were really wiser and better. I will tell you the tale of my wanderings and of the "Herculean" labours, as I may call them, which I endured only to find at last the oracle irrefutable. After the politicians, I went to the poets; tragic, dithyrambic, and all sorts. And there, I said to myself, you will be instantly detected; now you will find out that you are more ignorant than they are. Accordingly I took them some of the most elaborate passages in their own writings, and asked what was the meaning of them—thinking that they would teach me something. Will you believe me? I am almost ashamed to confess the truth, but I must say that there is hardly a person present who would not have talked better about their poetry than they did themselves. Then I knew that not by wisdom do poets write poetry, but by a sort of genius and inspiration; they are like diviners or soothsayers who also say many fine things, but do not understand the meaning of them. The poets appeared to me to be much in the same case; and I further observed that upon the strength of their poetry they believed themselves to be the wisest of men in other things in which they were not wise. So I departed, conceiving myself to be superior to them for the same reason that I was superior to the politicians.

At last I went to the artisans. I was conscious that I knew nothing at all, as I may say, and I was sure that they knew many fine things; and here I was not mistaken, for they did know many things of which I was ignorant, and in this they certainly were wiser than I was. But I observed that even the good artisans fell into the same error as the poets;—because they were good workmen they thought that they also knew all sorts of high matters, and this defect in them overshadowed their wisdom; and therefore I asked myself on behalf of the oracle, whether I would like to be as I was, neither having their knowledge nor their ignorance, or like them in both; and I made answer to myself and to the oracle that I was better off as I was.

This inquisition has led to my having many enemies of the worst and most dangerous kind, and has given occasion also to many calumnies. And I am called wise, for my hearers always imagine that I myself possess the wisdom which I find wanting in others: but the truth is, O men of Athens, that God only is wise; and by his answer he intends to show that the wisdom of men is worth little or nothing; he is not speaking of Socrates, he is only using my name by way of illustration, as if he said, He, O men, is the wisest, who, like Socrates, knows that his wisdom is in truth worth nothing. And so I go about the world obedient to the god, and search and make enquiry into the wisdom of any one, whether citizen or stranger, who appears to be wise; and if he is not wise, then in vindication of the oracle I show him he is not wise; and my occupation quite absorbs me, and I have no time to give either to any public matter of interest or to any concern of my own, but I am in utter poverty by reason of my devotion to the god.

There is another thing:—young men of the richer classes, who have not much to do, come about me of their own accord; they like to hear the pretenders examined, and they often imitate me, and proceed to examine others; there are plenty of persons, as they quickly discover, who think that they know something, but really know little or nothing; and then those who are examined by them instead of being angry with themselves are angry with me: This confounded Socrates, they say; this villainous misleader of youth!—and then if somebody asks them, Why, what evil does he practice or teach? they do not know, and cannot tell; but in order that they may not appear to be at a loss, they repeat the ready-made charges which are used against all philosophers about teaching things up in the clouds and under the earth, and having no gods, and making the worse appear the better cause; for they do not like to confess that their presence of knowledge has been detected—which is the truth; and as they are numerous and ambitious and energetic, and are drawn up in battle array and have persuasive tongues, they have filled your ears with their loud and inveterate calumnies. And this is the reason why my three accusers, Meletus and Anytus and Lycon, have set upon me; Meletus, who has a quarrel with me on behalf of the poets; Anytus, on behalf of the craftsmen and politicians; Lycon, on behalf of the rhetoricians: and, as I said at the beginning, I cannot expect to get rid of such a mass of calumny all in a moment. And this, O men of Athens, is the truth and the whole truth; I have concealed nothing, I have dissembled nothing. And yet, I know that my plainness of speech makes them hate me, and what is their hatred but a proof that I am speaking the truth? Hence has arisen the prejudice against me; and this is the reason of it, as you will find out either in this or in any future enquiry.

I have said enough in my defence against the first class of my accusers; I turn to the second class. They are headed by Meletus, that good man and true lover of his country, as he calls himself. Against these, too, I must try to make a defence:—Let their affidavit be read: it contains something of this kind: It says that Socrates is a doer of evil, who corrupts the youth; and who does not believe in the gods of the State, but has other new divinities of his own. Such is the charge; and now let us examine the particular counts. He says that I am a doer of evil, and corrupt the youth; but I say, O men of Athens, that Meletus is a doer of evil, in that he pretends to be in earnest when he is only in jest, and is so eager to bring men to trial from a pretended zeal and interest about matters in which he really never had the smallest interest. And the truth of this I will endeavour to prove to you.

Come hither, Meletus, and let me ask a question of you. You think a great deal about the improvement of youth?

Yes, I do.

Tell the judges, then, who is their improver; for you must know, as you have taken the pains to discover their corrupter, and are citing and accusing me before them. Speak, then, and tell the judges who their improver is.—Observe, Meletus, that you are silent, and have nothing to say. But is not this rather disgraceful, and a very considerable proof of what I was saying, that you have no interest in the matter? Speak up, friend, and tell us who their improver is.

The laws.

But that, my good sir, is not my meaning. I want to know who the person is, who, in the first place, knows the laws.

The judges, Socrates, who are present in court.

What, do you mean to say, Meletus, that they are able to instruct and improve youth?

Certainly they are.

What, all of them, or some only and not others?

All of them.

By the goddess. Here, that is good news! There are plenty of improvers, then. And what do you say of the audience,—do they improve them?

Yes, they do.

And the senators?

Yes, the senators improve them.

But perhaps the members of the assembly corrupt them?—or do they improve them?

They improve them.

Then every Athenian improves and elevates them; all with the exception of myself; and I alone am their corrupter? Is that what you affirm?

That is what I stoutly affirm.

I am very unfortunate if you are right. But suppose I ask you a question: How about horses? Does one man do them harm and all the world good? Is not the exact opposite the truth? One man is able to do them good, or at least not many;—the trainer of horses, that is to say, does them good, and others who have to do with them rather injure them? Is not that true, Meletus, of horses, or of any other animals? Most assuredly it is; whether you and Anytus say yes or no. Happy indeed would be the condition of youth if they had one corrupter only, and all the rest of the world were their improvers. But you, Meletus, have sufficiently shown that you never had a thought about the young: your carelessness is seen in your not caring about the very things which you bring against me.

And now, Meletus, I will ask you another question—by Zeus I will: Which is better, to live among bad citizens, or among good ones? Answer, friend, I say; the question is one which may be easily answered. Do not the good do their neighbours good, and the bad do them evil?

Certainly.

And is there any one who would rather be injured than benefited by those who live with him? Answer, my good friend, the law requires you to answer—does any one like to be injured?

Certainly not.

And when you accuse me of corrupting and deteriorating the youth, do you allege that I corrupt them intentionally or unintentionally?

Intentionally, I say.

But you have just admitted that the good do their neighbours good, and the evil do them evil. Now, is that a truth which your superior wisdom has recognized thus early in life, and am I, at my age, in such darkness and ignorance as not to know that if a man with whom I have to live is corrupted by me, I am very likely to be harmed by him; and yet I corrupt him, and intentionally, too—so you say, although neither I nor any other human being is ever likely to be convinced by you. But either I do not corrupt them, or I corrupt them unintentionally; and on either view of the case you lie. If my offence is unintentional, the law has no cognizance of unintentional offences: you ought to have taken me privately, and warned and admonished me; for if I had been better advised, I should have left off doing what I only did unintentionally—no doubt I should; but you would have nothing to say to me and refused to teach me. And now you bring me up in this court, which is a place not of instruction, but of punishment.

It will be very clear to you, Athenians, as I was saying, that Meletus has no care at all, great or small, about the matter. But still I should like to know, Meletus, in what I am affirmed to corrupt the young. I suppose you mean, as I infer from your indictment, that I teach them not to acknowledge the gods which the State acknowledges, but some other new divinities or spiritual agencies in their stead. These are the lessons by which I corrupt the youth, as you say.

Yes, that I say emphatically.

Then, by the gods, Meletus, of whom we are speaking, tell me and the court, in somewhat plainer terms, what you mean! For I do not as yet understand whether you affirm that I teach other men to acknowledge some gods, and therefore that I do believe in gods, and am not an entire atheist—this you do not lay to my charge,—but only you say that they are not the same gods which the city recognizes—the charge is that they are different gods. Or, do you mean that I am an atheist simply, and a teacher of atheism?

I mean the latter—that you are a complete atheist.

What an extraordinary statement! Why do you think so, Meletus? Do you mean that I do not believe in the godhead of the sun or moon, like other men?

I assure you, judges, that he does not: for he says that the sun is stone, and the moon earth.

Friend Meletus, you think that you are accusing Anaxagoras: and you have but a bad opinion of the judges, if you fancy them illiterate to such a degree as not to know that these doctrines are found in the books of Anaxagoras the Clazomenian, which are full of them. And so, forsooth, the youth are said to be taught them by Socrates, when there are not infrequently exhibitions of them at the theatre (price of admission one drachma at the most); and they might pay their money, and laugh at Socrates if he pretends to father these extraordinary views. And so, Meletus, you really think that I do not believe in any god?

I swear by Zeus that you believe absolutely in none at all.

Nobody will believe you, Meletus, and I am pretty sure that you do not believe yourself. I cannot help thinking, that he has written this indictment in a spirit of mere wantonness and youthful bravado. Has he not compounded a riddle, thinking to try me? He said to himself; —I shall see whether the wise Socrates will discover my facetious contradiction, or whether I shall be able to deceive him and the rest of them. For he certainly does appear to me to contradict himself in the indictment as much as if he said that Socrates is guilty of not believing in the gods, and yet of believing in them—but this is not like a person who is in earnest.

I should like you, O men of Athens, to join me in examining what I conceive to be his inconsistency; and do you, Meletus, answer. And I must remind the audience of my request that they would not make a disturbance if I speak in my accustomed manner:

Did ever man, Meletus, believe in the existence of human things, and not of human beings? . . . I wish, men of Athens, that he would answer, and not be always trying to get up an interruption. Did ever any man believe in horsemanship, and not in horses, or in flute-playing, and not in flute-players? No, my friend; I will answer to you and to the court, as you refuse to answer for yourself. There is no man who ever did. But now please to answer the next question: Can a man believe in spiritual and divine agencies, and not in spirits or demigods?

He cannot.

How lucky I am to have extracted that answer, by the assistance of the court! But then you swear in the indictment that I teach and believe in divine or spiritual agencies (new or old, no matter for that); at any rate, I believe in spiritual agencies—so you say and swear in the affidavit; and yet if I believe in divine beings, how can I help believing in spirits or demigods;—must I not? To be sure I must; and therefore I may assume that your silence gives consent. Now what are spirits or demigods? are they not either gods or the sons of gods?

Certainly they are.

But this is what I call the facetious riddle invented by you: the demigods or spirits are gods, and you say first that I do not believe in gods, and then again that I do believe in gods; that is, if I believe in demigods. For if the demigods are the illegitimate sons of gods, whether by the nymphs or by any other mothers, of whom they are said to be the sons—what human being will ever believe that there are no gods if they are the sons of gods? You might as well affirm the existence of mules, and deny that of horses and asses. Such nonsense, Meletus, could only have been intended by you to make trial of me. You have put this into the indictment because you had nothing real of which to accuse me. But no one who has a particle of understanding will ever be convinced by you that the same men can believe in divine and superhuman beings, and yet not believe that there are gods and demigods and heroes.

I have said enough in answer to the charge of Meletus: any elaborate defence is unnecessary; but I know only too well how many are the enmities which I have incurred, and this is what will be my destruction if I am destroyed; —not Meletus, nor yet Anytus, but the envy and detraction of the world, which has been the death of many good men, and will probably be the death of many more; there is no danger of my being the last of them.

Some one will say: And are you not ashamed, Socrates, of a course of life which is likely to bring you to an untimely end? To him I may fairly answer: There you are mistaken: a man who is good for anything ought not to calculate the chance of living or dying; he ought only to consider whether in doing anything he is doing right or wrong—acting the part of a good man or a bad. Whereas, upon your view, the son of Thetis above all, who altogether despised danger in comparison with disgrace; and when he was so eager to slay Hector, his goddess mother said to him, that if he avenged his companion Patroclus, and slew Hector, he would die himself—"Fate," she said, in these or the like words, "waits for you next after Hector"; he, receiving this warning, utterly depised danger and death, and instead of fearing them, feared rather to live in dishonour, and not to avenge his friend. "Let me die forthwith," he replies, "and be avenged of my enemy, rather than abide here by the beaked ships, a laughing stock and a burden of the earth." Had Achilles any thought of death and danger? For wherever a man's place is, whether the place which he has chosen or that in which he has been placed by a commander, there he ought to remain in the hour of danger; he should not think of death or of anything but of disgrace. And this, O men of Athens, is a true saying.

Strange, indeed, would be my conduct, O men of Athens, if I, who, when I was ordered by the generals whom you chose to command me at Potidaea and Amphipolis and Delium, remained where they placed me, like any other man, facing death—if now, when, as I conceive and imagine, God orders me to fulfil the philosopher's mission of searching into myself and other men, I were to desert my post through fear of death, or any other fear; that would indeed be strange, and I might justly be arraigned in court for denying the existence of the gods, if I disobeyed the oracle because I was afraid of death, fancying that I was wise when I was not wise. For the fear is indeed the pretence of wisdom, and not real wisdom, being a pretence of knowing the unknown; and no one knows whether death, which men in their fear apprehend to be the greatest evil, may not be the greatest good. Is not this ignorance of a disgraceful sort, the ignorance which is the conceit that a man knows what he does not know? And in this respect only I believe myself to differ from men in general, and may perhaps claim to be wiser than they are:—that whereas I know but little of the world below, I do not suppose that I know: but I do know that injustice and disobedience to a better, whether God or man, is evil and dishonourable, and I will never fear or avoid a possible good rather than a certain evil. And therefore if you let me go now, and are not convinced by Anytus, who said that since I had been prosecuted I must be put to death; (or if not that I ought never to have been prosecuted at all); and that if I escape now, your sons will all be utterly ruined by listening to my words—if you say to me, Socrates, this time we will not mind Anytus, and you shall be let off, but upon one condition, that you are not to enquire and speculate in this way any more, and that if you are caught doing so again you shall die;—if this was the condition on which you let me go, I should reply: Men of Athens, I honour and love you; but I shall obey God rather than you, and while I have life and strength I shall never cease from the practice and teaching of philosophy, exhorting any one whom I meet and saying to him after my manner: You, my friend,— a citizen of the great and mighty and wise city of Athens,— are you not ashamed of heaping up the greatest amount of money and honour and reputation, and caring so little about wisdom and truth and the greatest improvement of the soul, which you never regard or heed at all? And if the person with whom I am arguing, says: Yes, but I do care; then I do not leave him or let him go at once; but I proceed to interrogate and examine him, and if I think that he has no virtue in him, but only says that he has, I reproach him with undervaluing the greater, and overvaluing the less. And I shall repeat the same words to every one whom I meet, young and old, citizen and alien, but especially to the citizens, inasmuch as they are my brethren. For know that this is the command of God; and I believe that no greater good has ever happened in the State than my service to the God. For I do nothing but go about persuading you all, old and young alike, not to take thought for your persons or your properties, but first and chiefly to care about the greatest improvement of the soul. I tell you that virtue is not given by money, but that from virtue comes money and every other good of man, public as well as private. This is my teaching, and if this is the doctrine which corrupts the youth, I am a mischievous person. But if any one says that this is not my teaching, he is speaking an untruth. Wherefore, O men of Athens, I say to you, do as Anytus bids or not as Anytus bids, and either acquit me or not; but whichever you do, understand that I shall never alter my ways, not even if I have to die many times.

Men of Athens, do not interrupt, but hear me; there was an understanding between us that you should hear me to the end: I have something more to say, at which you may be inclined to cry out; but I believe that to hear me will be good for you, and therefore I beg that you will not cry out. I would have you know, that if you kill such an one as I am, you will injure yourselves more than you will injure me. Nothing will injure me, not Meletus nor yet Anytus—they cannot, for a bad man is not permitted to injure a better than himself. I do not deny that Anytus may, perhaps, kill him, or drive him into exile, or deprive him of civil rights; and he may imagine, and others may imagine, that he is inflicting a great injury upon him: but there I do not agree. For the evil of doing as he is doing—the evil of unjustly taking away the life of another—is greater far.

And, now, Athenians, I am not going to argue for my own sake, as you may think, but for yours, that you may not sin against the God by condemning me, who am his gift to you. **For if you kill me you will not easily find a successor to me, who, if I may use such a ludicrous figure of speech, am a sort of gadfly, given to the State by God; and the State is a great and noble steed who is tardy in his motions owing to his very size, and requires to be stirred into life.** I am that gadfly which God has attached to the State, and all day long and in all places am always fastening upon you, arousing and persuading and reproaching you. You will not easily find another like me, and therefore I would advise you to spare me. I dare say that you may feel out of temper (like a person who is suddenly awakened from sleep), and you think that you might easily strike me dead as Anytus advises, and then you would sleep on for the remainder of your lives, unless God in his care of you sent you another gadfly. When I say that I am given to you by God, the proof of my mission is this:—if I had been like other men, I should not have neglected all my own concerns or patiently seen the neglect of them during all these years, and have been doing yours, coming to you individually like a father or elder brother, exhorting you to regard virtue; such conduct, I say, would be unlike human nature. If I had gained anything, or if my exhortations had been paid, there would have been some sense in my doing so; but now, as you will perceive, not even the impudence of my accusers dares to say that I have ever extracted or sought pay of any one; of that they have no witness. And I have a sufficient witness to the truth of what I say—my poverty.

Some one may wonder why I go about in private giving advice and busying myself with the concerns of others, but do not venture to come forward in public and advise the State. I will tell you why. You have heard me speak at sundry times and in divers places of an oracle or sign which comes to me, and this is the divinity which Meletus ridicules in the indictment. This sign, which is a kind of voice, first began to come to me when I was a child; it always forbids but never commands me to do anything which I am going to do. This is what deters me from being a politician. And rightly, as I think. For I am certain, O men of Athens, that if I had engaged in politics, I should have perished long ago, and done no good either to you or to myself. And do not be offended at my telling you the truth; for the truth is, that no man who goes to war with you or any other multitude, honestly striving against the many lawless and unrighteous deeds which are done in a State, will save his life; he who will fight for the right, if he would live even for a brief space, must have a private station and not a public one.

I can give you convincing evidence of what I say, not words only, but what you value far more—actions. Let me relate to you a passage of my own life which will prove to you that I should never have yielded to injustice from any fear of death and that "as I should have refused to yield" I must have died at once. I will tell you a tale of the courts, not very interesting perhaps, but nevertheless true. The only office of State which I ever held, O men of Athens, was that of senator: the tribe Antiochis, which is my tribe, had the presidency at the trial of the generals who had not taken up the bodies of the slain after the battle of Arginusae; and you proposed to try them in a body, contrary to law, as you all thought afterwards; but at the time I was the only one of the Prytanes who was opposed to the illegality, and I gave my vote against you; and when the orators threatened to impeach and arrest me, and you called and shouted, I made up my mind that I would run the risk, having law and justice with me, rather than take part in your injustice because I feared imprisonment and death. This happened in the days of the democracy. But when the oligarchy of the Thirty was in power, they sent for me and four others into the rotunda, and bade us bring Leon the Salaminian from Salamis, as they wanted to put him to death. This was a specimen of the sort of commands which they were always giving with the view of implicating as many as possible in their crimes; and then I showed, not in word only but in deed, that, if I may be allowed to use such an expression, I cared not a straw for death, and that my great and only care was lest I should do an unrighteous or unholy thing. For the strong arm of that oppressive power did not frighten me into doing wrong; and when we came out of the rotunda the other four went to Salamis and fetched Leon, but I went quietly home. For which I might have lost my life, had not the power of the Thirty shortly afterwards come to an end. And many will witness to my words.

Now, do you really imagine that I could have survived all these years, if I had led a public life, supposing that like a good man I had always maintained the right and had made justice, as I ought, the first thing? No, indeed, men of Athens, neither I nor any other man. But I have been always the same in all my actions, public as well as private, and never have I yielded any base compliance to those who are slanderously termed my disciples, or to any other. Not that I have any regular disciples. But if any one likes to come and hear me while I am pursuing my mission, whether he be young or old, he is not excluded. Nor do I converse only with those who pay; but any one, whether he be rich or poor, may ask and answer me and listen to my words; and whether he turns out to be a bad man or a good one, neither result can be justly imputed to me; for I never taught or professed to teach him anything. And if any one says that he has ever learned or heard anything from me in private which all the world has not heard, let me tell you that he is lying.

But I shall be asked, Why do people delight in continually conversing with you? I have told you already, Athenians, the whole truth about this matter: they like to hear the cross-examination of the pretenders to wisdom; there is amusement in it. Now, this duty of cross-examining other men has been imposed upon me by God; and has been signified to me by oracles, visions, and in every way in which the will of divine power was ever intimated to any one. This is true, O Athenians; or, if not true, would be soon refuted. If I am or have been corrupting the youth, those of them who are now grown up and have become sensible that I gave them bad advice in the days of their youth should come forward as accusers, and take their revenge; or if they do not like to come themselves, some of their relatives, fathers, brothers, or other kinsmen, should say what evil their families have suffered at my hands. Now is their time. Many of them I see in the court. There is Crito, who is of the same age of the same deme with myself, and there is Critobulus his son, whom I also see. Then again there is Lysanias of Sphettus, who is the father of Aeschines—he is present; and also there is Antiphon of Cephisus, who is the father of Epigenes; and there are the brothers of several who have associated with me. There is Nicostratus the son of Theosdotides, and the brother of Theodotus (now Theodotus himself is dead, and therefore he, at any rate, will not seek to stop him); and there is Paralus the son of Demodocus, who had a brother Theages; and Adeimantus the son of Ariston, whose brother Plato is present; and Aeantodorus, who is the brother of Appollodorus, whom I also see. I might mention a great many others, some of whom Meletus should have produced as witnesses in the course of his speech; and let him still produce them, if he has forgotten—I will make way for him. And let him say, if he has any testimony of the sort which he can produce. Nay, Athenians, the very opposite is the truth. For all these are ready to witness on behalf of the corrupter, of the injurer of their kindred, as Meletus and Anytus call me; not the corrupted youth only—there might have been a motive for that—but their uncorrupted elder relatives. Why should they too support me with their testimony? Why, indeed, except for the sake of truth and justice, and because they know that I am speaking the truth, and that Meletus is a liar.

Well, Athenians, this and the like of this is all the defence which I have to offer. Yet a word more. Perhaps there may be some one who is offended at me, when he calls to mind how he himself on a similar, or even a less serious occasion, prayed and entreated the judges with many tears, and how he produced his children in court, which was a moving spectacle, together with a host of relations and friends; whereas I, who am probably in danger of my life, will do none of these things. The contrast may occur to his mind, and he may be set against me, and vote in anger because he is displeased at me on this account. Now, if there be such a person among you,—mind, I do not say that there is,—to him I may fairly reply: My friend, I am a man, and like other men, a creature of flesh and blood, and not "of wood or stone," as Homer says; and I have a family, yes, and sons, O Athenians, three in number, one almost a man, and two others who are still young; and yet I will not bring any of them hither in order to petition you for an acquittal. And why not? Not from any self-assertion or want of respect for you. Whether I am or am not afraid of death is another question, of which I will not now speak. But, having regard to public opinion, I feel that such conduct would be discreditable to myself, and to you, and to the whole State. One who has reached my years, and who has a name for wisdom, ought not to demean himself. Whether this opinion of me be deserved or not, at any rate the world has decided that Socrates is in some way superior to other men. And if those among you who are said to be superior in wisdom and courage, and any other virtue, demean themselves in this way, how shameful is their conduct! I have seen men of reputation, when they have been condemned, behaving in the strangest manner: they seemed to fancy that they were going to suffer something dreadful if they died, and that they could be immortal if you only allowed them to live; and I think that such are a dishonour to the State, and that any stranger coming in would have said to them that the most eminent men of Athens, to whom the Athenians themselves give honour and command, are no better than women. And I say that these things ought not to be done by those of us who have a reputation; and if they are done, you ought not to permit them; you ought rather to show that you are far more disposed to condemn the man who gets up a doleful scene and makes the city ridiculous, than him who holds his peace.

But, setting aside the question of public opinion, there seems to be something wrong in asking a favour of a judge, and thus procuring an acquittal, instead of informing and convincing him. For his duty is, not to make a present of justice, but to give judgment; and he has sworn that he will judge according to the laws, and not according to his own good pleasure; and we ought not to encourage you, nor should you allow yourselves to be encouraged, in this habit of perjury—there can be no piety in that. Do not then require me to do what I consider dishonourable and impious and wrong, especially now, when I am being tried for impiety on the indictment of Meletus. For if, O men of Athens, by force of persuasion and entreaty I could overpower your oaths, then I should be teaching you to believe that there are no gods, and in defending should simply convict myself of the charge of not believing in them. But that is not so—far otherwise. For I do believe that there are gods, and in a sense higher than that in which any of my accusers believe in them. And to you and to God I commit my cause, to be determined by you as is best for you and me....

A majority of the jurors then found Socrates guilty: 281 votes against 220. The condemned man was allowed to propose a penalty in lieu of the death penalty proposed by Meletus. Socrates again spoke:

There are many reasons why I am not grieved, O men of Athens, at the vote of condemnation. I expected it, and am only surprised that the votes are so nearly equal; for I had thought that the majority against me would have been far larger; but now, had thirty votes gone over to the other side, I should have escaped Meletus. I may say more; for without the assistance of Anytus and Lycon, any one may see that he would not have had a fifth part of the votes, as the law requires, in which case he would have incurred a fine of a thousand drachmae.

And so he proposes death as the penalty. And what shall I propose on my part, O men of Athens? Clearly that which is my due. And what is my due? What returns shall be made to the man who has never had the wit to be idle during his whole life; but has been careless of what the many care for—wealth, and family interests, and military offices, and speaking in the assembly, and magistracies, and plots, and parties. Reflecting that

I was really too honest a man to be a politician and live, I did not go where I could do no good to you or to myself; but where I could do the greatest good privately to every one of you, thither I went, and sought to persuade every man among you that he must look to himself, and seek virtue and wisdom before he looks to his private interests, and look to the State before he looks to the interests of the State; and that this should be the order which he observes in all his actions. What shall be done to such an one? Doubtless some good thing, O men of Athens, if he has his reward; and the good should be of a kind suitable to him. What would be a reward suitable to a poor man who is your benefactor, and who desires leisure that he may instruct you? There can be no reward so fitting as maintenance in the Prytaneum, O men of Athens, a reward which he deserves far more than the citizen who has won the prize at Olympia in the horse or chariot race, whether the chariots were drawn by two horses or by many. For I am in want, and he has enough; and he only gives you the appearance of happiness, and I give you the reality. And if I am to estimate the penalty fairly, I should say that maintenance in the Prytaneum is the just return.

Perhaps you think that I am braving you in what I am saying now, as in what I said before about the tears and prayers. But this is not so. I speak rather because I am convinced that I never intentionally wronged any one, although I cannot convince you—the time has been too short; if there were a law at Athens, as there is in other cities, that a capital cause should not be decided in one day, then I believe that I should have convinced you. But I cannot in a moment refute great slanders; and, as I am convinced that I never wronged another, I will assuredly not wrong myself. I will not say of myself that I serve any evil, or propose any penalty. Why should I? Because I am afraid of the penalty of death which Meletus proposes? When I do not know whether death is a good or an evil, why should I propose a penalty which would certainly be an evil? Shall I say imprisonment? And why should I live in prison, and be the slave of the magistrate of the year—of the Eleven? Or shall the penalty be a fine, and imprisonment until the fine is paid? There is the same objection. I should have to lie in prison, for money I have none, and cannot pay. And if I say exile (and this may possibly be the penalty which you will affix), I must indeed be blinded by the love of life, if I am so irrational as to expect that when you, who are my own citizens, cannot endure my discourses and words, and have found them so grievous and odious that you will have no more of them, others are likely to endure me. No, indeed, men of

Athens, that is not very likely. And what a life should I lead, at my age, wandering from city to city, ever changing my place of exile, and always being driven out! For I am quite sure that wherever I go, there, as here, the young men will flock to me; and if I drive them away, their elders will drive me out at their request; and if I let them come, their fathers and friends will drive me out for their sakes.

Some one will say: Yes, Socrates, but cannot you hold your tongue, and then you may go into a foreign city, and no one will interfere with you? Now, I have great difficulty in making you understand my answer to this. For if I tell you that to do as you say would be a disobedience to the God, and therefore that I cannot hold my tongue, you will not believe that I am serious; and if I say again that daily to discourse about virtue, and of those other things about which you hear me examining myself and others, is the greatest good of man, and that **the unexamined life is not worth living,** you are still less likely to believe me. Yet I say what is true, although a thing of which it is hard for me to persuade you. Also, I have never been accustomed to think that I deserve to suffer any harm. Had I money I might have estimated the offence at what I was able to pay, and not have been much the worse. But I have none, and therefore I must ask you to proportion the fine to my means. Well, perhaps I could afford a mina, and therefore I propose that penalty: Plato, Crito, Critobulus, and Apollodorus, my friends here, bid me say thirty minae, and they will be the sureties. Let thirty minae be the penalty; for which sum they will be ample security to you....

Another vote was taken and the death penalty was passed. Socrates then made his final statement:

Not much time will be gained, O Athenians, in return for the evil name which you will get from the detractors of the city, who will say that you killed Socrates, a wise man; for they will call me wise, even although I am not wise, when they want to reproach you. If you had waited a little while, your desire would have been fulfilled in the course of nature. For I am far advanced in years, as you may perceive, and not far from death. I am speaking now not to all of you, but only to those who have condemned me to death. And I have another thing to say to them: You think that I was convicted because I had not words of the sort which would have procured my acquittal—I mean, if I had thought fit to leave nothing undone or unsaid. Not so; the deficiency which led to my conviction was not of words—certainly not. But I had not the boldness or impudence or inclination to address you as you would have liked me to do, weeping and wailing and lamenting, and saying and doing many things which you have been accustomed to hear from others, and which, as I maintain, are unworthy of me. I thought at the time that I ought not to do anything common or mean when in danger: nor do I now repent of the style of my defence; I would rather die having spoken after my manner, than speak in your manner and live. For neither in war nor yet at law ought I or any man to use every way of escaping death. Often in battle there can be no doubt that if a man will throw away his arms, and fall on his knees before his pursuers, he may escape death; and in other dangers there are other ways of escaping death, if a man is willing to say and do anything. The difficulty, my friends, is not to avoid death, but to avoid unrighteousness; for that runs faster than death. I am old and move slowly, and the slower runner has overtaken me, and my accusers are keen and quick, and the faster runner, who is unrighteousness, has overtaken them. And now I depart hence condemned by you to suffer the penalty of death, —they too go their ways condemned by the truth to suffer the penalty of villainy and wrong; and I must abide by my award—let them abide by my award—let them abide by theirs. I suppose that these things may be regarded as fated,—and I think that they are well.

And now, O men who have condemned me, I would fain prophesy to you; for I am about to die, and in the hour of death men are gifted with prophetic power. And I prophesy to you who are my murderers, that immediately after my departure punishment far heavier than you have inflicted on me will surely await you. Me you have killed because you wanted to escape the accuser, and not to give an account of your lives. But that will not be as you suppose: far otherwise. For I say that there will be more accusers of you than there are now; accusers whom hitherto I have restrained: and as they are younger they will be more inconsiderate with you, and you will be more offended at them. If you think that by killing men you can prevent some one from censuring your evil lives, you are mistaken; that is not a way of escape which is either possible or honorable; the easiest and the noblest way is not to be disabling others, but to be improving yourselves. This is the prophecy which I utter before my departure to the judges who have condemned me.

Friends, who would have acquitted me, I would like also to talk with you about the thing which has come to pass, while the magistrates are busy, and before I go to the place at which I must die. Stay then a little, for we may as well talk with one another while there is time. You are my friends, and I should like to show you the meaning of this event which has happened to me. O my judges—for you I may truly call judges—I should like to tell you a wonderful circumstance. Hitherto the divine faculty of which the internal oracle is the source has constantly been in the habit of opposing me even about trifles, if I was going to make a slip or error in any matter; and now as you see there has come upon me that which may be thought, and is generally believed to be, the last and worst evil. But the oracle made no sign of opposition, either when I was leaving my house in the morning, or when I was on my way to the court, or while I was speaking, at anything which I was going to say; and yet I have often been stopped in the middle of a speech, but now in nothing I either said or did touching the matter in hand has the oracle opposed me. What do I take to be the explanation of this silence? I will tell you. It is an intimation that what has happened to me is a good, and that those of us who think that death is an evil are in error. For the customary sign would surely have opposed me had I been going to evil and not to good.

Let us reflect in another way, and we shall see that there is great reason to hope that death is a good; for one of two things—either death is a state of nothingness and utter unconsciousness, or, as men say, there is a change and migration of the soul from this world to another. Now, if you suppose that there is no consciousness, but a sleep like the sleep of him who is undisturbed even by dreams, death will be an unspeakable gain. For if a person were to select the night in which his sleep was undisturbed even by dreams, and were to compare with this the other days and nights of his life, and then were to tell us how many days and nights he had passed in the course of his life better and more pleasantly than this one, I think that any man, I will not say a private man, but even the great king will not find many such days or nights, when compared with the others. Now, if death be of such a nature, I say that to die is gain; for eternity is then only a single night. But if death is the journey to another place, and there, as men say, all the dead abide, what good, O my friends and judges, can be greater than this? If, indeed, when the pilgrim arrives in the world below, he is delivered from the professors of justice in this world, and finds the true judges who are said to give judgment there, Minos and Rhadamanthus and Aeacus and Triptolemus, and other sons of God who were righteous in their own life, that pilgrimage will be worth making. What would not a man give if he might converse with Orpheus and

Musaeus and Hesiod and Homer? Nay, if this be true, let me die again and again. I myself, too, shall have a wonderful interest in there meeting and conversing with Palamedes, and Ajax the son of Telamon, and any other ancient hero who has suffered death through an unjust judgment; and there will be no small pleasure, as I think, in comparing my own sufferings with theirs. Above all, I shall then be able to continue my search into true and false knowledge; as in this world, so also in the next; and I shall find out who is wise, and who pretends to be wise, and is not. What would not a man give, O judges, to be able to examine the leader of the great Trojan expedition; or Odysseus or Sisyphus, or numberless others, men and women too! What infinite delight would there be in conversing with them and asking them questions! In another world they do not put a man to death for asking questions: assuredly not. For besides being happier than we are, they will be immortal, if what is said is true.

Wherefore, O judges, be of good cheer about death, and **know of a certainty, that no evil can happen to a good man, either in life or after death**. He and his are not neglected by the gods; nor has my own approaching end happened by mere chance. But I see clearly that the time had arrived when it was better for me to die and be released from trouble; wherefore the oracle gave no sign. For which reason, also, I am not angry with my condemners, or with my accusers; they have done me no harm, although they did not mean to do me any good; and for this I may gently blame them.

Still, I have a favour to ask of them. When my sons are grown up, I would ask you, O my friends, to punish them; and I would have you trouble them, as I have troubled you, if they seem to care about riches, or anything, more than about virtue; or if they pretend to be something when they are really nothing,—then reprove them, as I have reproved you, for not caring about that for which they ought to care, and thinking that they are something when they are really nothing. And if you do this, both I and my sons will have received justice at your hands.

The hour of departure has arrived, and we go our ways—I to die, and you to live. Which is better God only knows.

Life in the Woods

Henry David Thoreau

When I wrote the following pages, or rather the bulk of them, I lived alone, in the woods, a mile from any neighbour, in a house which I had built myself, on the shore of Walden Pond, in Concord, Massachusetts, and earned my living by the labour of my hands only. I lived there two years and two months. At present I am a sojourner in civilised life again.

I should not obtrude my affairs so much on the notice of my readers if very particular inquiries had not been made by my townsmen concerning my mode of life, which some would call impertinent, though they do not appear to me at all impertinent, but, considering the circumstances, very natural and pertinent. Some have asked what I got to eat; if I did not feel lonesome; if I was not afraid; and the like. Others have been curious to learn what portion of my income I devoted to charitable purposes; and some, who have large families, how many poor children I maintained. I will therefore ask those of my readers who feel no particular interest in me to pardon me if I undertake to answer some of these questions in this book. In most books, the *I*, or first person, is omitted; in this it will be retained; that, in respect to egotism, is the main difference. We commonly do not remember that it is, after all, always the first person that is speaking. I should not talk so much about myself if there were anybody else whom I knew as well. Unfortunately, I am confined to this theme by the narrowness of my experience. Moreover, I, on my side, require of every writer, first or last, a simple and sincere account of his own life, and not merely what he has heard of other men's lives; some such account as he would send to his kindred from a distant land; for if he has lived sincerely, it must have been in a distant land to me. Perhaps these pages are more particularly addressed to poor students. As for the rest of my readers, they will accept such portions as apply to them. I trust that none will stretch the seams in putting on the coat, for it may do good service to him whom it fits. . . .

Most men, even in this comparatively free country, through mere ignorance and mistake, are so occupied with the factitious cares and superfluously coarse labours of life that its finer fruits cannot be plucked by them. Their fingers, from excessive toil, are too clumsy and tremble too much for that. Actually, the labouring man has not leisure for a true integrity day by day; he cannot afford to sustain the manliest relations to men; his labour would be depreciated in the market. He has no time to be anything but a machine. How can he remember well his ignorance— which his growth requires —who has so often to use his knowledge? We should feed and clothe him gratuitously sometimes, and recruit him with our cordials, before we judge of him. The finest qualities of our nature, like the bloom on fruits, can be preserved only by the most delicate handling. Yet we do not treat ourselves nor one another thus tenderly. . . .

The mass of men lead lives of quiet desperation. What is called resignation is confirmed desperation. From the desperate city you go into the desperate country, and have to console yourself with the bravery of minks and muskrats. A stereotyped but unconscious despair is concealed even under what are called the games and amusements of mankind. There is no play in them, for this comes after work. But it is a characteristic of wisdom not to do desperate things.

When we consider what, to use the words of the catechism, is the chief end of man, and what are the true necessaries and means of life, it appears as if men had deliberately chosen the common mode of living because they preferred it to any other. Yet they honestly think there is no choice left. But alert and healthy natures remember that the sun rose clear. It is never too late to give up our prejudices. No way of thinking or doing, however ancient, can be trusted without proof. What everybody echoes or in silence passes by as true to-day may turn out to be falsehood to-morrow, mere smoke of opinion, which some had trusted for a cloud that would sprinkle fertilising rain on their fields. What old people say you cannot do you try and find that you can. Old deeds for old people, and new deeds for new. Old people did not know enough once, perchance, to fetch fuel to keep the fire a-going; new people put a little dry wood under a pot, and are whirled round the globe with the speed of birds, in a way to kill old people, as the phrase is. Age is no better, hardly so well, qualified for an instructor as youth, for it has not profited so much as it has lost. One may almost doubt if the wisest man has learned anything of absolute value by living. Practically, the old have no very important advice to give the young, their own experience has been so partial, and their lives have been such miserable failures, for private reasons, as they must believe; and it may be that they have some faith left which belies that experience, and they are only less young than they were. I have lived some thirty years on this planet, and I have yet to hear the first syllable of valuable or even earnest advice from my seniors. They have told me nothing, and probably cannot tell me anything, to the purpose. Here is life, an experiment to a great extent untried by me; but it does not avail me that they have tried it. If I have any experience which I think valuable, I am sure to reflect that this my Mentors said nothing about. . . .

The greater part of what my neighbours call good I believe in my soul to be bad, and if I repent of anything, it is very likely to be my good behaviour. What demon possessed me that I behaved so well? You may say the wisest thing you can, old man,—you who have lived seventy years, not without honour of a kind, —I hear an irresistible voice which invites me away from all that. One generation abandons the enterprises of another like stranded vessels.

I think that we may safely trust a good deal more than we do. We may waive just so much care of ourselves as we honestly bestow elsewhere. Nature is as well adapted to our weakness as to our strength. The incessant anxiety and strain of some is a well-nigh incurable form of disease. We are made to exaggerate the importance of what work we do; and yet how much is not done by us! or, what if we had been taken sick? How vigilant we are! determined not to live by faith if we can avoid it; all the day long on the alert, at night we unwillingly say our prayers and commit ourselves to uncertainties. So thoroughly and sincerely are we compelled to live, reverencing our life, and denying the possibility of change. This is the only way, we say; but there are as many ways as there can be drawn radii from one centre. All change is a miracle to contemplate; but it is a miracle which is taking place every instant. Confucius said, "To know that we know what we know, and that we do not know what we do not know, that is true knowledge." When one man has reduced a fact of the imagination to be a fact to his understanding, I foresee that all men will at length establish their lives on that basis.

Let us consider for a moment what most of the trouble and anxiety which I have referred to is about, and how much it is necessary that we be troubled, or at least, careful. It would be some advantage to live a primitive and frontier life, though in the midst of an outward civilisation, if only to learn what are the gross necessaries of life and what methods have been taken to obtain them; or even to look over the old day-books of the merchants, to see what it was that the men most commonly bought at the stores, what they stored, that is, what are the grossest groceries. For the improvements of ages have had but little influence on the essential laws of man's existence: as our skeletons, probably, are not to be distinguished from those of our ancestors.

By the words, *necessary of life,* I mean whatever, of all that man obtains by his own exertions, has been from the first, or from long use has become, so important to human life that few, if any, whether from savageness, or poverty, or philosophy, ever attempt to do without it. To many creatures there is in this sense but one necessary of life—Food. To the bison of the prairie it is a few inches of palatable grass, with water to drink; unless he seeks the Shelter of the forest or the mountain's shadow. None of the brute creation requires more than Food and Shelter. The necessaries of life for man in this climate may, accurately enough, be distributed under the several heads of Food, Shelter, Clothing, and Fuel; for not till we have secured these are we prepared to entertain the true problems of life with freedom and a prospect of success. Man has invented, not only houses, but clothes and cooked food; and possibly from the accidental discovery of the warmth of fire, and the consequent use of it, at first a luxury, arose the present necessity to sit by it. We observe cats and dogs acquiring the same second nature....

Most of the luxuries, and many of the so-called comforts of life, are not only indispensable, but positive hindrances to the elevation of mankind. With respect to luxuries and comforts, the wisest have ever lived a more simple and meagre life than the poor. The ancient philosophers, Chinese, Hindoo, Persian, and Greek, were a class than which none has been poorer in outward riches, none so rich in inward. We know not much about them. It is remarkable that *we* know so much of them as we do. The same is true of the more modern reformers and benefactors of their race. None can be an impartial or wise observer of human life but from the vantage ground of what *we* should call voluntary poverty. Of a life of luxury the fruit is luxury, whether in agriculture, or commerce, or literature, or art. There are nowadays professors of philosophy, but not philosophers. Yet it is admirable to profess because it was once admirable to live. To be a philosopher is not merely to have subtle thoughts, nor even to found a school, but so to love wisdom as to live according to its dictates, a life of simplicity, independence, magnanimity, and trust. It is to solve some of the problems of life, not only theoretically, but practically....

When first I took up my abode in the woods, that is, began to spend my nights as well as days there, which, by accident, was on Independence

Day, on the 4th of July, 1845, my house was not finished for winter, but was merely a defence against the rain, without plastering or chimney, the walls being of rough weatherstained boards, with wide chinks, which made it cool at night. The upright white hewn studs and freshly planed door and window-casings gave it a clean and airy look, especially in the morning, when its timbers were saturated with dew, so that I fancied that by noon some sweet gum would exude from them. To my imagination it retained throughout the day more or less of this auroral character, reminding me of a certain house on a mountain which I had visited the year before. This was an airy, an unplastered cabin, fit to entertain a travelling god, and where a goddess might trail her garments. The winds which passed over my dwelling were such as sweep over the ridges of mountains, bearing the broken strains, or celestial parts, only, of terrestrial music. The morning wind forever blows, the poem of creation is uninterrupted; but few are the ears that hear it. Olympus is but the outside of the earth everywhere. . . .

I was seated by the shore of a small pond, about a mile and a half south of the village of Concord and somewhat higher than it, in the midst of an extensive wood between that town and Lincoln, and about two miles south of that our only field known to fame, Concord battle ground; but I was so low in the woods that the opposite shore, half a mile off, like the rest, covered with wood, was my most distant horizon. For the first week, whenever I looked out on the pond, it impressed me like a tarn high up on the one side of a mountain, its bottom far above the surface of other lakes, and, as the sun arose, I saw it throwing off its nightly clothing of mist, and here and there, by degrees, its soft ripples or its smooth reflecting surface was revealed, while the mists, like ghosts, were stealthily withdrawing in every direction into the woods, as at the breaking up of some nocturnal conventicle. The very dew seemed to hang upon the trees later into the day than usual, as on the sides of mountains. . . .

I went to the woods because I wished to live deliberately, to front only the essential facts of life, and see if I could not learn what it had to teach, and not, when I came to die, discover that I had not lived. I did not wish to live what was not life, living is so dear; nor did I wish to practice resignation, unless it was quite necessary. I wanted to live deep and suck out all the marrow of life, to live so sturdily and Spartan-like as to put to rout all that was not life, to cut a broad swath and shave close, to drive life into a corner, and reduce it to its lowest terms, and, if it proved to be mean, why then to get the whole and genuine meanness of it, and publish its meanness to the world; or if it were sublime, to know it by experience, and be able to give a true account of it in my next excursion. For most men, it appears to me, are in a strange uncertainty about it, whether it is of the devil or of God, and have *somewhat hastily* concluded that it is the chief end of man here to "glorify God and enjoy Him forever."

Still we live meanly, like ants; though the fable tells us that we were long ago changed into men; like pygmies we fight with cranes; it is error upon error, and clout upon clout, and our best virtue has for its occasion a superfluous and evitable wretchedness. Our life is frittered away by detail. An honest man has hardly need to count more than his ten fingers, or in extreme cases he may add his ten toes, and lump the rest. Simplicity, simplicity, simplicity! I say, let your affairs be as two or three, and not a hundred or a thousand; instead of a million count half-a-dozen, and keep your accounts on your thumb-nail. In the midst of this chopping sea of civilised life, such are the clouds and storms and quicksands and thousand-and-one items to be allowed for, that a man has to live, if he would not founder and go to the bottom and not make his port at all, by dead reckoning, and he must be a great calculator indeed who succeeds. Simplify, simplify. Instead of three meals a-day, if it be necessary eat but one; instead of a hundred dishes, five; and reduce other things in proportion. . . .

Every morning was a cheerful invitation to make my life of equal simplicity, and I may say innocence, with Nature herself. I have been as sincere a worshipper of Aurora as the Greeks. I got up early and bathed in the pond: that was a religious exercise, and one of the best things which I did. They say that characters were engraved on the bathing tub of king Tching-thang to this effect: "Renew thyself completely each day; do it again, and again, and forever again." I can understand that. Morning brings back the heroic ages. I was as much affected by the faint hum of a mosquito making its invisible and unimaginable tour through my apartment at earliest dawn, when I was sitting with door and windows open, as I could be by any trumpet that ever sang of fame. . . . All poets and heroes, like Memnon, are the children of Aurora, and emit their music at sunrise. To him whose elastic and vigorous thought keeps pace with the sun, the day is a perpetual morning. It matters not what the clocks say or the attitudes and labours of men. Morning is when I am awake and there is a dawn in me. Moral reform is the effort to throw off sleep. Why is it that men give so poor an account of their day if they have not been slumbering? They are not such poor calculators. If they had not been overcome with drowsiness they would have performed something. The millions are awake enough for physical labour; but only one in a million is awake enough for effective intellectual exertion, only one in a hundred million to a poetic or divine life. To be awake is to be alive. I have never yet met a man who was quite awake. How could I have looked him in the face?

We must learn to reawaken and keep ourselves awake, not by mechanical aids, but by an infinite expectation of the dawn, which does not forsake us in our soundest sleep. I know of no more encouraging fact than the unquestionable ability of man to elevate his life by a conscious endeavour. It is something to be able to paint a particular picture, or to carve a statue, and so to make a few objects beautiful; but it is far more glorious to carve and paint the very atmosphere and medium through which we look, which morally we can do. To affect the quality of the day, that is the highest of arts. Every man is tasked to make his life, even in its details, worthy of the contemplation of his most elevated and critical hour. . . .

Let us spend one day as deliberately as Nature, and not be thrown off the track by every nutshell and mosquito's wing that falls on the rails. Let us rise early and fast, or break fast, gently and without perturbation; let company come and let company go, let the bells ring and the children cry,—determined to make a day of it. . . . Let us settle ourselves, and work and wedge our feet downward through the mud and slush of opinion, and prejudice, and tradition, and delusion, and appearance, that alluvion which covers the globe, through Paris and London, through New York and Boston and Concord, through church and state, through poetry and philosophy and religion, till we come to a hard bottom and rocks in place, which we can call *reality*, and say, This is, and no mistake; and then begin, having a *point d'appui*, below freshet and frost and fire, a place where you might found a wall or a state, or set a lamp-post safely, or perhaps a gauge, not a Nilometer, but a Realometer, that future ages might know how deep a freshet of shams and appearances had gathered from time to time. If you stand right fronting and face to face to a fact, you will see the sun glimmer on both its surfaces, as if it were a cimeter, and feel its sweet edge dividing you through the heart and marrow, and so you will happily conclude your mortal career. Be it life or death, we crave only reality. If we are really dying, let us hear the rattle in our throats and feel cold in the extremities; if we are alive, let us go about our business.

Time is but the stream I go a-fishing in. I drink at it; but while I drink I see the sandy bottom and detect how shallow it is. Its thin current slides away, but eternity remains. I would drink deeper; fish in the sky, whose bottom is pebbly with stars. I cannot count one. I know not the first letter of the alphabet. I have always been regretting that I was not as wise as the day I was born. The intellect is a cleaver; it discerns and rifts its way into the secret of things. I do not wish to be any more busy with my hands than is necessary. My head is hands and feet. I feel all my best faculties concentrated in it. My instinct tells me that my head is an organ for burrowing, as some creatures use their snout and forepaws, and with it I would mine and burrow my way through these hills. I think that the richest vein is somewhere hereabouts; so by the divining rod and thin rising vapours I judge; and here I will begin to mine. . . .

If one listens to the faintest but constant suggestions of his genius, which are certainly true, he sees not to what extremes, or even insanity, it may lead him; and yet that way, as he grows more resolute and faithful, his road lies. The faintest assured objection which one healthy man feels will at length prevail over the arguments and customs of mankind. No man ever followed his genius till it misled him. Though the result were bodily weakness, yet perhaps no one can say that the consequences were to be regretted, for these were a life of conformity to higher principles. If the day and the night are such that you greet them with joy, and life emits a fragrance like flowers and sweet scented herbs, is more elastic, more starry, more immortal,—that is your success. All nature is your congratulation, and you have cause momentarily to bless yourself. The greatest gains and values are farthest from being appreciated. We easily come to doubt if they exist. We soon forget them. They are the highest reality. Perhaps the facts most astounding and most real are never communicated by man to man. The true harvest of my daily life is somewhat as intangible and indescribable as the tints of morning or evening. It is a little star-dust caught, a segment of the rainbow which I have clutched. . . .

I left the woods for as good a reason as I went there. Perhaps it seemed to me that I had several more lives to live, and could not spare any more time for that one. It is remarkable how easily and insensibly we fall into a particular route, and make a beaten track for ourselves. I had not lived there a week before my feet wore a path from my door to the pondside; and though it is five or six years since I trod it, it is still quite distinct. It is true I fear that others may have fallen into it, and so helped to keep it open. The surface of the earth is soft and impressible by the feet of men; and so with the paths which the mind travels. How worn and dusty, then, must be the highways of the world—how deep the ruts of tradition and conformity! I did not wish to take a cabin passage, but rather to go before the mast and on the deck of the world, for there I could best see the moonlight amid the mountains. I do not wish to go below now.

I learned this, at least, by my experiment: that if one advances confidently in the direction of his dreams, and endeavours to live the life which he has imagined, he will meet with a success unexpected in common hours. He will put some things behind, will pass an invisible boundary; new, universal, and more liberal laws will begin to establish themselves around and within him; or the old laws be expanded, and interpreted in his favour in a more liberal sense, and he will live with the license of a higher order of beings. In proportion as he simplifies his life, the laws of the universe will appear less complex, and solitude will not be solitude, nor poverty poverty, nor weakness weakness. If you have built castles in the air, your work need not be lost; that is where they should be. Now put the foundations under them.

Feminism, Feelings, and Philosophy

Morwenna Griffiths

Women are more emotional than men, or such is the commonly held belief in present day Western society. But is the belief true? And does it matter? The answers are not easy ones to find because the meaning of the statement is so unclear. It might mean, for instance, that women are less in control of their emotions, or it might mean that they feel things more deeply, or that they are more irrational than men. None of these statements necessarily implies any of the rest—though they often come as a package. Indeed, the statement that women are more emotional than men has no clear meaning. However, it has a considerable political force because it is used to justify or explain the position of women. The usual justification/explanation runs: since women are more emotional they are less suited to public life. But this is not the only possible political use of the statement. It has been taken up recently by some feminists and used in celebration of women's values and as a criticism of men and their personal, moral, or social arrangements. In other words, feminists have stood the argument on its head. It now goes: since men are so unemotional, they are unfit to run public life.

Feminist writing questions and challenges the assumption that emotion, feeling, nature, and bodies are in opposition to rationality, mind, and freedom, such that the relationship between them is one of hierarchical control. This challenge is implicit in a wide variety of feminist concerns. Feminism is not monolithic and feminists do not all speak with one voice. It is all the more striking then that the different concerns expressed in feminist writing and the variety of different voices which make themselves heard, all point, time and again, in a similar direction with regard to emotion and reason.

Quite rightly, women have not begun their criticism of masculinism with the abstract categories found useful to describe masculine viewpoints. They have begun with the concrete and particular, for instance, rape, depression, abortion, pay. Out of these concrete, particular concerns, abstractions are generated. One which keeps recurring is the close relationship between feelings and thought, emotion and reason, mind and body, and the need to break down current dualism in thinking about them. An extension of all this is the kind of relationship we perceive ourselves to have with the rest of the natural world, and the damage that is done to us and to it if that relationship is misconceived. How these concerns are theorised varies. But however deep the differences they are focused on a shared concern, that of the fundamental significance of feeling.... The production of feminist knowledge is grounded in feeling. So far from feelings being seen as mere subjectivity, something to be overcome in the search for objectivity, they are seen to be a source of knowledge. The knowledge gained is distorted, however, unless power relations deriving from personality, race, class, etc., are acknowledged and allowed for. All of this can be seen directly in the theory and practice of the activity known as "consciousness-raising" in which feelings are the subject matter, and their expression is a means of arriving at the truth, a truth about public, political life rather than about individual personalities. Feelings and their expression are likely to be a part of the process of obtaining rational objective knowledge, rather than being a hindrance to it.

Further, **truth and knowledge become distorted when feelings are not acknowledged.** Most seriously, one way in which distortion has occurred is in the conceptualisation of truth and knowledge themselves. Evelyn Fox Keller has discussed this process for science. She argues that the kinds of rational objectivity and technical control taken to be constitutive of science are distortions introduced by unacknowledged and unexamined myths of masculinity which have their roots in typically masculine ways of feeling and which pervade scientific thought.

• • •

Feminist views on feeling constitute a significant criticism of much mainstream Western philosophy of mind, and . . . these criticisms need to be taken into account if a better understanding of ourselves, both men and women, is to be reached. I have been summarising the way in which feminist writing implicitly questions and challenges assumptions about feeling and its relationship to reason, bodies and objectivity, assumptions which have been widely accepted in modern Western societies and by modern Western philosophers. I shall focus on three ways in which feminist writing challenges these assumptions. . . .

The first two criticisms are to do with the concepts used to describe people and the third is to do with the focus of attention. The first criticism is that human beings have been discussed in terms of just the two categories of mind and body (or of embodied minds), so feelings and emotions have been thought to be some uneasy mixture of the two. Secondly, the relationship between mind and body (and feelings where they have been noticed at all) has been thought to be one of hierarchical control. Thirdly, the contradictions inherent in this view of people as embodied minds remain unnoticed because feelings have largely been ignored in philosophical discussions. If feelings were taken more seriously as feminism suggests they should be, the view would be harder to maintain.

The first implied criticism that arises from feminist views is that the conceptualisation of human beings has generally been into just two categories. This criticism seems justified. Philosophy of mind has been dominated by considerations of minds as rational, reasonable, reasoning or, sometimes, rationalising. Philosophers also notice bodies, but they have little to say about feeling or emotions as a separate category. This lack of attention can be obscured by the way it is sometimes simply assumed that feelings and emotions are of the body or of the mind.

This dualism is particularly obvious in the analytical tradition where one of the famous, and intractable, problems in philosophy of mind is the "mind-body" problem, that is, the problematic nature of the relationship of minds to bodies. In this respect it is not much of an exaggeration to say that philosophy is less a series of footnotes to Plato than a series of footnotes to Descartes, whom Mary Daly calls "modern philosophy's severed head." Many contemporary philosophers now find themselves thinking of an even more disembodied phenomenon, the "brain in a vat." It is true that the similarity is disguised. In analytical philosophy the language has changed from Descartes's pineal gland, corporeal and thinking substances to neurons, intentional objects and physical matter, or to the metaphors of computer programs, software and hardware. . . . Of course, I do not want to suggest that any particular details of Descartes's system are accepted by those philosophers who try to solve the "mind-body" problem: my point here is that Descartes set the terms in which the discussion is conducted.

Descartes paid some attention to feelings and emotions, trying to fit them into the structure of his philosophy. In his book, *The Passions of the Soul*, Descartes begins by noting that the passions affect and are affected by both soul and body. He defines the passions of the soul as:

> The perceptions, feelings, or emotions of the soul which we relate specially to it, and which are caused, maintained, and fortified by some movement of the spirits. (Art. 27)

The "spirits" are "animal spirits," i.e. of the body. He continues:

> Of all the kinds of thought which it [the soul] may have, there are no others which so powerfully agitate and disturb it as do these passions. (Art. 28)

He is making clear that the passions are not a perception of an outside object like sound, scent or colour, nor of a state of body like hunger, thirst or pain, but neither are they a pure activity of the soul, because the most proximate cause is the spirits. He seems unable to sustain this initial position within the framework of his dualism. By the end of his account he is describing a split between *intellectual* emotions and *bodily* ones. For instance, he distinguishes the passion "joy" from purely intellectual "joy." The latter has an obscure relationship with the body. He says:

> It is true that while the soul is united to the body this intellectual joy can hardly fail to be accompanied by that which is passion. (Art. 91)

But he does not explain what is meant by the phrase "can hardly fail to." In effect he abandoned his original definition but did not replace it with another. Feelings and emotions do not fit easily into a two-category system consisting of mind and body, and Descartes failed to solve the problem of making them do so.

Descartes's dualism has been much criticised. Many writers on emotions and feelings begin by criticising him. They declare themselves to be in reaction against him. It is striking though that these critics end up by adopting a very similar solution to Descartes to the problems of fitting feelings and emotions into the philosophy of mind. It is rare nowadays in philosophical circles for emotions to be thought of as pure physical prompting of the body. More often, emotions are defined as "intentional," that is, of the mind. Feelings are then contrasted with them and are said to be of the body. We end up with emotions (of the mind, rational) contrasted with feelings (of the body, natural).

• • •

Hofstadter and Dennett say succinctly:

> Emotions are an automatic by-product of the ability to think. They are implied by the nature of thought.

In this dualist conception of the mind, it is this insistence that emotions are of the mind that make them rational. Since to be rational is to have choice and to be free, it then becomes clear that in so far as emotions are rational they are under the control of reason. They are contrasted with "feelings," which being of the body are not reasonable, but like the rest of the physical world can be controlled indirectly by the exercise of intelligence.

Beginning with the assumptions that bodies and minds are the only fundamental categories and that they are separate and different, the Cartesian solution is not a surprising one. There are other solutions. For instance, if emotions and feelings are taken to be of the body, the controlling relationship may be reversed, and the rational mind controlled by the bodily promptings of feelings. However, none of these dualist solutions are satisfactory. Feelings and emotions do not fit comfortably into a twofold division. This is true both of the "bodily feelings" and of the "mental emotions." The feelings of sexuality and hunger, for instance, are dependent on understanding as well as on physical promptings. The emotions of fear, love, ambition and pride have associated feeling as well as judgment, and it is not at all clear that all of them are rational. And even if all this were resolved, a whole range of other psychological terms associated with feeling such as mood and character are left unaccounted for and unexplained. These problems have been noted by a number of commentators but they remain unresolved.

My first criticism of philosophy of mind, a criticism which is implicit in feminist writing, was that human beings have been wrongly described in terms of minds and bodies only. It is clear from the above summary that the second criticism, that the relationship between them is taken to be one of hierarchical control, appears to be justified too. . . .

I turn now to the third criticism, that feelings have largely been ignored as a focus of attention in philosophy. The question as to why feelings and emotions are not taken to be of much significance is an interesting one. Feeling and emotion present intractable problems to arguments that assume minds and bodies to be the only categories necessary to describe human beings, so it would seem that they should attract attention. They do not. Broadly speaking, feelings are ignored as a serious topic of discussion. . . .

An adequate account of emotion has to take into consideration the process by which feelings come into being, the process by which our feelings become human feelings. To say that our feelings are human feelings is to draw attention to the fact, on the one hand, that they will be different from those of other species simply because of our different genetic inheritance. On the other hand, they will reflect the way human beings create themselves through their social interactions. That is, we have to take into account the history of an individual, and the time and place in which she lives her life. A snapshot of one instant in her life is insufficient to give any depth of understanding. To say this is firstly to emphasis both "nature" and "culture" rather than one at the expense of the other, and secondly to look at whole lives. The suggestion that I am making here about human feelings depends on both of these.

It is common enough to discuss either social relationships or genetically given feelings as constrained by each other, but this is usually done with respect to adults. By contrast, I begin by looking at the development of the individual from babyhood, and this makes my account significantly different. The feelings of newborn babies may be genetically given, but from the moment of birth they interact with the understandings and perceptions of the growing baby. Until they do so they are not fully human—but human feelings develop out of the feelings of babies. The process of coming to have human feelings comes about as a result of the interactions of those not yet quite human feelings inherent in human babies with the knowledge, understanding, perceptions and beliefs that people develop as a result of growing up and living in the world. As these feelings interact and reinteract with all the other understandings and perceptions of the individual, new feelings are formed which may be only partly conscious. That is, they are intelligent and the result of intelligence, but they are not necessarily susceptible to cool calculation. In sum, coming to have human feelings involves the understanding of the individual agent: the feelings are her own feelings. But they are not hers quite independently of the rest of the world. The feelings she has also depend on the kinds of understanding available to her: she lives her life in specific historical and geographical circumstances. Finally, they depend on the physical ground of her being: she has a human body.

The account I have outlined has implications for our understanding of how people conduct themselves. Rather than fill in the outline I shall describe some of the claims that follow from it. If the account is right, it suggests *both* that human understanding and actions are essential to human feelings and *also* that human feelings are essential to human understanding and actions. The first of these two claims is easy to see, I think, given what I have said about learning and feelings. A few examples may help to make it clear. Depression about the arms race, fear of going into debt, love of landscape, and the pain of losing a friend are all examples of human feelings that are dependent on being born a human being but that are incomprehensible without human understanding. In nonhumans depression, fear, love, or the pain of losing a friend may be as sharply felt but must be significantly different.

My claim that understanding is essential to feelings applies to all feelings, not only to those feelings that are sometimes called emotions. In particular, it is true of those feelings that are often called sensations. Pain, hunger, and tiredness all vary with the meaning they have to the individual experiencing them. This conclusion gets support from medical descriptions and psychological research into pain in which there is evidence that pain varies with the meaning it has to the sufferer. The pain of battle wounds, the pain of amputated limbs, the pain of torture or the pain of an infection are not explicable only in terms of physiology—though they are not independent of physiology either. . . .

The process I am describing is dialectical. Our feelings prompt the articulation of our beliefs about the world, and the pattern of conceptualisation of it. They reflect both factual and evaluative judgments. The articulations are learnt in social interactions. But the articulation also molds the feelings. The process is a continuing one which is why an ahistorical snapshot approach, looking at feelings at just one particular moment, must be distorting.

If the foregoing is correct, it is evident that people's feelings are not simply private and individual. They could not be anything other than social. This follows from the fact that the understandings which help determine feelings are shared in a large part with other groups of people. Understanding about the world depends on access to information about it, and to experiences within it. It also depends, of course, on sharing public language with others.

One particularly influential effect is the social world. The understandings and therefore the feelings of people are systematically related to the person's position in society. An obvious example here is class. People who share a class position will share a particular set of viewpoints, that is, have easy access to certain information and language in which to discuss it. Of course, there are many factors influencing anyone's point of view and they may intersect in a variety of ways. Nothing I have said suggests that points of view are entailed by class position, only that they are influenced by it.

Similarly, human understandings and feelings are systematically related to differences in biology, in so far as human beings have different biologies. A clear example here is that of age. The different ways of understanding and acting available to different age groups affect their feelings about the world. Children the world over share feelings unavailable to their grandparents, and, possibly, vice versa.

Both of the factors I have described, the effect of society and the effect of biology, combine to make feelings gender-related. The understandings and perceptions available to females are different from those available to males. Males and females are treated differently from each other and perceive themselves differently. Physiological differences, such as menstruation, pregnancy and the menopause in women, and erections and ejaculation in men, will also give the two sexes different understandings and feelings about the world.

The argument that physiological differences are likely to remain significant in the lives of future generations should not be taken as implying that "biology is destiny." For instance, at present, it is often argued that the facts of pregnancy and lactation imply that women ought to care for young infants. The opposite implications could be drawn just as straightforwardly, with the significance of the sex difference being kept. The argument could run: women have to take the responsibility of nine months of pregnancy, and, moreover, are in some danger during childbirth. It follows, in the name of justice, if for no other reason, that men should take primary responsibility for the infant.

• • •

Trying to explain adult human beings as though they are embodiments of rational understanding is a futile activity. The feelings of adults cannot be understood in terms of brute sensations acted upon by rational thoughts. Nor can emotions be understood as by-products of thought, independent of human sensations or bodies. An altogether more complex model is needed. The one I have suggested is an interactive one in which feelings and emotions have to be understood in terms of the history of an individual's life, and in terms of the social context in which that life is lived. Clearly, if this suggestion is right, the concepts of rationality and of mind would change accordingly.

Following from this is another implication for philosophy, that feelings are a source of knowledge and should be treated seriously as such since both need to be taken into account in coming to understand the world. In effect, feelings are a route to truth: they both provide us with our beliefs about the world and also provide a basis for assessing these beliefs. Control of feelings and emotions by the rational mind is a wrong understanding of how human beings ought to conduct themselves. In other words, a rational agent is required to attend to and reflect on feelings, not to attempt to control them, except in so far as a rearticulation of feelings might be appropriate in the light of reflection. The complex interactions of feelings in ourselves are open to reflection and change. One part does not dominate the other. We must be "in harmony with" our feelings, rather than "in control of" them.

There are implications for feminist theory as well as for philosophy. The idea that we can shrug off our patriarchal straitjackets and find our presocial selves is misleading. It is particularly misleading, over the way sexism relates to the issues of class and race. The model I have gestured at in this article helps to explain why feminists must take account of class and race. It shows how the issue of sex/gender is similar to them and also why it is different because it is rooted in physiology.

Philosophical Thinking in India, China, and Japan

Michael C. Brannigan

India

The people of India are no strangers to suffering, and philosophical activity is born of suffering. In this past year alone, floods have left millions of her inhabitants homeless and a devastating earthquake has claimed the lives of over 30,000 people. As seen throughout her history, a sense of pathos continues to fill India's landscape. And in this setting, ultimate questions are inevitably raised. Given the inherent condition of suffering, does existence have a purpose, and if so, what is it? More specifically, what is the meaning and purpose of my life? Who am I? Is freedom from suffering possible? If so, how? What is the ideal of life? How can I attain it? An awareness of the tragic sense of life stimulates such questions.

These questions have produced two of the world's most prominent philosophical traditions: Hindu and Buddhist. In both systems, philosophical activity originates from an elementary dissatisfaction with the human condition. Both traditions address issues of meaning, purpose, and salvation. Within the context of this inquiry into liberation from suffering, we find three characteristic traits in Indian philosophy:

- It aims to discover our true nature.
- It is transformative.
- It is religious.

Finding Our True Nature

Philosophy in India is essentially concerned with self-deliverance. This quest for deliverance is intimately bound up with the discovery of our true nature. For example, the aim in Hindu thought is to achieve enlightenment, or *moksha*. And the experience of enlightenment comes about only with the realization of our true identity. For the Buddhist, liberation is called nirvana. Nirvana occurs when we realize our true nature. Therefore, in Indian philosophy, salvation and self-discovery are intimately linked with each other.

The whole of Indian thought, whether Hindu or Buddhist, centers around the task of self-discovery. This can properly occur only when our total personality is involved. Self-awakening transcends the confining boundaries of a pure intellectual pursuit and demands a complete engagement. There are many references in Hindu and Buddhist thought that warn us against relying too heavily upon the intellect for self-realization. Hindu and Buddhist theories of knowledge unceasingly emphasize the inherent limits to our ordinary ways of knowing.

Questioning Transforms the Questioner

This leads us to our second assertion: Indian philosophy is essentially transformative. It naturally transforms us because we are engaged in this radical questioning concerning our liberation and self-discovery. These questions are radical because they intimately and ultimately involve who we are in essence.

In this respect, the goal and the process are not separate, and self-transformation occurs in the act of questioning. This is why philosophical activity exercises more than just the intellect. Philosophy is not simply a way of thinking, but, more importantly, a way of being. It involves not just a search for truth, but a *life* of truth. At the same time, because it originates from a basic dissatisfaction with the human condition, it inspires a way of life that is profoundly concerned with deliverance. It is precisely this salvific intent of philosophy that makes it so deeply religious.

Philosophy as a Religious Activity

From all of this we see that philosophy in India bears a strongly religious character. By this we mean religion in its more fundamental senses:

- distinguishing the sacred from the profane
- pointing to a higher and deeper reality behind appearances
- showing a way to personal salvation

Philosophy and religion in India share these major elements. First, they partake of the same goal of salvation. They each seek both a genuine liberation from the transitory and freedom from suffering. Second, this salvific intent involves a deep excursion into one's innermost being. True freedom can only be accompanied by an authentic quest for self. Third, within this quest, the individual undergoes various degrees of transformation.

An example of the religious nature of Indian philosophy lies in the teachings of the philosopher Sankara. Although multitudes were drawn to his teachings, he specified a number of guidelines for those desiring to study under him:

1. They must be able to distinguish the abiding from the fleeting.
2. They must have a degree of detachment from this world (and any other world), knowing that all worlds are transitory.
3. They must have already cultivated such virtues as poise, truthfulness, and so on.
4. They must have a strong desire for liberation from the wheel of life.[1]

All of this has nothing to do with unquestioning allegiance to a set of creeds. Instead, it portrays a liberating profile of the philosophical-religious quest, a quest that is most intimate.

In Western cultures, religion and philosophy have developed into separate disciplines, as evidenced in colleges and universities, where they exist as separate departments. Even though many Indian thinkers acknowledge this distinction, they also maintain that, in essence, they are interdependent.

The religious character of Indian philosophy does not preclude its own philosophical rigor. Indeed, some Hindu schools of philosophy, such as Nyaya, combine logical subtlety and conceptual analyses. Yet, their investigations are conducted in light of achieving the inseparable goals of insight and liberation. Despite its many intricacies and varieties, Indian philosophy possesses a unique unitive aspect. All the different schools of thought are bound together in the common search for deliverance in and through insight into one's true identity. Indian philosophy pursues this quest through a radical questioning that transforms the questioner in the very process of examining the question.

Wisdom as Knowledge and Compassion

To conclude, let us examine the meaning of *darshana*, the closest equivalent to "philosophy" in Sanskrit. *Darshana* means a type of "seeing" or "viewing." It refers to both the activity of having a point of view and the outlook itself. In any case, *darshana* does not mean an absolute or totally comprehensive way of knowing.

What is interesting to note within our present context is that this "point of view" that we assume is not simply an intellectual, academic exercise. It exacts our full involvement in the act of perceiving. *Darshana*, "seeing," is more than an intellectualization, which in itself is only one type of seeing. Philosophical activity demands seeing with the heart as well as with the mind. This harmony of mind and heart constitutes the pulse of wisdom.

This kind of seeing incorporates two key terms: *prajna* and *karuna*. *Prajna* refers to the intellectual basis of wisdom. In this respect, it can mean knowledge. *Karuna*, on the other hand, means "love" or "compassion." True intelligence is wisdom and comprises a synthesis of knowledge and compassion. True wisdom is the harmony of mind and heart. This is beautifully portrayed in the Buddhist ideal of the *bodhisattva*. The *bodhisattva* represents one who has attained "awakening," or "enlightenment" and dedicates his or her life to sharing this wisdom with others. This ideal epitomizes the union of *prajna* and *karuna*.

China

Within the intellectual climate of China, three major streams of thought have nurtured the historical, cultural, and social life of its peoples: Taoism, Confucianism, and Buddhism. However, as with India, an assessment of Chinese philosophical activity remains limited if we confine ourselves within our own Western perspectives. To begin with, consider the Chinese language and its worldview.

In Chinese, characters replace the alphabet used by most other languages. These characters are ideographic representations within an experiential context. Therefore, the language lacks grammatical precision.

As for worldview, events are essentially viewed by the Chinese as interconnected phenomena. Each person and every activity is influenced by the harmonious working together of Heaven and Earth. Heaven and Earth are not diametrically separate realities. Material existence is infused with a profound spirituality. There is no natural versus supernatural, no spiritual opposed to physical, no divine in contrast to human. Rather, a principle of harmony, a confluence of apparent contrasts, characterizes existence. There is this balance between the two primordial and enduring forces of yin and yang. This vision of harmony provides a setting with which to examine the nature of philosophical activity.

In order to grasp the nature of Chinese philosophy, we need to understand it within this context of language and worldview. In this fashion, we discover that philosophy, religion, culture, and politics all interact. For instance, not only were many Chinese philosophers scholars and teachers, but they were actively involved socially and politically. The total cultural and intellectual milieu of Chinese thought reveals an intimate rapport between philosophy and its actualization in society.

Harmony: Intuition and Reason

All this leads us to one of the most vital aspects of Chinese philosophical activity: its attempt to achieve a harmonious balance between reason and intuition. We are not claiming that intuition is stressed in China at the expense of rationality or logic. Chinese philosophy does exhibit various degrees of analytic sophistication. **The key idea in Chinese philosophical thought, however, is harmony**—harmony between reason and feeling, between rationality and intuition.

For example, let us look at the relationship between Taoism and Confucianism. They have often been viewed as opposing schools of thought. Indeed, they differ with respect to emphases and styles of teaching. Taoism, the earlier of the two, emphasizes our rapport with nature and highlights our intuitive faculties. On the other hand, Confucianism stresses our relationship within the social fabric. It seeks to sustain communal harmony, and it heralds reason.

Despite these differences, they generally represent two complementary aspects within human nature. Complementarity, in this sense, allows for disagreement and even conflict. Although there are points upon which Taoism and Confucianism are at odds, they emphasize different paths to the essential goal of harmony. Taken as a whole, they produce a more unified picture. Taoism reflects our most personal and intuitive aspect, assuming our essential oneness with nature. Taoism thereby appeals to the deepest forces within us. It addresses this question: How can we live in harmony with ourselves and with nature? On the other hand, Confucianism represents our more social and reasonable character and addresses the reality of our collective existence. It asks the question: How can we properly live in harmony with others?

The fundamental point is this: Their complementarity reflects the needed balance between a more personally creative and a socially ordered lifestyle. The Chinese sage incorporates both in a creative symmetry. Chinese philosophy, therefore, does not exaggerate the importance of reason and intellect; nor does it overemphasize the level of feelings or intuition. As a whole, Chinese thought, as manifested in Taoism and Confucianism, seeks a synthesis of both intuition and reason, and its goal is harmony.

How to Be Truly Human: Moral Cultivation

The Chinese quest for harmony encompasses the need for self-cultivation. Self-cultivation and moral development, or the "rectification of the heart," work together. This is most apparent in Confucian thought, whose goal is attaining full humanness, called *jen. Jen* is considered the highest virtue, the essence of moral cultivation. For the Confucian, the person is involved in the cardinal task of learning how to be truly human.

What does this mean in Confucian terms? As indicated above, the attainment of full humanness comes about only when we achieve an interior balance. Learning to become human calls for a harmony of the two dimensions of self and other. On the other hand, for Taoists, being fully human requires an inner harmony and oneness with nature. Thus Taoists and Confucians define what it means to be human in different ways. Nevertheless, for both, harmony is essential. Let us look further at some Confucian ideas.

Harmony: Self and Other

Confucians view the self as the center of a nexus of connections of family, friends, society, and state. These connections, viewed as a series of concentric circles, define the self. And, particularly because the self is at the center of these relationships, the evolving of that same self in turn affects those various relations. In other words, the individual self and the social self interact in a way in which each defines the other.

This inherent reciprocity of self and other is illustrated by the Confucian teaching of the Five Cardinal Relationships. These associations are the concentric circles that define the self of the person (as well as the self of the community). They concern the ties between the following people:

- son and father
- government official and ruler
- younger brother and elder brother
- friends and friends
- wife and husband

Self-cultivation is necessarily a communal affair.

Sagehood

In Chinese philosophy, our various goals—harmony, inner peace, learning to be fully human, moral cultivation, external harmony—are all closely linked. All are steps in the process of achieving "sagehood." The Chinese believe that we bear the potential for sagehood. It is primarily a matter of developing a seed that has always been within us. Generally, the Chinese have a wonderfully optimistic view of human nature. All of us, no matter what our status, have the capacities to become sages.

Japan

Tokyo and Kyoto symbolize two contrasting images in modern Japan. A highly advanced technology has overtaken Tokyo, one of the world's business capitals. Meanwhile, Kyoto sustains the presence of tradition with its temples and other monuments of Japan's past. Japan remains a conspicuous example of a meeting between the forces of modernization and the spirit of tradition.

In view of this, how does this affect Japanese thought and philosophy? In order to address this question, we must have a clear understanding of what we mean by Japanese "philosophy." This incurs a special difficulty in trying to comprehend what may well be one of the most puzzling of cultures. Yet our attempt at understanding is certainly timely in light of our trade relations with Japan.

Japanese thought has often been viewed as being essentially unphilosophical in both nature and expression. Some scholars have felt that, with few exceptions, Japanese thought has lacked any strict philosophical foundations. Is this true? This text shows that there is, in fact, a strong philosophical tradition in Japanese thinking. Yet Japanese philosophy, as well as religion, is understood in a unique way. As with India and China, Japanese "philosophy" cannot be viewed solely according to Western philosophical categories.

Language and Philosophical Thinking

The Japanese written language possesses some features that appear to make it less conducive to logical and abstract thought: It is immediate, emotive, and relational. These three traits typify Japanese philosophical activity and provide a foundation for establishing the way of thinking for the Japanese. Because these qualities make abstract, analytic expression and thought all the more difficult, philosophical activity in general is approached in a different way. Let us look at each aspect.

Immediacy

When we claim that the Japanese language possesses immediacy, we refer to its ability to encapsulate a particular experience with a minimum of rationalization about that same experience. The idea is to express a specific situation or event in its unanalyzed, immediate form. A recent film by the renown director Akira Kurasawa, entitled *Ran*, depicts this tendency through its protagonist, the aging king Hidetora. Betrayed by one of his sons and trapped within a castle, his entire entourage is destroyed. He miraculously survives the devastation and roams the countryside for some days, encountering visions and voices. Upon being discovered by his loyal retainers, his immediate response is *"samui."* *Samui* literally means "cold," and it encapsulates the entirety of his experience with the least amount of reflection and analysis. Here, a single word becomes a lens through which to view a particular experience. Too much reflection and analysis dilutes the meaning of the experience.

It is this trait of immediacy that partly accounts for a diminished emphasis on formal logical analysis in Japan as a substructure for philosophic expression. This seems strange in light of Japan's highly developed interest in mathematics. And this is especially remarkable given their sophistication in computer technology. After all, both mathematics and computers share a logical foundation. This compels us to hold that although a formal system of logic has not developed as such in Japan, it still has its own "logical" way of thinking.

Much of Japanese philosophy stresses the importance of immediacy and direct experience. This means the simple, direct encounter with reality. "To the things themselves" is a common Japanese expression. To illustrate, Zen Buddhism, though imported from China (Ch'an Buddhism), is uniquely Japanese and stresses the primacy of the immediate, prereflective, "pure" experience. The main reason for its appeal to Japanese is probably its emphasis on the primacy of the experience. When Zen first came to Japan, it found favor with both monks and samurai. The samurai especially found it to be a unique method for mental discipline. Often confronted with life-and-death situations, the samurai could learn to practice their swordsmanship without interference from the thinking mind. Zen instructs us to go straight to the experience itself.

Emotiveness

Another peculiarity of the Japanese language is that its expressions are often primarily emotive in character. The vocabulary is richly laden with expressions of sensitivity. Rational analysis is secondary to capturing the emotions that naturally flow in and through a given experience.

The Japanese language originated from the Chinese, and it was systematized after the third century. Terms such as *risei* ("reason") were not part of the original language structure. The same holds true for *gainen*, which means "concept." These terms were absent from the original system because the original vocabulary tended to emphasize feelings and emotions. The original characters were less conducive for indicating abstract, philosophical concepts.

To illustrate, here are the Japanese *kanji* (Chinese characters) for "love" and "hate." They demonstrate this emotive orientation inherent in the language. "Love" is represented by combining the characters for "woman," [女] and "child," [子]. The result is [女子]. On the other hand, "hate" is represented as the "increasing," [曽], of one's "heart" or "state of mind," [忄]. It is written as [憎].

Relationality

Probably the most unique characteristic of the Japanese language lies in its expression of relationships. Ideas, feelings, and objects are depicted in light of their connections with other ideas, feelings, and objects. This perfectly accords with the Japanese view of reality in which all things act and interact in relationship with each other.

For example, the use of certain pronouns in speech depends on their specific context, within which the Japanese have time-honored rules of propriety. Respect for one's superiors—whether they are parents, grandparents, teachers, the company boss, and so on—expresses itself in the forms of speech elicited through the use of certain pronouns. It is important to remember that for the Japanese there is no clear conception of the individual as *individual*. After the introduction of Western logic, the term *kobutsu* ("individual") was coined. Nevertheless, the individual is still defined within the web of human relationships.

This is often depicted in regular sentence structures in which the subject of the sentence is often omitted, for an emphasis on the subject could convey the idea of an independent, objective individual being. The subject is often omitted to indicate further that there is no sharp delineation between the subject and the predicate, between the actor and the act. This will become clearer when we more closely examine Japanese Buddhist philosophy.

This expression of relationality is clearly illustrated through many of its *kanji*. The character [月] sometimes takes on the meaning of "flesh" or "part of the body." By doubling this same character, "companion" comes about, [月月]. Here we have a literal notion of the idea of relationality. The character for "elder brother" takes a bit more imagination. If we place the "mouth," [口] over the pair of "human legs," [儿], then we have the symbol for the sibling in the family who traditionally has the last say, [兄]. The Chinese depicted the "woman" as pregnant with her arms outstretched, as in comforting. The Japanese adopted this more simplistically as [母]. A good example of relationship lies in the character for "peace," which is represented by a "woman," [女], under a "roof" of a house, [宀]. Thus "peace," [安] occurs with the comforting, nurturing mother within the home.

In all this we see the strong link between linguistic expression and thought. And this carries itself into philosophical activity. It is clear that the structure of the Japanese language is such that it inhibits the expression of logical, abstract thinking. Yet, from the start, we need to use caution in applying a Western philosophical frame of reference to assess non-Western patterns of thought. It is quite the case that the Japanese do think philosophically in their own fashion. And **their philosophy is typified by its concern for immediacy, sensitivity, and relationship**. As we will see, the intellectual and cultural history of the Japanese conveys a unique philosophical tradition centering around these traits.

Note

[1] This is mentioned in Troy Wilson Organ, *Western Approaches to Eastern Philosophy* (Athens, Ohio: Ohio University Press, 1975), 21.

Is There an African Philosophy?

Innocent Onyewuenyi

In conversation with professors and students in America who knew I was teaching African philosophy, the question always put to me was: Are there African philosophers and what have they written? I have not heard or read of any. In other words, if there are no known academic philosophers in Africa, then there is no African philosophy.

Remember that I am in no way conceding that there are no academic philosophers in Africa. There are several of them, but their accounts were purposely withheld from history of philosophy books.... When they are mentioned they are grouped with Greco-Oriental philosophers. Little do some of us know that Plotinus, who wrote works on philosophy and opened a school in Rome, was from Lycon in Egypt. He made an attempt to travel to Persia and India to study their philosophies, but the expedition failed. Little do some of us know that the first woman philosopher, Hypatia, was from Alexandria and was murdered by Christians. Names like St. Augustine, Origen, Cyril, and Tertulian are not unfamiliar; they are black Africans. More pertinent to our subject is the fact that what today we call Greek or Western philosophy is copied from indigenous African philosophy of the "Mystery System." All the values of the mystery system were adopted by the Greeks and Ionians who came to Egypt to study; or studied elsewhere under Egyptian-trained teachers. These included Herodotus, Socrates, Hypocrates, Anaxagoras, Plato, Aristotle, and others. Are we not taught that Socrates is the first man to say "Man know thyself?" Yet, this expression was found commonly inscribed on Egyptian temple doors centuries before Socrates was born. Aristotle not only received his education in Africa, but he took over an entire library of works belonging to the Egyptian mystery system when he entered Egypt with Alexander the Great, after which we hear of the Corpus Aristotelium. Plato's alleged Theory of Ideas is borrowed from Egypt. Parmenides's references to "charioteers" and "winged steeds" were already dramatized in the *Judgement Scene* of the Egyptian *Book of the Dead*.

One would have to read *The Stolen Legacy* by George G. M. James to get some idea of the apprenticeship of the so-called Greek philosophers under Egyptian Mystery Priests. From his reading of Herodotus, Pliny,

Diogenes Laertius, and early historians of philosophy, James noted about Pythagoras: "We are also further informed through Herodotus and Pliny, that after severe trials, including circumcision, had been imposed upon him by Egyptian priests, he was finally initiated into all their secrets. That he learnt the doctrine of metempsychosis, of which there was no trace before in the Greek religion; that his knowledge of medicine and strict system of diethetics rules, distinguished him as a product of Egypt . . . and that his attainment in geometry corresponded with the ascertained fact that Egypt was the birth place of that science."[1]

A contemporary African author, Willie E. Abraham, in his *Mind of Africa*, gives an account of a Ghanaian philosopher by the name Amo Anton, born near Axim about the year 1700. He went to Holland, entered the University of Thalle and in 1729 publicly defended his dissertation. He moved on to Wittenberg, and while Kant was still a boy, became Master of Philosophy there. In 1734 he defended a work in which he argued that sensation was not a mental faculty. (Amo was a rationalist philosopher after Leibniz, whom as a boy he met at the Duke of Brunswick's.) His performance was greatly praised. And the chairman and faculty members described him as a most noble and renowned man from Africa, extraordinarily honest, diligent, and so erudite that he stood above his mates. In 1738 he produced his magnum opus, a book on logic, theory of knowledge and metaphysics.[2]

There were philosophers in the university towns of Timbucktu and Jene in West Africa who wrote works on the subject. Basil Davidson quotes the historian Leo Africanus, who wrote around 1520 concerning African scholars in the Mali and Songhai empires, "By the sixteenth century, West African writers were at work on historical, legal, moral and religious subjects."[3] Alexis Kagame has written on the concept of being among the Ruanda-Urundis. Adesany Adebayo has written on Yoruba metaphysical thinking. Placide Tempels sketched the worldview and ethics of the Congo. Joseph B. Danquah in Ghana did extensive work on the concept of God among the Akans.

Philosophizing: A Universal Experience

Be that as it may, my contention is that the philosophy of a people has little or nothing to do with the academic exponents of that philosophy. **Philosophizing is a universal experience. Every culture has its own worldview.** If you study the history of philosophy, you will find there is no agreement on the definition of philosophy. Some say it is the love of wisdom, others, the search for truth, and still others, the sense of wonder. What is generally agreed about philosophy is that it seeks to establish order among the various phenomena of the surrounding world, and it traces their unity by reducing them to their simplest elements. What are these various phenomena? They are things, facts, events, an intelligible world, an ethical world, and a metaphysical world.

These various phenomena of the surrounding world are the same in all cultures and societies. The themes dealt with in philosophy are universal. How each culture traces the unity of these themes, synthesizes, or organizes them into a totality is based on each culture's concept of life, namely the interrelationship between objects and persons and between persons and persons themselves. Hence it is that the order or unity the people of a culture establish is their own order relative to their own conception of life in which everything around them becomes meaningful. No culture has *the* order or *the* last word. Hence the establishment of various truths of a spontaneous, logical, ethical, aesthetical, and metaphysical nature, not one of them being of absolute or universal validity.

This is the basis for calling a philosophy European, Asian, Indian, or American. If what we have said is true, we can and should talk of African philosophy, because the African culture has its own way of establishing order. It has its own view of life. And "life" according to Dilthey, is the starting point of philosophy. Georg Misch summarizes him thus: "Dilthey regarded 'life' as the starting point of philosophy; life as actually lived and embodied or 'objectified' in the spiritual world we live in. Life, according to Dilthey, is a subject for scientific investigation insofar as history and moral philosophy or the human sciences deal with it; but our knowledge of life is, above all, contained in certain cultural or personal views of the world—which plays a prominent part in philosophy as well as in religion and poetry."[4]

Hegel underscored the cultural and relative aspect of philosophy when he said: "But men do not at certain epochs merely philosophize in general. For there is a definite philosophy which arises among a people and the definite character which permeates all the other historical sides of the Spirit of the people, which is most intimately related to them, and which constitutes their foundation. The particular form of a philosophy is thus contemporaneous with a particular constitution of the people amongst whom it makes its appearance, with their institutions and forms of government, their morality, their social life and their capabilities, customs and enjoyments of the same."[5] The notion of philosophy itself for Hegel, as can be deduced from his words, is a factor in the life history of the human experience of the individual mind and is subject to the conditions of race, culture, and civilization. A further support to the issue of philosophical relativity was given by Victor Uchendu in his monograph *The Igbo of Southeast Nigeria*. He said, "To know how a people view the world around them is to understand how they evaluate life, and a people's evaluation of life, both temporal and non-temporal, provides them with a 'charter' of action, a guide to Behaviour."[6]

The African has an unwritten timeless code of behavior and attitudes which have persisted for centuries. The condition for the possibility of this, its explanation, lies in the presence of a corpus of coordinated mental or intellectual concepts. Placide Tempels puts it better: "Behaviour can be neither universal nor permanent unless it is based upon a concatenation of ideas, a logical system of thought, a complete positive philosophy of the universe, of man and of the things which surround him, of existence, life, death and the life beyond."[7]

Having shown that there can be and there certainly is an African philosophy, I now expose the content of this philosophy as briefly as possible. We are going to treat the core areas of philosophy, any philosophy—namely, metaphysics or ontology, epistemology, and ethics.

African Metaphysics or Ontology

Henry Alpern in his *March of Philosophy* said: "Metaphysics by the very definition that it is a study of reality, of that which does not appear to our senses, of truth in the absolute sense, is the groundwork of any theory concerning all phases of human behavior. David Hume, whom no one can charge of shutting his eyes to experience, said that metaphysics is necessary for art, morality, religion, economics, sociology; for the abstract sciences, as well as for every branch of human endeavour considered from the practical angle. It is the foundation upon which one builds one's career consciously and unconsciously; it is the guide; the author of the human interests; upon its truth or falsity depends what type of man you may develop into."[8]

The ideas from this quotation explain adequately the singular and unique importance of African ontology in the overall treatment and understanding of African philosophy. In recent decades, studies that were made of the scientific, religious, and practical human endeavor of Africans have accepted their foundation as consisting in ancestor worship, animism, totemism, and magic. These are only vague ideas, because no well-founded definitions of animism, totemism, and magic have been laid down, and the roots of these conceptions have not been explored. The root is in the fundamental concept of African ontology. When we understand this ontology, the concepts of magic, ancestor worship, totemism, and sorcery, as ethnologists apply them to Africa, become ridiculous if not foolish.

What then is ontology? It is the science of "being as such," "the reality that is." The metaphysics of Western philosophy has generally been based upon a static conception of being. In the African philosophical thought, being is dynamic. Existence-in-relation sums up the African conception of life and reality. The African does not separate being from force as its attribute. Rather "the Africans speak, act, live, as if for them beings were forces. . . . Force, for them, is the nature of being, force is being, being is force." When you say, in terms of Western philosophy, that beings are differentiated by their essences or nature; Africans say that forces differ in their essences or nature. There is the divine force, terrestrial or celestial forces, human forces, and vegetable and even mineral forces.[9] When Western metaphysics defines "being" as "that which is" or "the thing insofar as it is," the African definition reads: "that which is force," or "an existent force." God of course is the Great Force. There is a hierarchy of forces starting from God, spirits, founding fathers, the dead, according to the order of primogeniture; then the living according to their rank in terms of seniority. After living men come animals, vegetables, and minerals, which are in turn categorized on their relative importance in their own classes.

The Interaction Forces: One Being Influences Another

The concept of separate beings, of substances, to use a scholastic term, which exist side by side, independent one of another, is foreign to African thought.[10] I might add parenthetically that I am not so sure that this concept of separate substances might not be the ontological basis for so much individualism and personal freedom in the Western world. The African thought holds that created beings preserve a bond one with another, an intimate ontological relationship. There is interaction of being with being, that is to say of force with force. This is more so among rational beings known as *Muntu*, a term which includes the living and the dead, Orishas, and God. *Muntu* is a force endowed with intelligence, a force which has control over irrational creatures known as *bintu*. Because of this ontological relationship among beings, the African knows and feels himself to be in intimate and personal relationship with other forces acting above or below him in the hierarchy of forces. "The human being, apart from the ontological hierarchy and interaction of forces, has no existence in the conception of the Bantu."[11] So much for the ontology—sketchy though it may be.

African Epistemology or Theory of Knowledge

Theory of knowledge follows closely upon ontology. The view adopted by the African theory of knowledge is consonant with its metaphysics. Knowledge or wisdom for the African consists in how deeply he understands the nature of forces and their interaction. "True wisdom," Tempels tells us, "lies in ontological knowledge; it is the intelligence of forces, of their hierarchy, their cohesion and their interaction."[12] We said earlier that God is Force; God is also wisdom in that He knows all forces, their ordering, their dependence, their potential, and their mutual interaction. A person is said to know or have wisdom inasmuch as he approaches divine wisdom. One approaches divine knowledge when one's flesh becomes less fleshy, to use Léopold Senghor's expression, that is, the older a person gets, the more wisdom he has. The same note of hierarchy comes into play here. The ancestors have more wisdom, followed by the elders, dead or living.

Distinction must be made here of the two levels of human intelligence. Intelligence can be either *practical* or *habitual*. Practical intelligence is cleverness, slyness in dealing with the contingent aspects of forces. Habitual intelligence is active knowledge of the nature of forces, their relationship. And this includes how man, the being with intelligence, makes use of things and activates the forces asleep in them. This kind of wisdom is different from book knowledge, which is not regarded as wisdom in the strict traditional sense. "Study and personal search for knowledge does not give wisdom. One can learn to read, to write; but all that has nothing in common with 'wisdom.' It gives no ontological knowledge of the nature of beings. There are many talents and clever skills that remain far short of wisdom."[13] Having a college degree does not qualify an African as a wise person in the community. This in part explains why there has been confusion in Africa since the colonial era, because the colonial administrators regarded the educated as the wise people, and consequently and arbitrarily appointed them legislators and leaders in the community, contrary to African political philosophy, which took the eldest of the community, to be, by divine law, the repository of wisdom and the link between God, the ancestors, and the living. He is divine. Swailem Sidhom in his article, "The Theological Estimate of Man" lamented the state of things when he said: "Power is conceived by the

African as something pertaining to the divine. Hence it cannot be placed into unexercised hands. But the hands are rarely exercised nowadays. Scheduled education has replaced experience and has toppled the accepted standards. Seniority of age does not mean much anymore, and a father may now be instructed by the child of his bowels. Nevertheless, power is dangerous and it kills. Like a live coal from upon the very altar of God, it can only be cared for by those who have been graduated into maturity."[14] This despair is understandable if you grasp the African's conception of existence and his philosophy of vital forces.

African Ethical Theory

Some foreign observers of the African scene have declared that the African has no sense of sin. An example is Edwin Smith, who said in his *African Ideas of God*: "It would seem that in general Africans are not conscious of any direct relation between their theism and their ethic of dynamism."[15] Others maintain that Africans have but a vague idea of the Supreme Being, that he always keeps his distance and does not associate himself with the daily lives of men. All these and more are mere prejudices. The Nigerian writer, E. Adeolu Adegbola, said about African morality: "Everywhere African morality is hinged on many sanctions. But the most fundamental sanction is the fact that God's all-seeing eyes scan the total area of human behaviour and personal relationships. God is spoken of as having eyes all over like a sieve."[16] Placide Tempels, who questioned Africans closely on this point, informs us that, "the influence of God in the daily life of man is recognized in many African proverbs and sayings. . . ."[17] He says that such authors, as I mentioned above, are speaking under the influence of Western moral theory, according to which the social order is mere conformity with conventionalized behavior. On the contrary, African morality and moral law are filled with fixed beliefs, unshakable principles held from conviction. They surely know the distinction between good and evil. They refer to moral evil as "stinking"; they feel it deeply in their spirit.

The norms of good and evil are objective and of universal validity; no room for subjectivism or solipsism and situation ethics. African ethical truths are not relative. Except for cases of ignorance, there are little or no mitigating circumstances.

The root of their knowledge of good and evil is bound up with their philosophy. The Africans see a relationship between morality and the ontological order. Everything is associated and coordinated under the all-embracing unity of "vital force." In his judgment of his conduct the African takes into consideration the fact that he is not alone; that he is a cog in a wheel of interacting forces. He knows that the most important thing in his action is not how it affects him personally, but how it affects the world order, the spiritual republic, outside of which he does not exist as a *Muntu*, outside of which he is a planet off its orbit, meaningless and nonexisting. His life is not his own in a selfish manner. It belongs to God. The strengthening of this life and its preservation are in the hands of his ancestors and elders. In the life of the community each person has his place and each has his right to well-being and happiness. Therefore, what to do and what to avoid in order to preserve, increase, and strengthen vital force in himself and others of his clan constitute morality. "Objective morality to the Bantu is ontological, immanent and intrinsic morality. Bantu moral standards depend essentially on things ontologically understood."[18]

It follows that an act will be accounted ethically good if it can be judged ontologically good and by deduction be assessed as juridically just. The same idea is introduced by Plato in the *Republic*. The individual Greek citizen is to interpret an action good or evil, not in reference to selfish interests, but in reference to the community of which he is a part. The African ethical theory is what I would like to call metaphysical ethics in one sense and ethical communalism in another sense—where an individual takes into consideration the community of vital forces in deciding the goodness or evil of his proper actions.

Human positive or customary laws are made in reference to the growth or preservation of *Muntu*'s vital force; otherwise they are meaningless. All customary law that is worthy of the name is inspired, animated, and justified from the African's point of view, by the philosophy of living forces, or growth, of influence, and of the vital hierarchy. The validity and strength of the customary law of indigenous peoples reside in its foundation in their philosophy. This is why we say in African ethical theory that an act which is characterized as ontologically good "will therefore be accounted *ethically good*; and at length, be assessed as *juridically just*."[19] "In contrast to the European sense of justice, which measures liability by material damage, it is according to African philosophy the loss in force, in joy of life that is evaluated, independently of material considerations."[20]

Conclusion

The rediscovery of African philosophy has influenced African scholars in writing about African personality or what the French-speaking Africans call Negritude. Kwame Nkrumah, Julius Nyerere, Léopold Senghor, Aimé Césaire, Nnamdi Azikiwe, and Chinua Achebe have written prose and verse to celebrate this philosophy—a philosophy of unity and complete encounter of all things and beings, which by reason of the dynamic character of African ontology, has surfaced on the communal structure of our society based on the division of labor and rights; in which man attains growth and recognition by how well he fulfills a function for the overall well-being of the community. We African's have not yet yielded to the subtlety (and I pray we shall never) which would allow our traditional lawmakers and judges to design customary laws divorced from our philosophy, from the nature of beings, as we understand them, and from our view of the world.

Notes

[1] James, *The Stolen Legacy* (New, York, 1954), p. 43.
[2] Abraham, *The Mind of Africa* (Chicago, 1966), p. 129.
[3] Davidson, *A History of West Africa* (New York, 1966), p. 166.
[4] Misch, *The Dawn of Philosophy* (London, 1950), p. 47.
[5] Hegel, *Lectures on the History of Philosophy* (London, 1968), 1: 53.
[6] Uchendu, *The Igbo of Southeast Nigeria* (New York, 1965), p. 12.
[7] Tempels, *Bantu Philosophy* (Paris: Présence Africaine, 1969), p. 19.
[8] Alpern, *The March of Philosophy* (New York, 1934), p. 99.
[9] Tempels, *Bantu Philosophy*, pp. 51 and 52.
[10] Ibid., p. 58.
[11] Ibid., p. 104.
[12] Ibid., p. 73.
[13] Ibid., p. 74.
[14] Sidhom, "The Theological Estimate of Man," in *Biblical Revelation and African Beliefs*, ed. Kwesi Dickinson (London, 1969), p. 115.
[15] Smith, *African Ideas of God* (London, 1950), p. 22.
[16] Dickinson, *Biblical Revelation*, p. 116.
[17] Tempels, *Bantu Philosophy*, p. 117.
[18] Ibid., p. 121.
[19] Ibid.
[20] Janheinz Jahn, *Muntu: An Outline of the New African Culture* (New York, 1961), p. 117.

The Value of Philosophy

Bertrand Russell

Having now come to the end of our brief and very incomplete review of the problems of philosophy, it will be well to consider, in conclusion, what is the value of philosophy and why it ought to be studied. It is the more necessary to consider this question, in view of the fact that many men, under the influence of science or of practical affairs, are inclined to doubt whether philosophy is anything better than innocent but useless trifling, hair-splitting distinctions, and controversies on matters concerning which knowledge is impossible.

This view of philosophy appears to result, partly from a wrong conception of the ends of life, partly from a wrong conception of the kind of goods which philosophy strives to achieve. Physical science, through the medium of inventions, is useful to innumerable people who are wholly ignorant of it; thus the study of physical science is to be recommended, not only, or primarily, because of the effect on mankind in general. This utility does not belong to philosophy. If the study of philosophy has any value at all for others than students of philosophy, it must be only indirectly, through its effects upon the lives of those who study it. It is in these effects, therefore, if anywhere, that the value of philosophy must be primarily sought.

But further, if we are not to fail in our endeavour to determine the value of philosophy, we must first free our minds from the prejudices of what are wrongly called "practical" men. The "practical" man, as this word is often used, is one who recognizes only material needs, who realizes that men must have food for the body, but is oblivious of the necessity of providing food for the mind. If all men were well off, if poverty and disease had been reduced to their lowest possible point, there would still remain much to be done to produce a valuable society; and even in the existing world the goods of the mind are at least as important as the goods of the body. It is exclusively among the goods of the mind that the value of philosophy is to be found; and only those who are not indifferent to these goods can be persuaded that the study of philosophy is not a waste of time.

Philosophy, like all other studies, aims primarily at knowledge. The knowledge it aims at is the kind of knowledge which gives unity and system to the body of the sciences, and the kind which results from a critical examination of the grounds of our convictions, prejudices, and beliefs. But it cannot be maintained that philosophy has had any very great measure of success in its attempts to provide definite answers to its questions. If you ask a mathematician, a mineralogist, a historian, or any other man of learning, what definite body of truths has been ascertained by his science, his answer will last as long as you are willing to listen. But if you put the same question to a philosopher, he will, if he is candid, have to confess that his study has not achieved positive results such as have been achieved by other sciences. It is true that this is partly accounted for by the fact that, as soon as definite knowledge concerning any subject becomes possible, this subject ceases to be called philosophy, and becomes a separate science. The whole study of the heavens, which now belongs to astronomy, was once included in philosophy; Newton's great work was called "the mathematical principles of natural philosophy." Similarly, the study of the human mind, which was, until very lately, a part of philosophy, has now been separated from philosophy and has become the science of psychology. Thus, to a great extent, the uncertainty of philosophy is more apparent than real: those questions which are already capable of definite answers are placed in the sciences, while those only to which, at present, no definite answer can be given, remain to form the residue which is called philosophy.

This is, however, only a part of the truth concerning the uncertainty of philosophy. There are many questions—and among them those that are of the profoundest interest to our spiritual life—which, so far as we can see, must remain insoluble to the human intellect unless its powers become of quite a different order from what they are now. Has the universe any unity of plan or purpose, or is it a fortuitous concourse of atoms? Is consciousness a permanent part of the universe, giving hope of indefinite growth in wisdom, or is it a transitory accident on a small planet on which life must ultimately become impossible? Are good and evil of importance to the universe or only to man? Such questions are asked by philosophy, and variously answered by various philosophers. But it would seem that, whether answers be otherwise discoverable or not, the answers suggested by philosophy are none of them demonstrably true. Yet, however slight may be the hope of discovering an answer, it is part of the business of philosophy to continue the consideration of such questions, to make us aware of their importance, to examine all the approaches to them, and to keep alive that speculative interest in the universe which is apt to be killed by confining ourselves to definitely ascertainable knowledge.

Many philosophers, it is true, have held that philosophy could establish the truth of certain answers to such fundamental questions. They have supposed that what is of most importance in religious beliefs could be proved by strict demonstration to be true. In order to judge of such attempts, it is necessary to take a survey of human knowledge, and to form an opinion as to its methods and its limitations. On such a subject it would be unwise to pronounce dogmatically; but if the investigations of our previous chapters have not led us astray, we shall be compelled to renounce the hope of finding philosophical proofs of religious beliefs. We cannot, therefore, include as part of the value of philosophy any definite set of answers to such questions. Hence, once more, the value of philosophy must not depend upon any supposed body of definitely ascertainable knowledge to be acquired by those who study it.

The value of philosophy is, in fact, to be sought largely in its very uncertainty. The man who has no tincture of philosophy goes through life imprisoned in the prejudices derived from common sense, from the habitual beliefs of his age or his nation, and from convictions which have grown up in his mind without the co-operation or consent of his deliberate reason. To such a man the world tends to become definite, finite, obvious; common objects rouse no questions, and unfamiliar possibilities are contemptuously rejected. As soon as we begin to philosophise, on the contrary, we find, as we saw in our opening chapters, that even the most everyday things lead to problems to which only very incomplete answers can be given. Philosophy, though unable to tell us with certainty what is the true answer to the doubts which it raises, is able to suggest many possibilities which enlarge our thoughts and free them from the tyranny of custom. **Thus, while diminishing our feeling of certainty as to what things are, it greatly increases our knowledge as to what they may be; it removes the somewhat arrogant dogmatism of those who have never travelled into the region of liberating doubt, and it keeps alive our sense of wonder by showing familiar things in an unfamiliar aspect.**

Apart from its utility in showing unsuspected possibilities, philosophy has a value—perhaps its chief value—through the greatness of the objects which it contemplates, and the freedom from narrow and personal aims resulting from this contemplation. The life of the instinctive man is shut up within the circle of his private interests: family and friends may be included, but the outer world is not regarded except as it may help or hinder what comes within the circle of instinctive wishes. In such a life there is something feverish and confined, in comparison with which the philosophic life is calm and free. The private world of instinctive interests is a small one, set in the midst of a great and powerful world which must, sooner or later, lay our private world in ruins. Unless we can so enlarge our interests as to include the whole outer world, we remain like a garrison in a beleaguered fortress, knowing that the enemy prevents escape and that ultimate surrender is inevitable. In such a life there is no peace, but a constant strife between the insistence of desire and the powerlessness of will. In one way or another, if our life is to be great and free, we must escape this prison and this strife.

One way of escape is by philosophic contemplation. Philosophic contemplation does not, in its widest survey, divide the universe into two hostile camps—friends and foes, helpful and hostile, good and bad—it views the whole impartially. Philosophic contemplation, when it is unalloyed does not aim at proving that the rest of the universe is akin to man. All acquisition of knowledge is an enlargement of the Self, but this enlargement is best attained when it is not directly sought. It is obtained when the desire for knowledge is alone operative, by a study which does not wish in advance that its objects should have this or that character but adapts the Self to the characters which it finds in its objects. This enlargement of Self is not obtained when, taking the Self as it is, we try to show that the world is so similar to this Self that knowledge of it is possible without any admission of what seems alien. The desire to prove this is a form of self-assertion, and like all self-assertion, it is an obstacle to the growth of Self which it desires, and of which the Self knows that it is capable. Self-assertion, in philosophic speculation as elsewhere, views the world as a means to its own ends; thus it makes the world of less account than Self, and the Self sets bounds to the greatness of its goods. In contemplation, on the contrary, we start from the not-Self, and through its greatness the boundaries of Self are enlarged, through the infinity of the universe the mind which contemplates it achieves some share in infinity.

For this reason greatness of soul is not fostered by those philosophies which assimilate the universe to Man. Knowledge is a form of union of Self and not-Self; like all union, it is impaired by dominion, and therefore by any attempt to force the universe into conformity with what we find in ourselves. There is a widespread philosophical tendency towards the view which tells us that man is the measure of all things, that truth is man-made, that space and time and the world of universals are properties of the mind, and that, if there be anything not created by the mind, it is unknowable and of no account for us. This view, if our previous discussions were correct, is untrue; but in addition to being untrue, it has the effect of robbing philosophic contemplation of all that gives it value, since it fetters contemplation to Self. What it calls knowledge is not a union with the not-Self, but a set of prejudices, habits, and desires, making an impenetrable veil between us and the world beyond. The man who finds pleasure in such a theory of knowledge is like the man who never leaves the domestic circle for fear his word might not be law.

The true philosophic contemplation, on the contrary, finds its satisfaction in every enlargement of the not-Self, in everything that magnifies the objects contemplated, and thereby the subject contemplating. Everything, in contemplation, that is personal or private, everything that depends upon habit, self-interest, or desire, distorts the object, and hence impairs the union which the intellect seeks. By thus making a barrier between subject and object, such personal and private things become a prison to the intellect. The free intellect will see as God might see, without a *here* and *now*, without hopes and fears, without the trammels of customary beliefs and traditional prejudices, calmly, dispassionately, in the sole and exclusive desire of knowledge—knowledge as impersonal, as purely contemplative, as it is possible for man to attain. Hence also the free intellect will value more the abstract and universal knowledge into which the accidents of private history do not enter, than the knowledge brought by the senses, and dependent, as such knowledge must be, upon an exclusive and personal point of view and a body whose sense-organs distort as much as they reveal.

The mind which has become accustomed to the freedom and impartiality of philosophic contemplation will preserve something of the same freedom and impartiality in the world of action and emotion. It will view its purposes and desires as parts of the whole, with the absence of insistence that results from seeing them as infinitesimal fragments in a world of which all the rest is unaffected by any one man's deeds. The impartiality which, in contemplation, is the unalloyed desire for truth, is the very same quality of mind which, in action, is justice, and in emotion is that universal love which can be given to all, and not only to those who are judged useful or admirable. Thus contemplation enlarges not only the objects of our thoughts, but also the objects of our actions and our affections: it makes us citizens of the universe, not only of one walled city at war with all the rest. In this citizenship of the universe consists man's true freedom, and his liberation from the thraldom of narrow hopes and fears.

Thus, to sum up our discussion of the value of philosophy: Philosophy is to be studied, not for the sake of any definite answers to its questions, since no definite answers can, as a rule, be known to be true, but rather for the sake of the questions themselves; because these questions enlarge our conception of what is possible, enrich our intellectual imagination, and diminish the dogmatic assurance which closes the mind against speculation; but above all because, through the greatness of the universe which philosophy contemplates, the mind also is rendered great, and becomes capable of that union with the universe which constitutes its highest good.

Chapter II: Being

Why is there something rather than nothing? What is the nature of being? Can we know the structure of reality that underlies appearances? Is there some basic "stuff" from which all things ultimately derive their being? Is reality one or many? How is change possible? That is, how is it that things pass from non-being to being and from being to non-being? Is the structure of the universe such that human freedom is possible? Do time and space exist? The above questions about being are all related to the fundamental question: "What does it mean to be?"

Metaphysics is the branch of philosophy that inquires into the nature of that which is ultimately real. Metaphysics is commonly called "first philosophy." It deals with "first principles" or, in Greek philosophy, *arche* that lie at the basis of any inquiry. Metaphysical questions, that is, those questions that inquire into the nature of Being itself, call forth and organize our most basic and original thinking.

The philosopher Martin Heidegger believed that poetic thinking afforded human beings access to the very source of their being; i.e., Being itself. To enter into Being requires, among other qualities, patience and courage. He wrote:

> All our heart's courage is the
> echoing response to the
> first call of Being which
> gathers our thinking into the
> play of the world.

The essays in this section will help us in our attempt to begin to think deeply about Being.

In the excerpt from *Siddhartha*, Hermann Hesse presents his thinking about Buddhism. "We suffer the illusion that time is something real." Hesse continues, ". . . and if time is not real, then the dividing line that seems to lie between this world and eternity, between suffering and bliss, between good and evil, is also an illusion." In the smile of Siddhartha one "sees" the timeless presence of flowing forms.

Lao Tzu's *Tao-Te Ching* is a Chinese classic and perhaps the world's most translated book, with the exception of the Bible. This work is the foundation of Taoism. The Tao is the way. It is the way of ultimate reality and it is the way of nature. The Tao is also the way that humans should live. That is to say, one ought to harmonize one's life and actions with nature and, as a result, one's life will flow with the way of ultimate reality. The Tao is often compared with flowing water and Taoism is referred to as "The Watercourse Way."

Thales (ca. 640–546 B.C.E.) was the first recognized philosopher in the Western tradition. He was interested in the nature and structure of the universe and the problem of change. This chapter contains philosophical fragments from all the major "Pre-Socratic Philosophers" from Thales to Pythagoras. These thinkers were largely metaphysicians that dealt with fundamental questions concerning ultimate reality and the nature of Being.

In "Two Tables," Sir Arthur Eddington discusses the metaphysical problem of appearance versus reality. He contrasts the "familiar" world in which we live and the scientific world. The latter, it is claimed is the real world and the former is the world as it appears. Contrary to common sense, Eddington argues that familiar objects, like tables, are largely constructions of the human mind.

Bishop Berkeley was an idealist. Idealism holds that ideas are ultimately real. For Berkeley *esse* is *percipi* (i.e., "to be is to be perceived"). According to Berkeley, ". . . certainly no idea, whether faint or strong, can exist otherwise than in a mind perceiving it." Berkeley's analysis claims that material objects consist solely of ideas, whether in the mind of God or in the conscious agents God created.

Shankara's work presents the Hindu view of the universe. "The Crest-Jewel of Discrimination" shows that the permanent reality of Atman-Brahman is covered by layers of appearance, Maya. That one qualified to seek Brahman is one who has discrimination and can distinguish between the eternal and the non-eternal. Atman is the individual soul. Brahman is the world soul or the universal soul. The great truth of reality that frees one from the bonds of ignorance and leads to the attainment of liberation is this: Atman is Brahman.

from Siddhartha

Hermann Hesse

Govinda

Govinda once spent a rest period with some other monks in the pleasure grove which Kamala, the courtesan, had once presented to the followers of Gotama. He heard talk of an old ferryman who lived by the river, a day's journey away, and whom many considered to be a sage. When Govinda moved on, he chose the path to the ferry, eager to see this ferryman, for although he had lived his life according to the rule and was also regarded with respect by the younger monks for his age and modesty, there was still restlessness in his heart and his seeking was unsatisfied.

He arrived at the river and asked the old man to take him across. When they climbed out of the boat on the other side, he said to the old man: "You show much kindness to the monks and pilgrims; you have taken many of us across. Are you not also a seeker of the right path?"

There was a smile in Siddhartha's old eyes as he said: "Do you call yourself a seeker, O venerable one, you who are already advanced in years and wear the robe of Gotama's monks?"

"I am indeed old," said Govinda, "but I have never ceased seeking. I will never cease seeking. That seems to be my destiny. It seems to me that you also have sought. Will you talk to me a little about it, my friend?"

Siddhartha said: "What could I say to you that would be of value, except that perhaps you seek too much, that as a result of your seeking you cannot find."

"How is that?" asked Govinda.

"When someone is seeking," said Siddhartha, "it happens quite easily that he only sees the thing that he is seeking; that he is unable to find anything, unable to absorb anything, because he is only thinking of the thing he is seeking, because he has a goal, because he is obsessed with his goal. **Seeking means: to have a goal; but finding means: to be free, to be receptive, to have no goal.** You, O worthy one, are perhaps indeed a seeker, for in striving towards your goal, you do not see many things that are under your nose."

"I do not yet quite understand," said Govinda. "How do you mean?"

Siddhartha said: "Once, O worthy one, many years ago, you came to this river and found a man sleeping there. You sat beside him to guard him while he slept, but you did not recognize the sleeping man, Govinda."

Astonished and like one bewitched the monk gazed at the ferryman.

"Are you Siddhartha?" he asked in a timid voice. "I did not recognize you this time, too. I am very pleased to see you again, Siddhartha, very pleased. You have changed very much, my friend. And have you become a ferryman now?"

Siddhartha laughed warmly. "Yes, I have become a ferryman. Many people have to change a great deal and wear all sorts of clothes. I am one of those, my friend. You are very welcome, Govinda, and I invite you to stay the night in my hut."

Govinda stayed the night in the hut and slept in the bed that had once been Vasudeva's. He asked the friend of his youth many questions and Siddhartha had a great deal to tell him about his life.

When it was time for Govinda to depart the following morning, he said with some hesitation: "Before I go on my way, Siddhartha, I should like to ask you one more question. Have you a doctrine, belief or knowledge which you uphold, which helps you to live and do right?"

Siddhartha said: "You know, my friend, that even as a young man, when we lived with the ascetics in the forest, I came to distrust doctrines and teachers and to turn my back on them. I am still of the same turn of mind, although I have, since that time, had many teachers. A beautiful courtesan was my teacher for a long time, and a rich merchant and a dice player. On one occasion, one of the Buddha's wandering monks was my teacher. He halted in his pilgrimage to sit beside me when I fell asleep in the forest. I also learned something from him and I am grateful to him, very grateful. But most of all, I have learned from this river and from my predecessor, Vasudeva. He was a simple man; he was not a thinker, but he realized the essential as well as Gotama. He was a holy man, a saint."

Govinda said: "It seems to me, Siddhartha, that you still like to jest a little. I believe you and know that you have not followed any teacher, but have you not yourself, if not a doctrine, certain thoughts? Have you not discovered certain knowledge yourself that has helped you to live? It would give me great pleasure if you would tell me something about this."

Siddhartha said: "Yes, I have had thoughts and knowledge here and there. Sometimes, for an hour or for a day, I have become aware of knowledge, just as one feels life in one's heart. I have had many thoughts, but it would be difficult for me to tell you about them. But this is one thought that has impressed me, Govinda. Wisdom is not communicable. The wisdom which a wise man tries to communicate always sounds foolish."

"Are you jesting?" asked Govinda.

"No, I am telling you what I have discovered. **Knowledge can be communicated, but not wisdom. One can find it, live it, be fortified by it, do wonders through it, but one cannot communicate and teach it.** I suspected this when I was still a youth and it was this that drove me away from teachers. There is one thought I have had, Govinda, which you will again think is a jest or folly: that is, in every truth the opposite is equally true. For example, a truth can only be expressed and enveloped in words if it is one-sided. Everything that is thought and expressed in words is one-sided, only half the truth; it all lacks totality, completeness, unity. When the Illustrious Buddha taught about the world, he had to divide it into Samsara and Nirvana, into illusion and truth, into suffering and salvation. One cannot do otherwise, there is no other method for those who teach. But the world itself, being in and around us, is never one-sided. Never is a man or a deed wholly Samsara or wholly Nirvana; never is a man wholly a saint or a sinner. This only seems so because we suffer the illusion that time is something real. **Time is not real**, Govinda. I have realized this repeatedly. And if time is not real, then the dividing line that seems to lie between this world and eternity, between suffering and bliss, between good and evil, is also an illusion."

"How is that?" asked Govinda, puzzled.

"Listen, my friend! I am a sinner and you are a sinner, but someday the sinner will be Brahma again, will someday attain Nirvana, will someday become a Buddha. Now this 'someday' is illusion; it is only a comparison. The sinner is not on the way to a Buddha-like state; he is not evolving, although our thinking cannot conceive things otherwise. No, the potential Buddha already exists in the sinner; his future is already there. The potential hidden Buddha must be recognized in him, in you, in everybody. The world, Govinda, is not imperfect or slowly evolving along a long path to perfection. No, it is perfect at every moment; every sin already carries grace within it, all small children are potential old men, all sucklings have death within them, all dying people—eternal life. It is not possible for one person to see how far another is on the way; the Buddha exists in the robber and dice player; the robber exists in the Brahmin. During deep meditation it is possible to dispel time, to see simultaneously all the past, present and future, and then everything is good, everything is perfect, everything is Brahman. Therefore, it seems to me that everything that exists is good—death as well as life, sin as well as holiness, wisdom as well as folly. Everything is necessary, everything needs only my agreement, my assent, my loving understanding; then all is well with me and nothing can harm me. I learned through my body and soul that it was necessary for me to sin, that I needed lust, that I had to strive for property and experience nausea and the depths of despair in order to learn not to resist them, in order to learn to love the world, and no longer compare it with some kind of desired imaginary world, some imaginary vision of perfection, but to leave it as it is, to love it and be glad to belong to it. These, Govinda, are some of the thoughts that are in my mind."

Siddhartha bent down, lifted a stone from the ground and held it in his hand.

"This," he said, handling it, "is a stone, and within a certain length of time it will perhaps be soil and from the soil it will become plant, animal or man. Previously I should have said: This stone is just a stone; it has no value, it belongs to the world of Maya, but perhaps because within the cycle of change it can also become man and spirit, it is also of importance. That is what I should have thought. But now I think: This stone is stone; it is also animal, God and Buddha. I do not respect and love it because it was one thing and will become something else, but because it has already long been everything and always is everything. I love it just because it is a stone, because today and now it appears to me a stone. I see value and meaning in each one of its fine markings and cavities, in the yellow, in the grey, in the hardness and the sound of it when I knock it, in the dryness or dampness of its surface. There are stones that feel like oil or soap, that look like leaves or sand, and each one is different and worships Om in its own way; each one is Brahman. At the same time it is very much stone, oily or soapy, and that is just what pleases me and seems wonderful and worthy of worship. But I will say no more about it. Words do not express thoughts very well. They always become a little different immediately they are expressed, a little distorted, a little foolish. And yet it also pleases me and seems right that what is of value and wisdom to one man seems nonsense to another."

Govinda had listened in silence.

"Why did you tell me about the stone?" he asked hesitatingly after a pause.

"I did so unintentionally. But perhaps it illustrates that I just love the stone and the river and all these things that we see and from which we can learn. I can love a stone, Govinda, and a tree or a piece of bark. These are things and one can love things. But one cannot love words. Therefore teachings are of no use to me; they have no hardness, no softness, no colors, no corners, no smell, no taste—they have nothing but words. Perhaps that is what prevents you from finding peace, perhaps there are too many words, for even salvation and virtue. Sansara and Nirvana are only words, Govinda. Nirvana is not a thing; there is only the word Nirvana."

Govinda said: "Nirvana is not only a word, my friend; it is a thought."

Siddhartha continued: "It may be a thought, but I must confess, my friend, that I do not differentiate very much between thoughts and words. Quite frankly, I do not attach great importance to thoughts either. I attach more importance to things. For example, there was a man at this ferry who was my predecessor and teacher. He was a holy man who for many years believed only in the river and nothing else. He noticed that the river's voice spoke to him. He learned from it; it educated and taught him. The river seemed like a god to him and for many years he did not know that every wind, every cloud, every bird, every beetle is equally divine and knows and can teach just as well as the esteemed river. But when this holy man went off into the woods, he knew everything; he knew more than you and I, without teachers, without books, just because he believed in the river."

Govinda said: "But what you call thing, is it something real, something intrinsic? Is it not only the illusion of Maya, only image and appearance? Your stone, your tree, are they real?"

"This also does not trouble me much," said Siddhartha. "If they are illusion, then I also am illusion, and so they are always of the same nature as myself. It is that which makes them so lovable and venerable. That is why I can love them. And here is a doctrine at which you will laugh. It seems to me, Govinda, that love is the most important thing in the world. It may be important to great thinkers to examine the world, to explain and despise it. But I think it is only important to love the world, not to despise it, not for us to hate each other, but to be able to regard the world and ourselves and all beings with love, admiration and respect."

"I understand that," said Govinda, "but that is just what the Illustrious One called illusion. He preached benevolence, forbearance, sympathy, patience—but not love. He forbade us to bind ourselves to earthly love."

"I know that," said Siddhartha smiling radiantly, "I know that, Govinda, and here we find ourselves within the maze of meanings, within the conflict of words, for I will not deny that my words about love are in apparent contradiction to the teachings of Gotama. That is just why I distrust words so much, for I know that this contradiction is an illusion. I know that I am at one with Gotama. How, indeed, could he not know love, he who has recognized all humanity's vanity and transitoriness, yet loves humanity so much that he has devoted a long life solely to help and teach people? Also with this great teacher, the thing to me is of greater importance than the words; his deeds and life are more important to me than his talk, the gesture of his hand is more important to me than his opinions. Not in speech or thought do I regard him as a great man, but in his deeds and life."

The two old men were silent for a long time. Then as Govinda was preparing to go, he said: "I thank you, Siddhartha, for telling me something of your thoughts. Some of them are strange thoughts. I cannot grasp them all immediately. However, I thank you, and I wish you many peaceful days."

Inwardly, however, he thought: Siddhartha is a strange man and he expresses strange thoughts. His ideas seem crazy. How different do the Illustrious One's doctrines sound! They are clear, straightforward, comprehensible; they contain nothing strange, wild or laughable. But Siddhartha's hands and feet, his eyes, his brow, his breathing, his smile, his greeting, his gait affect me differently from his thoughts. Never, since the time our Illustrious Gotama passed into Nirvana, have I ever met a man with the exception of Siddhartha about whom I felt: This is a holy man! His ideas may be strange, his words may sound foolish, but his glance and his hand, his skin and his hair, all radiate a purity, peace, serenity, gentleness and saintliness which I have never seen in any man since the recent death of our illustrious teacher.

While Govinda was thinking these thoughts and there was conflict in his heart, he again bowed to Siddhartha, full of affection towards him. He bowed low before the quietly seated man.

"Siddhartha," he said, "we are now old men. We may never see each other again in this life. I can see, my dear friend, that you have found peace. I realize that I have not found it. Tell me one more word, my esteemed friend, tell me something that I can conceive, something I can understand! Give me something to help me on my way, Siddhartha. My path is often hard and dark."

Siddhartha was silent and looked at him with his calm, peaceful smile. Govinda looked steadily in his face, with anxiety, with longing. Suffering, continual seeking and continual failure were written in his look.

Siddhartha saw it and smiled.

"Bend near to me!" he whispered in Govinda's ear. "Come, still nearer, quite close! Kiss me on the forehead, Govinda."

Although surprised, Govinda was compelled by a great love and presentiment to obey him; he leaned close to him and touched his forehead with his lips. As he did this, something wonderful happened to him. While he was still dwelling on Siddhartha's strange words, while he strove in vain to dispell the conception of time, to imagine Nirvana and Sansara as one, while even a certain contempt for his friend's words conflicted with a tremendous love and esteem for him, this happened to him.

He no longer saw the face of his friend Siddhartha. Instead he saw other faces, many faces, a long series, a continuous stream of faces—hundreds, thousands, which all came and disappeared and yet all seemed to be there at the same time, which all continually changed and renewed themselves and which were yet all Siddhartha. He saw the face of a fish, of a carp, with tremendous painfully opened mouth, a dying fish with dimmed eyes. He saw the face of a newly born child, red and full of wrinkles, ready to cry. He saw the face of a murderer, saw him plunge a knife into the body of a man; at the same moment he saw this criminal kneeling down, bound, and his head cut off by an executioner. He saw the naked bodies of men and women in the postures and transports of passionate love. He saw corpses stretched out, still, cold, empty. He saw the heads of animals, boars, crocodiles, elephants, oxen, birds. He saw Krishna and Agni. He saw all these forms and faces in a thousand relationships to each other, all helping each other, loving, hating and destroying each other and become newly born. Each one was mortal, a passionate, painful example of all that is transitory. Yet none of them died, they only changed, were always reborn, continually had a new face: only time stood between one face and another. And all these forms and faces rested, flowed, reproduced, swam past and merged into each other, and over them all there was continually something thin, unreal and yet existing, stretched across like thin glass or ice, like a transparent skin, shell, form or mask of water—and this mask was Siddhartha's smiling face which Govinda touched with his lips at that moment. And Govinda saw that this mask-like smile, this smile of unity over the flowing forms, this smile of simultaneousness over the thousands of births and deaths—this smile of Siddhartha—was exactly the same as the calm, delicate, impenetrable, perhaps gracious, perhaps mocking, wise, thousand-fold smile of Gotama the Buddha, as he had perceived it with awe a hundred times. It was in such a manner, Govinda knew, that the Perfect One smiled.

No longer knowing whether time existed, whether this display had lasted a second or a hundred years, whether there was a Siddhartha or a Gotama, a Self and others, wounded deeply by a divine arrow which gave him pleasure, deeply enchanted and exalted, Govinda stood yet a while bending over Siddhartha's peaceful face which he had just kissed, which had just been the stage of all present and future forms. His countenance was unchanged after the mirror of the thousand-fold forms had disappeared from the surface. He smiled peacefully and gently, perhaps very graciously, perhaps very mockingly, exactly as the Illustrious One had smiled.

Govinda bowed low. Incontrollable tears trickled down his old face. He was overwhelmed by a feeling of great love, of the most humble veneration. He bowed low, right down to the ground, in front of the man sitting there motionless, whose smile reminded him of everything that he had ever loved in his life, of everything that had ever been of value and holy in his life.

Tao-Te Ching

Lao Tzu

1

The Tao that can be told of is not the eternal Tao;
The name that can be named is not the eternal name.
The Nameless is the origin of Heaven and Earth;
The Named is the mother of all things.

Therefore let there always be non-being, so we may see their
subtlety,And let there always be being, so we may see their outcome.
The two are the same,
But after they are produced, they have different names.
They both may be called deep and profound.
Deeper and more profound,
The door of all subtleties!

2

When the people of the world all know beauty as beauty,
   There arises the recognition of ugliness.
When they all know the good as good,
   There arises the recognition of evil.
Therefore:

   Being and non-being produce each other;
   Difficult and easy complete each other;
   Long and short contrast each other;
   High and low distinguish each other;
   Sound and voice harmonize each other;
   Front and behind accompany each other.

Therefore the sage manages affairs without action
And spreads doctrines without words.
All things arise, and he does not turn away from them.
He produces them but does not take possession of them.
He acts but does not rely on his own ability.

He accomplishes his task but does not claim credit for it.
It is precisely because he does not claim credit that his accomplishment remains with him.

4

Tao is empty (like a bowl).
It may be used but its capacity is never exhausted.
It is bottomless, perhaps the ancestor of all things.
It blunts its sharpness,
It unties its tangles.
It softens its light.
It becomes one with the dusty world.
Deep and still, it appears to exist forever.
I do not know whose son it is.
It seems to have existed before the Lord.

6

The spirit of the valley never dies.
　It is called the subtle and profound female.
The gate of the subtle and profound female
　Is the root of Heaven and Earth.
It is continuous, and seems to be always existing.
Use it and you will never wear it out.

8

The best (man) is like water.
Water is good; it benefits all things and does not compete with them.
It dwells in (lowly) places that all disdain.
This is why it is so near to Tao.

(The best man) in his dwelling loves the earth.
In his heart, he loves what is profound.
In his associations, he loves humanity.
In his words, he loves faithfulness.
In government, he loves order.
In handling affairs, he loves competence.
In his activities, he loves timeliness.
It is because he does not compete that he is without reproach.

11

Thirty spokes are united around the hub to make a wheel,
   But it is on its non-being that the utility of the carriage depends.
Clay is molded to form a utensil,
   But it is on its non-being that the utility of the utensil depends.
Doors and windows are cut out to make a room,
   But it is on its non-being that the utility of the room depends.
Therefore turn being into advantage, and turn non-being into utility.

14

We look at it and do not see it;
   Its name is The Invisible.
We listen to it and do not hear it;
   Its name is The Inaudible.
We touch it and do not find it;
   Its name is The Subtle (formless).
These three cannot be further inquired into,
And hence merge into one.
Going up high, it is not bright, and coming down low, it is not dark.
Infinite and boundless, it cannot be given any name;
It reverts to nothingness.
This is called shape without shape,
Form without objects.
It is The Vague and Elusive.
Meet it and you will not see its head.
Follow it and you will not see its back.
Hold on to the Tao of old in order to master the things of the present.
From this one may know the primeval beginning (of the universe).
This is called the bond of Tao.

21

The all-embracing quality of the great virtue follows alone from the Tao.
The thing that is called Tao is eluding and vague.
   Vague and eluding, there is in it the form.
   Eluding and vague, in it are things.
Deep and obscure, in it is the essence.
The essence is very real; in it are evidences.

From the time of old until now, its name (manifestations) ever remains.
By which we may see the beginning of all things.
How do I know that the beginnings of all things are so?
Through this (Tao).

28

He who knows the male and keeps to the female
Becomes the ravine of the world.
Being the ravine of the world,
He will never depart from eternal virtue,
But returns to the state of infancy.
He who knows the white and yet keeps to the black
Becomes the model for the world.
Being the model for the world,
He will never deviate from eternal virtue,
But returns to the state of the non-ultimate.
He who knows glory but keeps to humility
Becomes the valley of the world.
Being the valley of the world,
He will be proficient in eternal virtue,
And returns to the state of simplicity (uncarved wood).
When the uncarved wood is broken up, it is turned into concrete things.
But when the sage uses it, he becomes the leading official.
Therefore the great ruler does not cut up.

38

The man of superior virtue is not (conscious of) his virtue,
   And in this way he really possesses virtue.
The man of inferior virtue never loses (sight of) his virtue,
   And in this way he loses his virtue.
The man of superior virtue takes no action, but has no ulterior motive
       to do so.
The man of inferior virtue takes action, and has an ulterior motive to do
       so.
The man of superior humanity takes action, but has no ulterior motive
       to do so.
The man of superior righteousness takes action, but has no ulterior
       motive to do so.
The man of superior propriety takes action,
And when people do not respond to it, he will stretch his arms and
       force it on them.

Therefore when Tao is lost, only then does the doctrine of virtue arise.
When virtue is lost, only then does the doctrine of humanity arise.
When humanity is lost, only then does the doctrine of righteousness arise.
When righteousness is lost, only then does the doctrine of propriety arise.
Now, propriety is a superficial expression of loyalty and faithfulness, and the beginning of disorder.
Those who are the first to know have the flowers of Tao but are the beginning of ignorance.
For this reason the great man dwells in the thick, and does not rest with the thin.
He dwells in the fruit, and does not rest with the flower.
Therefore he rejects the one, and accepts the other.

43

The softest things in the world overcome the hardest things in the world.
Non-being penetrates that in which there is no space.
Through this I know the advantage of taking no action.
Few in the world can understand the teaching without words and the advantage of taking no action.

81

True words are not beautiful;
   Beautiful words are not true.
A good man does not argue;
   He who argues is not a good man.
A wise man has no extensive knowledge;
   He who has extensive knowledge is not a wise man.

The sage does not accumulate for himself.
The more he uses for others, the more he has himself.
The more he gives to others, the more he possesses of his own.
The Way of Heaven is to benefit others and not to injure.
The Way of the sage is to act but not to compete.

The Pre-Socratic Philosophers

Thales

1. **Water is the basis for all things.**
2. The earth floats upon water.
3. **Gods are in all things.**
4. Soul is present in the lodestone (that is, in the magnet) because it causes iron to move.

Anaximander

1. **The apeiron (that is, the "infinite unbounded") is the primary principle of all things.** From the apeiron come all things. To it, they return when they cease to be. They come into being and pass out of being by necessity, according to the order of time, in order to right the injustice they have done.

Anaximenes

1. **Our souls, which are pneuma (that is, air) keep us together as the pneuma binds together the cosmos.**

Heraclitus

1. Although the logos is eternal, people have not understood it. Even after hearing it, they do not understand. All things are known through the logos, yet people seem to be without knowledge of it as you can see from the following test: Everything must be spoken of according to its nature, both how it comes to be and how it grows. Men speak of things without being attentive, as if they were asleep and not awake.
2. That which is common to all should guide us. Yet, while the logos is common to all, each person acts as though intelligence is private and his or hers alone.

3. Those who love wisdom should seek to learn about the world in its particulars.
4. Those who seek gold must dig up much earth to find it.
5. All people should know themselves and practice temperance.
6. What I most revere are those things which can be seen and those which can be heard.
7. Eyes are more accurate than ears.
8. Those who are awake have a world in common. The sleepers live in private worlds of their own.
9. Nature loves to hide.
10. Expect the unexpected. Otherwise, you will never find the truth.
11. **Everything flows and nothing remains fixed.**
12. **No one steps twice into the same river since the waters flow on and on.**
13. What is cold becomes hot; what is hot becomes cold. What is wet becomes dry; what is dry becomes wet.
14. War is father and king of all that is.
15. War is common to all things. Strife is justice.
16. Homer erred when he wished that strife would cease between gods and men. Were that to occur, all things would cease to exist.
17. **Change alone does not change.**
18. All things become fire and from fire all things are born as in the eternal exchange of money and goods.
19. The universe, which is the same for all, has always been and always will be. Unmade by god or man, it is eternal fire, always being kindled, always going out.
20. Fire changes. First it is the sea, and of the sea, half becomes earth and half the lightning flash.
21. Fire lives the death of earth, air the death of fire, water the death of air, and earth the death of water.

22. The sun is no wider than a person's foot.
23. The most beautiful universe is no more than a random heap of rubbish.
24. No boundaries exist for the soul, such are its depths.
25. Soul is a fine mist out of which comes all else. It is made of the smallest of all particles and it moves forever. The moving universe can only be known by that in motion.
26. Souls rise from what is moist.
27. The best souls are dry.
28. Souls yearn to become damp.
29. Souls die when they become wet, and it is death to water to become earth. Water is born out of the earth, and souls out of the water.
30. Desire buys what it wants at the cost of the soul.
31. Bigotry is the sacred disease.
32. If all that is were made of smoke, it is by smell we would know all.
33. Understanding is divine. Human nature has no real understanding.
34. Humans are not rational; intelligence exists only in what encompasses them.
35. Although humans are intimately connected with the Logos, they persist in setting themselves against it.
36. Gods become humans; humans become gods. Each one lives in the other's death and dies in the other's life.
37. Character is destiny.
38. People should speak with reason and thereby share a body of thought in common as the people of a city share laws. All human laws participate in divine law which penetrates as it will into the affairs of people but is greater by far than human law.
39. Fight for law as you would for the city wall.
40. In law, all share a single will to obey.
41. Extinguish pride more quickly than you would a fire.

42. To toil at the same things continuously is not only wearisome; it is to be ruled by what you do.
43. Dogs bark at strangers.
44. In opposition there is concord; from discord comes harmony.
45. We know health by sickness, good by evil, fullness by hunger, rest by weariness.
46. The daemon (spirit) regards an adult as childish just as a child is regarded by an adult.
47. All things are beautiful and good to God; to humans some things seem right and others wrong.
48. Doctors cut, burn, and torture the sick. Then they send the bill.
49. The way up and the way down are one and the same.
50. A person's bones and joints are both unified and disunited. To agree is to differ. Discord is harmony. Out of the many, one; from one comes the many.
51. The living become the dead, the dead become the living. Those awake become sleepers, the sleepers become awake. The young become old, the old become young.
52. The unheard harmony of things is sweeter than the heard.
53. Most do not understand that which is at war with itself agrees with itself. Consider the bow and the lyre.
54. Listen not to me but to the Logos; all is one.
55. Wisdom is one and unique. It is both willing and unwilling to be called Zeus.
56. All things come in seasons.
57. Even the sleepers accomplish their purpose in the cosmos.

Parmenides

1. The horses of my chariot sped me to the farthest reaches of my desire, bringing me at last to the road of the Goddess on which travel those who know through all cities. The wise horses pulled my chariot while maidens led the way. The axle, spun by the wheels on

either side, glowed in its sockets and hummed. From the realms of night, the maidens of the Sun threw back their veils from their faces and led the chariot swiftly toward the light. We arrived at the gates of night and day, which have a stone lintel above and a threshold below. The gates are of the aether but are stronger than iron when closed. Inexorable Justice bolts them securely with rewards and punishment. But, the maidens charmed the Goddess with gentle words, persuading her to shoot back the bolts. The gates swung back on their hinges, nailed to bronze posts, to reveal a wide expanse, a broad avenue down which the maidens led my horses and chariot. The Goddess greeted me warmly. Taking my hand in hers, she spoke these words:

> Welcome my son who comes here with immortal maidens at the reins. No evil has brought you here. Righteousness and Justice have conveyed you to me, far from the beaten paths of humans. You must learn of all matters, both the unflinching heart of complete truth and the opinions of mortals which lack truth. It is needful, too, that you should review all and learn how to judge of mere seeming.

The Way of Truth

2. No one can ever prove that non-being is. Restrain your mind from that way. Do not let habit lead your eyes to be aimless, your ear and tongue to be echoes. Reason should be your judge, not custom. When left alone, the heart will take the wrong road.

3. Look toward what is distant yet present to the mind. You cannot sever being from being.

4. It matters not where I begin. In any event, I must return where I set out.

5. Heed my words: there are two paths which the mind can take. One path is that It Is and cannot not-be. This is the way of truth. The other path is that It Is Not and that Non-Being Is. This cannot be thought. **You cannot know or say that which is Not.**

6. That being is is necessary since being is possible and not being is not possible. Many confused people maintain that to be and not to be are the same and are not the same and that all is in a state of change, some things coming into being and some things going out of being.

7. The only truth path is expressed by the one word: IS. What is has no beginning and has no end. It is whole, indestructible, and continuous. How could you proceed to learn about its birth? How and why it has grown? I shall not permit you to say it came from not-being, for it is impossible to even think that non-being is. What could have caused it to arise from non-being at one time rather than at another? Of necessity is either Is or it Is Not. Nothing can spring from Being except Being itself. Justice will not allow Being to be born or destroyed. Thus we must decide whether It Is or Is Not. We must agree that it is necessary to reject the unthinkable and unsayable. How could What Is be said to come to be in the future? How could this occur? For if it were coming into being, then at one time it must have not been. How could it move? It is without beginning and end. It remains fixed in place where it is. Natural Law prohibits that Being should be anything less than perfectly complete. If it needed anything at all to complete it, it would need everything. Thinking and what is thought are the same. Thought does not exist apart from Being, nor either thought or being apart from saying. All the usual beliefs mortals have about things coming to be and perishing, about things being and not-being, about movement and the like are nothing more than names. Since limit is necessary, Being must be complete on every side, like a perfectly rounded sphere. It is not greater in any direction than in any other.

8. **Thought and Being are one and the same.**

The Way of Opinion

9. Here ends my (that is the Goddess') rational discourse on truth. Next, learn about the opinions of mortals. Mortals have the habit of naming two thought-forms, one of which should not be named. They oppose these forms in properties and character. On one side is the fire of the upper sky; on the other side there is heavy darkness. I shall tell you of these appearances, as mortals understand it, so that you will know of such matters.

10. When all things have been named light and night, based on the differences that appear to exist between them, then everything must be full of both things at once since neither has anything in common with the other.

11. You shall learn about the sky and the unseen wonders of the torch of the sun and how they came into being. You shall learn about the moon and its works. You shall learn also about the heavens and how they came to be, and how Necessity fixed the limits of the stars.

12. The smaller orbits are filled with pure fire. Next, the orbits are mixed with darkness and light. In the middle is the divinity who rules all. She is who rules over eros and birth everywhere, prompting female to join with male and male with female.

13. The first god she made was Eros.

14. The mind of a mortal is made up according to the mixing of bodily parts. In all, it is the same: thinking consists in the composition of the body's parts. It is an excess of body that constitutes thought.

15. Thus according to common opinion things come into being and thus they are now. Thus after a time they will perish. To each kind of thing names are assigned by mortals.

Zeno

1. If things are many, they are finite in number since they must be as many as they are and not more or less. However, if things are many, they must be infinite in number for there are always other things between any two things. Between those things there are still other things.

2. If a thing is said to be moving, it must be moving either in the place in which it is or in a place in which it is not. But, it is impossible for it to move in the place in which it is since it fills that place and there is, consequently, no room in which it might move. Nor is it possible for it to move in the place in which it is not since it does not occupy that place. Therefore, it is impossible that things move.

3. (From Aristotle's account in the sixth book of the *Physics*) Achilles can never overtake a tortoise in a foot race if the tortoise has even a small headstart, for Achilles will first have to reach the point from which the tortoise started out. But, by that time, the tortoise will have advanced. Then Achilles will have to reach the point to which the tortoise has advanced. But, by that time, the tortoise will have advanced still farther. **Achilles, thus, can never catch the tortoise.**

Empedocles

1. Come now, with all your powers, see how each thing appears. Do not trust your eyes more than your ears or your ears more than your taste. Reject nothing that the body proclaims that might serve to bring knowledge. Pay attention to each particular manifestation.

2. Foolish men are they who cannot reach out with their thoughts, who believe that what Was Not could somehow come into Being or that what is in Being could be utterly destroyed and vanish into Nothingness.

3. There is no birth among all mortal things; there is no annihilation in death. Elements are mingled and interchanged, and this is called Nature.

4. When elements combine to form a man or a bird or a plant, we call it "birth." When these things are separated into their elements, we call it "death."

5. In the Cosmos, nothing is empty and nothing overfull.

6. **The sources from which all has come are earth, water, air, and fire.**

7. Earth, at anchor in the harbor of Aphrodite, mixes in proper proportion with fire, moisture, and air to form blood.

8. Long ago there came to be a single One out of many. At another time, it chided itself to make many out of One. Double-sided is the birth of transient things, and double-sided their death. Uniting things both creates and destroys; separating them involves growth and scattering as things become individuals. This process never ceases. At time, **Love brings scattered things together. At another time Strife rends them apart.** From this process have arisen all things that were, are, or shall be: trees, men, women, animals, birds, fishes, even such revered things as the long-lived gods. Reality consists of the basic elements that mixing with one another assume different characteristics.

9. There arose long ago on the earth heads without necks, arms without shoulders, and eyes wandering about in search of heads. Things came together by pure chance, with many novelties coming to be.

10. The heart lives in a sea of blood flowing back and forth around it. The flowing blood is what we know as "thought."

11. As people live differently, their thoughts are different.
12. The lawful is not binding on some but not on others. The law extends everywhere.
13. Do not wish for a crown of laurel.

Anaxagoras

1. Because our senses are weak, we cannot judge the truth.
2. What we see is but a glimpse of the unseen.
3. Others do not understand what they call coming-to-be and perishing. A thing does not come-to-be or perish; things simply come about from the mixing of elements and cease when the elements are separated out.
4. We must imagine that composite beings contain ingredients of every variety. The seeds of everything, with all kinds of colors, characteristics, and ways of affecting the senses are contained in each composite being.
5. In everything there is a portion of everything else with the exception that some things have no mind.
6. Whatever there is most of in a particular composite thing determines the apparent nature that we assign to it.
7. The great and the small share equally the number of parts they possess. Nothing exists apart, everything has a portion of everything else. Since there is no smallest amount, no total isolation can occur. It is similarly impossible for something to come to exist out of nothing. Thus things must be now as they were in the beginning. Each thing contains a multiplicity of other things.
8. In small things there is no least thing, but always lesser things.
9. When all things were mixed together, before any things had separated out, nothing was discernable, not even color. The variety of all things we see today was present in the original whole.
10. Although other things have a portion of everything else in them, **Mind is unlimited, autonomous, and pure.** It is unmixed with anything else. If this were not so, then it would be part of all that exists and it could not have command over all else as it now does. Mind,

because it is fine and pure knows all that is and has the greatest power.
11. All Mind, from the greatest to the smallest, is alike; for other things, nothing is completely like anything else.
12. Mind commanded the cosmos, causing the universe to rotate. **Mind set in order all that was, is, and will be.** When it first set the cosmos in motion, things began to separate from the rotating mass.
13. The denser things, the water, the cold, and the dark, gathered where the earth now is. The less dense things, the light, dryness, and warmth went to the farthest reaches of the aether.
14. It is possible that there are other worlds where people exist. They may have their sun and moon and stars as we do. It may be that the separating and individuation process we see occurs not only in our own world but in other worlds as well.

Democritus

The Atoms and the Void

According to this new system of nature philosophy, all the "things" of experience consist of very minute indivisible particles of matter ("atoms"), more or less widely separated in empty space. **"In truth, nothing exists but atoms and the void,"** said Democritus. By this proposition, to us so simple-sounding, two innovations were introduced into the conception of nature.

1. What truly exists is no longer identified exclusively with corporeal, space-occupying substance; for space unoccupied also exists. It will be recalled that Parmenides had found empty space "unthinkable," and that this finding had been a chief occasion for his stumbling into the error of denying that motion is an actual fact in the world. Empedocles and Anaxagoras, by their doctrine of the coming together and separation of the elements, had indeed reasserted the fact of movement; but they seem not to have felt necessary thereto the existence of space wholly unoccupied by any of the elements. Leucippus, apparently, was the first thinker clearly to discern that existence is not coextensive with corporeality, and that no inconsistency is involved in the conception of space void of all material content. A later writer thus states Leucippus' case: "He held that *what is* is no more real than

what is not, and that both alike are factors in the explanation of the things that come into being; for he asserted that the substance of the atoms was compact and full, and these he designated *what is*, while they move in the void, which he designated *what is not* but asserted to be quite as real as *what is*." The void, then, is a reality.

2. No less novel is the conception of a strictly *indivisible particle* of matter. A small piece of wood, cork, chalk, or other substance may, of course, be divided. But, if one could carry the process of division far enough, one must in the end come upon certain ultimate indivisible particles, "atoms." (The term "atom" means, in its strict etymology, simply "the indivisible.") Such a notion as this is diametrically opposed to Anaxagoras' assertions that "it is impossible for there to be a least thing" and that "all things were together infinite both in number and in smallness." Indeed, all previous thinkers had, however vaguely, supposed matter to be a *continuous* mass, such as by its own intrinsic nature to set no limits to dismemberment. The atomic particle of this new theory is of course very minute, far smaller than any possible perceptible thing. Yet it is *not* "infinitely small," nor a mere mathematical point; it has size, a right half and a left. It is indivisible because its halves, though distinguishable by thought, are not in reality separated by empty space. An atom is the absolutely "full." Hereupon it becomes apparent that these two novel ideas of this system, the atom and the void, are as conceptions closely connected.

Properties of the Atom in Isolation

The traits of the individual atom must be more completely described. As one might expect, the atoms are *eternal, indestructible, unchangeable;* so far do they comply with the Parmenidean criteria of *what is*. The permanence of an atom is grounded in its simplicity. The atom has no internal structure; there is no diversity of substance within it. Physically it is not complex, but a simple unit. The only change that can befall an atom is in the company it keeps, in its changing associations with other atoms; but throughout all the combinings and separatings of atoms, whereby "things" arise and perish, each atom remains its own unaltered self.

Pythagoras

1. In the cosmos, all is harmonized from the limitless and limited.
2. If everything were limitless, we could not recognize particular things.
3. Whatever the mind knows, it knows by number; it is not possible for the mind to know except by number. Nothing about things could be known except by number. It is number which seizes upon the things we know by sense perception and brings them in harmony into the soul where they are recognized and compared with each other.
4. The real essence of things is eternal. Thus nature partakes of the divine rather than the merely human intellect. It would be impossible for us to know any thing, unless each thing in the cosmos has a real essence.
5. The One is the first principle of all else.
6. Harmony consists of the unification of mixed elements, an agreement among what does not agree.
7. The ancients taught that the soul, in being implanted in the body as though it were in a tomb, is being punished for past misdeeds.
8. **Number is the ruling principle that maintains the eternal stability, of things in the universe.**

Two Tables

Sir Arthur Eddington

I have settled down to the task of writing these lectures and have drawn up my chairs to my two tables. Two tables! Yes; there are duplicates of every object about me—two tables, two chairs, two pens.

This is not a very profound beginning to a course which ought to reach transcendent levels of scientific philosophy. But we cannot touch bedrock immediately; we must scratch a bit at the surface of things first. And whenever I begin to scratch; the first thing I strike is—my two tables.

One of them has been familiar to me from earliest years. It is a commonplace object of that environment which I call the world. How shall I describe it? It has extension; it is comparatively permanent; it is colored; above all it is *substantial*. By substantial I do not merely mean that it does not collapse when I lean up on it; I mean that it is constituted of "substance," and by that word I am trying to convey to you some conception of its intrinsic nature. It is a *thing*; not like space, which is a mere negation; nor like time, which is—Heaven knows what! But that will not help you to my meaning because it is the distinctive characteristic of a "thing" to have this substantiality, and I do not think substantiality can be described better than by saying that it is the kind of nature exemplified by an ordinary table. And so we go round in circles. After all if you are a plain commonsense man, not too much worried with scientific scruples, you will be confident that you understand the nature of an ordinary table. I have even heard of plain men who had the idea that they could better understand the mystery of their own nature if scientists would discover a way of explaining it in terms of the easily comprehensible nature of a table.

Table no. 2 is my scientific table. It is a more recent acquaintance and I do not feel so familiar with it. It does not belong to the world previously mentioned—that world which spontaneously appears around me when I open my eyes, though how much of it is objective and how much subjective I do not here consider. It is part of a world which in more devious ways has forced itself on my attention. My scientific table is mostly emptiness. Sparsely scattered in that emptiness are numerous electric charges rushing about with great speed; but their combined bulk amounts to less than a billionth of the bulk of the table itself. Notwithstanding its strange construction it turns out to be an entirely efficient table. It supports my writing paper as satisfactorily as table no. 1; for when I lay the paper on it the little electric particles with their headlong speed keep on hitting the underside, so that the paper is maintained in shuttlecock fashion at a nearly steady level. If I lean upon this table I shall not go through; or, to be strictly accurate, the chance of my scientific elbow going through my scientific table is so excessively small that it can be neglected in practical life. Reviewing their properties one by one, there seems to be nothing to choose between the two tables for ordinary purposes; but when abnormal circumstances befall, then my scientific table shows to advantage. If the house catches fire my scientific table will dissolve quite naturally into scientific smoke, whereas my familiar table undergoes a metamorphosis of its substantial nature which I can only regard as miraculous.

There is nothing *substantial* about my second table. It is nearly all empty space—space pervaded, it is true, by fields of force, but these are assigned to the category of, "influences," not of "things." Even in the minute part which is not empty we must not transfer the old notion of substance. In dissecting matter into electric charges we have travelled far from that picture of it which first gave rise to the conception of substance, and the meaning of that conception—if it ever had any—has been lost by the way. **The whole trend of modern scientific views is to break down the separate categories of "things," "influences," "forms," etc., and to substitute a common background of all experience.** Whether we are studying a material object, a magnetic field, a geometrical figure, or a duration of time, our scientific information is summed up in measures; neither the apparatus of measurement nor the mode of using it suggests that there is anything essentially different in these problems. The measures themselves afford no ground for a classification by categories. We feel it necessary to concede some background to the measures—an external world; but the attributes of this world, except insofar as they are reflected in the measures, are outside scientific scrutiny. Science has at last revolted against attaching the exact knowledge contained in these measurements to a traditional picture-gallery of conceptions which convey no authentic information of the background and obtrude irrelevancies into the scheme of knowledge.

I will not here stress further the nonsubstantiality of electrons, since it is scarcely necessary to the present line of thought. Conceive them as substantially as you will, there is a vast difference between my scientific table with its substance (if any) thinly scattered in specks in a region mostly empty and the table of everyday conception which we regard as the type of solid reality—an incarnate protest against Berkeleian subjectivism. It makes all the difference in the world whether the paper before me is poised as it were on a swarm of flies and sustained in shuttlecock fashion by a series of tiny blows from the swarm underneath, or whether it is supported because there is substance below it, it being the intrinsic nature of substance to occupy space to the exclusion of other substance; all the difference in conception at least, but no difference to my practical task of writing on the paper.

I need not tell you that modern physics has by delicate test and remorseless logic assured me that my second scientific table is the only one which is really there—wherever "there" may be. On the other hand I need not tell you that modern physics will never succeed in exorcising that first table—strange compound of external nature, mental imagery, and inherited prejudice—which lies visible to my eyes and tangible to my grasp. We must bid good-bye to it for the present, for we are about to turn from the familiar world to the scientific world revealed by physics. This is, or is intended to be, a wholly external world.

"You speak paradoxically of two worlds. Are they not really two aspects or two interpretations of one and the same world?"

Yes, no doubt they are ultimately to be identified after some fashion. But the process by which the external world of physics is transformed into a world of familiar acquaintance in human consciousness is outside the scope of physics. And so the world studied according to the methods of physics remains detached from the world familiar to consciousness, until after the physicist has finished his labors upon it. Provisionally, therefore, we regard the table which is the subject of physical research as altogether separate from the familiar table, without prejudging the question of their ultimate identification. It is true that the whole scientific inquiry starts from the familiar world and in the end it must return to the familiar world; but the part of the journey over which the physicist has charge is in foreign territory.

Until recently there was a much closer linkage; the physicist used to borrow the raw material of his world from the familiar world, but he does so no longer. His raw materials are ether, electrons, quanta, potentials, Hamiltonian functions, etc., and he is nowadays scrupulously careful to guard these from contamination by conceptions borrowed from the other world. There is a familiar table parallel to the scientific table, but there is no familiar electron, quantum, or potential parallel to the scientific electron, quantum, or potential. We do not even desire to manufacture a familiar counterpart to these things or, as we should commonly say, to "explain" the electron. After the physicist has quite finished his world-building a linkage or identification is allowed; but premature attempts at linkage have been found to be entirely mischievous.

Reality Consists of Ideas

George Berkeley

It is evident to anyone who takes a survey of the *objects of human knowledge* that they are either *ideas* actually imprinted on the senses, or else such as are perceived by attending to the passions and operations of the mind; or lastly, *ideas* formed by help of memory and imagination—either compounding, dividing, or barely representing those originally perceived in the aforesaid ways. By sight I have the ideas of light and colours, with their several degrees and variations. By touch I perceive hard and soft, heat and cold, motion and resistance; and of all these more and less either as to quantity or degree. Smelling furnishes me with odours; the palate with tastes; and hearing conveys sounds to the mind in all their variety of tone and composition.

And as several of these are observed to accompany each other, they come to be marked by one name, and so to be reputed as one *thing*. Thus, for example, a certain colour, taste, smell, figure, and consistence having been observed to go together, are accounted one distinct thing, signified by the name apple; other collections of ideas constitute a stone, a tree, a book, and the like sensible things; which as they are pleasing or disagreeable excite the passions of love, hatred, joy, grief, and so forth. . . .

2. But, besides all that endless variety of ideas or objects of knowledge, there is likewise something which knows or perceives them, and exercises divers operations, as willing, imagining, remembering, about them. This perceiving, active being is what I call *mind, spirit, soul,* or *myself*: By which words I do not denote any one of my ideas, but a thing entirely distinct from them, wherein they exist, or, which is the same thing, whereby they are perceived—for the existence of an idea consists in being perceived.

3. That neither our thoughts, nor passions, nor ideas formed by the imagination exist without the mind is what everybody will allow. And to me it is no less evident that the various sensations or ideas imprinted on the sense, however blended or combined together (that is, whatever objects they compose), cannot exist otherwise than in a mind perceiving them. I think an intuitive knowledge may be obtained of this by any one that shall attend to what is meant by the term *exist* when applied to sensible

things. The table I write on I say exists, that is, I see and feel it; and if I were out of my study I should say it existed—meaning thereby that if I was in my study I might perceive it, or that some other spirit actually does perceive it. There was an odour, that is, it was smelt; there was a sound, that is, it was heard; a colour or figure, and it was perceived by sight or touch. This is all that I can understand by these and the like expressions. **For as to what is said of the absolute existence of unthinking things without any relation to their being perceived, that is to me perfectly unintelligible. Their *esse* is *percipi*, nor is it possible they should have any existence out of the minds or thinking things which perceive them.**

4. It is indeed an opinion strangely prevailing amongst men, that houses, mountains, rivers, and in a word all sensible objects, have an existence, natural or real, distinct from their being perceived by the understanding. But, with how great an assurance and acquiescence soever this principle may be entertained in the world, yet whoever shall find in his heart to call it in question may, if I mistake not, perceive it to involve a manifest contradiction. For, what are the forementioned objects but the things we perceive by sense? and what do we perceive besides our own ideas or sensations? and is it not plainly repugnant that any one of these, or any combination of them, should exist unperceived?

5. If we thoroughly examine this tenet it will, perhaps, be found at bottom to depend on the doctrine of *abstract ideas*. For can there be a nicer strain of abstraction than to distinguish the existence of sensible objects from their being perceived, so as to conceive them existing unperceived? Light and colours, heat and cold, extension and figures—in a word the things we see and feel—what are they but so many sensations, notions, ideas, or impressions on the sense? and is it possible to separate, even in thought, any of these from perception? For my part, I might as easily divide a thing from itself. I may, indeed, divide in my thoughts, or conceive apart from each other, those things which, perhaps, I never perceived by sense so divided. Thus, I imagine the trunk of a human body without the limbs, or conceive the smell of a rose without thinking on the rose itself. So far, I will not deny, I can abstract—if that may properly be called *abstraction* which extends only to the conceiving separately such objects as it is possible may really exist or be actually perceived asunder. But my conceiving or imagining power does not extend beyond the possibility of real existence or perception. Hence, as it is impossible for me to see or feel

anything without an actual sensation of that thing, so is it impossible for me to conceive in my thoughts any sensible thing or object distinct from the sensation or perception of it. [In truth, the object and the sensation are the same thing, and cannot therefore be abstracted from each other.]

6. Some truths there are so near and obvious to the mind that a man need only open his eyes to see them. Such I take this important one to be, viz. that all the choir of heaven and furniture of the earth, in a word all those bodies which compose the mighty frame of the world, have not any subsistence without a mind, that their *being* is to be perceived or known; that consequently, so long as they are not actually perceived by me, or do not exist in my mind or that of any other created spirit, they must either have no existence at all, or else subsist in the mind of some Eternal Spirit—it being perfectly unintelligible, and involving all the absurdity of abstraction, to attribute to any single part of them an existence independent of a spirit. [To be convinced of which, the reader need only reflect, and try to separate in his own thoughts the *being* of a sensible thing from its *being perceived*.]

7. From what has been said it is evident there is not any other Substance than *Spirit*, or that which perceives. But, for the fuller demonstration of this point, let it be considered the sensible qualities are colour, figure, motion, smell, taste, etc., i.e., the ideas perceived by sense. Now, for an idea to exist in an unperceiving thing is a manifest contradiction, for to have an idea is all one has to perceive; that therefore wherein colour, figure, etc., exist must perceive them; hence it is clear there can be no unthinking substance or *substratum* of those ideas.

8. But, say you, though the ideas themselves do not exist without the mind, yet there may be things like them, whereof they are copies or resemblances, which things exist without the mind in an unthinking substance. I answer, an idea can be like nothing but an idea; a colour or figure can be like nothing but another colour or figure. If we look but never so little into our thoughts, we shall find it impossible for us to conceive a likeness except only between our ideas. Again, I ask whether those supposed originals or external things, of which our ideas are the pictures or representations, be themselves perceivable or no? If they are, then they are ideas and we have gained our point; but if you say they are not, I appeal to any one whether it be sense to assert a colour is like something which is invisible; hard or soft, like something which is intangible; and so of the rest.

9. Some there are who make a distinction betwixt *primary* and *secondary* qualities. By the former they mean extension, figure, motion, rest, solidity or impenetrability, and number; by the latter they denote all other sensible qualities, as colours, sounds, tastes, and so forth. The ideas we have of these they acknowledge not to be the resemblances of anything existing without the mind, or unperceived, but they will have our ideas of the primary qualities to be patterns or images of things which exist without the mind, in an unthinking substance which they call Matter. By Matter, therefore, we are to understand an inert, senseless substance, in which extension, figure, and motion do actually subsist. But it is evident, from what we have already shown, that extension, figure, and motion are only ideas existing in the mind, and that an idea can be like nothing but another idea, and that consequently neither they nor their archetypes can exist in an unperceiving substance. Hence, it is plain that the very notion of what is called *Matter or corporeal substance*, involves a contradiction in it. . . .

25. All our ideas, sensations, notions, or the things which we perceive, by whatsoever names they may be distinguished, are visibly inactive—there is nothing of power or agency included in them. So that one idea or object of thought cannot produce or make any alteration in another. To be satisfied of the truth of this, there is nothing else requisite but a bare observation of our ideas. For, since they and every part of them exist only in the mind, it follows that there is nothing in them but what is perceived: but whoever shall attend to his ideas, whether of sense or reflection, will not perceive in them any power or activity; there is, therefore, no such thing contained in them. A little attention will discover to us that the very being of an idea implies passiveness and inertness in it, insomuch that it is impossible for an idea to do anything, or, strictly speaking, to be the cause of anything: neither can it be the resemblance or pattern of any active being, as is evident from [paragraph] 8. Whence it plainly follows that extension, figure, and motion cannot be the cause of our sensations. To say, therefore, that these are the effects of powers resulting from the configuration, number, motion, and size of corpuscles, must certainly be false.

26. We perceive a continual succession of ideas, some are anew excited, others are changed or totally disappear. There is therefore some cause of these ideas, whereon they depend, and which produces and changes them. That this cause cannot be any quality or idea or combination of ideas, is clear from the preceding section. It must therefore be a substance; but it has been shown that there is no . . . material substance: it

remains, therefore that the cause of ideas is an [immaterial] active substance or Spirit.

27. A Spirit is one simple, undivided, active being—as it perceives ideas it is called the *understanding*, and as it produces or otherwise operates about them it is called the *will*. Hence there can be no *idea* formed of a soul or spirit; for all ideas whatever, being passive and inert (vid. sec. 25), they cannot represent unto us, by way of image or likeness, that which acts. A little attention will make it plain to anyone that to have an idea which shall be like that active principle of motion and change of ideas is absolutely impossible. Such is the nature of *spirit*, or that which acts, that it cannot be of itself perceived, but only by the effects which it produceth. If any man shall doubt of the truth of what is here delivered, let him but reflect and try if he can frame the idea of any power or active being; and whether he has ideas of two principal powers, marked by the names *will* and *understanding*, distinct from each other as well as from a third idea of Substance or Being in general, with a relative notion of its supporting or being the subject of the aforesaid powers—which is signified by the name *soul* or *spirit*. This is what some hold; but, so far as I can see, the words *will, [understanding, mind,] soul, spirit*, do not stand for different ideas, or, in truth, for any idea at all, but for something which is very different from ideas, and which, being an agent, cannot be like unto, or represented by, any idea whatsoever. [Though it must be owned at the same time that we have some *notion* of soul, spirit, and the operations of the mind; such as willing, loving, hating—inasmuch as we know or understand the meaning of these words.]

28. I find I can excite ideas in my mind at pleasure, and vary and shift the scene as oft as I think fit. It is no more than willing, and straightway this or that idea arises in my fancy; and by the same power it is obliterated and makes way for another. This making and unmaking of ideas doth very properly denominate the mind active. Thus much is certain and grounded on experience: but when we talk of unthinking agents, or of exciting ideas exclusive of volition, we only amuse ourselves with words.

29. But, whatever power I may have over my own thoughts, I find the ideas actually perceived by Sense have not a like dependence on my will. When in broad daylight I open my eyes, it is not in my power to choose whether I shall see or no, or to determine what particular objects shall present themselves to my view; and so likewise as to the hearing and other senses, the ideas imprinted on them are not creatures of my will. There is therefore some *other* Will or Spirit that produces them.

30. The ideas of Sense are more strong, lively, and distinct than those of the imagination; they have likewise a steadiness, order, and coherence, and are not excited at random, as those which are the effects of human wills often are, but in a regular train or series—the admirable connexion whereof sufficiently testifies the wisdom and benevolence of its Author. Now the set rules or established methods wherein the Mind we depend on excites in us the ideas of sense, are called the *laws of nature*; and these we learn by experience, which teaches us that such and such ideas are attended with such and such other ideas, in the ordinary course of things.

31. This gives us a sort of foresight which enables us to regulate our actions for the benefit of life. And without this we should be eternally at a loss; we could not know how to act anything that might procure us the least pleasure, or remove the least pain of sense. That food nourishes, sleep refreshes, and fire warms us; that to sow in the seed-time is the way to reap in the harvest; and in general that to obtain such or such ends, such or such means are conducive—all this we know, not by discovering any necessary connexion between our ideas, but only by the observation of the settled laws of nature, without which we should be all in uncertainty and confusion, and a grown man no more know how to manage himself in the affairs of life than an infant just born.

32. And yet this consistent uniform working, which so evidently displays the goodness and wisdom of that Governing Spirit whose Will constitutes the laws of nature, is so far from leading our thoughts to Him, that it rather sends them wandering after second causes. For, when we perceive certain ideas of Sense constantly followed by other ideas, and we know this is not of our own doing, we forthwith attribute power and agency to the ideas themselves, and make one the cause of another, than which nothing can be more absurd and unintelligible. Thus, for example, having observed that when we perceive by sight a certain round luminous figure we at the same time perceive by touch the idea or sensation called heat, we do from thence conclude the sun to be the cause of heat. And in like manner perceiving the motion and collision of bodies to be attended with sound, we are inclined to think the latter the effect of the former.

33. The ideas imprinted on the Senses by the Author of nature are called *real things*: and those excited in the imagination being less regular, vivid, and constant, are more properly termed *ideas*, or *images of things*, which they copy and represent. But then our sensations, be they never so vivid and distinct, are nevertheless ideas, that is, they exist in the mind, or are perceived by it, as truly as the ideas of its own framing. The ideas of

Sense are allowed to have more reality in them, that is, to be more strong, orderly, and coherent than the creatures of the mind; but this is no argument that they exist without the mind. They are also less dependent on the spirit, or thinking substance which perceives them, in that they are excited by the will of another and more powerful spirit; yet still they are *ideas,* and **certainly no idea, whether faint or strong, can exist otherwise than in a mind perceiving it.**

The Crest-Jewel of Discrimination

Shankara

A man should be intelligent and learned, with great powers of comprehension, and able to overcome doubts by the exercise of his reason. One who has these qualifications is fitted for knowledge of the Atman.

He alone may be considered qualified to seek Brahman who has discrimination, whose mind is turned away from all enjoyments, who possesses tranquillity and the kindred virtues, and who feels a longing for liberation.

In this connection, the sages have spoken of four qualifications for attainment. When these are present, devotion to the Reality will become complete. When they are absent, it will fail.

First is mentioned discrimination between the eternal and the non-eternal. Next comes renunciation of the enjoyment of the fruits of action, here and hereafter. Then come the six treasures of virtue, beginning with tranquillity. And last, certainly, is the longing for liberation.

Brahman is real; the universe is unreal. A firm conviction that this is so is called *discrimination* between the eternal and the non-eternal.

Renunciation is the giving-up of all the pleasures of the eyes, the ears, and the other senses, the giving-up of the desire for a physical body as well as for the highest kind of spirit-body of a god.

To detach the mind from all objective things by continually seeing their imperfection, and to direct it steadfastly toward Brahman, its goal—this is called *tranquillity*.

To detach both kinds of sense-organs—those of perception and those of action—from objective things, and to withdraw them to rest in their respective centers—this is called *self-control*. True *mental poise* consists in not letting the mind react to external stimuli.

To endure all kinds of afflictions without rebellion, complaint or lament—this is called *forbearance*.

A firm conviction, based upon intellectual understanding that the teachings of the scriptures and of one's master are true—this is called by the sages the *faith* which leads to realization of the Reality.

To concentrate the intellect repeatedly upon the pure Brahman and to keep it fixed there always—this is called *self-surrender*. This does not mean soothing the mind, like a baby, with idle thoughts.

Longing for liberation is the will to be free from the fetters forged by ignorance—beginning with the ego-sense and so on, down to the physical body itself—through the realization of one's true nature.

Even though this longing for liberation may be present in a slight or moderate degree, it will grow intense through the grace of the teacher, and through the practice of renunciation and of virtues such as tranquillity, etc.: And it will bear fruit.

When renunciation and the longing for liberation are present to an intense degree within a man, then the practice of tranquillity and the other virtues will bear fruit and lead to the goal.

Where renunciation and longing for liberation are weak, tranquillity and the other virtues are a mere appearance, like the mirage in the desert.

Among all means of liberation, devotion is supreme. To seek earnestly to know one's real nature—this is said to be devotion.

In other words, devotion can be defined as the search for the reality of one's own Atman. The seeker after the reality of the Atman, who possesses the above-mentioned qualifications, should approach an illumined teacher from whom he can learn the way to liberation from all bondage. . . .

Now I shall tell you the nature of the Atman. If you realize it, you will be freed from the bonds of ignorance, and attain liberation.

There is a self-existent Reality, which is the basis of our consciousness of ego. That Reality is the witness of the three states of our consciousness, and is distinct from the five bodily coverings.[1]

That Reality is the knower in all states of consciousness—waking, dreaming and dreamless sleep. It is aware of the presence or absence of the mind and its functions. It is the Atman.

That Reality sees everything by its own light. No one sees it. It gives intelligence to the mind and the intellect, but no one gives it light.

That Reality pervades the universe, but no one penetrates it. It alone shines. The universe shines with its reflected light.

Because of its presence, the body, senses, mind and intellect apply themselves to their respective functions, as though obeying its command.

Its nature is eternal consciousness. It knows all things, from the sense of ego to the body itself. It is the knower of pleasure and pain and of the sense-objects. It knows everything objectively—just as a man knows the objective existence of a jar.

This is the Atman, the Supreme being, the ancient. It never ceases to experience infinite joy. It is always the same. It is consciousness itself. The organs and vital energies function under its command.

Here, within this body, in the pure mind, in the secret chamber of intelligence, in the infinite universe within the heart, the Atman shines in its captivating splendour, like a noonday sun. By its light, the universe is revealed.

It is the knower of the activities of the mind and of the individual man. It is the witness of all the actions of the body, the sense-organs and the vital energy. It seems to be identified with all these, just as fire appears identified with an iron ball. But it neither acts nor is subject to the slightest change.

The Atman is birthless and deathless. It neither grows nor decays. It is unchangeable, eternal. It does not dissolve when the body dissolves. Does the ether cease to exist when the jar that enclosed it is broken?

The Atman is distinct from Maya,[2] the primal cause, and from her effect, the universe. The nature of the Atman is pure consciousness. The Atman reveals this entire universe of mind and matter. It cannot be defined. In and through the various states of consciousness—the waking, the dreaming and the sleeping—it maintains our unbroken awareness of identity. It manifests itself as the witness of the intelligence.

The Mind

With a controlled mind and an intellect which is made pure and tranquil, you must realize the Atman directly, within yourself. Know the Atman as the real I. Thus you cross the shoreless ocean of worldliness, whose waves are birth and death. Live always in the knowledge of identity with Brahman, and be blessed.

Man is in bondage because he mistakes what is non-Atman for his real Self. This is caused by ignorance. Hence follows the misery of birth and death. Through ignorance, man identifies the Atman with the body, taking the perishable for the real. Therefore he nourishes this body, and anoints it, and guards it carefully. He becomes enmeshed in the things of the senses like a caterpillar in the threads of its cocoon.

Deluded by his ignorance, a man mistakes one thing for another. Lack of discernment will cause a man to think that a snake is a piece of rope. When he grasps it in this belief he runs a great risk. The acceptance of the unreal as real constitutes the state of bondage. Pay heed to this, my friend.

The Atman is indivisible, eternal, one without a second. It is eternally made manifest by the power of its own knowledge. Its glories are infinite. The veil of tamas[3] hides the true nature of the Atman, just as an eclipse hides the rays of the sun.

When the pure rays of the Atman are thus concealed, the deluded man identifies himself with his body, which is non-Atman. Then rajas, which has the power of projecting illusory forms, afflicts him sorely. It binds him with chains of lust, anger and the other passions.

His mind becomes perverted. His consciousness of the Atman is swallowed up by the shark of total ignorance. Yielding to the power of rajas, he identifies himself with the many motions and changes of the mind. Therefore he is swept hither and thither, now rising, now sinking, in the boundless ocean of birth and death, whose waters are full of the poison of sense-objects. This is indeed a miserable fate.

The sun's rays bring forth layers of cloud. By them, the sun is concealed; and so it appears that the clouds alone exist. In the same way, the ego, which is brought forth by the Atman, hides the true nature of the Atman; and so it appears that the ego alone exists.

On a stormy day the sun is swallowed up by thick clouds; and these clouds are attacked by sharp, chill blasts of wind. So, when the Atman is enveloped in the thick darkness of tamas, the terrible power of rajas attacks the deluded man with all kinds of sorrows.

Man's bondage is caused by the power of these two—tamas and rajas. Deluded by these, he mistakes the body for the Atman and strays on to the path that leads to death and rebirth.

Man's life in this relative world may be compared to a tree. Tamas is the seed. Identification of the Atman with the body is its sprouting forth. The cravings are its leaves. Work is its sap. The body is its trunk. The vital forces are its branches. The sense-organs are its twigs. The sense-objects are its flowers. Its fruits are the sufferings caused by various actions. The individual man is the bird who eats the fruit of the tree of life.

The Atman's bondage to the non-Atman springs from ignorance. It has no external cause. It is said to be beginningless. It will continue indefinitely until a man becomes enlightened. As long as a man remains in this bondage it subjects him to a long train of miseries—birth, death, sickness, decrepitude, and so forth.

This bondage cannot be broken by weapons, or by wind, or by fire, or by millions of acts. Nothing but the sharp sword of knowledge can cut through this bondage. It is forged by discrimination and made keen by purity of heart, through divine grace.

A man must faithfully and devotedly fulfill the duties of life as the scriptures prescribe. This purifies his heart. A man whose heart is pure realizes the supreme Atman. Thereby he destroys his bondage to the world, root and all.

Wrapped in its five coverings, beginning with the physical, which are the products of its own Maya, the Atman remains hidden, as the water of a pond is hidden by a veil of scum.

When the scum is removed, the pure water is clearly seen. It takes away a man's thirst, cools him immediately and makes him happy.

When all the five coverings are removed, the pure Arman is revealed. It is revealed as God dwelling within; as unending, unalloyed bliss; as the supreme and self-luminous Being.

The wise man who seeks liberation from bondage must discriminate between Atman and non-Atman. In this way, he can realize the Atman, which is Infinite Being, Infinite Wisdom and Infinite Love. Thus he finds happiness.

The Atman dwells within, free from attachment and beyond all action. A man must separate this Atman from every object of experience, as a stalk of grass is separated from its enveloping sheath. Then he must dissolve into the Atman all those appearances which make up the world of name and form. He is indeed a free soul who can remain thus absorbed in the Atman alone.

The Body

This body is the "physical covering." Food made its birth possible; on food it lives; without food it must die. It consists of cuticle, skin, flesh, blood, bone and water. It cannot be the Atman, the ever-pure, the self-existent.

It did not exist before birth, it will not exist after death. It exists for a short while only, in the interim between them. Its very nature is transient, and subject to change. It is a compound, not an element. Its vitality is only a reflection. It is a sense-object, which can be perceived, like a jar. How can it be the Atman—the experiencer of all experiences?

The body consists of arms, legs and other limbs. It is not the Atman—for when some of these limbs have been cut off, a man may continue to live and function through his remaining organs. The body is controlled by another. It cannot be the Atman, the controller.

The Atman watches the body, with its various characteristics, actions and states of growth. That this Atman, which is the abiding reality, is of another nature than the body, must be self-evident.

The body is a bundle of bones held together by flesh. It is very dirty and full of filth. The body can never be the same as the self-existent Atman, the knower. The nature of the Atman is quite different from that of the body.

It is the ignorant man who identifies himself with the body, which is compounded of skin, flesh, fat, bone and filth. The man of spiritual discrimination knows the Atman, his true being, the one supreme reality, as distinct from the body.

The fool thinks, "I am the body." The intelligent man thinks, "I am an individual soul united with the body." But the wise man, in the greatness of his knowledge and spiritual discrimination, sees the Atman as reality and thinks, "I am Brahman."

O fool, stop identifying yourself with this lump of skin, flesh, fat, bones and filth. Identify yourself with Brahman, the Absolute, the Atman in all beings. That is how you can attain the supreme peace.

The intelligent man may be learned in Vedanta and the moral laws. But there is not the least hope of his liberation until he stops mistakenly identifying himself with the body and the sense-organs. This identification is caused by delusion.

You never identify yourself with the shadow cast by your body, or with its reflection, or with the body you see in a dream or in your imagination. Therefore you should not identify yourself with this living body, either.

Those who live in ignorance identify the body with the Atman. This ignorance is the root-cause of birth, death and rebirth. Therefore you must strive earnestly to destroy it. When your heart is free from this ignorance, there will no longer be any possibility of your rebirth. You will reach immortality.

That covering of the Atman which is called "the vital covering" is made up of the vital force and the five organs of action. The body is called "the physical covering." It comes to life when it is enveloped by the vital covering. It is thus that the body engages in action.

This vital covering is not the Atman—for it is merely composed of the vital airs. Air-like, it enters and leaves the body. It does not know what is good or bad for itself, or for others. It is always dependent upon the Atman.

Purification

The mind, together with the organs of perception, forms the "mental covering." It causes the sense of "I" and "mine." It also causes us to discern objects. It is endowed with the power and faculty of differentiating objects by giving them various names. It is manifest, enveloping the "vital covering."

The mental covering may be compared to the sacrificial fire. It is fed by the fuel of many desires. The five organs of perception serve as priests. Objects of desire are poured upon it like a continuous stream of oblations. Thus it is that this phenomenal universe is brought forth.

Ignorance is nowhere, except in the mind. The mind is filled with ignorance, and this causes the bondage of birth and death. When, in the enlightenment of the Atman, a man transcends the mind, the phenomenal universe disappears from him. When a man lives in the domain of mental ignorance, the phenomenal universe exists for him.

In dream, the mind is emptied of the objective universe, but it creates by its own power a complete universe of subject and object. The waking state is only a prolonged dream. The phenomenal universe exists in the mind.

In dreamless sleep, when the mind does not function, nothing exists. This is our universal experience. Man seems to be in bondage to birth and death. This is a fictitious creation of the mind, not a reality.

The wind collects the clouds, and the wind drives them away again. Mind creates bondage, and mind also removes bondage.

The mind creates attachment to the body and the things of this world. Thus it binds a man, as a beast is tied by a rope. But it is also the mind which creates in a man an utter distaste for sense-objects, as if for poison. Thus it frees him from his bondage.

The mind, therefore, is the cause of man's bondage and also of his liberation. It causes bondage when it is darkened by rajas. It causes liberation when it is freed from rajas and tamas, and made pure.

If discrimination and dispassion are practiced, to the exclusion of everything else, the mind will become pure and move toward liberation. Therefore the wise man who seeks liberation must develop both these qualities within himself.

That terrible tiger called an impure mind prowls in the forest of the sense-objects. The wise man who seeks liberation must not go there.

The mind of the experiencer creates all the objects which he experiences, while in the waking or the dreaming state. Ceaselessly, it creates the differences in men's bodies, color, social condition and race. It creates the variations of the gunas. It creates desires, actions and the fruits of actions.

Man is pure spirit, free from attachment. The mind deludes him. It binds him with the bonds of the body, the sense-organs and the life-breath. It creates in him the sense of "I" and "mine." It makes him wander endlessly among the fruits of the actions it has caused.

The error of identifying Atman with non-Atman is the cause of man's birth, death and rebirth. This false identification is created by the mind. Therefore, it is the mind that causes the misery of birth, death and rebirth for the man who has no discrimination and is tainted by rajas and tamas.

Therefore the wise, who know Reality, have declared that the mind is full of ignorance. Because of this ignorance, all the creatures of the universe are swept helplessly hither and thither, like masses of cloud before the wind.

Therefore, the seeker after liberation must work carefully to purify the mind. When the mind has been made pure, liberation is as easy to grasp as the fruit which lies in the palm of your hand.

Seek earnestly for liberation, and your lust for sense-objects will be rooted out. Practice detachment toward all actions. Have faith in the Reality. Devote yourself to the practice of spiritual disciplines, such as hearing the word of Brahman, reasoning and meditating upon it. Thus the mind will be freed from the evil of rajas.

The "mental covering," therefore, cannot be the Atman. It has a beginning and an end, and is subject to change. It is the abode of pain. It is an object of experience. The seer cannot be the thing which is seen.

The Covering of Intellect

The discriminating faculty with its powers of intelligence, together with the organs of perception, is known as the "covering of intellect." To be the doer is its distinguishing characteristic. It is the cause of man's birth, death and rebirth.

The power of intelligence that is in the "covering of intellect" is a reflection of the Atman, the pure consciousness. The "covering of intellect" is an effect of Maya. It possesses the faculty of knowing and acting. It always identifies itself entirely with the body, sense-organs, etc.

It has no beginning. It is characterized by its sense of ego. It constitutes the individual man. It is the initiator of all actions and undertakings. Impelled by the tendencies and impressions formed in previous births, it performs virtuous or sinful actions and experiences their results.

It gathers experiences by wandering through many wombs of higher or lower degree. The states of waking and dreaming belong to this '"covering of intellect." It experiences joy and sorrow.

Because of its sense of "I" and "mine," it constantly identifies itself with the body, and the physical states, and with the duties pertaining to the different stages and orders of life. This "covering of intellect" shines with a bright light because of its proximity to the shining Atman. It is a garment of the Atman, but man identifies himself with it and wanders around the circle of birth, death and rebirth because of his delusion.

The Atman, which is pure consciousness, is the light that shines in the shrine of the heart, the center of all vital force. It is immutable, but it becomes the "doer" and "experiencer" when it is mistakenly identified with the "covering of intellect."

The Atman assumes the limitations of the "covering of intellect" because it is mistakenly identified with that covering, which is totally different from itself. This man, who is the Atman, regards himself as being separate from it, and from Brahman, who is the one Atman in all creatures. An ignorant man, likewise, may regard a jar as being different from the clay of which it was made.

By its nature, the Atman is forever unchanging and perfect. But it assumes the character and nature of its coverings because it is mistakenly identified with them. Although fire is formless, it will assume the form of red-hot iron. . . .

Atman Is Brahman

The Disciple: Master, if we reject these five coverings as unreal, it seems to me that nothing remains but the void. How, then, can there be an existence which the wise man may realize as one with his Atman?

The Master: That is a good question, O prudent one. Your argument is clever. Nevertheless, there must be an existence, a reality which perceives the ego-sense and the coverings and is also aware of the void which is their absence. This reality by itself remains unperceived. Sharpen your discrimination that you may know this Atman, which is the knower.

He who experiences is conscious of himself. Without an experiencer, there can be no self-consciousness.

The Atman is its own witness, since it is conscious of itself. The Atman is no other than Brahman.

The Atman is pure consciousness, clearly manifest as underlying the states of waking, dreaming and dreamless sleep. It is inwardly experienced as unbroken consciousness, the consciousness that I am I. It is the unchanging witness that experiences the ego, the intellect and the rest, with their various forms and changes. It is realized within one's own heart as existence, knowledge and bliss absolute. Realize this Atman within the shrine of your own heart.

The fool sees the reflection of the sun in the water of a jar, and thinks it is the sun. Man in the ignorance of his delusion sees the reflection of Pure Consciousness upon the coverings, and mistakes it for the real I.

In order to look at the sun, you must turn away from the jar, the water, and the sun's reflection in the water. The wise know that these three are only revealed by the reflection of the self-luminous sun. They are not the sun itself.

The body, the covering of intellect, the reflection of consciousness upon it—none of these is the Atman. The Atman is the witness, infinite consciousness, revealer of all things but distinct from all, no matter whether they be gross or subtle. It is the eternal reality, omnipresent, all-pervading, the subtlest of all subtleties. It has neither inside nor outside. It is the real I, hidden in the shrine of the heart. Realize fully the truth of the Atman. Be free from evil and impurity, and you shall pass beyond death.

Know the Atman, transcend all sorrows, and reach the fountain of joy. Be illumined by this knowledge, and you have nothing to fear. If you wish to find liberation, there is no other way of breaking the bonds of rebirth.

What can break the bondage and misery of this world? The knowledge that the Atman is Brahman. Then it is that you realize Him who is one without a second, and who is the absolute bliss.

Realize Brahman, and there will be no more returning to this world—the home of all sorrows. You must realize absolutely that the Atman is Brahman.

Then you will win Brahman for ever. He is the truth. He is existence and knowledge. He is absolute. He is pure and self-existent. He is eternal, unending joy. He is none other than the Atman.

The Atman is one with Brahman: this is the highest truth. Brahman alone is real. There is none but He. When He is known as the supreme reality there is no other existence but Brahman.

The Universe

Brahman is the realty—the one existence, absolutely independent of human thought or idea. Because of the ignorance of our human minds, the universe seems to be composed of diverse forms. It is Brahman alone.

A jar made of clay is not other than clay. It is clay essentially. The form of the jar has no independent existence. What, then, is the jar? Merely an invented name!

The form of the jar can never be perceived apart from the clay. What, then, is the jar? An appearance! The reality is the clay itself.

This universe is an effect of Brahman. It can never be anything else but Brahman. Apart from Brahman, it does not exist. There is nothing beside Him. He who says that this universe has an independent existence is still suffering from delusion. He is like a man talking in his sleep.

"The universe is Brahman"—so says the great seer of the Atharva Veda. The universe, therefore, is nothing but Brahman. It is superimposed upon Him. It has no separate existence, apart from its ground.

If the universe, as we perceive it, were real, knowledge of the Atman would not put an end to our delusion. The scriptures would be untrue. The revelations of the Divine Incarnations would make no sense. These alternatives cannot be considered either desirable or beneficial by any thinking person.

Sri Krishna, the Incarnate Lord, who knows the secret of all truths, says in the Gita: "Although I am not within any creature, all creatures exist within me. I do not mean that they exist within me physically. That is my divine mystery. My Being sustains all creatures and brings them to birth, but has no physical contact with them."

If this universe were real, we should continue to perceive it in deep sleep. But we perceive nothing then. Therefore it is unreal, like our dreams.

The universe does not exist apart from the Atman. Our perception of it as having an independent existence is false, like our perception of blueness in the sky. How can a superimposed attribute have any existence, apart from its substratum? It is only our delusion which causes this misconception of the underlying reality.

No matter what a deluded man may think he is perceiving, he is really seeing Brahman and nothing else but Brahman. He sees mother-of-pearl and imagines that it is silver. He sees Brahman and imagines that it is the universe.

But this universe, which is superimposed upon Brahman, is nothing but a name.

I Am Brahman

Brahman is supreme. He is the reality—the one without a second. He is pure consciousness, free from any taint. He is tranquillity itself. He has neither beginning nor end. He does not change. He is joy for ever.

He transcends the appearance of the manifold, created by Maya. He is eternal, for ever beyond reach of pain, not to be divided, not to be measured, without form, without name, undifferentiated, immutable. He shines with His own light. He is everything that can be experienced in this universe.

The illumined seers know Him as the uttermost reality, infinite, absolute, without parts—the pure consciousness. In Him they find that knower, knowledge and known have become one.

They know Him as the reality which can neither be cast aside (since He is ever-present within the human soul) nor grasped (since He is beyond the power of mind and speech). They know Him immeasurable, beginningless, endless, supreme in glory. They realize the truth: "I am Brahman."

Notes

[1] [The five bodily coverings will be discussed later. They are the physical, the vital, the mental, the intellectual, and the covering of bliss. These are called "coverings" because Shankara pictures them as progressively thinner bodies or sheaves (like those dolls within dolls) that cover the *Atman*. This is based on the idea that matter extends from a gross level (the physical body as we think of it) to subtler or finer levels. Notice that things like mind and intellect, which in the West have usually been thought of as immaterial, are here thought of as material (but matter of a finer sort).—Ed.]

[2] [*Maya* is sometimes translated as "illusion" and sometimes as "appearance." It refers to the illusions done by magicians and Shankara uses this analogy to indicate the process by which Brahman produces the universe. In general, *Maya* is the impermanent which appears to be real but is not. It stands in contrast to the permanence of *Atman-Brahman*, which is what is truly real.—Ed.]

[3] [*Tamas* are one of the three *gunas* that make up all material things. *Gunas* are qualities. In ancient Hindu cosmology it was thought that everything material is made up of some combination or mixture of the *gunas*. *Tamas* is the quality of stupor, laziness, stupidity, heaviness, and inaction in general. *Rajas*, another *guna*, is the active principle and hence the opposite of *tamas*. *Sattva*, the third *guna*, is associated with the pure, the fine, and the calm.—Ed.]

Chapter III: Knowledge

The most fundamental question that can be asked concerning human knowledge is a question of meaning; namely, "What does it mean to know (e.g., something/anything at all)?" How is it possible for the human understanding to distinguish between truth and error? What is the nature of knowledge? What is the source of human knowledge? What kinds of things can we know? Do we really know anything at all? What are the limits of human knowledge?

The branch of philosophy that investigates the problems associated with knowledge is called epistemology. The term derives from the Greek word *episteme* that is translated "knowledge." The word epistemology is commonly taken to mean "theory of knowledge." In his well-known work, *An Essay Concerning Human Understanding*, John Locke declares that his purpose is ". . . to inquire into the original, certainty, and extent of human knowledge, together with the grounds and degrees of belief, opinions, and assent. . . ." This, in sum, is also the basic purpose and aim of epistemology.

In Plato's "Knowledge Is Recollection" the philosopher Socrates presents the view that all learning is simply recollection of innate ideas. This thesis implies the pre-existence of the soul. By asking a series of skillful questions, Socrates is able to assist an uneducated slave boy to demonstrate his "innate" knowledge of geometry. Since the boy was never "taught" but merely "questioned," Plato asserts that this is proof that the soul is always possessed with knowledge and that the soul is immortal.

The companion pieces, "The Divided Line" and "The Allegory of the Cave," are two of the most significant writings in Western thought. Plato's "Cave" is perhaps the most powerful figure in philosophy. The purpose of the "Allegory," according to Plato, is "to show in a figure how far our nature is enlightened or unenlightened." Both the "Line" and the "Cave" lead the thinker beyond the realm of opinion generated by the senses to the realm of knowledge. Different or perhaps varying degrees of reality are known in different ways. The highest form of knowledge is the product of pure thought. The majority of humankind, the *hoi polloi*, are held prisoners by the senses and spend their lives in the ever-changing realm of opinion.

René Descartes was both a first-rate philosopher and an innovative mathematician. He is known as the "Father of Modern Philosophy." Reprinted in this volume are "Meditation I" and "Meditation II" from Descartes's *Meditations on First Philosophy* and his "What Is Indubitable?" from his *Discourse on Method*. The aim of Descartes's philosophical project was to find a certain foundation for knowledge. In order to achieve his goal of certainty Descartes employed a method of systematic or radical doubt. According to this method, Descartes vowed to withhold assent from all matters that are not entirely certain and indubitable as well as from those propositions that are manifestly false. Insofar as Descartes doubted the "truths" of the senses, even to the point of denying the external world, he was a sceptic. Descartes's certain truth was expressed in his famous *Cogito*; namely, "I *think, therefore I am*." From the indubitable certainty of his own existence, as a "thinking-thing," he constructed, by way of the ontological argument, a metaphysical bridge through God to the external world and thereby placed all knowledge on a firm foundation.

Philosophically, Descartes was a rationalist. Rationalism is the view that the mind contains or generates knowledge independent of sense experience, *a priori*. This position maintains that all knowledge is ultimately derived from innate ideas or is found by comparing ideas. In contrast, philosophers like John Locke, George Berkeley, and David Hume are empiricists. Empiricism is the view that all knowledge is derived from experience.

David Hume saw scepticism as an appropriate method for the study of philosophy. In "Scepticism," Hume tells us that scepticism helps preserve impartiality in judgment and weans the mind of prejudice.

In the next selection, "An Empiricist Theory of Knowledge," John Locke sets forth the basic tenets of empiricism. Locke begins the selection with a critique of innate ideas and asserts that, at birth, the mind is a *tabula rasa*, or "blank slate." "Let us suppose the mind to be, as we say, white paper, void of all characters, without any ideas—how comes it to be furnished?" Locke's answer to this question defines not only empiricism, but is the beginning point for a new theory of education. Locke continues, "To this I answer, in one word, from *experience*. In that all our knowledge is founded; and from that it ultimately derives itself."

David Hume's essay, "The Problem of Induction," is a philosophical classic. The essay begins with Hume's famous and useful distinction: "All the objects of human reason or inquiry may naturally be divided into two kinds, to wit, 'Relations of Ideas,' and 'Matters of Fact.'" The former are analytic truths of reason and, as such, are true necessarily. However, Hume points out that all of our thinking dealing with matters of fact is dependent on the relationship of *cause* and *effect*. The problem of induction is that there is no necessary connection between cause and effect. Rather, the relationship of cause and effect is established by custom whereby the mind associates two events on the basis of constant and regular conjunction. Since induction is the primary method of science, Hume has demonstrated that certainty is not possible for science. He states, "All inferences from experience, therefore, are effects of custom, not of reasoning."

In "Is the Sex of the Knower Epistemologically Significant?" Lorraine Code maintains that these are good reasons for asking who the knower is. Standard epistemology has uncritically treated the knower as a "featureless abstraction." Code argues that "the sex of the knower is epistemologically significant." Gender-related factors, she asserts play a "critical role" in the construction of knowledge. Her feminist epistemology is both critical and creative. As a critical epistemology it uproots and examines those assumptions that have guided the field for centuries. As a creative epistemology it broadens the range of epistemological considerations that have gone unnoticed because the field was needlessly, but narrowly, restricted.

In "Practice and Contradiction," Mao Tse-Tung is clear, "There can be no knowledge apart from practice." In crafting his epistemology Mao draws on two main sources—traditional Chinese thought and the writings of Karl Marx. China, as a civilization, has always valued practical concerns above theoretical concerns. Chinese cosmology described an ever-changing cosmos of particulars that must always be harmonized in appropriate ways. From Marx, Mao imported the idea of struggle and contradiction. For Mao,

> If you want to know a certain thing or a certain class of things directly, you must personally participate in the practical struggle to change reality, to change that thing or class of things, for only thus can you come into contact with them as phenomena; only through personal participation in the practical struggle to change reality can you uncover the essence of the thing or class of things and comprehend them.

Knowledge Is Recollection

Plato

Meno: O Socrates, I used to be told, before I knew you, that you were always doubting yourself and making others doubt; and now you are casting your spells over me, and I am simply getting bewitched and enchanted, and am at my wits' end. And if I may venture to make a jest upon you, **you seem to me both in your appearance and in your power over others to be very like the flat torpedo fish, who torpifies those who come near him and touch him, as you have now torpified me, I think**. For my soul and my tongue are really torpid, and I do not know how to answer you; and though I have been delivered of an infinite variety of speeches about virtue before now, and to many persons—and very good ones they were, as I thought—at this moment I cannot even say what virtue is. And I think that you are very wise in not voyaging and going away from home, for if you did in other places as you do in Athens, you would be cast into prison as a magician.

Soc.: You are a rogue, Meno, and had all but caught me. . . .

. . . As to my being a torpedo, if the torpedo is torpid as well as the cause of torpidity in others, then indeed I am a torpedo, but not otherwise; for **I perplex others, not because I am clear, but because I am utterly perplexed myself.** And now I know not what virtue is, and you seem to be in the same case, although you did once perhaps know before you touched me. However, I have no objection to join with you in the enquiry.

Meno: And how will you enquire, Socrates, into that which you do not know? What will you put forth as the subject of enquiry? And if you find what you want, how will you ever know that this is the thing which you did not know?

Soc.: I know, Meno, what you mean; but just see what a tiresome dispute you are introducing. You argue that a man cannot enquire either about that which he knows, or about that which he does not know; for if he knows, he has no need to enquire; and if not, he cannot; for he does not know the very subject about which he is to enquire.

Meno: Well, Socrates, and is not the argument sound?

Soc.: I think not.

Meno: Why not?

Soc.: I will tell you why: I have heard from certain wise men and women who spoke of things divine that—

Meno: What did they say?

Soc.: They spoke of a glorious truth, as I conceive.

Meno: What was it? and who were they?

Soc.: Some of them were priests and priestesses, who had studied how they might be able to give a reason of their profession: there have been poets also, who spoke of these things by inspiration, like Pindar, and many others who were inspired. And they say—mark, now, and see whether their words are true—they say that the soul of man is immortal, and at one time has an end, which is termed dying, and at another time is born again, but is never destroyed. And the moral is, that a man ought to live always in perfect holiness. *'For in the ninth year Persephone sends the souls of those from whom she has received the penalty of ancient crime back again from beneath into the light of the sun above, and these are they who become noble kings and mighty men and great in wisdom and are called saintly heroes in after ages.'* The soul, then, as being immortal, and having been born again many times, and having seen all things that exist, whether in this world or in the world below, has knowledge of them all; and it is no wonder that she should be able to call to remembrance all that she ever knew about virtue, and about everything; for as all nature is akin, and the soul has learned all things, there is no difficulty in her eliciting or as men say learning, out of a single recollection all the rest, if a man is strenuous and does not faint; for all enquiry and **all learning is but recollection**. And therefore we ought not to listen to this sophistical argument about the impossibility of enquiry: for it will make us idle, and is sweet only to the sluggard; but the other saying will make us active and inquisitive. In that confiding, I will gladly enquire with you into the nature of virtue.

Meno: Yes, Socrates; but what do you mean by saying that we do not learn, and that what we call learning is only a process of recollection? Can you teach me how this is?

Soc.: I told you, Meno, just now that you were a rogue, and now you ask whether I can teach you, when I am saying that there is no teaching, but only recollection; and thus you imagine that you will involve me in a contradiction.

Meno: Indeed, Socrates, I protest that I had no such intention. I only asked the question from habit; but if you can prove to me that what you say is true, I wish that you would.

Soc.: It will be no easy matter, but I will try to please you to the utmost of my power. Suppose that you call one of your numerous attendants; that I may demonstrate on him.

Meno: Certainly. Come hither, boy.

Soc.: He is Greek, and speaks Greek, does he not?

Meno: Yes, indeed; he was born in the house.

Soc.: Attend now to the questions which I ask him, and observe whether he learns of me or only remembers.

Meno: I will.

Soc.: Tell me, boy, do you know that a figure like this is a square?

Boy: I do.

Soc.: And you know that a square figure has these four lines equal?

Boy: Certainly.

Soc.: And these lines which I have drawn through the middle of the square are also equal?

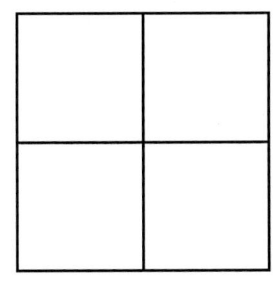

Boy: Yes.

Soc.: A square may be of any size?

Boy: Certainly.

Soc.: And if one side of the figure be of two feet, and the other side be of two feet, how much will the whole be? Let me explain: if in one direction the space was of two feet, and in the other direction of one foot, the whole would be of two feet taken once?

Boy: Yes.

Soc.: But since this side is also of two feet, there are twice two feet?

Boy: There are.

Soc.: Then the square is of twice two feet?

Boy: Yes.

Soc.: And how many are twice two feet? count and tell me.

Boy: Four, Socrates.

Soc.: And might there not be another square twice as large as this, and having like this the lines equal?

Boy: Yes.

Soc.: And of how many feet will that be?

Boy: Of eight feet.

Soc.: And now try and tell me the length of the line which forms the side of that double square: this is two feet—what will that be?

Boy: Clearly, Socrates, it will be double.

Soc.: Do you observe, Meno, that I am not teaching the boy anything, but only asking him questions; and now he fancies that he knows how long a line is necessary in order to produce a figure of eight square feet; does he not?

Meno: Yes.

Soc.: And does he really know?

Meno: Certainly not.

Soc.: He only guesses that because the square is double, the line is double.

Meno: True.

Soc.: Observe him while he recalls the steps in regular order. *(To the Boy.)* Tell me, boy, do you assert that a double space comes from a double line? Remember that I am not speaking of an oblong, but of a figure equal every way, and twice the size of this—that is to say of eight feet; and I want to know whether you still say that a double square comes from a double line?

Boy: Yes.

Soc.: But does not this line become doubled if we add another such line here?

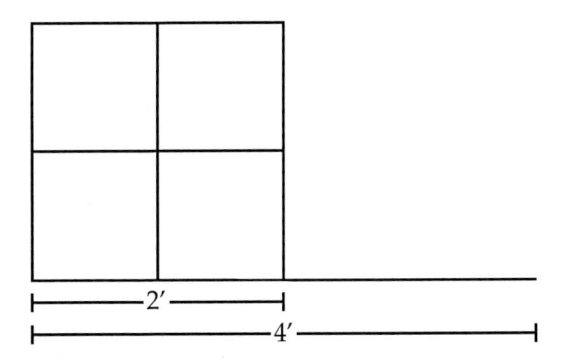

Boy: Certainly.

Soc.: And four such lines will make a space containing eight feet?

Boy: Yes.

Soc.: Let us describe such a figure: Would you not say that this is the figure of eight feet?

Boy: Yes.

Soc.: And are there not these four divisions in the figure, each of which is equal to the figure of four feet?

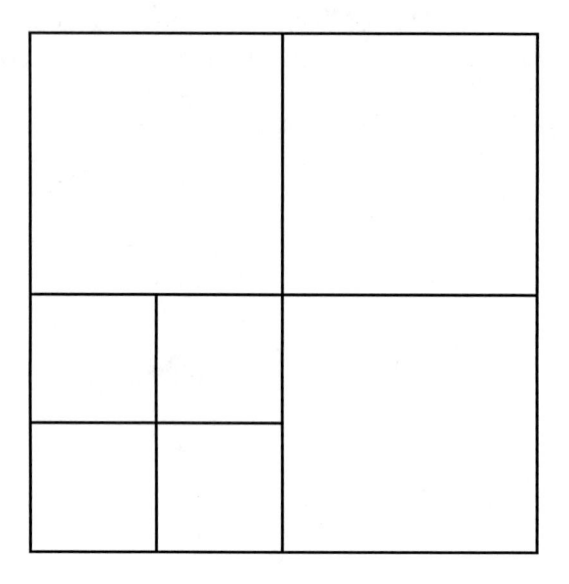

Boy: True.

Soc.: And is not that four times four?

Boy: Certainly.

Soc.: And four times is not double?

Boy: No, indeed.

Soc.: But how much?

Boy: Four times as much.

Soc.: Therefore the double line, boy, has given a space, not twice, but four times as much.

Boy: True.

Soc.: Four times four are sixteen—are they not?

Boy: Yes.

Soc.: What line would give you a space of eight feet, as this gives one of sixteen feet;— do you see?

Boy: Yes.

Soc.: And the space of four feet is made from this half line?

Boy: Yes.

Soc.: Good; and is not a space of eight feet twice the size of this, and half the size of the other?

Boy: Certainly.

Soc.: Such a space, then, will be made out of a line greater than this one, and less than that one?

Boy: Yes; I think so.

Soc.: Very good; I like to hear you say what you think. And now tell me, is not this a line of two feet and that of four?

Boy: Yes.

Soc.: Then the line which forms the side of eight feet ought to be more than this line of two feet, and less than the other of four feet?

Boy: It ought.

Soc.: Try and see if you can tell me how much it will be.

Boy: Three feet.

Soc.: Then if we add a half to this line of two, that will be the line of three. Here are two and there is one; and on the other side, here are two also and there is one: and that makes the figure of which you speak?

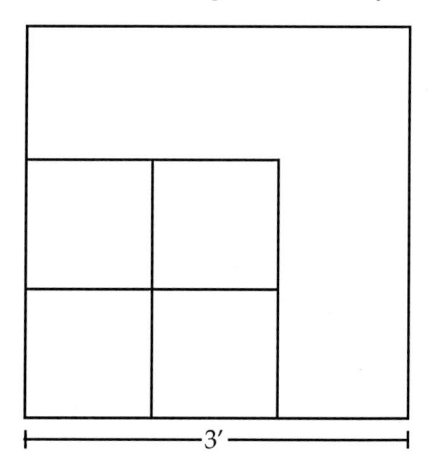

Boy: Yes.

Soc.: But if there are three feet this way and three feet that way, the whole space will be three times three feet?

Boy: That is evident.

Soc.: And how much are three times three feet?

Boy: Nine.

Soc.: And how much is the double of four?

Boy: Eight.

Soc.: Then the figure of eight is not made out of a line of three?

Boy: No.

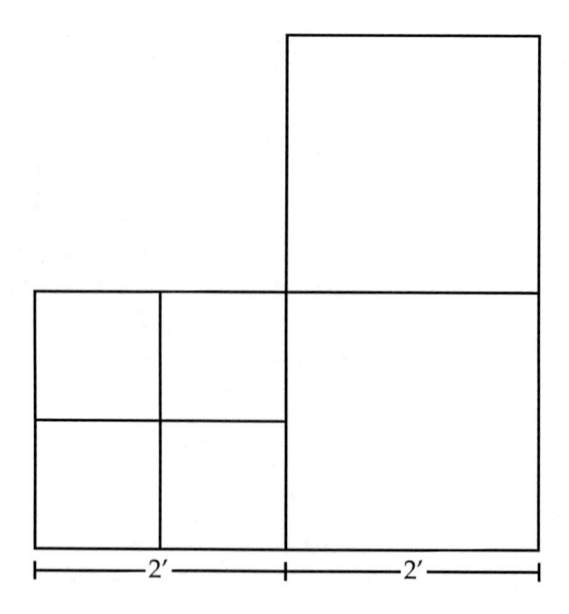

Soc.: But from what line?—tell me exactly; and if you would rather not reckon, try and show me the line.

Boy: Indeed, Socrates, I do not know.

Soc.: Do you see, Meno, what advances he has made in his power of recollection? He did not know at first, and he does not know now, what is the side of a figure of eight feet: but then he thought that he knew, and answered confidently as if he knew, and had no difficulty; now he has a difficulty, and neither knows nor fancies that he knows.

Meno: True.

Soc.: Is he not better off in knowing his ignorance?

Meno: I think that he is.

Soc.: If we have made him doubt, and given him the 'torpedo's shock,' have we done him any harm?

Meno: I think not.

Soc.: We have certainly, as would seem, assisted him in some degree to the discovery of the truth; and now he will wish to remedy his ignorance, but then he would have been ready to tell all the world again and again that the double space should have a double side.

Meno: True.

Soc.: But do you suppose that he would ever have enquired into or learned what he fancied that he knew, though he was really ignorant of it, until he had fallen into perplexity under, the idea that he did not know, and had desired to know?

Meno: I think not, Socrates.

Soc.: Then he was the better for the torpedo's touch?

Meno: I think so.

[Although the slave boy has never been educated, he possesses innate knowledge of geometry. Socrates claims that all he is doing is helping the slave bring to consciousness that which he already knows. That is, education is recollection of innate ideas.]

Soc.: Mark now the farther development. I shall only ask him, and not teach him, and he shall share the enquiry with me: and do you watch and see if you find me telling or explaining anything to him, instead of eliciting his opinion. Tell me, boy, is not this a square of four feet which I have drawn?

Boy: Yes.

Soc.: And now I add another square equal to the former one?

Boy: Yes.

Soc.: And a third, which is equal to either of them?

Boy: Yes.

Soc.: Suppose that we fill up the vacant corner?

Boy: Very good.

Soc.: Here, then, there are four equal spaces?

Boy: Yes.

Soc.: And how many times larger is this space than this other?

Boy: Four times.

Soc.: But it ought to have been twice only, as you will remember.

Boy: True.

Soc.: And does not this line, reaching from corner to corner, bisect each of these spaces? [BDEF]

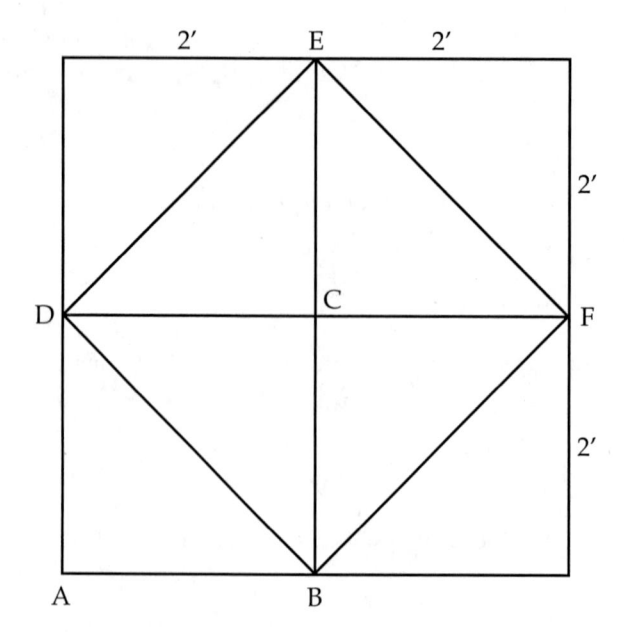

Boy: Yes.

Soc.: And are there not here four equal lines which contain this space? [BD, DE, EF, and FB]

Boy: There are.

Soc.: Look and see how much this space is.

Boy: I do not understand.

Soc.: Has not each interior line cut off half of the four spaces? [BD, DE, EF, and FB]

Boy: Yes.

Soc.: And how many spaces are there in this section? [BDEF]

Boy: Four.

Soc.: And how many in this? [ABCD]

Boy: Two.

Soc.: And four is how many times two?

Boy: Twice.

Soc.: And this space is of how many feet? [BDEF]

Boy: Of eight feet.

Soc.: And from what line do you get this figure?

Boy: From this. [BDEF]

Soc.: That is, from the line which extends from corner to corner of the figure of four feet?

Boy: Yes.

Soc.: And that is the line which the learned call the diagonal. And if this is the proper name, then you, Meno's slave, are prepared to affirm that the double space is the square of the diagonal?

Boy: Certainly, Socrates.

Soc.: What do you say of him, Meno? Were not all these answers given out of his own head?

Meno: Yes, they were all his own.

Soc.: And yet, as we were just now saying, he did not know?

Meno: True.

Soc.: But still he had in him those notions of his—had he not?

Meno: Yes.

Soc.: Then he who does not know may still have true notions of that which he does not know?

Meno: He has.

Soc.: And at present these notions have just been stirred up in him, as in a dream; but if he were frequently asked the same questions, in different forms, he would know as well as any one at last?

Meno: I dare say.

Soc.: Without any one teaching him he will recover his knowledge for himself, if he is only asked questions?

Meno: Yes.

Soc.: And this spontaneous recovery of knowledge in him is recollection?

Meno: True.

Soc.: And this knowledge which he now has must he not either have acquired or always possessed?

Meno: Yes.

Soc.: But if he always possessed this knowledge he would always have known; or if he has acquired the knowledge he could not have acquired it in this life, unless he has been taught geometry; for he may be made to do the same with all geometry and every other branch of knowledge. Now, has any one ever taught him all this? You must know about him, if, as you say, he was born and bred in your house.

Meno: And I am certain that no one ever did teach him.

Soc.: And yet he has the knowledge?

Meno: The fact, Socrates, is undeniable.

Soc.: But if he did not acquire the knowledge in this life, then he must have had and learned it at some other time?

Meno: Clearly he must.

Soc.: Which must have been the time when he was not a man?

Meno: Yes.

Soc.: And if there have been always true thoughts in him, both at the time when he was and was not a man, which only need to be awakened into knowledge by putting questions to him, his soul must have always possessed this knowledge, for he always either was or was not a man?

Meno: Obviously.

Soc.: And if the truth of all things always existed in the soul, then the soul is immortal. Wherefore be of good cheer, and try to recollect what you do not know, or rather what you do not remember.

Meno: I feel, somehow, that I like what you are saying.

Soc.: And I, Meno, like what I am saying. Some things I have said of which I am not altogether confident. But that we shall be better and braver and less helpless if we think that we ought to enquire, than we should have been if we indulged in the idle fancy that there was no knowing and no use in seeking to know what we do not know;—that is a theme upon which I am ready to fight, in word and deed, to the utmost of my power.

The Divided Line

Plato

Knowledge versus Opinion

Gl.: Who then are the true philosophers?

Soc.: **Those who are lovers of the vision of truth.**

Gl.: That is also good; but I should like to know what you mean?

Soc.: To another I might have a difficulty in explaining; but I am sure that you will admit a proposition which I am about to make.

Gl.: What is the proposition?

Soc.: That since beauty is the opposite of ugliness, they are two?

Gl.: Certainly.

Soc.: And inasmuch as they are two, each of them is one?

Gl.: True again.

Soc.: And of just and unjust, good and evil, and of every other class, the same remark holds; taken singly, each of them is one; but from the various combinations of them with actions and things and with one another, they are seen in all sorts of lights and appear many?

Gl.: Very true.

Soc.: And this is the distinction which I draw between the sight-loving, art-loving, practical class and those of whom I am speaking, and who are alone worthy of the name of philosophers.

Gl.: How do you distinguish them?

Soc.: The lovers of sounds and sights are, as I conceive, fond of tones and colors and forms and all the artificial products that are made out of them, but their mind is incapable of seeing or loving absolute beauty.

Gl.: True.

Soc.: Few are they who are able to attain to the sight of this. And the man who believes in beautiful things but does not believe in absolute beauty, nor is able to follow if one lead him to an understanding of it—do you think that his life is real or a dream? Is it not a dream? For whether a man be asleep or awake is it not dream-like to mistake the image for the real thing?

Gl.: I should certainly say that such an one was dreaming.

Soc.: But take the case of the other, who recognizes the existence of absolute beauty and is able to distinguish the idea from the objects which participate in the idea, neither putting the objects in the place of the idea nor the idea in the place of the objects—is he a dreamer, or is he awake?

Gl.: He is wide awake.

Soc.: And may we not say that the mind of the one who knows has knowledge and that the mind of the other, who opines only, has opinion?

Gl.: Certainly.

Soc.: But suppose that the latter should quarrel with us and dispute our statement, can we administer any soothing cordial or advice to him, without revealing to him that there is sad disorder in his wit?

Gl.: We must certainly offer him some good advice.

Soc.: Come, then, and let us think of something to say to him. Shall we begin by assuring him that he is welcome to any knowledge which he may have, and that we rejoice at his having it? But we should like to ask him a question: Does he who has knowledge know something or nothing?

Gl.: I answer that he knows something.

Soc.: Something that is or is not?

Gl.: Something that is; for how can that which is not ever be known?

Soc.: And are we assured, after looking at the matter from many points of view, that absolute being is or may be absolutely known, but that the utterly non-existent is utterly unknown?

Gl.: Nothing can be more certain.

Soc.: Good. But if there be anything which is of such a nature as to be and not to be, that will have a place intermediate between pure being and the absolute negation of being?

Gl.: Yes, between them.

Soc.: And, as knowledge corresponds to being and ignorance of necessity to not-being, we must find something intermediate between ignorance and knowledge for that which lies between them, if there is such a thing.

Gl.: Yes.

Soc.: Would you admit the existence of opinion?

Gl.: No question.

Soc.: Is opinion the same faculty as knowledge or is it a different faculty?

Gl.: A different faculty.

Soc.: Then opinion and knowledge have to do with different kinds of matter corresponding to this difference of faculties?

Gl.: Yes.

Soc.: And knowledge is relative to being and knows being. But before I proceed further I will make a division. I will begin by placing faculties in a class by themselves: they are powers in us, and in all other things, by which we do as we do. Sight and hearing, for example, I should call faculties. Have I clearly explained the class which I mean?

Gl.: Yes, I quite understand.

Soc.: Then let me tell you my view about them. I do not see the faculties, and therefore the distinctions of shape, color, and the like, which enable me to discern the differences of some things, do not apply to them. In speaking of a faculty I think only of its sphere and its result; and that which has the same sphere and the same result I call the same faculty, but that which has another sphere and another result I call different. Would that be your way of speaking?

Gl.: Yes.

Soc.: Would you say that knowledge is a faculty, or in what class would you place it?

Gl.: Certainly knowledge is a faculty, and the mightiest of all faculties.

Soc.: And is opinion also a faculty?

Gl.: Certainly; for opinion is that with which we are able to form an opinion.

Soc.: And yet you were acknowledging a little while ago that knowledge is not the same as opinion?

Gl.: Why, yes; how can any reasonable being ever identify that which is infallible with that which errs?

Soc.: An excellent answer, proving that we are quite conscious of a distinction between them.

Gl.: Yes.

Soc.: Then knowledge and opinion having distinct powers have also distinct spheres or subject-matters?

Gl.: That is certain.

Soc.: Being is the sphere or subject-matter of knowledge, and knowledge is to know the nature of being?

Gl.: Yes.

Soc.: And opinion is to have an opinion?

Gl.: Yes.

Soc.: And do we know what we opine? or is the subject-matter of opinion the same as the subject-matter of knowledge?

Gl.: Nay, that has been already disproven; if difference in faculty implies difference in the sphere or subject-matter, and if, as we were saying, opinion and knowledge are distinct faculties, then the sphere of knowledge and of opinion can not be the same.

Soc.: Then if being is the subject-matter of knowledge, something else must be the subject-matter of opinion?

Gl.: Yes, something else.

Soc.: Well then, is not-being the subject-matter of opinion? or, rather, how can there be an opinion at all about not-being? Reflect; when a man has an opinion, has he not an opinion about something? Can he have an opinion which is an opinion about nothing?

Gl.: Impossible.

Soc.: He who has an opinion has an opinion about some one thing?

Gl.: Yes.

Soc.: And not-being is not one thing but, properly speaking, nothing?

Gl.: True.

Soc.: Of not-being, ignorance was assumed to be the necessary correlative; of being, knowledge?

Gl.: True.

Soc.: Then opinion is not concerned either with being or with not-being?

Gl.: Not with either.

Soc.: And can therefore neither be ignorance nor knowledge?

Gl.: That seems to be true.

Soc.: But is opinion to be sought without and beyond either of them, in a greater clearness than knowledge, or in a greater darkness than ignorance?

Gl.: In neither.

Soc.: Then I suppose that opinion appears to you to be darker than knowledge, but lighter than ignorance?

Gl.: Both; and in no small degree.

Soc.: And also to be within and between them?

Gl.: Yes.

Soc.: Then you would infer that opinion is intermediate?

Gl.: No question.

Soc.: But were we not saying before, that if anything appeared to be of a sort which is and is not at the same time, that sort of thing would appear also to lie in the interval between pure being and absolute not-being; and that the corresponding faculty is neither knowledge nor ignorance, but will be found in the interval between them?

Gl.: True.

Soc.: And in that interval there has now been discovered something which we call opinion?

Gl.: There has.

Soc.: Then what remains to be discovered is the object which partakes equally of the nature of being and not-being, and can not rightly be termed either, pure and simple; this unknown term, when discovered, we may truly call the subject of opinion, and assign each to their proper faculty,—the extremes to the faculties of the extremes and the mean to the faculty of the mean.

Gl.: True.

Soc.: This being premised, I would ask the gentleman who is of opinion that there is no absolute or unchangeable idea of beauty—in whose opinion the beautiful is the manifold— he, I say, your lover of beautiful sights, who can not bear to be told that the beautiful is one, and the just is one, or that anything is one—to him I would appeal, saying, Will you be so very kind, sir, as to tell us whether, of all these beautiful things, there is one which will not be found ugly; or of the just, which will not be found unjust; or of the holy, which will not also be unholy?

Gl.: No; the beautiful will in some point of view be found ugly; and the same is true of the rest.

Soc.: And may not the many which are doubles be also halves?—doubles, that is, of one thing, and halves of another?

Gl.: Quite true.

Soc.: And things great and small, heavy and light, as they are termed, will not be denoted by these any more than by the opposite names?

Gl.: True; both these and the opposite names will always attach to all of them.

Soc.: And can any one of those many things which are called by particular names be said to be this rather than not to be this?

Gl.: They are like the punning riddles which are asked at feasts or the children's puzzle about the eunuch aiming at the bat, with what he hit him, as they say in the puzzle, and upon what the bat was sitting. The individual objects of which I am speaking are also a riddle, and have a double sense: nor can you fix them in your mind, either as being or not-being, or both, or neither.

Soc.: Then what will you do with them? Can they have a better place than between being and not-being? For they are clearly not in greater darkness or negation than not-being, or more full of light and existence than being.

Gl.: That is quite true.

Soc.: Thus then we seem to have discovered that the many ideas which the multitude entertain about the beautiful and about all other things are tossing about in some region which is half-way between pure being and pure not-being?

Gl.: We have.

Soc.: Yes; and we had before agreed that anything of this kind which we might find was to be described as matter of opinion, and not as matter of knowledge; being the intermediate flux which is caught and detained by the intermediate faculty.

Gl.: Quite true.

Soc.: Then those who see the many beautiful, and who yet neither see absolute beauty, nor can follow any guide who points the way thither; who see the many just, and not absolute justice, and the like,—such persons may be said to have opinion but not knowledge?

Gl.: That is certain.

Soc.: But those who see the absolute and eternal and immutable may be said to know, and not to have opinion only?

Gl.: Neither can that be denied.

Soc.: The one love and embrace the subjects of knowledge, the other those of opinion? The latter are the same, as I dare say you will remember, who listened to sweet sounds and gazed upon fair colors, but would not tolerate the existence of absolute beauty.

Gl.: Yes, I remember.

Soc.: Shall we then be guilty of any impropriety in calling them lovers of opinion rather than lovers of wisdom, and will they be very angry with us for thus describing them?

Gl.: I shall tell them not to be angry; no man should be angry at what is true.

Soc.: But those who love the truth in each thing are to be called lovers of wisdom and not lovers of opinion.

Gl.: Assuredly.

The Objects of Knowledge

Soc.: . . . I must first come to an understanding with you, and remind you of what I have mentioned in the course of this discussion, and at many other times.

Gl.: What?

Soc.: The old story, that there is a many beautiful and a many good, and so of other things which we describe and define; to all of them the term "many" is applied.

Gl.: True.

Soc.: And there is an absolute beauty and an absolute good, and of other things to which the term "many" is applied there is an absolute; for they may be brought under a single idea, which is called the essence of each.

Gl.: Very true.

Soc.: The many, as we say, are seen but not known, and the ideas are known but not seen.

Gl.: Exactly.

Soc.: And what is the organ with which we see the visible things?

Gl.: The sight.

Soc.: And with the hearing, we hear, and with the other senses perceive the other objects of sense?

Gl.: True.

Soc.: But have you remarked that sight is by far the most costly and complex piece of workmanship which the artificer of the senses ever contrived?

Gl.: No, I never have.

Soc.: Then reflect: has the ear or voice need of any third or additional nature in order that the one may be able to hear and the other to be heard?

Gl.: Nothing of the sort.

Soc.: No, indeed; and the same is true of most, if not all, the other senses—you would not say that any of them requires such an addition?

Gl.: Certainly not.

Soc.: But you see that without the addition of some other nature there is no seeing or being seen?

Gl.: How do you mean?

Soc.: Sight being, as I conceive, in the eyes, and he who has eyes wanting to see; color being also present in them, still unless there be a third nature specially adapted to the purpose, the owner of the eyes will see nothing and the colors will be invisible.

Gl.: Of what nature are you speaking?

Soc.: Of that which you term light.

Gl.: True.

Soc.: Noble, then, is the bond which links together sight and visibility, and great beyond other bonds by no small difference of nature; for light is their bond, and light is no ignoble thing?

Gl.: Nay, the reverse of ignoble.

Soc.: And which of the gods in heaven would you say was the lord of this element? Whose is that light which makes the eye to see perfectly and the visible to appear?

Gl.: You mean the sun, as you and all mankind say.

Soc.: May not the relation of sight to this deity be described as follows?

Gl.: How?

Soc.: Neither sight nor the eye in which sight resides is the sun?

Gl.: No.

Soc.: Yet of all the organs of sense the eye is the most like the sun?

Gl.: By far the most like.

Soc.: And the power which the eye possesses is a sort of effluence which is dispensed from the sun?

Gl.: Exactly.

Soc.: Then the sun is not sight, but the author of sight who is recognized by sight?

Gl.: True.

Soc.: And this is he whom I call the child of the good, whom the good begat in his own likeness, to be in the visible world, in relation to sight and the things of sight, what the good is in the intellectual world in relation to mind and the things of mind:

Gl.: Will you be a little more explicit?

Soc.: Why, you know, that the eyes, when a person directs them towards objects on which the light of day is no longer shining, but the moon and stars only, see dimly, and are nearly blind; they seem to have no clearness of vision in them?

Gl.: Very true.

Soc.: But when they are directed towards objects on which the sun shines, they see clearly and there is sight in them?

Gl.: Certainly.

Soc.: And the soul is like the eye: when resting upon that on which truth and being shine, the soul perceives and understands, and is radiant with intelligence; but when turned towards the twilight of becoming and perishing, then she has opinion only, and goes blinking about, and is first of one opinion and then of another, and seems to have no intelligence?

Gl.: Just so.

Soc.: Now, that which imparts truth to the known and the power of knowing to the knower is what I would have you term the idea of good, and this you will deem to be the cause of science, and of truth in so far as the latter becomes the subject of knowledge; beautiful too, as are both truth and knowledge, you will be right in esteeming this other nature as more beautiful than either; and, as in the previous instance, light and sight may be truly said to be like the sun, and yet not to be the sun, so in this other sphere, science and truth may be deemed to be like the good, but not the good; the good has a place of honor yet higher.

Gl.: What a wonder of beauty that must be, which is the author of science and truth, and yet surpasses them in beauty; for you surely can not mean to say that pleasure is the good?

Soc.: God forbid; but may I ask you to consider the image in another point of view?

Gl.: In what point of view?

Soc.: You would say, would you not, that the sun is not only the author of visibility in all visible things, but of generation and nourishment and growth, though he himself is not generation?

Gl.: Certainly.

Soc.: In like manner the good may be said to be not only the author of knowledge to all things known, but of their being and essence, and yet the good is not essence, but far exceeds essence in dignity and power.

Gl.: (With a ludicrous earnestness) By the light of heaven, how amazing!

The Line

D
Ideas: *Reason*

C
Mathematics: *Intelligence*

B
Physical Phenomena: *Belief*

A
Images: *Imagination*

The Four Levels of Knowledge: The Line

Soc.: You have to imagine that there are two ruling powers, and that one of them, the good, is set over the intellectual world, the other, the Sun, over the visible world. May I suppose that you have this distinction of the visible and intelligible fixed in your mind?

Gl.: I have.

Soc.: Now take a line which has been cut into two unequal parts; and divide each of them again in the same proportion, and suppose the two main divisions to answer, one to the visible and the other to the intelligible, and then compare the subdivisions in respect to their clearness and want of clearness, and you will find that the first section (A) in the sphere of the visible consists of images. And by images I mean, in the first place, shadows, and in the second place, reflections in water and in solid, smooth and polished bodies and the like. Do you understand?

Gl.: Yes, I understand.

Soc.: Imagine now, the other section (B), of which this is only the resemblance, to include the animals which we see, and everything that grows or is made. **Would you not admit that both the sections of this division have different degrees of truth, and that the copy is to the original as the sphere of opinion is to the sphere of knowledge?**

Gl.: Most undoubtedly.

Soc.: Next we proceed to consider the manner in which the sphere of the intellectual is to be divided. There are two subdivisions, in the lower (C) of which the soul uses the figures given by the former division as images; the inquiry can only be hypothetical, and instead of going upwards to a principle descends to the other end; in the higher of the two (D), the soul passes out of hypotheses, and goes up to a principle which is above hypotheses, making no use of images as in the former case, but proceeding only in and through the ideas themselves.

Gl.: I do not quite understand your meaning.

Soc.: Then I will try again; you will understand me better when I have made some preliminary remarks. [Regarding C], you are aware that students of geometry, arithmetic, and the kindred sciences assume the odd and the even and the figures and three kinds of angles and the like in their several branches of science; these are their hypotheses, which they and everybody are supposed to know, and therefore they do not deign to give any account of them either to themselves or others; but they begin with them, and go on until they arrive at last, and in a consistent manner, at their conclusion.

Gl.: Yes, I know.

Soc.: And do you not know also that although they make use of the visible forms and reason about them, they are thinking not of these, but of the ideals which they resemble; not of the figures which they draw, but of the absolute square and the absolute diameter, and so on. The forms which they draw or make are actual things, which have shadows and reflections in water of their own, but now they serve in turn as images, but the soul is really seeking to behold the things themselves, which can only be seen with the eye of the mind.

Gl.: That is true.

Soc.: And of this I spoke as the intelligible (C), although in the search after it the soul is compelled to use hypotheses; not ascending to a first principle, because she is unable to rise above the region of hypothesis, but employing the objects of which the shadows below are resemblances in their turn as images, they having in relation to the shadows and reflections of them a greater distinctness, and therefore a higher value.

Gl.: I understand, that you are speaking of the province of geometry and the sister arts.

Soc.: When I speak of the other division of the intelligible (D), you will understand me to speak of that other sort of knowledge which reason herself attains by the power of dialectic, using the hypotheses not as first principles, but only as hypotheses—that is to say, as steps and points of departure into a world which is above hypotheses, in order that she may soar beyond them to the first principle of the whole; and clinging to this and then to that which depends on this, by successive steps she descends again without the aid of any sensible object, from ideas, through ideas, and in ideas she ends.

Gl.: I understand you. Not perfectly, for you seem to me to be describing a task which is really tremendous; but at any rate, I understand you to say that knowledge and being, which the science of dialectic contemplates, are clearer than the notions of the arts, as they are termed, which proceed from hypotheses only. These are also contemplated by the understanding, and not by the senses: yet, because they start from hypotheses and do not ascend to a principle, those who contemplate them appear to you not to exercise the higher reason upon them, although when a first principle is added to them they are cognizable by the higher reason. And the habit which is concerned with geometry and the cognate sciences I suppose that you would term understanding and not reason, as being intermediate between opinion and reason.

Soc.: You have quite conceived my meaning; and now, corresponding to these four divisions, let there be four faculties in the soul—Reason answering to the highest (D), Understanding to the second (C), Belief (or conviction) to the third (B), and Imaging (or perception of shadows) to the last (A). And let us suppose that the several faculties have clearness in the same degree that their objects have truth.

Gl.: I understand and give my assent, and accept this arrangement of the matter.

The Allegory of the Cave

Plato

Soc.: **And now, let me show in a figure how far our nature is enlightened or unenlightened**:—Behold! human beings living in an underground den, which has a mouth open towards the light and reaching all along the den; here they have been from their childhood, and have their legs and necks chained so that they can not move, and can only see before them, being prevented by the chains from turning round their heads. Above and behind them a fire is blazing at a distance, and between the fire and the prisoners there is a raised way; and you will see, if you look, a low wall built along the way, like the screen which marionette players have in front of them, over which they show the puppets.

Gl.: I see.

Soc.: And do you see men passing along the wall carrying all sorts of vessels, and statues and figures of animals made of wood and stone and various materials, which appear over the wall? Some of them are talking, others silent.

Gl.: You have shown me a strange image, and they are strange prisoners.

Soc.: Like ourselves; and they see only their own shadows, or the shadows of one another, which the fire throws on the opposite wall of the cave?

Gl.: True; how could they see anything but the shadows if they were never allowed to move their heads?

Soc.: And of the objects which are being carried in like manner they would only see the shadows?

Gl.: Yes.

Soc.: And if they were able to converse with one another, would they not suppose that they were naming what was actually before them?

Gl.: Very true.

Soc.: And suppose further that the prison had an echo which came from the other side, would they not be sure to fancy when one of the passers-by spoke that the voice which they heard came from the passing shadow?

Gl.: No question.

Soc.: To them, the truth would be literally nothing but the shadows of the images.

Gl.: That is certain.

Soc.: And now look again, and see what will naturally follow if the prisoners are released and disabused of their error. At first, when any of them is liberated and compelled suddenly to stand up and turn his neck round and walk and look towards the light, he will suffer sharp pains; the glare will distress him, and he will be unable to see the realities of which in his former state he had seen the shadows; and then conceive some one saying to him, that what he saw before was an illusion, but that now, when he is approaching nearer to being and his eye is turned towards more real existence, he has a clearer vision,—what will be his reply? And you may further imagine that his instructor is pointing to the objects as they pass and requiring him to name them,—will he not be perplexed? Will he not fancy that the shadows which he formerly saw are truer than the objects which are now shown to him?

Gl.: Far truer.

Soc.: And if he is compelled to look straight at the light, will he not have a pain in his eyes which will make him turn away to take refuge in the objects of vision which he can see, and which he will conceive to be in reality clearer than the things which are now being shown to him?

Gl.: True.

Soc.: And suppose once more, that he is reluctantly dragged up a steep and rugged ascent, and held fast until he is forced into the presence of the sun himself, is he not likely to be pained and irritated? When he approaches the light his eyes will be dazzled, and he will not be able to see anything at all of what are now called realities.

Gl.: Not all in a moment.

Soc.: He will require to grow accustomed to the sight of the upper world. And first he will see the shadows best, next the reflections of men and other objects in the water, and then the objects themselves; then he will gaze upon the light of the moon and the stars and the spangled heaven;

and he will see the sky and the stars by night better than the sun or the light of the sun by day?

Gl.: Certainly.

Soc.: Last of all he will be able to see the sun, and not mere reflections of him in the water, but he will see him in his own proper place, and not in another; and he will contemplate him as he is.

Gl.: Certainly.

Soc.: He will then proceed to argue that this is he who gives the season and the years, and is the guardian of all that is in the visible world, and in a certain way the cause of all things which he and his fellows have been accustomed to behold?

Gl.: Clearly, he would first see the sun and then reason about him.

Soc.: And when he remembered his old habitation, and the wisdom of the den and his fellow-prisoners, do you not suppose that he would felicitate himself on the change, and pity them?

Gl.: Certainly, he would.

Soc.: And if they were in the habit of conferring honors among themselves on those who were quickest to observe the passing shadows and to remark which of them went before, and which followed after, and which were together; and who were therefore best able to draw conclusions as to the future, do you think that he would care for such honors and glories, or envy the possessors of them? Would he not say with Homer,

> *Better to be the poor servant of a poor master,*

and to endure anything, rather than think as they do and live after their manner?

Gl.: Yes, I think that he would rather suffer anything than entertain these false notions and live in this miserable manner.

Soc.: Imagine once more, such an one coming suddenly out of the sun to be replaced in his old situation; would he not be certain to have his eyes full of darkness?

Gl.: To be sure.

Soc.: And if there were a contest, and he had to compete in measuring the shadows with the prisoners who had never moved out of the den, while his sight was still weak, and before his eyes had become steady (and the time which would be needed to acquire this new habit of sight might be very considerable), would he not be ridiculous? Men would say of him that up he went and down he came without his eyes; and that it was better not even to think of ascending; and if any one tried to loose another and lead him up to the light, let them only catch the offender, and they would put him to death.

Gl.: No question.

Soc.: This entire allegory you may now append, dear Glaucon, to the previous argument; the prison-house is the world of sight, the light of the fire is the sun, and **you will not misapprehend me if you interpret the journey upwards to be the ascent of the soul into the intellectual world** according to my poor belief, which, at your desire, I have expressed—whether rightly or wrongly God knows. But, whether true or false, my opinion is that in the world of knowledge **the idea of good appears last of all, and is seen only with an effort; and, when seen, is also inferred to be the universal author of all things beautiful and right, parent of light and of the lord of light in this visible world, and the immediate source of reason and truth in the intellectual; and that this is the power upon which he who would act rationally either in public or private life must have his eye fixed.**

Gl.: I agree, as far as I am able to understand you.

Soc.: Moreover, you must not wonder that those who attain to this beatific vision are unwilling to descend to human affairs; for their souls are ever hastening into the upper world where they desire to dwell; which desire of theirs is very natural, if our allegory may be trusted.

Gl.: Yes, very natural.

Soc.: And is there anything surprising in one who passes from divine contemplations to the evil state of man, misbehaving himself in a ridiculous manner; if, while his eyes are blinking and before he has become accustomed to the surrounding darkness, he is compelled to fight in courts of law, or in other places, about the images or the shadows of images of justice, and is endeavouring to meet the conceptions of those who have never yet seen absolute justice?

Gl.: Anything but surprising.

Soc.: Any one who has common sense will remember that the bewilderments of the eyes are of two kinds, and arise from two causes, either from coming out of the light or from going into the light, which is true of the mind's eye, quite as much as of the bodily eye; and he who remembers this when he sees any one whose vision is perplexed and weak, will not be too ready to laugh; he will first ask whether that soul of man has come out of the brighter life, and is unable to see because unaccustomed to the dark, or having turned from darkness to the day is dazzled by excess of light. And he will count the one happy in his condition and state of being, and he will pity the other; or, if he have a mind to laugh at the soul which comes from below into the light, there will be more reason in this than in the laugh which greets him who returns from above out of the light into the den.

Gl.: That is a very just distinction.

Soc.: But then, if I am right, certain professors of education must be wrong when they say that they can put a knowledge into the soul which was not there before, like sight into blind eyes.

Gl.: They undoubtedly say this.

Soc.: **Whereas, our argument shows that the power and capacity of learning exists in the soul already**; and that just as the eye was unable to turn from darkness to light without the whole body, so too the instrument of knowledge can only by the movement of the whole soul be turned from the world of becoming into that of being, and learn by degrees to endure the sight of being, and of the brightest and best of being, or in other words, of the good.

Gl.: Very true.

Soc.: And must there not be some art which will effect conversion in the easiest and quickest manner; not implanting the faculty of sight, for that exists already, but has been turned in the wrong direction, and is looking away from the truth?

Gl.: Yes, such an art may be presumed.

Soc.: And whereas the other so-called virtues of the soul seem to be akin to bodily qualities, for even when they are not originally innate they can be implanted later by habit and exercise, the virtue of wisdom more than anything else contains a divine element which always remains, and by this conversion is rendered useful and profitable; or, on the other hand, hurtful and useless. Did you never observe the narrow intelligence flashing from the keen eye of a clever rogue—how eager he is, how clearly his paltry soul sees the way to his end; he is the reverse of blind, but his keen eye-sight is forced into the service of evil, and he is mischievous in proportion to his cleverness? . . .

from Meditations on First Philosophy

René Descartes

Meditation I

Of the Things Which May Be Brought Within the Sphere of the Doubtful

It is now some years since I detected how many were the false beliefs that I had from my earliest youth admitted as true, and how doubtful was everything I had since constructed on this basis; and from that time I was convinced that I must once for all seriously undertake to rid myself of all the opinions which I had formerly accepted, and commence to build anew from the foundation, if I wanted to establish any firm and permanent structure in the sciences. But as this enterprise appeared to be a very great one, I waited until I had attained an age so mature that I could not hope that at any later date I should be better fitted to execute my design. This reason caused me to delay so long that I should feel that I was doing wrong were I to occupy in deliberation the time that yet remains to me for action. Today, then, since very opportunely for the plan I have in view I have delivered my mind from every care [and am happily agitated by no passions] and since I have procured for myself an assured leisure in a peaceable retirement, I shall at last seriously and freely address myself to the general upheaval of all my former opinions.

Now for this object it is not necessary that I should show that all of these are false—I shall perhaps never arrive at this end. But inasmuch as reason already persuades me that I ought no less carefully to withhold my assent from matters which are not entirely certain and indubitable than from those which appear to me manifestly to be false, if I am able to find in each one some reason to doubt, this will suffice to justify my rejecting the whole. And for that end it will not be requisite that I should examine each in particular, which would be an endless undertaking; for owing to the fact that the destruction of the foundations of necessity brings with it the downfall of the rest of the edifice, I shall only in the first place attack those principles upon which all my former opinions rested.

All that up to the present time I have accepted as most true and certain I have learned either from the senses or through the senses; but it is sometimes proved to me that these senses are deceptive, and it is wiser not to trust entirely to any thing by which we have once been deceived.

But it may be that although the senses sometimes deceive us concerning things which are hardly perceptible, or very far away, there are yet many others to be met with as to which we cannot reasonably have any doubt, although we recognise them by their means. For example, there is the fact that I am here, seated by the fire, attired in a dressing gown, having this paper in my hands and other similar matters. And how could I deny that these hands and this body are mine, were it not perhaps that I compare myself to certain persons, devoid of sense, whose cerebella are so troubled and clouded by the violent vapours of black bile, that they constantly assure us that they think they are kings when they are really quite poor, or that they are clothed in purple when they are really without covering, or who imagine that they have an earthenware head or are nothing but pumpkins or are made of glass. But they are mad, and I should not be any the less insane were I to follow examples so extravagant.

At the same time I must remember that I am a man, and that consequently I am in the habit of sleeping, and in my dreams representing to myself the same things or sometimes even less probable things, than do those who are insane in their waking moments. How often has it happened to me that in the night I dreamt that I found myself in this particular place, that I was dressed and seated near the fire, whilst in reality I was lying undressed in bed! At this moment it does indeed seem to me that it is with eyes awake that I am looking at this paper; that this head which I move is not asleep, that it is deliberately and of set purpose that I extend my hand and perceive it; what happens in sleep does not appear so clear nor so distinct as does all this. But in thinking over this I remind myself that on many occasions I have in sleep been deceived by similar illusions, and in dwelling carefully on this reflection I see so manifestly that there are no certain indications by which we may clearly distinguish wakefulness from sleep that I am lost in astonishment. And my astonishment is such that it is almost capable of persuading me that I now dream.

Now let us assume that we are asleep and that all these particulars, e.g. that we open our eyes, shake our head, extend our hands, and so on, are but false delusions; and let us reflect that possibly neither our hands nor our whole body are such as they appear to us to be. At the same time we must at least confess that the things which are represented to us in sleep are like painted representations which can only have been formed as the counterparts of something real and true, and that in this way those general things at least, i.e. eyes, a head, hands, and a whole body, are not imaginary things, but things really existent. For, as a matter of fact, painters, even when they study with the greatest skill to represent sirens and satyrs by forms the most strange and extraordinary, cannot give them natures which are entirely new, but merely make a certain medley of the members of different animals; or if their imagination is extravagant enough to invent something so novel that nothing similar has ever before been seen, and that then their work represents a thing purely fictitious and absolutely false, it is certain all the same that the colours of which this is composed are necessarily real. And for the same reason, although these general things, to wit, [a body], eyes, a head, hands, and such like, may be imaginary, we are bound at the same time to confess that there are at least some other objects yet more simple and more universal, which are real and true; and of these just in the same way as with certain real colours, all these images of things which dwell in our thoughts, whether true and real or false and fantastic, are formed.

To such a class of things pertains corporeal nature in general, and its extension, the figure of extended things, their quantity or magnitude and number, as also the place in which they are, the time which measures their duration, and so on.

That is possibly why our reasoning is not unjust when we conclude from this that Physics, Astronomy, Medicine and all other sciences which have as their end the consideration of composite things, are very dubious and uncertain; but that Arithmetic, Geometry and other sciences of that kind which only treat of things that are very simple and very general, without taking great trouble to ascertain whether they are actually existent or not, contain some measure of certainty and an element of the indubitable. For whether I am awake or asleep, two and three together always form five, and the square can never have more than four sides, and it does not seem possible that truths so clear and apparent can be suspected of any falsity [or uncertainty].

Nevertheless I have long had fixed in my mind the belief that an all-powerful God existed by whom I have been created such as I am. But how do I know that He has not brought it to pass that there is no earth, no heaven, no extended body, no magnitude, no place, and that nevertheless [I possess the perceptions of all these things and that] they seem to me to exist just exactly as I now see them? And, besides, as I sometimes imagine that others deceive themselves in the things which they think they know best, how do I know that I am not deceived every time that I add two and three, or count the sides of a square, or judge of things yet simpler, if anything simpler can be imagined? But possibly God has not desired that I should be thus deceived, for He is said to be supremely good. If, however, it is contrary to His goodness to have made me such that I constantly deceive myself, it would also appear to be contrary to His goodness to permit me to be sometimes deceived, and nevertheless I cannot doubt that He does permit this.

There may indeed be those who would prefer to deny the existence of a God so powerful, rather than believe that all other things are uncertain. But let us not oppose them for the present, and grant that all that is here said of a God is a fable; nevertheless in whatever way they suppose that I have arrived at the state of being that I have reached—whether they attribute it to fate or to accident, or make out that it is by a continual succession of antecedents, or by some other method—since to err and deceive oneself is a defect, it is clear that the greater will be the probability of my being so imperfect as to deceive myself ever, as is the Author to whom they assign my origin the less powerful. To these reasons I have certainly nothing to reply, but at the end I feel constrained to confess that there is nothing in all that I formerly believed to be true, of which I cannot in some measure doubt, and that not merely through want of thought or through levity, but for reasons which are very powerful and maturely considered; so that henceforth I ought not the less carefully to refrain from giving credence to these opinions than to that which is manifestly false, if I desire to arrive at any certainty [in the sciences].

But it is not sufficient to have made these remarks, we must also be careful to keep them in mind. For these ancient and commonly held opinions still revert frequently to my mind, long and familiar custom having given them the right to occupy my mind against my inclination and rendered them almost masters of my belief; nor will I ever lose the habit of deferring to them or of placing my confidence in them, so long as I consider them as they really are, i.e. opinions in some measure doubtful, as I have just shown, and at the same time highly probable, so that there is much more reason to believe in than to deny them. That is why I consider that I shall not be acting amiss, if, taking of set purpose a contrary belief, I allow myself to be deceived, and for a certain time pretend that all these opinions are entirely false and imaginary, until at last, having thus balanced my former prejudices with my latter [so that they cannot divert my opinions more to one side than to the other], my judgment will no longer be dominated by bad usage or turned away from the right knowledge of the truth. For I am assured that there can be neither peril nor error in this course, and that I cannot at present yield too much to distrust, since I am not considering the question of action, but only of knowledge.

I shall then suppose, not that God who is supremely good and the fountain of truth, but some evil genius not less powerful than deceitful, has employed his whole energies in deceiving me; I shall consider that the heavens, the earth, colours, figures, sound, and all other external things are nought but the illusions and dreams of which this genius has availed himself in order to lay traps for my credulity; I shall consider myself as having no hands, no eyes, no flesh, no blood, nor any senses, yet falsely believing myself to possess all these things; I shall remain obstinately attached to this idea, and if by this means it is not in my power to arrive at the knowledge of any truth, I may at least do what is in my power [i.e. suspend my judgment], and with firm purpose avoid giving credence to any false thing, or being imposed upon by this arch deceiver, however powerful and deceptive he may be. But this task is a laborious one, and insensibly a certain lassitude leads me into the course of my ordinary life. And just as a captive who in sleep enjoys an imaginary liberty, when he begins to suspect that his liberty is but a dream, fears to awaken, and conspires with these agreeable illusions that the deception may be prolonged, so insensibly of my own accord I fall back into my former opinions, and I dread awakening from this slumber, lest the laborious wakefulness which would follow the tranquillity of this repose should have to be spent not in daylight, but in the excessive darkness of the difficulties which have just been discussed.

Meditation II

Of the Nature of the Human Mind; and That It Is More Easily Known Than the Body

The Meditation of yesterday filled my mind with so many doubts that it is no longer in my power to forget them. And yet I do not see in what manner I can resolve them; and, just as if I had all of a sudden fallen into very deep water, I am so disconcerted that I can neither make certain of setting my feet on the bottom, nor can I swim and so support myself on the surface. **I shall nevertheless make an effort and follow anew the same path as that on which I yesterday entered, i.e. I shall proceed by**

setting aside all that in which the least doubt could be supposed to exist, just as if I had discovered that it was absolutely false; and I shall ever follow in this road until I have met with something which is certain, or at least, if I can do nothing else, until I have learned for certain that there is nothing in the world that is certain. Archimedes, in order that he might draw the terrestrial globe out of its place, and transport it elsewhere, demanded only that one point should be fixed and immoveable; in the same way I shall have the right to conceive high hopes if I am happy enough to discover one thing only which is certain and indubitable.

I suppose, then, that all the things that I see are false; I persuade myself that nothing has ever existed of all that my fallacious memory represents to me. I consider that I possess no senses; I imagine that body, figure, extension, movement and place are but the fictions of my mind. What, then, can be esteemed as true? Perhaps nothing at all, unless that there is nothing in the world that is certain.

But how can I know there is not something different from those things that I have just considered, of which one cannot have the slightest doubt? Is there not some God, or some other being by whatever name we call it, who puts these reflections into my mind? That is not necessary, for is it not possible that I am capable of producing them myself? I myself, am I not at least something? But I have already denied that I had senses and body. Yet I hesitate, for what follows from that? Am I so dependent on body and senses that I cannot exist without these? But I was persuaded that there was nothing in all the world, that there was no heaven, no earth, that there were no minds, nor any bodies: was I not then likewise persuaded that I did not exist? Not at all; of a surety I myself did exist since I persuaded myself of something [or merely because I thought of something]. But there is some deceiver or other, very powerful and very cunning, who ever employs his ingenuity in deceiving me. Then without doubt I exist also if he deceives me, and let him deceive me as much as he will, he can never cause me to be nothing so long as I think that I am something. So that after having reflected well and carefully examined all things, we must come to the definite conclusion that this proposition: I am, I exist, is necessarily true each time that I pronounce it, or that I mentally conceive it.

But I do not yet know clearly enough what I am, I who am certain that I am; and hence I must be careful to see that I do not imprudently take some other object in place of myself, and thus that I do not go astray in respect of this knowledge that I hold to be the most certain and most evident of all that I have formerly learned. That is why I shall now consider anew what I believed myself to be before I embarked upon these last reflections; and of my former opinions I shall withdraw all that might even in a small degree be invalidated by the reasons which I have just brought forward, in order that there may be nothing at all left beyond what is absolutely certain and indubitable.

What then did I formerly believe myself to be? Undoubtedly I believed myself to be a man. But what is a man? Shall I say a reasonable animal? Certainly not; for then I should have to inquire what an animal is, and what is reasonable; and thus from a single question I should insensibly fall into an infinitude of others more difficult; and I should not wish to waste the little time and leisure remaining to me in trying to unravel subtleties like these. But I shall rather stop here to consider the thoughts which of themselves spring up in my mind, and which were not inspired by anything beyond my own nature alone when I applied myself to the consideration of my being. In the first place, then, I considered myself as having a face, hands, arms, and all that system of members composed of bones and flesh as seen in a corpse which I designated by the name of body. In addition to this I considered that I was nourished, that I walked, that I felt, and that I thought, and I referred all these actions to the soul: but I did not stop to consider what the soul was, or if I did stop, I imagined that it was something extremely rare and subtle like a wind, a flame, or an ether, which was spread throughout my grosser parts. As to body I had no manner of doubt about its nature, but thought I had a very clear knowledge of it; and if I had desired to explain it according to the notions that I had then formed of it, I should have described it thus: By the body I understand all that which can be defined by a certain figure: something which can be confined in a certain place, and which can fill a given space in such a way that every other body will be excluded from it; which can be perceived either by touch, or by sight, or by hearing, or by taste, or by smell: which can be moved in many ways not, in truth, by itself, but by something which is foreign to it, by which it is touched [and from which it receives impressions]: for to have the power of self-movement, as also of feeling or of thinking, I did not consider to appertain to the nature of body: on the contrary, I was rather astonished to find that faculties similar to them existed in some bodies.

But what am I, now that I suppose that there is a certain genius which is extremely powerful, and, if I may say so, malicious, who employs all his powers in deceiving me? Can I affirm that I possess the least of all those things which I have just said pertain to the nature of body? I pause to consider, I revolve all these things in my mind, and I find none of which I can say that it pertains to me. It would be tedious to stop to enumerate them. Let us pass to the attributes of soul and see if there is any one which is in me? What of nutrition or walking [the first mentioned]? But if it is so that I have no body it is also true that I can neither walk nor take nourishment. Another attribute is sensation. But one cannot feel without body, and besides I have thought I perceived many things during sleep that I recognised in my waking moments as not having been experienced at all. What of thinking? I find here that thought is an attribute that belongs to me; it alone cannot be separated from me. I am, I exist, that is certain. But how often? Just when I think; for it might possibly be the case if I ceased entirely to think, that I should likewise cease altogether to exist. I do not now admit anything which is not necessarily true: to speak accurately I am not more than a thing which thinks, that is to say a mind or a soul, or an understanding, or a reason, which are terms whose significance was formerly unknown to me. I am, however, a real thing and really exist; but what thing? I have answered: a thing which thinks.

And what more? I shall exercise my imagination [in order to see if I am not something more]. I am not a collection of members which we call the human body: I am not a subtle air distributed through these members, I am not a wind, a fire, a vapour, a breath, nor anything at all which I can imagine or conceive; because I have assumed that all these were nothing. Without changing that supposition I find that I only leave myself certain of the fact that I am somewhat. But perhaps it is true that these same things which I supposed were nonexistent because they are unknown to me, are really not different from the self which I know. I am not sure about this, I shall not dispute about it now; I can only give judgment on things that are known to me. I know that I exist, and I inquire what I am, I whom I know to exist. But it is very certain that the knowledge of my existence taken in its precise significance does not depend on things whose existence is not yet known to me; consequently it does not depend on those which I can feign in imagination. And indeed the very term *feign* in imagination proves to me my error, for I really do this if I image myself a something, since to imagine is nothing else than to contemplate the figure or image of a corporeal thing. But I already know for certain that I am, and that it may be that all these images, and, speaking generally, all things that relate to the nature of body are nothing but dreams [and chimeras]. For this reason I see clearly that I have as little reason to say, 'I shall stimulate my imagination in order to know more distinctly what I am,' than if I were to say, 'I am now awake, and I perceive somewhat that is real and true: but because I do not yet perceive it distinctly enough, I shall go to sleep of express purpose, so that my dreams may represent the perception with greatest truth and evidence.' And, thus, I know for certain that nothing of all that I can understand by means of my imagination belongs to this knowledge which I have of myself, and that it is necessary to recall the mind from this mode of thought with the utmost diligence in order that it may be able to know its own nature with perfect distinctness.

But what then am I? A thing which thinks. What is a thing which thinks? It is a thing which doubts, understands, [conceives], affirms, denies, wills, refuses, which also imagines and feels.

Certainly it is no small matter if all these things pertain to my nature. But why should they not so pertain? Am I not that being who now doubts nearly everything, who nevertheless understands certain things, who affirms that one only is true, who denies all the others, who desires to know more, is averse from being deceived, who imagines many things, sometimes indeed despite his will, and who perceives many likewise, as by the intervention of the bodily organs? Is there nothing in all this which is as true as it is certain that I exist, even though I should always sleep and though he who has given me being employed all his ingenuity in deceiving me? Is there likewise any one of these attributes which can be distinguished from my thought, or which might be said to be separated from myself? For it is so evident of itself that it is I who doubts, who understands, and who desires, that there is no reason here to add anything to explain it. And I have certainly the power of imagining likewise; for although it may happen (as I formerly supposed) that none of the things which I imagine are true, nevertheless this power of imagining does not cease to be really in use, and it forms part of my thought. Finally, I am the same who feels, that is to say, who perceives certain things, as by the organs of sense, since in truth I see light, I hear noise, I feel heat. But it will be said that these phenomena are false and that I am dreaming. Let it be so; still it is at least quite certain that it seems to me that I see light, that I hear noise and that I feel heat. That cannot be false; properly speaking it is what is in me called feeling; and used in this precise sense that is no other thing than thinking.

From this time I begin to know what I am with a little more clearness and distinction than before; but nevertheless it still seems to me, and I cannot prevent myself from thinking, that corporeal things, whose images are framed by thought, which are tested by the senses, are much more distinctly known than that obscure part of me which does not come under the imagination. Although really it is very strange to say that I know and understand more distinctly these things whose existence seems to me dubious, which are unknown to me, and which do not belong to me, than others of the truth of which I am convinced, which are known to me and which pertain to my real nature, in a word, than myself. But I see clearly how the case stands: my mind loves to wander, and cannot yet suffer itself to be retained within the just limits of truth. Very good, let us once more give it the freest rein, so that, when afterwards we seize the proper occasion for pulling up, it may the more easily be regulated and controlled.

Let us begin by considering the commonest matters, those which we believe to be the most distinctly comprehended, to wit, the bodies which we touch and see; not indeed bodies in general, for these general ideas are usually a little more confused, but let us consider one body in particular. Let us take, for example, this piece of wax: it has been taken quite freshly from the hive, and it has not yet lost the sweetness of the honey which it contains; it still retains somewhat of the odour of the flowers from which it has been culled; its colour, its figure, its size are apparent; it is hard, cold, easily handled, and if you strike it with the finger, it will emit a sound. Finally all the things which are requisite to cause us distinctly to recognise a body, are met within it. But notice that while I speak and approach the fire what remained of the taste is exhaled, the smell evaporates, the colour alters, the figure is destroyed, the size increases, it becomes liquid, it heats, scarcely can one handle it, and when one strikes it, no sound is emitted. Does the same wax remain after this change? We must confess that it remains; none would judge otherwise. What then did I know so distinctly in this piece of wax? It could certainly be nothing of all that the senses brought to my notice, since all these things which fall under taste, smell, sight, touch, and hearing, are found to be changed, and yet the same wax remains.

Perhaps it was what I now think, viz. that this wax was not that sweetness of honey, nor that agreeable scent of flowers, nor that particular whiteness, nor that figure, nor that sound, but simply a body which a little while before appeared to me as perceptible under these forms, and which is now perceptible under others. But what, precisely, is it that I imagine when I form such conceptions? Let us attentively consider this, and, abstracting from all that does not belong to the wax, let us see what remains. Certainly nothing remains excepting a certain extended thing which is flexible and movable. But what is the meaning of flexible and movable? Is it not that I imagine that this piece of wax being round is capable of becoming square and of passing from a square to a triangular figure? No, certainly it is not that, since I imagine it admits of an infinitude of similar changes, and I nevertheless do not know how to compass the infinitude by my imagination, and consequently this conception which I have of the wax is not brought about by the faculty of imagination. What now is this extension? Is it not also unknown? For it becomes greater when the wax is melted, greater when it is boiled, and greater still when the heat increases; and I should not conceive [clearly] according to truth what wax is, if I did not think that even this piece that we are considering is capable of receiving more variations in extension than I have ever imagined. We must then grant that I could not even understand through the imagination what this piece of wax is, and that it is my mind alone which perceives it. I say this piece of wax in particular, for as to wax in general it is yet clearer. But what is this piece of wax which cannot be understood excepting by the [understanding or] mind? It is certainly the same that I see, touch, imagine, and finally it is the same which I have always believed it to be from the beginning. But what must particularly be observed is that its perception is neither an act of vision, nor of touch, nor of imagination, and has never been such although it may have appeared formerly to be so, but only an intuition of the mind, which may be imperfect and confused as it was formerly, or clear and distinct as it is at present, according as my attention is more or less directed to the elements which are found in it, and of which it is composed.

Yet in the meantime I am greatly astonished when I consider [the great feebleness of mind] and its proneness to fall [insensibly] into error; for although without giving expression to my thoughts I consider all this in my own mind, words often impede me and I am almost deceived by the terms of ordinary language. For we say that we see the same wax, if it is present, and not that we simply judge that it is the same from its having the same colour and figure. From this I should conclude that I knew the wax by means of vision and not simply by the intuition of the mind; unless by chance I remember that, when looking from a window and saying I see men who pass in the street, I really do not see them, but infer that what I see is men, just as I say that I see wax. And yet what do I see from the window but hats and coats which may cover automatic machines? Yet I judge these to be men. And similarly solely by the faculty of judgment which rests in my mind, I comprehend that which I believed I saw with my eyes.

A man who makes it his aim to raise his knowledge above the common should be ashamed to derive the occasion for doubting from the forms of speech invented by the vulgar; I prefer to pass on and consider whether I had a more evident and perfect conception of what the wax was when I first perceived it, and when I believed I knew it by means of the external senses or at least by the common sense as it is called, that is to say by the imaginative faculty, or whether my present conception is clearer now that I have most carefully examined what it is, and in what way it can be known. It would certainly be absurd to doubt as to this. For what was there in this first perception which was distinct? What was there which might not as well have been perceived by any of the animals? But when I distinguish the wax from its external forms, and when, just as if I had taken from it its vestments, I consider it quite naked, it is certain that although some error may still be found in my judgment, I can nevertheless not perceive it thus without a human mind.

But finally what shall I say of this mind, that is, of myself, for up to this point I do not admit in myself anything but mind? What then, I who seem to perceive this piece of wax so distinctly, do I not know myself, not only with much more truth and certainty, but also with much more distinctness and clearness? For if I judge that the wax is or exists from the fact that I see it, it certainly follows much more clearly that I am or that I exist myself from the fact that I see it. For it may be that what I see is not really wax, it may also be that I do not possess eyes with which to see anything; but it cannot be that when I see, or (for I no longer take account of the distinction) when I think I see, that I myself who think am nought. So if I judge that the wax exists from the fact that I touch it, the same thing will follow, to wit, that I am; and if I judge that my imagination, or some other cause, whatever it is, persuades me that the wax exists, I shall still conclude the same. And what I have here remarked of wax may be applied to all other things which are external to me [and which are met with outside of me]. And further, if the [notion or] perception of wax has seemed to me clearer and more distinct, not only after the sight or the touch, but also after many other causes have rendered it quite manifest to me, with how much more [evidence] and distinctness must it be said that I now know myself, since all the reasons which contribute to the knowledge of wax, or any other body whatever, are yet better proofs of the nature of my mind! And there are so many other things in the mind itself which may contribute to the elucidation of its nature, that those which depend on body such as these just mentioned, hardly merit being taken into account.

But finally here I am, having insensibly reverted to the point I desired, for, since it is now manifest to me that even bodies are not properly speaking known by the senses or by the faculty of imagination, but by the understanding only, and since they are not known from the fact that they are seen or touched, but only because they are understood, I see clearly that there is nothing which is easier for me to know than my mind. But because it is difficult to rid oneself so promptly of an opinion to which one was accustomed for so long, it will be well that I should halt a little at this point, so that by the length of my meditation I may more deeply imprint on my memory this new knowledge.

What Is Indubitable?

René Descartes

I do not know whether I ought to tell you about the first meditations I made there; for they are so metaphysical and so out of the ordinary, that perhaps they would not be to everyone's liking. Nevertheless, so that one might be able to judge whether the foundations I have laid are sufficiently firm, I am in some sense forced to speak. For a long time I have noticed that in moral matters one must sometimes follow opinions that one knows are quite uncertain, just as if they were indubitable, as has been said above; but since then I desired to attend only to the search for truth, I thought it necessary that I do exactly the opposite, and that I reject as absolutely false everything in which I could imagine the least doubt, so as to see whether, after this process, anything in my set of beliefs remains that is entirely indubitable. Thus, since our senses sometimes deceive us, I decided to suppose that nothing was exactly as our senses would have us imagine. And since there are men who err in reasoning, even in the simplest matters in geometry, and commit paralogisms, judging that I was just as prone to err as the next man, I rejected as false all the reasonings that I had previously taken for demonstrations. And finally, taking into account the fact that the same thoughts we have when we are awake can also come to us when we are asleep, without any of the latter thoughts being true, I resolved to pretend that everything that had ever entered my mind was no more true than the illusions of my dreams. But immediately afterward I noticed that, during the time I wanted thus to think that everything was false, it was necessary that I, who thought thus, be something. **And noticing that this truth—*I think, therefore I am*—was so firm and so certain that the most extravagant suppositions of the sceptics were unable to shake it, I judged that I could accept it without scruple as the first principle of the philosophy I was seeking.**

Then, examining with attention what I was, and seeing that I could pretend that I had no body and that there was no world nor any place where I was, but that I could not pretend, on that account, that I did not exist; and that, on the contrary, from the very fact that I thought about doubting the truth of other things, it followed very evidently and very certainly that I existed. On the other hand, had I simply stopped thinking, even if all the rest of what I have ever imagined were true, I would have no reason to believe that I existed. From this I knew that I was a substance the whole essence or nature of which was merely to think, and which, in order to exist, needed no place and depended on no material thing. Thus this "I," that is, the soul through which I am what I am, is entirely distinct from the body, and is even easier to know than the body, and even if there were no body, the soul would not cease to be all that it is.

After this, I considered in a general way what is needed for a proposition to be true and certain; for since I had just found a proposition that I knew was true, I thought I ought also know in what this certitude consists. And having noticed that there is nothing in all of this—*I think, therefore I am*—that assures me that I am uttering the truth, except that I see very clearly that, in order to think, one must exist; I judged that I could take as a general rule that the things we conceive very clearly and very distinctly are all true, but that there only remains some difficulty in properly discerning which are the ones that we distinctly conceive.

Following this, reflecting upon the fact that I doubted and that, as a consequence, my being was not utterly perfect (for I saw clearly that it is a greater perfection to know than to doubt), I decided to search for the source from which I had learned to think of a thing more perfect than myself; and I readily knew that this ought to originate from some nature that was in effect more perfect. As to those thoughts of mine that were of many other things outside me—such as the sky, the earth, light, heat, and a thousand other things—I was not quite so anxious to know where they came from, since, having noticed nothing in them that seemed to me to make them superior to me, I could believe that, if they were true, they were dependencies of my nature, to the extent that it had any perfection; and that if they were not true, I received them from nothing, that is, they were in me because I had some defect. But the same could not hold for the idea of a being more perfect than my own; for the receiving of this idea from nothing is a manifest impossibility; and since it is no less a contradiction that something more perfect should follow from and depend upon something less perfect than that something can come from nothing, I certainly could not obtain it from myself. It thus remained that this idea was placed in me by a nature truly more perfect than I was, and even that it had within itself all the perfections of which I could have any idea, that is, to put my case in a single word, that this nature was God. To this I added that, since I knew of some perfections that I did not possess, I was not the only being in existence (here, if you please, I shall use freely the language of the School), but that of necessity it must be the case that there is something else more perfect, upon which I depended, and from which I acquired all that I had. For, had I been alone and independent of everything else, so as to have derived from myself all of that small allotment of perfection I had through participation in the perfect being, I would have been able for the same reason to give myself the remainder of what I knew was lacking in me; and thus I would be infinite, eternal, unchanging, all-knowing, all-powerful—in short, I would have all the perfections I could discern in God. For, following from the reasonings I have just given, to know the nature of God, as far as my own nature was able, I had only to consider each thing about which I found an idea in myself, whether or not it was a perfection to have them, and I was certain that none of those that were marked by any imperfection were in this nature, but that all other perfections were. So I observed that doubt, inconstancy, sadness and the like could not be in him, given the fact that I would have been happy to be exempt from them. Now, over and above that, I had ideas of several sensible and corporeal things; for even supposing that I was dreaming and that everything I saw or imagined was false, I still could not deny that the ideas were not truly in my thought. But since I had already recognized very clearly in my case that intelligent nature is distinct from corporeal nature, taking into consideration that all composition attests to dependence and that dependence is manifestly a defect, I therefore judged that being composed of these two natures cannot be a perfection in God and that, as a consequence, God is not thus composed. But, if there are bodies in the world, or intelligences, or other natures that were not entirely perfect, their being ought to depend on God's power, inasmuch as they cannot subsist without God for a single moment.

After this, I wanted to search for other truths, and, having set before myself the object dealt with by geometricians, which I conceived to be like a continuous body or a space indefinitely extended in length, breadth, and height or depth, divisible into various parts which could have various shapes and sizes and be moved or transposed in all sorts of ways (for all this the geometricians take for granted in their object), I ran through some of their simplest proofs. And having noticed that this great certitude that everyone attributes to them is founded only on the fact that one conceives them evidently conforming to the rule that I mentioned earlier, I also noted that there had been nothing in them that assured me of the existence of their object. For I saw very well that by supposing, for example, a triangle, it is necessary for its three angles to be equal to two right angles; but I did not see anything in all this which would assure me that any triangle existed. On the other hand, returning to an examination of the idea I had of a perfect being, I found that existence was contained in it, in the same way as the fact that its three angles are equal to two right angles is contained in the idea of a triangle, or that, in the case of a sphere, all its parts are equidistant from its center, or even more evidently so; and consequently, it is, at the very least, just as certain that God, who is a perfect being, is or exists, as any demonstration in geometry could be.

But what makes many people become persuaded that it is difficult to know this (i.e., the existence of the perfect being), and also even to know what kind of thing their soul is, is that they never lift their minds above sensible things and that they are so much in the habit of thinking about only what they can imagine (which is a particular way of thinking appropriate only for material things), that whatever is not imaginable seems to them to be unintelligible. This is obvious enough from what even the philosophers in the Schools take as a maxim: that there is nothing in the understanding that has not first been in the senses (where obviously the ideas of God and the soul have never been). And it seems to me that those who want to use their imagination to comprehend these things are doing the same as if, to hear sounds or to smell odors, they wanted to use their eyes, except for this difference: the sense of sight assures us no less of the truth of its objects than do the senses of smell or hearing, whereas neither our imagination nor our sense could ever assure us of anything if our understanding did not intervene.

Finally, if there are men who have not yet been sufficiently persuaded of the existence of God and their soul by means of the reasons I have brought forward, I would very much like them to know that all the other things they thought perhaps to be more certain—such as having a body, there being stars and an earth, and the like—are less certain. For although one might have a moral certainty about these things, which is such that it seems outrageous for anyone to doubt it, yet, while it is a question of metaphysical certitude, it seems unreasonable for anyone to deny that there is a sufficient basis for one's not being completely certain about the subject, given that one can, in the same fashion, imagine that while asleep one has a different body and that one sees different stars and a different earth, without any of it being the case. For how does one know that the thoughts that come to us in our dreams are more false than the others, given that often they are no less vivid or express? Let the best minds study this as much as they please, I do not believe they can give any reason that would suffice to remove this doubt, were they not to presuppose the existence of God. For first of all, even what I have already taken for a rule—namely that all the things we very clearly and very distinctly conceive are true—is certain only because God is or exists, and is a perfect being, and because all that is in us comes from him. Thus it follows that our ideas or our notions, being real things and coming from God, insofar as they are clear and distinct, cannot to this extent fail to be true. Thus, if we have ideas sufficiently often that contain falsity, this can only be the case with respect to things that have something confused or obscure about them, since in this regard they participate in nothing; that is, they are thus in us in such a confusion only because we are not perfect. And it is evident that there is no less a contradiction that falsity or imperfection, as such, proceed from God, than that truth or perfection proceed from nothing. But if we did not know that all that is real and true in us comes from a perfect and infinite being, however clear and distinct our ideas may be, we would have no reason that assured us that they had the perfection of being true.

But after the knowledge of God and the soul has thus rendered us certain of this rule, it is very easy to know that the dreams we imagine while asleep ought in no way make us doubt the truth of the thoughts we have while awake. For if it should happen, even while one is asleep; that someone has a very distinct idea, as, for example, when a geometrician invents a new demonstration, his being asleep does not impede its being true. And as to the most common error of our dreams, which consists in the fact that they represent to us various objects in the same way as our exterior senses do, it is of no importance that it gives us the occasion to question the truth of such ideas, since they can also deceive us just as often without our being asleep—as when those with jaundice see everything as yellow-colored, or when the stars or other distant bodies appear to us a great deal smaller than they are. In short, whether awake or asleep, we should never allow ourselves to be persuaded except by the evidence of our reason. And it is to be noted that I said this of our reason, and not of our imagination or our senses. For, although we see the sun very clearly, we should not on that account judge that it is only as large as we see it; and we can very well imagine distinctly the head of a lion grafted on the body of a goat, without necessarily concluding for that reason that there existed a chimera; for reason does not suggest to us that what we thus see or imagine is true. But it does suggest to us that all our ideas or notions ought to have some foundation in truth; for it would not be possible that

God, who is all perfect and entirely truthful, would have put them in us without that. And because our reasonings are never so evident nor so complete while we are asleep as they are while we are awake, even though our imaginations are sometimes just as, or even more, vivid and express when asleep, reason also suggests to us that our thoughts are unable all to be true, since we are not all-perfect; what truth there is in them ought infallibly to be found in those we have when awake rather than those we have in our dreams.

Scepticism

David Hume

There is a species of scepticism, *antecedent* to all study and philosophy, which is much inculcated by Des Cartes and others, as a sovereign preservative against error and precipitate judgment. It recommends an universal doubt, not only of all our former opinions and principles, but also of our very faculties; of whose veracity, say they, we must assure ourselves, by a chain of reasoning, deduced from some original principle, which cannot possibly be fallacious or deceitful. But neither is there any such original principle, which has a prerogative above others, that are self-evident and convincing: or if there were, could we advance a step beyond it, but by the use of those very faculties, of which we are supposed to be already diffident. The Cartesian doubt, therefore, were it ever possible to be attained by any human creature (as it plainly is not) would be entirely incurable; and no reasoning could ever bring us to a state of assurance and conviction upon any subject.

It must, however, be confessed, that this species of scepticism, when more moderate, may be understood in a very reasonable sense, and is a necessary preparative to the study of philosophy, by preserving a proper impartiality in our judgements, and weaning our mind from all those prejudices, which we may have imbibed from education or rash opinion. **To begin with clear and self-evident principles, to advance by timorous and sure steps, to review frequently our conclusions, and examine accurately all their consequences; though by these means we shall make both a slow and a short progress in our systems; are the only methods, by which we can ever hope to reach truth, and attain a proper stability and certainty in our determinations.**

There is another species of scepticism, *consequent* to science and enquiry, when men are supposed to have discovered, either the absolute fallaciousness of their mental faculties, or their unfitness to reach any fixed determination in all those curious subjects of speculation, about which they are commonly employed. Even our very senses are brought into dispute, by a certain species of philosophers; and the maxims of common life are subjected to the same doubt as the most profound principles or conclusions of metaphysics and theology. As these paradoxical tenets (if they may be called tenets) are to be met with in some philosophers, and the refutation of them in several, they naturally excite our curiosity and make us enquire into the arguments on which they may be founded.

I need not insist upon the more trite topics, employed by the sceptics in all ages, against the evidence of *sense*; such as those which are derived from the imperfection and fallaciousness of our organs, on numberless occasions; the crooked appearance of an oar in water; the various aspects of objects, according to their different distances; the double images which arise from the pressing of one eye; with many other appearances of a like nature. These sceptical topics, indeed, are only sufficient to prove, that the senses alone are not implicitly to be depended on; but that we must correct their evidence by reason, and by considerations, derived from the nature of the medium, the distance of the object, and the disposition of the organ, in order to render them, within their sphere, the proper *criteria* of truth and falsehood. There are other more profound arguments against the senses, which admit not of so easy a solution.

It seems evident that men are carried, by a natural instinct or prepossession, to repose faith in their senses; and that, without any reasoning, or even almost before the use of reason, we always suppose an external universe, which depends not on our perception, but would exist, though we and every sensible creature were absent or annihilated. Even the animal creations are governed by a like opinion, and preserve this belief of external objects, in all their thoughts, designs, and actions.

It seems also evident that, when men follow this blind and powerful instinct of nature, they always suppose the very images presented by the senses, to be the external objects, and never entertain any suspicion that the one are nothing but representations of the other. This very table, which we see white and which we feel hard, is believed to exist, independent of our perception, and to be something external to our mind, which perceives it. Our presence bestows not being on it: our absence does not annihilate it. It preserves its existence uniform and entire, independent of the situation of intelligent beings, who perceive or contemplate it.

But this universal and primary opinion of all men is soon destroyed by the slightest philosophy, which teaches us that nothing can ever be present to the mind but an image or perception, and that the senses are only the inlets, through which these images are conveyed, without being able to produce any immediate intercourse between the mind and the object.

The table, which we see, seems to diminish as we remove farther from it: but the real table, which exists independent of us, suffers no alteration: it was, therefore, nothing but its image, which was present to the mind. These are the obvious dictates of reason; and no man, who reflects, ever doubted that the existences which we consider when we say *this house* and *that tree*, are nothing but perceptions in the mind, and fleeting copies or representations of other existences, which remain uniform and independent.

So far, then, are we necessitated by reasoning to contradict or depart from the primary instincts of nature, and to embrace a new system with regard to the evidence of our senses. But here philosophy finds herself extremely embarrassed, when she would justify this new system, and obviate the cavils and objections of the sceptics. She can no longer plead the infallible and irresistible instinct of nature: for that led us to a quite different system, which is acknowledged fallible and even erroneous. And to justify this pretended philosophical system, by a chain of clear and convincing argument, or even any appearance of argument, exceeds the power of all human capacity.

By what argument can it be proved, that the perceptions of the mind must be caused by external objects, entirely different from them, though resembling them (if that be possible) and could not arise either from the energy of the mind itself, or from the suggestion of some invisible and unknown spirit, or from some other cause still more unknown to us? It is acknowledged, that, in fact, many of these perceptions arise not from anything external, as in dreams, madness, and other diseases. And nothing can be more inexplicable than the manner in which body should so operate upon mind as ever to convey an image of itself to a substance, supposed of so different, and even contrary a nature.

It is a question of fact, whether the perceptions of the senses be produced by external objects, resembling them: how shall this question be determined? By experience surely; as all other questions of a like nature. But here experience is, and must be entirely silent. The mind has never any thing present to it but the perceptions, and cannot possibly reach any experience of their connexion with objects. The supposition of such a connexion is, therefore, without any foundation in reasoning. . . .

Thus the first philosophical objection to the evidence of sense or to the opinion of external existence consists in this, that such an opinion, if rested on natural instinct, is contrary to reason, and if referred to reason, is contrary to natural instinct, and at the same time carries no rational evidence with it, to convince an impartial enquirer. The second objection goes farther, and represents this opinion as contrary to reason: at least, if it be a principle of reason, that all sensible qualities are in the mind, not in the object. Bereave matter of all its intelligible qualities, both primary and secondary, you in a manner annihilate it, and leave only a certain unknown, inexplicable *something*, as the cause of our perceptions; a notion so imperfect, that no sceptic will think it worth while to contend against it. . . .

It is needless to insist farther on this head. These objections are but weak. For as, in common life, we reason every moment concerning fact and existence, and cannot possibly subsist, without continually employing this species of argument, any popular objections, derived from thence, must be insufficient to destroy that evidence. The great subverter of *Pyrrhonism* or the excessive principles of scepticism is action, and employment, and the occupations of common life. These principles may flourish and triumph in the schools; where it is, indeed, difficult, if not impossible, to refute them. But as soon as they leave the shade, and by the presence of the real objects, which actuate our passions and sentiments, are put in opposition to the more powerful principles of our nature, they vanish like smoke, and leave the most determined sceptic in the same condition as other mortals.

The sceptic, therefore, had better keep within his proper sphere, and display those *philosophical* objections, which arise from more profound researches. Here he seems to have ample matter of triumph; while he justly insists, that all our evidence for any matter of fact, which lies beyond the testimony of sense or memory, is derived entirely from the relation of cause and effect; that we have no other idea of this relation than that of two objects, which have been frequently *conjoined* together; that we have no argument to convince us, that objects, which have, in our experience, been frequently conjoined, will likewise, in other instances, be conjoined in the same manner; and that nothing leads us to this inference but custom or a certain instinct of our nature; which it is indeed difficult to resist, but which, like other instincts, may be fallacious and deceitful. While the sceptic insists upon these topics, he shows his force, or rather, indeed, his own and our weakness; and seems, for the time at least, to destroy all assurance and conviction. These arguments might be displayed at greater length, if any durable good or benefit to society could ever be expected to result from them.

For here is the chief and most confounding objection to *excessive* scepticism, that no durable good can ever result from it; while it remains in its full force and vigour. . . . A Pyrrhonian cannot expect that his philosophy will have any constant influence on the mind: or if it had, that its influence would be beneficial to society. On the contrary, he must acknowledge, if he will acknowledge anything, that all human life must perish, were his principles universally and steadily to prevail. All discourse, all action would immediately cease; and men remain in a total lethargy, till the necessities of nature, unsatisfied, put an end to their miserable existence. . . .

There is, indeed, a more *mitigated* scepticism or *academical* philosophy, which may be both durable and useful, and which may, in part, be the result of this Pyrrhonism, or *excessive* scepticism, when its undistinguished doubts are, in some measure, corrected by common sense and reflection. The greater part of mankind are naturally apt to be affirmative and dogmatical in their opinions; and while they see objects only on one side, and have no idea of any counterpoising argument, they throw themselves precipitately into the principles, to which they are inclined; nor have they any indulgence for those who entertain opposite sentiments. To hesitate or balance perplexes their understanding, checks their passion, and suspends their action. They are, therefore, impatient till they escape from a state which to them is so uneasy: and they think that they could never remove themselves far enough from it, by the violence of their affirmations and obstinacy of their belief. But could such dogmatical reasoners become sensible of the strange infirmities of human understanding, even in its most perfect state, and when most accurate and cautious in its determinations; such a reflection would naturally inspire them with more modesty and reserve, and diminish their fond opinion of themselves, and their prejudice against antagonists. . . .

Another species of *mitigated* scepticism which may be of advantage to mankind, and which may be the natural result of the Pyrrhonian doubts and scruples, is the limitation of our enquiries to such subjects as are best adapted to the narrow capacity of human understanding. The *imagination* of man is naturally sublime, delighted with whatever is remote and extraordinary, and running, without control, into the most distant parts of space and time in order to avoid the objects, which custom has rendered too familiar to it. A correct *Judgment* observes a contrary method, and avoiding all distant and high enquiries, confines itself to common life, and to such subjects as fall under daily practice and experience; leaving the more sublime topics to the embellishment of poets and orators, or to the arts of priests and politicians. To bring us to so salutary a determination, nothing can be more serviceable, than to be once thoroughly convinced of the force of the Pyrrhonian doubt, and of the impossibility, that anything, but the strong power of natural instinct, could free us from it. Those who have a propensity to philosophy, will still continue their researches; because they reflect that, besides the immediate pleasure, attending such an occupation, philosophical decisions are nothing but the reflections of common life, methodized and corrected. But they will never be tempted to go beyond common life, so long as they consider the imperfection of those faculties which they employ, their narrow reach, and their inaccurate operations.

An Empiricist Theory of Knowledge

John Locke

Introduction

An inquiry into the understanding is pleasant and useful. Since it is the *understanding* that sets man above the rest of sensible beings, and gives him all the advantage and dominion which he has over them; it is certainly a subject, even for its nobleness, worth our labour to inquire into. The understanding, like the eye, whilst it makes us see and perceive all other things, takes no notice of itself; and it requires art and pains to set it at a distance and make it its own object. But whatever be the difficulties that lie in the way of this inquiry; whatever it be that keeps us so much in the dark to ourselves; sure I am that all the light we can let in upon our minds, all the acquaintance we can make with our own understandings, will not only be very pleasant, but bring us great advantage, in directing our thoughts in the search of other things.

2. *Design.* **This, therefore, being my purpose—to inquire into the original, certainty, and extent of** *human knowledge*, **together with the grounds and degrees of** *belief, opinion,* **and** *assent;*—I shall not at present meddle with the physical consideration of the mind; or trouble myself to examine wherein its essence consists; or by what motions of our spirits or alterations of our bodies we come to have any *sensation* by our organs, or any *ideas* in our understandings; and whether those ideas do in their formation, any or all of them, depend on matter or not. These are speculations which, however curious and entertaining, I shall decline, as lying out of my way in the design I am now upon. It shall suffice to my present purpose, to consider the discerning faculties of a man, as they are employed about the objects which they have to do with. And I shall imagine I have not wholly misemployed myself in the thoughts I shall have on this occasion, if, in this historical, plain method, I can give any account of the ways whereby our understandings come to attain those notions of things we have; and can set down any measures of the certainty of our knowledge; or the grounds of those persuasions which are to be found amongst men, so various, different, and wholly contradictory; and yet asserted somewhere or other with such assurance and confidence, that he that shall take a view of the opinions of mankind, observe their opposi-

tion, and at the same time consider the fondness and devotion wherewith they are embraced, the resolution and eagerness wherewith they are maintained, may perhaps have reason to suspect, that either there is no such thing as truth at all, or that mankind hath no sufficient means to attain a certain knowledge of it.

3. *Method*. It is therefore worth while to search out the bounds between opinion and knowledge; and examine by what measures, in things whereof we have no certain knowledge, we ought to regulate our assent and moderate our persuasion. In order whereunto I shall pursue this following method:—

First, I shall inquire into the original of those *ideas,* notions, or whatever else you please to call them, which a man observes, and is conscious to himself he has in his mind; and the ways whereby the understanding comes to be furnished with them.

Secondly, I shall endeavour to show what *knowledge* the understanding hath by those ideas; and the certainty, evidence, and extent of it.

Thirdly, I shall make some inquiry into the nature and grounds of *faith* or *opinion*: whereby I mean that assent which we give to any proposition as true, of whose truth yet we have no certain knowledge. And here we shall have occasion to examine the reasons and degrees of *assent*.

Book I

Chapter I

1. It is an established opinion amongst some men, that there are in the understanding certain *innate principles;* some primary notions, κοιναι εννοιαι, characters, as it were stamped upon the mind of man; which the soul receives in its very first being, and brings into the world with it. It would be sufficient to convince unprejudiced readers of the falseness of this supposition, if I should only show (as I hope I shall in the following parts of this Discourse) how men, barely by the use of their natural faculties, may attain to all the knowledge they have, without the help of any innate impressions; and may arrive at certainty, without any such original notions or principles. For I imagine any one will easily grant that it would be impertinent to suppose the ideas of colours innate in a creature to whom God hath given sight, and a power to receive them by the eyes from external objects: and no less unreasonable would it be to attribute

several truths to the impressions of nature, and innate characters, when we may observe in ourselves faculties fit to attain as easy and certain knowledge of them as if they were originally imprinted on the mind.

But because a man is not permitted without censure to follow his own thoughts in the search of truth, when they lead him ever so little out of the common road, I shall set down the reasons that made me doubt of the truth of that opinion, as an excuse for my mistake, if I be in one; which I leave to be considered by those who, with me, dispose themselves to embrace truth wherever they find it.

2. There is nothing more commonly taken for granted than that there are certain *principles*, both *speculative* and *practical* (for they speak of both), universally agreed upon by all mankind: which therefore, they argue, must needs be the constant impressions which the souls of men receive in their first beings, and which they bring into the world with them, as necessarily and really as they do any of their inherent faculties.

3. This argument, drawn from universal consent, has this misfortune in it, that if it were true in matter of fact, that there were certain truths wherein all mankind agreed, it would not prove them innate, if there can be any other way shown how men may come to that universal agreement, in the things they do consent in, which I presume may be done.

4. But, which is worse, this argument of universal consent, which is made use of to prove innate principles, seems to me a demonstration that there are none such because there are none to which all mankind give an universal assent. I shall begin with the speculative, and instance in those magnified principles of demonstration, "Whatsoever is, is," and "It is impossible for the same thing to be and not to be"; which, of all others, I think have the most allowed title to innate. These have so settled a reputation of maxims universally received, that it will no doubt be thought strange if any one should seem to question it. But yet I take liberty to say, that these propositions are so far from having an universal assent, that there are a great part of mankind to whom they are not so much as known.

5. For, first, it is evident, that all children and idiots have not the least apprehension or thought of them. And the want of that is enough to destroy that universal assent which must needs be the necessary concomitant of all innate truths: it seeming to me near a contradiction to say, that there are truths imprinted on the soul, which it perceives or understands not: imprinting, if it signify anything, being nothing else but the

making certain truths to be perceived. For to imprint anything on the mind without the mind's perceiving it, seems to me hardly intelligible. If therefore children and idiots have souls, have minds, with those impressions upon them, *they* must unavoidably perceive them, and necessarily know and assent to these truths; which since they do not, it is evident that there are no such impressions. For if they are not notions naturally imprinted, how can they be innate? and if they are notions imprinted, how can they be unknown? To say a notion is imprinted on the mind, and yet at the same time to say that the mind is ignorant of it, and never yet took notice of it, is to make this impression nothing. No proposition can be said to be in the mind which it never yet knew, which it was never yet conscious of. For if any one may, then, by the same reason, all propositions that are true, and the mind is capable ever of assenting to, may be said to be in the mind, and to be imprinted: since, if any one can be said to be in the mind, which it never yet knew, it must be only because it is capable of knowing it; and so the mind is of all truths it ever shall know. Nay, thus truths may be imprinted on the mind which it never did, nor ever shall know; for a man may live long, and die at last in ignorance of many truths which his mind was capable of knowing, and that with certainty. So that if the capacity of knowing be the natural impression contended for, all the truths a man ever comes to know will, by this account, be every one of them innate; and this great point will amount to no more, but only to a very improper way of speaking; which, whilst it pretends to assert the contrary, says nothing different from those who deny innate principles. For nobody, I think, ever denied that the mind was *capable* of knowing several truths. The capacity, they say, is innate; the knowledge acquired. But then to what end such contest for certain innate maxims? If truths can be imprinted on the understanding without being perceived, I can see no difference there can be between any truths the mind is capable of knowing in respect of their original: they must all be innate or all adventitious: in vain shall a man go about to distinguish them. He therefore that talks of innate notions in the understanding, cannot (if he intend thereby any distinct sort of truths) mean such truths to be in the understanding as it never perceived, and is yet wholly ignorant of. For if these words "to be in the understanding" have any propriety, they signify to be understood. So that to be in the understanding, and not to be understood; to be in the mind and never to be perceived, is all one as to say anything is and is not in the mind or understanding. If therefore these two propositions, "Whatsoever is, is," and "It is impossible for the same thing to be and not to be," are by nature imprinted, children cannot be ignorant of them: infants, and all that have souls, must necessarily have them in their understandings, know the truth of them, and assent to it. . . .

Book II

Chapter I

1. Every man being conscious to himself that he thinks and that which his mind is applied about whilst thinking being the *ideas* that are there, it is past doubt that men have in their minds several ideas,—such as are those expressed by the words *whiteness, hardness, sweetness, thinking, motion, man, elephant, army, drunkenness*, and others: it is in the first place then to be inquired, *How he comes by them*?

I know it is a received doctrine, that men have native ideas, and original characters, stamped upon their minds in their very first being. This opinion I have at large examined already; and, I suppose what I have said in the foregoing Book will be much more easily admitted, when I have shown whence the understanding may get all the ideas it has; and by what ways and degrees they may come into the mind;—for which I shall appeal to every one's own observation and experience.

2. **Let us then suppose the mind to be, as we say, white paper, void of all characters, without any ideas:—How comes it to be furnished?** Whence comes it by that vast store which the busy and boundless fancy of man has painted on it with an almost endless variety? Whence has it all the *materials* of reason and knowledge? **To this I answer, in one word, from EXPERIENCE. In that all our knowledge is founded; and from that it ultimately derives itself.** Our observation employed either, about external sensible objects, or about the internal operations of our minds perceived and reflected on by ourselves, is that which supplies our understandings with all the *materials* of thinking. These two are the fountains of knowledge, from whence all the ideas we have, or can naturally have, do spring.

3. First, our Senses, conversant about particular sensible objects, do convey into the mind several distinct perceptions of things, according to those various ways wherein those objects do affect them. And thus we come by those *ideas* we have of *yellow, white, heat, cold, soft, hard, bitter, sweet*, and all those which we call sensible qualities; which when I say the senses convey into the mind, I mean, they from external objects convey into the mind what produces there those perceptions. This great source of

most of the ideas we have, depending wholly upon our senses, and derived by them to the understanding, I call SENSATION.

4. Secondly, the other fountain from which experience furnisheth the understanding with ideas is,—the perception of the operations of our own mind within us, as it is employed about the ideas it has got;—which operations, when the soul comes to reflect on and consider, do furnish the understanding with another set of ideas, which could not be had from things without. And such are *perception, thinking, doubting, believing, reasoning, knowing, willing,* and all the different actings of our own minds;—which we being conscious of, and observing in ourselves, do from these receive into our understandings as distinct ideas as we do from bodies affecting our senses. This source of ideas every man has wholly in himself, and though it be not sense, as having nothing to do with external objects, yet it is very like it, and might properly enough be called *internal sense*. But as I call the other Sensation, so I call this REFLECTION, the ideas it affords being such only as the mind gets by reflecting on its own operations within itself. By reflection then, in the following part of this discourse, I would be understood to mean, that notice which the mind takes of its own operations, and the manner of them, by reason whereof there come to be ideas of these operations in the understanding. These two, I say, viz. external material things, as the objects of SENSATION, and the operations of our own minds within, as the objects of REFLECTION, are to me the only originals from whence all our ideas take their beginnings. The term *operations* here I use in a large sense, as comprehending not barely the actions of the mind about its ideas, but some sort of passions arising sometimes from them, such as is the satisfaction or uneasiness arising from any thought.

5. The understanding seems to me not to have the least glimmering of any ideas which it doth not receive from one of these two. *External objects* furnish the mind with the ideas of sensible qualities, which are all those different perceptions they produce in us; and *the mind* furnishes the understanding with ideas of its own operations.

These, when we have taken a full survey of them, and their several modes, combinations, and relations, we shall find to contain all our whole stock of ideas; and that we have nothing in our minds which did not come in one of these two ways. Let any one examine his own thoughts, and thoroughly search into his understanding; and then let him tell me, whether all the original ideas he has there, are any other than of the objects of his senses, or of the operations of his mind, considered as objects of his reflection. And how great a mass of knowledge soever he imagines to be lodged there, he will, upon taking a strict view, see that he has not any idea in his mind but what one of these two have imprinted;—though perhaps, with infinite variety compounded and enlarged by the understanding, as we shall see hereafter.

6. He that attentively considers the state of a child, at his first coming into the world, will have little reason to think him stored with plenty of ideas, that are to be the matter of his future knowledge. It is *by degrees* he comes to be furnished with them. And though the ideas of obvious and familiar qualities imprint themselves before the memory begins to keep a register of time or order, yet it is often so late before some unusual qualities come in the way, that there are few men that cannot recollect the beginning of their acquaintance with them. And if it were worth while, no doubt a child might be so ordered as to have but a very few, even of the ordinary ideas, till he were grown up to a man. But all that are born into the world, being surrounded with bodies that perpetually and diversely affect them, variety of ideas, whether care be taken of it or not, are imprinted on the minds of children. Light and colours are busy at hand everywhere, when the eye is but open; sounds and some tangible qualities fail not to solicit their proper senses, and force an entrance to the mind;—but yet, I think, it will be granted easily, that if a child were kept in a place where he never saw any other but black and white till he were a man, he would have no more ideas of scarlet or green, than he that from his childhood never tasted an oyster, or a pineapple, has of those particular relishes. . . .

Chapter VIII

. . . 8. Whatsoever the mind perceives *in itself,* or is the immediate object of perception, thought, or understanding, that I call *idea;* and the power to produce any idea in our mind, I call *quality* of the subject wherein that power is. Thus a snowball having the power to produce in us the ideas of white, cold, and round,—the power to produce those ideas in us, as they are in the snowball, I call qualities; and as they are sensations or perceptions in our understandings, I call them ideas; which *ideas,* if I speak of sometimes as in the things themselves, I would be understood to mean those qualities in the objects which produce them in us.

9. Qualities thus considered in bodies are, *First,* such as are utterly inseparable from the body, in what state soever it be; and such as in all the

alterations and changes it suffers, all the force can be used upon it, it constantly keeps; and such as sense constantly finds in every particle of matter which has bulk enough to be perceived; and the mind finds inseparable from every particle of matter, though less than to make itself single be perceived by our senses: e.g. Take a grain of wheat, divide it into two parts; each part has still solidity, extension, figure, and mobility: divide it again, and it retains still the same qualities; and so divide it on, till the parts become insensible; they must retain still each of them all those qualities. For division (which is all that a mill, or pestle, or any other body, does upon another, in reducing it to insensible parts) can never take away either solidity, extension, figure, or mobility from any body, but only makes two or more distinct separate masses of matter, of that which was but one before; all which distinct masses, reckoned as so many distinct bodies, after division, make a certain number.

These I call *original* or *primary qualities* of body, which I think we may observe to produce simple ideas in us, viz. solidity, extension, figure, motion or rest, and number.

10. *Secondly,* such qualities which in truth are nothing in the objects themselves but powers to produce various sensations in us by their primary qualities, i.e. by the bulk, figure, texture, and motion of their insensible parts, as colours, sounds, tastes, etc. These I call *secondary qualities.* To these might be added a *third* sort, which are allowed to be barely powers; though they are as much real qualities in the subject as those which I, to comply with the common way of speaking, call qualities, but for distinction, secondary qualities. For the power in fire to produce a new colour, or consistency, in *wax* or *clay,*—by its primary qualities, is as much a quality in fire, as the power it has to produce in *me* a new idea or sensation of warmth or burning, which I felt not before,—by the same primary qualities, viz. the bulk, texture, and motion of its insensible parts. . . .

13. . . . let us suppose at present that the different motions and figures, bulk and number, of such particles, affecting the several organs of our senses, produce in us those different sensations which we have from the colours and smells of bodies; v.g. that a violet, by the impulse of such insensible particles of matter, of peculiar figures and bulks, and in different degrees and modifications of their motions, causes the ideas of the blue colour, and sweet scent of that flower to be produced in our minds. It being no more impossible to conceive that God should annex such ideas to such motions, with which they have no similitude, than that he

should annex the idea of pain to the motion of a piece of steel dividing our flesh, with which that idea hath no resemblance.

14. What I have said concerning colours and smells may be understood also of tastes and sounds, and the other like sensible qualities; which, whatever reality we by mistake attribute to them, are in truth nothing in the objects themselves, but powers to produce various sensations in us; and depend on those primary qualities, viz. bulk, figure, texture, and motion of parts as I have said.

15. From whence I think it easy to draw this observation,—that the ideas of primary qualities of bodies are resemblances of them, and their patterns do really exist in the bodies themselves, but the ideas produced in us by these secondary qualities have no resemblance of them at all. There is nothing like our ideas, existing in the bodies themselves. They are, in the bodies we denominate from them, only a power to produce those sensations in us: and what is sweet, blue, or warm in idea, is but the certain bulk, figure, and motion of the insensible parts, in the bodies themselves, which we call so.

16. Flame is denominated hot and light; snow, white and cold; and manna, white and sweet, from the ideas they produce in us. Which qualities are commonly thought to be the same in those bodies that those ideas are in us, the one the perfect resemblance of the other, as they are in a mirror, and it would by most men be judged very extravagant if one should say otherwise. And yet he that will consider that the same fire that, at one distance produces in us the sensation of warmth, does, at a nearer approach, produce in us the far different sensation of pain, ought to bethink himself what reason he has to say—that this idea of warmth, which was produced in him by the fire, is *actually in the fire;* and his idea of pain, which the same fire produced in him the same way, is *not* in the fire. Why are whiteness and coldness in snow, and pain not, when it produces the one and the other idea in us; and can do neither, but by the bulk, figure, number, and motion of its solid parts? . . .

21. Ideas being thus distinguished and understood, we may be able to give an account how the same water, at the same time, may produce the idea of cold by one hand and of heat by the other: whereas it is impossible that the same water, if those ideas were really in it, should at the same time be both hot and cold. For, if we imagine *warmth,* as it is in our hands, to be nothing but a certain sort and degree of motion in the minute particles of our nerves or animal spirits, we may understand how it is possi-

ble that the same water may, at the same time, produce the sensations of heat in one hand and cold in the other; which yet *figure* never does, that never producing the idea of a square by one hand which has produced the idea of a globe by another. But if the sensation of heat and cold be nothing but the increase or diminution of the motion of the minute parts of our bodies, caused by the corpuscles of any other body, it is easy to be understood, that if that motion be greater in one hand than in the other; if a body be applied to the two hands, which has in its minute particles a greater motion than in those of one of the hands, and a less than in those of the other, it will increase the motion of the one hand and lessen it in the other; and so cause the different sensations of heat and cold that depend thereon. . . .

8. When children have, by repeated sensations, got ideas fixed in their memories, they begin by degrees to learn the use of signs. And when they have got the skill to apply the organs of speech to the framing of articulate sounds, they begin to make use of words, to signify their ideas to others. These verbal signs they sometimes borrow from others, and sometimes make themselves, as one may observe among the new and unusual names children often give to things in the first use of language.

9. The use of words then being to stand as outward marks of our internal ideas, and those ideas being taken from particular things, if every particular idea that we take in should have a distinct name, names must be endless. To prevent this, the mind makes the particular ideas received from particular objects to become general; which is done by considering them as they are in the mind such appearances,—separate from all other existences, and the circumstances of real existence, as time, place, or any other concomitant ideas. This is called ABSTRACTION, whereby ideas taken from particular beings become general representatives of all of the same kind; and their names general names, applicable to whatever exists conformable to such abstract ideas. Such precise, naked appearances in the mind, without considering how, whence, or with what others they came there, the understanding lays up (with names commonly annexed to them) as the standards to rank real existences into sorts, as they agree with these patterns, and to denominate them accordingly. Thus the same colour being observed to-day in chalk or snow, which the mind yesterday received from milk, it considers that appearance alone, makes it a representative of all of that kind; and having given it the name *whiteness*, it by that sound signifies the same quality wheresoever to be imagined or met with; and thus universals, whether ideas or terms, are made. . . .

Book IV

Chapter XI *Of Our Knowledge of the Existence of Other Things*

1. The knowledge of our own being we have by intuition. The existence of a God, reason clearly makes known to us, as has been shown.

The knowledge of the existence of *any other thing* we can have only by *sensation:* for there being no necessary connexion of real existence with any *idea* a man hath in his memory; nor of any other existence but that of God with the existence of any particular man: no particular man can know the existence of any other being, but only when, by actual operating upon him, it makes itself perceived by him. For, the having the idea of anything in our mind, no more proves the existence of that thing, than the picture of a man evidences his being in the world, or the visions of a dream make thereby a true history.

2. It is therefore the *actual receiving* of ideas from without that gives us notice of the existence of other things, and makes us know, that something doth exist at that time without us, which causes that idea in us; though perhaps we neither know nor consider how it does it. For it takes not from the certainty of our senses, and the ideas we receive by them, that we know not the manner wherein they are produced: v.g. whilst I write this, I have, by the paper affecting my eyes, that idea produced in my mind, which, whatever object causes, I call *white;* by which I know that that quality or accident (i.e. whose appearance before my eyes always causes that idea) doth really exist, and hath a being without me. And of this, the greatest assurance I can possibly have, and to which my faculties can attain, is the testimony of my eyes, which are the proper and sole judges of this thing; whose testimony I have reason to rely on as so certain, that I can no more doubt, whilst I write this, that I see white and black, and that something really exists that causes that sensation in me, than that I write or move my hand; which is a certainty as great as human nature is capable of, concerning the existence of anything, but a man's self alone, and of God.

3. The notice we have by our senses of the existing of things without us, though it be not altogether so certain as our intuitive knowledge, or the deductions of our reason employed about the clear abstract ideas of our own minds; yet it is an assurance that deserves the name of *knowledge.* If we persuade ourselves that our faculties act and inform us right concerning the existence of those objects that affect them, it cannot pass for

an ill-grounded confidence: for I think nobody can, in earnest, be so sceptical as to be uncertain of the existence of those things which he sees and feels. At least, he that can doubt so far (whatever he may have with his own thoughts), will never have any controversy with me; since he can never be sure I say anything contrary to his own opinion. As to myself, I think God has given me assurance enough of the existence of things without me: since, by their different application, I can produce in myself both pleasure and pain, which is one great concernment of my present state. This is certain: the confidence that our faculties do not herein deceive us, is the greatest assurance we are capable of concerning the existence of material beings. For we cannot act anything but by our faculties; nor talk of knowledge itself, but by the help of those faculties which are fitted to apprehend even what knowledge is.

But besides the assurance we have from our senses themselves, that they do not err in the information they give us of the existence of things without us, when they are affected by them, we are further confirmed in this assurance by other concurrent reasons:—

4. I. It is plain those perceptions are produced in us by exterior causes affecting our senses: because those that want the *organs* of any sense, never can have the ideas belonging to that sense produced in their minds. This is too evident to be doubted: and therefore we cannot but be assured that they come in by the organs of that sense, and no other way. The organs themselves, it is plain, do not produce them: for then the eyes of a man in the dark would produce colours, and his nose smell roses in the winter: but we see nobody gets the relish of a pineapple, till he goes to the Indies, where it is, and tastes it.

5. II. Because sometimes I find that *I cannot avoid the having those ideas produced in my mind.* For though, when my eyes are shut, or windows fast, I can at pleasure recall to my mind the ideas of light, or the sun, which former sensations had lodged in my memory; so I can at pleasure lay by *that* idea, and take into my view that of the smell of a rose, or taste of sugar. But, if I turn my eyes at noon towards the sun, I cannot avoid the ideas which the light or sun then produces in me. So that there is a manifest difference between the ideas laid up in my memory (over which, if they were there only, I should have constantly the same power to dispose of them, and lay them by at pleasure), and those which force themselves upon me, and I cannot avoid having. And therefore it must needs be some exterior cause, and the brisk acting of some objects without me,

whose efficacy I cannot resist, that produces those ideas in my mind, whether I will or no. Besides, there is nobody who doth not perceive the difference in himself between contemplating the sun, as he hath the idea of it in his memory, and actually looking upon it: of which two, his perception is so distinct, that few of his ideas are more distinguishable one from another. And therefore he hath certain knowledge that they are not *both* memory, or the actions of his mind, and fancies only within him; but that actual seeing hath a cause without. . . .

Chapter XV Of Probability

1. As *demonstration* is the showing the agreement or disagreement of two ideas, by the intervention of one or more proofs, which have a constant, immutable, and visible connexion one with another; so *probability* is nothing but the appearance of such an agreement or disagreement, by the intervention of proofs, whose connexion is not constant and immutable, or at least is not perceived to be so, but is, or appears for the most part to be so, and is enough to induce the mind to judge the proposition to be true or false, rather than the contrary. For example: in the demonstration of it a man perceives the certain, immutable connexion there is of equality between the three angles of a triangle, and those intermediate ones which are made use of to show their equality to two right ones; and so, by an intuitive knowledge of the agreement or disagreement of the intermediate ideas in each step of the progress, the whole series is continued with an evidence, which clearly shows the agreement or disagreement of those three angles in equality to two right ones: and thus he has certain knowledge that it is so. But another man, who never took the pains to observe the demonstration, hearing a mathematician, a man of credit, affirm the three angles of a triangle to be equal to two right ones, assents to it, i.e. receives it for true: in which case the foundation of his assent is the probability of the thing; the proof being such as for the most part carries truth with it: the man on whose testimony he receives it, not being wont to affirm anything contrary to or besides his knowledge, especially in matters of this kind: so that that which causes his assent to this proposition, that the three angles of a triangle are equal to two right ones, that which makes him take these ideas to agree, without knowing them to do so, is the wonted veracity of the speaker in other cases, or his supposed veracity in this.

2. Our knowledge, as has been shown, being very narrow, and we not happy enough to find certain truth in everything which we have occasion

to consider; most of the propositions we think, reason, discourse—nay, act upon, are such as we cannot have undoubted knowledge of their truth: yet some of them border so near upon certainty, that we make no doubt at all about them; but assent to them as firmly, and act, according to that assent, as resolutely as if they were infallibly demonstrated, and that our knowledge of them was perfect and certain. But there being degrees herein, from the very neighbourhood of certainty and demonstration, quite down to improbability and unlikeness, even to the confines of impossibility; and also degrees of assent from full assurance and confidence, quite down to conjecture, doubt, and distrust: I shall come now (having, as I think, found out *the bounds of human knowledge and certainty*), in the next place, to consider *the several degrees and grounds of probability, and assent or faith*. . . .

5. Probability wanting that intuitive evidence which infallibly determines the understanding and produces certain knowledge, the mind, if it *will proceed rationally*, ought to examine all the grounds of probability, and see how they make more or less for or against any proposition, before it assents to or dissents from it; and, upon a due balancing the whole, reject or receive it, with a more or less firm assent, proportionately to the preponderancy of the greater grounds of probability on one side or the other.

The Problem of Induction

David Hume

Skeptical Doubts Concerning the Operations of the Understanding

Part I

All the objects of human reason or inquiry may naturally be divided into two kinds, to wit, "Relations of Ideas," and "Matters of Fact." Of the first kind are the sciences of Geometry, Algebra, and Arithmetic, and, in short, every affirmation which is either intuitively or demonstratively certain. *That the square of the hypotenuse is equal to the square of the two sides* is a proposition which expresses a relation between these figures. *That three times five is equal to the half of thirty* expresses a relation between these numbers. Propositions of this kind are discoverable by the mere operation of thought, without dependence on what is anywhere existent in the universe. Though there never were a circle or triangle in nature, the truths demonstrated by Euclid would forever retain their certainty and evidence.

Matters of fact, which are the second objects of human reason, are not ascertained in the same manner, nor is our evidence of their truth, however great, of a like nature with the foregoing. The contrary of every matter of fact is still possible, because it can never imply a contradiction and is conceived by the mind with the same facility and distinctness as if ever so conformable to reality. *That the sun will not rise tomorrow* is no less intelligible a proposition and implies no more contradiction than the affirmation *that it will rise*. We should in vain, therefore, attempt to demonstrate its falsehood. Were it demonstratively false, it would imply a contradiction and could never be distinctly conceived by the mind.

It may, therefore, be a subject worthy of curiosity to inquire what is the nature of that evidence which assures us of any real existence and matter of fact beyond the present testimony of our senses or the records of our memory. This part of philosophy, it is observable, had been little cultivated either by the ancients or moderns; and, therefore, our doubts and errors in the prosecution of so important an inquiry may be the more excusable while we march through such difficult paths without any guide or direction. They may even prove useful by exciting curiosity and destroying that implicit faith and security which is the bane of all reasoning and free inquiry. The discovery of defects in the common philosophy, if any such there be, will not, I presume, be a discouragement, but rather an incitement, as is usual, to attempt something more full and satisfactory than has yet been proposed to the public.

All reasonings concerning matter of fact seem to be founded on the relation of *cause* and *effect*. By means of that relation alone we can go beyond the evidence of our memory and senses. If you were to ask a man why he believes any matter of fact which is absent, for instance, that his friend is in the country or in France, he would give you a reason, and this reason would be some other fact: as a letter received from him or the knowledge of his former resolutions and promises. A man finding a watch or any other machine in a desert island would conclude that there had once been men in that island. All our reasonings concerning fact are of the same nature. And here it is constantly supposed that there is a connection between the present fact and that which is inferred from it. Were there nothing to bind them together, the inference would be entirely precarious. The hearing of an articulate voice and rational discourse in the dark assures us of the presence of some person. Why? Because these are the effects of the human make and fabric, and closely connected with it. If we anatomize all the other reasonings of this nature, we shall find that they are founded on the relation of cause and effect, and that this relation is either near or remote, direct or collateral. Heat and light are collateral effects of fire, and the one effect may justly be inferred from the other.

If we would satisfy ourselves, therefore, concerning the nature of that evidence which assures us of matters of fact, we must inquire how we arrive at the knowledge of cause and effect.

I shall venture to affirm, as a general proposition which admits of no exception, that the knowledge of this relation is not, in any instance, attained by reasonings *a priori*,[1] but arises entirely from experience, when we find that any particular objects are constantly conjoined with each other. Let an object be presented to a man of ever so strong natural reason and abilities—if that object be entirely new to him, he will not be able, by the most accurate examination of its sensible qualities, to discover any of its causes or effects. Adam, though his rational faculties be supposed, at the very first, entirely perfect, could not have inferred from the fluidity and transparency of water that it would suffocate him, or from the light and warmth of fire that it would consume him. No object ever discovers, by the qualities which appear to the senses, either the causes which produced it or the effects which will arise from it; nor can our reason, unassisted by experience, ever draw any inference concerning real existence and matter of fact.

This proposition, *that causes and effects are discoverable, not by reason, but by experience,* will readily be admitted with regard to such objects as we remember to have once been altogether unknown to us, since we must be conscious of the utter inability which we then lay under of foretelling what would arise from them. Present two smooth pieces of marble to a man who has no tincture of natural philosophy; he will never discover that they will adhere together in such a manner as to require great force to separate them in a direct line, while they make so small a resistance to a lateral pressure. Such events as bear little analogy to the common course of nature are also readily confessed to be known only by experience, nor does any man imagine that the explosion of gunpowder or the attraction of a loadstone could ever be discovered by arguments *a priori*. In like manner, when an effect is supposed to depend upon an intricate machinery or secret structure of parts, we make no difficulty in attributing all our knowledge of it to experience. Who will assert that he can give the ultimate reason why milk or bread is proper nourishment for a man, not for a lion or tiger?

But the same truth may not appear at first sight to have the same evidence with regard to events which have become familiar to us from our first appearance in the world, which bear a close analogy to the whole course of nature, and which are supposed to depend on the simple qualities of objects without any secret structure of parts. We are apt to imagine that we could discover these effects by the mere operation of our reason without experience. We fancy that, were we brought on a sudden into this world, we could at first have inferred that one billiard ball would communicate motion to another upon impulse, and that we needed not to have waited for the event in order to pronounce with certainty concerning it. Such is the influence of custom that where it is strongest it not only covers our natural ignorance but even conceals itself, and seems not to take place, merely because it is found in the highest degree.

But to convince us that all the laws of nature and all the operations of bodies without exception are known only by experience, the following reflections may perhaps suffice. Were any object presented to us, and were we required to pronounce concerning the effect which will result from it without consulting past observation, after what manner, I beseech you, must the mind proceed in this operation? It must invent or imagine some event which it ascribes to the object as its effect; and it is plain that this invention must be entirely arbitrary. The mind can never possibly find the effect in the supposed cause by the most accurate scrutiny and examination. For the effect is totally different from the cause, and consequently can never be discovered in it. Motion in the second billiard ball is a quite distinct event from motion in the first, nor is there anything in the one to suggest the smallest hint of the other. A stone or piece of metal raised into the air and left without any support immediately falls. But to consider the matter *a priori*, is there anything we discover in this situation which can beget the idea of a downward rather than an upward or any other motion in the stone or metal?

And as the first imagination or invention of a particular effect in all natural operations is arbitrary where we consult not experience, so must we also esteem the supposed tie or connection between the cause and effect which binds them together and renders it impossible that any other effect could result from the operation of that cause. When I see, for instance, a billiard ball moving in a straight line toward another, even suppose motion in the second ball should by accident be suggested to me as the result of their contact or impulse, may I not conceive that a hundred different events might as well follow from that cause? May not both these balls remain at absolute rest? May not the first ball return in a straight line or leap off from the second in any line or direction? All these suppositions are consistent and conceivable. Why, then, should we give the preference to one which is no more consistent or conceivable than the rest? All our reasonings *a priori* will never be able to show us any foundation for this preference.

In a word, then, every effect is a distinct event from its cause. It could not, therefore, be discovered in the cause, and the first invention or conception of it, *a priori*, must be entirely arbitrary. And even after it is suggested, the conjunction of it with the cause must appear equally arbitrary, since there are always many other effects which, to reason, must seem fully as consistent and natural. In vain, therefore, should we pretend to determine any single event or infer any cause or effect without the assistance of observation and experience.

Hence we may discover the reason why no philosopher who is rational and modest has ever pretended to assign the ultimate cause of any natural operation, or to show distinctly the action of that power which produces any single effect in the universe. It is confessed that the utmost effort of human reason is to reduce the principles productive of natural phenomena to a greater simplicity, and to resolve the many particular effects into a few general causes, by means of reasonings from analogy, experience, and observation. But as to the causes of these general causes, we should in vain attempt their discovery, nor shall we ever be able to satisfy ourselves by any particular explication of them. These ultimate springs and principles are totally shut up from human curiosity and inquiry. Elasticity, gravity, cohesion of parts, communication of motion by impulse—these are probably the ultimate causes and principles which we shall ever discover in nature; and we may esteem ourselves sufficiently happy if, by accurate inquiry and reasoning, we can trace up the particular phenomena to, or near to, these general principles. The most perfect philosophy of the natural kind only staves off our ignorance a little longer, as perhaps the most perfect philosophy of the moral or metaphysical kind serves only to discover larger portions of it. Thus the observation of human blindness and weakness is the result of all philosophy, and meets us, at every turn, in spite of our endeavors to elude or avoid it.

Nor is geometry, when taken into the assistance of natural philosophy, ever able to remedy this defect or lead us into the knowledge of ultimate causes by all that accuracy of reasoning for which it is so justly celebrated. Every part of mixed mathematics proceeds upon the supposition that certain laws are established by nature in her operations, and abstract reasonings are employed either to assist experience in the discovery of these laws or to determine their influence in particular instances where it depends upon any precise degree of distance and quantity. Thus it is a law of motion, discovered by experience, that the moment or force of any body in motion is in the compound ratio or proportion of its solid contents and its velocity, and, consequently, that a small force may remove the greatest obstacle or raise the greatest weight if by any contrivance or machinery we can increase the velocity of that force so as to make it an overmatch for its antagonist. Geometry assists us in the application of this law by giving us the just dimensions of all the parts and figures which can enter into any species of machine, but still the discovery of the law itself is owing merely to experience; and all the abstract reasonings in the world could never lead us one step toward the knowledge of it. When we reason *a priori* and consider merely any object or cause as it appears to the mind, independent of all observation, it never could suggest to us the notion of any distinct object, such as its effect, much less show us the inseparable and inviolable connection between them. A man must be very sagacious who could discover by reasoning that crystal is the effect of heat, and ice of cold, without being previously acquainted with the operation of these qualities.

Part II

But we have not yet attained any tolerable satisfaction with regard to the question first proposed. Each solution still gives rise to a new question as difficult as the foregoing and leads us on to further inquiries. When it is asked, *What is the nature of all our reasonings concerning matter of fact?* the proper answer seems to be, That they are founded on the relation of cause and effect. When again it is asked, *What is the foundation of all our reasonings and conclusions concerning that relation?* it may be replied in one word, *experience*. But if we still carry on our sifting humor and ask, *What is the foundation of all conclusions from experience?* this implies a new question which may be of more difficult solution and explication. Philosophers that give themselves airs of superior wisdom and sufficiency have a hard task when they encounter persons of inquisitive dispositions, who push them from every corner to which they retreat, and who are sure at last to bring them to some dangerous dilemma. The best expedient to prevent this confusion is to be modest in our pretensions and even to discover the difficulty ourselves before it is objected to us. By this means we may make a kind of merit of our very ignorance.

I shall content myself in this section with an easy task and shall pretend only to give a negative answer to the question here proposed. I say, then, that even after we have experience of the operations of cause and effect, our conclusions from that experience are *not* founded on reasoning or any process of the understanding. This answer we must endeavor both to explain and to defend.

It must certainly be allowed that nature has kept us at a great distance from all her secrets and has afforded us only the knowledge of a few superficial qualities of objects, while she conceals from us those powers and principles on which the influence of these objects entirely depends. Our senses inform us of the color, weight, and consistency of bread, but neither sense nor reason can ever inform us of those qualities which fit it for the nourishment and support of the human body. Sight or feeling conveys an idea of the actual motion of bodies, but as to that wonderful force or power which would carry on a moving body forever in a continued change of place, and which bodies never lose but by communicating it to others, of this we cannot form the most distant conception. But notwithstanding this ignorance of natural powers and principles, we always presume when we see like sensible qualities that they have like secret powers, and expect that effects similar to those which we have experienced will follow from them. If a body of like color and consistency with that bread which we have formerly eaten be presented to us, we make no scruple of repeating the experiment and foresee with certainty like nourishment and support. Now this is a process of the mind or thought of which I would willingly know the foundation. It is allowed on all hands that there is no known connection between the sensible qualities and the secret powers, and, consequently, that the mind is not led to form such a conclusion concerning their constant and regular conjunction by anything which it knows of their nature. As to past *experience*, it can be allowed to give *direct* and *certain* information of those precise objects only, and that precise period of time which fell under its cognizance: But why this experience should be extended to future times and to other objects which, for aught we know, may be only in appearance similar, this is the main question on which I would insist. The bread which I formerly ate nourished me; that is, a body of such sensible qualities was, at that time, endued with such secret powers. But does it follow that other bread must also nourish me at another time, and that like sensible qualities must always be attended with like secret powers? The consequence seems nowise necessary. At least, it must be acknowledged that there is here a consequence drawn by the mind that there is a certain step taken, a process of thought, and an inference which wants to be explained. These two propositions are far from being the same: *I have found that such an object has always been attended with such an effect, and I foresee that other objects which are in appearance similar will be attended with similar effects.* I shall allow, if you please, that the one proposition may justly be inferred from the other: I know, in fact, that it always is inferred. But if you insist that the inference is made by a chain of reasoning, I desire you to produce that reasoning. The connection between these propositions is not intuitive. There is required a medium which may enable the mind to draw such an inference, if indeed it be drawn by reasoning and argument. What that medium is I must confess passes my comprehension; and it is incumbent on those to produce it who assert that it really exists and is the original of all our conclusions concerning matter of fact.

This negative argument must certainly, in process of time, become altogether convincing if many penetrating and able philosophers shall turn their inquiries this way, and no one be ever able to discover any connecting proposition or intermediate step which supports the understanding in this conclusion. But as the question is yet new, every reader may not trust so far to his own penetration as to conclude, because an argument escapes his inquiry, that therefore it does not really exist. For this reason it may be requisite to venture upon a more difficult task, and, enumerating all the branches of human knowledge, endeavor to show that none of them can afford such an argument.

All reasonings may be divided into two kinds, namely, demonstrative reasoning, or that concerning relations of ideas, and moral reasoning, or that concerning matter of fact and existence. That there are no demonstrative arguments in the case seems evident, since it implies no contradiction that the course of nature may change and that an object, seemingly like those which we have experienced, may be attended with different or contrary effects. May I not clearly and distinctly conceive that a body, falling from the clouds and which in all other respects resembles snow, has yet the taste of salt or feeling of fire? Is there any more intelligible proposition than to affirm that all the trees will flourish in December and January, and will decay in May and June? Now, whatever is intelligible and can be distinctly conceived implies no contradiction and can never be proved false by any demonstrative argument or abstract reasoning *a priori*.

If we be, therefore, engaged by arguments to put trust in past experience and make it the standard of our future judgment, these arguments must be probable only, or such as regard matter of fact and real existence, according to the division above mentioned. But that there is no argument of this kind must appear if our explication of that species of reasoning be admitted as solid and satisfactory. We have said that all arguments concerning existence are founded on the relation of cause and effect, that our knowledge of that relation is derived entirely from experience, and that all our experimental conclusions proceed upon the supposition that the future will be conformable to the past. To endeavor, therefore, the proof of this last supposition by probable arguments, or arguments regarding existence, must be evidently going in a circle and taking that for granted which is the very point in question.

In reality, all arguments from experience are founded on the similarity which we discover among natural objects, and by which we are induced to expect effects similar to those which we have found to follow from such objects. And though none but a fool or madman will ever pretend to dispute the authority of experience or to reject that great guide of human life, it may surely be allowed a philosopher to have so much curiosity at least as to examine the principle of human nature which gives this mighty authority to experience and makes us draw advantage from that similarity which nature has placed among different objects. From causes which appear similar, we expect similar effects. This is the sum of all our experimental conclusions. Now it seems evident that, if this conclusion were formed by reason, it would be as perfect at first, and upon one instance, as after ever so long a course of experience; but the case is far otherwise. Nothing so like as eggs, yet no one, on account of this appearing similarity, expects the same taste and relish in all of them. It is only after a long course of uniform experiments in any kind that we attain a firm reliance and security with regard to a particular event. Now, where is that process of reasoning which, from one instance, draws a conclusion so different from that which it infers from a hundred instances that are nowise different from that single one? This question I propose as much for the sake of information as with an intention of raising difficulties. I cannot find, I cannot imagine any such reasoning. But I keep my mind still open to instruction if anyone will vouchsafe to bestow it on me.

Should it be said that, from a number of uniform experiments, we *infer* a connection between the sensible qualities and the secret powers, this, I must confess, seems the same difficulty, couched in different terms. The question still occurs, On what process of argument is this *inference* founded? Where is the medium, the interposing ideas which join propositions so very wide of each other? It is confessed that the color, consistency, and other sensible qualities of bread appear not of themselves to have any connection with the secret powers of nourishment and support; for otherwise we could infer these secret powers from the first appearance of these sensible qualities without the aid of experience, contrary to the sentiment of all philosophers, and contrary to plain matter of fact. Here, then, is our natural state of ignorance with regard to the powers and influence of all objects. How is this remedied by experience? It only shows us a number of uniform effects resulting from certain objects, and teaches us that those particular objects, at that particular time, were endowed with such powers and forces. When a new object endowed with similar sensible qualities is produced, we expect similar powers and forces, and look for a like effect. From a body of like color and consistency with bread, we expect like nourishment and support. But this surely is a step or progress of the mind which wants to be explained. When a man says, *I have found, in all past instances, such sensible qualities, conjoined with such secret powers, and when he says, similar sensible qualities will always be conjoined with similar secret powers,* he is not guilty of a tautology, nor are these propositions in any respect the same. You say that the one proposition is an inference from the other; but you must confess that the inference is not intuitive, neither is it demonstrative. Of what nature is it then? To say it is experimental is begging the question. For all inferences from experience suppose, as their foundation, that the future will resemble the past and that similar powers will be conjoined with similar sensible qualities. If there be any suspicion that the course of nature may change, and that the past may be no rule for the future, all experience becomes useless and can give rise to no inference or conclusion. It is impossible, therefore, that any arguments from experience can prove this resemblance of the past to the future, since all these arguments are founded on the supposition of that resemblance. Let the course of things be allowed hitherto ever so regular, that alone, without some new argument or inference, proves not that for the future it will continue so. In vain do you pretend to have learned the nature of bodies from your past experience. Their secret nature, and consequently all their effects and influence, may change without any change in their sensible qualities. This happens sometimes, and with regard to some objects. Why may it not happen always, and with regard to all objects? What logic, what process of argument secures you against this supposition? My practice, you say, refutes my doubts. But you mistake the purport of my question. As an agent, I am quite satisfied in the point; but as a philosopher who has some share of curiosity, I will not say skepticism, I want to learn the foundation of this inference. No reading, no inquiry has yet been able to remove my difficulty or give me satisfaction in a matter of such importance. Can I do better than propose the difficulty to the public, even though, perhaps, I have small hopes of obtaining a solution? We shall at least, by this means, be sensible of our ignorance, if we do not augment our knowledge.

I must confess that a man is guilty of unpardonable arrogance who concludes, because an argument has escaped his own investigation, that therefore it does not really exist. I must also confess that, though all the learned, for several ages, should have employed themselves in fruitless search upon any subject, it may still, perhaps, be rash to conclude positively that the subject must therefore pass all human comprehension. Even though we examine all the sources of our knowledge and conclude them unfit for such a subject, there may still remain a suspicion that the enumeration is not complete or the examination not accurate. But with regard to the present subject, there are some considerations which seem to remove all this accusation of arrogance or suspicion of mistake.

It is certain that the most ignorant and stupid peasants, nay infants, nay even brute beasts, improve by experience and learn the qualities of natural objects by observing the effects which result from them. When a child has felt the sensation of pain from touching the flame of a candle, he will be careful not to put his hand near any candle, but will expect a similar effect from a cause which is similar in its sensible qualities and appearance. If you assert, therefore, that the understanding of the child is led into this conclusion by any process of argument or ratiocination, I may justly require you to produce that argument, nor have you any pretense to refuse so equitable a demand. You cannot say that the argument is abstruse and may possibly escape your inquiry, since you confess that it is obvious to the capacity of a mere infant. If you hesitate, therefore, a moment or if, after reflection, you produce an intricate or profound argument, you, in a manner, give up the question and confess that it is not reasoning which engages us to suppose the past resembling the future, and to expect similar effects from causes which are to appearance similar. This is the proposition which I intended to enforce in the present section. If I be right, I pretend not to have made any mighty discovery. And if I be wrong, I must acknowledge myself to be indeed a very backward scholar, since I cannot now discover an argument which, it seems, was perfectly familiar to me long before I was out of my cradle.

Skeptical Solution of These Doubts

Part I

The passion for philosophy, like that for religion, seems liable to this inconvenience, that though it aims at the correction of our manners and extirpation of our vices, it may only serve, by imprudent management, to foster a predominant inclination and push the mind with more determined resolution toward that side which already *draws* too much by the bias and propensity of the natural temper. It is certain that, while we aspire to the magnanimous firmness of the philosophic sage and endeavor to confine our pleasures altogether within our own minds, we may, at last, render our philosophy, like that of Epictetus and other Stoics, only a more refined system of selfishness, and reason ourselves out of all virtue as well as social enjoyment. While we study with attention the vanity of human life and turn all our thoughts toward the empty and transitory nature of riches and honors, we are, perhaps, all the while flattering our natural indolence which, hating the bustle of the world and drudgery of business, seeks a pretense of reason to give itself a full and uncontrolled indulgence. There is, however, one species of philosophy which seems little liable to this inconvenience, and that because it strikes in with no disorderly passion of the human mind, nor can mingle itself with any natural affection or propensity; and that is the Academic or Skeptical philosophy. The Academics always talk of doubt and suspense of judgment, of danger in hasty determinations, of confining to very narrow bounds the inquiries of the understanding, and of renouncing all speculations which lie not within the limits of common life and practice. Nothing, therefore, can be more contrary than such a philosophy to the supine indolence of the mind, its rash arrogance, its lofty pretensions, and its superstitious credulity. Every passion is mortified by it, except the love of truth; and that passion never is nor can be carried to too high a degree. It is surprising, therefore, that this philosophy, which in almost every instance must be harmless and innocent, should be the subject of so much groundless reproach and obloquy. But, perhaps, the very circumstance which renders it so innocent is what chiefly exposes it to the public hatred and resentment. By flattering no irregular passion, it gains few partisans. By opposing so many vices and follies, it raises to itself abundance of enemies who stigmatize it as libertine, profane, and irreligious.

Nor need we fear that this philosophy, while it endeavors to limit our inquiries to common life, should ever undermine the reasonings of common life and carry its doubts so far as to destroy all action as well as speculation. Nature will always maintain her rights and prevail in the end over any abstract reasoning whatsoever. Though we should conclude, for instance, as in the foregoing section, that in all reasonings from experience there is a step taken by the mind which is not supported by any argument or process of the understanding, there is no danger that these reasonings, on which almost all knowledge depends, will ever be affected by such a discovery. If the mind be not engaged by argument to make this step, it must be induced by some other principle of equal weight and authority; and that principle will preserve its influence as long as human nature remains the same. What that principle is may well be worth the pains of inquiry.

Suppose a person, though endowed with the strongest faculties of reason and reflection, to be brought on a sudden into this world; he would, indeed, immediately observe a continual succession of objects and one event following another, but he would not be able to discover anything further. He would not at first, by any reasoning, be able to reach the idea of cause and effect, since the particular powers by which all natural operations are performed never appear to the senses; nor is it reasonable to conclude, merely because one event in one instance precedes another, that therefore the one is the cause, the other the effect. The conjunction may be arbitrary and casual. There may be no reason to infer the existence of one from the appearance of the other: and, in a word, such a person without more experience could never employ his conjecture or reasoning concerning any matter of fact or be assured of anything beyond what was immediately present to his memory or senses.

Suppose again that he has acquired more experience and has lived so long in the world as to have observed similar objects or events to be constantly conjoined together—what is the consequence of this experience? He immediately infers the existence of one object from the appearance of the other, yet he has not, by all his experience, acquired any idea or knowledge of the secret power by which the one object produces the other, nor is it by any process of reasoning he is engaged to draw this inference; but still he finds himself determined to draw it, and though he should be convinced that his understanding has no part in the operation, he would nevertheless continue in the same course of thinking. There is some other principle which determines him to form such a conclusion.

This principle is *custom* or *habit*. For wherever the repetition of any particular act or operation produces a propensity to renew the same act or operation without being impelled by any reasoning or process of the understanding, we always say that this propensity is the effect of *custom*. By employing that word we pretend not to have given the ultimate reason of such a propensity. We only point out a principle of human nature which is universally acknowledged, and which is well known by its effects. Perhaps we can push our inquiries no further or pretend to give the cause of this cause, but must rest contented with it as the ultimate principle which we can assign of all our conclusions from experience. It is sufficient satisfaction that we can go so far without repining at the narrowness of our faculties, because they will carry us no further. And it is certain we here advance a very intelligible proposition at least, if not a true one, when we assert that after the constant conjunction of two objects, heat and flame, for instance, weight and solidity, we are determined by custom alone to expect the one from the appearance of the other. This hypothesis seems even the only one which explains the difficulty why we draw from a thousand instances an inference which we are not able to draw from one instance that is in no respect different from them. Reason is incapable of any such variation. The conclusions which it draws from considering one circle are the same which it would form upon surveying all the circles in the universe. But no man, having seen only one body move after being impelled by another, could infer that every other body will move after a like impulse. **All inferences from experience, therefore, are effects of custom, not of reasoning.**

Custom, then, is the great guide of human life. It is that principle alone which renders our experience useful to us and makes us expect, for the future, a similar train of events with those which have appeared in the past. Without the influence of custom we should be entirely ignorant of every matter of fact beyond what is immediately present to the memory and senses. We should never know how to adjust means to ends or to employ our natural powers in the production of any effect. There would be an end at once of all action as well as of the chief part of speculation.

But here it may be proper to remark that though our conclusions from experience carry us beyond our memory and senses and assure us of matters of fact which happened in the most distant places and most remote ages, yet some fact must always be present to the senses or memory from which we may first proceed in drawing these conclusions. A man who should find in a desert country the remains of pompous buildings would conclude that the country had, in ancient times, been cultivated by civilized inhabitants; but did nothing of this nature occur to him, he could never form such an inference. We learn the events of former ages from history, but then we must peruse the volume in which this instruction is contained, and thence carry up our inferences from one testimony to another, till we arrive at the eyewitnesses and spectators of these distant events. In a word, if we proceed not upon some fact present to the memory or senses, our reasonings would be merely hypothetical; and however the particular links might be connected with each other, the whole chain of inferences would have nothing to support it, nor could we ever, by its means, arrive at the knowledge of any real existence. If I ask why you believe any particular matter of fact which you relate, you must tell me some reason; and this reason will be some other fact connected with it. But as you cannot proceed after this manner *in infinitum*,[2] you must at last terminate in some fact which is present to your memory or senses or must allow that your belief is entirely without foundation.

What, then, is the conclusion of the whole matter? A simple one, though, it must be confessed, pretty remote from the common theories of philosophy. All belief of matter of fact or real existence is derived merely from some object present to the memory or senses and a customary conjunction between that and some other object; or, in other words, having found, in many instances, that any two kinds of objects, flame and heat, snow and cold, have always been conjoined together: if flame or snow be presented anew to the senses, the mind is carried by custom to expect heat or cold, and to *believe* that such a quality does exist and will discover itself upon a nearer approach. This belief is the necessary result of placing the mind in such circumstances. It is an operation of the soul, when we are so situated, as unavoidable as to feel the passion of love, when we receive benefits; or hatred, when we meet with injuries. All these operations are a species of natural instincts, which no reasoning or process of the thought and understanding is able either to produce or to prevent.

• • •

Notes

[1] Independent of particular experience.
[2] To infinity.

Is the Sex of the Knower Epistemologically Significant?

Lorraine Code

A question that focuses on the knower, as the title of this chapter does, claims that there are good reasons for asking who that knower is. Uncontroversial as such a suggestion would be in ordinary conversations about knowledge, academic philosophers commonly treat "the knower" as a featureless abstraction. Sometimes, indeed, she or he is merely a place holder in the proposition "S knows that p." Epistemological analyses of the proposition tend to focus on the "knowing that," to determine conditions under which a knowledge claim can legitimately be made. Once discerned, it is believed, such conditions will hold across all possible utterances of the proposition. Indeed, throughout the history of modern philosophy the central "problem of knowledge" has been to determine necessary and sufficient conditions for the possibility and justification of knowledge claims. Philosophers have sought ways of establishing a relation of correspondence between knowledge and "reality" and/or ways of establishing the coherence of particular knowledge claims within systems of already-established truths. They have proposed methodologies for arriving at truth, and criteria for determining the validity of claims to the effect that "S knows that p." Such endeavors are guided by the putatively self-evident principle that truth once discerned, knowledge once established, claim their status *as* truth and knowledge by virtue of a grounding in or coherence within a permanent, objective, ahistorical, and circumstantially neutral framework or set of standards.

The question "Who is S?" is regarded neither as legitimate nor as relevant in these endeavors. As inquirers into the nature and conditions of human knowledge, epistemologists commonly work from the assumption that they need concern themselves only with knowledge claims that meet certain standards of *purity*. . . .

The only thing that is clear about S from the standard proposition "S knows that p" is that S is a (would-be) knower. Although the question "Who is S?" rarely arises, certain assumptions about S as knower permeate epistemological inquiry. Of special importance for my argument is the assumption that knowers are self-sufficient and solitary individuals, at least in their knowledge-seeking activities. This belief derives from a long and venerable heritage, with its roots in Descartes's quest for a basis of perfect certainty on which to establish his knowledge. The central aim of Descartes's endeavors is captured in this claim: "I shall have the right to conceive high hopes if I am happy enough to discover one thing only which is certain and indubitable." That "one thing," Descartes believed, would stand as the fixed pivotal, Archimedean point on which all the rest of his knowledge would turn. Because of its systematic relation to that point, his knowledge would be certain and indubitable.

Most significant for this discussion is Descartes's conviction that his quest will be conducted in a private, introspective examination of the contents of his own mind. It is true that, in the last section of the *Discourse on the Method*, Descartes acknowledges the benefit "others may receive from the communication of [his] reflection," and he states his belief that combining "the lives and labours of many" is essential to progress in scientific knowledge. It is also true that this individualistically described act of knowing exercises the aspect of the soul that is common to and alike in all knowers: namely, the faculty of reason. Yet his claim that knowledge seeking is an introspective activity of an individual mind accords no relevance either to a knower's embodiment or to his (or her) intersubjective relations. For each knower, the Cartesian route to knowledge is through private, abstract thought, through the efforts of reason unaided either by the senses or by consultation with other knowers. It is this individualistic, self-reliant, private aspect of Descartes's philosophy that has been influenced in shaping subsequent epistemological ideals.

Reason is conceived as autonomous in the Cartesian project in two ways, then. Not only is the quest for certain knowledge an independent one, undertaken separately by each rational being, but it is a journey of reason alone, unassisted by the senses. For Descartes believed that sensory experiences had the effect of distracting reason from its proper course.

The custom of formulating knowledge claims in the "S knows that p" formula is not itself of Cartesian origin. The point of claiming Cartesian inspiration for an assumption implicit in the formulation is that the knower who is commonly presumed to be the subject of that proposition is modeled, in significant respects, on the Cartesian pure inquirer. For epistemological purposes, all knowers are believed to be alike with respect both to their cognitive capacities and to their methods of achieving knowledge. In the empiricist tradition this assumption is apparent in the belief that simple, basic observational data can provide the foundation of knowledge just because perception is invariant from observer to observer, in standard observation conditions. In fact, a common way of filling the places in the "S knows that p" proposition is with substitutions such as "Peter knows that the door is open" or "John knows that the book is red." It does not matter who John or Peter is.

Such knowledge claims carry implicit beliefs not only about would-be knowers but also about the knowledge that is amenable to philosophical analysis. Although (Cartesian) rationalists and empiricists differ with respect to what kinds of claim count as foundational, they endorse similar assumptions about the relation of foundational claims to the rest of a body of knowledge. With "S knows that p" propositions, the belief is that such propositions stand as paradigms for knowledge in general. Epistemologists assume that knowledge is analyzable into prepositional "simples" whose truth can be demonstrated by establishing relations of correspondence to reality, or coherence within a system of known truths. These relatively simple knowledge claims (i.e., John knows that the book is red) could indeed be made by most "normal" people who know the language and are familiar with the objects named. Knowers would seem to be quite self-sufficient in acquiring such knowledge. Moreover, no one would claim to know "a little" that the book is red or to be in the process of acquiring knowledge about the openness of the door. Nor would anyone be likely to maintain that S knows better than W does that the door is open or that the book is red. Granting such examples paradigmatic status creates the mistaken assumption that all knowledge worthy of the name will be like this. . . .

In proposing that **the sex of the knower is epistemologically significant**, I am claiming that the scope of epistemological inquiry has been too narrowly defined. . . . There are numerous questions to be asked about knowledge whose answers matter to people who are concerned to know well. Among them are questions that bear not just on criteria of evidence, justification, and warrantability, but on the "nature" of cognitive agents: questions about their character; their material, historical, cultural circumstances; their interests in the inquiry at issue. These are questions about how credibility is established, about connections between knowledge and power, about the place of knowledge in ethical and aesthetic judgments, and about political agendas and the responsibilities of knowers. I am claiming that all of these questions are epistemologically significant. . . .

Although it has rarely been spelled out prior to the development of feminist critiques, it has long been tacitly assumed that S is male. Nor could S be just any man, the apparently infinite substitutability of the "S" term notwithstanding. The S who could count as a model, paradigmatic knower has most commonly—if always tacitly—been an adult (but not *old*), white, reasonably affluent (latterly middle-class) educated man of status, property, and publicly acceptable accomplishments. In theory of knowledge he has been allowed to stand for all men. This assumption does not merely derive from habit or coincidence, but is a manifestation of engrained philosophical convictions. Not only has it been taken for granted that knowers properly so-called are male, but when male philosophers have paused to note this fact, as some indeed have done, they have argued that things are as they should be. Reason may be alike in all men, but it would be a mistake to believe that "man," in this respect, "embraces woman." Women have been judged incapable, for many reasons, of achieving knowledge worthy of the name. It is no exaggeration to say that anyone who wanted to *count* as a knower has commonly had to be male.

In the *Politics*, Aristotle observes: "The freeman rules over the slave after another manner from that in which the male rules over the female, or the man over the child; although the parts of the soul are present in all of them, they are present in different degrees. For the slave has no deliberative faculty at all; the woman has, but it is without authority, and the child has, but it is immature." Aristotle's assumption that a woman will naturally be ruled by a man connects directly with his contention that a woman's deliberative faculty is "without authority." Even if a woman could, in her sequestered, domestic position, acquire deliberative skills, she would remain reliant on her husband for her sources of knowledge and information. She must be ruled by a man because, in the social structure of the *polis*, she enjoys neither the autonomy nor the freedom to put into visible practice the results of the deliberations she may engage in, in private. If she can claim no authority for her rational, deliberative endeavors, then her chances of gaining recognition as a knowledgeable citizen are seriously limited, whatever she may do.

Aristotle is just one of a long line of western thinkers to declare the limitations of women's cognitive capacities. Rousseau maintains that young men and women should be educated quite differently because of women's inferiority in reason and their propensity to be dragged down by their sensual natures. For Kierkegaard, women are merely aesthetic beings; men alone can attain the (higher) ethical and religious levels of existence. And for Nietzsche, the Apollonian (intellectual) domain is the male preserve, whereas women are Dionysian (sensuous) creatures.

Is the Sex of the Knower Epistemologically Significant?   239

Nineteenth-century philosopher and linguist Wilhelm von Humboldt, who writes at length about women's knowledge, sums up the central features of this line of thought as follows: "A sense of truth exists in [women] quite literally as a sense: . . . their nature also contains a lack or a failing of analytic capacity which draws a strict line of demarcation between ego and world; therefore, they will not come as close to the ultimate investigation of truth as man." The implication is that women's knowledge, if ever the products of their projects deserve that label, is inherently and inevitably *subjective*—in the most idiosyncratic sense—by contrast with the best of men's knowledge.

Objectivity, quite precisely construed, is commonly regarded as a defining feature of knowledge per se. So if women's knowledge is declared to be *naturally* subjective, then a clear answer emerges to my question. The answer is that if the would-be knower is female, then her sex is indeed epistemologically significant, for it disqualifies her as a knower in the fullest sense of that term. Such disqualifications will operate differently for women of different classes, races, ages, and allegiances, but in every circumstance they will operate asymmetrically for women and for men. Just what is to be made of these points—how their epistemological significance is to be construed—is the subject of this book.

The presuppositions I have just cited claim more than the rather simple fact that many kinds of knowledge and skill have, historically, been inaccessible to women on a purely practical level. It is true, historically speaking, that even women who were the racial and social "equals" of standard male knowers were only rarely able to become learned. The thinkers I have cited (and others like them) claim to find a rationale for this state of affairs through appeals to dubious "facts" about women's natural incapacity for rational thought. Yet deeper questions still need to be asked: Is there knowledge that is, quite simply, inaccessible to members of the female, or the male, sex? Are there kinds of knowledge that only men, or only woman, can acquire? Is the sex of the knower crucially determining in this respect, across all other specificities? The answers to these questions should not address only the *practical* possibilities that have existed for members of either sex. Such practical possibilities are the constructs of complex social arrangements that are themselves constructed out of historically specific choices, and are, as such, open to challenge and change.

Knowledge, as it achieves credence and authoritative status at any point in the history of the male-dominated mainstream, is commonly held to be a product of the individual efforts of human knowers. References to Pythagoras's theorem, Copernicus's revolution, and Newtonian and Einsteinian physics signal an epistemic community's attribution of pathbreaking contributions to certain of its individual members. The implication is that *that* person, single-handedly, has effected a leap of progress in a particular field of inquiry. In less publicly spectacular ways, other cognitive agents are represented as contributors to the growth and stability of public knowledge.

Now any contention that such contributions are the results of independent endeavor is highly contestable. . . . A complex of historical and other socio-cultural factors produces the conditions that make "individual" achievement possible, and "individuals" themselves are socially constituted. The claim that individual *men* are the creators of the authoritative . . . landmarks of western intellectual life is particularly interesting for the fact that the contributions—both practical and substantive—of their lovers, wives, children, servants, neighbors, friends, and colleagues rarely figure in analyses of their work.

The historical attribution of such achievements to specific cognitive agents does, nonetheless, accord a significance to individual efforts which raises questions pertinent to my project. It poses the problem, in another guise, of whether aspects of human specificity could, in fact, constitute conditions for the existence of knowledge or determine the kinds of knowledge that a knower can achieve. It would seem that such incidental physical attributes as height, weight, or hair color would not count among factors that would determine a person's capacities to know (though the arguments that skin color *does* count are too familiar). It is not necessary to consider how much Archimedes weighed when he made his famous discovery, nor is there any doubt that a thinner or a fatter person could have reached the same conclusion. But in cultures in which sex differences figure prominently in virtually every mode of human interaction, being female or male is far more fundamental to the construction of subjectivity than are such attributes as size or hair color. So the question is whether femaleness or maleness are the kinds of subjective factor (i.e., factors about the circumstances of a knowing subject) that are constitutive of the form and content of knowledge. Attempts to answer this question are complicated by the fact that sex/gender, then, always risks abstraction and is limited in its scope by the abstracting process. Further, the question seems to imply that sex and gender are themselves constants, thus obscuring the processes of *their* socio-cultural construction.

Hence the formulation of adequately nuanced answers is problematic and necessarily partial.

Even if it should emerge that gender-related factors play a crucial role in the construction of knowledge, then, the inquiry into the epistemological significance of the sex of the knower would not be complete. The task would remain of considering whether a distinction between "natural" and socialized capacity can retain any validity. The equally pressing question as to how the hitherto devalued products of *women's* cognitive projects can gain acknowledgment as "knowledge" would need to be addressed so as to uproot entrenched prejudices about knowledge, epistemology, and women. "The epistemological project" will look quite different once its tacit underpinnings are revealed. . . .

Feminist philosophy simply did not exist until philosophers learned to perceive the near-total absence of women in philosophical writings from the very beginning of western philosophy, to stop assuming that "man" could be read as a generic term. Explicit denigrations of women, which became the focus of philosophical writing in the early years of the contemporary women's movement, were more readily perceptible. The authors of derogatory views about women in classical texts clearly needed power to be able to utter their pronouncements with impunity: a power they claimed from a "received" discourse that represented women's nature in such a way that women undoubtedly merited the negative judgments that Aristotle or Nietzsche made about them. Women are now in a position to recognize and refuse these overt manifestations of contempt.

The covert manifestations are more intransigent. Philosophers, when they have addressed the issue at all, have tended to group philosophy with science as the most gender-neutral of disciplines. But feminist critiques reveal that this alleged neutrality masks a bias in favor of institutionalizing stereotypical masculine values into the fabric of the discipline—its methods, norms, and contents. In so doing, it suppresses values, styles, problems, and concerns stereotypically associated with femininity. Thus, whether by chance or by design, it creates a hegemonic philosophical practice in which the sex of the knower is, indeed, epistemologically significant.

Practice and Contradiction

Mao Tse-Tung

On Practice

On the Relation between Knowledge and Practice, between Knowing and Doing

Before Marx, materialism examined the problem of knowledge apart from the social nature of man and apart from his historical development, and was therefore incapable of understanding the dependence of knowledge on social practice, that is, the dependence of knowledge on production and the class struggle.

Above all, Marxists regard man's activity in production as the most fundamental practical activity, the determinant of all his other activities. Man's knowledge depends mainly on his activity in material production, through which he comes gradually to understand the phenomena, the properties and the laws of nature, and the relations between himself and nature; and through his activity in production he also gradually comes to understand, in varying degrees, certain relations that exist between man and man. None of this knowledge can be acquired apart from activity in production. In a classless society every person, as a member of society, joins in common effort with the other members, enters into definite relations of production with them and engages in production to meet man's material needs. In all class societies, the members of the different social classes also enter, in different ways, into definite relations of production and engage in production to meet their material needs. This is the primary source from which human knowledge develops.

Man's social practice is not confined to activity in production, but takes many other forms—class struggle, political life, scientific and artistic pursuits; in short, as a social being, man participates in all spheres of the practical life of society. Thus man, in varying degrees, comes to know the different relations between man and man, not only through his material life but also through his political and cultural life (both of which are intimately bound up with material life.) Of these other types of social practice, class struggle in particular, in all its various forms, exerts a profound influence on the development of man's knowledge. In class society everyone lives as a member of a particular class, and every kind of thinking, without exception, is stamped with the brand of a class.

Marxists hold that man's social practice alone is the criterion of the truth of his knowledge of the external world. What actually happens is that man's knowledge is verified only when he achieves the anticipated results in the process of social practice (material production, class struggle or scientific experiment). If a man wants to succeed in his work, that is, to achieve the anticipated results, he must bring his ideas into correspondence with the laws of the objective external world; if they do not correspond, he will fail in his practice. After he fails, he draws his lessons, corrects his ideas to make them correspond to the laws of the external world, and can thus turn failure into success; this is what is meant by "failure is the mother of success" and "a fall into the pit, a gain in your wit." The dialectical-materialist theory of knowledge places practice in the primary position, holding that human knowledge can in no way be separated from practice and repudiating all the erroneous theories which deny the importance of practice or separate knowledge from practice. Thus Lenin said, *"Practice is higher than (theoretical) knowledge, for it has not only the dignity of universality, but also of immediate actuality."* The Marxist philosophy of dialectical materialism has two outstanding characteristics. One is its class nature: it openly avows that dialectical materialism is in the service of the proletariat. The other is its practicality: it emphasizes the dependence of theory on practice, emphasizes that theory is based on practice and in turn serves practice. The truth of any knowledge or theory is determined not by subjective feelings, but by objective results in social practice. Only social practice can be the criterion of truth. The standpoint of practice is the primary and basic standpoint in the dialectical-materialist theory of knowledge.

But how then does human knowledge arise from practice and in turn serve practice? This will become clear if we look at the process of development of knowledge.

In the process of practice, man at first sees only the phenomenal side, the separate aspects, the external relations of things. For instance, some people from outside come to Yenan on a tour of observation. In the first day or two, they see its topography, streets and houses; they meet many people, attend banquets, evening parties and mass meetings, hear talk of various kinds and read various documents, all these being the phenomena, the separate aspects and the external relations of things. This is called the perceptual stage of cognition, namely, the stage of sense perceptions and impressions. That is, these particular things in Yenan act on the sense organs of the members of the observation group, evoke sense perceptions and give rise in their brains to many impressions together with a rough sketch of the external relations among these impressions: this is the first stage of cognition. At this stage, man cannot as yet form concepts, which are deeper, or draw logical conclusions.

As social practice continues, things that give rise to man's sense perceptions and impressions in the course of his practice are repeated many times; then a sudden change (leap) takes place in the brain in the process of cognition and concepts are formed. Concepts are no longer the phenomena, the separate aspects and the external relations of things; they grasp the essence, the totality and the internal relations of things. Between concepts and sense perceptions there is not only a quantitative but also a qualitative difference. Proceeding further, by means of judgement and inference one is able to draw logical conclusions. The expression in *San Kuo Yen Yi*, "knit the brows and a stratagem comes to mind," or in everyday language, "let me think it over," refers to man's use of concepts in the brain to form judgements and inferences. This is the second stage of cognition. This stage of conception, judgement and inference is the more important stage in the entire process of knowing a thing; it is the stage of rational knowledge. The real task of knowing is, through perception, to arrive at thought, to arrive step by step at the comprehension of the internal contradictions of objective things, of their laws and of the internal relations between one process and another, that is, to arrive at logical knowledge. To repeat, logical knowledge differs from perceptual knowledge in that perceptual knowledge pertains to the separate aspects, the phenomena and the external relations of things, whereas logical knowledge takes a big stride forward to reach the totality, the essence and the internal relations of things and discloses the inner contradictions in the surrounding world. Therefore, logical knowledge is capable of grasping the development of the surrounding world in its totality, in the internal relations of all its aspects.

If you want to know a certain thing or a certain class of things directly, you must personally participate in the practical struggle to change reality, to change that thing or class of things, for only thus can you come into contact with them as phenomena; only through personal participation in the practical struggle to change reality can you uncover the essence of that thing or class of things and comprehend them. This is the path to knowledge which every man actually travels though some people, deliberately distorting matters, argue to the contrary. The most ridiculous person in the world is the "know-all" who picks up a smattering of hearsay knowledge and proclaims himself "the world's Number One authority"; this merely shows that he has not taken a proper measure of himself. Knowledge is a matter of science, and no dishonesty or conceit whatsoever is permissible. What is required is definitely the reverse—honesty and modesty. If you want knowledge, you must take part in the practice of changing reality. If you want to know the taste of a pear, you must change the pear by eating it yourself. If you want to know the structure and properties of the atom you must make physical and chemical experiments to change the state of the atom. If you want to know the theory and methods of revolution, you must take part in revolution. All genuine knowledge originates in direct experience. But one cannot have direct experience of everything; as a matter of fact, most of our knowledge comes from indirect experience, for example, all knowledge from past times and foreign lands. To our ancestors and to foreigners, such knowledge was—or is—a matter of direct experience, and this knowledge is reliable if in the course of their direct experience the requirement of "scientific abstraction," spoken of by Lenin, was—or is—fulfilled and objective reality scientifically reflected; otherwise it is not reliable. Hence a man's knowledge consists only of two parts, that which comes from direct experience and that which comes from indirect experience. Moreover, what is indirect experience for me is direct experience for other people. Consequently, considered as a whole, knowledge of any kind is inseparable from direct experience. All knowledge originates in perception of the objective external world through man's physical sense organs. Anyone who denies such perception, denies direct experience, or denies personal participation in the practice that changes reality, is not a materialist. That is why the "know-all" is ridiculous. There is an old Chinese saying, "How can you catch tiger cubs without entering the tiger's lair?" This saying holds true for man's practice and it also holds true for the theory of knowledge. **There can be no knowledge apart from practice.**

From the Marxist viewpoint, theory is important, and its importance is fully expressed in Lenin's statement, "Without revolutionary theory there can be no revolutionary movement." But Marxism emphasizes the importance of theory precisely and only because it can guide action. If we have a correct theory but merely prate about it, pigeonhole it and do not put it into practice, then that theory, however good, is of no significance.

Knowledge begins with practice, and theoretical knowledge is acquired through practice, and must then return to practice. The active function of knowledge manifests itself not only in the active leap from perceptual to rational knowledge, but—and this is more important—it must manifest itself in the leap from rational knowledge to revolutionary practice. The knowledge which grasps the laws of the world, must be redirected to the practice of changing the world, must be applied anew in the practice of production, in the practice of revolutionary class struggle and revolutionary national struggle and in the practice of scientific experiment. This is the process of testing and developing theory, the continuation of the whole process of cognition. The problem of whether theory corresponds to objective reality is not, and cannot be, completely solved in the movement of knowledge from the perceptual to the rational, mentioned above. The only way to solve this problem completely is to redirect rational knowledge to social practice, apply theory to practice and see whether it can achieve the objectives one has in mind.

In the present epoch of the development of society, the responsibility of correctly knowing and changing the world has been placed by history upon the shoulders of the proletariat and its party. The struggle of the proletariat and the revolutionary people to change the world comprises the fulfillment of the following tasks to change the objective world and, at the same time, their own subjective world—to change their cognitive ability and change the relations between the subjective and the objective world.

On Contradiction

The law of contradiction in things, that is, the law of the unity of opposites, is the basic law of materialist dialectics. Lenin said, "Dialectics in the proper sense is the study of contradiction *in the very essence of objects.*" Lenin often called this law the essence of dialectics; he also called it the kernel of dialectics. In studying this law, therefore, we cannot but touch upon a variety of questions, upon a number of philosophical problems. If we can become clear on all these problems, we shall arrive at a fundamental understanding of materialist dialectics. The problems are: the two world outlooks, the universality of contradiction, the particularity of contradiction, the principal contradiction and the principal aspect of a contradiction, the identity and struggle of the aspects of a contradiction, and the place of antagonism in contradiction.

The Two World Outlooks

Throughout the history of human knowledge, there have been two conceptions concerning the law of development of the universe, the metaphysical conception and the dialectical conception, which form two opposing world outlooks.

In China another name for metaphysics is *hsuan-hsueh*. For a long period in history whether in China or in Europe, this way of thinking, which is part and parcel of the idealist world outlook, occupied a dominant position in human thought. In Europe, the materialism of the bourgeoisie in its early days was also metaphysical.

The metaphysical or vulgar evolutionist world outlook sees things as isolated, static and one-sided. It regards all things in the universe, their forms and their species, as eternally isolated from one another and immutable. Such change as there is can only be an increase or decrease in quantity or a change of place. Moreover, the cause of such an increase or decrease or change of place is not inside things but outside them, that is, the motive force is external.

As opposed to the metaphysical world outlook, the world outlook of materialist dialectics holds that in order to understand the development of a thing we should study it internally and in its relations with other things; in other words, the development of things should be seen as their internal and necessary self-movement, while each thing in its movement is interrelated with and interacts on the things around it. The fundamental cause of the development of a thing is not external but internal; it lies in the contradictoriness within the thing. There is internal contradiction in every single thing, hence its motion and development. Contradictoriness within a thing is the fundamental cause of its development, while its interrelations and interactions with other things are secondary causes. Thus materialist dialectics effectively combats the theory of external causes, or of an external motive force, advanced by metaphysical mechanical materialism and vulgar evolutionism. It is evident that purely external causes can only give rise to mechanical motion, that is, to changes in scale or quantity, but cannot explain why things differ qualitatively in thousands of ways and why one thing changes into another.

In order to reveal the particularity of the contradictions in any process in the development of a thing, in their totality or interconnections, that is, in order to reveal the essence of the process, it is necessary to reveal the particularity of the two aspects of each of the contradictions in that process; otherwise it will be impossible to discover the essence of the process. This likewise requires the utmost attention in our study.

There are many contradictions in the course of development of any major thing. For instance, in the course of China's bourgeois-democratic revolution, where the conditions are exceedingly complex, there exist the contradiction between all the oppressed classes in Chinese society and imperialism, the contradiction between the great masses of the people and feudalism, the contradiction between the proletariat and the bourgeoisie, the contradiction between the peasantry and the urban petty bourgeoisie on the one hand and the bourgeoisie on the other, the contradiction between the various reactionary ruling groups, and so on. These contradictions cannot be treated in the same way since each has its own particularity; moreover, the two aspects of each contradiction cannot be treated in the same way since each aspect has its own characteristics. We who are engaged in the Chinese revolution should not only understand the particularity of these contradictions in their totality, that is, in their interconnections, but should also study the two aspects of each contradiction as the only means of understanding the totality. When we speak of understanding each aspect of a contradiction, we mean understanding what specific position each aspect occupies, what concrete forms it assumes in its interdependence and in its contradiction with its opposite, and what concrete methods are employed in the struggle with its opposite, when the two are both interdependent and in contradiction, and also after the interdependence breaks down. Lenin said:

> ... in order really to know an object we must embrace, study, all its sides, all connections and "mediations." We shall never achieve this completely, but the demand for all-sidedness is a safeguard against mistakes and rigidity.

We should remember his words. To be superficial means to consider neither the characteristics of a contradiction in its totality nor the characteristics of each of its aspects; it means to deny the necessity for probing deeply into a thing and minutely studying the characteristics of its contradiction, but instead merely to look from afar and, after glimpsing the rough outline, immediately to try to resolve the contradiction (to answer a question, settle a dispute, handle work, or direct a military operation). This way of doing things is bound to lead to trouble.

Without concrete analysis there can be no knowledge of the particularity of any contradiction. We must always remember Lenin's words, the concrete analysis of concrete conditions.

Marx and Engels were the first to provide us with excellent models of such concrete analysis.

When Marx applied this law to the study of the economic structure of capitalist society, he discovered that the basic contradiction of this society is the contradiction between the social character of production and the private character of ownership. This contradiction manifests itself in the contradiction between the organized character of production in individual enterprises and the anarchic character of production in society as a whole. In terms of class relations, it manifests itself in the contradiction between the bourgeoisie and the proletariat.

The Principal Contradiction and the Principal Aspect of a Contradiction

There are still two points in the problem of the particularity of contradiction which must be singled out for analysis, namely, the principal contradiction and the principal aspect of a contradiction.

There are many contradictions in the process of development of a complex thing, and one of them is necessarily the principal contradiction whose existence and development determine or influence the existence and development of the other contradictions.

For instance, in capitalist society the two forces in contradiction, the proletariat and the bourgeoisie, form the principal contradiction. The other contradictions, such as those between the non-monopoly capitalists and the monopoly capitalists, between bourgeois democracy and bourgeois fascism, among the capitalist countries and between imperialism and the colonies, are all determined or influenced by this principal contradiction.

But whatever happens, there is no doubt at all that at every stage in the development of a process, there is only one principal contradiction which plays the leading role.

Hence, if in any process there are a number of contradictions, one of them must be the principal contradiction playing the leading and decisive role, while the rest occupy a secondary and subordinate position. Therefore, in studying any complex process in which there are two or more contradictions, we must devote every effort to finding its principal contradiction. Once this principal contradiction is grasped, all problems can be readily solved.

But, in any given contradiction, whether principal or secondary, should the two contradictory aspects be treated as equal? Again, no. In any contradiction the development of the contradictory aspects is uneven. Sometimes they seem to be in equilibrium, which is however only temporary and relative, while unevenness is basic. Of the two contradictory aspects, one must be principal and the other secondary. The principal aspect is the one playing the leading role in the contradiction. The nature of a thing is determined mainly by the principal aspect of a contradiction, the aspect which has gained the dominant position.

We often speak of "the new superseding the old." The supersession of the old by the new is a general, eternal and inviolable law of the universe. The transformation of one thing into another, through leaps of different forms in accordance with its essence and external conditions—this is the process of the new superseding the old. In each thing there is contradiction between its new and its old aspects, and this gives rise to a series of struggles with many twists and turns.

In capitalist society, capitalism has changed its position from being a subordinate force in the old feudal era to being the dominant force, and the nature of society has accordingly changed from feudal to capitalist. In the new, capitalist era, the feudal forces changed from their former dominant position to a subordinate one, gradually dying out. Such was the case, for example, in Britain and France. With the development of the productive forces, the bourgeoisie changes from being a new class playing a progressive role to being an old class playing a reactionary role, until it is finally overthrown by the proletariat and becomes a class deprived of privately owned means of production and stripped of power, when it, too, gradually dies out.

The Identity and Struggle of the Aspects of a Contradiction

When we understand the universality and the particularity of contradiction, we must proceed to study the problem of the identity and struggle of the aspects of a contradiction.

Identity, unity, coincidence, interpenetration, interpermeation, interdependence (or mutual dependence for existence), interconnection or mutual cooperation—all these different terms mean the same thing and refer to the following two points: first, the existence of each of the two aspects of a contradiction in the process of the development of a thing presupposes the existence of the other aspect, and both aspects coexist in a single entity; second, in given conditions, each of the two contradictory aspects transforms itself into its opposite. This is the meaning of identity.

The fact is that no contradictory aspect can exist in isolation. Without its opposite aspect, each loses the condition for its existence. Just think, can any one contradictory aspect of a thing or of a concept in the human mind exist independently? Without life, there would be no death; without death, there would be no life. Without "above," there would be no "below"; without "below," there would be no "above." Without misfortune, there would be no good fortune; without good fortune, there would be no misfortune. Without facility, there would be no difficulty; without difficulty, there would be no facility. Without landlords, there would be no tenant-peasants; without tenant-peasants, there would be no landlords. Without the bourgeoisie, there would be no proletariat; without the proletariat, there would be no bourgeoisie. Without imperialist oppression of nations, there would be no colonies or semi-colonies; without colonies or semi-colonies, there would be no imperialist oppression of nations. It is so with all opposites; in given conditions, on the one hand they are opposed to each other, and on the other they are interconnected, interpenetrating, interpermeating and interdependent, and this character is described as identity. In given conditions, all contradictory aspects possess the character of non-identity and hence are described as being in contradiction. But they also possess the character of identity and hence are interconnected. This is what Lenin means when he says that dialectics studies "how *opposites* can be . . . *identical*." How then can they be identical? Because each is the condition for the other's existence. This is the first meaning of identity.

But is it enough to say merely that each of the contradictory aspects is the condition for the other's existence, that there is identity between them and that consequently they can coexist in a single entity? No, it is not. The matter does not end with their dependence on each other for their existence; what is more important is their transformation into each other. That is to say, in given conditions, each of the contradictory aspects within a thing transforms itself into its opposite, changes its position to that of its opposite. This is the second meaning of the identity of contradiction

Chapter IV: Truth

What does it mean for a belief or for a claim about the world to be true? What are the standards or criteria by which one can determine whether a particular belief or claim is true? Philosophical theories of truth, most notably the correspondence theory, the coherence theory, and the pragmatic theory, attempt to answer the above questions.

However, other philosophers point out that there are more basic questions to be investigated that concern the nature of truth itself: e.g., "What is truth?" According to the ancients, "truth" (Gk. *aletheia*) is essentially a disclosure. It is reality showing itself, from within itself, as itself. It is the revealed reality that lays at the basis of all appearance. The view that truth is a disclosure raises other interesting questions concerning whether this disclosure is personal or impersonal.

This section not only examines the traditional theories of truth but considers truth as subjectivity and attempts to get behind the various theories of truth to the essence of truth.

In "Truth as Correspondence," Bertrand Russell claims that any theory of truth must account for its opposite; namely, falsehood. The nature of truth rests on the correspondence of belief with fact. According to Russell, ". . . a belief is true when there is a corresponding fact, and is false when there is no corresponding fact."

In "Truth Is Established by Coherence," Francis Bradley tells us the test for truth is that of system. On Bradley's view,

> Truth is an ideal expression of the universe, at once coherent and comprehensive. It must not conflict with itself, and there must be no suggestion which fails to fall inside it. Perfect truth in short must realize the idea of a systematic whole.

Thus, Bradley's two criteria for truth are coherence and comprehensiveness.

"Truth," says William James, "happens to be an idea." "Pragmatism's conception of truth" presents a distinctive, American philosophy that is rooted in practical experience. In other words, pragmatism evaluates statements solely on the basis of their practical consequences and bearing on human interests. James puts pragmatism's truth test in the form of a question: "What, in short, is the truth's cash value in experiential terms?"

Søren Kierkegaard is often referred to as the "Father of Existentialism." For an existentialist, the problem of being logically precedes and must take precedence over questions of human knowledge. Thus, being is not a legitimate subject of objective enquiry because it is disclosed to the existing individual only by reflection on his/her unique and existence in time and space. According to Kierkegaard, "Subjectivity is the truth."

In "On the Essence of Truth," Martin Heidegger stresses the ultimate relationship of being and truth. Human existence (*Dasein*) is the open space where beings are disclosed in many and various ways. According to Heidegger, "The essence of truth reveals itself as freedom." Freedom is "letting beings be." But, human beings often conceal truth and in exchange for security accept a multitude of "truths." In fact, in the name of religion, science, politics and academics some of these "truths" become "eternal truths."

In the reading from "Cultural Gaps: Why Do We Misunderstand?" the Japanese philosopher Isamu Nagami takes a phenomenological look at the communication between individuals and cultures which he calls "intersubjectivity." By focusing on intersubjectivity, he mediates the dichotomy between subjectivity and objectivity with regard to truth. Since many cross-cultural misunderstandings occur, Nagami's work is important because it dismisses relativism on the one hand and epistemic-ethical imperialism on the other hand. The former option claims "truth" is a relative concept and the later holds that truth is somehow the possession of a particular conceptual framework, culture, or group and this Truth should be universally imposed. Through a consideration of intersubjectivity, language and taken-for-grantedness, Nagami moves toward a "fusion of horizons" made possible by a comportment of "openness and listening." He states:

> We are living in a constant transformative process within the horizon of encounters between different people. If we are open and responsive to other people in dialogue, then mystery can lead humans to learn to trust and find a way of reconciling the differences of culture and existence.

Truth as Correspondence

Bertrand Russell

Our knowledge of truths, unlike our knowledge of things, has an opposite, namely *error*. So far as things are concerned, we may know them or not know them, but there is no positive state of mind which can be described as erroneous knowledge of things, so long, at any rate, as we confine ourselves to knowledge by acquaintance. Whatever we are acquainted with must be something: we may draw wrong inference from our acquaintance, but the acquaintance itself cannot be deceptive. Thus there is no dualism as regards acquaintance. But as regards knowledge of truths, there is a dualism. We may believe what is false as well as what is true. We know that on very many subjects different people hold different and incompatible opinions: hence some beliefs must be erroneous. Since erroneous beliefs are often held just as strongly as true beliefs, it becomes a difficult question how they are to be distinguished from true beliefs. How are we to know, in a given case, that our belief is not erroneous? That is a question of the very greatest difficulty, to which no completely satisfactory answer is possible. There is, however, a preliminary question which is rather less difficult, and that is: What do we *mean* by truth and falsehood? It is this preliminary question which is to be considered in this chapter.

. . . We are not asking how we can know whether a belief is true or false: we are asking what is meant by the question whether a belief is true or false. It is to be hoped that a clear answer to this question may help us to obtain an answer to the question what beliefs are true, but for the present we ask only "What is truth?" and "What is falsehood?" not "What beliefs are true?" and "What beliefs are false?" It is very important to keep these different questions entirely separate, since any confusion between them is sure to produce an answer which is not really applicable to either.

There are three points to observe in the attempt to discover the nature of truth, three requisites which any theory must fulfill.

1. Our theory of truth must be such as to admit of its opposite, falsehood. A good many philosophers have failed adequately to satisfy this condition: they have constructed theories according to which all our thinking ought to have been true, and have then had the greatest difficulty

in finding a place for falsehood. In this respect our theory of belief must differ from our theory of acquaintance, since in the case of acquaintance it was not necessary to take account of any opposite.

2. It seems fairly evident that if there were no beliefs there could be no falsehood, and no truth either, in the sense in which truth is correlative to falsehood. If we imagine a world of mere matter, there would be no room for falsehood in such a world, and although it would contain what may be called "facts," it would not contain any truths, in the sense in which truths are things of the same kind as falsehoods. In fact, truth and falsehood are properties of beliefs and statements: hence a world of mere matter, since it would contain no beliefs or statements, would also contain no truth or falsehood.

3. But, as against what we have just said, it is to be observed that the truth or falsehood of a belief always depends upon something which lies outside the belief itself. If I believe that Charles I died on the scaffold, I believe truly, not because of any intrinsic quality of my belief, which could be discovered by merely examining the belief, but because of an historical event which happened two and a half centuries ago. If I believe that Charles I died in his bed, I believe falsely: no degree of vividness in my belief, or of care in arriving at it, prevents it from being false, again because of what happened long ago, and not because of any intrinsic property of my belief. Hence, although truth and falsehood are properties of beliefs, they are properties dependent upon the relations of the beliefs to other things, not upon any internal quality of the beliefs.

The third of the above requisites leads us to adopt the view—which has on the whole been commonest among philosophers—that truth consists in some form of correspondence between belief and fact. It is, however, by no means an easy matter to discover a form of correspondence to which there are no irrefutable objections. By this partly—and partly by the feeling that, if truth consists in a correspondence of thought with something outside thought, thought can never know when truth has been attained—many philosophers have been led to try to find some definition of truth which shall not consist in relation to something wholly outside belief. The most important attempt at a definition of this sort is the theory that truth consists in *coherence*. It is said that the mark of falsehood is failure to cohere in the body of our beliefs, and that it is the essence of a truth to form part of the completely rounded system which is The Truth.

There is, however, a great difficulty in this view, or rather two great difficulties. The first is that there is no reason to suppose that only *one* coherent body of beliefs is possible. It may be that, with sufficient imagination, a novelist might invent a past for the world that would perfectly fit on to what we know, and yet be quite different from the real past. In more scientific matters, it is certain that there are often two or more hypotheses which account for all the known facts on some subject, and although, in such cases, men of science endeavor to find the facts which will rule out all the hypotheses except one, there is no reason why they should always succeed.

In philosophy, again, it seems not uncommon for two rival hypotheses to be both able to account for all the facts. Thus, for example, it is possible that life is one long dream, and that the outer world has only that degree of reality that the objects of dreams have; but although such a view does not seem inconsistent with known facts, there is no reason to prefer it to the common-sense view, according to which other people and things do really exist. Thus coherence as the definition of truth fails because there is no proof that there can be only one coherent system.

The other objection to this definition of truth is that it assumes the meaning of "coherence" known, whereas, in fact, "coherence" presupposes the truth of the laws of logic. Two propositions are coherent when both may be true, and are incoherent when one at least must be false. Now in order to know whether two propositions can both be true, we must know such truths as the law of contradiction. For example, the two propositions "this tree is a beech" and "this tree is not a beech," are not coherent, because of the law of contradiction. But if the law of contradiction itself were subjected to the test of coherence, we should find that, if we choose to suppose it false, nothing will any longer be incoherent with anything else. Thus the laws of logic supply the skeleton or framework within which the test of coherence applies, and they themselves cannot be established by this test.

For the above two reasons, coherence cannot be accepted as giving the *meaning* of truth, though it is often a most important *test* of truth after a certain amount of truth has become known.

Hence we are driven back to *correspondence with fact* as constituting the nature of truth. It remains to define precisely what we mean by "fact," and what is the nature of the correspondence which must subsist between belief and fact, in order that belief may be true.

In accordance with our three requisites, we have to seek a theory of truth which (1) allows truth to have an opposite, namely falsehood, (2) makes truth a property of beliefs, but (3) makes it a property wholly dependent upon the relation of the beliefs to outside things.

The necessity of allowing for falsehood makes it impossible to regard belief as a relation of the mind to a single object, which could be said to be what is believed. If belief were so regarded, we should find that, like acquaintance, it would not admit of the opposition of truth and falsehood, but would have to be always true. This may be made clear by examples. Othello believes falsely that Desdemona loves Cassio. We cannot say that this belief consists in a relation to a single object, "Desdemona's love for Cassio," for if there were such an object, the belief would be true. There is in fact no such object, and therefore Othello cannot have any relation to such an object. Hence his belief cannot possibly consist in a relation to this object.

It might be said that his belief is a relation to a different object, namely "that Desdemona loves Cassio"; but it is almost as difficult to suppose that there is such an object as this, when Desdemona does not love Cassio, as it was to suppose that there is "Desdemona's love for Cassio." Hence it will be better to seek for a theory of belief which does not make it consist in a relation of the mind to a single object.

It is common to think of relations as though they always held between *two* terms, but in fact this is not always the case. Some relations demand three terms, some four, and so on. Take, for instance, the relation "between." So long as only two terms come in, the relation "between" is impossible: three terms are the smallest number that render it possible. York is between London and Edinburgh; but if London and Edinburgh were the only places in the world, there could be nothing which was between one place and another. Similarly *jealousy* requires three people: there can be no such relation that does not involve three at least. Such a proposition as "A wishes B to promote C's marriage with D" involves a relation of four terms; that is to say, A and B and C and D all come in, and the relation involved cannot be expressed otherwise than in a form involving all four. Instances might be multiplied indefinitely, but enough has been said to show that there are relations which require more than two terms before they can occur.

The relation involved in *judging* or *believing* must, if falsehood is to be duly allowed for, be taken to be a relation between several terms, not between two. When Othello believes that Desdemona loves Cassio, he must not have before his mind a single object, "Desdemona's love for Cassio," or "that Desdemona loves Cassio," for that would require that there should be objective falsehoods, which subsist independently of any minds; and this, though not logically refutable, is a theory to be avoided if possible. Thus it is easier to account for falsehood if we take judgment to be a relation in which the mind and the various objects concerned all occur severally; that is to say, Desdemona and loving and Cassio must all be terms in the relation which subsists when Othello believes that Desdemona loves Cassio. This relation, therefore, is a relation of four terms, since Othello also is one of the terms of the relation. When we say that it is a relation of four terms, we do not mean that Othello has a certain relation to Desdemona, and has the same relation to loving and also to Cassio. This may be true of some other relation than believing; but believing, plainly, is not a relation which Othello has to *each* of the three terms concerned, but to *all* of them together: there is only one example of the relation of believing involved, but this one example knits together four terms. Thus the actual occurrence, at the moment when Othello is entertaining his belief, is that the relation called "believing" is knitting together into one complex whole the four terms Othello, Desdemona, loving, and Cassio. What is called belief or judgment is nothing but this relation of believing or judging, which relates a mind to several things other than itself. An *act* of belief or of judgment in the occurrence between certain terms at some particular time, of the relation of believing or judging.

We are now in a position to understand what it is that distinguishes a true judgment from a false one. For this purpose we will adopt certain definitions. In every act of judgment there is a mind which judges, and there are terms concerning which it judges. We will call the mind the *subject* in the judgment, and the remaining terms the *objects*. Thus, when Othello judges that Desdemona loves Cassio, Othello is the subject, while the objects are Desdemona and loving and Cassio. The subject and the objects together are called the *constituents* of the judgment. It will be observed that the relation of judging has what is called a "sense" or "direction." We may say, metaphorically, that it puts its objects in a certain *order*, which we may indicate by means of the order of the words in the sentence. (In an inflected language, the same thing will be indicated by inflections, e.g., by the difference between nominative and accusative.) Othello's judgment that Cassio loves Desdemona differs from his judgment that Desdemona loves Cassio, in spite of the fact that it consists of the same constituents, because the relation of judging places the constituents in a different order in the two cases. Similarly, if Cassio judges that Desdemona loves Othello, the constituents of the judgment are still the same, but their order is different. This property of having a "sense" or "direction" is one which the relation of judging shares with all other relations. The "sense" of relations is the ultimate source of order and series and a host of mathematical concepts; but we need not concern ourselves further with this aspect.

We spoke of the relation called "judging" or "believing" as knitting together into one complex whole the subject and the objects. In this respect, judging is exactly like every other relation. Whenever a relation holds between two or more terms, it unites the terms into a complex whole. If Othello loves Desdemona, there is such a complex whole as "Othello's love for Desdemona." The terms united by the relation may be themselves complex, or may be simple, but the whole which results from their being united must be complex. Wherever there is a relation which relates certain terms, there is a complex object formed of the union of those terms; and conversely, wherever there is a complex object, there is a relation which relates its constituents. When an act of believing occurs, there is a complex, in which "believing" is the uniting relation, and subject and objects are arranged in a certain order by the "sense" of the relation of believing. Among the objects, as we saw in considering "Othello believes that Desdemona loves Cassio," one must be a relation—in this instance, the relation "loving." But this relation, as it occurs in the act of believing, is not the relation which creates the unity of the complex whole consisting of the subject and the objects. The relation "loving," as it occurs in the act of believing, is one of the objects—it is a brick in the structure, not the cement. The cement is the relation "believing." When the belief is *true*, there is another complex unity, in which the relation which was one of the objects of the belief relates the other objects. Thus, e.g., if Othello believes *truly* that Desdemona loves Cassio, then there is a complex unity, "Desdemona's love for Cassio," which is composed exclusively of the *objects* of the belief, in the same order as they had in the belief, with the relation which was one of the objects occurring now as the cement that binds together the other objects of the belief. On the other hand, when a belief is *false*, there is no such complex unity composed only of the objects of the belief. If Othello believes *falsely* that Desdemona loves Cassio, then there is no such complex unity as "Desdemona's love for Cassio."

Thus a belief is *true* when it *corresponds* to a certain associated complex, and *false* when it does not. Assuming, for the sake of definiteness, that the objects of the belief are two terms and a relation, the terms being put in a certain order by the "sense" of the believing, then if the two terms in that order are united by the relation into a complex, the belief is true; if not, it is false. This constitutes the definition of truth and falsehood that we were in search of. Judging or believing is a certain complex unity of which a mind is a constituent; if the remaining constituents, taken in the order which they have in the belief, form a complex unity, then the belief is true; if not, it is false.

Thus although truth and falsehood are properties of beliefs, yet they are in a sense extrinsic properties, for the condition of the truth of a belief is something not involving beliefs, or (in general) any mind at all, but only the *objects* of the belief. A mind, which believes, believes truly when there is a *corresponding* complex not involving the mind, but only its objects. This correspondence ensures truth, and its absence entails falsehood. Hence we account simultaneously for the two facts that beliefs (a) depend on minds for their *existence*, (b) do not depend on minds for their *truth*.

We may restate our theory as follows: If we take such a belief as "Othello believes that Desdemona loves Cassio," we will call Desdemona and Cassio the *object-terms*, and loving the *object-relation*. If there is a complex unity "Desdemona's love for Cassio," consisting of the object-terms related by the object relation in the same order as they have in the belief, then this complex unity is called the *fact corresponding to the belief*. **Thus a belief is true when there is a corresponding fact, and is false when there is no corresponding fact.**

... Minds do not *create* truth or falsehood. They create beliefs, but when once the beliefs are created, the mind cannot make them true or false, except in the special case where they concern future things which are within the power of the person believing, such as catching trains. What makes a belief true is a *fact*, and this fact does not (except in exceptional cases) in any way involve the mind of the person who has the belief.

Truth Is Established by Coherence

Francis H. Bradley

What I maintain is that in the case of facts of perception and memory the test [of truth] which we do apply, and which we must apply, is that of system. I contend that this test works satisfactorily, and that no other test will work. And I argue in consequence that there are no judgements of sense which are in principle infallible. . . .

The reason for maintaining independent facts and infallible judgements, as I understand it, is twofold. (1) Such data, it may be said, can be actually shown. And (2) in any case they must exist, since without them the intelligence cannot work. . . .

1. I doubt my ability to do justice to the position of the man who claims to show ultimate given facts exempt from all possible error. In the case of any datum of sensation or feeling, to prove that we have this wholly unmodified by what is called "apperception" seems a hopeless undertaking. And how far it is supposed that such a negative can be proved I do not know. What, however, is meant must be this, that we somehow and somewhere have verifiable facts of perception and memory, and also judgements, free from all chance of error. I will begin hereby recalling a truth familiar but often forgotten. . . . In your search for independent facts and for infallible truths you may go so low that, when you have descended beyond the level of error, you find yourself below the level of any fact or of any truth which you can use. What you seek is particular facts of perception or memory, but what you get may be something not answering to that character. I will go on to give instances of what I mean, and I think that in every case we shall do well to ask this question, "What on the strength of our ultimate fact are we able to contradict?"

a. If we take the instance of simple unrelated sensations or feelings, a, b, c—supposing that there are such things—what judgement would such a fact enable us to deny? We could on the strength of this fact deny the denial that a, b and c exist in any way, manner or sense. But surely this is not the kind of independent fact of which we are in search.

b. From this let us pass to the case of a complex feeling containing, at once and together, both a and b. On the ground of this we can deny the statement that a and b cannot or do not ever anyhow co-exist in feeling. This is an advance, but it surely leaves us far short of our goal.

c. What we want, I presume, is something that at once is infallible and that also can be called a particular fact of perception or memory. And we want, in the case of perception, something that would be called a fact for observation. We do not seem to reach this fact until we arrive somewhere about the level of "I am here and now having a sensation or complex of sensations of such or such a kind." The goal is reached; but at this point, unfortunately, the judgement has become fallible, so far at least as it really states particular truth.

(a) In such a judgement it is in the first place hard to say what is meant by the "I." If, however, we go beyond feeling far enough to mean a self with such or such a real existence in time, then memory is involved, and the judgement at once, I should urge, becomes fallible. . . . Thus the statement made in the judgement is liable to error, or else the statement does not convey particular truth.

(b) And this fatal dilemma holds good when applied to the "now" and "here." If these words mean a certain special place in a certain special series or order, they are liable to mistake. But, if they fall short of this meaning, then they fail to state individual fact. My feeling is, I agree, not subject to error in the proper sense of that term, but on the other side my feeling does not of itself deliver truth. And the process which gets from it a deliverance as to individual fact is fallible.

Everywhere such fact depends on construction. And we have here to face not only the possibility of what would commonly be called mistaken interpretation. We have in addition the chance of actual sense-hallucination. And, worse than this, we have the far-reaching influence of abnormal suggestion and morbid fixed idea. This influence may stop short of hallucination, and yet may vitiate the memory and the judgement to such an extent that there remains no practical difference between idea and perceived fact. And, in the face of these possibilities, it seems idle to speak of perceptions and memories secure from all chance of error. Or on the other side banish the chance of error, and with what are you left? You then have something which (as we have seen) goes no further than to warrant the assertion that such and such elements can and do co-exist—somehow and somewhere, or again that such or such a judgement happens—without any regard to its truth and without any specification of its psychical context. And no one surely will contend that with this we have particular fact.

The doctrine that perception gives us infallible truth rests on a foundation which in part is sound and in part fatally defective. That what is felt is felt, and cannot, so far as felt, be mistaken—so much as this must be accepted. But the view that, when I say "this," "now," "here," or "my," what I feel, when so speaking, is carried over intact into my judgement, and that my judgement in consequence is exempt from error, seems wholly indefensible. It survives, I venture to think, only because it never has understood its complete refutation.

That which I designate is not and cannot be carried over into my judgement. The judgement may in a sense answer to that which I feel, but none the less it fails to contain and to convey my feeling. And on the other hand, so far as it succeeds in expressing my meaning, the judgement does this in a way which makes it liable to error. Or, to put it otherwise, the perceived truth, to be of any use, must be particularized. So far as it is stated in a general form, it contains not only that which you meant to say but also, and just as much, the opposite of that which you meant. And to contend for the infallibility of such a truth seems futile. On the other side so far as your truth really is individualized, so far as it is placed in a special construction and vitally related to its context, to the same extent the element of interpretation or implication is added. And, with this element obviously comes the possibility of mistake. As we have seen above that, viewed psychologically, particular judgements of perception immune from all chance of error seem hardly tenable.

2. I pass now to the second reason for accepting infallible data of perception. Even if we cannot show these (it is urged) we are bound to assume them. For in their absence our knowledge has nothing on which to stand, and this want of support results in total scepticism.

It is possible of course here to embrace both premises and conclusion, and to argue that scepticism is to be preferred to an untrue assumption. And such a position I would press on the notice of those who uphold infallible judgements of sense and memory. But personally I am hardly concerned in this issue, for I reject both the conclusion and the premises together. Such infallible and incorrigible judgements are really not required for our knowledge, and, since they cannot be shown, we must not say that they exist. . . .

I agree that we depend vitally on the sense-world, that our material comes from it, and that apart from it knowledge could not begin. To this world, I agree, we have for ever to return, not only to gain new matter but to confirm and maintain the old. I agree that to impose order from without on sheer disorder would be wholly impracticable, and that, if my sense-world were disorderly beyond a certain point, my intelligence would not exist. And further I agree that we cannot suppose it possible that *all* the judgements of perception and memory which for me come first, could in fact for me be corrected. I cannot, that is, imagine the world of my experience to be so modified that in the end none of these accepted facts should be left standing. But so far, I hasten to add, we have not yet come to the real issue. There is still a chasm between such admissions and the conclusion that there are judgements of sense which possess truth absolute and infallible.

We meet here a false doctrine largely due to a misleading metaphor. My known world is taken to be a construction built upon such and such foundations. It is argued, therefore, to be in principle a superstructure which rests upon these supports. You can go on adding to it no doubt, but only so long as the supports remain; and, unless they remain, the whole building comes down. But the doctrine, I have to contend, is untenable, and the metaphor ruinously inapplicable. The foundation in truth is provisional merely. In order to begin my construction I take the foundation as absolute—so much certainly is true. But that my construction continues to rest on the beginnings of my knowledge is a conclusion which does not follow. It does not follow that, if these are allowed to be fallible, the whole building collapses. For it is in another sense that my world rests upon the data of perception.

My experience is solid, not so far as it is a superstructure but so far as in short it is a system. My object is to have a world as comprehensive and coherent as possible, and, in order to attain this object, I have not only to reflect but perpetually to have recourse to the materials of sense. I must go to this source both to verify the matter which is old and also to increase it by what is new. And in this way I must depend upon the judgements of perception. Now it is agreed that, if I am to have an orderly world, I cannot possibly accept all "facts." Some of these must be relegated, as they are, to the world of error, whether we succeed or fail in modifying and correcting them. And the view which I advocate takes them all as in principle fallible. On the other hand, that view denies that there is any necessity for absolute facts of sense. Facts for it are true, we may say, just so far as they work, just so far as they contribute to the order of experience. If by taking certain judgements of perception as true, I can get more system into my world, then these "facts" are so far true, and if by taking certain "facts" as errors I can order my experience better, then so far these "facts" are errors. And there is no "fact" which possesses an absolute right. Certainly there are truths with which I begin and which I personally never have to discard, and which therefore remain in fact as members of my known world. And of some of these certainly it may be said that without them I should not know how to order my knowledge. But it is quite another thing to maintain that every single one of these judgements is in principle infallible. The absolute indispensable fact is in my view the mere creature of false theory. Facts are valid so far as, when taken otherwise than as "real," they bring disorder into my world. And there are today for me facts such that, if I take them as mistakes, my known world is damaged and, it is possible, ruined. But how does it follow that I cannot tomorrow on the strength of new facts gain a wider order in which these old facts can take a place as errors? The supposition may be improbable, but what you have got to show is that it is in principle impossible. A foundation used at the beginning does not in short mean something fundamental at the end, and there is no single "fact" which in the end can be called fundamental absolutely. It is all a question of relative contribution to my known world-order.

"Then no judgement of perception will be more than probable?" Certainly that is my contention. "Facts" are justified because and as far as, while taking them as real, I am better able to deal with the incoming new "facts" and in general to make my world wider and more harmonious. The higher and wider my structure, and the more that any particular fact or set of facts is implied in that structure, the more certain are the structure and the facts. And, if we could reach an all-embracing ordered whole, then our certainty would be absolute. But, since we cannot do this, we have to remain content with relative probability. Why is this or that fact of observation taken as practically certain? It is so taken just so far as it is *not* taken in its own right. (i) Its validity is due to such and such a person perceiving it under such and such conditions. This means that a certain intellectual order in the person is necessary as a basis, and again that nothing in the way of sensible or mental distortion intervenes between this order and what is given. And (ii) the observed fact must agree with our world as already arranged, or at least must not upset this. If the fact is too much contrary to our arranged world we provisionally reject it. We eventually accept the fact only when after confirmation the hypothesis of its error becomes still more ruinous. We are forced then more or less to rearrange our world, and more or less perhaps to reject some previous "facts." The question throughout is as to what is better or worse for our order as a whole.

Why again to me is a remembered fact certain, supposing that it is so? Assuredly not because it is infallibly delivered by the faculty of Memory, but because I do not see how to reconcile the fact of its error with my accepted world. Unless I go on the principle of trusting my memory, apart from any special reason to the contrary, I cannot order my world so well, if indeed I can order it at all. The principle here again is system. . . .

The same account holds with regard to the facts of history. For instance, the guillotining of Louix XVI is practically certain because to take this as error would entail too much disturbance of my world. Error is possible here of course. Fresh facts conceivably might come before me such as would compel me to modify in part my knowledge as so far arranged. And in this modified arrangement the execution of Louis would find its place as an error. But the reason for such a modification would have to be considerable, while, as things are, no reason exists. . . . To take memory as in general trustworthy, where I have no special reason for doubt, and to take the testimony of those persons, whom I suppose to view the world as I view it, as being true, apart from special reason on the other side—these are principles by which I construct my ordered world, such as it is. And because by any other method the result is worse, therefore for me these principles are true. On the other hand to suppose that any "fact" or perception or memory is so certain that no possible experience could justify me in taking it as error seems to me injurious if not ruinous. On such a principle my world of knowledge would be ordered worse, if indeed it could be ordered at all. For to accept all the "facts," as they offer themselves, seems obviously impossible; and, if it is we who have to decide as to which facts are infallible, then I ask how we are to decide. The ground of validity, I maintain, consists in successful contribution. That is a principle of order, while any other principle, so far as I see, leads to chaos.

"But," it may still be objected, "my fancy is unlimited. I can therefore invent an imaginary world even more orderly than my known world. And further this fanciful arrangement might possibly be made so wide that the world of perception would become for me in comparison small and inconsiderable. Hence, my perceived world, so far as not supporting my fancied arrangement, might be included within it as *error*. Such a consequence would or might lead to confusion in theory and to disaster in practice. And yet the result follows from your view inevitably, unless after all you fall back upon the certainty of perception."

To this possible objection, I should reply first, that it has probably failed to understand rightly the criterion which I defend. The aspect of comprehensiveness has not received here its due emphasis. The idea of system demands the inclusion of all possible material. Not only must you include everything to be gained from immediate experience and perception, but you must also be ready to act on the same principle with regard to fancy. But this means that you cannot confine yourself within the limits of this or that fancied world, as suits your pleasure or private convenience. You are bound also, so far as is possible, to recognize and to include the opposite fancy.

This consideration to my mind ruins the above hypothesis on which the objection was based. The fancied arrangement not only has opposed to it the world of perception. It also has against it any opposite arrangement and any contrary fact which I can fancy. And, so far as I can judge, these contrary fancies will balance the first. Nothing, therefore, will be left to outweigh the world as perceived, and the imaginary hypothesis will be condemned by our criterion.

. . . I may state the view which has commended itself to my mind. **Truth is an ideal expression of the Universe, at once coherent and comprehensive.** It must not conflict with itself, and there must be no suggestion which fails to fall inside it. Perfect truth in short must realize the idea of a systematic whole. And such a whole . . . possesses essentially the two characters of coherence and comprehensiveness.

Pragmatism's Conception of Truth

William James

Truth, as any dictionary will tell you, is a property of certain of our ideas. It means their 'agreement,' as falsity means their disagreement, with 'reality.' Pragmatists and intellectualists both accept this definition as a matter of course. They begin to quarrel only after the question is raised as to what may precisely be meant by the term 'agreement,' and what by the term 'reality,' when reality is taken as something for our ideas to agree with.

In answering these questions the pragmatists are more analytic and painstaking, the intellectualists more offhand and irreflective. The popular notion is that a true idea must copy its reality. Like other popular views, this one follows the analogy of the most usual experience. Our true ideas of sensible things do indeed copy them. Shut your eyes and think of yonder clock on the wall, and you get just such a true picture or copy of its dial. But your idea of its 'works' (unless you are a clock-maker) is much less of a copy, yet it passes muster, for it in no way clashes with the reality. Even though it should shrink to the mere word 'works,' that word still serves you truly; and when you speak of the 'time-keeping function' of the clock, or of its spring's 'elasticity,' it is hard to see exactly what your ideas can copy.

You perceive that there is a problem here. Where our ideas cannot copy definitely their object, what does agreement with that object mean? Some idealists seem to say that they are true whenever they are what God means that we ought to think about that object. Others hold the copy-view all through, and speak as if our ideas possessed truth just in proportion as they approach to being copies of the Absolute's eternal way of thinking.

These views, you see, invite pragmatistic discussion. But the great assumption of the intellectualists is that truth means essentially an inert static relation. When you've got your true idea of anything, there's an end of the matter. You're in possession; you *know;* you have fulfilled your thinking destiny. You are where you ought to be mentally; you have obeyed your categorical imperative; and nothing more need follow on that climax of your rational destiny. Epistemologically you are in stable equilibrium.

Pragmatism, on the other hand, asks its usual question. "Grant an idea or belief to be true," it says, "what concrete difference will its being true make in any one's actual life? How will the truth be realized? What experiences will be different from those which would obtain if the belief were false? **What, in short, is the truth's cash-value in experiential terms?"**

The moment pragmatism asks this question, it sees the answer: *True ideas are those that we can assimilate, validate, corroborate and verify. False ideas are those that we can not.* That is the practical difference it makes to us to have true ideas; that, therefore, is the meaning of truth, for it is all that truth is known-as.

This thesis is what I have to defend. The truth of an idea is not a stagnant property inherent in it. **Truth *happens* to an idea.** It *becomes* true, is *made* true by events. Its verity *is* in fact an event, a process: the process namely of its verifying itself, its veri-*fication*. Its validity is the process of its valid*ation*.

But what do the words verification and validation themselves pragmatically mean? They again signify certain practical consequences of the verified and validated idea. It is hard to find any one phrase that characterizes these consequences better than the ordinary agreement-formula—just such consequences being what we have in mind whenever we say that our ideas 'agree' with reality. They lead us, namely, through the acts and other ideas which they instigate, into or up to, or towards, other parts of experience with which we feel all the while—such feeling being among our potentialities—that the original ideas remain in agreement. The connexions and transitions come to us from point to point as being progressive, harmonious, satisfactory. This function of agreeable leading is what we mean by an idea's verification. Such an account is vague and it sounds at first quite trivial, but it has results which it will take the rest of my [lecture] to explain.

Let me begin by reminding you of the fact that the possession of true thoughts means everywhere the possession of invaluable instruments of action; and that our duty to gain truth, so far from being a blank command from out of the blue, or a 'stunt' self-imposed by our intellect, can account for itself by excellent practical reasons.

The importance to human life of having true beliefs about matters of fact is a thing too notorious. We live in a world of realities that can be infinitely useful or infinitely harmful. Ideas that tell us which of them to expect count as the true ideas in all this primary sphere of verification, and the pursuit of such ideas is a primary human duty. The possession of truth, so far from being here an end in itself, is only a preliminary means towards other vital satisfactions. If I am lost in the woods and starved, and find what looks like a cow-path, it is of the utmost importance that I should think of a human habitation at the end of it, for if I do so and follow it, I save myself. The true thought is useful here because the house which is its object is useful. The practical value of true ideas is thus primarily derived from the practical importance of their objects to us. Their objects are, indeed, not important at all times. I may on another occasion have no use for the house; and then my idea of it, however verifiable, will be practically irrelevant, and had better remain latent. Yet since almost any object may some day become temporarily important, the advantage of having a general stock of *extra* truths, of ideas that shall be true of merely possible situations, is obvious. We store such extra truths away in our memories, and with the overflow we fill our books of reference. Whenever such an extra truth becomes practically relevant to one of our emergencies, it passes from cold-storage to do work in the world and our belief in it grows active. You can say of it then either that 'it is useful because it is true' or that 'it is true because it is useful.' Both these phrases mean exactly the same thing, namely that here is an idea that gets fulfilled and can be verified. True is the name for whatever idea starts the verification-process, useful is the name for its completed function in experience. True ideas would never have been singled out as such, would never have acquired a class-name, least of all a name suggesting value, unless they had been useful from the outset in this way.

From this simple cue pragmatism gets her general notion of truth as something essentially bound up with the way in which one moment in our experience may lead us towards other moments which it will be worth while to have been led to. Primarily, and on the common-sense level, the truth of a state of mind means this function of *a leading that is worth while*. When a moment in our experience, of any kind whatever, inspires us with a thought that is true, that means that sooner or later we dip by that thought's guidance into the particulars of experience again and make advantageous connexion with them. This is a vague enough statement, but I beg you to retain, for it is essential.

Our experience meanwhile is all shot through with regularities. One bit of it can warn us to get ready for another bit, can 'intend' or be 'significant of' that remoter object. The object's advent is the significance's verification. Truth, in these cases, meaning nothing but eventual verification, is manifestly incompatible with waywardness on our part. Woe to him whose beliefs play fast and loose with the order which realities follow in his experience; they will lead him nowhere or else make false connexions.

By 'realities' or 'objects' here, we mean either things of common sense sensibly present, or else common-sense relations, such as dates, places distances, kinds, activities. Following our mental image of a house along the cow-path, we actually come to see the house; we get the image's full verification. *Such simply and fully verified leadings are certainly the originals and prototypes of the truth-process.* Experience offers indeed other forms of truth-process, but they are all conceivable as being primary, verifications arrested, multiplied or substituted one for another.

Take, for instance, yonder object on the wall. You and I consider it to be a 'clock,' altho no one of us has seen the hidden works that make it one. We let our notion pass for true without attempting to verify. If truths mean verification-process essentially, ought we then to call such unverified truths as this abortive? No, for they form the overwhelmingly large number of the truths we live by. Indirect as well as direct verifications pass muster. Where circumstantial evidence is sufficient, we can go without eye-witnessing. Just as we here assume Japan to exist without ever having been there, because it *works* to do so, everything we know conspiring with the belief, and nothing interfering, so we assume that thing to be a clock. We *use* it as a clock regulating the length of our lecture by it. The verification of the assumption here means its leading to no frustration or contradiction. *Verifiability* of wheels and weights and pendulum is as good as verification. For one truth-process completed there are a million in our lives that function in this state of nascency. They turn us *towards* direct verification; lead us into the *surroundings* of the objects they envisage; and then, if everything runs on harmoniously, we are so sure that verification is possible that we omit it, and are usually justified by all that happens.

Truth lives, in fact, for the most part on a credit system. Our thoughts and beliefs 'pass,' so long as nothing challenges them, just as bank-notes pass so long as nobody refuses them. But this all points to direct face-to-face verifications somewhere, without which the fabric of truth collapses like a financial system with no cash-basis whatever. You accept my verification of one thing, I yours of another. We trade on each other's truth. But belief verified concretely by *somebody* are the posts of the whole superstructure.

Another great reason—beside economy of time—for waiving complete verification in the usual business of life is that all things exist in kinds and not singly. Our world is found once for all to have that peculiarity. So that when we have once directly verified our ideas about one specimen of a kind, we consider ourselves free to apply them to other specimens without verification. A mind that habitually discerns the kind of thing before it, and acts by the law of the kind immediately, without pausing to verify, will be a 'true' mind in ninety-nine out of a hundred emergencies, proved so by its conduct fitting everything it meets, and getting no refutation.

Indirectly or only potentially verifying processes may thus be true as well as full verification-processes. They work as true processes would work, give us the same advantages, and claim our recognition for the same reasons. All this on the common-sense level of matters of fact, which we are alone considering.

But matters of fact are not our only stock in trade. *Relations among purely mental ideas* form another sphere where true and false beliefs obtain, and here the beliefs are absolute, or unconditional. When they are true they bear the name either of definitions or of principles. It is either a principle or a definition that 1 and 1 make 2, that 2 and 1 make 3, and so on; that white differs less from gray than it does from black; that when the cause begins to act the effect also commences. Such propositions hold of all possible 'ones,' of all conceivable 'whites' and 'grays' and 'causes.' The objects here are mental objects. Their relations are perceptually obvious at a glance, and no sense-verification is necessary. Moreover, once true, always true, of those same mental objects. Truth here has an 'eternal' character. If you can find a concrete thing anywhere that is 'one' or 'white' or 'gray' or 'effect,' then your principles will everlastingly apply to it. It is but a case of ascertaining the kind, and then applying the law of its kind to the particular object. You are sure to get truth if you can but name the kind rightly, for your mental relations hold good of everything of that kind without exception. If you then, nevertheless, failed to get truth concretely, you would say that you had classed your real objects wrongly.

In this realm of mental relations, truth again is an affair of leading. We relate one abstract idea with another, framing in the end great systems of logical and mathematical truth, under the respective terms of which the sensible facts of experience eventually arrange themselves, so that our eternal truths hold good of realities also. This marriage of fact and theory is endlessly fertile. What we say is here already true in advance of special verification, *if we have subsumed our objects rightly.* Our ready-made ideal framework for all sorts of possible objects follows from the very structure of our thinking. We can no more play fast and loose with these abstract relations than we can do so with our sense-experiences. They coerce us; we must treat them consistently, whether or not we like the results. The rules of addition apply to our debts as rigorously as to our assets. The hundredth decimal of π, the ratio of the circumference to its diameter, is predetermined ideally now, tho no one may have computed it. If we should ever need the figure in our dealings with an actual circle we should need to have it given rightly, calculated by the usual rules; for it is the same kind of truth that those rules elsewhere calculate.

Between the coercions of the sensible order and those of the ideal order, our mind is thus wedged tightly. Our ideas must agree with realities, be such realities concrete or abstract, be they facts or be they principles, under penalty of endless inconsistency and frustration.

So far, intellectualists can raise no protest. They can only say that we have barely touched the skin of the matter.

Realities mean, then, either concrete facts, or abstract kinds of thing and relations perceived intuitively between them. They furthermore and thirdly mean, as things that new ideas of ours must no less take account of, the whole body of other truths already in our possession. But what now does 'agreement' with such threefold realities mean?—to use again the definition that is current.

Here it is that pragmatism and intellectualism begin to part company. Primarily, no doubt, to agree means to copy, but we saw that the mere word 'clock' would do instead of a mental picture of its works, and that of many realities our ideas can only be symbols and not copies. 'Past time,' 'power,' 'spontaneity,'—how can our mind copy such realities?

To 'agree' in the widest sense with a reality *can only mean to be guided either straight up to it or into its surroundings, or to be put into such working touch with it as to handle either it or something connected with it better than if we disagreed.* Better either intellectually or from the quarter of that reality come to interfere with the way in which our ideas guide us elsewhere. To copy a reality is, indeed, one very important way of agreeing with it, but it is far from being essential. The essential thing is the process of being guided. Any idea that helps us to *deal* whether practically or intellectually, with either the reality or its belongings, that doesn't entangle our progress in frustrations, that *fits*, in fact, and adapts our life to the reality's whole setting, will agree sufficiently to meet the requirement. It will hold true of that reality.

Thus, *names* are just as 'true' or 'false' as definite mental pictures are. They set up similar verification-processes, and lead to fully equivalent practical results.

All human thinking gets discursified; we exchange ideas; we lend and borrow verifications, get them from one another by means of social intercourse. All truth thus gets verbally built out, stored up, and made available for every one. Hence, we must *talk* consistently just as we must *think* consistently: for both in talk and thought we deal with kinds. Names are arbitrary, but once understood they must be kept to. We mustn't now call Abel 'Cain' or Cain 'Abel.' If we do, we ungear ourselves from the whole book of Genesis, and from all its connexions with the universe of speech and fact down to the present time. We throw ourselves out of whatever truth that entire system of speech and fact may embody.

The overwhelming majority of our true ideas admit of no direct or face-to-face verification—those of past history, for example, as of Cain and Abel. The stream of time can be remounted only verbally, or verified indirectly by the present prolongations or effects of what the past harbored. Yet if they agree with these verbalities and effects, we can know that our ideas of the past are true. *As true as past time itself was,* so true was Julius Caesar, so true were antediluvian monsters, all in their proper dates and settings. That past time itself was, is guaranteed by its coherence with everything that's present. True as the present *is*, the past *was* also.

Agreement thus turns out to be essentially an affair of leading—leading that is useful because it is into quarters that contain objects that are important. True ideas lead us into useful verbal and conceptual quarters as well as directly up to useful sensible termini. They lead to consistency, stability and flowing human intercourse. They lead away from excentricity and isolation, from foiled and barren thinking. The untrammelled flowing of the leading-process, its general freedom from clash and contradiction, passes for its indirect verification; but all roads lead to Rome, and in the end and eventually, all true processes must lead to the face of directly verifying sensible experiences *somewhere*, which sombody's ideas have copied.

Such is the large loose way in which the pragmatist interprets the word agreement. He treats it altogether practically. He lets it cover any process of conduction from a present idea to a future terminus, provided only it run prosperously. It is only thus that 'scientific' ideas, flying as they do beyond common sense, can be said to agree with their realities. It is, as I have already said, *as if* reality were made of ether, atoms or electrons, but we mustn't think so literally. The term 'energy' doesn't even pretend to stand for anything 'objective.' It is only a way of measuring the surface of phenomena so as to string their changes on a simple formula.

Yet in the choice of these man-made formulas we can not be capricious with impunity any more than we can be capricious on the common-sense practical level. We must find a theory that will *work;* and that means something extremely difficult; for our theory must mediate between all previous truths and certain new experiences. It must derange common sense and previous belief as little as possible, and it must lead to some sensible terminus or other that can be verified exactly. To 'work' means both these things; and the squeeze is so tight that there is little loose play for any hypothesis. Our theories are wedged and controlled as nothing else is. Yet sometimes alternative theoretic formulas are equally compatible with all the truths we know, and then we choose between them for subjective reasons. We choose the kind of theory to which we are already partial; we follow 'elegance' or 'economy.' Clerk-Maxwell somewhere says it would be 'poor scientific taste' to choose the more complicated of two equally well evidenced conceptions; and you will all agree with him. Truth in science is what gives us the maximum possible sum of satisfactions, taste included, but consistency both with previous truth and with novel fact is always the most imperious claimant.

I have led you through a very sandy desert. But now, if I may be allowed so vulgar an expression, we begin to taste the milk in the coconut. Our rationalist critics here discharge their batteries upon us, and to reply to them will take us out from all this dryness into full sight of a momentous philosophical alternative.

Our account of truth is an account of truths in the plural, of processes of leading, realized *in rebus* [in things themselves], and having only this quality in common, that they *pay.* They pay by guiding us into or towards some part of a system that dips at numerous points into sense-precepts, which we may copy mentally or not, but with which at any rate we are now in the kind of commerce vaguely designated as verification. Truth for us is simply a collective name for verification-processes, just as health, wealth, strength, etc., are names for other processes connected with life, and also pursued because it pays to pursue them. Truth is *made,* just as health, wealth, and strength are made, in the course of experience.

Here rationalism is instantaneously up in arms against us. I can imagine a rationalist to talk as follows:

"Truth is not made," he will say; "it absolutely obtains, being a unique relation that does not wait upon any process, but shoots straight over the head of experience, and hits its reality every time. Our belief that yon thing on the wall is a clock is true already, altho no one in the whole history of the world should verify it. The bare quality of standing in that transcendent relation is what makes any thought true that possesses it, whether or not there be verification. You pragmatists put the cart before the horse in making truth's being reside in verification-processes. These are merely signs of its being, merely our lame ways of ascertaining after the fact, which of our ideas already has possessed the wondrous quality. The quality itself is timeless, like all essences and natures. Thoughts partake of it directly, as they partake of falsity or of irrelevancy. It can't be analyzed away into pragmatic consequences."

The whole plausibility of this rationalist tirade is due to the fact to which we have already paid so much attention. In our world, namely, abounding as it does in things of similar kinds and similarly associated, one verification serves for others of its kind, and one great use of knowing things is to be led not so much to them as to their associates, especially to human talk about them. The quality of truth, obtaining *ante rem* [prior to an examination of particular things in the world], pragmatically means, then, the fact that in such a world innumerable ideas work better by their indirect or possible than by their direct and actual verification. Truth *ante rem* means only verifiability, then; or else it is a case of the stock rationalist trick of treating the *name* of a concrete phenomenal reality as an independent prior entity, and placing it behind the reality as its explanation.

In the case of 'wealth' we all see the fallacy. We know that wealth is but a name for concrete processes that certain men's lives play a part in, and not a natural excellence found in Messrs. Rockefeller and Carnegie, but not in the rest of us.

Like wealth, health also lives *in rebus*. It is a name for processes, as digestion, circulation, sleep, etc., that go on happily, tho in this instance we are more inclined to think of it as a principle and to say the man digests and sleeps so well *because* he is so healthy.

With 'strength' we are, I think, more rationalistic still, and decidedly inclined to treat it as an excellence pre-existing in the man and explanatory of the herculean performances of his muscles.

With 'truth' most people go over the border entirely, and treat the rationalistic account as self-evident. But really all these words in *th* are exactly similar. Truth exists *ante rem* just as much and as little as the other things do.

The scholastics, following Aristotle, made much of the distinction between habit and act. Health *in actu* [fully realized and actual] means, among other things, good sleeping and digesting. But a healthy man need not always be sleeping, or always digesting, any more than a wealthy man need be always handling money, or a strong man always lifting weights. All such qualities sink to the status of 'habits' between their times of exercise; and similarly truth becomes a habit of certain of our ideas and beliefs in their intervals of rest from their verifying activities. But those activities are the root of the whole matter, and the condition of there being any habit to exist in the intervals.

'The true,' to put it very briefly, is only the expedient in the way of our thinking, just as 'the right' is only the expedient in the way of our behaving. Expedient in almost any fashion; and expedient in the long run and on the whole of course; for what meets expediently all the experience in sight won't necessarily meet all farther experiences equally satisfactorily. Experience, as we know, has ways of *boiling over,* and making us correct our present formulas.

The 'absolutely' true, meaning what no farther experience will ever alter, is that ideal vanishing-point towards which we imagine that all our temporary truths will some day converge. It runs on all fours with the perfectly wise man, and with the absolutely complete experience; and, if these ideals are ever realized, they will all be realized together. Meanwhile we have to live to-day by what truth we can get to-day, and be ready to-morrow to call it falsehood. Ptolemaic astronomy, euclidean space, aristotelian logic, scholastic metaphysics, were expedient for centuries, but human experience has boiled over those limits, and we now call these things only relatively true, or true within those borders of experience. 'Absolutely' they are false; for we know that those limits were casual, and might have been transcended by past theorists just as they are by present thinkers.

When new experiences lead to retrospective judgments, using the past tense, what these judgments utter *was* true, even tho no past thinker had been led there. We live forwards, a Danish thinker has said, but we understand backwards. The present sheds a backward light on previous processes. They may have been truth-processes for the actors in them. They are not so for one who knows the later revelations of the story.

This regulative notion of a potential better truth to be established later, possibly to be established some day absolutely, and having powers of retroactive legislation, turns its face, like all pragmatist notions, towards concreteness of fact, and towards the future. Like the half-truths, the absolute truth will have to be *made*, made as a relation incidental to the growth of a mass of verification-experience, to which the half-true ideas are all along contributing their quota.

I have already insisted on the fact that truth is made largely out of previous truths. Men's beliefs at any time are so much experience *funded*. But the beliefs are themselves parts of the sum total of the world's experience and become matter, therefore, for the next day's funding operations. So far as reality means experienceable reality, both it and the truths men gain about it are everlastingly in proccess of mutation—mutation towards a definite goal, it may be—but still mutation.

Mathematicians can solve problems with two variables. On the Newtonian theory, for instance, acceleration varies with distance, but distance also varies with acceleration. In the realm of truth-processes facts come independently and determine our beliefs provisionally. But these beliefs make us act, and as fast as they do so, they bring into sight or into existence new facts which re-determine the beliefs accordingly. So the whole coil and ball of truth, as it rolls up, is the product of a double influence. Truths emerge from facts; but they dip forward into facts again and add to them; which facts again create or reveal new truth (the word is indifferent) and so on indefinitely. The 'facts' themselves meanwhile are not *true*. They simply *are*. Truth is the function of the beliefs that start and terminate among them.

The most fateful point of difference between being a rationalist and being a pragmatist is now fully in sight. Experience is in mutation, and our psychological ascertainments of truth are in mutation—so much rationalism will allow; but never that either reality itself or truth itself is mutable. Reality stands complete and ready-made from all eternity, rationalism insists, and the agreement of our ideas with it is that unique unanalyzable virtue in them of which she has already told us. As that intrinsic excellence, their truth has nothing to do with our experiences. It adds nothing to the content of experience. It makes no difference to reality itself; it is supervenient, inert, static, a reflexion merely. It doesn't *exist*, it *holds* or *obtains*, it belongs to another dimension from that of either facts or fact-relations, belongs, in short, to the epistemological dimension—and with that big word rationalism closes the discussion.

Thus, just as pragmatism faces forward to the future, so does rationalism here again face backward to a past eternity. True to her inveterate habit, rationalism reverts to 'principles,' and thinks that when an abstraction once is named, we own an oracular solution.

The Subjective Truth

Søren Kierkegaard

When the question of truth is raised in an objective manner, reflection is directed objectively to the truth, as an object to which the knower is related. Reflection is not focused upon the relationship, however, but upon the question of whether it is the truth to which the knower is related. If only the object to which he is related is the truth, the subject is accounted to be in the truth. When the question of the truth is raised subjectively, reflection is directed subjectively to the nature of the individual's relationship: if only the mode of this relationship is in the truth, the individual is in the truth, even if he should happen to be thus related to what is not true.[1] Let us take as an example the knowledge of God. Objectively, reflection is directed to the problem of whether this object is the true God; subjectively, reflection is directed to the question whether the individual is related to a something *in such a manner* that his relationship is in truth a God-relationship. On which side is the truth now to be found? Ah, may we not here resort to a mediation, and say: It is on neither side, but in the mediation of both? Excellently well said, provided we might have it explained how an existing individual manages to be in a state of mediation. For to be in a state of mediation is to be finished, while to exist is to become. Nor can an existing individual be in two places at the same time—he cannot be an identity of subject and object. When he is nearest to being in two places at the same time he is in passion; but passion is merely momentary, and passion is also the highest expression of subjectivity.

The existing individual who chooses to pursue the objective way enters upon the entire approximation-process by which it is proposed to bring God to light objectively. But this is in all eternity impossible, because God is a subject, and therefore exists only for subjectivity in inwardness. The existing individual who chooses the subjective way apprehends instantly the entire dialectical difficulty involved in having to use some time, perhaps a long time, in finding God objectively; and he feels this dialectical difficulty in all its painfulness, because he must use God at that very moment, since every moment is wasted in which he does not have God.[2] That very instant he has God, not by virtue of any objective deliberation but by virtue of the infinite passion of inwardness. The objective inquirer, on the other hand, is not embarrassed by such dialectical difficulties as

281

are involved in devoting an entire period of investigation to finding God—since it is possible that the inquirer may die tomorrow; and if he lives he can scarcely regard God as something to be taken along if convenient, since God is precisely that which one takes *a tout prix*, which in the understanding of passion constitutes the true inward relationship to God.

It is at this point, so difficult dialectically, that the way swings off for everyone who knows what it means to think, and to think existentially; which is something very different from sitting at a desk like a fantastical being and writing about what one has never done, something very different from writing *de omnibus dubitandum*, and at the same time being as existentially credulous as the most sensuous of men. Here is where the way swings off, and the change is marked by the fact that, while objective knowledge rambles comfortably on by way of the long road of approximation without being impelled by the urge of passion, subjective knowledge counts every delay a deadly peril, and the decision so infinitely important and so instantly pressing that it is as if the opportunity had already passed unutilized.

Now when the problem is to reckon up on which side there is most truth, whether on the side of one who seeks the true God objectively, and pursues the approximate truth of the God-idea; or on the side of one who, driven by the infinite passion of his need of God, feels an infinite concern for his own relationship to God in truth (and to be at one and the same time on both sides equally is, as we have noted, not possible for an existing individual, but is merely the happy delusion of an imaginary I-am-I): the answer cannot be in doubt for anyone who has not been demoralized with the aid of science. If one who lives in the midst of Christianity goes up to the house of God, the house of the true God, with the true conception of God in his knowledge, and prays, but prays in a false spirit; and one who lives in an idolatrous community prays with the entire passion of the infinite, although his eyes rest upon the image of an idol: where is there most truth? The one prays in truth to God though he worships an idol; the other prays falsely to the true God, and hence worships in fact an idol.

When one man investigates objectively the problem of immortality, and another embraces an uncertainty with the passion of the infinite: where is there most truth, and who has the greater certainty? The one has entered upon a never-ending approximation, for the certainty of immortality lies precisely in the subjectivity of the individual; the other is immortal, and fights for his immortality by struggling with the uncertainty. Let us consider Socrates. Nowadays everyone dabbles in a few proofs; some have several such proofs, others fewer. But Socrates! He puts the question objectively in a problematic manner: *if* there is an immortality. Must he therefore be accounted a doubter in comparison with one of our modern thinkers with the three proofs? By no means. On this "if" he risks his entire life, he has the courage to meet death, and he has with the passion of the infinite so determined the pattern of his life that it must be found acceptable—*if* there is an immortality. Can any better proof be given for the immortality of the soul? But those who have the three proofs do not at all determine their lives in conformity therewith; if there is an immortality, it must feel disgust over their manner of life: can any better refutation be given of the three proofs? The "bit" of uncertainty that Socrates had helped him, because he himself contributed the passion of the infinite; the three proofs that the others have do not profit them at all, because they are and remain dead to spirit and enthusiasm, and their three proofs, in lieu of proving anything else, prove just this. A young girl may enjoy all the sweetness of love on the basis of what is merely a weak hope; but she is beloved, because she rests everything on this weak hope; but many a wedded matron more than once subjected to the strongest expressions of love has in so far indeed had proofs, but strangely enough has not enjoyed *quod erat demonstrandum*. The Socratic ignorance, which Socrates held fast with the entire passion of his inwardness, was thus an expression for the principle that the eternal truth is related to an existing individual, and that this truth must therefore be a paradox for him as long as he exists; and yet it is possible that there was more truth in the Socratic ignorance as it was in him, than in the entire objective truth of the System, which flirts with what the times demand and accommodates itself to *Privatdocents*.

The objective accent falls on WHAT is said, the subjective accent on HOW it is said. This distinction holds even in the aesthetic realm, and receives definite expression in the principle that what is in itself true may in the mouth of such and such a person become untrue. In these times this distinction is particularly worthy of notice for, if we wish to express in a single sentence the difference between ancient times and our own, we should doubtless have to say: "In ancient times only an individual here and there knew the truth; now all know it, but the inwardness of its appropriation stands in an inverse relationship to the extent of its dissemination. Aesthetically the contradiction that truth becomes untruth in this or that person's mouth is best construed comically. In the ethico-religious sphere, the accent is again on the "how." But this is not to be understood as referring to demeanor, expression, delivery, or the like; rather it refers to the relationship sustained by the existing individual, in his own existence, to the content of his utterance. Objectively the interest is focused merely on the thought-content, subjectively on the inwardness. At its maximum this inward "how" is the passion of the infinite, and the passion of the infinite is the truth. But the passion of the infinite is precisely subjectivity, and thus subjectivity becomes the truth. Objectively there is no infinite decision, and hence it is objectively in order to annul the difference between good and evil, together with the principle of contradiction, and therewith also the infinite difference between the true and the false. Only in subjectivity is there decision, to seek objectivity is to be in error. It is the passion of the infinite that is the decisive factor and not its content, for its content is precisely itself. In this manner subjectivity and the subjective "how" constitute the truth.

But the "how" which is thus subjectively accentuated, precisely because the subject is an existing individual, is also subject to a dialectic with respect to time. In the passionate moment of decision, where the road swings away from objective knowledge, it seems as if the infinite decision were thereby realized. But in the same moment the existing individual finds himself in the temporal order, and the subjective "how" is transformed into a striving, a striving which receives indeed its impulse and a repeated renewal from the decisive passion of the infinite, but is nevertheless a striving.

When subjectivity is the truth, the conceptual determination of the truth must include an expression for the antithesis to objectivity, a memento of the fork in the road where the way swings off; this expression will also indicate the tension of the subjective inwardness. Here is such a definition of truth: *An objective uncertainty held fast in an appropriation-process of the most passionate inwardness is the truth*, the highest truth attainable for an *existing individual*. At the point where the way swings off (and where this is cannot be specified objectively, since it is a matter of subjectivity), there objective knowledge is placed in abeyance. Thus the subject merely has, objectively, the uncertainty; but it is this which precisely increases the tension of that infinite passion which constitutes his inwardness. The truth is precisely the venture which chooses an objective uncertainty with the passion of the infinite. I contemplate nature in the hope of finding God, and I see omnipotence and wisdom; but I also see much else that disturbs my mind and excites anxiety. The sum of all this is an objective uncertainty. But it is for this very reason that the inwardness becomes as intense as it is, for it embraces this objective uncertainty with the entire passion of the infinite. In the case of a mathematical proposition the objectivity is given, but for this reason the truth of such a proposition is also an indifferent truth.

But the above definition of truth is an equivalent expression for faith. Without risk there is no faith. Faith is precisely the contradiction between the infinite passion of the individual's inwardness and the objective uncertainty. If I am capable of grasping God objectively, I do not believe, but precisely because I cannot do this I must believe. If I wish to preserve myself in faith I must constantly be intent upon holding fast the objective uncertainty, so that in the objective uncertainty I am out "upon the seventy thousand fathoms of water," and yet believe.

In the principle that subjectivity, inwardness, is the truth, there is comprehended the Socratic wisdom, whose everlasting merit it was to have become aware of the essential significance of existence, of the fact that the knower is an existing individual. For this reason Socrates was in the truth by virtue of his ignorance, in the highest sense in which this was possible within paganism. To attain to an understanding of this, to comprehend that the misfortune of speculative philosophy is again and again to have forgotten that the knower is an existing individual, is in our objective age difficult enough. "But to have made an advance upon Socrates, without even having understood what he understood, is at any rate not Socratic." Compare the "Moral" of the *Fragments*.[3]

Let us now start from this point and, as was attempted in the *Fragments*, seek a determination of thought which will really carry us further. I have nothing here to do with the question of whether this proposed thought-determination is true or not, since I am merely experimenting; but it must at any rate be clearly manifest that the Socratic thought is understood within the new proposal, so that at least I do not come out behind Socrates.

When subjectivity, inwardness, is the truth, the truth objectively defined becomes a paradox; and the fact that the truth is objectively a paradox shows in its turn that subjectivity is the truth. For the objective situation is repellent; and the expression for the objective repulsion constitutes the tension and the measure of the corresponding inwardness. The paradoxical character of the truth is its objective uncertainty; this uncertainty is an expression for the passionate inwardness, and this passion is precisely the truth. So far the Socratic principle. The eternal and essential truth, the truth which has an essential relationship to an existing individual because it pertains essentially to existence (all other knowledge being from the Socratic point of view accidental, its scope and degree a matter of indifference), is a paradox. But the eternal essential truth is by no means in itself a paradox; it becomes paradoxical by virtue of its relationship to an existing individual. The Socratic ignorance is the expression for the objective uncertainty; the inwardness of the existing individual is the truth. To anticipate here what will be developed later, let me make the following remark: the Socratic ignorance is an analogue to the category of the absurd, only that there is still less of objective certainty in the repellent effect that the absurd exercises. It is certain only that it is absurd, and precisely on that account it incites to an infinitely greater tension in the corresponding inwardness. The Socratic inwardness in existing is an analogue to faith; only that the inwardness of faith, corresponding as it does, not to the repulsion of the Socratic ignorance, but to the repulsion exerted by the absurd, is infinitely more profound.

Socratically the eternal essential truth is by no means in its own nature paradoxical, but only in its relationship to an existing individual. This finds expression in another Socratic proposition, namely, that all knowledge is recollection. This proposition is not for Socrates a cue to the speculative enterprise, and hence he does not follow it up; essentially it becomes a Platonic principle. Here the way swings off: Socrates essentially accentuates existence, while Plato forgets this and loses himself in speculation. Socrates' infinite merit is to have been an *existing* thinker, not a speculative philosopher who forgets what it means to exist. For Socrates therefore the principle that all knowledge is recollection has at the moment of his leave-taking, and as the constantly rejected possibility of engaging in speculation, the following two-fold significance: (1) that the knower is essentially *integer*, and that with respect to the knowledge of the eternal truth he is confronted with no other difficulty than the circumstance that he exists; which difficulty, however, is so essential and decisive for him that it means that existing, the process of transformation to inwardness in and by existing, the deepening in and through existing, is the truth; (2) that existence in time does not have any decisive significance, because the possibility of taking oneself back into eternity through recollection is always there, though this possibility is constantly nullified by the fact that the deepening in existence utilizes the time, not for speculation, but for the transformation to inwardness in existing.

The Subjective Truth

The infinite merit of the Socratic position was precisely to accentuate the fact that the knower is an existing individual, and that the task of existing is his essential task. Making an advance upon Socrates by failing to understand this is quite a mediocre achievement. This Socratic principle we must therefore bear in mind, and then inquire whether the formula may not be so altered as really to make an advance beyond the Socratic position.

Subjectivity, inwardness, has been posited as the truth; can any expression for the truth be found which has a still *higher degree of inwardness*? Aye, there is such an expression, provided the principle that subjectivity or inwardness is the truth begins by positing the opposite principle: that subjectivity is untruth. Let us not be overhasty. Speculative philosophy also says that subjectivity is untruth, but says it exactly conversely, by saying that objectivity is the truth. Speculative philosophy determines subjectivity negatively as tending toward objectivity. This second determination of ours, however, places a hindrance in its own way while proposing to begin, which precisely makes the inwardness far more intensive. Socratically speaking, subjectivity is untruth if it refuses to understand that subjectivity is truth, but, for example, desires to become objective. Here, on the other hand, subjectivity, in beginning upon the task of becoming the truth through a subjectifying process, is in the difficulty that it is already untruth. Thus the labor of the task is thrust backward, backward, that is, in inwardness. So far is it from being the case that the way tends in the direction of objectivity, that the beginning merely lies still deeper in subjectivity.

But the subject cannot be untruth eternally, or eternally be presupposed as having been untruth; it must have been brought to this condition in time, or here become untruth in time. The Socratic paradox consisted in the fact that the eternal truth was related to an existing individual, but now existence has stamped itself upon the existing individual a second time. There has taken place so essential an alteration in him that he cannot now possibly take himself back Socratically into the eternal by way of recollection. To do this is to speculate; to be able to do this, but to reject the possibility by apprehending the task of life as a realization of inwardness in existing, is the Socratic position. But now the difficulty is that what followed Socrates on his way as a rejected possibility has become an impossibility. If engaging in speculation was a dubious merit, even from the point of view of the Socratic, it is now neither more nor less than confusion.

The paradox emerges when the eternal truth and existence are placed in juxtaposition with one another; each time the fact of existence is realized, the paradox becomes more clearly evident. Viewed Socratically the knower was simply an existing individual, but now the existing individual bears the stamp of having been essentially altered by existence.

Let us now call the untruth of the individual *Sin*. Viewed eternally he cannot be in sin, nor can he be eternally presupposed as having been in sin. By coming into existence therefore (for the beginning was that subjectivity is untruth) he becomes a sinner. He is not born as a sinner in the sense that he is presupposed as being a sinner before he is born, but he is born in sin and as a sinner. This we might call *Original Sin*. But if existence has in this manner acquired a power over him, he is prevented from taking himself back into the eternal by way of recollection. If it was paradoxical to posit the eternal truth in relationship to an existing individual, it is now absolutely paradoxical to posit it in relationship to such an individual as we have here defined. But the more difficult it is made for him to take himself out of existence by way of recollection, the more profound is the inwardness that his existence may have in existence; and when it is made impossible for him, when he is held so fast in existence that the back door of recollection is forever closed to him, then his inwardness will be the most profound possible. But let us never forget that the Socratic merit was to stress the fact that the knower is an existing individual; for the more difficult the matter becomes, the greater the temptation to hasten along the easy road of speculation, away from fearful dangers and crucial decisions, to the winning of renown and honors and prosperity, and so forth. If even Socrates understood the dubiety of taking himself speculatively out of existence back into the eternal, although no other difficulty confronted the existing individual except that he existed, and that existing was his essential task: now it is impossible. Forward he must, backward he cannot go.

Subjectivity is the truth. By virtue of the relationship subsisting between the eternal, essential truth and the existing individual, the paradox came into being. Let us now go further, let us suppose that the eternal essential truth is itself a paradox. How does the paradox come into being? By putting the eternal essential truth into juxtaposition with existence. Hence when we posit such a conjunction within the truth itself, the truth becomes a paradox. The eternal truth has come into being in time: this is the paradox. If, in accordance with the determinations just posited, the subject is prevented by sin from taking himself back into the eternal, now he need not trouble himself about this; for now the eternal essential truth is not behind him but in front of him, through its being in existence or having existed, so that, if the individual does not existentially and in existence lay hold of the truth, he will never lay hold of it.

Existence can never be more sharply accentuated than by means of these determinations. The evasion by which speculative philosophy attempts to recollect itself out of existence has been made impossible. Here the only question is about understanding this impossibility; every speculative attempt which insists upon being speculative shows *eo ipso* that it has not been understood. The individual may thrust all this away from him, and take refuge in speculation; but it is impossible first to accept it, and then to wish to revoke it by means of speculation, since it is definitely calculated to prevent speculation.

When the eternal truth is related to an existing individual, it becomes a paradox. The paradox repels in the inwardness of the existing individual, through the objective uncertainty and the corresponding Socratic ignorance. But since the paradox is not in the first instance itself paradoxical (but only in its relationship to the existing individual), it does not repel with a sufficient intensive inwardness. For without risk there is no faith, and the greater the risk, the greater the faith; the more objective security, the less inwardness (for inwardness is precisely subjectivity), and the less objective security, the more profound the possible inwardness. When the paradox is paradoxical in itself, it repels the individual by virtue of its absurdity, and the corresponding passion of inwardness is faith. But subjectivity, inwardness, is the truth; for otherwise we have forgotten what the merit of the Socratic position is. But there can be no stronger expression for inwardness than when the retreat out of existence into the eternal by way of recollection is impossible: when, with truth confronting the individual as a paradox, gripped in the anguish and pain of sin, facing the tremendous risk of the objective insecurity, the individual believes. But without risk no faith, not even the Socratic form of faith, much less the form of which we here speak.

When Socrates believed that there was a God, he held fast to the objective uncertainty with the whole passion of his inwardness, and it is precisely in this contradiction and in this risk, that faith is rooted. Now it is otherwise. Instead of the objective uncertainty, there is here a certainty, namely, that objectively it is absurd; and this absurdity, held fast in the passion of inwardness, is faith. The Socratic ignorance is like a witty jest in comparison with the earnestness of facing the absurd; and the Socratic existential inwardness is like Greek lightmindedness in comparison with the grave strenuosity of faith.

What now is the absurd? The absurd is—that the eternal truth has come into being in time, that God has come into being, has been born, has grown up, and so forth, has come into being precisely like any other individual human being, quite indistinguishable from other individuals. For every assumption of immediate recognizability is preSocratic paganism, and from the Jewish point of view, idolatry; and every determination of what really makes an advance beyond the Socratic must essentially bear the stamp of having a relationship to God's having come into being; for faith *sensu strictissimo*, as was developed in the *Fragments*,[4] refers to becoming. When Socrates believed that there was a God, he saw very well that where the way swings off there is also an objective way of approximation, for example, by the contemplation of nature and human history, and so forth. His merit was precisely to shun this way, where the quantitative siren song enchants the mind and deceives the existing individual.

In relation to the absurd, the objective approximation-process is like the comedy, *Misunderstanding upon Misunderstanding*,[5] which is generally played by *Privatdocents* and speculative philosophers. The absurd is precisely by its objective repulsion the measure of the intensity of faith in inwardness. Suppose a man who wishes to acquire faith; let the comedy begin. He wishes to have faith, but he wishes also to safeguard himself by means of an objective inquiry and its approximation-process. What happens? With the help of the approximation-process the absurd becomes something different: it becomes probable, it becomes increasingly probable, it becomes extremely and emphatically probable. Now he is ready to believe it, and he ventures to claim for himself that he does not believe as shoemakers and tailors and simple folk believe, but only after long deliberation. Now he is ready to believe it; and lo, now it has become precisely impossible to believe it. Anything that is almost probable, or probable, or extremely and emphatically probable, is something he can almost know, or as good as know, or extremely and emphatically almost *know*—but it is impossible to *believe*. For the absurd is the object of faith, and the only object that can be believed.

Notes

[1] The reader will observe that the question here is about essential truth, or about the truth which is essentially related to existence, and that it is pre-

cisely for the sake of clarifying it as inwardness or as subjectivity that this contrast is drawn. (K)

2. In this manner God certainly becomes a postulate, but not in the otiose manner in which this word is commonly understood. It becomes clear rather that the only way in which an existing individual comes into relation with God is when the dialectical contradiction brings his passion to the point of despair, and helps him to embrace God with the "category of despair" (faith). Then the postulate is so far from being arbitrary that it is precisely a life-necessity. It is then not so much that God is a postulate as that the existing individual's postulation of God is a necessity.

3. English edition, p. 93.
4. English edition, pp. 68–70.
5. The title of a comedy by Overskou.

On the Essence of Truth

Martin Heidegger

Our topic is the *essence* of truth. The question regarding the essence of truth is not concerned with whether truth is a truth of practical experience or of economic calculation, the truth of a technical consideration or of political sagacity, or, in particular, a truth of scientific research or of artistic composition, or even the truth of thoughtful reflection or of cultic belief. The question of essence disregards all this and attends to the one thing that in general distinguishes every "truth" as truth.

Yet with this question concerning essence do we not soar too high into the void of generality which deprives all thinking of breath? Does not the extravagance of such questioning bring to light the groundlessness of all philosophy? A radical thinking that turns to what is actual must surely from the first insist bluntly on establishing the actual truth which today gives us a measure and a stand against the confusion of opinions and reckonings. In the face of this actual need what use is the question concerning the essence of truth, this "abstract" question that disregards everything actual? Is not the question of essence the most inessential and superfluous that could be asked?

No one can evade the evident certainty of these considerations. None can lightly neglect their compelling seriousness. But what is it that speaks in these considerations? "Sound" common sense. It harps on the demand for palpable utility and inveighs against knowledge of the essence of beings, which essential knowledge has long been called "philosophy."[1]

Common sense has its own necessity; it asserts its rights with the weapon peculiarly suitable to it, namely, appeal to the "obviousness" of its claims and considerations. However, philosophy can never refute common sense, for the latter is deaf to the language of philosophy. Nor may it even wish to do so, since common sense is blind to what philosophy sets before its essential vision.

Moreover, we ourselves remain within the sensibleness of common sense to the extent that we suppose ourselves to be secure in those multiform "truths" of practical experience and action, of research, composition, and belief. We ourselves intensify that resistance which the "obvious" has to every demand made by what is questionable.

Therefore even if some questioning concerning truth is necessary, what we then demand is an answer to the question as to where we stand today. We want to know what our situation is today. We call for the goal which should be posited for man in and for his history. We want the actual "truth." Well then—truth!

But in calling for the actual "truth" we must already know what truth as such means. Or do we know this only by "feeling" and "in a general way"? But is not such vague "knowing" and our indifference regarding it more desolate than sheer ignorance of the essence of truth?

1. The Usual Concept of Truth

What do we ordinarily understand by "truth"? This elevated yet at the same time worn and almost dulled word "truth" means what makes a true thing true. What is a true thing? We say, for example, "It is a true joy to cooperate in the accomplishment of this task." We mean that it is purely and actually a joy. The true is the actual. Accordingly, we speak of true gold in distinction from false. False gold is not actually what it appears to be. It is merely a "semblance" and thus is not actual. What is not actual is taken to be the opposite of the actual. But what merely seems to be gold is nevertheless something actual. Accordingly, we say more precisely: actual gold is genuine gold. Yet both are "actual," the circulating counterfeit no less than the genuine gold. What is true about genuine gold thus cannot be demonstrated merely by its actuality. The question recurs: what do "genuine" and "true" mean here? Genuine gold is that actual gold the actuality of which is in accordance [*in der Übereinstimmung steht*] with what, always and in advance, we "properly" mean by "gold." Conversely, wherever we suspect false gold, we say: "Here something is not in accord" [*stimmt nicht*]. On the other hand, we say of whatever is "as it should be": "It is in accord." The *matter* is in accord [*Die S a c h e stimmt*].

However, we call true not only an actual joy, genuine gold, and all beings of such kind, but also and above all we call true or false our statements about beings, which can themselves be genuine or not with regard to their kind, which can be thus or otherwise in their actuality. A statement is true if what it means and says is in accordance with the matter about which the statement is made. Here too we say, "It is in accord." Now, though, it is not the matter that is in accord but rather the *proposition*.

The true, whether it be a matter or a proposition, is what accords, the accordant [*das Stimmende*]. Being true and truth here signify accord, and that in a double sense: on the one hand, the consonance [*Einstimmigkeit*] of a matter with what is supposed in advance regarding it and, on the other hand, the accordance of what is meant in the statement with the matter.

This dual character of the accord is brought to light by the traditional definition of truth: *veritas est adaequatio rei et intellectūs*. This can be taken to mean: truth is the correspondence [*Angleichung*] of the matter to knowledge. But it can also be taken as saying: truth is the correspondence of knowledge to the matter. Admittedly, the above definition is usually stated only in the formula *veritas est adaequatio intellectūs ad rem* [truth is the adequation of intellect to thing]. Yet truth so conceived, propositional truth, is possible only on the basis of material truth [*Sachwahrheit*], of *adaequatio rei ad intellectum* [adequation of thing to intellect]. Both concepts of the essence of *veritas* have continually in view a conforming to . . . [*Sichrichten nach* . . .], and hence think truth as *correctness* [*Richtigheit*].

Nonetheless, the one is not the mere inversion of the other. On the contrary, in each case *intellectūs* and *res* are thought differently. In order to recognize this we must trace the usual formula for the ordinary concept of truth back to its most recent (i.e., the medieval) origin. *Veritas* as *adaequatio rei ad intellectum* does not imply the later transcendental conception of Kant—possible only on the basis of the subjectivity of man's essence— that "objects conform to our knowledge." Rather, it implies the Christian theological belief that, with respect to what it is and whether it is, a matter, as created *(ens creatum)*, is only insofar as it corresponds to the idea preconceived in the *intellectus divinus*, i.e., in the mind of God, and thus measures up to the idea (is correct) and in this sense is "true." The *intellectus humanus* too is an *ens creatum*. As a capacity bestowed upon man by God, it must satisfy its *idea*. But the understanding measures up to the idea only by accomplishing in its propositions the correspondence of what is thought to the matter, which in its turn must be in conformity with the *idea*. If all beings are "created," the possibility of the truth of human knowledge is grounded in the fact that matter and proposition measure up to the idea in the same way and therefore are fitted to each other on the basis of the unity of the divine plan of creation. *Veritas* as *adaequatio rei (creandae) ad intellectum (divinum)* guarantees *veritas* as *adaequatio intellectūs (human) ad rem (creatam)*. Throughout, *veritas* essentially implies *convenientia*, the coming of beings themselves, as created, into agreement with the Creator, an "accord" with regard to the way they are determined in the order of creation.

But this order, detached from the notion of creation, can also be represented in a general and indefinite way as a world-order. The theologically conceived order of creation is replaced by the capacity of all objects to be planned by means of a worldly reason [*Weltvernunft*] which supplies the law for itself and thus also claims that its procedure is immediately intelligible (what is considered "logical"). That the essence of propositional truth consists in the correctness of statements needs no further special proof. Even where an effort is made—with a conspicuous lack of success —to explain how correctness is to occur, it is already presupposed as being the essence of truth. Likewise, material truth always signifies the consonance of something at hand with the "rational" concept of its essence. The impression arises that this definition of the essence of truth is independent of the interpretation of the essence of the Being of all beings, which always includes a corresponding interpretation of the essence of man as the bearer and executor of *intellectus*. Thus the formula for the essence of truth (*veritas est adaequatio intellectūs et rei*) comes to have its general validity as something immediately evident to everyone. Under the domination of the obviousness which this concept of truth seems to have but which is hardly attended to as regards its essential grounds, it is considered equally obvious that truth has an opposite, and that there is untruth. The untruth of the proposition (incorrectness) is the non-accordance of the statement with the matter. The untruth of the matter (non-genuineness) signifies non-agreement of a being with its essence. In each case untruth is conceived as a non-accord. The latter falls outside the essence of truth. Therefore when it is a question of comprehending the pure essence of truth, untruth, as such an opposite of truth, can be put aside.

But then is there any further need at all for a special unveiling of the essence of truth? Is not the pure essence of truth already adequately represented in the generally accepted concept, which is upset by no theory and is secured by its obviousness? Moreover, if we take the tracing back of propositional truth to material truth to be what in the first instance it shows itself to be, namely a theological explanation, and if we then keep the philosophical definition completely pure of all admixture of theology and limit the concept of truth to propositional truth, then we encounter an old— though not the oldest—tradition of thinking, according to which truth is the accordance (*homoiōsis*) of a statement (*logos*) with a matter (*pragma*). What is it about statements that here remains still worthy of question—granted that we know what is meant by accordance of a statement with the matter? Do we know that?

2. The Inner Possibility of Accordance

We speak of accordance in various senses. We say, for example, considering two five-mark coins lying on the table: they are in accordance with one another. They come into accord in the oneness of their outward appearance. Hence they have the latter in common, and thus they are in this regard alike. Furthermore, we speak of accordance whenever, for example, we state regarding one of the five-mark coins: this coin is round. Here the statement is in accordance with the thing. Now the relation obtains, not between thing and thing, but rather between a statement and a thing. But wherein are the thing and the statement supposed to be in accordance, considering that the *relata* are manifestly different in their outward appearance? The coin is made of metal. The statement is not material at all. The coin is round. The statement has nothing at all spatial about it. With the coin something can be purchased. The statement about it is never a means of payment. But in spite of all their dissimilarity the above statement, as true, is in accordance with the coin. And according to the usual concept of truth this accord is supposed to be a correspondence. How can what is completely dissimilar, the statement, correspond to the coin? It would have to become the coin and in this way relinquish itself entirely. The statement never succeeds in doing that. The moment it did, it would no longer be able as a statement to be in accordance with the thing. In the correspondence the statement must remain—indeed even first become—what it is. In what does its essence, so thoroughly different from every thing, consist? How is the statement able to correspond to something else, the thing, precisely by persisting in its own essence?

Correspondence here cannot signify a thing-like approximation between dissimilar kinds of things. The essence of the correspondence is determined rather by the kind of relation that obtains between the statement and the thing. As long as this "relation" remains undetermined and is not grounded in its essence, all dispute over the possibility and impossibility, over the nature and degree, of the correspondence loses its way in a void. But the statement regarding the coin relates "itself" to this thing in that it presents [*vor-stellt*] it and says of the presented how, according to the particular perspective that guides it, it is disposed. What is stated by the presentative statement is said of the presented thing in just such manner *as* that thing, as presented, is. The "such-as" has to do with the presenting and its presented. Disregarding all "psychological" preconceptions as well as those of any "theory of consciousness," to present here means to let the thing stand opposed as object. As thus placed, what stands opposed must traverse an open field of opposedness [*Entgegen*] and nevertheless must maintain its stand as a thing and show itself as something withstanding [*ein Ständiges*]. This appearing of the thing in traversing a field of opposedness takes place within an open region, the openness of which is not first created by the presenting but rather is only entered into and taken over as a domain of relatedness. The relation of the presentative statement to the thing is the accomplishment of that *bearing* [*Verhältnis*] which originally and always comes to prevail as a comportment [*Verhalten*]. But all comportment is distinguished by the fact that, standing in the open region, it adheres to something opened up *as such*.[2] What is thus opened up, solely in this strict sense, was experienced early in Western thinking as "what is present" and for a long time has been named "being."

Comportment stands open to beings. Every open relatedness is a comportment. Man's open stance varies depending on the kind of beings and the way of comportment. All working and achieving, all action and calculation, keep within an open region within which beings, with regard to what they are and how they are, can properly take their stand and become capable of being said. This can occur only if beings present themselves along with the presentative statement so that the latter subordinates itself to the directive that it speak of beings *such-as* they are. In following such a directive the statement conforms to beings. Speech that directs itself accordingly is correct (true). What is thus said is the correct (the true).

A statement is invested with its correctness by the openness of comportment; for only through the latter can what is opened up really become the standard for the presentative correspondence. Open comportment must let itself be assigned this standard. This means that it must take over a pregiven standard for all presenting. This belongs to the openness of comportment. But if the correctness (truth) of statements becomes possible only through this openness of comportment, then what first makes correctness possible must with more original right be taken as the essence of truth.

Thus the traditional assignment of truth exclusively to statements as the sole essential locus of truth falls away. Truth does not originally reside in the proposition. But at the same time the question arises of the ground of the inner possibility of the open comportment which pregives a standard, which possibility alone lends to propositional correctness the appearance of fulfilling the essence of truth at all.

3. The Ground of the Possibility of Correctness

Whence does the presentative statement receive the directive to conform to the object and to accord by way of correctness? Why is this accord involved in determining the essence of truth? How can something like the accomplishment of a pregiven directedness occur? And how can the initiation into an accord occur? Only if this pregiving has already entered freely into an open region for something opened up which prevails there and which binds every presenting. To free oneself for a binding directedness is possible only by *being free* for what is opened up in an open region. Such being free points to the heretofore uncomprehended essence of freedom. The openness of comportment as the inner condition of the possibility of correctness is grounded in freedom. *The essence of truth is freedom.*

But does not this proposition regarding the essence of correctness substitute one obvious item for another? In order to be able to carry out any act, and therefore one of presentative stating and even of according or not according with a "truth," the actor must of course be free. However, the proposition in question does not really mean that an unconstrained act belongs to the execution of the statement, to its pronouncement and reception; rather, the proposition says that freedom is the *essence* of truth itself. In this connection "essence" is understood as the ground of the inner possibility of what is initially and generally admitted as known. Nevertheless, in the concept of freedom we do not think truth, and certainly not at all its essence. The proposition that the essence of truth (correctness of statements) is freedom must consequently seem strange.

To place the essence of truth in freedom—doesn't this mean to submit truth to human caprice? Can truth be any more radically undermined than by being surrendered to the arbitrariness of this "wavering reed"? What forced itself upon sound judgment again and again in the previous discussion now all the more clearly comes to light: truth is here driven back to the subjectivity of the human subject. Even if an objectivity is also accessible to this subject, still such objectivity remains along with subjectivity something human and at man's disposal.

Certainly deceit and dissimulation, lies and deception, illusion and semblance—in short, all kinds of untruth—are ascribed to man. But of course untruth is also the opposite of truth. For this reason, as the non-essence of truth, it is appropriately excluded from the sphere of the question concerning the pure essence of truth. This human origin of untruth indeed only serves to confirm by contrast the essence of truth "in itself" as holding sway "beyond" man. Metaphysics regards such truth as the imperishable and eternal, which can never be founded on the transitoriness and fragility that belong to man's essence. How then can the essence of truth still have its subsistence and its ground in human freedom?

Resistance to the proposition that the essence of truth is freedom is based on preconceptions, the most obstinate of which is that freedom is a property of man. The essence of freedom neither needs nor allows any further questioning. Everyone knows what man is.

4. The Essence of Freedom

However, indication of the essential connection between truth as correctness and freedom uproots those preconceptions—granted of course that we are prepared for a transformation of thinking. Consideration of the essential connection between truth and freedom leads us to pursue the question of the essence of man in a regard which assures us an experience of a concealed essential ground of man (of Dasein), and in such a manner that the experience transposes us in advance into the originally essential domain of truth. But here it becomes evident also that freedom is the ground of the inner possibility of correctness only because it receives its own essence from the more original essence of uniquely essential truth. Freedom was first determined as freedom for what is opened up in an open region. How is this essence of freedom to be thought? That which is opened up, that to which a presentative statement as correct corresponds, are beings opened up in an open comportment. Freedom for what is opened up in an open region lets beings be the beings they are. Freedom now reveals itself as letting beings be.

Ordinarily we speak of letting be whenever, for example, we forgo some enterprise that has been planned. "We let something be" means we do not touch it again, we have nothing more to do with it. To let something be has here the negative sense of letting it alone, of renouncing it, of indifference and even neglect.

However, the phrase required now—to let beings be—does not refer to neglect and indifference but rather the opposite. To let be is to engage oneself with beings. On the other hand, to be sure, this is not to be understood only as the mere management, preservation, tending, and planning of the beings in each case encountered or sought out. To let be—that is, to let beings be as the beings which they are—means to engage oneself with the open region and its openness into which every being comes to stand, bringing that openness, as it were, along with itself. Western thinking in its beginning conceived this open region as *ta alēthea*, the unconcealed. If we translate *alētheia* as "unconcealment" rather than "truth," this translation is not merely more literal; it contains the directive to rethink the ordinary concept of truth in the sense of the correctness of statements and to think it back to that still uncomprehended disclosedness and disclosure of beings. To engage oneself with the disclosedness of beings is not to lose oneself in them; rather, such engagement withdraws in the face of beings in order that they might reveal themselves with respect to what and how they are and in order that presentative correspondence might take its standard from them. As this letting-be it exposes itself to beings as such and transposes all comportment into the open region. Letting-be, i.e., freedom, is intrinsically exposing, ek-sistent.[3] Considered in regard to the essence of truth, the essence of freedom manifests itself as exposure to the disclosedness of beings.

Freedom is not merely what common sense is content to let pass under this name: the caprice, turning up occasionally in our choosing, of inclining in this or that direction. Freedom is not mere absence of constraint with respect to what we can or cannot do. Nor is it on the other hand mere readiness for what is required and necessary (and so somehow a being). Prior to all this ("negative" and "positive" freedom), freedom is engagement in the disclosure of beings as such. Disclosedness itself is conserved in ek-sistent engagement, through which the openness of the open region, i.e., the "there" ["*Da*"], is what it is.

In Da-sein the essential ground, long ungrounded, on the basis of which man is able to ek-sist, is preserved for him. Here "existence" does not mean *existentia* in the sense of occurring or being at hand. Nor on the other hand does it mean, in an "existentiell" fashion, man's moral endeavor in behalf of his "self," based on his psychophysical constitution. Ek-sistence, rooted in truth as freedom, is exposure to the disclosedness of beings as such. Still uncomprehended, indeed, not even in need of an essential grounding, the ek-sistence of historical man begins at that moment when the first thinker takes a questioning stand with regard to the unconcealment of beings by asking: what are beings? In this question unconcealment is experienced for the first time. Being as a whole reveals itself as *physis*, "nature," which here does not yet mean a particular sphere of beings but rather beings as such as a whole, specifically in the sense of emerging presence [*aufgehendes Anwesen*]. History begins only when beings themselves are expressly drawn up into their unconcealment and conserved in it, only when this conservation is conceived on the basis of questioning regarding beings as such. The primordial disclosure of being as a whole, the question concerning beings as such, and the beginning of Western history are the same; they occur together in a "time" which, itself unmeasurable, first opens up the open region for every measure.

But if ek-sistent Da-sein, which lets beings be, sets man free for his "freedom" by first offering to his choice something possible (a being) and by imposing on him something necessary (a being), human caprice does not then have freedom at its disposal. Man does not "possess" freedom as a property. At best, the converse holds: freedom, ek-sistent, disclosive Da-sein, possesses man—so originally that only *it* secures for humanity that distinctive relatedness to being as a whole as such which first founds all history. Only ek-sistent man is historical. "Nature" has no history.

Freedom, understood as letting beings be, is the fulfillment and consummation of the essence of truth in the sense of the disclosure of beings. "Truth" is not a feature of correct propositions which are asserted of an "object" by a human "subject" and then "are valid" somewhere, in what sphere we know not; rather, truth is disclosure of beings through which an openness essentially unfolds [*west*]. All human comportment and bearing are exposed in its open region. Therefore man *is* in the manner of ek-sistence.

Because every mode of human comportment is in its own way open and plies itself to that toward which it comports itself, the restraint of letting-be, i.e., freedom, must have granted it its endowment of that inner directive for correspondence of presentation to beings. That man ek-sists now means that for historical humanity the history of its essential possibilities is conserved in the disclosure of beings as a whole. The rare and the simple decisions of history arise from the way the original essence of truth essentially unfolds.

However, because truth is in essence freedom, historical man can, in letting beings be, also *not* let beings be the beings which they are and as they are. Then beings are covered up and distorted. Semblance comes to power. In it the non-essence of truth comes to the fore. However, because ek-sistent freedom as the essence of truth is not a property of man; because on the contrary man ek-sists and so becomes capable of history only as the property of this freedom; the non-essence of truth cannot first arise subsequently from mere human incapacity and negligence. Rather, untruth must derive from the essence of truth. Only because truth and untruth are, *in essence, not* irrelevant to one another but rather belong together is it possible for a true proposition to enter into pointed opposition to the corresponding untrue proposition. The question concerning the essence of truth thus first reaches the original domain of what is at issue when, on the basis of a prior glimpse of the full essence of truth, it has included a consideration of untruth in its unveiling of that essence. Discussion of the non-essence of truth is not the subsequent filling of a gap but rather the decisive step toward an adequate posing of the *question* concerning the essence of truth. Yet how are we to comprehend the non-essence in the essence of truth? If the essence of truth is not exhausted by the correctness of statements, then neither can untruth be equated with the incorrectness of judgments.

5. The Essence of Truth

The essence of truth reveals itself as freedom. The latter is ek-sistent, disclosive letting beings be. Every mode of open comportment flourishes in letting beings be and in each case is a comportment to this or that being. As engagement in the disclosure of being as a whole as such, freedom has already attuned all comportment to being as a whole. However, being attuned (attunement)[4] can never be understood as "experience" and "feeling," because it is thereby simply deprived of its essence. For here it is interpreted on the basis of something ("life" and "soul") that can maintain the semblance of the title of essence only as long as it bears in itself the distortion and misinterpretation of being attuned. Being attuned, i.e., ek-sistent exposedness to beings as a whole, can be "experienced" and "felt" only because the "man who experiences," without being aware of the essence of the attunement, is always engaged in being attuned in a way that discloses beings as a whole. Every mode of historical man's comportment—whether accentuated or not, whether understood or not—is attuned and by this attunement is drawn up into beings as a whole. The openedness of being as a whole does not coincide with the sum of all immediately familiar beings. On the contrary: where beings are not very familiar to man and are scarcely and only roughly known by science, the openedness of beings as a whole can prevail more essentially than it can where the familiar and wellknown has become boundless, and nothing is any longer able to withstand the business of knowing, since technical mastery over things bears itself without limit. Precisely in the leveling and planing of this omniscience, this mere knowing, the openedness of beings gets flattened out into the apparent nothingness of what is no longer even a matter of indifference but rather is simply forgotten.

Letting beings be, which is an attuning, a bringing into accord, prevails throughout and anticipates all the open comportment that flourishes in it. Man's comportment is brought into definite accord throughout by the openedness of being as a whole. However, from the point of view of everyday calculations and preoccupations this "as a whole" appears to be incalculable and incomprehensible. It cannot be understood on the basis of the beings opened up in any given case, whether they belong to nature or to history. Although it ceaselessly brings everything into definite accord, still it remains indefinite, indeterminable; it then coincides for the most part with what is most fleeting and most unconsidered. However, what brings into accord is not nothing but rather a concealing of beings as a whole. Precisely because letting be always lets beings be in a particular comportment which relates to them and thus discloses them, it conceals beings as a whole. Letting-be is intrinsically at the same time a concealing. In the ek-sistent freedom of Da-sein a concealing of being as a whole comes to pass [*ereignet sich*]. Here there *is* concealment.

6. Untruth as Concealing

Concealment deprives *alētheia* of disclosure yet does not render it *sterēsis* (privation); rather, concealment preserves what is most proper to *alētheia* as its own. Considered with respect to truth as disclosedness, concealment is then undisclosedness and accordingly the untruth that is most proper to the essence of truth. The concealment of beings as a whole does not first show up subsequently as a consequence of the fact that knowledge of beings is always fragmentary. The concealment of beings as a whole, untruth proper, is older than every openedness of this or that being. It is also older than letting-be itself which in disclosing already holds concealed and comports itself toward concealing. What conserves letting-be in this relatedness to concealing? Nothing less than the concealing of what is concealed as a whole, of beings as such, i.e., the mystery; not a particular mystery regarding this or that, but rather the one mystery—that, in general, mystery (the concealing of what is concealed) as such holds sway throughout man's Da-sein.

In letting beings as a whole be, which discloses and at the same time conceals, it happens that concealing appears as what is first of all concealed. Insofar as it ek-sists, Da-sein conserves the first and broadest undisclosedness, untruth proper. The proper non-essence of truth is the mystery. Here non-essence does not yet have the sense of inferiority to essence in the sense of what is general (*koinon, genos*), its *possibilitas* and the ground of its possibility. Non-essence is here what in such a sense would be a pre-essential essence. But "non-essence" means at first and for the most part the deformation of that already inferior essence. Indeed, in each of these significations the non-essence remains always in its own way essential to the essence and never becomes inessential in the sense of irrelevant. But to speak of non-essence and untruth in this manner goes very much against the grain of ordinary opinion and looks like a dragging up of forcibly contrived *paradoxa*. Because it is diffcult to eliminate this impression, such a way of speaking, paradoxical only for ordinary *doxa* (opinion), is to be renounced. But surely for those who know about such matters the "non-" of the primordial non-essence of truth, as untruth, points to the still unexperienced domain of the truth of Being (not merely of beings).

As letting beings be, freedom is intrinsically the resolutely open bearing that does not close up in itself.[5] All comportment is grounded in this bearing and receives from it directedness toward beings and disclosure of them. Nevertheless, this bearing toward concealing conceals itself in the process, letting a forgottenness of the mystery take precedence and disappearing in it. Certainly man takes his bearings [*verhält sich*] constantly in his comportment toward beings; but for the most part he acquiesces in this or that being and its particular openedness. Man clings to what is readily available and controllable even where ultimate matters are concerned. And if he sets out to extend, change, newly assimilate, or secure the openedness of the beings pertaining to the most various domains of his activity and interest, then he still takes his directives from the sphere of readily available intentions and needs.

However, to reside in what is readily available is intrinsically not to let the concealing of what is concealed hold sway. Certainly among readily familiar things there are also some that are puzzling, unexplained, undecided, questionable. But these self-certain questions are merely transitional, intermediate points in our movement within the readily familiar and thus not essential. Wherever the concealment of beings as a whole is conceded only as a limit that occasionally announces itself, concealing as a fundamental occurrence has sunk into forgottenness.

But the forgotten mystery of Dasein is not eliminated by the forgottenness; rather, the forgottenness bestows on the apparent disappearance of what is forgotten a peculiar presence [*Gegenwart*]. By disavowing itself in and for forgottenness, the mystery leaves historical man in the sphere of what is readily available to him, leaves him to his own resources. Thus left, humanity replenishes its "world" on the basis of the latest needs and aims, and fills out that world by means of proposing and planning. From these man then takes his standards, forgetting being as a whole. He persists in them and continually supplies himself with new standards, yet without considering either the ground for taking up standards or the essence of what gives the standard. In spite of his advance to new standards and goals, man goes wrong as regards the essential genuineness of his standards. He is all the more mistaken the more exclusively he takes himself, as subject, to be the standard for all beings. The inordinate forgetfulness of humanity persists in securing itself by means of what is readily available and always accessible. This persistence has its unwitting support in that *bearing* by which Dasein not only ek-sists but also at the same time *in-sists*, i.e., holds fast to what is offered by beings, as if they were open of and in themselves.

As ek-sistent, Dasein is insistent. Even in insistent existence the mystery holds sway, but as the forgotten and hence "inessential" essence of truth.

7. Untruth as Errancy

As insistent, man is turned toward the most readily available beings. But he insists only by being already ek-sistent, since, after all, he takes beings as his standard. However, in taking its standard, humanity is turned away from the mystery. The insistent turning toward what is readily available and the ek-sistent turning away from the mystery belong together. They are one and the same. Yet turning toward and away from is based on a turning to and fro proper to Dasein. Man's flight from the mystery toward what is readily available, onward from one current thing to the next, passing the mystery by—this is *erring*.[6]

Man errs. Man does not merely stray into errancy. He is always astray in errancy, because as ek-sistent he in-sists and so already is caught in errancy. The errancy through which man strays is not something which, as it were, extends alongside man like a ditch into which he occasionally stumbles; rather errancy belongs to the inner constitution of the Da-sein into which historical man is admitted. Errancy is the free space for that turning in which insistent ek-sistence adroitly forgets and mistakes itself constantly anew. The concealing of the concealed being as a whole holds sway in that disclosure of specific beings, which, as forgottenness of concealment, becomes errancy.

Errancy is the essential counter-essence to the primordial essence of truth. Errancy opens itself up as the open region for every opposite to essential truth. Errancy is the open site for and ground of *error*. Error is not just an isolated mistake but rather the realm (the domain) of the history of those entanglements in which an kinds of erring get interwoven.

In conformity with its openness and its relatedness to beings as a whole, every mode of comportment has its mode of erring. Error extends from the most ordinary wasting of time, making a mistake, and miscalculating, to going astray and venturing too far in one's essential attitudes and decisions. However, what is ordinarily and even according to the teachings of philosophy recognized as error, incorrectness of judgments and falsity of knowledge, is only one mode of erring and, moreover, the most superficial one. The errancy in which any given segment of historical humanity must proceed for its course to be errant is essentially connected with the openness of Dasein. By leading him astray, errancy dominates man through and through. But, as leading astray, errancy at the same time contributes to a possibility that man is capable of drawing up from his ek-sistence—the possibility that, by experiencing errancy itself and by not mistaking the mystery of Da-sein, he *not* let himself be led astray.

Because man's in-sistent ek-sistence proceeds in errancy, and because errancy as leading astray always oppresses in some manner or other and is formidable on the basis of this oppression of the mystery, specifically as something forgotten, in the ek-sistence of his Dasein man is *especially* subjected to the rule of the mystery and the oppression of errancy. He is in the *needful condition of being constrained* by the one and the other. The full essence of truth, including its most proper non-essence, keeps Dasein in need by this perpetual turning to and fro. Dasein is a turning into need. From man's Dasein and from it alone arises the disclosure of necessity and, as a result, the possibility of being transposed into what is inevitable.

The disclosure of beings as such is simultaneously and intrinsically the concealing of being as a whole. In the simultaneity of disclosure and concealing errancy holds sway. Errancy and the concealing of what is concealed belong to the primordial essence of truth. Freedom, conceived on the basis of the in-sistent ek-sistence of Dasein, is the essence of truth (in the sense of the correctness of presenting) only because freedom itself originates from the primordial essence of truth, the rule of the mystery in errancy. Letting beings be takes its course in open comportment. However, letting beings as such be as a whole occurs in a way befitting its essence only when from time to time it gets taken up in its primordial essence. Then resolute openness toward the mystery [*Ent-schlossenheit zum Geheimnis*] is under way into errancy as such. Then the question of the essence of truth gets asked more originally. Then the ground of the intertwining of the essence of truth with the truth of essence reveals itself. The glimpse into the mystery out of errancy is a question—in the sense of that unique question of what being as such is as a whole. This questioning thinks the question of the *Being* of beings, a question that is essentially misleading and thus in its manifold meaning is still not mastered. The thinking of Being, from which such questioning primordially originates, has since Plato been understood as "philosophy" and later received the title "metaphysics."

8. Philosophy and the Question of Truth

In the thinking of Being the liberation of man for ek-sistence, the liberation that grounds history, is put into words. These are not just the "expression" of an opinion but are always already the ably conserved articulation of the truth of being as a whole. How many have ears for these words matters not. Who those are that can hear them determines man's standpoint in history. However, in the same period in which the beginning of philosophy takes place, the *marked* domination of common sense (sophistry) also begins.

Sophistry appeals to the unquestionable character of the beings that are opened up and interprets all thoughtful questioning as an attack on, an unfortunate irritation of, common sense.

However, what philosophy is according to the estimation of common sense, which is quite justified in its own domain, does not touch on the essence of philosophy, which can be determined only on the basis of relatedness to the original truth of being as such as a whole. But because the full essence of truth contains the non-essence and above all holds sway as concealing, philosophy as a questioning into this truth is intrinsically discordant. Philosophical thinking is gentle releasement that does not renounce the concealment of being as a whole. Philosophical thinking is especially the stern and resolute openness that does not disrupt the concealing but entreats its unbroken essence into the open region of understanding and thus into its own truth.

In the gentle sternness and stern gentleness with which it lets being as such be as a whole, philosophy becomes a questioning which does not cling solely to beings yet which also can allow no externally imposed decree. Kant presaged this innermost need that thinking has. For he says of philosophy:

> Here philosophy is seen in fact to be placed in a precarious position which is supposed to be stable—although neither in heaven nor on earth is there anything on which it depends or on which it is based. It is here that it has to prove its integrity as the keeper of its laws [*Selbsthalterin ihrer Gesetze*], not as the mouthpiece of laws secretly communicated to it by some implanted sense or by who knows what tutelary nature. (*Grundlegung zur Metaphysik der Sitten. Werke,* Akademieausgabe IV, 425.)

With this essential interpretation of philosophy, Kant, whose work introduces the final turning of Western metaphysics, envisions a domain which to be sure he could understand only on the basis of his fundamental metaphysical position, founded on subjectivity, and which he had to understand as the keeping of its laws. This essential view of the determination of philosophy nevertheless goes far enough to renounce every subjugation of philosophical thinking, the most destitute kind of which lets philosophy still be of value as an "expression" of "culture" (Spengler) and as an ornament of productive mankind.

However, whether philosophy as "keeper of its laws" fulfills its primordially decisive essence, or whether it is not itself first of all kept and appointed to its task as keeper by the truth of that to which its laws pertain—this depends on the primordiality with which the original essence of truth becomes essential for thoughtful questioning.

The present undertaking takes the question of the essence of truth beyond the confines of the ordinary definition provided in the usual concept of essence and helps us to consider whether the question of the essence of truth must not be, at the same time and even first of all, the question concerning the truth of essence. But in the concept of "essence" philosophy thinks Being. In tracing the inner possibility of the correctness of statements back to the ek-sistent freedom of letting-be as its "ground," likewise in pointing to the essential commencement of this ground in concealing and in errancy, we want to show that the essence of truth is not the empty "generality" of an "abstract" universality but rather that which, self-concealing, is unique in the unremitting history of the disclosure of the "meaning" of what we call Being—what we for a long time have been accustomed to considering only as being as a whole.

9. Note

The question of the essence of truth arises from the question of the truth of essence. In the former question essence is understood initially in the sense of whatness (*quidditas*) or material content (*realitas*), whereas truth is understood as a characteristic of knowledge. In the question of the truth of essence, essence is understood verbally; in this word, remaining still within metaphysical presentation, Being is thought as the difference that holds sway between Being and beings. Truth signifies sheltering that lightens [*lichtendes Bergen*] as the basic characteristic of Being. The question of the essence of truth finds its answer in the proposition *the essence of truth is the truth of essence*. After our explanation it can easily be seen that the proposition does not merely reverse the word order so as to conjure the specter of paradox. The subject of the proposition—if this unfortunate grammatical category may still be used at all—is the truth of essence. Sheltering that lightens is—i.e., lets essentially unfold—accordance between knowledge and beings. The proposition is not dialectical. It is no proposition at all in the sense of a statement. The answer to the question of the essence of truth is the saying of a turning [*die Sage einer Kehre*] within the history of Being. Because sheltering that lightens belongs to it, Being appears primordially in the light of concealing withdrawal. The name of this lighting [*Lichtung*] is *alētheia*.

Already in the original project the lecture "On the Essence of Truth" was to have been completed by a second lecture "On the Truth of Essence." The latter failed for reasons that are now indicated in the "Letter on Humanism" [Reading V, below].

The decisive question (in *Being and Time*, 1927) of the meaning, i.e., of the project-domain (cf. p. 151), i.e., of the openness, i.e., of the truth of Being and not merely of beings, remains intentionally undeveloped. Our thinking apparently remains on the path of metaphysics. Nevertheless, in its decisive steps, which lead from truth as correctness to ek-sistent freedom, and from the latter to truth as concealing and as errancy, it accomplishes a change in the questioning that belongs to the overcoming of metaphysics. The thinking attempted in the lecture comes to fulfillment in the essential experience that a nearness to the truth of Being is first prepared for historical man on the basis of the Da-sein into which man can enter. Every kind of anthropology and all subjectivity of man as subject is not merely left behind—as it was already in *Being and Time*—and the truth of Being sought as the ground of a transformed historical position; rather, the movement of the lecture is such that it sets out to think from this other ground (Dasein). The course of the questioning is intrinsically the way of a thinking which, instead of furnishing representations and concepts, experiences and tries itself as a transformation of its relatedness to Being.

Notes

[1] Throughout the translation *das Seiende* is rendered as "being" or "beings," *ein Seiendes* as "a being," *Sein* as "Being," *das Seiende im Ganzen* as either "being as a whole" or "beings as a whole" depending on the context—Tr.

[2] The text reads, "ein Offenbares *als ein solches*." In ordinary German *offenbar* means "evident," "manifest." However, the context which it has here through its link with "open region" (*das Offene*), "open stance" (*Offenständigkeit*), and "openness" (*Offenheit*) already suggests the richer sense that the word has for Heidegger: that of something's being so opened up as to reveal itself, to be manifest (as, for example, a flower in bloom), in contrast to something's being so closed or sealed up within itself that it conceals itself.—Tr.

[3] This variant of the word *Existenz* indicates the ecstatic character of freedom, its standing outside itself.—Tr.

[4] The text reads, "*Die Gestimmtheit (Stimmung)....*" *Stimmung* refers not only to the kind of attunement which a musical instrument receives by being tuned but also to the kind of attunement that constitutes a mood or a disposition of Dasein. The important etymological connection between *Stimmung* and the various formations based on *stimmen* (to accord) is not retained in the translation.—Tr.

[5] "Resolutely open bearing" seeks to translate *das entschlossene Verhältnis*. *Entschlossen* is usually rendered as "resolute," but such a translation fails to retain the word's structural relation to *verschlossen*, "closed" or "shut up." Significantly, this connection is what makes it possible for Heidegger to transform the sense of the word: he takes the prefix as a privation rather than as indicating establishment of the condition designated by the word to which it is affixed. Thus, as the text here makes quite clear, *entschlossen* signifies just the opposite of that kind of "resolve" in which one makes up his mind in

such fashion as to close off all other possibilities: it is rather a kind of keeping *un-closed*.—TR.

6 "To err" may translate *irren* only if it is understood in its root sense derived from the Latin *errare*, "to wander from the right way," and only secondarily in the sense "to fall into error."—TR.

from Cultural Gaps: Why Do We Misunderstand?

Isamu Nagami

A well-known Japanese psychologist, Takeo Doi, expressed his frustration and puzzlement with American ways of life in his book, *The Anatomy of Dependence*:

> From time to time I began to feel an awkwardness arising from the difference between my ways of thinking and feeling and those of my hosts (that is, Americans). For example, not long after my arrival in America I visited the house of someone to whom I had been introduced by a Japanese acquaintance, and was talking to him when he asked me, "Are you hungry? We have some ice cream if you'd like it. " As I remember, I was rather hungry, but finding myself asked point-blank if I was hungry by someone whom I was visiting for the first time, I could not bring myself to admit it, and ended by denying the suggestion. I probably cherished a mild hope that he would press me again; but my host, disappointingly, said "I see " with no further ado, leaving me regretting that I had not replied more honestly. And I found myself thinking that a Japanese would almost never ask a stranger unceremoniously if he was hungry, but would produce something to give him without asking.

Those who have lived in foreign countries have experienced more or less the sort of cultural shock Doi expressed so well. These kinds of intercultural experiences have led many thinkers to probe into the core elements of culture for comparative study. In Japan, for example, we find many popular writers who explain the difference between Japanese culture and that of the Western nations including the U.S.A. in terms of group orientation and individual identity. The thesis for this type of argument is that while Japanese behavior in general can be explained by orientation within the group, Americans behave on the basis of individual freedom. There is no doubt that this reveals a meaningful comparison between the two cultures to those who have journalistic interests. But if we start by inquiring into various modalities of the experiential world of daily life in culture, we find we cannot follow the above approach primarily for three reasons. 1) Those who accept the group versus individual thesis tend to explain every cultural phenomenon in terms of this and as a result they conceal many other rich possibilities which every culture may contain. 2) Certain features are common to all social worlds. In this respect every culture can share a kind of symbolic common denominator through which we can compare differences. Yet, this approach of contrast ignores the universality in human existence. 3) The very fact that people understand and describe different cultures reveals a kind of cultural ethos in which their thinking is embedded. That is to say, their ways of thinking are inescapably and necessarily cultural. This thought process is not self-critically oriented in the sense that it is not able to show its historico-cultural character and, therefore, tends to be ideological.

The most striking characteristic of these approaches is based on their inability to provide any critical perspective and at the same time on a sort of false legitimacy in our actual human life. Thus it is crucial for us to find another way to understand culture in its most sensible manners. In this respect, we would propose a method of phenomenological reflection, for phenomenology can reveal the various dimensions of human life which, I believe, symbolize culture and thereby can help us to overcome the aforementioned difficulties.

• • •

Intersubjectivity, Language and Taken-for-Grantedness

When, for instance a boy and his mother see a cedar, she is most likely to call it a tree rather than a cedar. After a while if he happens to see an oak tree and asks her "What's that?" she will call it a tree. At that time he might be very confused with that term simply because there is a difference between a cedar and an oak and yet they partake of the same name, tree. But gradually he realizes that the word or sound "tree" implies a certain group of characteristics which belong to the same category. It is clear that a word "tree" signifies an abstract expression in the sense that it represents certain characteristics and ignores others such as those that belong to the category "flower." In this respect, concreteness in common sense is not concrete in reality, but rather abstract. The reason why people mistake abstract expressions for concrete reality is due to the fact that they unconsciously accept the expressions as taken-for-granted, rooted in a specific temporal world. Hence some concrete meanings in one culture are not concrete but very enigmatic, non-concrete expressions in another. In English, people distinguish tree from parts of tree which are used for architectural and other purposes, that is "wood." But in Japanese we don't do so. We express the idea of tree and wood both with one term, *Ki*. Yet, the dictionary usually describes *Ki* as having the same meaning as tree. Languages also differ in their built-in grammatical signals, that is in semantics, syntax and phonetics. In English people are very conscious of specifying the number of people involved in what they are discussing. But in Japanese the contrary is often true. Here we can see that the very nature of language through which we comprehend the world and understand ourselves inevitably involves us in the cultural context of language. Hence languages differ immensely from one another not only in pronunciation, vocabulary and grammar, but also in the way they recognize certain things and ignore others, thereby reflecting the society and culture they serve. Experience and language are reciprocal in the sense that human beings can experience outside reality only in terms of the meanings disclosed by language. Human beings are thrown into language worlds in which they learn to identify things as well as to understand reality. In this sense it is obvious that our ways of understanding and interpreting reality are already conditioned by the socially given knowledge.

If we accept that our knowledge is socially given, it seems that we are caught in the relativistic position of suggesting that there is no such thing as objectivity. Hence, we may ask a further question: How can we affirm something as an objective entity on which everybody can agree? In this question we again need to reflect on what I will call the intersubjective world which language as well as our everyday life thinking always presupposes. Situationally we unconsciously put ourselves as the center of spatio-temporal coordinates in the world. This means that I usually see the position I occupy as "here," distinguished from "there" taken by a fellow human being. Yet we can interchange our positions freely, as if we can place ourselves in the other's situation. A saying such as "Do unto others as you would have them do unto you," implies this interchangeability. This interchangeability is possible because there is an intersubjectively acknowledged spatio-temporal world in which both s/he and I are embedded and therefore can exchange, as well as share, our positions in essentially the same fashion with essentially the same possibilities and consequences. The concept of intersubjectivity signifies this intersubjectively acknowledged spatio-temporal world. Each socio-cultural environment presupposes an intersubjective world which historically develops various conceptions of the world as symbolized in language. Those who have been living in American society share various typicalities as a horizon of familiarity and of unquestioned pre-experience. Through the use of these we can converse with one another and understand the objects of the world as the reality of the taken-for-granted. The meanings of words such as tree or flower are simply taken for granted and therefore are self-evident. In other words, we are speaking, acting and understanding within an intersubjective world in which we share our perspectives through knowledge gained by previous experience. The fact that I am able to express my thinking to a fellow human being already presupposes an intersubjective world in which both s/he and I are embedded and, therefore, s/he can share my thinking and I hers/his. This sharing is the very basis with which we can affirm objective reality for we are able to identify an entity within the same perspective. Understanding, hence, always presupposes a common social heritage of an intersubjective world with the participation of Mystery. It is in this intersubjectivity that we can understand our ways of perceiving outside reality as the objective one.

The Problem of Intersubjectivity

Up till this point in our discussion, intersubjectivity has not seemed to present a crucial problem to our cultural concerns. However, when we consider cases in which there are two distinctive groups responding differently according to their own intersubjective worlds, the problem of intersubjectivity can be seen. In order to reveal this problem, let me follow Alfred Schutz's notion of "in-group" and "out-group." The in-group, as defined by Schutz, are those who accept the ready-made standardized scheme of a socio-cultural environment, that is, an intersubjective world as an unquestioned and unquestionable system of knowledge. For them the system of knowledge in everyday life situation as manifested in language, tradition, habits and various social systems appears to have sufficient coherence, clarity and consistency. In contrast those who stand outside of that world are defined as the out-group. Members of the out-group sometimes feel that what is taken-for-granted by the in-group is actually an ambiguous and enigmatic reality since the out-group have not had any sharing experience with the in-group's historical traditions. Suppose, for instance, that an American who has never lived in any foreign country has to live in Japan, without first learning about the culture or studying the language, and to work at a Japanese factory in a Japanese style. Being astonished by the Japanese employee's daily singing of the company's song or quoting the company's slogan in a militaristic manner, s/he would as a result have considerable difficulty in understanding the Japanese way of life simply because s/he does not share his/her intersubjective world with that of the Japanese. The self-evidence of everyday life for the members of an ingroup may not be self-evident for those of the out-group. It is this gap that creates misunderstandings.

I explained a sharing world of an in-group in distinction to that of out-groups. Actually this characterization does not really indicate the true meaning of sharing because the sharing world of an in-group eventually destroys the sharing world in the global sense. A sharing world of an in-group becomes a kind of confinement in which we tend to glorify ourselves as a sharing people, as exemplified in Germany and Japan during the Second World War. As long as we understand "sharing a world" in terms of in-group and out-group, we in a sense validate a dualism of the human condition in which in-group stands apart from out-group. This does not really signify the true meaning of sharing. To share various human concerns in the world means not to differentiate in-group from out-group, but to take part in every possible activity in the world. This participation can create a sort of "fusion of horizons" in which the differences between in-group and out-group eventually disappear, creating a new horizon of understanding which involves a broadening of the present horizon.

Fusion of Horizon: Openness and Listening

The encounter between in-group and out-group usually creates tension. How can we overcome this tension and at the same time attain a respectful understanding of each other, allowing every individual and every culture to their own dignity? Indeed this is an important question. Let us recall Gadamer's attempt to explain the encounter between text and interpreter in his *magnum opus*, *Truth and Method*, for his analysis is helpful in understanding the question of the encounter between in-group and out-group. He states:

> The concept of the 'horizon' suggests itself because it expresses the wide, superior vision that the person who is seeking to understand must have. To acquire a horizon means that one learns to look beyond what is close at hand—not in order to look away from it, but to see it better within a larger whole and in truer proportion.

"To acquire a horizon means that one learns to look beyond what is close at hand." What does that mean? It means that we need to learn to understand the out-group's own dignity enabling them to disclose their true nature. This requires from us an openness towards out-groups, a willingness to listen to what the members of out-groups would say. Earlier I discussed the example of the notions of tree and *Ki*; so long as we are caught up within the taken-for-grantedness of our notions in language, we will never be able to understand the real meanings of out-groups' expressions. But if we are able to admit that our understanding is historically conditioned and therefore to allow ourselves to be open to what an outgroup says, then a new horizon between us may come into being in the sense that everybody will become able to realize the limitedness of both tree and *Ki* in a larger context. Openness and listening are keys to understanding other cultures as well as other human beings. It is true that an understanding of other cultures involves issues more complex than the difference between tree and *Ki*. Yet, if we lose a sense of listening and openness, there is no possibility for us to understand different cultures and people.

At present we are confronted by the nuclear crisis. This came about because we lost the attitude of listening to others, because we forgot that human beings are rooted in the common destiny of the world, because we manipulated others at our disposal, and because we lost the original meaning of the Biblical story about human beings on earth: human beings were created to bring to light and to protect the world in the context of relationships within which different people and things belong together with mutual dependency.

In the question of fusion of horizons between different cultures and people, language reveals very mysterious powers. Since every language is tied up to a particular historical setting, various languages differ from one another. Language is also the medium through which human beings are able to identify various historico-cultural phenomena in their settings. Hence, historico-cultural differences can be understood as differences among languages. In this regard, language always discloses particular characteristics of its own historico-cultural setting.

But how can we mediate these differences of language? Clearly it is also through language that differences can be fused or compared. In this respect, language discloses the universal dimension through which differences can be overcome. It is true that the English language is different from Japanese. But if English discloses totally different characteristics from Japanese, is it possible for any Japanese to understand the various meanings of English? The very fact that I can translate different English expressions into Japanese already presupposes that there are universally shared meanings between the two languages. Thus language discloses not only particular modes of being, but also the universal dimensions of our existence.

Language, furthermore, has the immanently transcending power by which I mean that language is able to overcome its own limited meaning in its historical condition. Here, paradoxically speaking, our fateful situation is not fateful when we reflect on, and open ourselves to, the fatefulness of our existence. When I say that the tree of the English language is different from the *Ki* of Japanese, I note that the meanings of tree and *Ki* are limited. Yet, in so pointing out, language can open much larger possibilities than those of tree and *Ki*. Because any society signifies linguistically its historical heritage in which human relationality dwells, human relationships, too, disclose particular modes of being as well as universality. Human relationality contains something common to all humanity. Everywhere we find language, cultural objects, playthings for children, family life through which human beings live and celebrate such great events of life as birth, initiation, marriage and death. These are given universally. Human beings are different and yet we share various dimensions of human existence as universally shared meanings. It is in this human sharing that we can appreciate and understand different people.

We cannot escape the "taken-for-grantedness" of our world. We are fatefully thrown into that world where we must find meanings for our existence. It is impossible for us to have meaningful dialogue with others if we do not take our language for granted. For example, it is impossible for us to bring our sick baby to a doctor if we do not take some medical knowledge for granted. In this regard "taken-for-grantedness" discloses appreciative human meanings in addition to its ideological dimensions. One of the fundamental mistakes utopian theorists often make is to assume that they themselves are the vanguard as they claim *a-priori* powers to transcend the ideological power of culture. But, in so doing, they themselves become ideological in the sense that they negate the ultimate human condition: human beings are historical beings who disclose a fateful as well as a transformative mode of life and thought. It seems to me that every human being at certain points has to share in the ideological power of existence. We are, in a sense, living within original sin. However, this does not mean that we cannot transcend various modes of ideological power in our respective cultures. **We are living in a constant transformative process within the horizon of encounters between different people. If we are open and responsive to other people in dialogue, then Mystery can lead humans to learn to trust and find a way**

of reconciling the differences of culture and existence. This awareness opens up much richer possibilities of shaping various modes of our existence in more meaningful ways. The genuine work of education, it seems to me, is to provide and teach this dialogical-critical ability to human beings so that we can create and develop meaningful societies in a global sense.

Chapter V: Goodness

What is the nature of goodness and what does it mean to be a good person? Practically, how can I become a good person and how can I lead a good life? What is the relationship of goodness to happiness? Is the good life, in fact, the happy life? How does happiness differ from pleasure? From self-gratification? Can one become good simply by following moral rules or by obeying the law? In other words, is the performance of certain actions or types of actions sufficient to make one good? Does becoming good involve doing or not doing certain things? Or, does goodness involve being or becoming a certain type of individual and cultivating a certain character or habits of character called virtues?

Normative thinking about how we, as human beings, are to dwell in this world constitutes that branch of philosophy known as ethics. Ethics is thinking philosophically about the moral dimension of human existence. This branch of philosophy involves an investigation into the nature of good and evil, the nature of right, and the essence of justice. In his famous work, *Utilitarianism*, the philosopher John Stuart Mill states:

> The question is often asked, and properly so, in regard to any supposed moral standard—what is its sanction? What are the motives to obey? Or, whence does it derive its binding force? It is a necessary part of moral philosophy to provide the answer to this question. . . .

The essays in this section attempt to answer the question concerning the nature of moral force and, in doing so, they provide us with insight into the above questions and offer guidance for life.

In the "Story of a Good Brahman," Voltaire deals with the philosophical problem of knowledge versus happiness. If the issue is "being happy," what does it matter how much knowledge one has? Many have pointed out that the quest for knowledge often results in futility. In fact, the search for knowledge often leads to doubt and disappointment in contrast to firm convictions that allow individuals to lead happy lives.

The selection on Hindu philosophy from the *Bhagavad Gita* or *Song of God* calls the readers' attention to the intrinsic value of work. Life itself is work and work ought to be performed free of attachment and without concern for results. According to the *Bhagavad Gita*, "To action alone hast thou a right and never to its fruit; let not the fruits of action be thy motive; neither let there be in thee any attachment to inaction."

Confucius is rightly referred to as China's "first teacher." For over two millennia his teachings have ranked first in importance and have shaped the character of the peoples of East Asia. One of the things we learn from the master is that true learning takes an entire lifetime. The superior or exemplary person aims to be a person of complete virtue. One becomes great not through self-promotion but by promoting and benefiting others. Reciprocity, Confucius taught, is one word that can serve as a rule of practice for a lifetime. The, so-called, "Silver Rule" states, "What you do not want done to yourself, do not do to others."

According to the Arabic philosopher Yahyā ibn ᶜAdī, "Character is the state of the soul by which man performs his acts without either foresight or choice." It becomes incumbent upon individuals to so cultivate their character and human development so as to attire the soul in the "garments of goodness." Moral perfection or completeness is accomplished by developing virtuous habits of character and abandoning vice.

Xunzi was one of the "Hundred Philosophers" who established the intellectual heritage of China. Master Xun wrote in the Confucian tradition. According to Xunzi, "the nature of man is evil; his goodness is the result of his activities." He believed that humans are basically feeling-oriented and, as such, are naturally inclined to seek the satisfaction of personal, generally selfish, desires. Left unchecked, the necessary consequence of desire is evil. Xunzi's writings stress the cosmic principle of propriety (*li*) as a means of moral cultivation and external social control. It is by way of public ritual (*li*) that a prosperous, civilized, and peaceful culture may be attained.

Philosophically, the history of Western ethical thinking revolves around the works of Aristotle, Immanuel Kant, and John Stuart Mill. According to Aristotle, happiness is the highest good, the supreme good, or life's *summum bonum*. Happiness is the only good that individuals seek for its own sake and never for the sake of something else. For Aristotle, "happiness is an activity of the soul in accordance with complete or perfect virtue." The pursuit of happiness takes a whole lifetime.

Immanuel Kant was both a product of and leading architect of the Enlightenment. Kant's moral philosophy is grounded in reason and in the logical form of moral imperatives. The person of moral worth acts from a good will, one that is "good in itself," and therefore acts solely from the motive of doing what is right. Because humans are rational beings, they have the capacity to distinguish right from wrong. Kant's categorical imperative states: "I am never to act otherwise than so that I could also will that my maxim should become a universal law." Since humans are free beings, life offers choices and the good person freely chooses what is right simply because *they* know it is right.

Utilitarianism views the notions of "right" and "wrong" in relationship to an action's consequences. John Stuart Mill defines utilitarianism as follows:

> The creed which accepts as the foundation of moral's "utility" or the "greatest happiness principle" holds that actions are right in proportion as they tend to promote happiness; wrong as they tend to produce the reverse of happiness.

Utilitarianism has strong practical and psychological appeal because most people like to believe that right actions count towards the fulfillment of life's highest good.

In "The Idea of a Female Ethic," Jean Grimshaw challenges the bedrock assumptions about ethics that are prevalent in mainstream moral philosophy and, arguably, in the whole history of ethical thought. For Grimshaw,

> The idea that virtue is in some way *gendered*, that the standards and criteria of morality are different for women and men, is one that has been central to the ethical thinking of a great many philosophers.

This work is important for several reasons: First, Grimshaw's article calls into question any gendered view of ethics that devalues women or assigns to women a subordinate role. Secondly, this article opens possible ways to critically examine moral and social structures. Thirdly, this piece opens discussions about hierarchies, networks, the place of care, and the structure of the workplace—to name a few examples.

Although ambition is often talked about as a desirable human quality, Jiddu Krishnamurti did not share this view. Krishnamurti, in fact, saw ambition as one of the causes of fear. Ambitious people, according to Krishnamurti, are the "most frightened" people and they are dangerous. The purpose of education is to help individuals grow and thereby free them from the ugliness of ambition so they might find their true vocation. Krishnamurti put it this way, "The ambitious man has never found his true vocation; if he had, he would not be ambitious."

Finally, the position of ethical relativism is set forth in Ruth Benedict's famous essay, "Ethics Are Relative." Benedict states that "morality differs in every society, and it is a convenient term for socially approved habits." This view is opposed by the position of cultural universalism that claims there are universal moral principles that are absolute and thus morally binding on all individuals, at all times and in all cultures.

Story of a Good Brahman

Voltaire

I met on my travels an old Brahman, a very wise man, full of wit and very learned; moreover he was rich, and consequently even wiser; for, lacking nothing, he had no need to deceive anyone. His family was very well governed by three beautiful wives who schooled themselves to please him; and when he was not entertaining himself with his wives, he was busy philosophizing.

Near his house, which was beautiful, well decorated, and surrounded by charming gardens, lived an old Indian woman, bigoted, imbecilic, and rather poor.

The Brahman said to me one day: "I wish I had never been born."

I asked him why. He replied:

"I have been studying for forty years, which is forty years wasted; I teach others, and I know nothing; this situation brings into my soul so much humiliation and disgust that life is unbearable to me. I was born, I live in time, and I do not know what time is; I find myself in a point between two eternities, as our sages say, and I have no idea of eternity. I am composed of matter; I think, and I have never been able to find out what produces thought; I do not know whether my understanding is a simple faculty in me like that of walking or of digesting, and whether I think with my head, as I take with my hands. Not only is the principle of my thinking unknown to me, but the principle of my movements is equally hidden from me. I do not know why I exist. However, people every day ask me questions on all these points; I have to answer; I have nothing any good to say; I talk much, and I remain confounded and ashamed of myself after talking.

"It is much worse yet when they ask me whether Brahma was produced by Vishnu or whether they are both eternal. God is my witness that I don't know a thing about it, and it certainly shows in my answers. 'Ah! Reverend Father,' they say to me, 'teach us how it is that evil inundates the whole world.' I am as much at a loss as those who ask me that question; I sometimes tell them that all is for the very best, but those who have been ruined and mutilated at war believe nothing of it, and neither do I;

I retreat to my house overwhelmed with my curiosity and my ignorance. I read our ancient books, and they redouble the darkness I am in. I talk to my companions: some answer that we must enjoy life and laugh at men; the others think they know something, and lose themselves in absurd ideas; everything increases the painful feeling I endure. I am sometimes ready to fall into despair, when I think that after all my seeking I know neither where I come from, nor what I am, nor where I shall go, nor what shall become of me."

The state of this good man caused me real pain; no one was either more reasonable or more honest than he. I perceived that the greater the lights of his understanding and the sensibility of his heart, the more unhappy he was.

That same day I saw the old woman who lived in his vicinity: I asked her whether she had ever been distressed not to know how her soul was made. She did not even understand my question: she had never reflected a single moment of her life over a single one of the points that tormented the Brahman; she believed with all her heart in the metamorphoses of Vishnu, and, provided she could sometimes have some water from the Ganges to wash in, she thought herself the happiest of women.

Struck by the happiness of this indigent creature, I returned to my philosopher and said to him:

"Aren't you ashamed to be unhappy at a time when right at your door there is an old automaton who thinks of nothing and who lives happily?"

"You are right," he answered; "I have told myself a hundred times that I would be happy if I was as stupid as my neighbor, and yet I would want no part of such a happiness."

This answer of my Brahman made a greater impression on me than all the rest. I examined myself and saw that indeed I would not have wanted to be happy on condition of being imbecilic.

I put the matter up to some philosophers, and they were of my opinion.

"There is, however," I said, "a stupendous contradiction in this way of thinking."

For after all, what is at issue? Being happy. What matters being witty or being stupid? What is more, those who are content with their being are quite sure of being content; those who reason are not so sure of reasoning well.

"So it is clear," I said, "that we should choose not to have common sense, if ever that common sense contributes to our ill-being."

Everyone was of my opinion, and yet I found no one who wanted to accept the bargain of becoming imbecilic in order to become content. From this I concluded that if we set store by happiness, we set even greater store by reason.

But, upon reflection, **it appears that to prefer reason to felicity is to be very mad.** Then how can this contradiction be explained? Like all the others. There is much to be said about it.

Work, Nonattachment, and Wisdom

from Bhagavad Gita

Work without Concern for the Results

To action alone hast thou a right and never at all to its fruit; let not the fruits of action be thy motive; neither let there be in thee any attachment to inaction.

Fixed in *yoga*, do thy work, O winner of wealth (Arjuna), abandoning attachment, with an even mind in success and failure, for evenness of mind is called *yoga*.

Far inferior indeed is mere action to the discipline of intelligence, O winner of wealth (Arjuna); seek refuge in intelligence. Pitiful are those who seek for the fruits of their action.

One who has yoked his intelligence [with the Divine] (or is established in his intelligence) casts away even here both good and evil. Therefore strive for *yoga*; *yoga* is skill in action.

The wise who have united their intelligence [with the Divine], renouncing the fruits which their action yields and freed from the bonds of birth, reach the sorrowless state.

When thine intelligence shall cross the whirl of delusion, then shalt thou become indifferent to what has been heard and what is yet to be heard.

When thine intelligence, which is bewildered by the Vedic texts, shall stand unshaken and stable in spirit (*samādhi*), then shalt thou attain to insight (yoga).

The Characteristics of the Perfect Sage

Arjuna said:

What is the description of the man who has this firmly founded wisdom, whose being is steadfast in spirit, O Keśava (Kṛṣṇa)? How does the man of settled intelligence speak; how does he sit; how does he walk?

Work, Nonattachment, and Wisdom

The Blessed Lord said:

When a man puts away all the desires of his mind, O Pārtha (Arjuna), and when his spirit is content in itself, then is he called stable in intelligence.

He whose mind is untroubled in the midst of sorrows and is free from eager desire amid pleasures, he from whom passion, fear, and rage have passed away—he is called a sage of settled intelligence.

He who is without affection on any side, who does not rejoice or loathe as he obtains good or evil—his intelligence is firmly set [in wisdom].

He who draws away the senses from the objects of sense on every side as a tortoise draws in his limbs into the shell—his intelligence is firmly set [in wisdom].

The objects of sense turn away from the embodied soul who abstains from feeding on them, but the taste for them remains. Even the taste turns away when the Supreme is seen.

Even though a man may ever strive [for perfection] and be ever so discerning, O Son of Kunti (Arjuna), his impetuous senses will carry off his mind by force.

Having brought all the senses under control, he should remain firm in *yoga*, intent on Me; for he, whose senses are under control, his intelligence is firmly set.

When a man dwells in his mind on the objects of sense, attachment to them is produced. From attachment springs desire, and from desire comes anger.

From anger arises bewilderment, from bewilderment loss of memory, and from loss of memory the destruction of intelligence; and from the destruction of intelligence he perishes.

But a man of disciplined mind, who moves among the objects of sense, with the senses under control and free from attachment and aversion—he attains purity of spirit.

And in that purity of spirit, there is produced for him an end of all sorrow; the intelligence of such a man of pure spirit is soon established [in the peace of the self].

For the uncontrolled, there is no intelligence; nor for the uncontrolled is there the power of concentration; and for him without concentration, there is no peace; and for the unpeaceful, how can there be happiness?

When the mind runs after the roving senses, it carries away the understanding, even as a wind carries away a ship on the waters.

Therefore, O Mighty-armed (Arjuna), he whose senses are all withdrawn from their objects—his intelligence is firmly set.

What is night for all beings is the time of waking for the disciplined soul; and what is the time of waking for all beings is night for the sage who sees (or the sage of vision).

He unto whom all desires enter as waters into the sea, which, though ever being filled, is ever motionless, attains to peace, and not he who hugs his desires.

He who abandons all the desires and acts free from longing, without any sense of mineness or egotism—he attains to peace.

This is the divine state, O Pārtha (Arjuna); having attained thereto, one is not again bewildered; fixed in that state at the end [at the hour of death] one can attain to the bliss of God.

Life Is Work; Unconcern for Results Is Needful

The Blessed Lord said:

O blameless One, in this world a twofold way of life has been taught of yore by Me, the path of knowledge for men of contemplation and that of works for men of action.

Not by abstention from work does a man attain freedom from action; nor by mere renunciation does he attain to his perfection.

For no one can remain even for a moment without doing work; everyone is made to act helplessly by the impulses born of nature.

He who restrains his organs of action but continues in his mind to brood over the objects of sense, whose nature is deluded, is said to be a hypocrite [a man of false conduct].

But he who controls the senses by the mind, O Arjuna, and without attachment engages to organs of action in the path of work, he is superior.

Be Satisfied in the Self

But the man whose delight is in the Self alone, who is content with the Self, who is satisfied with the Self—for him there exists no work that needs to be done.

Similarly, in this world he has no interest whatever to gain by the actions that he has done and none to be gained by the actions that he has not done. He does not depend on all these beings for any interest of his.

Therefore, without attachment, perform always the work that has to be done, for man attains to the highest by doing work without attachment.

Set an Example to Others

It was even by works that Janaka and others attained to perfection. Thou shouldst do works also with a view to the maintenance of the world.

Whatsoever a great man does, the same is done by others as well. Whatever standard he sets, the world follows.

There is not for me, O Pārtha (Arjuna), any work in the three worlds which has to be done or anything to be obtained which has not been obtained; yet I am engaged in work.

For, if ever I did not engage in work unwearied, O Pārtha (Arjuna), men would in every way follow my path.

If I should cease to work, these worlds would fall in ruin, and I should be the creator of disordered life and destroy these people.

As the unlearned act from attachment to their work, so should the learned also act, O Bhārata (Arjuna), but without any attachment, with the desire to maintain the world-order.

Let him not unsettle the minds of the ignorant who are attached to action. The enlightened man doing all works in a spirit of *yoga* should set others to act (as well).

The Self Is No Doer

While all kinds of work are done by the modes of nature (guṇas), he whose soul is bewildered by the self-sense thinks, "I am the doer."

But he who knows the true character of the distinction of the soul from the modes of nature and their works, O Mighty-armed (Arjuna), understanding that it is the modes which are acting on the modes themselves, does not get attached.

Those who are misled by the modes of nature get attached to the works produced by them. But let no one who knows the whole unsettle the minds of the ignorant who know only a part.

Resigning all thy works to Me, with thy consciousness fixed in the Self, being free from desire and egoism, fight, delivered, from thy fever.

Those men, too, who, full of faith and free from cavil, constantly follow this teaching of Mine are released from the bondage of works.

But those who slight My teaching and do not follow it, know them to be blind to all wisdom, lost and senseless.

Nature and Duty

Even the man of knowledge acts in accordance with his own nature. Beings follow their nature. What can repression accomplish?

For every sense-attachment and [every] aversion are fixed in regard to the objects of that sense. Let no one come under their sway, for they are his two enemies.

Better is one's own law though imperfectly carried out than the law of another carried out perfectly. Better is death in the fulfillment of one's own law, for to follow another's law is perilous.

Action and Inaction

What is action? What is inaction?—as to this even the wise are bewildered. I will declare to thee what action is, knowing which thou shalt be delivered from evil.

One has to understand what action is, and likewise one has to understand what is wrong action, and one has to understand about inaction. Hard to understand is the way of work.

He who in action sees inaction and action in inaction—he is wise among men, he is a *yogin*, and he has accomplished all his work.

He whose undertakings are all free from the will of desire, whose works are burned up in the fire of wisdom—him the wise call a man of learning.

Having abandoned attachment to the fruit of works, ever content, without any kind of dependence, he does nothing though he is ever engaged in work.

Having no desires, with his heart and self under control, giving up all possessions, performing action by the body alone, he commits no wrong.

He who is satisfied with whatever comes by chance, who has passed beyond the dualities (of pleasure and pain), who is free from jealousy, who remains the same in success and failure—even when he acts, he is not bound.

Wisdom and Work

Knowledge as a sacrifice is greater than any material sacrifice, O scourge of the foe (Arjuna), for all works without any exception culminate in wisdom

Learn that by humble reverence, by inquiry, and by service. The men of wisdom who have seen the truth will instruct thee in knowledge.

In Praise of Wisdom

When thou hast known it, thou shalt not fall again into this confusion, O Pāndava (Arjuna), for by this thou shalt see all existences without exception in the Self, then in Me.

Even if thou shouldst be the most sinful of all sinners, thou shalt cross over all evil by the boat of wisdom alone.

As the fire which is kindled turns its fuel to ashes, O Arjuna, even so does the fire of wisdom turn to ashes all work.

There is nothing on earth equal in purity to wisdom. He who becomes perfected by *yoga* finds is of himself, in his self [*ātman*] in course of time.

Faith Is Necessary for Wisdom

He who has faith, who is absorbed in it [i.e., wisdom], and who has subdued his senses, gains wisdom, and having gained wisdom he attains quickly the supreme peace.

But the man who is ignorant, who has no faith, who is of a doubting nature, perishes. For the doubting soul [*ātman*] there is neither this world nor the world beyond, nor any happiness.

Works do not bind him who has renounced all works by *yoga*, who has destroyed all doubt by wisdom, and who ever possesses his soul, O winner of wealth (Arjuna).

Therefore, having cut asunder with the sword of wisdom this doubt in thy heart that is born of ignorance, resort to *yoga* and stand up, O Bhārata (Arjuna).

The Enlightened Self

The embodied self who has controlled his nature, having renounced all actions by the mind [inwardly], dwells at ease in the city of nine gates,[1] neither working or causing work to be done.

The Sovereign Self does not create for the people agency, nor does He act. Nor does He connect works with their fruits. It is nature that works out these.

The All-pervading Spirit does not take on the sin or the merit of any. Wisdom is enveloped by ignorance; thereby creatures are bewildered.

But for those in whom ignorance is destroyed by wisdom—for them wisdom lights up the Supreme Self like the sun.

Thinking of That, directing one's whole conscious being to That, making That their whole aim, with That as the sole object of their devotion, they reach a state from which there is no return, their sins washed away by wisdom.

Sages see with an equal eye, a learned and humble *brāhmin*, a cow, an elephant, or even a dog, or an outcaste.

Even here on earth the created world is overcome by those whose mind is established in equality. God is flawless and the same in all. Therefore are these persons established in God.

One should not rejoice on obtaining what is pleasant or sorrow on obtaining what is unpleasant. He who is thus firm of understanding and unbewildered—such a knower of God is established in God.

When the self is no longer attached to external contacts [objects], one finds the happiness that is in the Self. Such a one who is in union with God enjoys undying bliss.

Whatever pleasures are born of contacts with objects are only sources of pain: they have a beginning and an end, O Son Kuntī (Arjuna); no wise man delights in them.

He who is able to resist the rush of desire and anger—even here before he gives up his body, he is a *yogin*, he is the happy man.

Peace from Within

He who finds his happiness within, his joy within, and likewise his light only within, that *yogin* becomes divine and attains to the beatitude of God.

The holy men whose sins are destroyed, whose doubts [dualities] are cut asunder, whose minds are disciplined, and who rejoice in doing good to all creatures attain to the beatitude of God.

To those austere souls who are delivered from desire and anger and who have subdued their minds and have knowledge of the Self—near to them lies the beatitude of God.

Shutting out all external objects, fixing the vision between the eyebrows, making even the inward and the outward breaths moving within the nostrils, the sage who has controlled the senses, mind, and understanding, who is intent on liberation, who has cast away desire, fear and anger—he is ever freed.

And having known Me as the Enjoyer of sacrifices and austerities, the Great Lord of all the worlds, the Friend of all beings, he [the sage] attains peace.

The Pathway and the Goal

Work is said to be the means of the sage who wishes to attain to *yoga*; when he has attained to *yoga*, serenity is said to be the means.

When one does not get attached to the objects of sense or to works, and has renounced all purposes, then he is said to have attained to *yoga*.

Let a man lift himself by himself; let him not degrade himself; for the Self alone is the friend of the self and the Self alone is the enemy of the self.

For him who has conquered his [lower] self by the [higher] Self his Self is a friend, but for him who has not possessed his [higher] Self, his very Self will act in emnity, like an enemy.

When one has conquered one's [lower] self and has attained to the calm of self-mastery, his Supreme Self abides ever concentrate: he is at peace in cold and heat, in pleasure and pain, in honor and dishonor.

The ascetic (*yogi*) whose soul is satisfied with wisdom and knowledge, who is unchanging and master of his senses, to whom a clod, a stone, and a piece of gold are the same, is said to be controlled [in *yoga*].

He who is equal-minded among friends, companions, and foes, among those who are neutral and impartial, among those who are hateful and related, among saints and sinners—he excels.

Note

[1] The nine gates are the two eyes, the two ears, the two nostrils, the mouth, and the two organs of excretion and generation.

from The Analects of Confucius

The Character of Confucius[1]

[2.4] The Master said, "At fifteen, I had my mind bent on learning. At thirty, I stood firm. At forty, I had no doubts. At fifty, I knew the decrees of Heaven.[2] At sixty, my ear was an obedient organ for the reception of truth. At seventy, I could follow what my heart desired, without transgressing what was right."

[7.1] The Master said, "A transmitter and not a maker, believing in and loving the ancients, I venture to compare myself with our old P'eng."[3]

The Master said, "The silent treasuring up of knowledge; learning without tiring; and instructing others without being wearied—which one of these things belongs to me?"

The Master said, "Leaving virtue without proper cultivation; not thoroughly discussing what is learned; not being able to move towards righteousness of which a knowledge is gained; and not being able to change what is not good—these are the things which cause me much concern."

When the Master was unoccupied with business, his manner was easy, and he looked pleased.

[5] The Master said, "My decline is extreme. For a long time, I have not dreamed, as I used to do, that I saw the duke of Chou."[4]

The Master said, "Let the will be set on the path of duty. Let every attainment in what is good be firmly grasped. Let perfect virtue be accorded with. Let relaxation and enjoyment be found in the arts."

The Master said, "From the man bringing his bundle of dried meat[5] for my teaching, or more than that, I have never refused instruction to any one."

The Master said, "I do not open up the truth to one who is not eager to get knowledge, nor help out any one who is not anxious to explain himself. When I have presented one corner of a subject to any one, and he cannot from it learn the other three, I do not repeat my lesson."

When the Master was eating by the side of a mourner, he never ate to the full. He did not sing on the same day in which he had been weeping. . . .

[19] The Master said, "I am not one who was born in the possession of knowledge; I am one who is fond of antiquity,[6] and earnest in seeking it there."

[20] The subjects on which the Master did not talk were extraordinary things,[7] feats of strength, disorder, and spiritual beings.

The Master said, "When I walk along with two others, they may serve me as my teachers. I will select their good qualities and follow them, their bad qualities and avoid them."

The Master said, "Heaven produced the virtue that is in me. Hwan T'ui[8]—what can he do to me?"

The Master said, "Do you think, my disciples, that I have any concealments? I conceal nothing from you. There is nothing which I do that is not shown to you, my disciples—that is my way."

There were four things which the Master taught—letters, ethics, devotion of soul, and truthfulness.

[10.1] Confucius, in his village, looked simple and sincere, and as if he were not able to speak. When he was in the prince's ancestral temple, or in the court, he spoke minutely on every point, but cautiously.

When he was on duty at court, in speaking with the great officers of the lower grade he spoke freely, but in a straightforward manner. In speaking with those of the higher grade, he did so mildly, but precisely. When the ruler was present, his manner displayed respectful uneasiness; it was serious, but self-possessed.

When the prince called on him to receive a visitor, his countenance appeared to change, and his legs to move forward with difficulty. He inclined himself to the other officers among whom he stood, moving his left or right arm, as their position required, but keeping the skirts of his robe before and behind evenly adjusted. He hastened forward, with his arms like the wings of a bird. When the guest had left, he would report to the prince, "The visitor is not looking back any more."

When he entered the palace gate, he seemed to bend his body, as if it were not sufficient to admit him. When he was standing, he did not occupy the middle of the gateway; when he passed in or out, he did not tread upon the threshold. When he was passing the vacant place of the prince, his countenance appeared to change, and his legs to bend under him, and his words came as if he hardly had breath to speak them. He ascended the reception hall, holding up his robe with both his hands, and his body bent. He held in his breath also, as if he dared not breathe.

[8] He liked to have his rice finely cleaned, and to have his minced meat cut quite small. He did not eat rice which had been injured by heat or damp and turned sour, nor fish or meat which was gone. He did not eat what was discolored, or what was of a bad flavor, nor anything which was badly cooked, or was not in season. He did not eat meat which was not cut properly, nor what was served without its proper sauce. Though there might be a large quantity of meat, he would not allow what he took to exceed the due proportion for the rice. It was only in wine that he laid down no limit for himself, but he did not allow himself to be confused by it. He did not partake of wine and dried meat bought in the market. He was never without ginger when he ate. He did not eat much. When he had been assisting at the prince's sacrifice, he did not keep the meat which he received overnight. The meat of his family sacrifice he did not keep over three days. If kept over three days, people could not eat it. When eating, he did not converse. When in bed, he did not speak. Although his food might be coarse rice and vegetable soup, he would offer a little of it in sacrifice with a serious, respectful air.

If his mat was not straight, he did not sit on it.

[10] When the villagers were drinking together, after those who carried walking staffs left, he went out immediately. When the villagers were going through their ceremonies to drive away pestilential influences, he put on his court robes and stood on the eastern steps.

When he was sending complimentary inquiries to any one in another state, he bowed twice as he escorted the messenger away.

When Chi K'ang sent him a present of medicine, he bowed and received it, saying, "I do not know it. I dare not taste it."

The stable burned down when he was at court, and on his return he said, "Has any person been hurt?" He did not ask about the horses.

The Virtues of the Superior Man[9]

[1.1] The Master said, "Is it not pleasant to learn with a constant perseverance and application? Is it not delightful to have friends coming from distant quarters? Is he not a man of complete virtue, who feels no discomposure though men may take no note of him?"

The philosopher Yu said, "Few are those who, being filial and fraternal, are fond of offending their superiors. There have been none, who, not liking to offend their superiors, have been fond of stirring up confusion. The superior man bends his attention to the foundation. That being established, all practical courses naturally grow up. Filial piety and fraternal submission—are they not the root of all benevolent actions?"

The Master said, "Fine words and an insinuating appearance are seldom associated with true virtue."

The philosopher Tsang said, "I daily examine myself on three points: whether, in transacting business for others, I have been faithful; whether, in dealings with friends, I have been sincere; whether I have mastered and practiced the instructions of my teacher." . . .

[6] The Master said, "A youth, when at home, should be filial, and away from home he should be respectful to his elders. He should be earnest and truthful. He should overflow in love to all, and cultivate the friendship of good people. When he has time and opportunity, after the performance of these things, he should employ them in the arts."

Tsze-hsia said, "If a man withdraws his mind from the love of beauty, and applies it as sincerely to the love of the virtuous; if, in serving his parents, he can exert his utmost strength; if, in serving his prince, he can devote his life; if, in his dealings with his friends, his words are sincere—although men say that he has not learned, I will certainly say that he has."

The Master said, "If the scholar is not serious, he will not call forth any veneration, and his learning will not be solid. Hold faithfulness and sincerity as first principles. Have no friends not equal to yourself. When you have faults, do not fear to abandon them."

The philosopher Tsang said, "Let there be a careful attention to perform the funeral rites to parents, and let them be followed when long gone with the ceremonies of sacrifice. Then the virtue of the people will resume its proper excellence." . . .

[14] The Master said, "He who aims to be a man of complete virtue in his food does not seek to gratify his appetite, nor in his dwelling place does he seek the appliances of ease. He is earnest in what he does, and careful in his speech. He frequents the company of men of principle that he may be rectified. Such a person may be said indeed to love to learn."

[15.17] The Master said, "The superior man considers righteousness to be essential in everything. He performs it according to the rules of propriety. He brings it forth in humility. He completes it with sincerity. This is indeed a superior man."

The Master said, "The superior man is distressed by his lack of ability. He is not distressed by his lack of fame."

The Master said, "The superior man dislikes the thought of his name not being mentioned after his death."

[20] The Master said, "What the superior man seeks is in himself. What the inferior man seeks is in others."

The Master said, "The superior man is dignified, but does not wrangle. He is sociable, but not a partisan."

The Master said, "The superior man does not promote a man simply on account of his words, nor does he put aside good words because of the man."

Tsze-kung asked, saying, **"Is there one word which may serve as a rule of practice for all one's life?" The Master said, "Is not Reciprocity[10] such a word? What you do not want done to yourself, do not do to others."**

Benevolence[11]

The Master said, "Virtuous manners constitute the excellence of a neighborhood. If a man in selecting a residence does not fix on one where such manners prevail, how can he be wise?"

The Master said, "Those who are without virtue cannot abide long either in a condition of poverty and hardship, or in a condition of enjoyment. The virtuous rest in virtue; the wise desire virtue."

The Master said, "It is only the [truly] virtuous man who can love, or who can hate, others."

The Master said, "If the will is set on virtue, there will be no practice of wickedness."

[5] The Master said, "Riches and honors are what men desire. If it cannot be obtained in the proper way, they should not be held. Poverty and a low condition are what men dislike. If it cannot be obtained in the proper way, they should not be avoided. If a superior man abandons virtue, how can he fulfill the requirements of that name? The superior man does not, even for the space of a single meal, act contrary to virtue. In moments of haste, he clings to it. In seasons of danger, he clings to it."

The Master said, "I have not seen a person who loved virtue, or one who hated what was not virtuous. He who loved virtue would esteem nothing above it. He who hated what is not virtuous would practice virtue in such a way that he would not allow anything that is not virtuous to approach his person. Is any one able for one day to apply his strength to virtue? I have not seen the case in which his strength would be sufficient. Should there possibly be any such case, I have not seen it."

The Actions of Filial Piety[12]

The sovereign king orders the chief minister to send down his lessons of virtue to the millions of the people. . . .

[4] [After getting properly] dressed [in the morning], [sons] should go to their parents and parents-in-law.[14] On getting to where they are, with bated breath and gentle voice they should ask if their clothes are too warm or too cold, whether they are ill or pained, or uncomfortable in any part. If they are, they should proceed reverently to stroke and scratch the place. They should in the same way, going before or following after, help and support their parents in leaving or entering the apartment. In bringing in the basin for them to wash, the younger will carry the stand and the elder the water. They will beg to be allowed to pour out the water, and when the washing is concluded, they will hand them the towel. They will ask whether they want anything, and then respectfully bring it. All this they will do with an appearance of pleasure to make their parents feel at ease. They should bring gruel, thick or thin, spirits or juice, soup with vegetables, beans, wheat, spinach, rice, millet, maize, and glutinous millet—whatever they wish, in fact. They should bring dates, chestnuts, sugar and honey to sweeten their dishes; the ordinary or the large-leaved violets, leaves of elm-trees, fresh or dry, and the most soothing rice-water to lubricate them; and fat and oil to enrich them. The parents will be sure to taste them, and when they have done so, the young people should withdraw. . . .

From the time that sons receive an official appointment,[15] they and their father occupy different parts of their residence. But at dawn, the son will pay his respects, and express his affection by the offer of pleasant delicacies. At sunrise he will retire, and he and his father will attend to their different duties. At sundown, the son will pay his evening visit in the same way. . . .

[10] While the parents are both alive, at their regular meals, morning and evening, the eldest son and his wife will encourage them to eat everything, and what is left after all, they themselves will eat. When the father is dead, and the mother still alive, the eldest son should wait upon her at her meals. The wives of the other sons will do with what is left as in the former case. The children should have the sweet, soft and oily things that are left.

When sons and their wives are ordered to do anything by their parents, they should immediately respond and reverently proceed to do it. In going forward or backward, or turning round, they should be careful and serious. While going out or coming in, while bowing or walking, they should not presume to belch, sneeze, or cough, to yawn or stretch themselves, to stand on one foot, or to lean against anything, or to look askance. They should not dare to spit or snivel, nor if it is cold to put on more clothes, nor if they itch anywhere, to scratch themselves. Unless for reverent attention to something, they should not presume to bare their [parents'] shoulders or chest. Unless it be in wading, they should not hold up their clothes. Of their private dress and coverlet, they should not display the inside. They should not allow the spittle or snivel of their parents to be seen. They should ask leave to rinse away any dirt on their caps or girdles, and to wash their clothes that are dirty with lye that has been prepared for the purpose; and to stitch together, with needle and thread, any tear. . . .

Sons and sons' wives, who are filial and reverential, when they receive an order from their parents should not refuse or delay executing it. When their parents give them anything to eat or drink, which they do not like, they will nevertheless taste it and wait for their further orders. When they give them clothes which are not to their liking, they will put them on, and wait in the same way. If their parents give them anything to do, and then employ another to take their place, although they do not like the arrangement, they will in the meantime give it into his hands and let him do it, doing it again, if it is not done well. . . .

When sons and their wives have not been filial and reverential, the parents should not be angry and resentful with them, but endeavor to instruct them. If they will not receive instruction, they should then be angry with them. If that anger does no good, they can then drive out the son, and send the wife away, yet not publicly showing why they have treated them so.

[15] If a parent has a fault, the son should with bated breath, and bland aspect, and gentle voice, admonish him. If the admonition does not take effect, he will be more reverential and more filial; and when the father seems pleased, he will repeat the admonition. If he should be displeased with this, rather than allow him to commit an offense against anyone in the neighborhood or countryside, the son should strongly protest. If the parent is angry and more displeased, and beat him till the blood flows, he should not presume to be angry and resentful, but be still more reverential and more filial.

The Attitude of Filial Piety[16]

[2.5] Mang asked what filial piety was. The Master said, "It is not being disobedient." Soon after, as Fan Ch'ih was driving him, the Master told him, saying, "Mang-sun asked me what filial piety was, and I answered him—'not being disobedient'." Fan Ch'ih said, "What did you mean?" The Master replied, "That parents, when alive, should be served according to propriety; that, when dead, they should be buried according to propriety; and that they should be sacrificed to according to propriety."

Mang Wu asked what filial piety was. The Master said, "Do not make your parents anxious about anything else than your being sick."

Tsze-yu asked what filial piety was. The Master said, "Filial piety nowadays means the support of one's parents. But dogs and horses likewise are able to do something in the way of support. Without reverence, what is there to distinguish the one support given from the other?"

Tsze-hsia asked what filial piety was. The Master said, "The difficulty is with the countenance. When their elders have any troublesome affairs and the young do their work, and when the young have plenty of wine and food to set before their elders, how can this be considered filial piety?"

[4.18] The Master said, "In serving his parents, a son may protest to them, but gently; when he sees that they do not incline to follow his advice, he shows an increased degree of reverence, but does not abandon his purpose; and should they punish him, he does not allow himself to murmur."

The Master said, "While his parents are alive, the son may not leave his home area to a far distance. If he does go away, he must have a fixed place to which he goes."[17]

[20] The Master said, "If the son for three years[18] does not alter from the way of his father, he may be called filial."

The Master said, "The age of one's parents should always be kept in the memory, as an reason for joy and for fear."

[13.18] The duke of Sheh informed Confucius, saying, "Among us here are those who may be styled upright in their conduct. If their father stole a sheep, they will bear witness to the fact." Confucius said, "Among us, in our part of the country, those who are upright are different from this. The father conceals the misconduct of the son, and the son conceals the misconduct of the father. Uprightness is to be found in this."

Propriety[19]

The Master said, "If a man lacks the virtues proper to humanity, what has he to do with the rites of propriety? If a man is without the virtues proper to humanity, what has he to do with music?"

Lin Fang asked what was the first thing to be attended to in ceremonies. The Master said, "A great question indeed! In festive ceremonies, it is better to be sparing than extravagant. In the ceremonies of mourning, it is better that there be deep sorrow than a minute attention to observances.". . .

[8] Tsze-hsia asked, "What is the meaning of the passage, 'The pretty dimples of her artful smile! The well-defined black and white of her eye! The plain ground for the colors'?"[20] The Master said, "The business of laying on the colors follows [the preparation of] the plain ground." "Ceremonies then are a subsequent thing?" The Master said, "It is you, Shang, who can bring out my meaning. Now I can begin to talk about the Odes with you."

The Master said, "I could describe the ceremonies of the Hsia dynasty, but Chi cannot sufficiently attest my words. I could describe the ceremonies of the Yin dynasty, but Sung cannot sufficiently attest my words. [They cannot do so] because of the insufficiency of their records and wise men. If those were sufficient, I could adduce them in support of my words.". . .

[12] He sacrificed to the dead as if they were present.[21] He sacrificed to the spirits as if the spirits were present. The Master said, "I consider my not being present at the sacrifice as if I did not sacrifice."

Wang-sun Chia asked, "What is the meaning of the saying, 'It is better to pay court to the furnace than to the southwest corner'?"[22] The Master said, "Not so. He who offends against Heaven has none to whom he can pray."

The Master said, "Chou had the advantage of viewing the two past dynasties. How complete and elegant are its regulations! I follow Chou."

[15] The Master, when he entered the Grand Temple,[23] asked about everything. Someone said, "Who says that the son of the man of Tsau knows the rules of propriety! He has entered the grand temple and asks about everything." The Master heard the remark, and said, "This [behavior of mine] is indeed a rule of propriety.". . .

[17] Tzu-kung wished to do away with the offering of a sheep connected with the inauguration of the first day of each month. The Master said, "Tzu, you love the sheep; I love the ceremony."[24]

The Master said, "The full observance of the rules of propriety in serving one's prince is accounted by people to be flattery."

The duke Ting asked how a prince should employ his ministers, and how ministers should serve their prince. Confucius replied, "A prince should employ his minister according to the rules of propriety; ministers should serve their prince with faithfulness."

The Way[25]

Confucius said, "When good government prevails in the empire, ceremonies, music, and punitive military expeditions proceed from the son of Heaven. When bad government prevails in the empire, ceremonies, music, and punitive military expeditions proceed from the princes. When these things proceed from the princes, as a rule, the cases will be few in which they do not lose their power in ten generations. When they proceed from the great officers of the princes, as a rule, the cases will be few in which they do not lose their power in five generations. When the subsidiary ministers of the great officers hold in their grasp the orders of the state, as a rule, the cases will be few in which they do not lose their power in three generations. When right principles prevail in the kingdom, government will not be in the hands of the great officers. When right principles prevail in the kingdom, there will be no discussions among the common people."

The Love of Learning[26]

The Master said, "Yu, have you heard the six words to which are attached six faults?" Yu replied, "I have not." "Sit down, and I will tell them to you. There is the love of being benevolent without the love of learning; the fault here leads to a foolish simplicity. There is the love of knowing without the love of learning; the fault here leads to dissipation of mind. There is the love of being sincere without the love of learning; the fault here leads to an injurious disregard of consequences. There is the love of straightforwardness without the love of learning; the fault here leads to rudeness. There is the love of boldness without the love the learning; the fault here leads to insubordination. There is the love of firmness without the love of learning; the fault here leads to extravagant conduct."

The Master said, "My children, why do you not study the *Book of Poetry*? The Odes serve to stimulate the mind. They may be used for purposes of self-contemplation. They teach the art of sociability. They show how to regulate feelings of resentment. From them you learn the more immediate duty of serving one's father, and the remoter duty of serving one's prince. From them we become largely acquainted with the names of birds, beasts, and plants.". . .

[12] The Master said, "He who puts on an appearance of stern firmness, while inwardly he is weak, is like one of the small, common people. Yes, is he not like the thief who breaks through, or climbs over, a wall?"

Notes

[1] *Analects* 2.4, 7.1–9, 19-24; 10.1–4, 8–12
[2] *decrees* (or "mandate") *of Heaven:* understood today by most Confucianists as the working of Nature in people and events, not primarily as the working of God.
[3] *old P'eng:* a sage from ancient times.
[4] *duke of Chou:* in the view of Confucius, one of the greatest of the early Chinese sage kings.
[5] *dried meat:* the smallest possible payment for instruction. Confucianism believes that learning and self-cultivation should be open to all who desire it.
[6] *antiquity:* Confucianists emphasize the Chinise custom of seeking direction from the ancient writings.

7. *extraordinary things:* strange events in nature
8. *Hwan T'ui:* an army officer who had attempted to kill Confucius.
9. *Analects* 1.1–4, 6–9, 14; 15.17–23
10. *Reciprocity:* the virtue *shu.*
11. *Analects* 4.1–6
12. *Classic of Rites* 10.1, 4, 7, 10–11, 13–15
13. Taken, with editing, from James Legge, trans., *The Sacred Books of China: The Texts of Confucianism,* part 3, *Sacred Books of the East,* vol. 27 (Oxford, Oxford University Press, 1885), pp. 449–457.
14. The passage presupposes that one's parents have an apartment or room in one's house, typically the case in traditional China.
15. *official appointment:* in a government position.
16. *Analects* 2.5–8; 4.18–21; 13.18
17. *a fixed place:* so his parents know where he is.
18. *for three years:* after the death of the father.
19. *Analects* 3.3–4, 8–9, 12–15, 17–19
20. A poem from the *Odes.*
21. A traditional saying.
22. A traditional saying, meaning that it is better to serve the gods of food than the ancestral spirits of the shrine (at the southwest corner of the Chinese house).
23. *the Grand Temple:* in the state of Lu.
24. Also translated, "Tzu, you love the sheep, but I love the sacrifice."
25. *Analects* 16.2
26. *Analects* 17.8–9, 12

On Cultivation of Character

Yaḥyā ibn ʿAdī

Know that man among all other animals is endowed with thought and judgment, and of all things, he always loves what is most excellent, of degrees, the noblest and of possessions, the most precious, as long as he does not swerve from judgment in his choice, and passion does not conquer him in the pursuit of his aims.

The most appropriate object a man may choose for himself, when he does not fall below attainment of his utmost nor remain satisfied with falling short of his end, is his own completion and perfection. It is inherent to man's completion and perfection that he be pleased with the noble traits and merits of good character and that he keep aloof from ignoble traits and repugnant qualities in his character, and that he take in all his circumstances the directives of virtues and avoid in all his actions the pathways of vice.

This being so, it is incumbent upon man to take as his goal the acquisition of every trait safe from defect and to direct his zeal towards obtaining every noble tendency that is devoid of flaw, and to give his effort to avoidance of every vicious reprehensible quality and to make every exertion to discard every base, blameworthy characteristic, so that he may attain perfection by means of cultivating his character and may attire himself in the garments of goodness . . . and vie by truth with those who are powerful and proud, and cling to the highest steps of vigilance and nobility.

Character is a state of the soul by which man performs his acts without either forethought or choice. Character may be innate and instinctive in some people while in others it may not occur except through training and effort. So, for example, generosity may exist in many people without training and effort, and bravery, equanimity, continence, justice and their like, among praiseworthy traits, may also occur. Among people are many in whom that exists, and so among them are those, too, who come to it by training; among them are those who remain entrenched in habits of virtue, and those who live a life based on ethical precepts.

Reprehensible traits exist in many people; for example, stinginess, cowardice, injustice and evil-doing. These habits are predominant in most people and are their usual, ingrained pattern of behavior. There are few people free from distasteful traits and free from all defects, but they contend with one another in [doing bad]. So, too, with laudable qualities of character: people may differ and contend with each other for superiority, but those who by their natures are good are very few, while the odious are numerous. As for those who by their natures are vicious, these are the majority of people since evil prevails over the nature of most people. This is because when man acts unconstrainedly from his inborn nature, he uses neither thought nor discernment, neither shame nor prudence, and the characteristics of the beasts dominate him. This is because man is distinguished from beasts solely by thought and discernment; whenever he does not employ these, he partakes with beasts of their habits. . . .

It remains for us now to mention the attributes of the perfect man which comprise the good qualities of character, as well as the way by which he arrives at perfection. Hence we say: The perfect man is he whom virtue has not abandoned and whom vice has not disfigured. A man rarely reaches this extreme but whenever man does reach this limit, he is more comparable to the angels than to men. For man is imprinted with varieties of defect; all sorts of evil overwhelm him in accord with his inmost nature; rarely does he ever purify himself from all of these or is his soul free from every defect and deficiency. . . .

Nevertheless, perfection, although precious and difficult to partake of, is possible. It is the ultimate toward which man strives and a final end which has a limit. Whenever human resolve is sincere and man gives his striving its due, he is worthy to reach to his final end, . . . and to arrive at his desire.

Human Nature Is Evil

Xunzi

The nature of man is evil; his goodness is the result of his activity.[1] Now, man's inborn nature is to seek for gain. If this tendency is followed, strife and rapacity result and deference and compliance disappear. By inborn nature one is envious and hates others. If these tendencies are followed, injury and destruction result and loyalty and faithfulness disappear. By inborn nature one possesses the desires of ear and eye and likes sound and beauty. If these tendencies are followed, lewdness and licentiousness result, and the pattern and order of propriety and righteousness disappear. Therefore to follow man's nature and his feelings will inevitably result in strife and rapacity, combine with rebellion and disorder, and end in violence. Therefore there must be the civilizing influence of teachers and laws and the guidance of propriety and righteousness, and then it will result in deference and compliance, combine with pattern and order, and end in discipline. From this point of view, it is clear that the nature of man is evil and that his goodness is the result of activity.

Crooked wood must be heated and bent before it becomes straight. Blunt metal must be ground and whetted before it becomes sharp. Now the nature of man is evil. It must depend on teachers and laws to become correct and achieve propriety and righteousness and then it becomes disciplined. Without teachers and laws, man is unbalanced, off the track, and incorrect. Without propriety and righteousness, there will be rebellion, disorder, and chaos. The sage-kings of antiquity, knowing that the nature of man is evil, and that it is unbalanced, off the track, incorrect, rebellious, disorderly, and undisciplined, created the rules of propriety and righteousness and instituted laws and systems in order to correct man's feelings, transform them, and direct them so that they all may become disciplined and conform with the Way (Tao). Now people who are influenced by teachers and laws, accumulate literature and knowledge, and follow propriety and righteousness are superior men, whereas those who give rein to their feelings, enjoy indulgence, and violate propriety and righteousness are inferior men. From this point of view, it is clear that the nature of man is evil and that his goodness is the result of his activity.

Comment. In the *Hsün Tzu*, rules of propriety and law are often spoken of together, giving the impression that, unlike Confucius and Mencius who advocated propriety (*li*) as inner control, Hsün Tzu advocated it for external control. Thus rules of propriety shifted from being a means of personal moral cultivation to one of social control.

Mencius said, "Man learns because his nature is good." This is not true. He did not know the nature of man and did not understand the distinction between man's nature and his effort. Man's nature is the product of Nature; it cannot be learned and cannot be worked for. Propriety and righteousness are produced by the sage. They can be learned by men and can be accomplished through work. What is in man but cannot be learned or worked for is his nature. What is in him and can be learned or accomplished through work is what can be achieved through activity. This is the difference between human nature and human activity. Now by nature man's eye can see and his ear can hear. But the clarity of vision is not outside his eye and the distinctness of hearing is not outside his ear. It is clear that clear vision and distinct hearing cannot be learned. Mencius said, "The nature of man is good; it [becomes evil] because man destroys his original nature." This is a mistake. By nature man departs from his primitive character and capacity as soon as he is born, and he is bound to destroy it. From this point of view, it is clear that man's nature is evil.

By the original goodness of human nature is meant that man does not depart from his primitive character but makes it beautiful, and does not depart from his original capacity but utilizes it, so that beauty being [inherent] in his primitive character and goodness being [inherent] in his will are like clear vision being inherent in the eye and distinct hearing being inherent in the ear. Hence we say that the eye is clear and the ear is sharp. Now by nature man desires repletion when hungry, desires warmth when cold, and desires rest when tired. This is man's natural feeling. But now when a man is hungry and sees some elders before him, he does not eat ahead of them but yields to them. When he is tired, he dares not seek rest because he wants to take over the work [of elders]. The son yielding to or taking over the work of his father, and the younger brother yielding to or taking over the work of his older brother—these two lines of action are contrary to original nature and violate natural feeling. Nevertheless, the way of filial piety is the pattern and order of propriety and righteousness. If one follows his natural feeling, he will have no deference or compliance. Deference and compliance are opposed to his natural feelings. From this point of view, it is clear that man's nature is evil and that his goodness is the result of his activity.

Someone may ask, "If man's nature is evil, whence come propriety and righteousness?" I answer that all propriety and righteousness are results of the activity of sages and not originally produced from man's nature. The potter pounds the clay and makes the vessel. This being the case, the vessel is the product of the artisan's activity and not the original product of man's nature. The artisan hews a piece of wood and makes a vessel. This being the case, the vessel is the product of the artisan's activity and not the original product of man's nature. The sages gathered together their ideas and thoughts and became familiar with activity, facts, and principles, and thus produced propriety and righteousness and instituted laws and systems. This being the case, propriety and righteousness, and laws and systems are the products of the activity of the sages and not the original products of man's nature.

As to the eye desiring color, the ear desiring sound, the mouth desiring flavor, the heart desiring gain, and the body desiring pleasure and ease—all these are products of man's original nature and feelings. They are natural reactions to stimuli and do not require any work to be produced. But if the reaction is not naturally produced by the stimulus but requires work before it can be produced, then it is the result of activity. Here lies the evidence of the difference between what is produced by man's nature and what is produced by his effort. Therefore the sages transformed man's nature and aroused him to activity. As activity was aroused, propriety and righteousness were produced, and as propriety and righteousness were produced, laws and systems were instituted. This being the case, propriety, righteousness, laws, and systems are all products of the sages. In his nature, the sage is common with and not different from ordinary people. It is in his effort that he is different from and superior to them.

It is the original nature and feelings of man to love profit and seek gain. Suppose some brothers are to divide their property. If they follow their natural feelings, they will love profit and seek gain, and thus will do violence to each other and grab the property. But if they are transformed by the civilizing influence of the pattern and order of propriety and righteousness, they will even yield to outsiders. Therefore, brothers will quarrel if they follow their original nature and feeling but, if they are transformed by righteousness and propriety, they will yield to outsiders.

People desire to be good because their nature is evil. If one has little, he wants abundance. If he is ugly, he wants good looks. If his circumstances are narrow, he wants them to be broad. If poor, he wants to be rich. And if he is in a low position, he wants a high position. If he does not have it himself, he will seek it outside. If he is rich, he does not desire more wealth, and if he is in a high position, he does not desire more power. If he has it himself, he will not seek it outside. From this point of view, [it is clear that] people desire to be good because their nature is evil.

Now by nature a man does not originally possess propriety and righteousness; hence he makes strong effort to learn and seeks to have them. By nature he does not know propriety and righteousness; hence he thinks and deliberates and seeks to know them. Therefore, by what is inborn alone, man will not have or know propriety and righteousness. There will be disorder if man is without propriety and righteousness. There will be violence if he does not know propriety and righteousness. Consequently by what is inborn alone, disorder and violence are within man himself. From this point of view, it is clear that the nature of man is evil and that his goodness is the result of his activity.

Mencius said, "The nature of man is good." I say that this is not true. By goodness at any time in any place is meant true principles and peaceful order, and by evil is meant imbalance, violence, and disorder. This is the distinction between good and evil. Now do we honestly regard man's nature as characterized by true principles and peaceful order? If so, why are sages necessary and why are propriety and righteousness necessary? What possible improvement can sages make on true principles and peaceful order?

Now this is not the case. Man's nature is evil. Therefore the sages of antiquity, knowing that man's nature is evil, that it is unbalanced and incorrect, and that it is violent, disorderly, and undisciplined, established the authority of rulers to govern the people, set forth clearly propriety and righteousness to transform them, instituted laws and governmental measures to rule them, and made punishment severe to restrain them, so that all will result in good order and be in accord with goodness. Such is the government of sage-kings and the transforming influence of propriety and righteousness.

But suppose we try to remove the authority of the ruler, do away with the transforming influence of propriety and righteousness, discard the rule of laws and governmental measure, do away with the restraint of punishment, and stand and see how people of the world deal with one another. In this situation, the strong would injure the weak and rob them, and the many would do violence to the few and shout them down. The whole world would be in violence and disorder and all would perish in an instant. From this point of view, It is clear that man's nature is evil and that his goodness is the result of his activity.

The man versed in ancient matters will certainly support them with evidences from the present, and he who is versed in [the principles of] Nature will certainly support them with evidences from the world of men. In any discussion, the important things are discrimination and evidence. One can then sit down and talk about things, propagate them, and put them into practice. But now Mencius said that man's nature is good. He had neither discrimination nor evidence. He sat down and talked about the matter but rose and could neither propagate it nor put it into practice. Is this not going too far? Therefore if man's nature is good, sage-kings can be done away with and propriety and righteousness can be stopped. But if his nature is evil, sage-kings are to be followed and propriety and righteousness are to be greatly valued. For bending came into existence because there was crooked wood, the carpenter's square and ruler came into existence because things are not straight, and the authority of rule is instituted and propriety and righteousness are made clear because man's nature is evil. From this point of view, it is clear that man's nature is evil and that his goodness is the result of his activity. Straight wood does not depend on bending to become straight; it is straight by nature. But crooked wood must be bent and heated before it becomes straight because by nature it is not straight. Now, the nature of man is evil. It has to depend on the government of sage-kings and the transforming influence of propriety and righteousness, and then all will result in good order and be in accord with goodness. From this point of view, it is clear that man's nature is evil and that his goodness the result of his activity. . . .

Note

1. According to Yang Liang, *wei* (artificial) is "man's activity." It means what is created by man and not a result of natural conditions. This is accepted by most commentators, including Hao I-hsing, who has pointed out that in ancient times *wei* (ordinarily mearung false or artificial) and *wei* (activity) were interchangeable.

Virtue and Happiness

Aristotle

Every art and every scientific inquiry, and similarly every action and purpose, may be said to aim at some good. Hence the good has been well defined as that at which all things aim. But it is clear that there is a difference in ends; for the ends are sometimes activities, and sometimes results beyond the mere activities. Where there are ends beyond the action, the results are naturally superior to the action.

As there are various actions, arts, and sciences, it follows that the ends are also various. Thus health is the end of the medical art, a ship of shipbuilding, victory of strategy, and wealth of economics. It often happens that a number of such arts or sciences combine for a single enterprise, as the art of making bridles and all such other arts as furnish the implements of horsemanship combine for horsemanship, and horsemanship and every military action for strategy; and in the same way, other arts or sciences combine for others. In all these cases, the ends of the master arts or sciences, whatever they may be, are more desirable than those of the subordinate arts or sciences, as it is for the sake of the former that the latter are pursued. It makes no difference to the argument whether the activities themselves are the ends of the action, or something beyond the activities, as in the above-mentioned sciences.

If it is true that in the sphere of action there is some end which we wish for its own sake, and for the sake of which we wish everything else, and if we do not desire everything for the sake of something else (for, if that is so, the process will go on *ad infinitum,* and our desire will be idle and futile), clearly this end will be good and the supreme good. Does it not follow then that the knowledge of this good is of great importance for the conduct of life? Like archers who have a mark at which to aim, shall we not have a better chance of attaining what we want? If this is so, we must endeavor to comprehend, at least in outline, what this good is, and what science or faculty makes it its object. . . .

As every science and undertaking aims at some good, what is in our view the good at which political science aims, and what is the highest of all practical goods? As to its name there is, I may say, a general agreement. The masses and the cultured classes agree in calling it happiness, and conceive that "to live well" or "to do well" is the same thing as "to be happy." But as to what happiness is they do not agree, nor do the masses give the same account of it as the philosophers. The former take it to be something visible and palpable, such as pleasure, wealth, or honor; different people, however, give different definitions of it, and often even the same man gives different definitions at different times. When he is ill, it is health, when he is poor, it is wealth; if he is conscious of his own ignorance, he envies people who use grand language above his own comprehension. Some philosophers, on the other hand, have held that, besides these various goods, there is an absolute good which is the cause of goodness in them all. [These were members of Plato's school of thought.] It would perhaps be a waste of time to examine all these opinions; it will be enough to examine such as are most popular or as seem to be more or less reasonable.

... Men's conception of the good or of happiness may be read in the lives they lead. Ordinary or vulgar people conceive it to be a pleasure, and accordingly choose a life of enjoyment. For there are, we may say, three conspicuous types of life, the sensual, the political, and, thirdly, the life of thought. Now the mass of men present an absolutely slavish appearance, choosing the life of brute beasts, but they have ground for so doing because so many persons in authority share the tastes of Sardanapalus. [A half legendary ruler of ancient Assyria, whose name to the Greeks stood for the extreme of Oriental luxury and extravagance.] Cultivated and energetic people, on the other hand, identify happiness with honor, as honor is the general end of political life. But this seems too superficial an idea for our present purpose; for honor depends more upon the people who pay it than upon the person to whom it is paid, and the good we feel is something which is proper to a man himself and cannot be easily taken away from him. Men too appear to seek honor in order to be assured of their own goodness. Accordingly, they seek it at the hands of the sage and of those who know them well, and they seek it on the ground of their virtue; clearly then, in their judgment at any rate, virtue is better than honor. Perhaps then we might look on virtue rather than honor as the end of political life. Yet even this idea appears not quite complete; for a man may possess virtue and yet be asleep or inactive throughout life, and not only so, but he may experience the greatest calamities and misfortunes. Yet no one would call such a life a life of happiness, unless he were maintaining a paradox. But we need not dwell further on this subject, since it is sufficiently discussed in popular philosophical treatises. The third life is the life of thought, which we will discuss later. [The discussion of the life of thought occurs in Book X.]

The life of money making is a life of constraint; and wealth is obviously not the good of which we are in quest; for it is useful merely as a means to something else. It would be more reasonable to take the things mentioned before—sensual pleasure, honor, and virtue—as ends than wealth, since they are things desired on their own account. Yet these too are evidently not ends, although much argument has been employed to show that they are. . . .

But leaving this subject for the present, let us revert to the good of which we are in quest and consider what it may be. For it seems different in different activities or arts; it is one thing in medicine, another in strategy, and so on. What is the good in each of these instances? It is presumably that for the sake of which all else is done. In medicine this is health, in strategy victory, in architecture a house, and so on. In every activity and undertaking it is the end, since it is for the sake of the end that all people do whatever else they do. If then there is an end for all our activity, this will be the good to be accomplished; and if there are several such ends, it will be these.

Our argument has arrived by a different path at the same point as before; but we must endeavor to make it still plainer. Since there are more ends than one, and some of these ends—for example, wealth, flutes, and instruments generally—we desire as means to something else, it is evident that not all are final ends. But the highest good is clearly something final. Hence if there is only one final end, this will be the object of which we are in search; and if there are more than one, it will be the most final. We call that which is sought after for its own sake more final than that which is sought after as a means to something else; we call that which is never desired as a means to something else more final than things that are desired both for themselves and as means to something else. Therefore, we call absolutely final that which is always desired for itself and never as a means to something else. Now happiness more than anything else answers to this description. For happiness we always desire for its own sake and never as a means to something else, whereas honor, pleasure, intelligence, and every virtue we desire partly for their own sakes (for we should desire them independently of what might result from them), but partly also as means to happiness, because we suppose they will prove instruments of happiness. Happiness, on the other hand, nobody desires for the sake of these things, nor indeed as a means to anything else at all. . . .

Perhaps, however, it seems a commonplace to say that happiness is the supreme good; what is wanted is to define its nature a little more clearly. The best way of arriving at such a definition will probably be to ascertain the function of man. For, as with a flute player, a sculptor, or any artist, or in fact anybody who has a special function or activity, his goodness and excellence seem to lie in his function, so it would seem to be with man, if indeed he has a special function. Can it be said that, while a carpenter and a cobbler have special functions and activities, man, unlike them, is naturally functionless? Or, as the eye, the hand, the foot, and similarly each part of the body has a special function, so may man be regarded as having a special function apart from all these? What, then, can this function be? It is not life; for life is apparently something that man shares with plants; and we are looking for something peculiar to him. We must exclude therefore the life of nutrition and growth. There is next what may be called the life of sensation. But this too, apparently, is shared by man with horses, cattle, and all other animals. There remains what I may call the active life of the rational part of man's being. Now this rational part is twofold; one part is rational in the sense of being obedient to reason, and the other in the sense of possessing and exercising reason and intelligence. The active life too may be conceived of in two ways, [In other words, life may be taken to mean either the mere possession of certain faculties or their active exercise.] either as a state of character, or as an activity; but we mean by it the life of activity, as this seems to be the truer form of the conception.

The function of man then is activity of soul in accordance with reason, or not apart from reason. Now, the function of a man of a certain kind, and of a man who is good of that kind—for example, of a harpist and a good harpist—are in our view the same in kind. This is true of all people of all kinds without exception, the superior excellence being only an addition to the function; for it is the function of a harpist to play the harp, and of a good harpist to play the harp well. This being so, if we define the function of man as a kind of life, and this life as an activity of the soul or a course of action in accordance with reason, and if the function of a good man is such activity of a good and noble kind, and if everything is well done when it is done in accordance with its proper excellence, it follows that the good of man is activity of soul in accordance with virtue, or, if there are more virtues than one, in accordance with the best and most complete virtue. But we must add the words "in a complete life." For as one swallow or one day does not make a spring, so one day or a short time does not make a man blessed or happy. . . .

Our account accords too with the view of those who hold that happiness is virtue or excellence of some sort; for activity in accordance with virtue is virtue. But there is plainly a considerable difference between calling the supreme good possession or use, a state of mind, or an activity. For a state of mind may exist without producing anything good—for example, if a person is asleep, or in any other way inert. Not so with an activity, since activity implies acting and acting well. As in the Olympic games it is not the most beautiful and strongest who receive the crown but those who actually enter the combat, for from those come the victors, so it is those who act that win rightly what is noble and good in life.

Their life too is pleasant in itself. For pleasure is a state of mind, and whatever a man is fond of is pleasant to him, as a horse is to a lover of horses, a show to a lover of spectacles, and, similarly, just acts to a lover of justice, and virtuous acts in general to a lover of virtue. Now most men find a sense of discord in their pleasures, because their pleasures are not all naturally pleasant. But the lovers of nobleness take pleasure in what is naturally pleasant, and virtuous acts are naturally pleasant. Such acts then are pleasant both to these persons and in themselves. Nor does the life of such persons need more pleasure attached to it as a sort of charm; it possesses pleasure in itself. For, it may be added, a man who does not delight in noble acts is not good; as nobody would call a man just who did not enjoy just action, or liberal who did not enjoy liberal action, and so on. If this is so, it follows that acts of virtue are pleasant in themselves. They are also good and noble, and good and noble in the highest degree, for the judgment of the virtuous man on them is right, and his judgment is as we have described. Happiness then is the best and noblest and pleasantest thing in the world. . . .

Still it is clear, as we said, that happiness requires the addition of external goods; for it impossible, or at least difficult, to do noble deeds with no outside means. For many things can be done only through the aid of friends or wealth or political power; and there are some things the lack of which spoils our felicity, such as good birth, wholesome children, and personal beauty. For a man who is extremely ugly in appearance or low born or solitary and childless can hardly be happy; perhaps still less so, if he has exceedingly bad children or friends, or has had good children or friends and lost them by death. As we said, then, happiness seems to need prosperity of this kind in addition to virtue. For this reason some persons identify happiness with good fortune, though others do so with virtue. . . .

It is reasonable then not to call an ox or a horse or any other animal happy; for none of them is capable of sharing in this activity. For the same reason no child can be happy, since the youth of a child keeps him for the time being from such activity; if a child is ever called happy, the ground of felicitation is his promise, rather than his actual performance. For happiness demands, as we said, a complete virtue and a complete life. And there are all sorts of changes and chances in life, and the most prosperous of men may in his old age fall into extreme calamities, as Priam did in the heroic legends. [The disastrous fate of Priam, king of Troy, was part of the well-known Homeric tales.] And a person who has experienced such chances and died a miserable death, nobody calls happy. . . .

If it is right to wait for the end, and only when the end has come, to call a man happy, not for being happy then but for having been so before, surely it is an extraordinary thing that, at the time when he is happy, we should not speak the truth about him, because we are unwilling to call the living happy in view of the changes to which they are liable, and because we have formed an idea of happiness as something permanent and exempt from the possibility of change, while every man is liable to many turns of fortune's wheel. . . .

The difficulty we have now discussed proves again the correctness of our definition. For there is no human function so constant as virtuous activities; . . . Among these activities too the most noble are the most permanent, and it is of them that the life of happiness chiefly and most continuously consists. This is apparently the reason why they are not likely to be forgotten. [Aristotle means that it is comparatively easy to forget scientific truths, when they have once been learned, but it is difficult, if not impossible, to lose the habit of virtuous activity. In other words, knowledge is less stable, and therefore less valuable, than character.] The element of durability then which is required will be found in the happy man, and he will preserve his happiness through life; for always or chiefly he will pursue such actions and thoughts as accord with virtue; nor will anyone bear the chances of life so nobly, with such a perfect composure, as he who is truly good. . . .

Now the events of chance are numerous and of different magnitudes. Small pieces of good fortune or the reverse do not turn the scale of life in any way, but great and numerous events make life happier if they turn out well, since they naturally give it beauty and the use of them may be noble and good. If, on the other hand, they turn out badly, they mar and mutilate happiness by causing pain and hinderances to many activities. Still, even in these circumstances, nobility shines out when a person bears with calmness the weight of accumulated misfortunes, not from insensibility but from dignity and greatness of spirit.

Then if activities determine the quality of life, as we said, no happy man can become miserable; for he will never do what is hateful and mean. For our idea of the truly good and wise man is that he bears all the chances of life with dignity and always does what is best in the circumstances, as a good general makes the best use of the forces at his command in war, or a good cobbler makes the best shoe with the leather given him, and so on through the whole series of the arts. If this is so, the happy man can never become miserable. I do not say that he will be fortunate if he meets such chances of life as Priam. Yet he will not be variable or constantly changing, for he will not be moved from his happiness easily or by ordinary misfortunes, but only by great and numerous ones; nor after them will he quickly regain his happiness. If he regains it at all, it will be only over a long and complete period of time and after great and notable achievement.

We may safely then define a happy man as one who is active in accord with perfect virtue and adequately furnished with external goods, not for some chance period of time but for his whole lifetime. . . .

Inasmuch as **happiness is an activity of soul in accordance with complete or perfect virtue,** it is necessary to consider virtue, as this will perhaps be the best way of studying happiness. . . .

Virtue or excellence being twofold, partly intellectual and partly moral, intellectual virtue is both originated and fostered mainly by teaching; it therefore demands experience and time. Moral virtue on the other hand is the outcome of habit, . . . From this fact it is clear that no moral virtue is implanted in us by nature; a law of nature cannot be altered by habituation. . . . It is neither by nature then nor in defiance of nature that virtues are implanted in us. Nature gives us the capacity of receiving them, and that capacity is perfected by habit. . . .

It is not enough to state merely that virtue is a moral state, we must also describe the character of that moral state.

It must be laid down then that every virtue or excellence has the effect of producing a good condition of that of which it is a virtue or excellence, and of enabling it to perform its function well. Thus the excellence of the eye makes the eye good and its function good, as it is by the excellence of the eye that we see well. Similarly, the excellence of the horse makes a horse excellent and good at racing, at carrying its rider and at facing the enemy.

If then this is universally true, the virtue or excellence of man will be such a moral state as makes a man good and able to perform his proper function well. We have already explained how this will be the case, but another way of making it clear will be to study the nature or character of this virtue.

Now in everything, whether it be continuous or discrete, it is possible to take a greater, a smaller, or an equal amount, and this either absolutely or in relation to ourselves, the equal being a mean between excess and deficiency. By the mean in respect of the thing itself, or the absolute mean, I understand that which is equally distinct from both extremes; and this is one and the same thing for everybody. By the mean considered relatively to ourselves I understand that which is neither too much nor too little; but this is not one thing, nor is it the same for everybody. Thus if 10 be too much and 2 too little we take 6 as a mean in respect of the thing itself; for 6 is as much greater than 2 as it is less than 10, and this is a mean in arithmetical proportion. But the mean considered relatively to ourselves must not be ascertained in this way. It does not follow that if 10 pounds of meat be too much and 2 be too little for a man to eat, a trainer will order him 6 pounds, as this may itself be too much or too little for the person who is to take it; it will be too little e.g. for Milo [the famous Crotoniate wrestler], but too much for a beginner in gymnastics. It will be the same with running and wrestling; the right amount will vary with the individual. This being so, everybody who understands his business avoids alike excess and deficiency; he seeks and chooses the mean, not the absolute mean, but the mean considered relatively to ourselves.

Every science then performs its function well, if it regards the mean and refers the works which it produces to the mean. This is the reason why it is usually said of successful works that it is impossible to take anything from them or to add anything to them, which implies that excess or deficiency is fatal to excellence but that the mean state ensures it. Good artists too, as we say, have an eye to the mean in their works. But virtue, like Nature herself, is more accurate and better than any art; virtue therefore will aim at the mean;—I speak of moral virtue, as it is moral virtue which is concerned with emotions and actions, and it is these which admit of excess and deficiency and the mean. Thus it is possible to go too far, or not to go far enough, in respect of fear, courage, desire, anger, pity, and pleasure and pain generally, and the excess and the deficiency are alike wrong; but to experience these emotions at the right times and on the right occasions and towards the right persons and for the right causes and in the right manner is the mean or the supreme good, which is characteristic of virtue. Similarly there may be excess, deficiency, or the mean, in regard to actions. But virtue is concerned with emotions and actions, and here excess is an error and deficiency a fault, whereas the mean is successful and laudable, and success and merit are both characteristics of virtue.

It appears then that virtue is a mean state, so far at least as it aims at the mean. . . .

Virtue then is a state of deliberate moral purpose consisting in a mean that is relative to ourselves, the mean being determined by reason, or as a prudent man would determine it. . . .

But it is not enough to lay down this as a general rule; it is necessary to apply it to particular cases. As in reasonings upon actions, general statements, although they are broader, are less exact than particular statements. For all action refers to particulars, and it is essential that our theories should harmonize with the particular cases to which they apply.

We must take particular virtues then from the catalogue of virtues.

In regard to feelings of fear and confidence, courage is a mean state. On the side of excess, he whose fearlessness is excessive has no name, as often happens, but he whose confidence is excessive is foolhardy, while he whose timidity is excessive and whose confidence is deficient is a coward.

In respect of pleasures and pains, although not indeed of all pleasures and pains, and to a less extent in respect of pains than of pleasures, the mean state is temperance, the excess is licentiousness. We never find people who are deficient in regard to pleasures; accordingly such people again have not received a name, but we may call them insensible.

As regards the giving and taking of money, the mean state is liberality, the excess and deficiency are prodigality and illiberality. . . .

In respect of honour and dishonour the mean state is highmindedness, the excess is what is called vanity, the deficiency littlemindedness. . . . Let us now discuss the other virtues in accordance with the method which we have followed hitherto.

Anger, like other emotions, has its excess, its deficiency, and its mean state. It may be said that they have no names, but as we call one who observes the mean gentle, we will call the mean state gentleness. Among the extremes, if a person errs on the side of excess, he may be called passionate and his vice passionateness, if on that of deficiency, he may be called impassive and his deficiency impassivity. . . .

It has now been sufficiently shown that moral virtue is a mean state, and in what sense it is a mean state; it is a mean state as lying between two vices, a vice of excess on the one side and a vice of deficiency on the other, and as aiming at the mean in the emotions and actions.

That is the reason why it is so hard to be virtuous; for it is always hard work to find the mean in anything, e.g., it is not everybody, but only a man of science, who can find the mean or centre of a circle. So too anybody can get angry—that is an easy matter—and anybody can give or spend money, but to give it to the right persons, to give the right amount of it and to give it at the right time and for the right cause and in the right way, this is not what anybody can do, nor is it easy. That is the reason why it is rare and laudable and noble to do well. . . .

If happiness consists of virtuous activity, it must be the activity of the highest virtue, or in other words, of the best part of our nature. Whether it is reason or something else that seems to exercise rule and authority over us by natural right and to reach up to things noble and divine—because it is itself either divine or the most divine part of us—the activity of this part in accordance with its proper virtue will be perfect happiness.

This . . . is an activity of thought or contemplation. Such a view would agree with our previous arguments and with the truth itself; for thought is the highest of our activities, as reason is the highest of our faculties, and the objects with which reason is concerned are the highest that can be known. Thought is also the most continuous, for it can more easily be continuous than any kind of action. We consider pleasure too an essential element of happiness; and we know there is no virtuous activity so pleasant as the activity of wisdom or philosophic reflection. Certainly philosophy is thought to offer pleasures of wonderful purity and certainty; and it is reasonable to suppose that people who know pass their time more pleasantly than people who are only searching.

Self-sufficiency too, of which we hear, is particularly a characteristic of thought activity. For while a philosopher, a just man, and everyone else needs the necessaries of life, after they are adequately provided with these things a just man still needs people to whom and with whom he may do justice, and a temperate man, a brave man, and everyone else needs others too. But the philosopher can contemplate truth by himself, and the wiser he is, the better he can do so. It is perhaps better for him to have fellow workers; nevertheless he is of all the most self-sufficient. It would seem too that this activity is the only one loved for its own sake, since it has no result but thinking; whereas from all practical action we gain something more or less besides the action itself. . . .

We conclude then that happiness reaches as far as the power of thought does, and that the greater a person's power of thought, the greater will be his happiness; not as something accidental but in virtue of his thinking, for that is noble in itself. Hence happiness must be a form of contemplation.

Man, nevertheless, being human, needs some external prosperity. His nature alone is not sufficient to support his thinking; it needs bodily health, food, and care of every kind. We must not however suppose that, because one cannot be happy without some external goods, a great variety of such goods is necessary for happiness. For neither self-sufficiency nor moral action demands excess of such things. We can do noble deeds without being lords of land and sea, for moderate means will enable a person to act virtuously. We may readily see this is so; for private persons are known to do good acts not less but actually more than their rulers. It is enough to have just as much as is needed for virtue. The man who lives in the active exercise of virtue will be happy. . . .

Friendship

Aristotle

It will be natural to discuss friendship or love next, for **friendship is a kind of virtue or implies virtue. It is also indispensable to life. For nobody would choose to live without friends, although he were in possession of every other good.** Nay, it seems that if people are rich and hold official and authoritative positions, they have the greatest need of friends; for what is the good of having this sort of prosperity if one is denied the opportunity of beneficence, which is never so freely or so admirably exercised as towards friends? Or how can it be maintained in safety and security without friends? For the greater a person's importance, the more liable it is to disaster. In poverty and other misfortunes we regard our friends as our only refuge. Again, friends are helpful to us, when we are young, as guarding us from error, and when we are growing old, as taking care of us, and supplying such deficiencies of action as are the consequences of physical weakness, and when we are in the prime of life, as prompting us to noble actions, according to the adage, "Two come together"; for two people have a greater power both of intelligence and of action *than either of the two by himself.*

It would seem that friendship or love is the natural instinct of a parent towards a child, and of a child towards a parent, not only among men, but among birds and animals generally, and among creatures of the same race towards one another, especially among men. This is the reason why we praise men who are the friends of their fellow-men or philanthropists. We may observe too in travelling how near and dear every man is to his fellow-man.

Again, it seems that friendship or love is the bond which holds states together, and that legislators set more store by it than by justice; for concord is apparently akin to friendship, and it is concord that they especially seek to promote, and faction, as being hostility to the state, that they especially try to expel.

If people are friends, there is no need of justice between them; but people may be just, and yet need friendship. Indeed it seems that justice, in its supreme form, assumes the character of friendship.

Nor is friendship indispensable only; it is also noble. We praise people who are fond of their friends, and it is thought to be a noble thing to have many friends, and there are some people who hold that to be a friend is the same thing as to be a good man.

But the subject of friendship or love is one that affords scope for a good many differences of opinion. Some people define it as a sort of likeness, and define people who are like each other as friends. Hence the sayings "Like seeks like," "Birds of a feather," and so on. Others on the contrary say that "two of a trade never agree." Upon this subject *some philosophical thinkers* indulge in more profound physical speculations; Euripides asserting that

> "the parched Earth loves the rain, And the great Heaven rain-laden loves to fall Earthwards";

Heraclitus that "the contending tends together," and that "harmony most beautiful is formed of discords," and that "all things are by strife engendered"; others, among whom is Empedocles, taking the opposite view and urging that "like desires like."

The physical questions we may leave aside as not being germane to the present enquiry. But let us investigate all such questions as are of human interest and relate to characters and emotions, e.g. whether friendship can be formed among all people, or it is impossible for people to be friends if they are vicious, and whether there is one kind of friendship or more than one. . . .

It is possible, I think, to elucidate the subject of friendship or love, by determining what it is that is lovable or an object of love. For it seems that it is not everything which is loved, but only that which is lovable, and that this is what is good or pleasant or useful. It would seem too that a thing is useful if it is a means of gaining something good or pleasant, and if so, it follows that what is good and what is pleasant will be lovable in the sense of being ends.

It may be asked then, Is it that which is good *in itself,* or that which is good relatively to us, that we love? For there is sometimes a difference between them; and the same question may be asked in regard to that which is pleasant. It seems then that everybody loves what is good relatively to himself, and that, while it is the good which is lovable in an absolute sense, it is that which is good relatively to each individual that is lovable in his eyes. It may be said that everybody loves not that which is good, but that which appears good relatively to himself. But this is not an objection that will make any difference; for in that case that which is lovable will be that which appears to be lovable.

There being three motives of friendship or love, it must be observed that we do not apply the term "friendship" or "love" to the affection felt for inanimate things. The reason is (1) that they are incapable of reciprocating affection, and (2) that we do not wish their good; for it would, I think, be ridiculous to wish the good e.g. of wine; if we wish it at all, it is only in the sense of wishing the wine to keep well, in the hope of enjoying it ourselves. But it is admitted that we ought to wish our friend's good for his sake, and not for our own. If we wish people good in this sense, we are called well-wishers, unless our good wishes are returned; such reciprocal well-wishing is called friendship or love.

But it is necessary, I think, to add, that the well-wishing must not be unknown. A person often wishes well to people whom he has not seen, but whom he supposes to be virtuous or useful; and it is possible that one of these persons may entertain the same feeling towards him. Such people then, it is clear, wish well to one another; but they cannot be properly called friends, as their disposition is unknown to each other. It follows that, if they are to be friends, they must be well-disposed to each other, and must wish each other's good, from one of the motives which have been assigned, and that each of them must know the fact of the other wishing him well.

But as the motives of friendship are specifically different, there will be a corresponding difference in the affections and friendships.

The kinds of friendship therefore will be three, being equal in number to the things which are lovable, *or are objects of friendship or love,* as every such object admits of a reciprocal affection between two persons, each of whom is aware of the other's love.

People who love each other wish each other's good in the point characteristic of their love. Accordingly those whose mutual love is based upon utility do not love each other for their own sakes, but only in so far as they derive some benefit one from another. It is the same with those whose love is based upon pleasure. Thus we are fond of witty people, not as possessing a certain character, but as being pleasant to ourselves. People then, whose love is based upon utility, are moved to affection by a sense of their own good, and people whose love is based upon pleasure, by a sense of their own pleasure; and they love a person not for being what he is in himself, but for being useful or pleasant to them. These friendships then are only friendships in an accidental sense; for the person loved is not loved as being what he is, but as being a source either of good or of pleasure. Accordingly, such friendships are easily dissolved, if the persons do not continue always the same; for they abandon their love if they cease to be pleasant or useful to each other. But utility is not a permanent quality; it varies at different times. Thus, when the motive of a friendship is done away, the friendship itself is dissolved, as it was dependent upon that motive. A friendship of this kind seems especially to occur among old people, as in old age we look to profit rather than pleasure, and among such people in the prime of life or in youth as have an eye to their own interest. Friends of this kind do not generally even live together; for sometimes they are not even pleasant to one another; nor do they need the intercourse of friendship, unless they bring some profit to one another, as the pleasure which they afford goes no further than they entertain hopes of deriving benefit from it. Among these friendships we reckon the friendship of hospitality, *i.e. the friendship which exists between a host and his guests.*

It would seem that the friendship of the young is based upon pleasure; for they live by emotion and are most inclined to pursue what is pleasant to them at the moment. But as their time of life changes, their pleasures are transformed. They are therefore quick at making friendships and quick at abandoning them; for the friendship changes with the object which pleases them, and friendship of this kind is liable to sudden change. Young men are amorous too, amorousness being generally a matter of emotion and pleasure; hence they fall in love and soon afterwards fall out of love, changing from one condition to another many times in the same day. But amorous people wish to spend their days and lives together, as it is thus that they attain the object of their friendship.

The perfect friendship or love is the friendship or love of people who are good and alike in virtue; for these people are alike in wishing each other's good, in so far as they are good, and they are good in themselves. But it is people who wish the good of their friends for their friends' sake that are in the truest sense friends, as their friendship is the consequence of their own character, and is not an accident. Their friendship therefore continues as long as their virtue, and virtue is a permanent quality.

Again, each of them is good in an absolute sense, and good in relation to his friend. For good men are not only good in an absolute sense, but serve each other's interest. They are pleasant too; for the good are pleasant in an absolute sense, and pleasant in relation to one another, as everybody finds pleasure in such actions as are proper to him, and the like, and all good people act alike or nearly alike.

Such a friendship is naturally permanent, as it unites in itself all the proper conditions of friendship. For the motive of all friendship or affection is good or pleasure, whether it be absolute or relative to the person who feels the affection, and it depends upon a certain similarity. In the friendship of good men all these specified conditions belong to the friends in themselves; for other friendships *only* bear a resemblance to the perfect friendship. That which is good in an absolute sense is also in an absolute sense pleasant. These are the principal objects of affection, and it is upon these that affectionate feeling, and affection in the highest and best sense, depend.

Friendships of this kind are likely to be rare; for such people are few. They require time and familiarity too; for, as the adage puts it, it is impossible for people to know one another until they have consumed the proverbial salt together; nor can people admit one another to friendship, or be friends at all, until each has been proved lovable and trustworthy to the other.

People, who are quick to treat one another as friends, wish to be friends but are not so really, unless they are lovable and know each other to be lovable; for the wish to be friends may arise in a minute, but not friendship. . . .

It is the friendship of the good which is friendship in the truest sense, as has been said several times. For it seems that, while that which is good or pleasant in an absolute sense is an object of love and desire, that which is good or pleasant to each individual is an object of love or desire to him; but the love or desire of one good man for another depends upon such goodness and pleasantness as are at once absolute and relative to the good.

Affection resembles a feeling but friendship resembles a moral state. For while affection may be felt for inanimate as much as for animate things, the love of friends for one another implies moral purpose, and such purpose is the outcome of a moral state.

Again, we wish the good of those whom we love for their own sake, and the wish is governed not by feeling but by the moral state. In loving our friend too, we love what is good for ourselves; as when a good man becomes a friend, he becomes a blessing to his friend. Accordingly each of two friends loves what is good for himself, and returns as much as he receives in good wishes and in pleasure; for, as the proverb says, equality is friendship.

A Good Will

Immanuel Kant

Nothing can possibly be conceived in the world, or even out of it, which can be called good without qualification, except a *good will*. Intelligence, wit, judgment, and the other *talents* of the mind, however they may be named, or courage, resolution, perseverance, as qualities of temperament, are undoubtedly good and desirable in many respects; but these gifts of nature may also become extremely bad and mischievous if the will which is to make use of them, and which, therefore, constitutes what is called *character*, is not good. It is the same with the *gifts of fortune*. Power, riches, honor, even health, and the general well-being and contentment with one's condition which is called *happiness*, inspire pride, and often presumption, if there is not a good will to correct the influence of these on the mind, and with this also to rectify the whole principle of acting, and adapt it to its end. The sight of a being who is not adorned with a single feature of a pure and good will, enjoying unbroken prosperity, can never give pleasure to an impartial rational spectator. Thus a good will appears to constitute the indispensable condition even of being worthy of happiness.

There are even some qualities which are of service to this good will itself, and may facilitate its action, yet which have no intrinsic unconditional value, but always presuppose a good will, and this qualifies the esteem that we justly have for them, and does not permit us to regard them as absolutely good. Moderation in the affections and passions, self-control, and calm deliberation are not only good in many respects, but even seem to constitute part of the intrinsic worth of the person; but they are far from deserving to be called good without qualification, although they have been so unconditionally praised by the ancients. For without the principles of a good will, they may become extremely bad; and the coolness of a villain not only makes him far more dangerous, but also directly makes him more abominable in our eyes than he would have been without it.

A good will is good not because of what it performs or effects, not by its aptness for the attainment of some proposed end, but simply by virtue of the volition—that is, it is good in itself, and considered by itself is to be esteemed much higher than all that can be brought about by it in favor of any inclination, nay, even of the sum-total of all inclinations. Even if it should happen that, owing to special disfavor of fortune, or the niggardly provision of a step-motherly nature, this will should wholly lack power to accomplish its purpose, if with its greatest efforts it should yet achieve nothing, and there should remain only the good will (not, to be sure, a mere wish, but the summoning of all means in our power), then, like a jewel, it would still shine by its own light, as a thing which has its whole value in itself. Its usefulness or fruitlessness can neither add to nor take away anything from this value. It would be, as it were, only the setting to enable us to handle it the more conveniently in common commerce, or to attract to it the attention of those who are not yet connoisseurs, but not to recommend it to true connoisseurs, or to determine its value. . . .

We have then to develop the notion of a will which deserves to be highly esteemed for itself, and is good without a view to anything further, a notion which exists already in the sound natural understanding, requiring rather to be cleared up than to be taught, and which in estimating the value of our actions always takes the first place and constitutes the condition of all the rest. In order to do this, we will take the notion of duty, which includes that of a good will, although implying certain subjective restrictions and hindrances. These, however, far from concealing it or rendering it unrecognizable, rather bring it out by contrast and make it shine forth so much the brighter.

I omit here all actions which are already recognized as inconsistent with duty, although they may be useful for this or that purpose, for with these the question whether they are done *from duty* cannot arise at all, since they even conflict with it. I also set aside those actions which really conform to duty, but to which men have *no* direct *inclination*, performing them because they are impelled thereto by some other inclination. For in this case we can readily distinguish whether the action which agrees with duty is done *from duty* or from a selfish view. It is much harder to make this distinction when the action accords with duty, and the subject has besides a *direct* inclination to it. For example, it is always a matter of duty that a dealer should not overcharge an inexperienced purchaser; and wherever there is much commerce the prudent tradesman does not overcharge, but keeps a fixed price for everyone, so that a child buys of him as well as any other. Men are thus *honestly* served; but this is not enough to make us believe that the tradesman has so acted from duty and from principles of honesty; his own advantage required it; it is out of the question in this case to suppose that he might besides have a direct inclination in favor of the buyers, so that, as it were, from love he should give no advantage to one over another. Accordingly the action was done neither from duty nor from direct inclination, but merely with a selfish view.

On the other hand, it is a duty to maintain one's life; and, in addition, everyone has also a direct inclination to do so. But on this account the often anxious care which most men take for it has no intrinsic worth, and their maxim has no moral import. They preserve their life *as duty requires*, no doubt, but not *because duty requires*. On the other hand, if adversity and hopeless sorrow have completely taken away the relish for life, if the unfortunate one, strong in mind, indignant at his fate rather than desponding or dejected, wishes for death, and yet preserves his life without loving it—not from inclination or fear, but from duty—then his maxim has a moral worth.

To be beneficent when we can is a duty; and besides this, there are many minds so sympathetically constituted that, without any other motive of vanity or self-interest, they find a pleasure in spreading joy around them, and can take delight in the satisfaction of others so far as it is their own work. But I maintain that in such a case an action of this kind, however proper, however amiable it may be, has nevertheless no true moral worth, but is on a level with other inclinations, for example, the inclination to honor, which, if it is happily directed to that which is in fact of public utility and accordant with duty, and consequently honorable, deserves praise and encouragement, but not esteem. For the maxim lacks the moral import, namely, that such actions be done *from duty*, not from inclination. Put the case that the mind of that philanthropist was clouded by sorrow of his own, extinguishing all sympathy with the lot of others, and that while he still has the power to benefit others in distress, he is not touched by their trouble because he is absorbed with his own; and now suppose that he tears himself out of this dead insensibility and performs the action without any inclination to it, but simply from duty, then first has his action its genuine moral worth. Further still, if nature has put little sympathy in the heart of this or that man, if he, supposed to be an upright man, is by temperament cold and indifferent to the sufferings of others, perhaps because in respect of his own he is provided with the special gift of patience and fortitude, and supposes, or even requires, that others should have the same—and such a man would certainly not be the meanest product of nature—but if nature had not specially framed him for a philanthropist, would he not still find in himself a source from whence to give himself a far higher worth than that of a good-natured temperament could be? Unquestionably. It is just in this that the moral worth of the character is brought out which is incomparably the highest of all, namely, that he is beneficent, not from inclination, but from duty. . . .

An action done from duty derives its moral worth, *not from the purpose* which is to be attained by it, but from the maxim by which it is determined, and therefore does not depend on the realization of the object of the action, but merely on the *principle of volition* by which the action has taken place, without regard to any object of desire. It is clear from what precedes that the purpose which we may have in view in our actions, or their effects regarded as ends and springs of the will, cannot give to actions any unconditional or moral worth. In what, then, can their worth lie if it is not to consist in the will and in reference to its expected effect? It cannot lie anywhere but in the *principle of the will* without regard to the ends which can be attained by the action. . . .

Thus the moral worth of an action does not lie in the effect expected from it, nor in any principle of action which requires to borrow its motive from this expected effect. For all these effects—agreeableness of one's condition, and even the promotion of the happiness of others—could have been also brought about by other causes, so that for this there would have been no need of the will of a rational being; whereas it is in this alone that the supreme and unconditional good can be found. The pre-eminent good which we call moral can therefore consist in nothing else than *the conception of law* in itself, *which certainly is only possible in a rational being*, in so far as this conception, and not the expected effect, determines the will. This is a good which is already present in the person who acts accordingly, and we have not to wait for it to appear first in the result.

But what sort of law can that be the conception of which must determine the will, even without paying any regard to the effect expected from it, in order that this will may be called good absolutely and without qualification? As I have deprived the will of every impulse which could arise to it from obedience to any law, there remains nothing but the universal conformity of its actions to law in general, which alone is to serve the will as a principle, that is, **I am never to act otherwise than so** *that I could also will that my maxim should become a universal law.* Here, now, it is the simple conformity to law in general, without assuming any particular law applicable to certain actions, that serves the will as its principle, and must so serve it if duty is not to be a vain delusion and a chimerical notion. The common reason of men in its practical judgments perfectly coincides with this, and always has in view the principle here suggested. Let the question be, for example: May I when in distress make a promise with the intention not to keep it? I readily distinguish here between the two significations which the question may have: whether it is prudent or whether it is right to make a false promise? The former may undoubtedly often be the case. I see clearly indeed that it is not enough to extricate myself from a present difficulty by means of this subterfuge, but it must be well considered whether there may not hereafter spring from this lie much greater inconvenience than that from which I now free myself, and as, with all my supposed *cunning,* the consequences cannot be so easily foreseen but that credit once lost may be much more injurious to me than any mischief which I seek to avoid at present, it should be considered whether it would not be more *prudent* to act herein according to a universal maxim, and to make it a habit to promise nothing except with the intention of keeping it. But it is soon clear to me that such a maxim will still only be based on the fear of consequences. Now it is a wholly different thing to be truthful from duty, and to be so from apprehension of injurious consequences. . . . For to deviate from the principle of duty is beyond all doubt wicked; but to be unfaithful to my maxim of prudence may often be very advantageous to me, although to abide by it is certainly safer. The shortest way, however, and an unerring one, to discover the answer to this question whether a lying promise is consistent with duty, is to ask myself, Should I be content that my maxim (to extricate myself from difficulty by a false promise) should hold good as a universal law, for myself as well as for others; and should I be able to say to myself, "Every one may make a deceitful promise when he finds himself in a difficulty from which he cannot otherwise extricate himself"? Then I presently become aware that, while I can will the lie, I can by no means will that lying should be a universal law. For with such a law there would be no promises at all, since it would be in vain to allege my intention in regard to my future actions to those who would not believe this allegation, or if they over-hastily did so, would pay me back in my own coin. Hence my maxim, as soon as it should be made a universal law, would necessarily destroy itself.

I do not, therefore, need any far-reaching penetration to discern what I have to do in order that my will may be morally good. Inexperienced in the course of the world, incapable of being prepared for all its contingencies, I only ask myself: Canst thou also will that thy maxim should be a universal law? If not, then it must be rejected, and that not because of a disadvantage accruing from it to myself or even to others, but because it cannot enter as a principle into a possible universal legislation, and reason extorts from me immediate respect for such legislation. I do not indeed as yet *discern* on what this respect is based . . . but at least I understand this . . . that the necessity of acting from *pure* respect for the practical law is what constitutes duty, to which every other motive must give place because it is the condition of a will being good *in itself,* and the worth of such a will is above everything. . . .

from Utilitarianism

John Stuart Mill

What Utilitarianism Is

A passing remark is all that needs be given to the ignorant blunder of supposing that those who stand up for utility as the test of right and wrong use the term in that restricted and merely colloquial sense in which utility is opposed to pleasure. An apology is due to the philosophical opponents of utilitarianism for even the momentary appearance of confounding them with anyone capable of so absurd a misconception; which is the more extraordinary, inasmuch as the contrary accusation, of referring everything to pleasure, and that, too, in its grossest form, is another of the common charges against utilitarianism: and, as has been pointedly remarked by an able writer, the same sort of persons, and often the very same persons, denounce the theory "as impracticably dry when the word 'utility' precedes the word 'pleasure,' and as too practically voluptuous when the word 'pleasure' precedes the word 'utility.'" Those who know anything about the matter are aware that every writer, from Epicurus to Bentham, who maintained the theory of utility meant by it, not something to be contradistinguished from pleasure, but pleasure itself, together with exemption from pain; and instead of opposing the useful to the agreeable or the ornamental, have always declared that the useful means these, among other things. Yet the common herd, including the herd of writers, not only in newspapers and periodicals, but in books of weight and pretension, are perpetually falling into this shallow mistake. Having caught up the word "utilitarian," while knowing nothing whatever about it but its sound, they habitually express by it the rejection or the neglect of pleasure in some of its forms: of beauty, of ornament, or of amusement. Nor is the term thus ignorantly misapplied solely in disparagement, but occasionally in compliment, as though it implied superiority to frivolity and the mere pleasures of the moment. And this perverted use is the only one in which the word is popularly known, and the one from which the new generation are acquiring their sole notion of its meaning. Those who introduced the word, but who had for many years discontinued it as a distinctive appellation, may well feel themselves called upon to resume it if by doing so they can hope to contribute anything toward rescuing it from this utter degradation.

The creed which accepts as the foundation of morals "utility" or the "greatest happiness principle" holds that actions are right in proportion as they tend to promote happiness; wrong as they tend to produce the reverse of happiness. By happiness is intended pleasure and the absence of pain; by unhappiness, pain and the privation of pleasure. To give a clear view of the moral standard set up by the theory, much more requires to be said; in particular, what things it includes in the ideas of pain and pleasure, and to what extent this is left an open question. But these supplementary explanations do not affect the theory of life on which this theory of morality is grounded—namely, that pleasure and freedom from pain are the only things desirable as ends; and that all desirable things (which are as numerous in the utilitarian as in any other scheme) are desirable either for pleasure inherent in themselves or as means to the promotion of pleasure and the prevention of pain.

Now such a theory of life excites in many minds, and among them in some of the most estimable in feeling and purpose, inveterate dislike. To suppose that life has (as they express it) no higher end than pleasure—no better and nobler object of desire and pursuit—they designate as utterly mean and groveling, as a doctrine worthy only of swine, to whom the followers of Epicurus were, at a very early period, contemptuously likened; and modern holders of the doctrine are occasionally made the subject of equally polite comparisons by its German, French, and English assailants.

When thus attacked, the Epicureans have always answered that it is not they, but their accusers, who represent human nature in a degrading light, since the accusation supposes human beings to be capable of no pleasures except those of which swine are capable. If this supposition were true, the charge could not be gainsaid, but would then be no longer an imputation; for if the sources of pleasure were precisely the same to human beings and to swine, the rule of life which is good enough for the one would be good enough for the other. The comparison of the Epicurean life to that of beasts is felt as degrading, precisely because a beast's pleasures do not satisfy a human being's conceptions of happiness. Human beings have faculties more elevated than the animal appetites and, when once made conscious of them, do not regard anything as happiness which does not include their gratification. I do not, indeed, consider the Epicureans to have been by any means faultless in drawing out their scheme of consequences from the utilitarian principle. To do this in any sufficient manner, many Stoic, as well as Christian, elements require to be included. But there is no known Epicurean theory of life which does not assign to the pleasures of the intellect, of the feelings and imagination, and of the moral sentiments a much higher value as pleasures than to those of mere sensation. It must be admitted, however, that utilitarian writers in general have placed the superiority of mental over bodily pleasures chiefly in the greater permanency, safety, uncostliness, etc., of the former—that is, in their circumstantial advantages rather than in their intrinsic nature. And on all these points utilitarians have fully proved their case; but they might have taken the other and, as it may be called, higher ground with entire consistency. It is quite compatible with the principle of utility to recognize the fact that some kinds of pleasure are more desirable and more valuable than others. It would be absurd that, while in estimating all other things quality is considered as well as quantity, the estimation of pleasure should be supposed to depend on quantity alone.

If I am asked what I mean by difference of quality in pleasures, or what makes one pleasure more valuable than another, merely as a pleasure, except its being greater in amount, there is but one possible answer. Of two pleasures, if there be one to which all or almost all who have experience of both give a decided preference, irrespective of any feeling of moral obligation to prefer it, that is the more desirable pleasure. If one of the two is, by those who are competently acquainted with both, placed so far above the other that they prefer it, even though knowing it to be attended with a greater amount of discontent, and would not resign it for any quantity of the other pleasure which their nature is capable of, we are justified in ascribing to the preferred enjoyment a superiority in quality so far outweighing quantity as to render it, in comparison, of small account.

Now it is an unquestionable fact that those who are equally acquainted with and equally capable of appreciating and enjoying both do give a most marked preference to the manner of existence which employs their higher faculties. Few human creatures would consent to be changed into any of the lower animals for a promise of the fullest allowance of a beast's pleasures; no intelligent human being would consent to be a fool, no instructed person would be an ignoramus, no person of feeling and conscience would be selfish and base, even though they should be persuaded that the fool, the dunce, or the rascal is better satisfied with his lot than they are with theirs. They would not resign what they possess more than he for the most complete satisfaction of all the desires which they have in common with him. If they ever fancy they would, it is only in cases of unhappiness so extreme that to escape from it they would exchange their lot for almost any other, however undesirable in their own eyes. A being of higher faculties requires more to make him happy, is capable probably of more acute suffering, and certainly accessible to it at more points, than one of an inferior type; but in spite of these liabilities, he can never really wish to sink into what he feels to be a lower grade of existence. We may give what explanation we please of this unwillingness; we may attribute it to pride, a name which is given indiscriminately to some of the most and to some of the least estimable feelings of which mankind are capable; we may refer it to the love of liberty and personal independence, an appeal to which was with the Stoics one of the most effective means for the inculcation of it; to the love of power or to the love of excitement, both of which do really enter into and contribute to it; but its most appropriate appellation is a sense of dignity, which all human beings possess in one form or other, and in some, though by no means in exact, proportion to their higher faculties, and which is so essential a part of the happiness of those in whom it is strong that nothing which conflicts with it could be otherwise than momentarily an object of desire to them. Whoever supposes that this preference takes place at a sacrifice of happiness—that the superior being, in anything like equal circumstances, is not happier than the inferior—confounds the two very different ideas of happiness and content. It is indisputable that the being whose capacities of enjoyment are low has the greatest chance of having them fully satisfied; and a highly endowed being will always feel that any happiness which he can look for, as the world is constituted, is imperfect. But he can learn to bear its imperfections, if they are at all bearable; and they will not make him envy the being who is indeed unconscious of the imperfections, but only because he feels not at all the good which those imperfections qualify. **It is better to be a human being dissatisfied than a pig satisfied; better to be Socrates dissatisfied than a fool satisfied.** And if the fool, or the pig, are of a different opinion, it is because they only know their own side of the question. The other party to the comparison knows both sides. . . .

I have dwelt on this point as being a necessary part of a perfectly just conception of utility or happiness considered as the directive rule of human conduct. But it is by no means an indispensable condition to the acceptance of the utilitarian standard; for that standard is not the agent's own greatest happiness, but the greatest amount of happiness altogether; and if it may possibly be doubted whether a noble character is always the happier for its nobleness, there can be no doubt that it makes other people happier, and that the world in general is immensely a gainer by it.

Utilitarianism, therefore, could only attain its end by the general cultivation of nobleness of character, even if each individual were only benefited by the nobleness of others, and his own, so far as happiness is concerned, were a sheer deduction from the benefit. But the bare enunciation of such an absurdity as this last renders refutation superfluous.

According to the greatest happiness principle, as above explained, the ultimate end, with reference to and for the sake of which all other things are desirable—whether we are considering our own good or that of other people—is an existence exempt as far as possible from pain, and as rich as possible in enjoyments, both in point of quantity and quality; the test of quality and the rule for measuring it against quantity being the preference felt by those who, in their opportunities of experience, to which must be added their habits of self-consciousness and self-observation, are best furnished with the means of comparison. This, being according to the utilitarian opinion the end of human action, is necessarily also the standard of morality, which may accordingly be defined "the rules and precepts for human conduct," by the observance of which an existence such as has been described might be, to the greatest extent possible, secured to all mankind; and not to them only, but, so far as the nature of things admits, to the whole sentient creation. . . .

Of What Sort of Proof the Principle of Utility is Susceptible

. . . (Q)uestions of ultimate ends do not admit of proof, in the ordinary acceptation of the term. To be incapable of proof by reasoning is common to all first principles, to the first premises of our knowledge, as well as to those of our conduct. But the former, being matters of fact, may be the subject of a direct appeal to the faculties which judge of fact—namely, our senses and our internal consciousness. Can an appeal be made to the same faculties on questions of practical ends? Or by what other faculty is cognizance taken of them?

Questions about ends are, in other words, questions what things are desirable. The utilitarian doctrine is that happiness is desirable, and the only thing desirable, as an end; all other things being only desirable as means to that end. What ought to be required of this doctrine, what conditions is it requisite that the doctrine should fulfill—to make good its claim to be believed?

The only proof capable of being given that an object is visible is that people actually see it. The only proof that a sound is audible is that people hear it; and so of the other sources of our experience. In like manner, I apprehend, the sole evidence it is possible to produce that anything is desirable is that people do actually desire it. If the end which the utilitarian doctrine proposes to itself were not, in theory and in practice, acknowledged to be an end, nothing could ever convince any person that it was so. No reason can be given why the general happiness is desirable, except that each person, so far as he believes it to be attainable, desires his own happiness. This, however, being a fact, we have not only all the proof which the case admits of, but all which it is possible to require, that happiness is a good, that each person's happiness is a good to that person, and the general happiness, therefore, a good to the aggregate of all persons. Happiness has made out its title as *one* of the ends of conduct and, consequently, one of the criteria of morality.

But it has not, by this alone, proved itself to be the sole criterion. To do that, it would seem, by the same rule, necessary to show, not only that people desire happiness, but that they never desire anything else. Now it is palpable that they do desire things which, in common language, are decidedly distinguished from happiness. They desire, for example, virtue and the absence of vice no less really than pleasure and the absence of pain. The desire of virtue is not as universal, but it is as authentic a fact as the desire of happiness. And hence the opponents of the utilitarian standard deem that they have a right to infer that there are other ends of human action besides happiness, and that happiness is not the standard of approbation and disapprobation.

But does the utilitarian doctrine deny that people desire virtue, or maintain that virtue is not a thing to be desired? The very reverse. It maintains not only that virtue is to be desired, but that it is to be desired disinterestedly, for itself. Whatever may be the opinion of utilitarian moralists as to the original conditions by which virtue is made virtue, however they may believe (as they do) that actions and dispositions are only virtuous because they promote another end than virtue, yet this being granted, and it having been decided, from considerations of this description, what *is* virtuous, they not only place virtue at the very head of the things which are good as means to the ultimate end, but they also recognize as a psychological fact the possibility of its being, to the individual, a good in itself, without looking to any end beyond it; and hold that the mind is not in a right state, not in a state conformable to utility, not in the state most conducive to the general happiness, unless it does love virtue in this manner—as a thing desirable in itself, even although, in the individual instance, it should not produce those other desirable consequences which it tends to produce, and on account of which it is held to be virtue. This opinion is not, in the smallest degree, a departure from the happiness principle. The ingredients of happiness are very various, and each of them is desirable in itself, and not merely when considered as swelling an aggregate. The principle of utility does not mean that any given pleasure, as music, for instance, or any given exemption from pain, as for example health, is to be looked upon as means to a collective something termed happiness, and to be desired, on that account. They are desired and desirable in and for themselves; besides being means, they are a part of the end. Virtue, according to the utilitarian doctrine, is not naturally and originally part of the end, but it is capable of becoming so; and in those who live it disinterestedly it has become so, and is desired and cherished, not as a means to happiness, but as a part of their happiness.

To illustrate this further, we may remember that virtue is not the only thing originally a means, and which if it were not a means to anything else would be and remain indifferent, but which by association with what it is a means to comes to be desired for itself, and that too with the utmost intensity. What, for example, shall we say of the love of money? There is nothing originally more desirable about money than about any heap of glittering pebbles. Its worth is solely that of the things which it will buy; the desires for other things than itself, which it is a means of gratifying. Yet the love of money is not only one of the strongest moving forces of human life, but money is, in many cases, desired in and for itself; the desire to possess it is often stronger than the desire to use it, and goes on increasing when all the desires which point to ends beyond it, to be compassed by it, are falling off. It may, then, be said truly that money is desired not for the sake of an end, but as part of the end. From being a means to happiness, it has come to be itself a principal ingredient of the individual's conception of happiness. The same may be said of the majority of the great objects of human life: power, for example, or fame, except that to each of these there is a certain amount of immediate pleasure annexed, which has at least the semblance of being naturally inherent in them—a thing which cannot be said of money. Still, however, the strongest natural attraction, both of power and of fame, is the immense aid they give to the attainment of our other wishes; and it is the strong association thus generated between them and all our objects of desire which gives to the direct desire of them the intensity it often assumes, so as in some characters to surpass in strength all other desires. In these cases the means have become a part of the end, and a more important part of it than any of the things which they are means to. What was once desired as an instrument for the attainment of happiness has come to be desired for its own sake. In being desired for its own sake it is, however, desired as *part* of happiness. The person is made, or thinks he would be made, happy by its mere possession; and is made unhappy by failure to obtain it. The desire of it is not a different thing from the desire of happiness any more than the love of music or the desire of health. They are included in happiness. They are some of the elements of which the desire of happiness is made up. Happiness is not an abstract idea but a concrete whole; and these are some of its parts. And the utilitarian standard sanctions and approves their being so. Life would be a poor thing, very ill provided with sources of happiness, if there were not this provision of nature by which things originally indifferent, but conducive to, or otherwise associated with, the satisfaction of our primitive desires, become in themselves sources of pleasure more valuable than the primitive pleasures, both in permanency, in the space of human existence that they are capable of covering, and even in intensity.

Virtue, according to the utilitarian conception, is a good of this description. There was no original desire of it, or motive to it, save its conduciveness to pleasure, and especially to protection from pain. But through the association thus formed it may be felt a good in itself, and desired as such with as great intensity as any other good; and with this difference between it and the love of money, of power, or of fame—that all of these may, and often do, render the individual noxious to the other members of the society to which he belongs, whereas there is nothing which makes him so much a blessing to them as the cultivation of the disinterested love of virtue. And consequently, the utilitarian standard, while it tolerates and approves those other acquired desires, up to the point beyond which they would be more injurious to the general happiness than promotive of it, enjoins and requires the cultivation of the love of virtue up to the greatest strength possible, as being above all things important to the general happiness.

It results from the preceding considerations that there is in reality nothing desired except happiness. Whatever is desired otherwise than as a means to some end beyond itself, and ultimately to happiness, is desired as itself a part of happiness, and is not desired for itself until it has become so. Those who desire virtue for its own sake desire it either because the consciousness of it is a pleasure, or because the consciousness of being without it is a pain, or for both reasons united; as in truth the pleasure and pain seldom exist separately, but almost always together—the same person feeling pleasure in the degree of virtue attained, and pain in not having attained more. If one of these gave him no pleasure, and the other no pain, he would not love or desire virtue, or would desire it only for the other benefits which it might produce to himself or to persons whom he cared for.

We have now, then, an answer to the question, of what sort of proof the principle of utility is susceptible. If the opinion which I have now stated is psychologically true—if human nature is so constituted as to desire nothing which is not either a part of happiness or a means of happiness—we can have no other proof, and we require no other, that these are the only things desirable. If so, happiness is the sole end of human action, and the promotion of it the test by which to judge of all human conduct; from whence it necessarily follows that it must be the criterion of morality, since a part is included in the whole.

And now to decide whether this is really so, whether mankind do desire nothing for itself but that which is a pleasure to them, or of which the absence is a pain, we have evidently arrived at a question of fact and experience, dependent, like all similar questions, upon evidence. It can only be determined by practiced self-consciousness and self-observation, assisted by observation of others. I believe that these sources of evidence, impartially consulted, will declare that desiring a thing and finding it pleasant, aversion to it and thinking of it as painful, are phenomena entirely inseparable or, rather, two parts of the same phenomenon—in strictness of language, two different modes of naming the same psychological fact; that to think of an object as desirable (unless for the sake of its consequences) and to think of it as pleasant are one and the same thing; and that to desire anything except in proportion as the idea of it is pleasant is a physical and metaphysical impossibility.

So obvious does this appear to me that I expect it will hardly be disputed; and the objection made will be, not that desire can possibly be directed to anything ultimately except pleasure and exemption from pain, but that the will is a different thing from desire; that a person of confirmed virtue or any other person whose purposes are fixed carries out his purposes without any thought of the pleasure he has in contemplating them or expects to derive from their fulfillment, and persists in acting on them, even though these pleasures are much diminished by changes in his character or decay of his passive sensibilities, or are outweighed by the pains which the pursuit of the purposes may bring upon him. All this I fully admit and have stated it elsewhere as positively and emphatically as anyone. Will, the active phenomenon, is a different thing from desire, the state of passive sensibility, and, though originally an offshoot from it, may in time take root and detach itself from the parent stock, so much so that in the case of a habitual purpose, instead of willing the thing because we desire it, we often desire it only because we will it. This, however, is but an instance of that familiar fact, the power of habit, and is nowise confined to the case of virtuous actions. Many indifferent things which men originally did from a motive of some sort they continue to do from habit. Sometimes this is done unconsciously, the consciousness coming only after the action; at other times with conscious volition, but volition which has become habitual and is put in operation by the force of habit, in opposition perhaps to the deliberate preference, as often happens with those who have contracted habits of vicious or hurtful indulgence. Third and last comes the case in which the habitual act of will in the individual instance is not in contradiction to the general intention prevailing at other times, but in fulfillment of it, as in the case of the person of confirmed virtue and of all who pursue deliberately and consistently any determinate end. The distinction between will and desire thus understood is an authentic and highly important psychological fact; but the fact consists solely in this—that will, like all other parts of our constitution, is amenable to habit, and that we may will from habit what we no longer desire for itself, or desire only because we will it. It is not the less true that will, in the beginning, is entirely produced by desire, including in that term the repelling influence of pain as well as the attractive one of pleasure. Let us take into consideration no longer the person who has a confirmed will to do right, but him in whom that virtuous will is still feeble, conquerable by temptation, and not to be fully relied on; by what means can it be strengthened? How can the will to be virtuous, where it does not exist in sufficient force, be implanted or awakened? Only by making the person *desire* virtue—by making him think of it in a pleasurable light, or of its absence in a painful one. It is by associating the doing right with pleasure, or the wrong with pain, or by eliciting and impressing and bringing home to the person's experience the pleasure naturally involved in the one or the pain in the other, that it is possible to call forth that will to be virtuous which, when confirmed, acts without any thought of either pleasure or pain. Will is the child of desire, and passes out of the dominion of its parent only to come under that of habit. That which is the result of habit affords no presumption of being intrinsically good; and there would be no reason for wishing that the purpose of virtue should become independent of pleasure and pain were it not that the influence of the pleasurable and painful associations which prompt to virtue is not sufficiently to be depended on for unerring constancy of action until it has acquired the support of habit. Both in feeling and in conduct, habit is the only thing which imparts certainty; and it is because of the importance to others of being able to rely absolutely on one's feelings and conduct, and to oneself of being able to rely on one's own, that the will to do right ought to be cultivated into this habitual independence. In other words, this state of the will is a means to good, not intrinsically a good; and does not contradict the doctrine that nothing is a good to human beings but in so far as it is either itself pleasurable or a means of attaining pleasure or averting pain.

But if this doctrine be true, the principle of utility is proved. Whether it is so or not, must now be left to the consideration of the thoughtful reader.

The Idea of a Female Ethic

Jean Grimshaw

Questions about gender have scarcely been central to mainstream moral philosophy this century. But **the idea that virtue is in some way *gendered*, that the standards and criteria of morality are different for women and men, is one that has been central to the ethical thinking of a great many philosophers**. It is to the eighteenth century that we can trace the beginnings of those ideas of a "female ethic," of "feminine" nature and specifically female forms of virtue, which have formed the essential background to a great deal of feminist thinking about ethics. The eighteenth century, in industrializing societies, saw the emergence of the concern about questions of femininity and female consciousness that was importantly related to changes in the social situation of women. Increasingly, for middle class women, the home was no longer also the workplace. The only route to security (of a sort) for a woman was a marriage in which she was wholly economically dependent, and for the unmarried women, the prospects were bleak indeed. At the same time, however, as women were becoming increasingly dependent on men in practical and material terms, the eighteenth century saw the beginnings of an idealization of family life and the married state that remained influential throughout the nineteenth century. A sentimental vision of the subordinate but virtuous and idealized wife and mother, whose specifically female virtues both defined and underpinned the "private" sphere of domestic life, came to dominate a great deal of eighteenth and nineteenth-century thought.

The idea that virtue is gendered is central, for example, to the philosophy of Rousseau. In *Emile*, Rousseau argued that those characteristics which would be faults in men are virtues in women. Rousseau's account of female virtues is closely related to his idealized vision of the rural family and simplicity of life which alone could counteract the evil manners of the city, and it is only, he thought, as wives and mothers that women can become virtuous. But their virtue is also premised on their dependence and subordination within marriage; for a woman to be independent, according to Rousseau, or for her to pursue goals whose aim was not the welfare of her family, was for her to lose those qualities which would make her estimable and desirable.

It was above all Rousseau's notion of virtue as "gendered" that Mary Wollstonecraft attacked in her *Vindication of the Rights of Woman*. Virtue, she argued, should mean the same thing for a woman as for a man, and she was a bitter critic of the forms of "femininity" to which women were required to aspire, and which, she thought, undermined their strength and dignity as human beings. Since the time of Wollstonecraft, there has always been an important strand in feminist thinking which has viewed with great suspicion, or rejected entirely, the idea that there are specifically female virtues. There are very good reasons for this suspicion. The idealization of female virtue, which perhaps reached its apogee in the effusions of many nineteenth-century male Victorian writers such as Rushkin, has usually been premised on female subordination. The "virtues" to which it was thought that women should aspire often reflect this subordination—a classic example is the "virtue" of selflessness, which was stressed by a great number of Victorian writers.

Despite this well-founded ambivalence about the idea of "female virtue," however, many women in the nineteenth century, including a large number who were concerned with the question of women's emancipation, remained attracted to the idea, not merely that there were specifically female virtues, but sometimes that women were morally superior to men, and to the belief that society could be morally transformed through the influence of women. What many women envisaged was, as it were, an *extension* throughout society of the "female values" of the private sphere of home and family. But, unlike many male writers, they used the idea of female virtue as a reason for women's entry into the "public" sphere rather than as a reason for their being restricted to the "private" one. And in a context where any sort of female independence was so immensely difficult to achieve, it is easy to see the attraction of any view which sought to re-evaluate and affirm those strengths and virtues conventionally seen as "feminine."

The context of contemporary feminist thought is of course very different. Most of the formal barriers to the entry of women into spheres other than the domestic have been removed, and a constant theme of feminist writing in the last twenty years has been a critique of women's restriction to the domestic role or the "private" sphere. Despite this, however, the idea of "a female ethic" has remained very important within feminist thinking. A number of concerns underlie the continued interest within feminism in the idea of a "female ethic." Perhaps most important is concern about the violent and destructive consequences to human life and to the planet of those fields of activity which have been largely male-dominated, such as war, politics, and capitalist economic domination. The view that the frequently destructive nature of these things is at least in part *due* to the fact that they are male-dominated is not of course new; it was common enough in many arguments for female suffrage at the beginning of the twentieth century. In some contemporary feminist thinking this has been linked to a view that many forms of aggression and destruction are closely linked to the nature of "masculinity" and the male psyche.

Such beliefs about the nature of masculinity and about the destructive nature of male spheres of activity are sometimes linked to "essentialist" beliefs about male and female nature. Thus, for example, in the very influential work of Mary Daly, all the havoc wreaked on human life and the planet tends to be seen as an undifferentiated result of the unchanging nature of the male psyche, and of the ways in which women themselves have been "colonized" by male domination and brutality. And contrasted with this havoc, in Daly's work, is a vision of an uncorrupted female psyche which might rise like a phoenix from the ashes of male-dominated culture and save the world. Not all versions of essentialism are quite as extreme or vivid as that of Daly; but it is not uncommon (among some supporters of the peace movement for example) to find the belief that women are "naturally" less aggressive, more gentle and nurturing, more co-operative, than men.

Such essentialist views of male and female nature are of course a problem if one believes that the "nature" of men and women is not something that is monolithic or unchanging, but is, rather, socially and historically constructed. And a great deal of feminist thinking has rejected any form of essentialism. But if one rejects the idea that any differences between male and female values and priorities can be ascribed to a fundamental male and female "nature," the question then arises as to whether the idea of a "female ethic" can be spelled out in a way that avoids essentialist assumptions. The attempt to do this is related to a second major concern of feminist thinking. This concern can be explained as follows. Women themselves have constantly tended to be devalued or inferiorized (frequently at the same time as being idealized). But this devaluation has not simply been of women themselves—their nature, abilities and characteristics. The "spheres" of activity with which they have particularly been associated have also been devalued. Again, paradoxically, they have also been idealized. Thus home, family, and domestic virtues, and women's role in the physical and emotional care of others have constantly been praised to the skies and seen as the bedrock of social life. At the same time, these things are commonly seen as a mere "backdrop" to the more "important" spheres of male activity, to which no self-respecting man could allow himself to be restricted; and as generating values which must always take second place if they conflict with values or priorities from elsewhere.

The second sort of approach to the idea of a "female ethic" results, then, both from a critique of essentialism, and from an attempt to see whether an alternative approach to questions about moral reasoning and ethical priorities can be derived from a consideration of those spheres of life and activity which have been regarded as paradigmatically female. Two things, in particular, have been suggested. The first is that there *are* in fact common or typical differences in the ways in which women and men think or reason about moral issues. This view of course, is not new. It has normally been expressed, however, in terms of a *deficiency* on the part of women; women are incapable of reason, of acting on principles; they are emotional, intuitive, too personal, and so forth. Perhaps, however, we might recognize *difference* without ascribing *deficiency*; and maybe a consideration of female moral reasoning can highlight the problems in the male forms of reasoning which have been seen as the norm?

The second important suggestion can be summarized as follows. It starts from the assumption that specific social practices generate their own vision of what is "good" or what is to be especially valued, their own concerns and priorities, and their own criteria for what is to be seen as a "virtue." Perhaps, then, the social practices, especially those of mothering and caring for others, which have traditionally been regarded as female, can be seen as generating ethical priorities and conceptions of "virtue" which should not only not be devalued but which can also provide a corrective to the more destructive values and priorities of those spheres of activity which have been dominated by men.

In her influential book *In A Different Voice: Psychological Theory and Women's Development* (1982) Carol Gilligan argued that those who have suggested that women typically reason differently from men about moral issues are right; what is wrong is their assumption of the inferiority or deficiency of female moral reasoning. The starting point for Gilligan's work was an examination of the work of Lawrence Kohlberg on moral development in children. Kohlberg attempted to identify "stages" in moral development, which could be analysed by a consideration of the responses children gave to questions about how they would resolve a moral dilemma. The "highest" stage, the stage at which, in fact, Kohlberg wanted to say that a specifically *moral* framework of reasoning was being used, was that at which moral dilemmas were resolved by an appeal to rules and principles; a logical decision about priorities, in the light of the prior acceptance of such rules or principles.

A much quoted example of Kohlberg's method, discussed in detail by Gilligan, is the case of two eleven-year-old children. "Jake" and "Amy," Jake and Amy were asked to respond to the following dilemma; a man called Heinz has a wife who is dying, but he cannot afford the drug she needs. Should he steal the drug in order to save his wife's life? Jake is clear that Heinz should steal the drug; and his answer revolves around a resolution of the rules governing life and poverty. Amy, however, responded very differently. She suggested that Heinz should go and talk to the druggist and see if they could not find some solution to the problem. Whereas Jake sees the situation as needing mediation through systems of logic or law, Amy, Gilligan suggests, sees a need for mediation through communication in relationships.

It is clear that Kohlberg's understanding of morality is based on the tradition that derives from Kant and moves through the work of such contemporary philosophers as John Rawls and R. M. Hare. The emphasis in this tradition is indeed on rules and principles, and Gilligan is by no means the only critic to suggest that any such understanding of morality will be bound to misrepresent women's moral reasoning and set up a typically male pattern of moral reasoning as a standard against which to judge women to be deficient. Nel Noddings, for example, in her book *Caring: A Feminine Approach to Ethics and Moral Education* (1984), argues that a morality based on rules or principles is in itself inadequate, and that it does not capture what is distinctive or typical about female moral thinking. She points out how, in a great deal of moral philosophy, it has been supposed that the moral task is, as it were, to abstract the "local detail" from a situation and see it as falling under a rule or principle. Beyond that, it is a question of deciding or choosing, in a case of conflict, how to order or rank one's principles in a hierarchy. And to rank as a *moral* one, a principle must be universalizable; that is to say, of the form "Whenever X, then do Y." Noddings argues that the posing of moral dilemmas in such a way misrepresents the nature of moral decision-making. Posing moral issues in the "desert-island dilemma" form, in which only the "bare bones" of a situation are described, usually serves to conceal rather than to reveal the sorts of questions to which only situational and contextual knowledge can provide an answer, and which are essential to moral judgement in the specific context.

But Noddings wants to argue, like Gilligan, not merely that this sort of account of morality is inadequate in general, but that women are less likely than men even to attempt to justify their moral decisions in this sort of way. Both of them argue that women do not tend to appeal to rules and principles in the same sort of way as men; that they are more likely to appeal to concrete and detailed knowledge of the situation, and to consider the dilemma in terms of the relationships involved.

Gilligan and Noddings suggest, therefore, that there are, as a matter of fact, differences in the ways in which women and men reason about moral issues. But such views of difference always pose great difficulties. The nature of the evidence involved is inevitably problematic; it would not be difficult to find two eleven-year-old children who reacted quite differently to Heinz's dilemma; and appeals to "common experience" of how women and men reason about moral issues can always be challenged by pointing to exceptions or by appealing to different experience.

The question, however, is not just one of empirical difficulty. Even if there *were* some common or typical differences between women and men, there is always a problem about how such differences are to be described. For one thing, it is questionable whether the sort of description of moral decision-making given by Kohlberg and others really does adequately represent its nature. Furthermore, the view that women do not act on principle, that they are intuitive and more influenced by "personal" considerations, has so often been used in contexts where women have been seen as deficient that it is as well to be suspicious of any distinction between women and men which seems to depend on this difference. It might, for example, be the case, not so much that women and men *reason differently* about moral issues, but that their ethical priorities differ, as that what is regarded as an important principle by women (such as maintaining relationships) is commonly seen by men as a *failure* of principle.

At best then, I think that the view that women "reason differently" over moral issues is difficult to spell out clearly or substantiate; at worst, it runs the risk of recapitulating old and oppressive dichotomies. But perhaps there is some truth in the view that women's ethical *priorities* may commonly differ from those of men? Again, is not easy to see how this could be very clearly established, or what sort of evidence would settle the question; but if it is correct to argue that ethical priorities will emerge from life experiences and from the ways these are socially articulated, then maybe one might assume that, given that the life experiences of women are commonly very different from those of men, their ethical priorities will differ too? Given, for instance, the experience of women in pregnancy, childbirth and the rearing of children, might there be, for example, some difference in the way they will view the "waste" of those lives in war. (This is not an idea that is unique to contemporary feminism; it was, for example, suggested by Olive Schreiner in her book *Woman and Labour*, which was published in 1911.)

There have been a number of attempts in recent feminist philosophy to suggest that the practices in which women engage, in particular the practices of childcare and the physical and emotional maintenance of other human beings, might be seen as generating social priorities and conceptions of virtue which are different from those which inform other aspects of social life. Sara Ruddick, for example, in an article entitled "Maternal thinking" (1980) argues that the task of mothering generates a conception of virtue which might provide a resource for a critique of those values and priorities which underpin much contemporary social life—including those of militarism. Ruddick does not want to argue that women can simply enter the public realm "as mothers" (as some suffragist arguments earlier in the twentieth century suggested) and transform it. She argues, nevertheless, that women's experience as mothers is central to their ethical life, and to the ways in which they might articulate a critique of dominant values and social mores. Rather similarly, Caroline Whitbeck has argued that the practices of caring for others, which have motherhood at their centre, provide an ethical model of the "mutual realization of people" which is very different from the competitive and individualistic norms of much social life (Whitbeck, 1983).

There are, however, great problems in the idea that female practices can generate an autonomous or coherent set of "alternative" values. Female practices are always socially situated and inflected by things such as class, race, material poverty or well-being, which have divided women and which they do not all share. Furthermore, practices such as childbirth and the education and rearing of children have been the focus of constant ideological concern and struggle; they have not just been developed by women in isolation from other aspects of the culture. The history of childcare this century, for example, has constantly been shaped by the (frequently contradictory) interventions both of "experts" in childcare (who have often been male) and by the state. Norms of motherhood have also been used in ways that have reinforced classist and racist assumptions about the "pathology" of working-class or black families. They have been used, too, by women themselves, in the service of such things as devotion to Hitler's "Fatherland" or the bitter opposition to feminism and equal rights in the USA. For all these reasons, if there is any usefulness at all in the idea of a "female ethic," I do not think it can consist in appealing to a supposedly autonomous realm of female values which can provide a simple corrective or alternative to the values of male-dominated spheres of activity.

Nevertheless, it is true that a great deal of the political theory and philosophy of the last two hundred years *has* operated with a distinction between the "public" and "private" spheres, and that the "private" sphere has been seen as the sphere of women. But that which is opposed to the "world" of the home, of domestic virtue and female self-sacrifice, is not just the "world" of war, or even of politics, it is also that of the "market." The concept of "the market" defines a realm of "public" existence which is contrasted with a private realm of domesticity and personal relations. The structure of individuality presupposed by the concept of the market is one which requires an instrumental rationality directed towards the abstract goal of production and profit, and a pervasive self-interest. The concept of "the market" precludes altruistic behaviour, or the taking of the well-being of another as the goal of one's activity.

The morality which might seem most appropriate to the marketplace is that of utilitarianism, which, in its classic forms, proposed a conception of happiness as distinct from the various activities which lead to this, of instrumental reason, and of an abstract individuality, as in the "felicific calculus" of Bentham, for example, whereby all subjects of pain or happiness are to be counted as equal and treated impersonally. But, as Ross Poole has argued, in "Morality, masculinity and the market" (1985), utilitarianism was not really able to provide an adequate morality, mainly because it could never provide convincing reasons why individuals should submit to a duty or obligation that was not in their interests in the short term. It is Kantianism, he suggests, that provides a morality that is more adequate to the market. Others have to figure in one's scheme of things not just as means to an end, but as agents, and the "individual" required by the market must be assumed to be equipped with a form of rationality that is not purely instrumental, and to be prepared to adhere to obligations and constraints that are experienced as duty rather than inclination. The sphere of the market, however, is contrasted with the "private" sphere of domestic and familial relations. Although of course men participate in this private sphere, it is the sphere in which female identity is found, and this identity is constructed out of care and nurturance and service for others. Since these others are known and particular, the "morality" of this sphere cannot be universal or impersonal; it is always "infected" by excess, partiality and particularity.

The first important thing to note about this contrast between the public sphere of the market and the private sphere of domestic relations is that it does not, and never has corresponded in any simple way to reality. Thus working-class women have worked outside the home since the earliest days of the Industrial Revolution, and the exclusive association of women with the domestic and private sphere has all but disappeared. Secondly, it is important to note that the morality of the marketplace and of the private sphere exist in a state of tension with each other. The marketplace could not exist without a sphere of domestic and familial relations which "supported" its own activities; yet the goals of the marketplace may on occasion be incompatible with the demands of the private sphere. The "proper" complementarity between them can only exist if the private sphere is subordinate to the public sphere, and that subordinancy has often been expressed by the dominance of men in the household as well as in public life. The practical subordinancy of the private sphere is mirrored by the ways in which, in much moral and political philosophy and social thought, the immediate and personal morality of the private sphere is seen as "inferior" to that which governs the exigencies of public life.

Furthermore, although, ideologically, the public and private spheres are seen as separate and distinct, in practice the private sphere is often governed by constraints and requirements deriving from the public sphere. A clear example of this is the ways in which views on how to bring up children and on what the task of motherhood entailed have so often been derived from broader social imperatives, such as the need to create a "fit" race for the task of ruling an empire, or the need to create a disciplined and docile industrial workforce.

The distinction between the public and the private has nevertheless helped to shape reality, and to form the experiences of people's lives. It is still commonly true, for example, that the tasks of the physical and emotional maintenance of other people largely devolve upon women, who often bear this responsibility as well as that of labour outside the home.

And the differences between male and female experience which follow from these things allow us to understand both why there may well often be differences between women and men in their perception of moral issues or moral priorities, and why these differences can never be summed up in the form of generalizations about women and men. Women and men commonly participate both in domestic and familial relations and in the world of labour and the marketplace. And the constraints and obligations experienced by individuals in their daily lives may lead to acute tensions and contradictions which may be both practically and morally experienced. (A classic example of this would be the woman who faces an acute conflict between the "impersonal" demands of her situation at work, as well as her own needs for activity outside the home, and the needs or demands of those such as children or aged parents whose care cannot easily be fitted into the requirements of the workplace.)

If ethical concerns and priorities arise from different forms of social life, then those which have emerged from a social system in which women have so often been subordinate to men must be suspect. Supposedly "female" values are not only the subject of little agreement among women; they are also deeply mired in conceptions of "the feminine" which depend on the sort of polarization between "masculine" and "feminine" which has itself been so closely related to the subordination of women. There is no autonomous realm of female values, or of female activities which can generate "alternative" values to those of the public sphere; and any conception of a "female ethic" which depends on these ideas cannot, I think, be a viable one.

But to say this is not necessarily to say that the lives and experiences of women cannot provide a source for a critique of the male-dominated public sphere. Experiences and perspectives which are articulated by gender cannot be sharply demarcated from those which are also articulated along other dimensions, such as race and class; and there is clearly no consensus among women as to how a critique of the priorities of the "public" world might be developed. Nevertheless taking seriously the experiences and perspectives of women—in childbirth and childcare for example—whilst not immediately generating any consensus about how things might be changed, generates crucial forms of questioning of social and moral priorities. It is often remarked, for example, that if men had the same sort of responsibility for children that women have, or if women had the same sorts of power as men to determine such things as priorities in work, or health care, or town planning, or the organization of domestic labour, many aspects of social life might be very different.

We cannot know in advance exactly what sorts of changes in moral and social priorities might result from radical changes in such things as the sexual division of labour or transformed social provision for the care of others; or from the elimination of the many forms of oppression from which women and men alike suffer. No appeal to current forms of social life can provide a blueprint. Nor should women be seen (as they are in some forms of feminist thinking) as "naturally" likely to espouse different moral or social priorities from men. Insofar as there are (or might be) differences in female ethical concerns, these can only emerge from, and will need to be painfully constructed out of, changes in social relationships and modes of living; and there is every reason to suppose that the process will be conflictual. But there is every reason, too, to suppose that in a world in which the activities and concerns which have traditionally been regarded as primarily female were given equal value and status, moral and social priorities would be very different from those of the world in which we live now.

References

Daly, M. *Gyn/Ecology: The Metaethics of Radical Feminism* (Boston: Beacon Press, 1978).

Gilligan, C. *In a Different Voice: Psychological Theory and Women's Development* (Cambridge, Mass.: Harvard University Press, 1982).

Kohlberg, L. *The Philosophy of Moral Development* (San Francisco: Harper and Row, 1981).

Noddings, N. *Caring: A Feminine Approach to Ethics and Education* (Berkeley: University of California Press, 1978).

Poole, R. "Morality, masculinity and the market," *Radical Philosophy*, 39 (1985).

Rousseau, J. J. *Emile* (London: Dent, Everyman's Library, 1974).

Ruddick, S. "Maternal thinking," *Feminist Studies*, 6 (Summer 1980).

Schreiner, C. *Woman and Labour* (1911); (London: Virago, 1978).

Whitbeck, C. "A different reality; feminist ontology," *Beyond Domination*, ed. C. Gould (Totowa, NJ: Rowman and Allanheld, 1983).

Wollstonecraft, M. *A Vindication of the Rights of Woman* (Harmondsworth: Pelican, 1975).

Ambition

J. Krishnamurti

You know I have been talking about fear; and it is very important for us to be conscious and aware of fear. Do you know how it comes into being? Throughout the world we can see that people are perverted by fear, twisted in their ideas, in their feelings, in their activities. So we ought to go into the problem of fear from every possible angle, not only from the moral and economic point of society, but also from the point of view of our inward, psychological struggles.

As I have said, fear for outward and inward security twists the mind and distorts our thinking. I hope you have thought a little about this, because the more clearly you consider this and see the truth of it, the freer you will be from all dependence. The older people have not brought about a marvellous society; the parents, the ministers, the teachers, the rulers, the priests have not created a beautiful world. On the contrary, they have created a frightful, brutal world in which everybody is fighting somebody; in which one group is against another, one class against another, one nation against another, one ideology or set of beliefs against another. The world in which you are growing up is an ugly world, a sorrowful world, where the older people try to smother you with their ideas, their beliefs, their ugliness; and if you are merely going to follow the ugly pattern of the older people who have brought about this monstrous society, what is the point of being educated, what is the point of living at all?

If you look around you will see that throughout the world there is appalling destruction and human misery. You may read about wars in history, but you do not know the actuality of it, how cities are completely destroyed, how the hydrogen bomb, when dropped on an island, causes the whole island to disappear. Ships are bombed and they go up into thin air. There is appalling destruction due to this so-called advancement, and it is in such a world you are growing up. You may have a good time while you are young, a happy time; but when you grow older, unless you are very alert, watchful of your thoughts, of your feelings, you will perpetuate this world of battles, of ruthless ambitions, a world where each one is competing with another, where there is misery, starvation, over-population and disease.

So, while you are young, is it not very important for you to be helped by the right kind of teacher to think about all these things, and not just be taught to pass some dull examinations? Life is sorrow, death, love, hate, cruelty, disease, starvation, and you have to begin to consider all these things. That is why I feel it is good that you and I should go into these problems together, so that your intelligence is awakened and you begin to have some real feeling about all these things. Then you will not grow up just to be married off and become a thoughtless clerk or a breeding machine, losing yourself in this ugly pattern of life like waters in the sands.

One of the causes of fear is ambition, is it not? And are you all not ambitious? What is your ambition? To pass some examination? To become a governor? Or, if you are very young, perhaps you just want to become an engine-driver, to drive engines across a bridge. But why are you ambitious? What does it mean? Have you ever thought about it? Have you noticed older people, how ambitious they are? In your own family, have you not heard your father or your uncle talk about getting more salary, or occupying some prominent position? In our society—and I have explained what our society is—everybody is doing that, trying to be on top. They all want to become somebody, do they not? The clerk wants to become the manager, the manager wants to become something bigger, and so on and so on—the continual struggle to become. If I am a teacher, I want to become the principal; if I am the principal, I want to become the manager. If you are ugly, you want to be beautiful. Or you want to have more money, more *saris,* more clothes, more furniture, houses, property—more and more and more. Not only outwardly, but also inwardly, in the so-called spiritual sense, you want to become somebody, though you cover that ambition by a lot of words. Have you not noticed this? And you think it is perfectly all right, don't you? You think it is perfectly normal, justifiable, right.

Now, what has ambition done in the world? So few of us have ever thought about it. When you see a man struggling to gain, to achieve, to get ahead of somebody else, have you ever asked yourself what is in his heart? If you will look into your own heart when you are ambitious, when you are struggling to become somebody, spiritually or in the wordly sense, you will find there the worm of fear. The ambitious man is the most frightened of men, because he is afraid to be what he is. He says, "If I remain what I am, I shall be nobody, therefore I must be somebody. I must become a magistrate, a judge, a minister." If you examine this process very closely, if you go behind the screen of words and ideas, beyond the wall of status and success, you will find there is fear; because the ambitious man is afraid to be what he is. He thinks that what he is in himself is insignificant, poor, ugly; he feels lonely, utterly empty, therefore he says, "I must go and achieve something." So either he goes after what he calls God, which is just another form of ambition, or he tries to become somebody in the world. In this way his loneliness, his sense of inward emptiness—of which he is really frightened—is covered up. He runs away from it, and ambition becomes the means through which he can escape.

So, what is happening in the world? Everybody is fighting somebody. One man feels less than another and struggles to get to the top. There is no love, there is no consideration, there is no deep thought. Our society is a constant battle of man against man. This struggle is born of the ambition to become somebody, and the older people encourage you to be ambitious. They want you to amount to something, to marry a rich man or a rich woman, to have influential friends. Being frightened, ugly in their hearts, they try to make you like themselves; and you in turn want to be like them, because you see the glamour of it all. When the governor comes, everybody bows down to the earth to receive him, they give him garlands, make speeches. He loves it, and you love it too. You feel honored if you know his uncle or his clerk, and you bask in the sunshine of his ambition, his achievements. So you are easily caught in the ugly web of the older generation, in the pattern of this monstrous society. Only if you are very alert, constantly watchful, only if you are not afraid and do not accept, but question all the time—only then will you not be caught, but go beyond and create a different world.

That is why it is very important for you to find your true vocation. Do you know what 'vocation' means? Something which you love to do, which is natural to you. After all, that is the function of education—to help you grow independently so that you are free of ambition and can find your true vocation. **The ambitious man has never found his true vocation; if he had, he would not be ambitious.**

So, it is the responsibility of the teachers, of the principal, to help you to be intelligent, unafraid, so that you can find your true vocation, your own way of life, the way you really want to live and earn your livelihood. This implies a revolution in thinking; because, in our present society, the man who can talk, the man who can write, the man who can rule, the man who has a big car, is thought to be in a marvellous position; and the man who digs in the garden, who cooks, who builds a house, is despised.

Are you aware of your own feelings when you look at a mason, at the man who mends the road, or drives a taxi, or pulls a cart? Have you noticed how you regard him with absolute contempt? To you he hardly even exists. You disregard him; but when a man has a title of some kind, or is a banker, a merchant, a *guru,* or a minister, you immediately respect him. But if you really find your true vocation, you will help to break down this rotten system completely; because then, whether you are a gardener, or a painter, or an engineer, you will be doing something which you love with your whole being; and that is not ambition. To do something marvellously well, to do it completely, truly, according to what you deeply think and feel—that is not ambition and in that there is no fear.

To help you to discover your true vocation is very difficult, because it means that the teacher has to pay a great deal of attention to each student to find out what he is capable of. He has to help him not to be afraid, but to question, to investigate. You may be a potential writer, or a poet, or a painter. Whatever it is, if you really love to do it, you are not ambitious; because in love there is no ambition.

So, is it not very important while you are young that you should be helped to awaken your own intelligence and thereby find your true vocation? Then you will love what you do, right through life, which means there will be no ambition, no competition, no fighting another for position, for prestige; and then perhaps you will be able to create a new world. In that new world all the ugly things of the older generation will cease to exist—their wars, their mischief, their separative gods, their rituals which mean absolutely nothing, their sovereign governments, their violence. That is why the responsibility of the teachers, and of the students, is very great.

Ethics Are Relative

Ruth Benedict

Modern social anthropology has become more and more a study of the varieties and common elements of cultural environment and the consequences of these in human behavior. For such a study of diverse social orders primitive peoples fortunately provide a laboratory not yet entirely vitiated by the spread of a standardized world-wide civilization. Dyaks and Hopis, Fijians and Yakuts are significant for psychological and sociological study because only among these simpler peoples has there been sufficient isolation to give opportunity for the development of localized social forms. In the higher cultures the standardization of custom and belief over a couple of continents has given a false sense of the inevitability of the particular forms that have gained currency, and we need to turn to a wider survey in order to check the conclusions we hastily base upon this near-universality of familiar customs. Most of the simpler cultures did not gain the wide currency of the one which, out of our experience, we identify with human nature, but this was for various historical reasons, and certainly not for any that gives us as its carriers a monopoly of social good or of social sanity. Modern civilization, from this point of view, becomes not a necessary pinnacle of human achievement but one entry in a long series of possible adjustments.

These adjustments, whether they are in mannerisms like the ways of showing anger, or joy, or grief in any society, or in major human drives like those of sex, prove to be far more variable than experience in any one culture would suggest. In certain fields, such as that of religion or of formal marriage arrangements, these wide limits of variability are well known and can be fairly described. In others it is not yet possible to give a generalized account, but that does not absolve us of the task of indicating the significance of the work that has been done and of the problems that have arisen.

One of these problems relates to the customary modern normal-abnormal categories and our conclusions regarding them. In how far are such categories culturally determined, or in how far can we with assurance regard them as absolute? In how far can we regard inability to function socially as diagnostic of abnormality, or in how far is it necessary to regard this as a function of the culture?

As a matter of fact, one of the most striking facts that emerge from a study of widely varying cultures is the ease with which our abnormals function in other cultures. It does not matter what kind of "abnormality" we choose for illustration, those which indicate extreme instability, or those which are more in the nature of character traits like sadism or delusions of grandeur or of persecution, there are well-described cultures in which these abnormals function at ease and with honor, and apparently without danger or difficulty to the society.

The most notorious of these is trance and catalepsy. Even a very mild mystic is aberrant in our culture. But most peoples have regarded even extreme psychic manifestations not only as normal and desirable, but even as characteristic of highly valued and gifted individuals. This was true even in our own cultural background in that period when Catholicism made the ecstatic experience the mark of sainthood. It is hard for us, born and brought up in a culture that makes no use of the experience, to realize how important a role it may play and how many individuals are capable of it, once it has been given an honorable place in any society. . . .

Cataleptic and trance phenomena are, of course, only one illustration of the fact that those whom we regard as abnormals may function adequately in other cultures. Many of our culturally discarded traits are selected for elaboration in different societies. Homosexuality is an excellent example, for in this case our attention is not constantly diverted, as in the consideration of trance, to the interruption of routine activity which it implies. Homosexuality poses the problem very simply. A tendency toward this trait in our culture exposes an individual to all the conflicts to which all aberrants are always exposed, and we tend to identify the consequences of this conflict with homosexuality. But these consequences are obviously local and cultural. Homosexuals in many societies are not incompetent, but they may be if the culture asks adjustments of them that would strain any man's vitality. Wherever homosexuality has been given an honorable place in any society, those to whom it is congenital have filled adequately the honorable roles society assigns to them. Plato's *Republic* is, of course, the most convincing statement of such a reading of homosexuality. It is presented as one of the major means to the good life, and it was generally so regarded in Greece at that time.

The cultural attitude toward homosexuals has not always been on such a high ethical plane, but it has been very varied. Among many American Indian tribes there exists the institution of the berdache, as the French called them. These men-women were men who at puberty or thereafter took the dress and the occupations of women. Sometimes they married other men and lived with them. Sometimes they were men with no inversion, persons of weak sexual endowment who chose this role to avoid the jeers of the women. The berdaches were never regarded as of first-rate supernatural power, as similar men-women were in Siberia, but rather as leaders in women's occupations, good healers in certain diseases, or, among certain tribes, as the genial organizers of social affairs. In any case, they were socially placed. They were not left exposed to the conflicts that visit the deviant who is excluded from participation in the recognized patterns of his society.

The most spectacular illustrations of the extent to which normality may be culturally defined are those cultures where an abnormality of our culture is the cornerstone of their social structure. It is not possible to do justice to these possibilities in a short discussion. A recent study of an island of northwest Melanesia by *Fortune* describes a society built upon traits which we regard as beyond the border of paranoia. In this tribe the exogamic groups look upon each other as prime manipulators of black magic, so that one marries always into an enemy group which remains for life one's deadly and unappeasable foes. They look upon a good garden crop as a confession of theft, for everyone is engaged in making magic to induce into his garden the productiveness of his neighbors'; therefore no secrecy in the island is so rigidly insisted upon as the secrecy of a man's harvesting of his yams. Their polite phrase at the acceptance of a gift is, "And if you now poison me, how shall I repay you this present?" Their preoccupation with poisoning is constant; no woman ever leaves her cooking pot for a moment untended. Even the great affinal economic exchanges that are characteristic of this Melanesian culture area are quite altered in Dobu since they are incompatible with this fear and distrust that pervades the culture. They go farther and people the whole world outside their own quarters with such malignant spirits that all-night feasts and ceremonials simply do not occur here. They have even rigorous religiously-enforced customs that forbid the sharing of seed even in one family group. Anyone else's food is deadly poison to you, so that communality of stores is out of the question. For some months before harvest the whole society is on the verge of starvation, but if one falls to the temptation and eats up one's seed yams, one is an outcast and a beachcomber for life. There is no coming back. It involves, as a matter of course, divorce and the breaking of all social ties.

Now in this society where no one may work with another and no one may share with another, *Fortune* describes the individual who was regarded by all his fellows as crazy. He was not one of those who periodically ran amok and, beside himself and frothing at the mouth, fell with a knife upon anyone he could reach. Such behavior they did not regard as putting anyone outside the pale. They did not even put the individuals who were known to be liable to these attacks under any kind of control. They merely fled when they saw the attack coming on and kept out of the way. "He would be all right tomorrow." But there was one man of sunny, kindly disposition who liked work and liked to be helpful. The compulsion was too strong for him to repress it in favor of the opposite tendencies of his culture. Men and women never spoke of him without laughing; he was silly and simple and definitely crazy. Nevertheless, to the ethnologist used to a culture that has, in Christianity, made his type the model of all virtue, he seemed a pleasant fellow. . . .

. . . Among the Kwakiutl it did not matter whether a relative had died in bed of disease, or by the hand of any enemy, in either case death was an affront to be wiped out by the death of another person. The fact that one had been caused to mourn was proof that one had been put upon. A chief's sister and her daughter had gone up to Victoria, and either because they drank bad whiskey or because their boat capsized they never came back. The chief called together his warriors. "Now I ask you, tribes, who shall wail? Shall I do it or shall another?" The spokesman answered, of course, "Not you, Chief. Let some other of the tribes." Immediately they set up the war pole to announce their intention of wiping out the injury, and gathered a war party. They set out, and found seven men and two children asleep and killed them. "Then they felt good when they arrived at Sebaa in the evening."

The point which is of interest to us is that in our society those who on that occasion would feel good when they arrived at Sebaa that evening would be the definitely abnormal. There would be some, even in our society, but it is not a recognized and approved mood under the circumstances. On the Northwest Coast those are favored and fortunate to whom that mood under those circumstances is congenial, and those to whom it is repugnant are unlucky. This latter minority can register in their own culture only by doing violence to their congenial responses and acquiring others that are difficult for them. The person, for instance, who, like a Plains Indian whose wife has been taken from him, is too proud to fight, can deal with the Northwest Coast civilization only by ignoring its strongest bents. If he cannot achieve it, he is the deviant in that culture, their instance of abnormality.

This head-hunting that takes place on the Northwest Coast after a death is no matter of blood revenge or of organized vengeance. There is no effort to tie up the subsequent killing with any responsibility on the part of the victim for the death of the person who is being mourned. A chief whose son has died goes visiting wherever his fancy dictates, and he says to his host, "My prince has died today, and you go with him." Then he kills him. In this, according to their interpretation, he acts nobly because he has not been downed. He has thrust back in return. The whole procedure is meaningless without the fundamental paranoid reading of bereavement. Death, like all the other untoward accidents of existence, confounds man's pride and can only be handled in the category of insults.

Behavior honored upon the Northwest Coast is one which is recognized as abnormal in our civilization, and yet it is sufficiently close to the attitudes of our own culture to be intelligible to us and to have a definite vocabulary with which we may discuss it. The megalomaniac paranoid trend is a definite danger in our society. It is encouraged by some of our major preoccupations, and it confronts us with a choice of two possible attitudes. One is to brand it as abnormal and reprehensible, and is the attitude we have chosen in our civilization. The other is to make it an essential attribute of ideal man, and this is the solution in the culture of the Northwest Coast.

These illustrations, which it has been possible to indicate only in the briefest manner, force upon us the fact that normality is culturally defined. An adult shaped to the drives and standards of either of these cultures, if he were transported into our civilization, would fall into our categories of abnormality. He would be faced with the psychic dilemmas of the socially unavailable. In his own culture, however, he is the pillar of society, the end result of socially inculcated mores, and the problem of personal instability in his case simply does not arise.

No one civilization can possibly utilize in its mores the whole potential range of human behavior. Just as there are great numbers of possible phonetic articulations, and the possibility of language depends on a selection and standardization of a few of these in order that speech communication may be possible at all, so the possibility of organized behavior of every sort, from the fashions of local dress and houses to the dicta of a people's ethics and religion, depends upon a similar selection among the possible behavior traits. In the field of recognized economic obligations or sex tabus this selection is as nonrational and subconscious a process as it is in the field of phonetics. It is a process which goes on in the group for long periods of time and is historically conditioned by innumerable accidents of isolation or of contact of peoples. In any comprehensive study of psychology, the selection that different cultures have made in the course of history within the great circumference of potential behavior is of great significance.

Every society, beginning with some slight inclination in one direction or another, carries its preference farther and farther, integrating itself more and more completely upon its chosen basis, and discarding those types of behavior that are uncongenial. Most of those organizations of personality that seem to us most uncontrovertibly abnormal have been used by different civilizations in the very foundations of their institutional life. Conversely the most valued traits of normal individuals have been looked on in differently organized cultures as aberrant. Normality, in short, within a very wide range, is culturally defined. It is primarily a term for the socially elaborated segment of human behavior in any culture; and abnormality, a term for the segment that that particular civilization does not use. The very eyes with which we see the problem are conditioned by the long traditional habits of our own society.

It is a point that has been made more often in relation to ethics than in relation to psychiatry. We do not any longer make the mistake of deriving the morality of our locality and decade directly from the inevitable constitution of human nature. We do not elevate it to the dignity of a first principle. We recognize that **morality differs in every society, and is a convenient term for socially approved habits.** Mankind has always preferred to say, "It is morally good," rather than "It is habitual," and the fact of this preference is matter enough for a critical science of ethics. But historically the two phrases are synonymous.

The concept of the normal is properly a variant of the concept of the good. It is that which society has approved. A normal action is one which falls well within the limits of expected behavior for a particular society. Its variability among different peoples is essentially a function of the variability of the behavior patterns that different societies have created for themselves, and can never be wholly divorced from a consideration of culturally institutionalized types of behavior.

Each culture is a more or less elaborate working-out of the potentialities of the segment it has chosen. In so far as a civilization is well integrated and consistent within itself, it will tend to carry farther and farther, accorded to its nature, its initial impulse toward a particular type of action, and from the point of view of any other culture those elaborations will include more and more extreme and aberrant traits.

Each of these traits, in proportion as it reinforces the chosen behavior patterns of that culture, is for that culture normal. Those individuals to whom it is congenial either congenitally, or as the result of childhood sets, are accorded prestige in that culture, and are not visited with the social contempt or disapproval which their traits would call down upon them in a society that was differently organized. On the other hand, those individuals whose characteristics are not congenial to the selected type of human behavior in that community are the deviants, no matter how valued their personality traits may be in a contrasted civilization.

The Dobuan who is not easily susceptible to fear of treachery, who enjoys work and likes to be helpful, is their neurotic and regarded as silly. On the Northwest Coast the person who finds it difficult to read life in terms of an insult contest will be the person upon whom fall all the difficulties of the culturally unprovided for. The person who does not find it easy to humiliate a neighbor, nor to see humiliation in his own experience, who is genial and loving, may, of course, find some unstandardized way of achieving satisfactions in his society, but not in the major patterned responses that his culture requires of him. If he is born to play an important role in a family with many hereditary privileges, he can succeed only by doing violence to his whole personality. If he does not succeed, he has betrayed his culture; that is, he is abnormal.

I have spoken of individuals as having sets toward certain types of behavior, and of these sets as running sometimes counter to the types of behavior which are institutionalized in the culture to which they belong. From all that we know of contrasting cultures it seems clear that differences of temperament occur in every society. The matter has never been made the subject of investigation, but from the available material it would appear that these temperament types are very likely of universal recurrence. That is, there is an ascertainable range of human behavior that is found wherever a sufficiently large series of individuals is observed. But the proportion in which behavior types stand to one another in different societies is not universal. The vast majority of the individuals in any group are shaped to the fashion of that culture. In other words, most individuals are plastic to the moulding force of the society into which they are born. In a society that values trance, as in India, they will have supernormal experience. In a society that institutionalizes homosexuality, they will be homosexual. In a society that sets the gathering of possessions as the chief human objective, they will amass property. The deviants, whatever the type of behavior the culture has institutionalized, will remain few in number, and there seems no more difficulty in moulding that vast malleable majority to the "normality" of what we consider an aberrant trait, such as delusions of reference, than to the normality of such accepted behavior patterns as acquisitiveness. The small proportion of the number of the deviants in any culture is not a function of the sure instinct with which that society has built itself upon the fundamental sanities, but of the universal fact that, happily, the majority of mankind quite readily take any shape that is presented to them. . . .

Chapter VI: Beauty

What is the essence of beauty? In what ways does the soul's contemplation of beauty allow the individual to transcend time and apprehend immorality? In the *Symposium*, Plato wonders:

> ... what if man had eyes to see the true beauty—the divine beauty, ... pure and clear and unalloyed, not clogged with the pollutions of mortality and all the colors and vanities of human life ... in that communion only, beholding beauty with the eye of the mind, he will be enabled to bring forth, not images of beauty, but realities (for he has hold not of an image but of a reality), and bringing forth and nourishing true virtue to become the friend of God and be immortal, if mortal man may.

How can we continually refine our perceptions so as to more clearly grasp the meaning of the beautiful?

The branch of philosophy that inquires into the nature of beauty is aesthetics. Although the nature of beauty and problems dealing with works of art have concerned philosophers since, at least, the time of Plato, the founder of aesthetics, as a branch of philosophy, was the eighteenth century German philosopher Baumgarten. "Aesthetics" means "sensuous perception" and, as a branch of philosophy, it investigates not only human responses to beauty but also experiences of art. According to Baumgarten, Truth is the Perfect or Absolute known through rational understanding, (i.e., perceived through mind's eye). Goodness, he held, is the Perfect or Absolute reached by the force of moral will, and Beauty is the Perfect or Absolute recognized through the senses.

Is Beauty a perfect form in itself or is it simply in the eye of the beholder? What is the value of creative works of art to a society? In what ways do works of art reinforce dominant values and beliefs? What is the relationship between art and moral character? Do works of art express truth? What is the relationship of the artist to the work of art itself? This section will help us think about the above questions and relationships.

In "Letters to a Young Poet," Rainer Maria Rilke encourages the poet to write "out of the depths of your own world, from the vastness of your own solitude." The poet, and by implication the artist, must go deep inside in order to authenticate the creative impulse. "What is necessary, after all, is only this: solitude, vast inner solitude. To walk inside yourself and meet no one for hours."

For Plato, beauty is an eternal form. Our senses are charmed, seduced and pleased by beautiful things (i.e., those things that participate in beauty itself). However, true beauty is apprehended by the mind, by inward sight. Plato said, "if . . . man's life is ever worth the living, it is when he attained this vision of the very soul of beauty."

In contrast to the view that beauty is a perfect form, Friedrich Nietzsche contends in "On Beauty and Ugliness," that nothing is more conditional than our feelings of beauty. The idea that anything is "beautiful in itself" is foreign to Nietzsche's way of thinking. Nietzsche tells us, "Nothing is beautiful, except man alone: all aesthetics rests upon this naivete, which is its *first* truth." He also argued, "the continuous development of art is bound up with the *Apollonian* and *Dionysian* duality."

In "What Is Art?" Count Leo Tolstoy argues that the true purpose of art is the communication of emotion. That is to say, genuine art must be rooted in human expression. Tolstoy contends, "the activity of art is based on the fact that a man, receiving through his sense of hearing or sight another man's expression of feeling, is capable of experiencing the emotion that moved the man who expressed it." The activity of art should unite human communities and art should be "of the people." His views are a condemnation of the elitist conceptions of the art of his time that stressed decoration and cultural ornamentation over simplicity and common feeling.

Walter Benjamin was a key figure in the Frankford School of Philosophy. In "The Work of Art in the Age of Mechanical Reproduction" he discusses the implications for works of art and related questions that must be addressed in an age of mass reproduction. He is concerned about the negative effects of technological reproduction on our understanding and appreciation of works of art. But he tells us that, "even the most perfect reproduction of a work of art is lacking in one element: its presence in time and space, its unique existence at the place where it happens to be." For Benjamin, "the presence of the original is the prerequisite to the concept of authenticity."

"The secret of infinity," according to Barbara Sandrisser, "then, can be said to be the moment in time when we perceive an elegant truth." In her essay, "On Elegance in Japan," Sandrisser provides a window to the Japanese world and Japanese ideas about elegance. She begins the discussion of elegance by considering a list of elegant things taken from Sei Shonagon's classic, *The Pillow Book*. Shonagon's insights about elegance as refined simplicity and cultivated taste are compared with Western attitudes that display a cultivated egotism and superficiality. A renewed appreciation of elegant objects is valuable because it can both enhance our daily activities and heighten our aesthetic appreciation.

Chinese aesthetics can be understood within the larger context of Chinese culture. Chinese culture itself presents an aesthetically ordered world, set within a dynamic cosmos, and the overriding aim is to achieve a grand harmony. In "Chinese Aesthetics," Kuang-Ming Wu states, "beauty is less a subject to be independently discussed than a pervasive attitude and atmosphere in which one moves and has one's being." The Chinese cosmos is immanent and therefore has no overriding universals like, for example, Plato's form of beauty. Chinese aesthetics reflects this cosmic attitude in that beauty is always thought and experienced in specific and concrete instances within a yin-yang constitutive involvement.

Letters to a Young Poet

Rainer Maria Rilke

You ask whether your verses are any good. You ask me. You have asked others before this. You send them to magazines. You compare them with other poems, and you are upset when certain editors reject your work. Now (since you have said you want my advice) I beg you to stop doing that sort of thing. You are looking outside, and that is what you should most avoid right now.

No one can advise or help you—no one. There is only one thing you should do. **Go into yourself.** Find out the reason that commands you to write; see whether it has spread its roots into the very depths of your heart; confess to yourself whether you would have to die if you were forbidden to write. This most of all: ask yourself in the most silent hour of your night: *must* I write? Dig into yourself for a deep answer. And if this answer rings out in assent, if you meet this solemn question with a strong, simple *"I must,"* then build your life in accordance with this necessity; your whole life, even into its humblest and most indifferent hour, must become a sign and witness to this impulse. Then come close to Nature. Then, as if no one had ever tried before, try to say what you see and feel and love and lose. Don't write love poems; avoid those forms that are too facile and ordinary: they are the hardest to work with, and it takes a great, fully ripened power to create something individual where good, even glorious, traditions exist in abundance. So rescue yourself from these general themes and write about what your everyday life offers you; describe your sorrows and desires, the thoughts that pass through your mind and your belief in some kind of beauty—describe all these with heartfelt, silent, humble sincerity and, when you express yourself, use the Things around you, the images from your dreams, and the objects that you remember. If your everyday life seems poor, don't blame *it*; blame yourself; admit to yourself that you are not enough of a poet to call forth its riches . . .

What is necessary, after all, is only this: solitude, vast inner solitude. To walk inside yourself and meet no one for hours—that is what you must be able to attain. To be solitary as you were when you were a child, when the grownups walked around involved with matters that seemed large and important because *they* looked so busy and because you didn't understand a thing about what they were doing.

And when you realize that their activities are shabby, that their vocations are petrified and no longer connected with life, why not then continue to look upon it all as a child would, as if you were looking at something unfamiliar, out of the depths of your own world, from the vastness of your own solitude, which is itself work and status and vocation? Why should you want to give up a child's wise not-understanding in exchange for defensiveness and scorn, since not-understanding is, after all, a way of being alone, whereas defensiveness and scorn are a participation in precisely what, by these means, you want to separate yourself from. . . .

The Form of Beauty

Plato

There are many spirits, and many kinds of spirits, too, and Love is one of them.

Then who were his parents? I asked.

I'll tell you, she said, though it's rather a long story. On the day of Aphrodite's birth the gods were making merry, and among them was Resource, the son of Craft. And when they had supped, Need came begging at the door because there was good cheer inside. Now, it happened that Resource, having drunk deeply of the heavenly nectar—for this was before the days of wine—wandered out into the garden of Zeus and sank into a heavy sleep, and Need, thinking that to get a child by Resource would mitigate her penury, lay down beside him and in time was brought to bed of Love. So Love became the follower and servant of Aphrodite because he was begotten on the same day that she was born, and further, he was born to love the beautiful since Aphrodite is beautiful herself.

Then again, as the son of Resource and Need, it has been his fate to be always needy; nor is he delicate and lovely as most of us believe, but harsh and arid, barefoot and homeless, sleeping on the naked earth, in doorways, or in the very streets beneath the stars of heaven, and always partaking of his mother's poverty. But, secondly, he brings his father's resourcefulness to his designs upon the beautiful and the good, for he is gallant, impetuous, and energetic, a mighty hunter, and a master of device and artifice—at once desirous and full of wisdom, a lifelong seeker after truth, an adept in sorcery, enchantment, and seduction.

He is neither mortal nor immortal, for in the space of a day he will be now, when all goes well with him, alive and blooming, and now dying, to be born again by virtue of his father's nature, while what he gains will always ebb away as fast. So Love is never altogether in or out of need, and stands, moreover, midway between ignorance and wisdom. You must understand that none of the gods are seekers after truth. They do not long for wisdom, because they are wise—and why should the wise be seeking the wisdom that is already theirs? Nor, for that matter, do the ignorant seek the truth or crave to be made wise. And indeed, what makes their case so hopeless is that, having neither beauty, nor goodness, nor intelligence, they are satisfied with what they are, and do not long for the virtues they have never missed.

. . . So much, then, for the nature and the origin of Love. You were right in thinking that he was the love of what is beautiful. But suppose someone were to say, Yes, my dear Socrates. Quite so, my dear Diotima. But what do you mean by the love of what is beautiful? Or, to put the question more precisely, what is it that the lover of the beautiful is longing for?

He is longing to make the beautiful his own, I said.

Very well, she replied, but your answer leads to another question. What will he gain by making the beautiful his own?

This, as I had to admit, was more than I could answer on the spur of the moment.

Well then, she went on, suppose that, instead of the beautiful, you were being asked about the good. I put it to you, Socrates. What is it that the lover of the good is longing for?

To make the good his own.

Then what will he gain by making it his own?

I can make a better shot at answering that, I said. He'll gain happiness.

Right, said she, for the happy are happy inasmuch as they possess the good, and since there's no need for us to ask why men should want to be happy, I think your answer is conclusive.

Absolutely, I agreed.

This longing, then, she went on, this love—is it common to all mankind? What do you think, do we all long to make the good our own?

Yes, I said, as far as that goes we're all alike.

Well then, Socrates, if we say that everybody always loves the same thing, does that mean that everybody is in love? Or do we mean that some of us are in love, while some of us are not?

I was a little worried about that myself, I confessed.

Oh, it's nothing to worry about, she assured me. You see, what we've been doing is to give the name of Love to what is only one single aspect of it; we make just the same mistake, you know, with a lot of other names.

For instance . . . ?

For instance, poetry. You'll agree that there is more than one kind of poetry in the true sense of the word—that is to say, calling something into existence that was not there before, so that every kind of artistic creation is poetry, and every artist is a poet.

True.

But all the same, she said, we don't call them all poets, do we? We give various names to the various arts, and only call the one particular art that deals with music and meter by the name that should be given to them all. And that's the only art that we call poetry, while those who practice it are known as poets.

Quite.

And that's how it is with Love. For "Love, that renowned and all-beguiling power," includes every kind of longing for happiness and for the good. Yet those of us who are subject to this longing in the various fields of business, athletics, philosophy, and so on, are never said to be in love, and are never known as lovers, while the man who devotes himself to what is only one of Love's many activities is given the name that should apply to all the rest as well.

Yes, I said, I suppose you might be right.

I know it has been suggested, she continued, that lovers are people who are looking for their other halves, but as I see it, Socrates, Love never longs for either the half or the whole of anything except the good. For men will even have their hands and feet cut off if they are once convinced that those members are bad for them. Indeed I think we only prize our own belongings in so far as we say that the good belongs to us, and the bad to someone else, for what we love is the good and nothing but the good. . . .

. . . And that being so, what course will Love's followers pursue, and in what particular field will eagerness and exertion be known as Love? In fact, what *is* this activity? Can you tell me that, Socrates?

If I could, my dear Diotima, I retorted, I shouldn't be so much amazed at *your* grasp of the subject, and I shouldn't be coming to you to learn the answer to that very question.

Well, I'll tell you, then, she said. To love is to bring forth upon the beautiful, both in body and in soul.

I'm afraid that's too deep, I said, for my poor wits to fathom.

I'll try to speak more plainly, then. We are all of us prolific, Socrates, in body and in soul, and when we reach a certain age our nature urges us to procreation. Nor can we be quickened by ugliness, but only by the beautiful. Conception, we know, takes place when man and woman come together, but there's a divinity in human propagation, an immortal something in the midst of man's mortality which is incompatible with any kind of discord. And ugliness is at odds with the divine, while beauty is in perfect harmony. In propagation, then, Beauty is the goddess of both fate and travail, and so when procreancy draws near the beautiful it grows genial and blithe, and birth follows swiftly on conception. But when it meets with ugliness it is overcome with heaviness and gloom, and turning away it shrinks into itself and is not brought to bed, but still labors under its painful burden. And so, when the procreant is big with child, he is strangely stirred by the beautiful, because he knows that beauty's tenant will bring his travail to an end. So you see, Socrates, that Love is not exactly a longing for the beautiful, as you suggested.

Well, what is it, then?

A longing not for the beautiful itself, but for the conception and generation that the beautiful effects.

Yes. No doubt you're right.

Of course I'm right, she said. And why all this longing for propagation? Because this is the one deathless and eternal element in our mortality. And since we have agreed that the lover longs for the good to be his own forever, it follows that we are bound to long for immortality as well as for the good—which is to say that Love is a longing for immortality.

So much I gathered, gentlemen, at one time and another from Diotima's dissertations upon Love.

And then one day she asked me, Well, Socrates, and what do you suppose is the cause of all this longing and all this love? Haven't you noticed what an extraordinary effect the breeding instinct has upon both animals and birds, and how obsessed they are with the desire, first to mate, and then to rear their litters and their broods, and how the weakest of them are ready to stand up to the strongest in defense of their young, and even die for them, and how they are content to bear the pinch of hunger and every kind of hardship, so long as they can rear their offspring?

With men, she went on, you might put it down to the power of reason, but how can you account for Love's having such remarkable effects upon the brutes? What do you say to that, Socrates?

Again I had to confess my ignorance.

Well, she said, I don't know how you can hope to master the philosophy of Love, if *that's* too much for you to understand.

But, my dear Diotima, I protested, as I said before, that's just why I'm asking you to teach me—because I realize how ignorant I am. And I'd be more than grateful if you'd enlighten me as to the cause not only of this, but of all the various effects of Love.

Well, she said, it's simple enough, so long as you bear in mind what we agreed was the object of Love. For here, too, the principle holds good that the mortal does all it can to put on immortality. And how can it do that except by breeding, and thus ensuring that there will always be a younger generation to take the place of the old?

Now, although we speak of an individual as being the same so long as he continues to exist in the same form, and therefore assume that a man is the same person in his dotage as in his infancy, yet, for all we call him the same, every bit of him is different, and every day he is becoming a new man, while the old man is ceasing to exist, as you can see from his hair, his flesh, his bones, his blood, and all the rest of his body. And not only his body, for the same thing happens to his soul. And neither his manners, nor his disposition, nor his thoughts, nor his desires, nor his pleasures, nor his sufferings, nor his fears are the same throughout his life, for some of them grow, while others disappear.

And the application of this principle to human knowledge is even more remarkable, for not only do some of the things we know increase, while some of them are lost, so that even in our knowledge we are not always the same, but the principle applies as well to every single branch of knowledge. When we say we are studying, we really mean that our knowledge is ebbing away. We forget, because our knowledge disappears, and we have to study so as to replace what we are losing, so that the state of our knowledge may seem, at any rate, to be the same as it was before.

This is how every mortal creature perpetuates itself. It cannot, like the divine; be still the same throughout eternity; it can only leave behind new life to fill the vacancy that is left in its species by obsolescence. This, my dear Socrates, is how the body and all else that is temporal partakes of the eternal; there is no other way. And so it is no wonder that every creature prizes its own issue, since the whole creation is inspired by this love, this passion for immortality.

Well, Diotima, I said, when she had done, that's a most impressive argument. I wonder if you're right.

Of course I am, she said with an air of authority that was almost professorial. Think of the ambitions of your fellow men, and though at first they may strike you as upsetting my argument, you'll see how right I am if you only bear in mind that men's great incentive is the love of glory, and that their one idea is "To win eternal mention in the deathless roll of fame."

For the sake of fame they will dare greater dangers, even, than for their children; they are ready to spend their money like water and to wear their fingers to the bone, and, if it comes to that, to die.

Do you think, she went on, that Alcestis would have laid down her life to save Admetus, or that Achilles would have died for the love he bore Patroclus, or that Codrus, the Athenian king, would have sacrificed himself for the seed of his royal consort, if they had not hoped to win "the deathless name for valor," which, in fact, posterity has granted them? No, Socrates, no. Every one of us, no matter what he does, is longing for the endless fame, the incomparable glory that is theirs, and the nobler he is, the greater his ambition, because he is in love with the eternal.

Well then, she went on, those whose procreancy is of the body turn to woman as the object of their love, and raise a family, in the blessed hope that by doing so they will keep their memory green, "through time and through eternity." But those whose procreancy is of the spirit rather than of the flesh—and they are not unknown, Socrates—conceive and bear the things of the spirit. And what are they? you ask. Wisdom and all her sister virtues; it is the office of every poet to beget them, and of every artist whom we may call creative.

Now, by far the most important kind of wisdom, she went on, is that which governs the ordering of society, and which goes by the names of justice and moderation. And if any man is so closely allied to the divine as to be teeming with these virtues even in his youth, and if, when he comes to manhood, his first ambition is to be begetting, he too, you may be sure, will go about in search of the loveliness—and never of the ugliness—on which he may beget. And hence his procreant nature is attracted by a comely body rather than an ill-favored one, and if, besides, he happens on a soul which is at once beautiful, distinguished, and agreeable, he is charmed to find so welcome an alliance. It will be easy for him to talk of virtue to such a listener, and to discuss what human goodness is and how the virtuous should live—in short, to undertake the other's education.

And, as I believe, by constant association with so much beauty, and by thinking of his friend when he is present and when he is away, he will be delivered of the burden he has labored under all these years. And what is more, he and his friend will help each other rear the issue of their friendship—and so the bond between them will be more binding, and their communion even more complete, than that which comes of bringing children up, because they have created something lovelier and less mortal than human seed.

And I ask you, who would not prefer such fatherhood to merely human propagation, if he stopped to think of Homer, and Hesiod, and all the greatest of our poets? Who would not envy them their immortal progeny, their claim upon the admiration of posterity? . . .

Well now, my dear Socrates, I have no doubt that even you might be initiated into these, the more elementary mysteries of Love. But I don't know whether you could apprehend the final revelation, for so far, you know, we are only at the bottom of the true scale of perfection.

Never mind, she went on, I will do all I can to help you understand, and you must strain every nerve to follow what I'm saying.

Well then, she began, the candidate for this initiation cannot, if his efforts are to be rewarded, begin too early to devote himself to the beauties of the body. First of all, if his preceptor instructs him as he should, he will fall in love with the beauty of one individual body, so that his passion may give life to noble discourse. Next he must consider how nearly related the beauty of any one body is to the beauty of any other, when he will see that if he is to devote himself to loveliness of form it will be absurd to deny that the beauty of each and every body is the same. Having reached this point, he must set himself to be the lover of every lovely body, and bring his passion for the one into due proportion by deeming it of little or of no importance.

Next he must grasp that the beauties of the body are as nothing to the beauties of the soul, so that wherever he meets with spiritual loveliness, even in the husk of an unlovely body, he will find it beautiful enough to fall in love with and to cherish—and beautiful enough to quicken in his heart a longing for such discourse as tends toward the building of a noble nature. And from this he will be led to contemplate the beauty of laws and institutions. And when he discovers how nearly every kind of beauty is akin to every other he will conclude that the beauty of the body is not, after all, of so great moment.

And next, his attention should be diverted from institutions to the sciences, so that he may know the beauty of every kind of knowledge. And thus, by scanning beauty's wide horizon, he will be saved from a slavish and illiberal devotion to the individual loveliness of a single boy, a single man, or a single institution. And, turning his eyes toward the open sea of beauty, he will find in such contemplation the seed of the most fruitful discourse and the loftiest thought, and reap a golden harvest of philosophy, until, confirmed and strengthened, he will come upon one single form of knowledge, the knowledge of the beauty I am about to speak of.

And here, she said, you must follow me as closely as you can.

Whoever has been initiated so far in the mysteries of Love and has viewed all these aspects of the beautiful in due succession, is at last drawing near the final revelation. And now, Socrates, there bursts upon him that wondrous vision which is the very soul of the beauty he has toiled so long for. It is an everlasting loveliness which neither comes nor goes, which neither flowers nor fades, for such beauty is the same on every hand, the same then as now, here as there, this way as that way, the same to every worshiper as it is to every other. Nor will his vision of the beautiful take the form of a face, or of hands, or of anything that is of the flesh. It will be neither words, nor knowledge, nor a something that exists in something else, such as a living creature, or the earth, or the heavens, or anything that is—but subsisting of itself and by itself in an eternal oneness, while every lovely thing partakes of it in such sort that, however much the parts may wax and wane, it will be neither more nor less, but still the same inviolable whole.

And so, when his prescribed devotion to boyish beauties has carried our candidate so far that the universal beauty dawns upon his inward sight, he is almost within reach of the final revelation. And this is the way, the only way, he must approach, or be led toward, the sanctuary of Love. Starting from individual beauties, the quest for the universal beauty must find him ever mounting the heavenly ladder, stepping from rung to rung—that is, from one to two, and from two to *every* lovely body, from bodily beauty to the beauty of institutions, from institutions to learning, and from learning in general to the special lore that pertains to nothing but the beautiful itself—until at last he comes to know what beauty is.

And if, my dear Socrates, Diotima went on, **man's life is ever worth the living, it is when he has attained this vision of the very soul of beauty**. And once you have seen it, you will never be seduced again by the charm of gold, of dress, of comely boys, or lads just ripening to manhood; you will care nothing for the beauties that used to take your breath away and kindle such a longing in you, and many others like you, Socrates, to be always at the side of the beloved and feasting your eyes upon him, so that you would be content, if it were possible, to deny yourself the grosser necessities of meat and drink, so long as you were with him.

But if it were given to man to gaze on beauty's very self—unsullied, unalloyed, and freed from the mortal taint that haunts the frailer loveliness of flesh and blood—if, I say, it were given to man to see the heavenly beauty face to face, would you call *his*, she asked me, an unenviable life, whose eyes had been opened to the vision, and who had gazed upon it in true contemplation until it had become his own forever?

And remember, she said, that it is only when he discerns beauty itself through what makes it visible that a man will be quickened with the true, and not the seeming, virtue for it is virtue's self that quickens him, not virtue's semblance. And when he has brought forth and reared this perfect virtue, he shall be called the friend of god, and if ever it is given to man to put on immortality, it shall be given to him.

On Beauty and Ugliness

Friedrich Nietzsche

19

*B*eautiful and ugly. Nothing is more conditional—or, let us say, narrower—than our feeling for beauty. Whoever would think of it apart from man's joy in man would immediately lose any foothold. "Beautiful in itself" is a mere phrase, not even a concept. In the beautiful, man posits himself as the measure of perfection; in special cases he worships himself in it. A species cannot do otherwise but thus affirm itself alone. Its *lowest* instinct, that of self-preservation and self-expansion, still radiates in such sublimities. Man believes the world itself to be overloaded with beauty—and he forgets himself as the cause of this. He alone has presented the world with beauty—alas! only with a very human, all-too-human beauty. At bottom, man mirrors himself in things; he considers everything beautiful that reflects his own image: the judgment "beautiful" is the *vanity of his species*. For a little suspicion may whisper this question into the skeptic's ear: Is the world really beautified by the fact that man thinks it beautiful? He has *humanized* it, that is all. But nothing, absolutely nothing, guarantees that man should be the model of beauty. Who knows what he looks like in the eyes of a higher judge of beauty? Daring perhaps? Perhaps even amusing? Perhaps a little arbitrary?

"O Dionysus, divine one, why do you pull me by my ears?" Ariadne once asked her philosophic lover during one of those famous dialogues on Naxos. "I find a kind of humor in your ears, Ariadne: why are they not even longer?"

Nothing is beautiful, except man alone: all aesthetics rests upon this naïvete, which is its *first* truth. Let us immediately add the second: nothing is ugly except the degenerating man—and with this the realm of aesthetic judgment is circumscribed. Physiologically, everything ugly weakens and saddens man. It reminds him of decay, danger, impotence; it actually deprives him of strength. One can measure the effect of the ugly with a dynamometer. Wherever man is depressed at all, he senses the proximity of something "ugly." His feeling of power, his will to power, his courage, his pride—all fall with the ugly and rise with the beautiful. In both cases we draw an inference: the premises for it are piled up in the greatest abundance in instinct. The ugly is understood as a sign and symptom of degeneration: whatever reminds us in the least of degeneration causes in us the judgment of "ugly." Every suggestion of exhaustion, of heaviness, of age, of weariness; every kind of lack of freedom, such as cramps, such as paralysis; and above all, the smell, the color, the form of dissolution, of decomposition— even in the ultimate attenuation into a symbol—all evoke the same reaction, the value judgment, "ugly." A *hatred* is aroused—but whom does man hate then? There is no doubt: the *decline of his type*. Here he hates out of the deepest instinct of the species; in this hatred there is a shudder, caution, depth, farsightedness—it is the deepest hatred there is. It is because of this that art is deep.

21

Schopenhauer. Schopenhauer, the last German worthy of consideration (who represents a *European* event like Goethe, like Hegel, like Heinrich Heine, and not merely a local event, a "national" one), is for a psychologist a first-rate case: namely, as a maliciously ingenious attempt to adduce in favor of a nihilistic total depreciation of life precisely the counter-instances, the great self affirmations of the "will to life," life's forms of exuberance. He has interpreted *art,* heroism, genius, beauty, great sympathy, knowledge, the will to truth, and tragedy, in turn, as consequences of "negation" or of the "will's" need to negate—the greatest psychological counterfeit in all history, not counting Christianity. On closer inspection, he is at this point merely the heir of the Christian interpretation: only he knew how to approve that which Christianity had repudiated, the great cultural facts of humanity—albeit in a Christian, that is, nihilistic, manner (namely, as ways of "redemption," as anticipations of "redemption," as stimuli of the need for "redemption").

22

I take a single case. Schopenhauer speaks of *beauty* with a melancholy fervor. Why? Because he sees in it a bridge on which one will go farther, or develop a thirst to go farther. Beauty is for him a momentary redemption from the "will"—a lure to eternal redemption. Particularly, he praises beauty as the redeemer from "the focal point of the will," from sexuality—in beauty he sees the negation of the drive toward procreation. Queer saint! Somebody seems to be contradicting you; I fear it is nature. To what end is there any such thing as beauty in tone, color, fragrance, or rhythmic movement in nature? What is it that beauty evokes? Fortunately, a philosopher contradicts him too. No lesser authority than that of the divine Plato (so Schopenhauer himself calls him) maintains a different proposition: that all beauty incites procreation, that just this is the *proprium* of its effect, from the most sensual up to the most spiritual.

23

Plato goes further. He says with an innocence possible only for a Greek, not a "Christian," that there would be no Platonic philosophy at all if there were not such beautiful youths in Athens: it is only their sight that transposes the philosopher's soul into an erotic trance, leaving it no peace until it lowers the seed of all exalted things into such beautiful soil. Another queer saint! One does not trust one's ears, even if one should trust Plato. At least one guesses that they philosophized differently in Athens, especially in public. Nothing is less Greek than the conceptual web-spinning of a hermit—*amor intellectualis dei*[1] after the fashion of Spinoza. Philosophy after the fashion of Plato might rather be defined as an erotic contest, as a further development and turning inward of the ancient agonistic gymnastics and of its *presuppositions*. What ultimately grew out of this philosophic eroticism of Plato? A new art form of the Greek agon: dialectics. Finally, I recall—against Schopenhauer and in honor of Plato—that the whole higher culture and literature of *classical* France too grew on the soil of sexual interest. Everywhere in it one may look for the amatory, the senses, the sexual contest, "the woman"—one will never look in vain.

24

L'art pour l'art. The fight against purpose in art is always a fight against the moralizing tendency in art, against its subordination to morality. *L'art pour l'art* means, "The devil take morality!" But even this hostility still betrays the overpowering force of the prejudice. When the purpose of moral preaching and of improving man has been excluded from art, it still does not follow by any means that art is altogether purposeless, aimless, senseless—in short, *l'art pour l'art*, a worm chewing its own tail. "Rather no purpose at all than a moral purpose!"—that is the talk of mere passion. A psychologist, on the other hand, asks: what does all art do? does it not praise? glorify? choose? prefer? With all this it strengthens or weakens certain valuations. Is this merely a "more-over"? an accident? something in which the artist's instinct had no share? Or is it not the very presupposition of the artist's ability? Does his basic instinct aim at art, or rather at the sense of art, at life? at a desirability of life? Art is the great stimulus to life: how could one understand it as purposeless, as aimless, as *l'art pour l'art*?

One question remains: art also makes apparent much that is ugly, hard, and questionable in life; does it not thereby spoil life for us? And indeed there have been philosophers who attributed this sense to it: "liberation from the will" was what Schopenhauer taught as the over-all end of art; and with admiration he found the great utility of tragedy in its "evoking resignation." But this, as I have already suggested, is the pessimist's perspective and "evil eye." We must appeal to the artists themselves. What does the tragic artist communicate of himself? Is it not precisely the state *without* fear in the face of the fearful and questionable that he is showing? This state itself is a great desideratum; whoever knows it, honors it with the greatest honors, He communicates it—*must* communicate it, provided he is an artist, a genius of communication. Courage and freedom of feeling before a powerful enemy, before a sublime calamity, before a problem that arouses dread—this triumphant state is what the tragic artist chooses, what he glorifies. Before tragedy, what is warlike in our soul celebrates its Saturnalia; whoever is used to suffering, whoever seeks out suffering, the heroic man praises his own being through tragedy—to him alone the tragedian presents this drink of sweetest cruelty.

Note

[1] "Intellectual love of God."

Apollo and Dionysus

Friedrich Nietzsche

We shall have gained much for the science of aesthetics, once we perceive not merely by logical inference, but with the immediate certainty of vision, that **the continuous development of art is bound up with the *Apollinian* and *Dionysian* duality**—just as procreation depends on the duality of the sexes, involving perpetual strife with only periodically intervening reconciliations, The terms Dionysian and Apollinian we borrow from the Greeks, who disclose to the discerning mind the profound mysteries of their view of art, not, to be sure, in concepts, but in the intensely clear figures of their gods. Through Apollo and Dionysus, the two art deities of the Greeks, we come to recognize that in the Greek world there existed a tremendous opposition, in origin and aims, between the Apollinian art of sculpture, and the nonimagistic, Dionysian art of music. These two different tendencies run parallel to each other, for the most part openly at variance; and they continually incite each other to new and more powerful births, which perpetuate an antagonism, only superficially reconciled by the common term "art"; till eventually, by a metaphysical miracle of the Hellenic "will" they appear coupled with each other, and through this coupling ultimately generate an equally Dionysian and Apollinian form of art—Attic tragedy.

In order to grasp these two tendencies, let us first conceive of them as the separate art worlds of *dreams* and *intoxication*. These physiological phenomena present a contrast analogous to that existing between the Apollinian and the Dionysian. It was in dreams, says Lucretius, that the glorious diving figures first appeared to the souls of men; in dreams the great shaper beheld the splendid bodies of superhuman beings; and the Hellenic poet, if questioned about the mysteries of poetic inspiration, would likewise have suggested dreams and he might have given an explanation like that of Hans Sachs in the *Meistersinger*:

> The poet's task is this, my friend,
> to read his dreams and comprehend.
> The truest human fancy seems
> to be revealed to us in dreams:
> all poems and versification
> are but true dreams' interpretation.

The beautiful illusion of the dream worlds, in the creation of which every man is truly an artist, is the prerequisite of all plastic art, and, as we shall see, of an important part of poetry also. In our dreams we delight in the immediate understanding of figures; all forms speak to us; there is nothing unimportant or superfluous. But even when this dream reality is most intense, we still have, glimmering through it, the sensation that it is *mere appearance*: at least this is my experience, and for its frequency—indeed, normality—I could adduce many proofs, including the sayings of the poets.

Philosophical men even have a presentiment that the reality in which we live and have our being is also mere appearance, and that another, quite different reality lies beneath it. Schopenhauer actually indicates as the criterion of philosophical ability the occasional ability to view men and things as mere phantoms or dream images. Thus the aesthetically sensitive man stands in the same relation to the reality of dreams as the philosopher does to the reality of existence; he is a close and willing observer, for these images afford him an interpretation of life, and by reflecting on these processes he trains himself for life.

It is not only the agreeable and friendly images that he experiences as something universally intelligible: the serious, the troubled, the sad, the gloomy, the sudden restraints, the tricks of accident, anxious expectations, in short, the whole divine comedy of life, including the inferno, also pass before him, not like mere shadows on a wall—for he lives and suffers with these scenes—and yet not without that fleeting sensation of illusion. And perhaps many will, like myself, recall how amid the dangers and terrors of dreams they have occasionally said to themselves in self-encouragement, and not without success: "It is a dream!" I have likewise heard of people who were able to continue one and the same dream for three and even more successive nights—facts which indicate clearly how our innermost being, our common ground, experiences dreams with profound delight and a joyous necessity.

This joyous necessity of the dream experience has been embodied by the Greeks in their Apollo: Apollo, the god of all plastic energies, is at the same time the soothsaying god. He, who (as the etymology of the name indicates) is the "shining one," the deity of light, is also ruler over the beautiful illusion of the inner world of fantasy. The higher truth, the perfection of these states in contrast to the incompletely intelligible everyday world, this deep consciousness of nature, healing and helping in sleep and dreams, is at the same time the symbolical analogue of the soothsaying faculty and of the arts generally, which make life possible and worth living. But we must also include in our image of Apollo that delicate boundary which the dream image must not overstep lest it have a pathological effect (in which case mere appearance would deceive us as if it were crude reality). We must keep in mind that measured restraint, that freedom from the wilder emotions, that calm of the sculptor god. His eye must be "sunlike," as befits his origin; even when it is angry and distempered it is still hallowed by beautiful illusion. And so, in one sense, we might apply to Apollo the words of Schopenhauer when he speaks of the man wrapped in the veil of *māyā* (*Welt als Wille and Vorstellung*, I, p. 416): "Just as in a stormy sea that, unbounded in all direction, raises and drops mountainous waves howling, a sailor sits in a boat and trusts in his frail bark: so in the midst of a world of torments the individual human being sits quietly, supported by and trusting in the *principium individuationis*." In fact, we might say of Apollo that in him the unshaken faith in this principium and the calm repose of the man wrapped up in it receive their most sublime expression; and we might call Apollo himself the glorious divine image of the *principium individuationis*, through whose gestures and eyes all the joy and wisdom of illusion," together with its beauty, speak to us.

In the same work Schopenhauer has depicted for us the tremendous *terror* which seizes man when he is suddenly dumfounded by the cognitive form of phenomena because the principle of sufficient reason, in some one of its manifestations, seems to suffer an exception. If we add to this terror the blissful ecstasy that wells from the innermost depths of man, indeed of nature, at this collapse of the *principium individuationis*, we steal a glimpse into the nature of the *Dionysian*, which is brought home to us most intimately by the analogy of intoxication.

Either under the influence of the narcotic draught, of which the songs of all primitive men and peoples speak; or with the potent coming if spring that penetrates all nature with joy, these Dionysian emotions awake, and as they grow in intensity everything subjective vanishes into complete self-forgetfulness. In the German Middle Ages, too, singing and dancing crowds, ever increasing in number, whirled themselves from place to place under this same Dionysian impulse. In these dancers of St. John and St. Vitus, we rediscover the Bacchic choruses of the Greeks, with their prehistory in Asia Minor, as far back as Babylon and the orgiastic Sacaea. There are some who, from obtuseness or lack of experience, turn away from such phenomena as from "folk-diseases," with contempt or pity born of the consciousness of their own "healthy-mindedness." But of course such poor wretches have no idea how corpselike and ghostly their so-called "healthy-mindedness" looks when the glowing life of the Dionysian revelers roars past them.

Under the charm of the Dionysian not only is the union between man and man reaffirmed, but nature which has become alienated, hostile, or subjugated, celebrates once more her reconciliation with her lost son, man. Freely, earth proffers her gifts, and peacefully the beasts of prey of the rocks and desert approach. The chariot of Dionysus is covered with flowers and garlands; panthers and tigers walk under its yoke. Transform Beethoven's "Hymn to Joy" into a painting; let your imagination conceive the multitudes bowing to the dust, awestruck—then you will approach the Dionysian. Now the slave is a free man; now all the rigid, hostile barriers that necessity, caprice, or "impudent convention" have fixed between man and man are broken. Now, with the gospel of universal harmony, each one feels himself not only united, reconciled, and fused with his neighbor, but as one with him, as if the veil of *māyā* had been torn aside and were now merely fluttering in tatters before the mysterious primordial unity.

In song and in dance man expresses himself as a member of a higher community; he has forgotten how to walk and speak and is on the way toward flying into the air, dancing. His very gestures express enchantment. Just as the animals now talk, and the earth yields milk and honey, supernatural sounds emanate from him, too: he feels himself a god, he himself now walks about enchanted, in ecstasy, like the gods he saw walking in his dreams. He is no longer an artist, he has become a work of art: in these paroxysms of intoxication the artistic power of all nature reveals itself to the highest gratification of the primordial unity. The noblest clay, the most costly marble, man, is here kneaded and cut, and to the sound of the chisel strokes of the Dionysian world-artist rings out the cry of the Eleusinian mysteries: "Do you prostate yourselves, millions? Do you sense your Maker, world?"

What Is Art?

Leo Tolstoy

Every work of art causes the receiver to enter into a certain kind of relationship both with him who produced, or is producing, the art, and with all those who, simultaneously, previously, or subsequently, receive the same artistic impression.

Speech, transmitting the thoughts and experiences of men, serves as a means of union among them, and art acts in a similar manner. The peculiarity of this latter means of intercourse, distinguishing it from intercourse by means of words, consists in this, that whereas by words a man transmits his thoughts to another, by means of art he transmits his feelings.

The activity of art is based on the fact that a man, receiving through his sense of hearing or sight another man's expression of feeling, is capable of experiencing the emotion which moved the man who expressed it. To take the simplest example: one man laughs, and another who hears becomes merry; or a man weeps, and another who hears feels sorrow. A man is excited or irritated, and another man seeing him comes to a similar state of mind. By his movements or by the sounds of his voice, a man expresses courage and determination or sadness and calmness, and this state of mind passes on to others. A man suffers, expressing his sufferings by groans and spasms, and this suffering transmits itself to other people; a man expresses his feeling of admiration, devotion, fear, respect, or love to certain objects, persons, or phenomena, and others are infected by the same feelings of admiration, devotion, fear, respect, or love to the same objects, persons, and phenomena.

And it is upon this capacity of man to receive another man's expression of feeling and experience those feelings himself, that the activity of art is based.

If a man infects another or others directly, immediately, by his appearance or by the sounds he gives vent to at the very time he experiences the feeling; if he causes another man to yawn when he himself cannot help yawning, or to laugh or cry when he himself is obliged to laugh or cry, or to suffer when he himself is suffering—that does not amount to art.

Art begins when one person, with the object of joining another or others to himself in one and the same feeling, expresses that feeling by certain external indications. To take the simplest example: a boy, having experienced, let us say, fear on encountering a wolf, relates that encounter; and, in order to evoke in others the feeling he has experienced, describes himself, his condition before the encounter, the surroundings, the wood, his own lightheartedness, and then the wolf's appearance, its movements, the distance between himself and the wolf, etc. All this, if only the boy, when telling the story, again experiences the feelings he had lived through and infects the hearers and compels them to feel what the narrator had experienced, is art. If even the boy had not seen a wolf but had frequently been afraid of one, and if, wishing to evoke in others the fear he had felt, he invented an encounter with a wolf and recounted it so as to make his hearers share the feelings he experienced when he feared the wolf, that also would be art. And just in the same way it is art if a man, having experienced either the fear of suffering or the attraction of enjoyment (whether in reality or in imagination), expresses these feelings on canvas or in marble so that others are infected by them. And it is also art if a man feels or imagines to himself feelings of delight, gladness, sorrow, despair, courage, or despondency and the transition from one to another of these feelings, and expresses these feelings by sounds so that the hearers are infected by them and experience them as they were experienced by the composer.

The feelings with which the artist infects others may be most various—very strong or very weak, very important or very insignificant, very bad or very good: feelings of love for one's own country, self-devotion and submission to fate or to God expressed in a drama, raptures of lovers described in a novel, feelings of voluptuousness expressed in a picture, courage expressed in a triumphal march, merriment evoked by a dance, humor evoked by a funny story, the feeling of quietness transmitted by an evening landscape or a lullaby, or the feeling of admiration evoked by a beautiful arabesque—it is all art.

If only the spectators or auditors are infected by the feelings which the author has felt, it is art.

To evoke in oneself a feeling one has experienced, and having evoked it in oneself, then, by means of movements, lines, colors, sounds, or forms expressed in words, so to transmit that feeling that others may experience the same feeling—that is the activity of art.

Art is a human activity consisting in this, that one man consciously, by means of certain external signs, hands on to others the feelings he has lived through, and that other people are infected by these feelings and also experience them.

For the great majority of working-people, our art, besides being inaccessible on account of its costliness, is strange in its very nature, transmitting as it does the feelings of people far removed from those conditions of laborious life which are natural to the great body of humanity. That which is enjoyment to a man of the rich classes is incomprehensible as a pleasure to a workingman, and evokes in him either no feeling at all or only a feeling quite contrary to that which it evokes in an idle and satiated man. Such feelings as form the chief subjects of present-day art—say, for instance, honor, patriotism, and amorousness—evoke in a workingman only bewilderment and contempt, or indignation. So that even if a possibility were given to the laboring classes in their free time to see, to read, and to hear all that forms the flower of contemporary art (as is done to some extent in towns by means of picture galleries, popular concerts, and libraries), the workingman (to the extent to which he is a laborer and has not begun to pass into the ranks of those perverted by idleness) would be able to make nothing of our fine art, and if he did understand it, that which he understood would not elevate his soul but would certainly, in most cases, pervert it. To thoughtful and sincere people there can, therefore, be no doubt that the art of our upper classes never can be the art of the whole people. But if art is an important matter, a spiritual blessing, essential for all men ("like religion," as the devotees of art are fond of saying), then it should be accessible to everyone. And if, as in our day, it is not accessible to all men, then one of two things: either art is not the vital matter it is represented to be or that art which we call art is not the real thing.

The unbelief of the upper classes of the European world had this effect—that instead of an artistic activity aiming at transmitting the highest feelings to which humanity has attained, those flowing from religious perception, we have an activity which aims at affording the greatest enjoyment to a certain class of society. And all of the immense domain of art, that part has been fenced off and is alone called art which affords enjoyment to the people of this particular circle.

Apart from the moral effects on European society of such a selection from the whole sphere of art of what did not deserve such a valuation, and the acknowledgment of it as important art, this perversion of art has weakened art itself and well-nigh destroyed it. The first great result was that art was deprived of the infinite, varied, and profound religious subject matter proper to it. The second result was that having only a small circle of people in view, it lost its beauty of form and became affected and obscure; and the third and chief result was that it ceased to be either natural or even sincere and became thoroughly artificial and brain-spun.

The Work of Art in the Age of Mechanical Reproduction

Walter Benjamin

In principle a work of art has always been reproducible. Man-made artifacts could always be imitated by men. Replicas were made by pupils in practice of their craft, by masters for diffusing their works, and, finally, by third parties in the pursuit of gain. Mechanical reproduction of a work of art, however, represents something new. Historically, it advanced intermittently and in leaps at long intervals, but with accelerated intensity. The Greeks knew only two procedures of technically reproducing works of art: founding and stamping. Bronzes, terra cottas, and coins were the only art works which they could produce in quantity. All others were unique and could not be mechanically reproduced. With the woodcut graphic art became mechanically reproducible for the first time, long before script became reproducible by print. The enormous changes which printing, the mechanical reproduction of writing, has brought about in literature are a familiar story. However, within the phenomenon which we are here examining from the perspective of world history, print is merely a special, though particularly important, case. During the Middle Ages engraving and etching were added to the woodcut; at the beginning of the nineteenth century lithography made its appearance.

With lithography the technique of reproduction reached an essentially new stage. This much more direct process was distinguished by the tracing of the design on a stone rather than its incision on a block of wood or its etching on a copperplate and permitted graphic art for the first time to put its products on the market, not only in large numbers as hitherto, but also in daily changing forms. Lithography enabled graphic art to illustrate everyday life, and it began to keep pace with printing. But only a few decades after its invention, lithography was surpassed by photography. For the first time in the process of pictorial reproduction, photography freed the hand of the most important artistic functions which henceforth devolved only upon the eye looking into a lens. Since the eye perceives more swiftly than the hand can draw, the process of pictorial reproduction was accelerated so enormously that it could keep pace with speech. A film operator shooting a scene in the studio captures the images at the speed of an actor's speech. Just as lithography virtually implied the illustrated newspaper, so did photography foreshadow the sound film. The technical reproduction of sound was tackled at the end of the last century. These convergent endeavors made predictable a situation which Paul Valéry pointed up in this sentence: "Just as water, gas, and electricity are brought into our houses from far off to satisfy our needs in response to a minimal effort, so we shall be supplied with visual or auditory images, which will appear and disappear at a simple movement of the hand, hardly more than a sign." . . . Around 1900 technical reproduction had reached a standard that not only permitted it to reproduce all transmitted works of art and thus to cause the most profound change in their impact upon the public; it also had captured a place of its own among the artistic processes. For the study of this standard nothing is more revealing than the nature of the repercussions that these two different manifestations—the reproduction of works of art and the art of the film—have had on art in its traditional form.

Even the most perfect reproduction of a work of art is lacking in one element: its presence in time and space, its unique existence at the place where it happens to be. This unique existence of the work of art determined the history to which it was subject throughout the time of its existence. This includes the changes which it may have suffered in physical condition over the years as well as the various changes in its ownership. The traces of the first can be revealed only by chemical or physical analyses which it is impossible to perform on a reproduction; changes of ownership are subject to a tradition which must be traced from the situation of the original.

The presence of the original is the prerequisite to the concept of authenticity. Chemical analyses of the patina of a bronze can help to establish this, as does the proof that a given manuscript of the Middle Ages stems from an archive of the fifteenth century. The whole sphere of authenticity is outside technical—and, of course, not only technical—reproducibility. Confronted with its manual reproduction, which was usually branded as a forgery, the original preserved all its authority; not so *vis à vis* technical reproduction. The reason is twofold. First, process reproduction is more independent of the original than manual reproduction. For example, in photography, process reproduction can bring out those aspects of the original that are unattainable to the naked eye yet accessible to the lens, which is adjustable and chooses its angle at will.

The Work of Art in the Age of Mechanical Reproduction

And photographic reproduction, with the aid of certain processes, such as enlargement or slow motion, can capture images which escape natural vision. Secondly, technical reproduction can put the copy of the original into situations which would be out of reach for the original itself. Above all, it enables the original to meet the beholder halfway, be it in the form of a photograph or a phonograph record. The cathedral leaves its locale to be received in the studio of a lover of art; the choral production, performed in an auditorium or in the open air, resounds in the drawing room.

The situations into which the product of mechanical reproduction can be brought may not touch the actual work of art, yet the quality of its presence is always depreciated. This holds not only for the art work but also, for instance, for a landscape which passes in review before the spectator in a movie. In the case of the art object, a most sensitive nucleus—namely, its authenticity—is interfered with whereas no natural object is vulnerable on that score. The authenticity of a thing is the essence of all that is transmissible from its beginning, ranging from its substantive duration to its testimony to the history which it has experienced. Since the historical testimony rests on the authenticity, the former, too, is jeopardized by reproduction when substantive duration ceases to matter. And what is really jeopardized when the historical testimony is affected is the authority of the object.

One might subsume the eliminated element in the term "aura" and go on to say: that which withers in the age of mechanical reproduction is the aura of the work of art. This is a symptomatic process whose significance points beyond the realm of art. One might generalize by saying: the technique of reproduction detaches the reproduced object from the domain of tradition. By making many reproductions it substitutes a plurality of copies for a unique existence. And in permitting the reproduction to meet the beholder or listener in his own particular situation, it reactivates the object reproduced. These two processes lead to a tremendous shattering of tradition which is the obverse of the contemporary crisis and renewal of mankind. Both processes are intimately connected with the contemporary mass movements. Their most powerful agent is the film. Its social significance, particularly in its most positive form, is inconceivable without its destructive, cathartic aspect, that is, the liquidation of the traditional value of the cultural heritage. This phenomenon is most palpable in the great historical films. It extends to ever new positions. In 1927 Abel Gance exclaimed enthusiastically: "Shakespeare, Rembrandt, Beethoven will make films . . . all legends, all mythologies and all myths, all founders of religion, and the very religions . . . await their exposed resurrection, and the heroes crowd each other at the gate." Presumably without intending it, he issued an invitation to a far-reaching liquidation.

. . . The concept of aura which was proposed above with reference to historical objects may usefully be illustrated with reference to the aura of natural ones. We define the aura of the latter as the unique phenomenon of a distance, however close it may be. If, while resting on a summer afternoon, you follow with your eyes a mountain range on the horizon or a branch which casts its shadow over you, you experience the aura of those mountains, of that branch. This image makes it easy to comprehend the social bases of the contemporary decay of the aura. It rests on two circumstances, both of which are related to the increasing significance of the masses in contemporary life. Namely, the desire of contemporary masses to bring things "closer" spatially and humanly, which is just as ardent as their bent toward overcoming the uniqueness of every reality by accepting its reproduction. Every day the urge grows stronger to get hold of an object at very close range by way of its likeness, its reproduction. Unmistakably, reproduction as offered by picture magazines and newsreels differs from the image seen by the unarmed eye. Uniqueness and permanence are as closely linked in the latter as are transitoriness and reproducibility in the former. To pry an object from its shell, to destroy its aura, is the mark of a perception whose "sense of the universal equality of things" has increased to such a degree that it extracts it even from a unique object by means of reproduction. Thus is manifested in the field of perception what in the theoretical sphere is noticeable in the increasing importance of statistics. The adjustment of reality to the masses and of the masses to reality is a process of unlimited scope, as much for thinking as for perception.

The uniqueness of a work of art is inseparable from its being imbedded in the fabric of tradition. This tradition itself is thoroughly alive and extremely changeable. An ancient statue of Venus, for example, stood in a different traditional context with the Greeks, who made it an object of veneration, than with the clerics of the Middle Ages, who viewed it as an ominous idol. Both of them, however, were equally confronted with its uniqueness, that is, its aura. Originally the contextual integration of art in tradition found its expression in the cult. We know that the earliest art works originated in the service of a ritual—first the magical, then the religious kind. It is significant that the existence of the work of art with reference to its aura is never entirely separated from its ritual function. In other words, the unique value of the "authentic" work of art has its basis in ritual, the location of its original use value. This ritualistic basis, however remote, is still recognizable as secularized ritual even in the most profane forms of the cult of beauty. The secular cult of beauty, developed during the Renaissance and prevailing for three centuries, clearly showed that ritualistic basis in its decline and the first deep crisis which befell it. With the advent of the first truly revolutionary means of reproduction, photography, simultaneously with the rise of socialism, art sensed the approaching crisis which has become evident a century later. At the time, art reacted with the doctrine of *l'art pour l'art,* that is, with a theology of art. This gave rise to what might be called a negative theology in the form of the idea of "pure" art, which not only denied any social function of art but also any categorizing by subject matter. (In poetry, Mallarmé was the first to take this position.)

An analysis of art in the age of mechanical reproduction must do justice to these relationships, for they lead us to an all-important insight: for the first time in world history, mechanical reproduction emancipates the work of art from its parasitical dependence on ritual. To an ever greater degree the work of art reproduced becomes the work of art designed for reproducibility. From a photographic negative, for example, one can make any number of prints; to ask for the "authentic" print makes no sense. But the instant the criterion of authenticity ceases to be applicable to artistic production, the total function of art is reversed. Instead of being based on ritual, it begins to be based on another practice—politics.

Works of art are received and valued on different planes. Two polar types stand out: with one, the accent is on the cult value; with the other, on the exhibition value of the work. Artistic production begins with ceremonial objects destined to serve in a cult. One may assume that what mattered was their existence, not their being on view. The elk portrayed by the man of the Stone Age on the walls of his cave was an instrument of magic. He did expose it to his fellow men, but in the main it was meant for the spirits. Today the cult value would seem to demand that the work of art remain hidden. Certain statues of gods are accessible only to the priest in the cella; certain Madonnas remain covered nearly all year round; certain sculptures on medieval cathedrals are invisible to the spectator on ground level. With the emancipation of the various art practices from ritual go increasing opportunities for the exhibition of their products. It is easier to exhibit a portrait bust that can be sent here and there than to exhibit the statue of a divinity that has its fixed place in the interior of a temple. The same holds for the painting as against the mosaic or fresco that preceded it. And even though the public presentability of a mass originally may have been just as great as that of a symphony, the latter originated at the moment when its public presentability promised to surpass that of the mass.

With the different methods of technical reproduction of a work of art, its fitness for exhibition increased to such an extent that the quantitative shift between its two poles turned into a qualitative transformation of its nature. This is comparable to the situation of the work of art in prehistoric times when, by the absolute emphasis on its cult value, it was, first and foremost, an instrument of magic. Only later did it come to be recognized as a work of art. In the same way today, by the absolute emphasis on its exhibition value the work of art becomes a creation with entirely new functions, among which the one we are conscious of, the artistic function, later may be recognized as incidental.

On Elegance in Japan

Barbara Sandrisser

During the last decade of the 10th Century in Japan, an accomplished, versatile lady-in-waiting, named Sei Shōnagon, wrote about elegance. She described six phenomena she believed to be truly elegant:

1. A white coat worn over a violet waistcoat.

2. Duck eggs.

3. Shaved ice mixed with liana syrup and put in a new silver bowl.

4. A rosary of rock crystal.

5. Wisteria blossoms. Plum blossoms covered with snow.

6. A pretty child eating strawberries.[1]

Today we, and perhaps some Japanese, would find it difficult to understand her interpretation of elegance. Our idea of what constitutes elegance most likely does not include any of Sei Shōnagon's preferences. Yet if we examine her selections carefully, we notice that they have certain attributes in common, and it is this kinship which provides us with a richer understanding of the elusive definition of elegance as perceived by the Japanese.

What strikes us immediately is that all the senses, even taste and sound, intermingle among her selections. We are also unable to dismiss the assuming elegance apparent in natural phenomena. Moreover, a kind of sixth sense emerges, a fusion of an intuitive response and an intellectual one which the Japanese call *kokoro*.[2]

Let us review her small inventory again in order to discover the significance of her selections.

A white coat worn over a violet waistcoat. In one of many highly descriptive vignettes, Sei Shōnagon, sitting in the shadows behind a translucent screen, observes a male caller entering the room:

> He looked magnificent as he came towards me. . . . He wore dark grape-colored trousers, boldly splashed with designs of wisteria branches; his

crimson under-robe was so glossy that it seemed to sparkle, while underneath one could make out layer upon layer of white and light violet robes.[3]

White, violet and lavender, much admired during Heian times, emit a decided potency, despite their seemingly fragile tones. Sei Shōnagon understood the inherent qualities of purity and cleanliness from her Shinto heritage and she enjoyed observing how brilliant flashes of white reflected neighboring colors.

From her description, one can easily imagine the visual impact. The interplay of color and pattern entices us just as it did one thousand years ago when Sei Shōnagon, Murasaki Shikibu and others carefully noted nuance of hue in their descriptive passages. If we imagine these colors in dim light against unpainted wood, which is how traditional Japanese perceived them indoors, their sensuous qualities become even more apparent. Moreover, we should try not to avoid the sensual aspects of Sei Shōnagon's image as it, too, touches upon the Japanese idea of elegance.

Duck eggs. Normally, Westerners refrain from referring to aspects of the natural world as elegant. We prefer to confine our concept of elegance to human endeavors. Duck eggs exhibit simplicity of form and delicacy of color. Their small and deceptively fragile appearance belies a remarkable inner strength. We imagine that Sei Shōnagon's fingers delighted in stroking their smooth surface as they sat in the palm of her hand. No doubt too they tasted splendid. In her time duck eggs evoked a subtle elegance; beautiful, modest and unequivocal. Their form expressed straightforward honesty and clarity.

Shaved ice mixed with liana syrup and put in a new silver bowl. During the winter ancient Japanese stored ice in special containers to be eaten during the hot, humid summer. Serving it in a silver bowl intensified the sensuous experience, for the melting green ice was beautiful to behold, cool to the touch while refreshing to one's palate. It was most likely the caviar of 10th Century Japan and of subsequent centuries. Smell and sound enhanced the experience of savoring the ice on one's tongue. Although we do not know if liana syrup was particularly fragrant, we know that ice "smells" cold and that the sound of eating can be pleasant to non-Westerners. The anticipation of eating something special and then actually consuming it is generally an accumulated response ultimately encompassing all our sensibilities.[4] Sei Shōnagon delighted in the exquisite taste of a small edible trifle placed in a beautiful but not ostentatious container, especially if the delicate item rapidly changed consistency. Enjoying ice with liana syrup on a hot day is surely a fleeting experience and, thus, to her an elegant moment in time.

A rosary of rock crystal. Possibly due to their flawed yet lovely appearance, Buddhist quartz beads seem to form an intimate relationship with the hand. Small and infinitely tactile, each irregular bead invites touch and contemplation. Thus, one could say that merely by glancing at or holding the rosary, one grasps a profound sense of elegance.

Wisteria blossoms. Plum blossoms covered with snow. The beauty of wisteria vines replete with cascading lavender and white blossoms borders on the erotic. In Sei Shōnagon's time they represented an invitation to one's beloved. Genji refers to the beauty of wisteria blossoms when courting one of his many ladies and we recall Sei Shōnagon's comment about wisteria sprays on the trousers of her male visitor. Traditional Japanese made a point of courting under wisteria arbors, and wisteria images found their way into virtually every art form.

Her image of plum blossoms covered with snow is surely nature's way of seducing us, while simultaneously alerting us to the temporal qualities of beauty. The snow will melt and both the plum blossoms and the wisteria will die. It is, then, again the beauty of the moment in time which is elegant, as well as the beautiful blossoms.

And finally, we wonder about the elegance of *a pretty child eating strawberries.* Possibly this image is the most elusive one to grasp. Indeed, it might be more appropriate to call it charming. Nonetheless, if we permit ourselves to abstract the image for a moment, we notice the harmony of form and color. The innate purity of the child's face is exemplified by its roundness and by the pale, creamy-white skin set against the smooth texture of exceedingly long blue-black hair. To this image of purity, one is compelled to add a touch of sensuousness of color, texture on the palate and flavor, all sensed vicariously: the delicate, red strawberry about to be enjoyed. Once again, it is a special moment in time. Here, too, the idea of *kokoro* emerges, for both the mind and heart realize the aesthetic and sensuous qualities inherent in the images Sei Shōnagon considered elegant.

Her choices are indeed beautiful ones. Beauty and elegance seem to flow into each other, creating a wave of responses. We sense that perhaps the Japanese value the beauty in elegance in ways which we have yet to decipher. Thus, exploring elegance as an aesthetic notion, both as we conceive it in the West and as the Japanese understand it, reveals fundamental yet intriguing truths for us to ponder. Throughout history, elegantly designed objects and expressions of ideas formed an intimate relationship with each of us by extending our knowledge of the world, by enhancing our daily activities and by heightening our aesthetic appreciation. Yet, in our society, this unique aspect of beauty is frequently ignored or misinterpreted. Elegance is oftentimes criticized as a superficial, dispensable quality. If we sense a paradox here, it is probably because one exists.

The etymology of the word elegance is worth exploring from its early Latin origins onward, as it reveals our peculiar cultural prejudices and also a certain Western cultivated egotism. For an idea or object to be considered elegant, it must first be chosen above others.[5] Thus in the etymological sense, it suggests choosing carefully or skillfully. However in early Latin, undoubtedly because of the social climate, the term elegant was used to ridicule those who were overly fastidious and foppish.

During classical times, the meaning of the word expanded to include the ideas of refined luxury and graceful propriety. Cicero, possibly the first true connoisseur of elegance as defined then, had this expanded meaning in mind when he referred to an *elegante vitae,* or elegant life. He found the decadent opulence enjoyed by many powerful Romans, including Julius Caesar, to be in poor taste. Integrity and elegance should not be, but often are, strangers to each other he felt. In his correspondence he refers to the elegant oratory, diction, and writing of others. Yet it was he who set the standard for both elegance and eloquence in this regard.

Sallust, born 20 years after Cicero in 86 BC (and unlike him, a friend of Julius Caesar) suggested that music, specifically melodies from a stringed instrument, and selected forms of dance could be described as elegant. This may be the first reference to elegance in the arts. These ideas of elegance, exemplified by grace of movement and refinement of sound, remain with us today. The fall of the Roman Empire undoubtedly caused the notion of elegance to recede into oblivion. Although difficult to document, the concept apparently remained dormant for centuries, resurfacing again during the Renaissance when the phrase "elegance of speech" returned to favor. Opulence in attire and in one's surrounding re-emerged, and with it, once again, dandyism and grandiosity.

In science the "elegant proof" gained recognition, that is, a scientific solution or theory that exhibits neatness, simplicity and ingenuity, a theory that does not necessarily follow a prescribed mathematical methodology. Indeed, this may be the most profound definition of elegance, one which

Cicero would undoubtedly endorse. Unlike other Western thinkers Renaissance scientists comprehended the significance of the relationship between elegance and beauty. Admiration for the elegant theory remains with us today, exemplified by Einstein's theory of relativity. Its supreme elegance and beauty continue to astonish us.

Thus by the 16th Century, elegance reflected early Latin and Classical notions, while simultaneously incorporating new dimensions, such as the notion of height. Tall buildings, statuesque people, high columns, were considered elegant. Graceful movement returned to favor, recalling Sallust's comment on dance. Luxurious attire, correctness of taste and refined manners, resulted in a "high class," in effect a "cultured" minority (the chosen few, one might say) turning back to the original definition of the word.

Today in Western society the word has fallen into disrepute. Elegance is now an affectation, in some ways similar to Roman times and the Renaissance. It is entangled with grandeur, ornateness, wealth, and physical appearance. We seem to have lost sight of the unique qualities inherent in the idea of elegance.

Perhaps we are confusing the *word* elegant with the *idea* of elegance. Oftentimes the word seems to substitute for the idea, image or object. We particularly notice this in advertising copy. Elegance describes virtually everything from clothing and cars to condominiums in Bermuda. But is it an actual component of the product being advertised? Evidence suggests that it is an overused, sexy, superficial word deliberately utilized to sell products, which then, presumably, will make us elegant (chic, tasteful, upper class, cultured) individuals. In short, purchasing such a product relieves us of our innate clumsiness, our coarseness, and perhaps most significantly, our seeming vulgarity.

Assuming we succumb to this onslaught, this never ending hype, do we then become elegant and if the answer is conceivably "yes," are we then beautiful too? The Latin origin of the word and its subsequent development suggests that in our society the two are completely separate. Generally beauty appears to be missing from elegance; one does not necessarily imply the other, although some, notably theoretical scientists, would suggest that beauty is assumed to be a part of elegance. Einstein frequently reserved his highest praise for an elegant theory by noting its beauty, and others, such as Hideki Yukawa, a Japanese physicist, note that Einstein himself "had a sense of beauty which is given to only a few theoretical physicists."[6]

Articulating how elegance applies to scientific theory is precarious at best. Rollo May interprets it as "The harmony of an internal form, the inner consistency of a theory, the character of beauty that touches your sensibilities."[7] In May's description elegance and beauty unite. Indeed, despite their differing etymologies, it is difficult (and unnecessary) to separate one from the other in order to isolate their parts. To extend this notion outside the realm of science, consider for a moment the elegance and beauty of Mozart's music, which we are told was notated by the composer directly as a unified whole, or Da Vinci's notebooks, Rembrandt's etchings, Rilke's poems: All offer us the exquisite harmony of internal form expressed in a unique way and all touch our sensibilities in a special way.

Yet, despite the creative work of the artists just cited our society appears to be reluctant to unify beauty and elegance overtly except in certain specific situations, such as the "elegant proof" referred to by scientists. Thus it is necessary to look at Japan where elegance is wedded to beauty linguistically and philosophically. One thousand years later, Kawabata, in his Nobel Prize acceptance speech, refers to the elegance of wisteria in much the same way as Shōnagon and Murasaki Shikibu:

> Wisteria sprays, as they trail in the breeze, suggest softness, gentleness, reticence. Disappearing and then appearing again in the early summer greenery, they have in them that feeling for the poignant beauty of things long characterized by the Japanese as *mono no aware*.[8]

Others translate *mono no aware* as the sadness of things, or sensitivity to things. Kawabata's interpretation "The poignant beauty of things" appears closest to Murasaki's idea of elegance. Both agree that our sensibilities and our mind/heart *(kokoro)* must be touched by the experience. Then and today, the phrase epitomizes the feeling which occurs at the precise moment the cherry blossoms are at their peak. Their brief transient glory, beautiful, yet sad, represents an elegant moment, a memorable interval.

The Heian era bequeathed a sophisticated aesthetic vocabulary to future generations due, in large part, to the emphasis placed on elegance. Admittedly, these arbiters of aesthetic nuance were mostly courtiers, the elite in Heian society, not the common people. Yet Sei Shōnagon describes the modest, rustic home of a local governor, lower on the social scale, who happened to be her maternal uncle. Her notion of rustic does not suggest crudeness or coarseness. She implies that the house was carefully designed to give an impression of quiet simplicity rather than ostentatious embellishment. Between the lines, she grudgingly admits that its simple qualities intrigue her. Buried between the snide reference to "poor and cramped" facilities lies a veiled compliment regarding its attractive characteristics.

There are many types of elegant beauty and beautiful elegance, and the Japanese have seemingly innumerable words to depict them. The most common word uniting the two is *miyabi*. How the character links with others suggests that it referred to poetry (*gago*, an elegant word), music (*gagaku*, ceremonial court music) and etiquette (*garyo*, magnanimity of behavior.) Too, it described the kind of elegance Sei Shōnagon appreciated in nature. The word *miyabi* was aristocratic in origin[9] and in application. Refinement of decorum, of costume, of virtually all aspects of daily life, including lovemaking, permeated the Heian Court.

Yubi, another word for elegance prevalent a thousand years ago, suggests a gentle, delicate beauty, exemplified perhaps by the child eating strawberries, the duck eggs, or by the lover who sends a perfectly worded poem, written on beautiful paper accompanied by a small branch of an appropriate blossom. Strength and passion hide behind the tender moment.

It is important then, to distinguish between the self-indulgent foppishness prevalent in Roman times and the ceremonial, almost ritualistic elegance of 10th Century Japan, which continued and expanded over the next centuries. Indeed, the Japanese prized elegance to such a degree that they seemed to nurture it and thus the fundamental notion of what elegance comprises—beauty, integrity of form, dignity, and profundity—intensified over time.

Other words incorporating essential qualities of elegance suggest further insights. During the Medieval period *Yugen* expressed an elegant profundity, an essence beyond words, particularly when referring to an ethereal, often silent, moment in a Nō performance. *Sabi*, and centuries later *Wabi* and *Shibui*, evolved out of the experience encountered in the tea ceremony. These words expressed the subtle nuance of an elegant beauty so profound that it touched the very core of one's being.

Significantly, virtually all Japanese words for beauty incorporating elegance into their meaning (and there are many) evoke an acute awareness of the relationship between time and space. **The secret of infinity, then,** can be said to be the moment in time when we perceive an elegant truth. Only then do we apprehend the dichotomy between the notion of perfection, which is inert, and the integrity of completeness. Perfection leaves us empty for there is literally nothing more.

Traditional Japanese perceived that, whether created by humans or by nature, objects need not be perfect in the Platonic sense, nor must they express aristocratic ideals. Acquiring the patina of age *(sabi)* exceeds merely becoming old and possibly antique. The modesty *(wabi)* of a simple wood dwelling or of objects used daily over a period of time, elicits an appreciative response. Understatement, even a touch of astringency, exemplified by the aesthetic notion of *shibui*, strongly influenced Japanese design. Less was not necessarily more; it was simply enough.

The Japanese spirit of elegance evokes a unique kind of aesthetic pride which developed from their long tradition of appreciating the grace and dignity inherent in everyday life. Aesthetic pride should not be misconstrued to mean condescension or vanity. Genuine elegance exists in essentiality. Nothing more can be eliminated without violating its meaning and thus everything essential remains and nothing unnecessary is added. Traditional Japanese perceived this essentiality in their environment. They esteemed elegant objects created by humans and elegance discovered in nature.

All cultures interpret themselves in many voices. Still, civilizations tend to echo the fundamental qualities of their cultural development through elegant ideas and through creative endeavors. The fact that animals design their environments, resulting in remarkably elegant solutions (i.e., bird nests, bee hives, beaver dams) only serves to remind us that we as human beings can perceive their elegance while they most likely cannot. The fundamental key which unites utility, comfort and beauty in all three cases is aesthetic appreciation of each as an elegant whole. Discovering elegance is a uniquely human ability, yet we malign the notion. This is merely one side of a paradox. The other side is that we incorporate the *word* elegance, rather than its meaning as evoked here, into a value system which emphasizes selling mediocre products, resulting in what might be called a "valueless system."

Traditional objects designed by the Japanese, such as folding fans, chopsticks, carpenter's tools and movable walls, to name a few, exemplify the concept of elegance in a meaningful way. These deceptively simple things suggest that elegance is not obvious. Occasionally it may even conceal itself, encouraging us to discover its subtleties, for elegance respects the essence of things. Indeed, the continuing value of apprehending and understanding elegance is that it simultaneously intensifies and refines our sensibilities and thus our human experiences.

Notes

[1] Sei Shōnagon, *The Pillow Book of Sei Shōnagon,* translated and edited by Ivan Morris, Penguin Books, 1967, pg. 69. In a footnote Ivan Morris tells us that the stems and leaves of the liana vine were used as mild sweeteners.
[2] Literally mind/heart.
[3] *The Pillow Book of Sei Shōnagon,* pg. 94.
[4] To repeat an old aphorism, eating is touch carried to the bitter end, according to Samuel Butler, a 17th Century British poet and satirist.
[5] See *Cassell's Latin Dictionary,* pg. 190.
[6] Hideki Yukawa, *Creativity and Intuition,* Kodansha, 1973, pg. 106.
[7] Rollo May, *The Courage to Create,* Bantam, 1975, pg. 159–160.
[8] Yasuneri Kawabata, *Japan, The Beautiful, and Myself,* Kodansha, 1969, pg. 48.
[9] Originally meaning courtliness.

Chinese Aesthetics

Kuang-Ming Wu

For the Chinese, beauty is the constitutive inter-involvement of many into one, and one with many, until the entire unison becomes both concrete-particular and cosmic-universal, both in scale and in substance. Here is a twofold characteristic—distinction and interchange, even on the level of the subject. As a result, **beauty is less of a subject to be independently discussed than a pervasive attitude and atmosphere in which one moves and has one's being.**

Yin-Yang Constitutive Involvement

Beauty is something poetic, which is *yin-yang* constitutive involvement. Originally meaning the shaded and the sunny, the *yin* and the *yang* are reciprocals, that is, counterparts and counterpoints. Counterpoints are contraries and contrasts such as yes and no, can and cannot, dark and bright, good and evil, comic and tragic, construction and destruction, and so on. Counterparts are mutuals such as this and that, form and content, will and desires, feeling and reason, body and mind, subject and object, husband and wife, writer and reader, composer, player and audience, the Five Elements (elementary ways of things), and so on.

When these reciprocals are constitutively involved one with another, the situation is "beautiful." It is mutual constitution, in which the one is so much a constituent of the other that when the one is taken away the other disappears. Positively put, these elements—counterpoints and counterparts—constitute together a self-involved unity, presenting a self-recursive integrity.

Since this is a unity of *counterpoints,* it is always a unity in polar motion; here dwell such phrases as "use of no use," "breath-bone," "the Way that is no way," "self-forgetting," and the like, describing the inscrutable vitality of beauty. Being creative constitution, it is called *poetic.* The entire world comes alive; things dwell therein without attachment, accommodated without being overwhelmed.

By the same token, as *counterparts* are constitutively involved, the form and the content, the natal and the actualized, and the like, realize their self-referential unity and consistency. It is then dispersed, and then realized again, in a dancing rhythm. This is the world of beauty.

In this atmosphere of poetic beauty, the "affective quality," "atmosphere of feeling," the subjective answer to the objective call, and the like, are included and transcended. We need no dichotomy here. . . .

Aesthetics as Cosmic Attitude

. . . What immediately strikes one, on mentioning "Chinese aesthetics," is that there is no such formal discipline in China. The Chinese neither raised theoretical problems (say, whether there is beauty in nature without the artist) and pursued them rigourously, nor erected metaphysical systems about the structure of beauty itself, nor even produced principles of aesthetic activities as a whole. Chinese thinking about beauty is always on the specific and the concrete, never abstract theorization.

Suppose we have a sketch of an apple. We can either stay there and enjoy the freshness of the apple, or leave it for the eternal form of Beauty of which it is a mere pointer and participant, or consider the relation among actuality, the art work and the subjects (the artist's feeling, intuition, sensuality; the viewer's reception through its revealment; adequacy to the apple-actuality), or, finally, classify all such considerations as exclusively in the realm of aesthetics, as the job of the philosopher of art, not of the artist himself or of the philosopher of politics.

In all this what is assumed are the separate entities—the artist, the idea, the art work, the intuition, the revealment or adequacy, the audience, the relation, the harmony, the event, the thing in itself, and all this as separate from other branches of philosophy.

In China such barriers break down. When considering the freshness of an apple, we see how the freshness emanates the breathing energies of the skies and the fields, of the breeze and the sun, of the smell and the colours and the atmosphere. The apple-freshness, glowing in such aura, energies, and smell, enhances the universe, and is enhanced by the universe; the apple and the universe dwell in each other and point to each other. The heaven-and-earth is the fresh apple and the freshness is cosmic, and the fresh is fresh, the cosmic, cosmic.

Without Dürer's sensuous colours and lines or Picasso's jagged abstractions and juxtapositions, the Chinese painting lures us on with rhythm-like natural dynamism, ebbing and flowing through the skies and fields, the cosmic joys and sorrows, the feelings and discernings, and all that amid daily hustle and bustle. The Chinese concrete universality unobtrusively nestles us in our world that is both ordinary and mysterious. The Chinese painterly accuracy is not exactly Italian; it is somehow transparent. In the painting shapes and colours invite us to *their* compellingly actual dynamism that pulses *throughout* the world. There is a diffusion which enhances the concrete. There in diffusion and enhancement is a cosmic significance in the particular. The poet/painter raises the brush, and the heaven-and-earth echo in anticipation. The cosmos-breath flows through the brush's beautiful execution into letters, calligraphy, and paintings, composing the very tapestry (*wen*) of the universe.

And in all this the artist and the viewer are involved. They in turn become the cosmic, while they remain themselves, glowing with the apple-fresh in the sunny autumn hills. They enter and are entered, while they engage in the activities of medicine, cooking, martial arts, politics. Thus every human activity is artistic, and every aesthetic act is cosmic; in everything we do, we utter the "language of ocean, language of sky" which cultivates our cosmic sense of justice, of truth.

All this is to say that we cannot define beauty, because its very definition depends on our attitude. Aesthetics is reflective sensibility, primarily attitude. We can think about aesthetic objects, and we can think about everything aesthetically. In the former our attitude is often that of objective analysis; in the latter, our attitude is not, and cannot be. We can have two attitudes in aesthetics, then: objective analysis and pervasive concord. . . .

Kongzi (Confucius) regarded music as one of the Six Arts to cultivate personality, as Plato regarded music as one of the powerful means of harmonizing personality. But whereas Plato wanted to inundate the soul with music in a planned geometric manner, Confucius wanted music to "perfume" the soul-chamber with its vapour, tuning the soul into a vital flexible whole.

Such natural oneness of the soul with the cosmic rhythm is apparent in painting. People usually say of a Chinese painter that the painter expresses himself, not the mountain, as he paints the mountain; after living in the mountain for months, absorbing it into himself, he goes home and paints.

Not so; the painter is instead at home in self-mountain. He paints as he moves and has his being in the world of the mountain; he neither paints the mountain nor expresses himself. He just is and behaves—he in the mountain and the mountain in him. He goes home because he goes home; have you seen anyone not going home? He neither purposely absorbs the mountain nor is he absorbed by it and disappears in it. He just is; the mountain just is. He paints as naturally as the mountain is there, naturally. He paints as naturally as he eats, sleeps, and dies. To paint is part of himself as he is, in the world as it is, in front of the mountain as it is.

. . . This is not mystical absorption of the self into the world in which the self and the mountain are abolished, or a pre-established harmony of the two, or their mutual reflection. All these descriptions are too fixated, too much categorized, missing that simple naturalness of the painter painting the world, rejoicing and singing the world as he lives at home in it. This is why the painter walks into his own painting; the painting is part of himself and the world. He can go into it because he is it; it is his world in which he lives.

Chapter VII: God

The question of whether God exists has occupied philosophers for centuries. It is not clear that the proposition, "God exists," can be conclusively proven or conclusively denied. Yet, the issue of God, regardless of the position one takes, has profound and real consequences upon every aspect of life. Whether one believes in God will affect how one views ultimate reality, self, others, world, time and history, moral foundations, meaning, truth, and beauty. To put it another way, it matters what one thinks about God.

In order to decide whether God in fact exists, one must first examine the meaning of the concept of God. That is, when an individual uses the term "God," just what does he or she mean? Who is God? What is God's nature? What are God's essential attributes? Which God/god are we talking about? A preliminary understanding of the concept is necessary if one is to speak meaningfully of the real existence or non-existence of God.

The essays in this section present the traditional proofs for the existence of God as well as attempts to show that God does not exist; most notably, the problem of evil. Still other essays explore possible responses to the "God problem" that arise in the face of inconclusive evidence concerning the issue of God's existence.

Saint Anselm's ontological argument begins with the concept of God as "a being greater than which nothing can be conceived." From this concept, Anselm reasons deductively to the necessary existence of God. Gaunilon's criticism and Anselm's response are also included.

William Paley's teleological argument is also referred to as "the design argument." He argued that as the physical existence of a watch is sufficient to make "the inference we think, is inevitable, that the watch must have had a maker," so too, the evidence of design in the universe is sufficient to conclude that there is a designer.

Saint Thomas believed that the existence of God could be proved in five ways. "The Five Ways" of Aquinas are also referred to as "the cosmological argument." Beginning from motion, causality, possible being, gradation and design, Aquinas reasons to the existence of God as Prime Mover, First Cause, Necessary Being, Absolute Standard and Designer.

For Blaise Pascal, the French mathematician, logician, inventor, philosopher and theologian, "The heart has reasons of which reason knows nothing. It is the heart which perceives God and not the reason." Because God's existence cannot be proved, Pascal says that one must wager.

Søren Kierkegaard held that existence takes precedence over knowledge. Proof, he contended, relates primarily to knowledge. To know whether God exists one must, he claimed, make a "leap of faith."

In "The Will to Believe," William James defends the individual's right to adopt a believing attitude in religious matters in spite of the absence of strictly logical grounds. Why? Because according to James the choice presented is a *genuine option*; i.e., one that is *living, forced,* and *momentous*. When presented with such options James contends that our passional nature not only may, but must, decide. Choosing to believe in God is reasonable in light of anticipated consequences, not reasonable on the grounds of independent evidence. In other words, we risk losing truth, despite the fact that we do not have compelling logical evidence. Here is what James says:

> *In concreto*, the freedom to believe can only cover living options which the intellect of the individual cannot by itself resolve, and living options never seem absurdities to him who has them to consider.

According to T. H. Huxley, agnosticism is a method that adheres to a single, time-tested principle. Huxley states the principle as follows, ". . . it is wrong for a man to say that he is certain of the objective truth of any proposition unless he can produce evidence which logically justifies that certainty." In other words, the agnostic feels that it is not intellectually honest to give assent to a belief without good grounds.

In "The Problem of Evil," John Hick presents what, he says, is to many "the most powerful positive objection to belief in God . . . the fact of evil." The problem traditionally takes the form of a dilemma. The problem of evil attempts to show that the following three propositions that are relevant to God's existence form an inconsistent set, (i.e., one in which it is logically impossible for all the propositions to be true at the same time). The three propositions are: "God is perfectly loving," "God is all powerful," and "Evil exists." The assumption that the proof makes is that the proposition "Evil exists" is self-evidently or experientially true. Therefore, God cannot be both omnipotent and perfectly loving. A stronger conclusion may also be derived; namely, "An all loving and all powerful God cannot exist."

In response to the problem of evil a number of theodicies (justifications of God's goodness in the face of evil) have been formulated. Among the often-cited theodicies are the greater good defense and the free-will defense. Both theodicies are related in various ways to the notion of "soul-making." Nevertheless, independently of the logical formation of the problem of evil, the fact of evil is a psychologically powerful barrier to belief in God for many people.

The Ontological Argument

Saint Anselm and *Gaunilon*

I. Saint Anselm

O Lord, who grants understanding to faith, make me, so far as is good for me, to understand that you exist, as we believe, and that you are what we believe you to be. Now we believe you to be something greater than which we can conceive of nothing. Could it be then that there is no such nature, since "the fool says in his heart. 'There is no God' " [Ps. 13:1]? But surely this same fool, when he hears me say this "something than which we can conceive of nothing greater," understands what he hears and what he understands is in his understanding even if he does not understand it to exist. For it is one thing for something to be in the understanding and quite another to understand that the thing in question exists. When a painter thinks of the work he will make beforehand, he has it in his understanding, but he does not think that what he has yet to make exists. But once he has painted it, he not only has it in his understanding but he understands that what he has made exists. Even the fool then must be convinced that in his understanding at least there is something than which nothing greater can be conceived, for when he hears this, he understands it and whatever is understood is in the understanding. But surely if the thing be such that we cannot conceive of something greater, it does not exist solely in the understanding. For if it were there only, one could also think of it as existing in reality and this is something greater. If the thing than which none greater can be thought were in the mind alone, then this same thing would both be and not be something than which nothing greater can be conceived. But surely this cannot be. Without doubt then there exists both in the understanding and in reality a being greater than which nothing can be conceived.

So truly does such a thing exist that it cannot be thought of as not existing. For we can think of something as existing which cannot be thought of as not existing, and such a thing is greater than what can be thought not to be. Wherefore, if the thing than which none greater can be thought could be conceived of as not existing then this very thing than which none greater can be thought is not a thing than which none greater can be thought. But this is not possible. **Hence, something greater than which**

nothing can be conceived so truly exists that it cannot be conceived not to be.

O Lord, our God, you are this being. So truly do you exist that you cannot even be thought of as nonexistent. And rightly so, for if some mind could think of something better than you, then the creature would rise above the Creator and would judge him, which is absurd. It is possible indeed to think of anything other than you as nonexistent. Of all beings then you alone have existence in the truest and highest sense, for nothing else so truly is or has existence in so great a measure. Why then does the fool "say in his heart, 'There is no God,' " when it is so evident to a reasoning mind that of all things you exist in a supreme degree? Why indeed save that he is stupid and a fool!

II. Gaunilon

If one doubts or denies there is some such nature that nothing greater than it can be conceived, he is told that the existence of this being is proved, first, from the fact that in doubting or denying such he already has such a being in his understanding, for in hearing about it, he understands what is said. Next he is told that what he understands must needs exist not only in the intellect but in reality as well. And the proof of this is that a thing is greater if it also exists in reality than if it were in the understanding alone. Were it only in the intellect, even something that once existed would be greater than it. And so what is greater than all is less than something and thus not really greater than everything, which is clearly contradictory. It is necessary then that something greater than all, already proved to exist in the understanding, exists in reality as well, for otherwise it could not be greater than all. To this he might reply: . . .

They say that somewhere in the ocean there is an island, which because of the difficulty, or better, the impossibility of finding what does not exist some call the lost island. And they say this island is inestimably wealthy, having all kinds of delights and riches in greater abundance even than the fabled "Fortunate Islands." And since it has no possessor or inhabitant, it excels all other inhabited countries in its possessions. Now should someone tell me that there is such an island, I could readily understand what he says, since there is no problem there. But suppose he adds, as though it were already implied: "You can't doubt any more that this island, which is more excellent than any land, really exists somewhere, since you don't doubt that it is in your understanding and that it is more excellent not to be in the understanding only. Hence it is necessary that it really exists, for if it did not, any land which does would excel it and consequently the island which you already understand to be more excellent would not be such." If one were to try to prove to me that this island in truth exists and its existence should no longer be questioned, either I would think he was joking or I would not know whether to consider him or me the greater fool, me for conceding his argument or him for supposing he had established with any certainty such an island's existence without first showing such excellence to be real and its existence indubitable rather than just a figment of my understanding, whose existence is uncertain.

This then is an answer the fool could make to your arguments against him. When he is first assured that this being is so great that its nonexistence is inconceivable, and that this in turn is established for no other reason than that otherwise it would not excel all things, he could counter the same way and say: "When have I admitted there really is any such thing, i.e. something so much greater than everything else that one could prove to me it is so real, it could not even be conceived as unreal?" What we need at the outset is a very firm argument to show there is some superior being, bigger and better than all else that exists, so that we can go on from this to prove all the other attributes such a bigger and better being has to have. As for the statement that it is inconceivable that the highest thing of all should not exist, it might be better to say its nonexistence or even its possibility of nonexistence is unintelligible. For according to the true meaning of the word, unreal things are not intelligible, but their existence is conceivable in the way that the fool thinks that God does not exist. I most certainly know I exist, but for all that, I know my nonexistence is possible. As for that supreme being which God is, I understand without doubt both his existence and the impossibility of his nonexistence. But whether I can conceive of my nonexistence as long as I most certainly know I exist, I don't know. But if I am able to, why can I not conceive of the nonexistence of whatever else I know with the same certainty? But if I cannot, then such an inability will not be something peculiar to God . . .

III. Saint Anselm

It was a fool against whom I argued in my little work. But since my critic is far from a fool, and is a Catholic speaking in the fool's behalf, it is enough for me if I can answer the Catholic . . .

But you claim our argument is on a par with the following. Someone imagines an island in the ocean which surpasses all lands in its fertility. Because of the difficulty, or rather impossibility, of finding what does not exist, he calls it "Lost Island." He might then say you cannot doubt that it really exists, because anyone can readily understand it from its verbal description. I assert confidently that if anyone finds something for me, besides that "than which none greater is conceivable," which exists either in reality or concept alone to which the logic of my argument can be applied, I will find and give him his "Lost Island," never to be lost again. But it now seems obvious that a thing such that none greater can be conceived cannot be thought of as nonexistent since it exists on such firm grounds of truth. For otherwise it would not exist at all. If anyone says he thinks it does not exist, then I declare that when he thinks this he either thinks of something than which a greater is inconceivable, or else he does not think at all. If he does not think, then neither does he think that what he is not thinking of is nonexistent. But if he does think, then he thinks of something which cannot be thought of as not existing. For if it could be conceived as nonexistent, it could be conceived as having a beginning and an end. Now this is impossible. Hence if anyone thinks of it, he thinks of something that cannot even be conceived to be nonexistent. Now whoever conceives it thus doesn't think of it as nonexistent, for if he did he would conceive what can't be conceived. Nonexistence is inconceivable, then, of something greater than which nothing can be conceived.

You claim moreover that when we say this supreme reality cannot be conceived of as nonexistent, it would be perhaps better to say that its nonexistence or even the possibility of its nonexistence is not understandable. But it is better to say it cannot be conceived. For had I said that the reality itself could not be understood not to exist, perhaps you, who insist that according to proper usage what is false cannot be understood, would object that nothing existing could be understood not to exist. For it is false to claim that what exists does not exist. Hence it would not be peculiar to God to be unable to be understood as nonexistent. If any one of the things that most certainly exist can be understood to be nonexistent, however, then other certain things can also be understood to be nonexistent. But this objection cannot be applied to "conceiving," if this is correctly understood. For though none of the things that exist can be understood not to exist, still they can all be conceived as nonexistent except the greatest. For all—and only—those things can be conceived as nonexistent which have a beginning or end or consist of parts or do not exist in their entirety in any time or place, as I have said. Only that being which cannot be conceived to be nonexistent must be conceived as having no beginning or end or composition of parts but is whole and entire always and everywhere.

Consequently you must realize that you can conceive of yourself as nonexistent, though you most certainly know that you exist. You surprise me when you say you are not sure of this. For we conceive of many things as nonexistent which we know to exist and of many things as existent which we know do not exist. And we conceive them thus not by judging but by imagining them so. We can indeed conceive of something as existent even while we know it does not exist, because we are able to conceive the one at the same time that we know the other. But we cannot conceive nonexistence while knowing existence, because we cannot conceive existence and nonexistence at the same time. If anyone distinguishes between the two senses of the statement in this fashion, then, he will understand that nothing, as long as it is known to be, can be conceived not to be, and that whatever exists, with the exception of a thing such that no greater is conceivable can be conceived of as nonexistent even when it is known to exist. This inability to be conceived of as nonexistent, then, is peculiar to God, even though there are many objects which cannot be conceived not to be while they are . . .

The Teleological Argument

William Paley

Statement of the Argument

In crossing a heath, suppose I pitched my foot against a *stone,* and were asked how the stone came to be there, I might possibly answer, that, for anything I knew to the contrary, it had lain there for ever; nor would it, perhaps, be very easy to show the absurdity of this answer. But suppose I found a *watch* upon the ground, and it should be inquired how the watch happened to be in that place, I should hardly think of the answer which I had given—that, for anything I knew, the watch might have always been there. Yet why should not this answer serve for the watch as well as for the stone? why is it not as admissible in the second case as in the first? For this reason, and for no other; viz., that, when we come to inspect the watch, we perceive (what we could not discover in the stone) that its several parts are framed and put together for a purpose, e.g. that they are so formed and adjusted as to produce motion, and that motion so regulated as to point out the hour of the day; that, if the different parts had been differently shaped from what they are, if a different size from what they are, or placed after any other manner, or in any other order than that in which they are placed, either no motion at all would have been carried on in the machine, or none which would have answered the use that is now served by it. To reckon up a few of the plainest of these parts, and of their offices, all tending to one result:—We see a cylindrical box containing a coiled elastic spring, which, by its endeavor to relax itself, turns round the box. We next observe a flexible chain (artificially wrought for the sake of flexure) communicating the action of the spring from the box to the fusee. We then find a series of wheels, the teeth of which catch in, and apply to, each other, conducting the motion from the fusee to the balance, and from the balance to the pointer, and, at the same time, by the size and shape of those wheels, so regulating that motion as to terminate in causing an index, by an equable and measured progression, to pass over a given space in a given time. We take notice that the wheels are made of brass, in order to keep them from rust; the springs of steel, no other metal being so elastic; that over the face of the watch there is placed a glass, a material employed in no other part of the work, but in the room of which, if there had been any other than a transparent substance, the hour could not be seen without opening the case. This mechanism being observed, (it requires indeed an examination of the instrument, and perhaps some previous knowledge of the subject, to perceive and understand it; but being once, as we have said, observed and understood,) **the inference, we think, is inevitable, that the watch must have had a maker;** that there must have existed, at some time, and at some place or other, an artificer or artificers who formed it for the purpose which we find it actually to answer; who comprehended its construction, and designed its use.

I. Nor would it, I apprehend, weaken the conclusion, that we had never seen a watch made; that we had never known an artist capable of making one; that we were altogether incapable of executing such a piece of workmanship ourselves, or of understanding in what manner it was performed; all this being no more than what is true of some exquisite remains of ancient art, of some lost arts, and, to the generality of mankind, of the more curious productions of modern manufacture. Does one man in a million know how oval frames are turned? Ignorance of this kind exalts our opinion of the unseen and unknown artist's skill, if he be unseen and unknown, but raises no doubt in our minds of the existence and agency of such an artist, at some former time, and in some place or other. Nor can I perceive that it varies at all the inference, whether the question arise concerning a human agent, or concerning an agent of a different species, or an agent possessing, in some respect, a different nature.

II. Neither, secondly, would it invalidate our conclusion, that the watch sometimes went wrong, or that it seldom went exactly right. The purpose of the machinery, the design, and the designer, might be evident, and, in the case supposed, would be evident, in whatever way we accounted for the irregularity of the movement, or whether we could account for it or not. It is not necessary that a machine be perfect, in order to show with what design it was made; still less necessary, where the only question is, whether it were made with any design at all.

III. Nor, thirdly, would it bring any uncertainty into the argument, if there were a few parts of the watch, concerning which we could not discover, or had not yet discovered, in what manner they conduced to the general effect; or even some parts, concerning which we could not ascertain whether they conduced to that effect in any manner whatever. For, as to the first branch of the case, if by the loss, or disorder, or decay of the parts in question, the movement of the watch were found in fact to be stopped, or disturbed, or retarded, no doubt would remain in our minds as to the utility or intention of these parts, although we should be unable to investigate the manner according to which, or the connection by which, the ultimate effect depended upon their action or assistance; and the more complex is the machine, the more likely is this obscurity to arise. Then, as to the second thing supposed, namely, that there were parts which might be spared without prejudice to the movement of the watch, and that he had proved this by experiment, these superfluous parts, even if we were completely assured that they were such, would not vacate the reasoning which we had instituted concerning other parts. The indication of contrivance remained, with respect to them, nearly as it was before.

IV. Nor, fourthly, would any man in his senses think the existence of the watch, with its various machinery, accounted for, by being told that it was one out of possible combinations of material forms; that whatever he had found in the place where he found the watch, must have contained some internal configuration or other; and that this configuration might be the structure now exhibited, viz., of the works of a watch, as well as a different structure.

V. Nor, fifthly, would it yield his inquiry more satisfaction, to be answered, that there existed in things a principle of order, which had disposed the parts of the watch into their present form and situation. He never knew a watch made by the principle of order; nor can he even form to himself an idea of what is meant by a principle of order, distinct from the intelligence of the watchmaker.

VI. Sixthly, he would be surprised to hear that the mechanism of the watch was no proof of contrivance, only a motive to induce the mind to think so.

VII. And not less surprised to be informed, that the watch in his hand was nothing more than the result of the laws of *metallic* nature. It is a perversion of language to assign any law as the efficient, operative cause of anything. A law presupposes an agent; for it is only the mode according to which an agent proceeds; it implies a power; for it is the order according to which that power acts. Without this agent, without this power, which are both distinct from itself, the *law* does nothing, is nothing. The expression, "the law of metallic nature," may sound strange and harsh to a philosophic ear; but it seems quite as justifiable as some others which are more familiar to him such as "the law of vegetable nature," "the law of animal nature," or, indeed, as "the law of nature" in general, when assigned as the cause of phenomena in exclusion of agency and power, or when it is substituted into the place of these.

VIII. Neither, lastly, would our observer be driven out of his conclusion, or from his confidence in this truth, by being told that he knew nothing at all about the matter. He knows enough for his argument: he knows the utility of the end: he knows the subserviency and adaptation of the means to the end. These points being known, his ignorance of other points, his doubts concerning other points, affect not the certainty of his reasoning. The consciousness of knowing little need not beget a distrust of that which he does know. . . .

Application of the Argument

Every indication of contrivance, every manifestation of design, which existed in the watch, exists in the works of nature; with the difference, on the side of nature, of being greater and more, and that in a degree which exceeds all computation. I mean that the contrivances of nature surpass the contrivances of art, in the complexity, subtilty, and curiosity of the mechanism; and still more, if possible, do they go beyond them in number and variety; yet in a multitude of cases, are not less evidently mechanical, not less evidently contrivances, not less evidently accommodated to their end, or suited to their office, than are the most perfect productions of human ingenuity. . . .

The Five Ways

Saint Thomas Aquinas

[Part I, Question 2, Article 3]

The existence of God can be proved in five ways.

The first and more manifest way is the argument from motion. It is certain, and evident to our senses, that in the world some things are in motion. Now whatever is moved is moved by another, for nothing can be moved except it is in potentiality to that towards which it is moved; whereas a thing moves inasmuch as it is in act. For motion is nothing else than the reduction of something from potentiality to actuality. But nothing can be reduced from potentiality to actuality, except by something in a state of actuality. Thus that which is actually hot, as fire, makes wood, which is potentially hot, to be actually hot, and thereby moves and changes it. Now it is not possible that the same thing should be at once in actuality and potentiality in the same respect, but only in different respects. For what is actually hot cannot simultaneously be potentially hot; but it is simultaneously potentially cold. It is therefore impossible that in the same respect and in the same way a thing should be both mover and moved, *i.e.*, that it should move itself. Therefore, whatever is moved must be moved by another. If that by which it is moved be itself moved, then this also must needs be moved by another, and that by another again. But this cannot go on to infinity, because then there would be no first mover, and consequently no other mover, seeing that subsequent movers move only inasmuch as they are moved by the first mover; as the staff moves only because it is moved by the hand. Therefore it is necessary to arrive at a first mover, moved by no other; and this everyone understands to be God.

The second way is from the nature of efficient cause. In the world of sensible things we find there is an order of efficient causes. There is no case known (neither is it, indeed, possible) in which a thing is found to be the efficient cause of itself; for so it would be prior to itself, which is impossible. Now in efficient causes it is not possible to go on to infinity, because in all efficient causes following in order, the first is the cause of the intermediate cause, and the intermediate is the cause of the ultimate cause, whether the intermediate cause be several, or one only. Now to take away the cause is to take away the effect. Therefore, if there be no first cause among efficient causes, there will be no ultimate, nor any intermediate, cause. But if in efficient causes it is possible to go on to infinity, there will be no first efficient cause, neither will there be an ultimate effect, nor any intermediate efficient causes; all of which is plainly false. Therefore it is necessary to admit a first efficient cause, to which everyone gives the name of God.

The third way is taken from possibility and necessity, and runs thus. We find in nature things that are possible to be and not to be, since they are found to be generated, and to be corrupted, and consequently, it is possible for them to be and not to be. But it is impossible for these always to exist, for that which can not-be at some time is not. Therefore, if everything can not-be, then at one time there was nothing in existence. Now if this were true, even now there would be nothing in existence, because that which does not exist begins to exist only through something already existing. Therefore, if at one time nothing was in existence, it would have been impossible for anything to have begun to exist; and thus even now nothing would be in existence—which is absurd. Therefore, not all beings are merely possible, but there must exist something the existence of which is necessary. But every necessary thing either has its necessity caused by another, or not. Now it is impossible to go on to infinity in necessary things which have their necessity caused by another, as has been already proved in regard to efficient causes. Therefore we cannot but admit the existence of some being having of itself its own necessity, and not receiving it from another, but rather causing in others their necessity. This all men speak of as God.

The fourth way is taken from the gradation to be found in things. Among beings there are some more and some less good, true, noble, and the like. But *more* and *less* are predicated of different things according as they resemble in their different ways something which is the maximum, as a thing is said to be hotter according as it more nearly resembles that which is hottest; so that there is something which is truest, something best, something noblest, and, consequently, something which is most being, for those things that are greatest in truth are greatest in being, as it is written in *Metaph.* ii.[1] Now the maximum in any genus is the cause of all in that genus, as fire, which is the maximum of heat, is the cause of all hot things, as is said in the same book.[2] Therefore there must also be something which is to all beings the cause of their being, goodness, and every other perfection; and this we call God.

The fifth way is taken from the governance of the world. We see that things which lack knowledge, such as natural bodies, act for an end, and this is evident from their acting always, or nearly always, in the same way, so as to obtain the best result. Hence it is plain that they achieve their end, not fortuitously, but designedly. Now whatever lacks knowledge cannot move towards an end, unless it be directed by some being endowed with knowledge and intelligence; as the arrow is directed by the archer. Therefore some intelligent being exists by whom all natural things are directed to their end; and this being we call God.

Notes

[1] Aquinas refers here to Aristotle's *Metaphysics*, Ia 1 (993b30).
[2] *Metaphysics*, Ia 1 (993b25).

The Wager

Blaise Pascal

Infinity–nothing. Our soul is cast into the body where it finds number, time, dimensions; it reasons about these things and calls them natural, or necessary, and can believe nothing else.

Unity added to infinity does not increase it at all, any more than a foot added to an infinite measurement: the finite is annihilated in the presence of the infinite and becomes pure nothingness. So it is with our mind before God, with our justice before divine justice. There is not so great a disproportion between our justice and God's as between unity and infinity.

God's justice must be as vast as his mercy. Now his justice towards the damned is less vast and ought to be less startling to us than his mercy towards the elect.

We know that the infinite exists without knowing its nature, just as we know that it is untrue that numbers are finite. Thus it is true that there is an infinite number, but we do not know what it is. It is untrue that it is even, untrue that it is odd, for by adding a unit it does not change its nature. Yet it is a number, and every number is even or odd. (It is true that this applies to every finite number.)

Therefore we may well know that God exists without knowing what he is.

Is there no substantial truth, seeing that there are so many true things which are not truth itself?

Thus we know the existence and nature of the finite because we too are finite and extended in space.

We know the existence of the infinite without knowing its nature, because it too has extension but unlike us no limits.

But we do not know either the existence or the nature of God, because he has neither extension nor limits.

But by faith we know his existence, through glory we shall know his nature.

Now I have already proved that it is quite possible to know that something exists without knowing its nature.

Let us now speak according to our natural lights.

If there is a God, he is infinitely beyond our comprehension, since, being indivisible and without limits, he bears no relation to us. We are therefore incapable of knowing either what he is or whether he is. That being so, who would dare to attempt an answer to the question? Certainly not we, who bear no relation to him.

Who then will condemn Christians for being unable to give rational grounds for their belief, professing as they do a religion for which they cannot give rational grounds? They declare that it is a folly, *stultitiam*, in expounding it to the world, and then you complain that they do not prove it. If they did prove it they would not be keeping their word. It is by being without proof that they show they are not without sense. "Yes, but although that excuses those who offer their religion as such, and absolves them from the criticism of producing it without rational grounds, it does not absolve those who accept it." Let us then examine this point, and let us say: "Either God is or he is not." But to which view shall we be inclined? Reason cannot decide this question. Infinite chaos separates us. At the far end of this infinite distance a coin is being spun which will come down heads or tails. How will you wager? Reason cannot make you choose either, reason cannot prove either wrong.

Do not then condemn as wrong those who have made a choice, for you know nothing about it. "No, but I will condemn them not for having made this particular choice, but any choice, for, although the one who calls heads and the other one are equally at fault, the fact is that they are both at fault: the right thing is not to wager at all."

Yes, but **you must wager**. There is no choice, you are already committed. Which will you choose then? Let us see: since a choice must be made, let us see which offers you the least interest. You have two things to lose: the true and the good; and two things to stake: your reason and your will, your knowledge and your happiness; and your nature has two things to avoid: error and wretchedness. Since you must necessarily choose, your reason is no more affronted by choosing one rather than the other. That is one point cleared up. But your happiness? Let us weigh up the gain and the loss involved in calling heads that God exists. Let us assess the two cases: if you win you win everything, if you lose you lose nothing. Do not hesitate then; wager that he does exist. "That is wonderful. Yes, I must wager, but perhaps I am wagering too much." Let us see: since there is an equal chance of gain and loss, if you stood to win only two lives for one you could still wager, but supposing you stood to win three?

You would have to play (since you must necessarily play) and it would be unwise of you, once you are obliged to play, not to risk your life in order to win three lives at a game in which there is an equal chance of losing and winning. But there is an eternity of life and happiness. That being so, even though there were an infinite number of chances, of which only one were in your favour, you would still be right to wager one in order to win two; and you would be acting wrongly, being obliged to play, in refusing to stake one life against three in a game, where out of an infinite number of chances there is one in your favour, if there were an infinity of infinitely happy life to be won. But here there is an infinity of infinitely happy life to be won, one chance of winning against a finite number of chances of losing, and what you are staking is finite. That leaves no choice; wherever there is infinity, and where there are not infinite chances of losing against that of winning, there is no room for hesitation, you must give everything. And thus, since you are obliged to play, you must be renouncing reason if you hoard your life rather than risk it for an infinite gain, just as likely to occur as a loss amounting to nothing.

For it is no good saying that it is uncertain whether you will win, that it is certain that you are taking a risk, and that the infinite distance between the certainty of what you are risking and the uncertainty of what you may gain makes the finite good you are certainly risking equal to the infinite good that you are not certain to gain. This is not the case. Every gambler takes a certain risk for an uncertain gain, and yet he is taking a certain finite risk for an uncertain finite gain without sinning against reason. Here there is no infinite distance between the certain risk and the uncertain gain: that is not true. There is, indeed, an infinite distance between the certainty of winning and the certainty of losing, but the proportion between the uncertainty of winning and the certainty of what is being risked is in proportion to the chances of winning or losing. And hence if there are as many chances on one side as on the other you are playing for even odds. And in that case the certainty of what you are risking is equal to the uncertainty of what you may win; it is by no means infinitely distant from it. Thus our argument carries infinite weight, when the stakes are finite in a game where there are even chances of winning and losing and an infinite prize to be won.

This is conclusive and if men are capable of any truth this is it.

"I confess, I admit it, but is there really no way of seeing what the cards are?"—"Yes. Scripture and the rest, etc."—"Yes, but my hands are tied and my lips are sealed; I am being forced to wager and I am not free; I am being held fast and I am so made that I cannot believe. What do you want me to do then?"—"That is true, but at least get it into your head that, if you are unable to believe, it is because of your passions, since reason impels you to believe and yet you cannot do so. Concentrate then not on convincing yourself by multiplying proofs of God's existence but by diminishing your passions. You want to find faith and you do not know the road. You want to be cured of unbelief and you ask for the remedy: learn from those who were once bound like you and who now wager all they have. These are people who know the road you wish to follow, who have been cured of the affliction of which you wish to be cured: follow the way by which they began. They behaved just as if they did believe, taking holy water, having masses said, and so on. That will make you believe quite naturally, and will make you more docile."[1]—"But that is what I am afraid of."— "But why? What have you to lose? But to show you that this is the way, the fact is that this diminishes the passions which are your great obstacles. . . ."

End of this address.

"Now what harm will come to you from choosing this course? You will be faithful, honest, humble, grateful, full of good works, a sincere, true friend. . . . It is true you will not enjoy noxious pleasures, glory and good living, but will you not have others?"

"I tell you that you will gain even in this life, and that at every step you take along this road you will see that your gain is so certain and your risk so negligible that in the end you will realize that you have wagered on something certain and infinite for which you have paid nothing."

"How these words fill me with rapture and delight!—"

"If my words please you and seem cogent, you must know that they come from a man who went down upon his knees before and after to pray this infinite and indivisible being, to whom he submits his own, that he might bring your being also to submit to him for your own good and for his glory: and that strength might thus be reconciled with lowliness."

Custom is our nature. Anyone who grows accustomed to faith believes it, and can no longer help fearing hell, and believes nothing else.

Anyone accustomed to believe that the king is to be feared. . . .

Who then can doubt that our soul, being accustomed to see number, " space, movement, believes in this and nothing else?

Do you believe that it is impossible for God to be infinite and indivisible?"—"Yes."—"Very well, I will show you something infinite and indivisible: it is a point moving everywhere at an infinite speed.

"For it is one and the same everywhere and wholly present in every place. From this natural phenomenon which previously seemed impossible to you you should realize that there may be others which you do not yet know. Do not conclude from your apprenticeship that there is nothing left for you to learn, but that you still have an infinite amount to learn."

It is untrue that we are worthy to be loved by others. It is unfair that we should want such a thing. If we were born reasonable and impartial, with a knowledge of ourselves and others, we should not give our wills this bias. However, we are born with it, and so we are born unfair.

For everything tends towards itself: this is contrary to all order.

The tendency should be towards the general, and the bias towards self is the beginning of all disorder, in war, politics, economics, in man's individual body.

The will is therefore depraved. If the members of natural and civil communities tend to the good of the whole body, the communities themselves should tend towards another more general body of which they are members. We should therefore tend towards the general. Thus we are born unfair and depraved.

No religion except our own has taught that man is born sinful, no philosophical sect has said so, so none has told the truth.

No sect and no religion has always existed on earth except Christianity.

We are greatly indebted to those who point out our faults, for they mortify us, they teach us that we have incurred contempt, but they do not prevent us incurring it in the future, for we have plenty of other faults to deserve it. They prepare us for the exercise of correcting and eradicating a given fault.

The heart has its reasons of which reason knows nothing: we know this in countless ways.

I say that it is natural for the heart to love the universal being or itself, according to its allegiance, and it hardens itself against either as it chooses. You have rejected one and kept the other. Is it reason that makes you love yourself?

It is the heart which perceives God and not the reason. That is what faith is: God perceived by the heart, not by the reason.

The only knowledge which is contrary alike to common sense and human nature is the only one always to have existed among men.

Only Christianity makes men both happy and lovable: the code of the gentleman does not allow you to be both happy and lovable.

Note

[1] *abêtira*. That is, the unbeliever will act unthinkingly and mechanically, and in this become more like the beasts, from whom man was differentiated, according to contemporary philosophy, by his faculty of reason.

The Leap of Faith

Søren Kierkegaard

In spite of the fact that Socrates studied with all diligence to acquire a knowledge of human nature and to understand himself, and in spite of the fame accorded him through the centuries as one who beyond all other men had an insight into the human heart, he has himself admitted that the reason for his shrinking from reflection upon the nature of such beings as Pegasus and the Gorgons was that he, the life-long student of human nature, had not yet been able to make up his mind whether he was a stranger monster than Typhon, or a creature of a gentler and simpler sort, partaking of something divine (*Phaedrus*, 229 E). This seems to be a paradox. However, one should not think slightingly of the paradoxical; for the paradox is the source of the thinker's passion, and the thinker without a paradox is like a lover without feeling: a paltry mediocrity. But the highest pitch of every passion is always to will its own downfall; and so it is also the supreme passion of the Reason to seek a collision, though this collision must in one way or another prove its undoing. The supreme paradox of all thought is the attempt to discover something that thought cannot think. This passion is at bottom present in all thinking, even in the thinking of the individual, in so far as in thinking he participates in something transcending himself. But habit dulls our sensibilities, and prevents us from perceiving it. So for example the scientists tell us that our walking is a constant falling. But a sedate and proper gentleman who walks to his office in the morning and back again at noon, probably thinks this to be an exaggeration, for his progress is clearly a case of mediation; how should it occur to him that he is constantly falling when he religiously follows his nose!

But in order to make a beginning, let us now assume a daring proposition; let us assume that we know what man is. Here we have that criterion of the Truth, which in the whole course of Greek philosophy was either *sought*, or *doubted*, or *postulated*, or *made fruitful*. Is it not remarkable that the Greeks should have borne us this testimony? And is it not an epitome, as it were, of the significance of Greek culture, an epigram of its own writing, with which it is also better served than with the frequently voluminous disquisitions sometimes devoted to it? Thus the proposition is well worth positing, and also for another reason, since we have already explained it in the two preceding chapters; while anyone who attempts to explain Socrates differently may well beware lest he fall into the snare of the earlier or later Greek scepticism. For unless we hold fast to the Socratic doctrine of Recollection, and to his principle that every individual man is Man, Sextus Empiricus stands ready to make the transition involved in "teaching" not only difficult but impossible; and Protagoras will begin where Sextus Empiricus leaves off, maintaining that man is the measure of all things, in the sense that the individual man is the measure for others, but by no means in the Socratic sense that each man is his own measure, neither more nor less.

So then we know what man is, and this wisdom, which I shall be the last to hold in light esteem, may progressively become richer and more significant, and with it also the Truth. But now the Reason stands still, just as Socrates did; for the paradoxical passion of the Reason is aroused and seeks a collision; without rightly understanding itself, it is bent upon its own downfall. This is like what happens in connection with the paradox of love. Man lives undisturbed a self-centered life, until there awakens within him the paradox of self-love, in the form of love for another, the object of his longing. (Self-love lies as the ground of all love or is the ground in which all love perishes; therefore if we conceive a religion of love, this religion need make but one assumption, as epigrammatic as true, and take its actuality for granted, namely, the condition that man loves himself, in order to command him to love his neighbor as himself.) The lover is so completely transformed by the paradox of love that he scarcely recognizes himself; so say the poets, who are the spokesmen of love, and so say also the lovers themselves, since they permit the poets merely to take the words from their lips, but not the passion from their hearts. In like manner the paradoxical passion of the Reason, while as yet a mere presentiment, retroactively affects man and his self-knowledge, so that he who thought to know himself is no longer certain whether he is a more strangely composite animal than Typhon, or if perchance his nature contains a gentler and diviner part. . . .

But what is this unknown something with which the Reason collides when inspired by its paradoxical passion, with the result of unsettling even man's knowledge of himself? It is the Unknown. It is not a human being, in so far as we know what man is; nor is it any other known thing. So let us call this unknown something: *the God*. It is nothing more than a name we assign to it. The idea of demonstrating that this unknown something (the God) exists, could scarcely suggest itself to the Reason. For if the God does not exist it would of course be impossible to prove it; and if he does exist it would be folly to attempt it. For at the very outset, in beginning my proof, I would have presupposed it, not as doubtful but as certain (a presupposition is never doubtful, for the very reason that it is a presupposition), since otherwise I would not begin, readily understanding that the whole would be impossible if he did not exist. But if when I speak of proving the God's existence I mean that I propose to prove that the Unknown, which exists, is the God, then I express myself unfortunately. For in that case I do not prove anything, least of all an existence, but merely develop the content of a conception. Generally speaking, it is a difficult matter to prove that anything exists; and what is still worse for the intrepid souls who undertake the venture, the difficulty is such that fame scarcely awaits those who concern themselves with it. The entire demonstration always turns into something very different and becomes an additional development of the consequences that flow from my having assumed that the object in question exists. Thus I always reason from existence, not toward existence, whether I move in the sphere of palpable sensible fact or in the realm of thought. I do not for example prove that a stone exists, but that some existing thing is a stone. The procedure in a court of justice does not prove that a criminal exists, but that the accused, whose existence is given, is a criminal. Whether we call existence an *accessorium* [something predicated] or the eternal *prius* [first given or assumed], it is never subject to demonstration. Let us take ample time for consideration. We have no such reason for haste as have those who from concern for themselves or for the God or for some other thing, must make haste to get existence demonstrated. Under such circumstances there may indeed be need for haste, especially if the prover sincerely seeks to appreciate the danger that he himself, or the thing in question, may be nonexistent unless the proof is finished and does not surreptitiously entertain the thought that it exists whether he succeeds in proving it or not.

If it were proposed to prove Napoleon's existence from Napoleon's deeds, would it not be a most curious proceeding? His existence does indeed explain his deeds, but the deeds do not prove *his* existence, unless I have already understood the word "his" so as thereby to have assumed his existence. But Napoleon is only an individual, and in so far there exists no absolute relationship between him and his deeds; some other person might have performed the same deeds. Perhaps this is the reason why I cannot pass from the deeds to existence. If I call these deeds the deeds of Napoleon the proof becomes superfluous, since I have already named him; if I ignore this, I can never prove from the deeds that they are Napoleon's, but only in a purely ideal manner that such deeds are the deeds of a great general, and so forth. But between the God and his works there is an absolute relationship; God is not a name but a concept. Is this perhaps the reason that his *essentia involvit existentiam* [essence entails existence]? The works of God are such that only the God can perform them. Just so, but where then are the works of the God? The works from which I would deduce his existence are not directly and immediately given. The wisdom in nature, the goodness, the wisdom in the governance of the world—are all these manifest, perhaps, upon the very face of things? Are we not here confronted with the most terrible temptations to doubt, and is it not impossible finally to dispose of all these doubts? But from such an order of things I will surely not attempt to prove God's existence; and even if I began I would never finish, and would in addition have to live constantly in suspense, lest something so terrible should suddenly happen that my bit of proof would be demolished. From what works then do I propose to derive the proof? From the works as apprehended through an ideal interpretation, i.e., such as they do not immediately reveal themselves. But in that case it is not from the works that I make the proof; I merely develop the ideality I have presupposed, and because of my confidence in *this* I make so bold as to defy all objections, even those that have not yet been made. In beginning my proof I presuppose the ideal interpretation, and also that I will be successful in carrying it through; but what else is this but to presuppose that the God exists, so that I really begin by virtue of confidence in him?

And how does the God's existence emerge from the proof? Does it follow straightway, without any breach of continuity? Or have we not here an analogy to the behaviour of the little Cartesian dolls? As soon as I let go of the doll it stands on its head. As soon as I let it go—I must therefore let it go. So also with the proof. As long as I keep my hold on the proof, i.e., continue to demonstrate, the existence does not come out, if for no other reason than that I am engaged in proving it; **but when I let the proof go, the existence is there. But this act of letting go is surely also something;** it is indeed a contribution of mine. Must not this also be taken into the account, this little moment, brief as it may be—it need not be long, for **it is a *leap*.** However brief this moment, if only an instantaneous now, this "now" must be included in the reckoning. If anyone wishes to have it ignored, I will use it to tell a little anecdote, in order to show that it nevertheless does exist. Chrysippus was experimenting with a sorites to see if he could not bring about a break in its quality, either progressively or retrogressively. But Carneades could not get it in his head when the new quality actually emerged. Then Chrysippus told him to try making a little pause in the reckoning, and so—so it would be easier to understand. Carneades replied: With the greatest pleasure, please do not hesitate on my account; you may not only pause, but even lie down to sleep, and it will help you just as little; for when you awake we will begin again where you left off. Just so; it boots as little to try to get rid of something by sleeping as to try to come into the possession of something in the same manner.

Whoever therefore attempts to demonstrate the existence of God (except in the sense of clarifying the concept, and without the *reservatio finalis* noted above, that the **existence emerges from the demonstration by a leap**) proves in lieu thereof something else, something which at times perhaps does not need a proof, and in any case needs none better; for the fool says in his heart that there is no God, but whoever says in his heart or to men: Wait just a little and I will prove it—what a rare man of wisdom is he![1] If in the moment of beginning his proof it is not absolutely undetermined whether the God exists or not, he does not prove it; and if it is thus undetermined in the beginning he will never come to begin, partly from fear of failure, since the God perhaps does not exist, and partly because he has nothing with which to begin.—A project of this kind would scarcely have been undertaken by the ancients. Socrates at least, who is credited with having put forth the physico-teleological proof for God's existence, did not go about it in any such manner. He always presupposes the God's existence, and under this presupposition seeks to interpenetrate nature with the idea of purpose. Had he been asked why he pursued this method, he would doubtless have explained that he lacked the courage to venture out upon so perilous a voyage of discovery without having made sure of the God's existence behind him. At the word of the God he casts his net as if to catch the idea of purpose; for nature herself finds many means of frightening the inquirer, and distracts him by many a digression.

The paradoxical passion of the Reason thus comes repeatedly into collision with this Unknown, which does indeed exist, but is unknown, and in so far does not exist. The Reason cannot advance beyond this point, and yet it cannot refrain in its paradoxicalness from arriving at this limit and occupying itself therewith. It will not serve to dismiss its relation to it simply by asserting that the Unknown does not exist, since this itself involves a relationship. But what then is the Unknown, since the designation of it as the God merely signifies for us that it is unknown? To say that it is the Unknown because it cannot be known, and even if it were capable of being known, it could not be expressed, does not satisfy the demands of passion, though it correctly interprets the Unknown as a limit; but a limit is precisely a torment for passion, though it also serves as an incitement. And yet the Reason can come no further, whether it risks an issue *via negationis* [by way of denying attributes] or *via eminentia* [by way of affirming attributes in the supreme degree].

What then is the Unknown? It is the limit to which the Reason repeatedly comes, and in so far, substituting a static form of conception for the dynamic, it is the different, the absolutely different. But because it is absolutely different, there is no mark by which it could be distinguished. When qualified as absolutely different it seems on the verge of disclosure, but this is not the case; for the Reason cannot even conceive an absolute unlikeness. The Reason cannot negate itself absolutely, but uses itself for the purpose, and thus conceives only such an unlikeness within itself as it can conceive by means of itself; it cannot absolutely transcend itself, and hence conceives only such a superiority over itself as it can conceive by means of itself. Unless the Unknown (the God) remains a mere limiting conception, the single idea of difference will be thrown into a state of confusion, and become many ideas of many differences. The Unknown is then in a condition of dispersion (διασπορά), and the Reason may choose at pleasure from what is at hand and the imagination may suggest (the monstrous, the ludicrous, etc.).

But it is impossible to hold fast to a difference of this nature. Every time this is done it is essentially an arbitrary act, and deepest down in the heart of piety lurks the mad caprice which knows that it has itself produced the God. If no specific determination of difference can be held fast, because there is no distinguishing mark, like and unlike finally become identified with one another, thus sharing the fate of all such dialectical opposites. The unlikeness clings to the Reason and confounds it, so that the Reason no longer knows itself and quite consistently confuses itself with the unlikeness. On this point paganism has been sufficiently prolific in fantastic inventions. As for the last named supposition, the self-irony of the Reason, I shall attempt to delineate it merely by a stroke or two, without raising any question of its being historical. There exists an individual whose appearance is precisely like that of other men; he grows up to manhood like others, he marries, he has an occupation by which he earns his livelihood, and he makes provision for the future as befits a man. For though it may be beautiful to live like the birds of the air, it is not lawful, and may lead to the sorriest of consequences: either starvation if one has enough persistence, or dependence on the bounty of others. This man is also the God. How do I know? I cannot know it, for in order to know it I would have to know the God, and the nature of the difference between the God and man; and this I cannot know, because the Reason has reduced it to likeness with that from which it was unlike. Thus the God becomes the most terrible of deceivers, because the Reason has deceived itself. The Reason has brought the God as near as possible, and yet he is as far away as ever.

Now perhaps someone will say: "You are certainly a crotcheteer, as I know very well. But you surely do not believe that I would pay any attention to such a crotchet, so strange or so ridiculous that it has doubtless never occurred to anyone, and above all so absurd that I must exclude from my consciousness everything that I have in it in order to hit upon it."—And so indeed you must. But do you think yourself warranted in retaining all the presuppositions you have in your consciousness, while pretending to think about your consciousness without presuppositions? Will you deny the consistency of our exposition: that the Reason, in attempting to determine the Unknown as the unlike, at last goes astray, and confounds the unlike with the like? From this there would seem to follow the further consequence, that if man is to receive any true knowledge about the Unknown (the God) he must be made to know that it is unlike him, absolutely unlike him. This knowledge the Reason cannot possibly obtain of itself; we have already seen that this would be a self-contradiction. It will therefore have to obtain this knowledge from the God. But even if it obtains such knowledge it cannot understand it, and thus is quite unable to possess such knowledge. For how should the Reason be able to understand what is absolutely different from itself? If this is not immediately evident, it will become clearer in the light of the consequences; for if the God is absolutely unlike man, then man is absolutely unlike the God; but how could the Reason be expected to understand this? Here we seem to be confronted with a paradox. Merely to obtain the knowledge that the God is unlike him, man needs the help of the God; and now he learns that the God is absolutely different from himself. But if the God and man are absolutely different, this cannot be accounted for on the basis of what man derives from the God, for in so far they are akin. Their unlikeness must therefore be explained by what man derives from himself, or by what he has brought upon his own head. But what can this unlikeness be? Aye, what can it be but sin; since the unlikeness, the absolute unlikeness, is something that man has brought upon himself. We have expressed this in the preceding by saying that man was in Error, and had brought this upon his head by his own guilt; and we came to the conclusion, partly in jest and yet also in earnest, that it was too much to expect of man that he should find this out for himself. Now we have again arrived at the same conclusion. The connoisseur in self-knowledge was perplexed over himself to the point of bewilderment when he came to grapple in thought with the unlike; he scarcely knew any longer whether he was a stranger monster than Typhon, or if his nature partook of something divine. What then did he lack? The consciousness of sin, which he indeed could no more teach to another than another could teach it to him, but only the God—if the God consents to become a Teacher. But this was his purpose, as we have imagined it. In order to be man's Teacher, the God proposed to make himself like the individual man, so that he might understand him fully. Thus our paradox is rendered still more appalling, or the same paradox has the double aspect which proclaims it as the Absolute Paradox; negatively by revealing the absolute unlikeness of sin, positively by proposing to do away with the absolute unlikeness in absolute likeness.

But can such a paradox be conceived? Let us not be over-hasty in replying; and since we strive merely to find the answer to a question, and not as those who run a race, it may be well to remember that success is to the accurate rather than to the swift. The Reason will doubtless find it impossible to conceive it, could not of itself have discovered it, and when it hears it announced will not be able to understand it, sensing merely that its downfall is threatened. In so far the Reason will have much to urge against it; and yet we have on the other hand seen that the Reason, in its paradoxical passion, precisely desires its own downfall. But this is what the Paradox also desires, and thus they are at bottom linked in understanding; but this understanding is present only in the moment of passion. Consider the analogy presented by love, though it is not a perfect one. Self-love lies as the ground of love; but the paradoxical passion of self-love when at its highest pitch wills precisely its own downfall. This is also what love desires, so that these two are linked in mutual understanding in the passion of the moment, and this passion is love. Why should not the lover find this conceivable? But he who in self-love shrinks from the touch of love can neither understand it nor summon the courage to venture it, since it means his downfall. Such is then the passion of love; self-love is indeed submerged but not annihilated; it is taken captive and becomes love's *spolia opima* [honorable spoils], but may again come to life, and this is love's temptation. So also with the Paradox in its relation to the Reason, only that the passion in this case has another name; or rather, we must seek to find a name for it.

Note

[1] What an excellent subject for a comedy of the higher lunacy!

The Will to Believe

William James

1

Let us give the name of *hypothesis* to anything that may be proposed to our belief; and just as the electricians speak of live and dead wires, let us speak of any hypothesis as either *live* or *dead*. A live hypothesis is one which appeals as a real possibility to him to whom it is proposed. If I ask you to believe in the Mahdi, the notion makes no electric connection with your nature—it refuses to scintillate with any credibility at all. As an hypothesis it is completely dead. To an Arab, however (even if he be not one of the Mahdi's followers), the hypothesis is among the mind's possibilities: it is alive. This shows that deadness and liveness in an hypothesis are not intrinsic properties, but relations to the individual thinker. They are measured by his willingness to act. The maximum of liveness in an hypothesis means willingness to act irrevocably. Practically, that means belief; but there is some believing tendency wherever there is willingness to act at all.

Next, let us call the decision between two hypotheses an *option*. Options may be of several kinds. They may be—first, *living* or *dead*; secondly, *forced* or *avoidable*; thirdly, *momentous* or *trivial*; and for our purposes we may call an option a *genuine* option when it is of the forced, living, and momentous kind.

(1) A living option is one in which both hypotheses are live ones. If I say to you: "Be a theosophist or be a Mohammedan," it is probably a dead option, because for you neither hypothesis is likely to be alive. But if I say: "Be an agnostic or be a Christian," it is otherwise: trained as you are, each hypothesis makes some appeal, however small, to your belief.

(2) Next, if I say to you: "Choose between going out with your umbrella or without it," I do not offer you a genuine option, for it is not forced. You can easily avoid it by not going out at all. Similarly, if I say, "Either love me or hate me," "Either call my theory true or call it false," your option is avoidable. You may remain indifferent to me, neither loving nor hating, and you may decline to offer any judgment as to my theory. But if I say, "Either accept this truth or go without it," I put on you a forced option, for there is no standing place outside of the alternative. Every dilemma

based on a complete logical disjunction, with no possibility of not choosing, is an option of this forced kind.

(3) Finally, if I were Dr. Nansen and proposed to you to join my North Pole expedition, your option would be momentous; for this would probably be your only similar opportunity, and your choice now would either exclude you from the North Pole sort of immortality altogether or put at least the chance of it into your hands. He who refuses to embrace a unique opportunity loses the prize as surely as if he tried and failed. *Per contra,* the option is trivial when the opportunity is not unique, when the stake is insignificant, or when the decision is reversible if it later prove unwise. Such trivial options abound in the scientific life. A chemist finds an hypothesis live enough to spend a year in its verification: he believes in it to that extent. But if his experiments prove inconclusive either way, he is quit for his loss of time, no vital harm being done. It will facilitate our discussion if we keep all these distinctions in mind. . . .

2

. . . The thesis I defend is . . . this: *Our passional nature not only lawfully may, but must, decide an option between propositions, whenever it is a genuine option that cannot by its nature be decided on intellectual grounds; for to say, under such circumstances, "Do not decide, but leave the question open," is itself a passional decision—just like deciding yes or no—and is attended with the same risk of losing the truth.* . . .

3

. . . . Wherever the option between losing truth and gaining it is not momentous, we can throw the chance of *gaining truth* away, and at any rate save ourselves from any chance of *believing falsehood,* by not making up our minds at all till objective evidence has come. In scientific questions, this is almost always the case; and even in human affairs in general, the need of acting is seldom so urgent that a false belief to act on is better than no belief at all. Law courts, indeed, have to decide on the best evidence attainable for the moment, because a judge's duty is to make law as well as to ascertain it, and (as a learned judge once said to me) few cases are worth spending much time over: the great thing is to have them decided on *any* acceptable principle, and got out of the way. But in our dealings with objective nature we obviously are recorders, not makers, of the truth; and decisions for the mere sake of deciding promptly and getting on to the next business would be wholly out of place. Throughout the breadth of physical nature facts are what they are quite independently of us, and seldom is there any such hurry about them that the risks of being duped by believing a premature theory need be faced. The questions here are always trivial options, the hypotheses are hardly living (at any rate not living for us spectators), the choice between believing truth or falsehood is seldom forced. The attitude of skeptical balance is therefore the absolutely wise one if we would escape mistakes. What difference, indeed, does it make to most of us whether we have or have not a theory of the Röntgen rays, whether we believe or not in mind-stuff, or have a conviction about the causality of conscious states? It makes no difference. Such options are not forced on us. On every account it is better not to make them, but still keep weighing reasons *pro et contra* with an indifferent hand.

I speak, of course, here of the purely judging mind. For purposes of discovery such indifference is to be less highly recommended, and science would be far less advanced than she is if the passionate desires of individuals to get their own faiths confirmed had been kept out of the game. . . . If you want an absolute duffer in an investigation, you must, after all, take the man who has no interest whatever in its results: he is the warranted incapable, the positive fool. The most useful investigator, because the most sensitive observer, is always he whose eager interest in one side of the question is balanced by an equally keen nervousness lest he become deceived. Science has organized this nervousness into a regular *technique*, her so-called method of verification; and she has fallen so deeply in love with the method that one may even say she has ceased to care for truth by itself at all. It is only truth as technically verified that interests her. The truth of truths might come in merely affirmative form, and she would decline to touch it. Such truth as that, she might repeat with Clifford, would be stolen in defiance of her duty to mankind. Human passions, however, are stronger than technical rules. *"Le coeur a ses raisons,"* as Pascal says, *"que la raison ne connait pas"* [1]; and however indifferent to all but the bare rules of the game the umpire, the abstract intellect, may be, the concrete players who furnish him the materials to judge of are usually, each one of them, in love with some pet "live hypothesis" of his own. Let us agree, however, that wherever there is no forced option, the dispassionately judicial intellect with no pet hypothesis, saving us, as it does, from dupery at any rate, ought be our ideal.

The question next arises: Are there not somewhere forced options in our speculative questions, and can we (as men who may be interested at least as much in positively gaining truth as in merely escaping dupery) always wait with impunity till the coercive evidence shall have arrived? It seems *a priori* improbable that the truth should be so nicely adjusted to our needs and powers as that. In the great boarding-house of nature, the cakes and the butter and the syrup seldom come out so even and leave the plates so clean. Indeed, we should view them with scientific suspicion if they did.

4

Moral questions immediately present themselves as questions whose solution cannot wait for sensible proof. A moral question is a question not of what sensibly exists, but of what is good, or would be good if it did exist. Science can tell us what exists; but to compare the *worths*, both of what exists and of what does not exist, we must consult not science, but what Pascal calls our heart. Science herself consults her heart when she lays it down that the infinite ascertainment of fact and correction of false belief are the supreme goods for man. Challenge the statement, and science can only repeat it oracularly, or else prove it by showing that such ascertainment and correction bring men all sorts of other goods which man's heart in turn declares. The question of having moral beliefs at all or not having them is decided by our will. Are our moral preferences true or false, or are they only odd biological phenomena, making things good or bad for *us*, but in themselves indifferent? How can your pure intellect decide? If your heart does not *want* a world of moral reality, your head will assuredly never make you believe in one. Mephistophelian scepticism, indeed, will satisfy the head's play-instincts much better than any rigorous idealism can. Some men (even at the student age) are so naturally cool-hearted that the moralistic hypothesis never has for them any pungent life, and in their supercilious presence the hot young moralist always feels strangely ill at ease. The appearance of knowingness is on their side, of *naivete* and gullibility on his. Yet, in the articulate heart of him, he clings to it that he is not a dupe, and that there is a realm in which (as Emerson says) all their wit and intellectual superiority is no better than the cunning of a fox. Moral scepticism can no more be refuted or proved by logic than intellectual scepticism can. When we stick to it that there *is* truth (be it of either kind), we do so with our whole nature, and resolve to stand or fall by the results. The sceptic with his whole nature adopts the doubting attitude; but which of us is the wiser, Omniscience only knows.

Turn now from these wide questions of good to a certain class of questions of fact, questions concerning personal relations, states of mind between one man and another. *Do you like me or not?*—for example. Whether you do or not depends, in countless instances, on whether I meet you half-way, am willing to assume that you must like me, and show you trust and expectation. The previous faith on my part in your liking's existence is in such cases what makes your liking come. But if I stand aloof, and refuse to budge an inch until I have objective evidence . . . ten to one your liking never comes. How many women's hearts are vanquished by the mere sanguine insistence of some man that they *must* love him! He will not consent to the hypothesis that they cannot. The desire for a certain kind of truth here brings about that special truth's existence; and so it is in innumerable cases of other sorts. Who gains promotions, boons, appointments, but the man in whose life they are seen to play the part of live hypotheses, who discounts them, sacrifices other things for their sake before they have come, and takes risks for them in advance? His faith acts on the powers above him as a claim, and creates its own verification.

A social organism of any sort whatever, large or small, is what it is because each member proceeds to his own duty with a trust that the other members will simultaneously do theirs. Wherever a desired result is achieved by the co-operation of many independent persons, its existence as a fact is a pure consequence of the precursive faith in one another of those immediately concerned. A government, an army, a commercial system, a ship, a college, an athletic team, all exist on this condition, without which not only is nothing achieved, but nothing is even attempted. A whole train of passengers (individually brave enough) will be looted by a few highwaymen, simply because the latter can count on one another, while each passenger fears that if he makes a movement of resistance, he will be shot before any one else backs him up. If we believed that the whole car-full would rise at once with us, we should each severally rise, and train-robbing would never even be attempted. There are, then, cases where a fact cannot come at all unless a preliminary faith exists in its coming. *And where faith in a fact can help create the fact*, that would be an insane logic which should say that faith running ahead of scientific evidence is the "lowest kind of immorality" into which a thinking being can fall. Yet such is the logic by which our scientific absolutists pretend to regulate our lives!

5

In truths dependent on our personal action, then, faith based on desire is certainly a lawful and possibly an indispensable thing.

But now, it will be said, these are all childish human cases, and have nothing to do with great cosmical matters, like the question of religious faith. Let us then pass on to that. Religions differ so much in their accidents that in discussing the religious question we must make it very generic and broad. What then do we now mean by the religious hypothesis? Science says things are; morality says some things are better than other things; and religion says essentially two things.

First, she says that the best things are the more eternal things, the overlapping things, the things in the universe that throw the last stone, so to speak, and say the final word. "Perfection is eternal"—this phrase of Charles Secretan seems a good way of putting this first affirmation of religion, an affirmation which obviously cannot yet be verified scientifically at all.

The second affirmation of religion is that we are better off even now if we believe her first affirmation to be true.

Now, let us consider what the logical elements of this situation are *in case the religious hypothesis in both its branches be really true*. (Of course, we must admit that possibility at the outset. If we are to discuss the question at all, it must involve a living option. If for any of you religion be a hypothesis that cannot, by any living possibility, be true, then you need go no farther. I speak to the "saving remnant" alone.) So proceeding, we see, first, that religion offers itself as a *momentous* option. We are supposed to gain, even now, by our belief, and to lose by our non-belief, a certain vital good. Secondly, religion is a *forced* option, so far as that good goes. We cannot escape the issue by remaining sceptical and waiting for more light, because, although we do avoid error in that way *if religion be untrue*, we lose the good, *if it be true*, just as certainly as if we positively chose to disbelieve. It is as if a man should hesitate indefinitely to ask a certain woman to marry him because he was not perfectly sure that she would prove an angel after he brought her home. Would he not cut himself off from that particular angel-possibility as decisively as if he went and married some one else? Scepticism, then, is not avoidance of option; it is option of a certain particular kind of risk. *Better risk loss of truth than chance of error*—that is your faith-vetoer's exact position. He is actively playing his stake as much as the believer is; he is backing the field against the religious hypothesis, just as the believer is backing the religious hypothesis against the field. To preach scepticism to us as a duty until "sufficient evidence" for religion be found, is tantamount therefore to telling us, when in presence of the religious hypothesis, that to yield to our fear of its being error is wiser and better than to yield to our hope that it may be true. It is not intellect against all passions, then; it is only intellect with one passion laying down its law. And by what, forsooth, is the supreme wisdom of this passion warranted? Dupery for dupery, what proof is there that dupery through hope is so much worse than dupery through fear? I, for one, can see no proof; and I simply refuse obedience to the scientist's command to imitate his kind of option, in a case where my own stake is important enough to give me the right to choose my own form of risk. If religion be true and the evidence for it be still insufficient, I do not wish, by putting your extinguisher upon my nature (which feels to me as if it had after all some business in this matter), to forfeit my sole chance in life of getting upon the winning side-that chance depending, of course, on my willingness to run the risk of acting as if my passional need of taking the world religiously might be prophetic and right.

All this is on the supposition that it really may be prophetic and right, and that, even to us who are discussing the matter, religion is a live hypothesis which may be true. Now, to most of us religion comes in a still further way that makes a veto on our active faith even more illogical. The more perfect and more eternal aspect of the universe is represented in our religions as having personal form. The universe is no longer a mere *It* to us, but a *Thou*, if we are religious; and any relation that may be possible from person to person might be possible here. For instance. although in one sense we are passive portions of the universe, in another we show a curious autonomy, as if we were small active centres on our own account. We feel, too, as if the appeal of religion to us were made to our own active good-will, as if evidence might be forever withheld from us unless we met the hypothesis half-way. To take a trivial illustration: just as a man who in a company of gentlemen made no advances, asked a warrant for every concession, and believed no one's word without proof, would cut himself off by such churlishness from all the social rewards that a more trusting spirit would earn—so here, one who should shut himself up in snarling logicality and try to make the gods extort his recognition willy-nilly, or not get it at all, might cut himself off forever from his only opportunity of making the gods' acquaintance. This feeling, forced on us we know not whence, that by obstinately believing that there are gods (although not to do so would be so easy both for our logic and our life) we are doing the universe the deepest service we can, seems part of the living essence of the religious hypothesis. If the hypothesis *were* true in all its parts, including this one, then pure intellectualism, with its veto on our making willing advances, would be an absurdity; and some participation of our sympathetic nature would be logically required. I, therefore, for one, cannot see my way to accepting the agnostic rules for truth-seeking, or wilfully agree to keep my willing nature out of the game. I cannot do so for this plain reason, *that a rule of thinking which would absolutely prevent me from acknowledging certain kinds of truth if those kinds of truth were really there, would be an irrational rule.*

That for me is the long and short of the formal logic of the situation, no matter what the kinds of truth might materially be.

I confess I do not see how this logic can be escaped. But sad experience makes me fear that some of you may still shrink from radically saying with me, *in abstracto*, that we have the right to believe at our own risk any hypothesis that is live enough to tempt our will. I suspect, however, that if this is so, it is because you have got away from the abstract logical point of view altogether, and are thinking (perhaps without realizing it) of some particular religious hypothesis which for you is dead. The freedom to "believe what we will" you apply to the case of some patent superstition; and the faith you think of is the faith defined by the schoolboy when he said, "Faith is when you believe something that you know ain't true." I can only repeat that this is misapprehension. ***In concreto*, the freedom to believe can only cover living options which the intellect of the individual cannot by itself resolve; and living options never seem absurdities to him who has them to consider.** When I look at the religious question as it really puts itself to concrete men, and when I think of all the possibilities which both practically and theoretically it involves, then this command that we shall put a stopper on our heart, instincts, and courage, and *wait*—acting of course meanwhile more or less as if religion were *not* true-till doomsday, or till such time as our intellect and senses working together may have raked in evidence enough—this command, I say, seems to me the queerest idol ever manufactured in the philosophic cave. Were we scholastic absolutists, there might be more excuse. If we had an infallible intellect with its objective certitudes, we might feel ourselves disloyal to such a perfect organ of knowledge in not trusting to it exclusively, in not waiting for its releasing word. But if we are empiricists, if we believe that no bell in us tolls to let us know for certain when truth is in our grasp, then it seems a piece of idle fantasticality to preach so solemnly our duty of waiting for the bell. Indeed we *may* wait if we will—I hope you do not think that I am denying that—but if we do so, we do so at our peril as much as if we believed. In either case we *act*, taking our life in our hands. No one of us ought to issue vetoes to the other, nor should we bandy words of abuse. We ought, on the contrary, delicately and profoundly to respect one another's mental freedom: then only shall we bring about the intellectual republic; then only shall we have that spirit of inner tolerance without which all our outer tolerance is soulless, and which is empiricism's glory; then only shall we live and let live, in speculative as well as in practical things.

Agnosticism

T. H. Huxley

Agnosticism . . . is not a creed, but a method, the essence of which lies in the rigorous application of a single principle. That principle is of great antiquity; it is as old as Socrates; as old as the writer who said, "Try all things, hold fast by that which is good"; it is the foundation of the Reformation, which simply illustrated the axiom that every man should be able to give a reason for the faith that is in him; it is the great principle of Descartes[1]; it is the fundamental axiom of modern science. Positively the principle may be expressed: In matters of the intellect, follow your reason as far as it will take you, without regard to any other consideration. And negatively: In matters of the intellect do not pretend that conclusions are certain which are not demonstrated or demonstrable. That I take to be the agnostic faith, which if a man keep whole and undefiled, he shall not be ashamed to look the universe in the face, whatever the future may have in store for him. . . .

The present discussion has arisen out of the use, which has become general in the last few years, of the terms "Agnostic" and "Agnosticism."

The people who call themselves "Agnostics" have been charged with doing so because they have not the courage to declare themselves "Infidels." It has been insinuated that they have adopted a new name in order to escape the unpleasantness which attaches to their proper denomination. To this wholly erroneous imputation, I have replied by showing that the term "Agnostic" did, as a matter of fact, arise in a manner which negatives it; and my statement has not been, and cannot be, refuted. Moreover, speaking for myself, and without impugning the right of any other person to use the term in another sense, I further say that Agnosticism is not properly described as a "negative" creed, nor indeed as a creed of any kind, except in so far as it expresses absolute faith in the validity of a principle, which is as much ethical as intellectual. **This principle may be stated in various ways, but they all amount to this: that it is wrong for a man to say that he is certain of the objective truth of any proposition unless he can produce evidence which logically justifies that certainty.** This is what Agnosticism asserts; and, in my opinion, it is all that is essential to Agnosticism. That which Agnostics deny and repudiate, as immoral, is the contrary doctrine, that there are propositions which men ought to believe, without logically satisfactory evidence; and that reprobation ought to attach to the profession of disbelief in such inadequately supported propositions. The justification of the Agnostic principle lies in the success which follows upon its application, whether in the field of natural, or in that of civil, history; and in the fact that, so far as these topics are concerned, no sane man thinks of denying its validity....

The extent of the region of the uncertain, the number of the problems the investigation of which ends in a verdict of not proven, will vary according to the knowledge and the intellectual habits of the individual Agnostic. I do not very much care to speak of anything as "unknowable." What I am sure about is that there are many topics about which I know nothing; and which, so far as I can see, are out of reach of my faculties. But whether these things are knowable by any one else is exactly one of those matters which is beyond my knowledge, though I may have a tolerably strong opinion as to the probabilities of the case....

It was inevitable that a conflict should arise between Agnosticism and Theology; or rather, I ought to say between Agnosticism and Ecclesiasticism. For Theology, the science, is one thing; and Ecclesiasticism, the championship of a foregone conclusion as to the truth of a particular form of Theology, is another. With scientific Theology, Agnosticism has no quarrel. On the contrary, the Agnostic, knowing too well the influence of prejudice and idiosyncrasy, even on those who desire most earnestly to be impartial, can wish for nothing more urgently than that the scientific theologian should not only be at perfect liberty to thresh out the matter in his own fashion; but that he should, if he can, find flaws in the Agnostic position; and, even if demonstration is not to be had, that he should put, in their full force, the grounds of the conclusions he thinks probable. The scientific theologian admits the Agnostic principle, however widely his results may differ from those reached by the majority of Agnostics.

But, as between Agnosticism and Ecclesiasticism, or, as our neighbours across the Channel call it, Clericalism, there can be neither peace nor truce. The Cleric asserts that it is morally wrong not to believe certain propositions, whatever the results of a strict scientific investigation of the evidence of these propositions. He tells us "that religious error is, in itself, of an immoral nature." He declares that he has prejudged certain conclusions, and looks upon those who show cause for arrest of judgment as emissaries of Satan. It necessarily follows that, for him, the attainment of faith, not the ascertainment of truth, is the highest aim of mental life. And, on careful analysis of the nature of this faith, it will too often be found to be, not the mystic process of unity with the Divine, understood by the religious enthusiast; but that which the candid simplicity of a Sunday scholar once defined it to be. "Faith," said this unconscious plagiarist of Tertullian,[2] "is the power of saying you believe things which are incredible."

Now I, and many other Agnostics, believe that faith, in this sense, is an abomination; and though we do not indulge in the luxury of self-righteousness so far as to call those who are not of our way of thinking hard names, we do feel that the disagreement between ourselves and those who hold this doctrine is even more moral than intellectual....

I trust that I have now made amends for any ambiguity, or want of fullness, in my previous exposition of that which I hold to be the essence of the Agnostic doctrine. Henceforward, I might hope to hear no more of the assertion that we are necessarily Materialists, Idealists, Atheists, Theists, or any other *ists*, if experience had led me to think that the proved falsity of a statement was any guarantee against its repetition. And those who appreciate the nature of our position will see, at once, that when Ecclesiasticism declares that we ought to believe this, that, and the other, and are very wicked if we don't, it is impossible for us to give any answer but this: We have not the slightest objection to believe anything you like, if you will give us good grounds for belief; but, if you cannot, we must respectfully refuse, even if that refusal should wreck morality and insure our own damnation several times over. We are quite content to leave that to the decision of the future. The course of the past has impressed us with the firm conviction that no good ever comes of falsehood, and we feel warranted in refusing even to experiment in that direction.

Notes

[1] A 17th century French philosopher.—Eds.
[2] An early church father and theologian who said, "I believe *because* it is absurd."—Eds.

The Problem of Evil

John Hick

To many, the most powerful positive objection to belief in God is the fact of evil. Probably for most agnostics it is the appalling depth and extent of human suffering, more than anything else, that makes the idea of a loving Creator seem so implausible and disposes them toward one or another of the various naturalistic theories of religion.

As a challenge to theism, the problem of evil has traditionally been posed in the form of a dilemma: **if God is perfectly loving, he must wish to abolish evil; and if he is all-powerful, he must be able to abolish evil. But evil exists; therefore God cannot be both omnipotent and perfectly loving.**

Certain solutions, which at once suggest themselves, have to be ruled out so far as the Judaic-Christian faith is concerned.

To say, for example (with contemporary Christian Science), that evil is an illusion of the human mind, is impossible within a religion based upon the stark realism of the Bible. Its pages faithfully reflect the characteristic mixture of good and evil in human experience. They record every kind of sorrow and suffering, every mode of man's inhumanity to man and of his painfully insecure existence in the world. There is no attempt to regard evil as anything but dark, menacingly ugly, heart-rending, and crushing. In the Christian scriptures, the climax of this history of evil is the crucifixion of Jesus, which is presented not only as a case of utterly unjust suffering, but as the violent and murderous rejection of God's Messiah. There can be no doubt, then, that for biblical faith, evil is unambiguously evil, and stands in direct opposition to God's will.

Again, to solve the problem of evil by means of the theory (sponsored, for example, by the Boston "Personalist" School)[1] of a finite deity who does the best he can with a material, intractable and co-eternal with himself, is to have abandoned the basic premise of Hebrew-Christian monotheism; for the theory amounts to rejecting belief in the infinity and sovereignty of God.

Indeed, any theory which would avoid the problem of the origin of evil by depicting it as an ultimate constituent of the universe, coordinate with good, has been repudiated in advance by the classic Christian teaching, first developed by Augustine, that evil represents the going wrong of something which in itself is good.[2] Augustine holds firmly to the Hebrew-Christian conviction that the universe is *good*—that is to say, it is the creation of a good God for a *good* purpose. He completely rejects the ancient prejudice, widespread in his day, that matter is evil. There are, according to Augustine, higher and lower, greater and lesser goods in immense abundance and variety; but everything which has being is good in its own way and degree, except in so far as it may have become spoiled or corrupted. Evil—whether it be an evil will, an instance of pain, or some disorder or decay in nature—has not been set there by God, but represents the distortion of something that is inherently valuable. Whatever exists is, as such, and in its proper place, good; evil is essentially parasitic upon good, being disorder and perversion in a fundamentally good creation. This understanding of evil as something negative means that it is not willed and created by God; but it does not mean (as some have supposed) that evil is unreal and can be disregarded. Clearly, the first effect of this doctrine is to accentuate even more the question of the origin of evil.

Theodicy,[3] as many modern Christian thinkers see it, is a modest enterprise, negative rather than positive in its conclusions. It does not claim to explain, nor to explain away, every instance of evil in human experience, but only to point to certain considerations which prevent the fact of evil (largely incomprehensible though it remains) from constituting a final and insuperable bar to rational belief in God.

In indicating these considerations it will be useful to follow the traditional division of the subject. There is the problem of *moral evil* or wickedness: why does an all-good and all-powerful God permit this? And there is the problem of the *non-moral evil* of suffering or pain, both physical and mental: why has an all-good and all-powerful God created a world in which this occurs?

Christian thought has always considered moral evil in its relation to human freedom and responsibility. To be a person is to be a finite center of freedom, a (relatively) free and self-directing agent responsible for one's own decisions. This involves being free to act wrongly as well as to act rightly. The idea of a person who can be infallibly guaranteed always to act rightly is self-contradictory. There can be no guarantee in advance that a genuinely free moral agent will never choose amiss. Consequently, the possibility of wrongdoing or sin is logically inseparable from the creation of finite persons, and to say that God should not have created beings who might sin amounts to saying that he should not have created people.

This thesis has been challenged in some recent philosophical discussions of the problem of evil, in which it is claimed that no contradiction is involved in saying that God might have made people who would be genuinely free and who could yet be guaranteed always to act rightly. A quotation from one of these discussions follows:

> If there is no logical impossibility in a man's freely choosing the good on one, or on several occasions, there cannot be a logical impossibility in his freely choosing the good on every occasion. God was not, then, faced with a choice between making innocent automata and making beings who, in acting freely, would sometimes go wrong: there was open to him the obviously better possibility of making beings who would act freely but always go right. Clearly, his failure to avail himself of this possibility is inconsistent with his being both omnipotent and wholly good.[4]

A reply to this argument is suggested in another recent contribution to the discussion.[5] If by a free action we mean an action which is not externally compelled but which flows from the nature of the agent as he reacts to the circumstances in which he finds himself, there is, indeed, no contradiction between our being free and our actions being "caused" (by our own nature) and therefore being in principle predictable. There is a contradiction, however, in saying that God is the cause of our acting as we do but that we are free beings in relation to God. There is, in other words, a contradiction in saying that God has made us so that we shall of necessity act in a certain way, and that we are genuinely independent persons in relation to him. If all our thoughts and actions are divinely predestined, however free and morally responsible we may seem to be to ourselves, we cannot be free and morally responsible in the sight of God, but must instead be his helpless puppets. Such "freedom" is like that of a patient acting out a series of posthypnotic suggestions: he appears, even to himself, to be free, but his volitions have actually been predetermined by another will, that of the hypnotist, in relation to whom the patient is not a free agent.

A different objector might raise the question of whether or not we deny God's omnipotence if we admit that he is unable to create persons who are free from the risks inherent in personal freedom. The answer that has always been given is that to create such beings is logically impossible. It is no limitation upon God's power that he cannot accomplish the logically impossible, since there is nothing here to accomplish, but only a meaningless conjunction of words[6]—in this case "person who is not a person." God is able to create beings of any and every conceivable kind; but creatures who lack moral freedom, however superior they might be to human beings in other respects, would not be what we mean by persons. They would constitute a different form of life which God might have brought into existence instead of persons. When we ask why God did not create such beings in place of persons, the traditional answer is that only persons could, in any meaningful sense, become "children of God," capable of entering into a personal relationship with their Creator by a free and uncompelled response to his love.

When we turn from the possibility of moral evil as a correlate of man's personal freedom to its actuality, we face something which must remain inexplicable even when it can be seen to be possible. For we can never provide a complete causal explanation of a free act; if we could, it would not be a free act. The origin of moral evil lies forever concealed within the mystery of human freedom.

The necessary connection between moral freedom and the possibility, now actualized, of sin throws light upon a great deal of the suffering which afflicts mankind. For an enormous amount of human pain arises either from the inhumanity or the culpable incompetence of mankind. This includes such major scourges as poverty, oppression and persecution, war, and all the injustice, indignity, and inequity which occur even in the most advanced societies. These evils are manifestations of human sin. Even disease is fostered to an extent, the limits of which have not yet been determined by psychosomatic medicine, by moral and emotional factors seated both in the individual and in his social environment. To the extent that all of these evils stem from human failures and wrong decisions, their possibility is inherent in the creation of free persons inhabiting a world which presents them with real choices which are followed by real consequences.

We may now turn more directly to the problem of suffering. Even though the major bulk of actual human pain is traceable to man's misused freedom as a sole or part cause, there remain other sources of pain which are entirely independent of the human will, for example, earthquake, hurricane, storm, flood, drought, and blight. In practice, it is often impossible to trace a boundary between the suffering which results from human wickedness and folly and that which falls upon mankind from without. Both kinds of suffering are inextricably mingled together in human experience. For our present purpose, however, it is important to note that the latter category does exist and that it seems to be built into the very structure of our world. In response to it, theodicy, if it is wisely conducted, follows a negative path. It is not possible to show positively that each item of human pain serves the divine purpose of good; but, on the other hand, it does seem possible to show that the divine purpose as it is understood in Judaism and Christianity could not be forwarded in a world which was designed as a permanent hedonistic paradise.

An essential premise of this argument concerns the nature of the divine purpose in creating the world. The skeptic's assumption is that man is to be viewed as a completed creation and that God's purpose in making the world was to provide a suitable dwelling-place for this fully-formed creature. Since God is good and loving, the environment which he has created for human life to inhabit is naturally as pleasant and comfortable as possible. The problem is essentially similar to that of a man who builds a cage for some pet animal. Since our world, in fact, contains sources of hardship, inconvenience, and danger of innumerable kinds, the conclusion follows that this world cannot have been created by a perfectly benevolent and all-powerful deity.[7]

Christianity, however, has never supposed that God's purpose in the creation of the world was to construct a paradise whose inhabitants would experience a maximum of pleasure and a minimum of pain. The world is seen, instead, as a place of "soul-making" in which free beings grappling with the tasks and challenges of their existence in a common environment, may become "children of God" and "heirs of eternal life." A way of thinking theologically of God's continuing creative purpose for man was suggested by some of the early Hellenistic Fathers of the Christian Church, especially Irenaeus. Following hints from St. Paul, Irenaeus taught that man has been made as a person in the image of God but has not yet been brought as a free and responsible agent into the finite likeness of God, which is revealed in Christ.[8] Our world, with all its rough edges, is the sphere in which this second and harder stage of the creative process is taking place.

This conception of the world (whether or not set in Irenaeus' theological framework) can be supported by the method of negative theodicy. Suppose, contrary to fact, that this world were a paradise from which all possibility of pain and suffering were excluded. The consequences would be very far-reaching. For example, no one could ever injure anyone else: the murderer's knife would turn to paper or his bullets to thin air; the bank safe, robbed of a million dollars, would miraculously become filled with another million dollars (without this device, on however large a scale, proving inflationary); fraud, deceit, conspiracy, and treason would somehow always leave the fabric of society undamaged. Again, no one would ever be injured by accident: the mountain-climber, steeplejack, or playing child falling from a height would float unharmed to the ground; the reckless driver would never meet with disaster. There would be no need to work, since no harm could result from avoiding work; there would be no call to be concerned for others in time of need or danger, for in such a world there could be no real needs or dangers.

To make possible this continual series of individual adjustments, nature would have to work by "special providences" instead of running according to general laws which men must learn to respect on penalty of pain or death. The laws of nature would have to be extremely flexible: sometimes gravity would operate, sometimes not; sometimes an object would be hard and solid, sometimes soft. There could be no sciences, for there would be no enduring world structure to investigate. In eliminating the problems and hardships of an objective environment, with its own laws, life would become like a dream in which, delightfully but aimlessly, we would float and drift at ease.

One can at least begin to imagine such a world. It is evident that our present ethical concepts would have no meaning in it. If, for example, the notion of harming someone is an essential element in the concept of a wrong action, in our hedonistic paradise there could be no wrong actions—nor any right actions in distinction from wrong. Courage and fortitude would have no point in an environment in which there is, by definition, no danger or difficulty. Generosity, kindness, the *agape* aspect of love, prudence, unselfishness, and all other ethical notions which presuppose life in a stable environment, could not even be formed. Consequently, such a world, however well it might promote pleasure, would be very ill adapted for the development of the moral qualities of human personality. In relation to this purpose it would be the worst of all possible worlds.

It would seem, then, that an environment intended to make possible the growth in free beings of the finest characteristics of personal life, must have a good deal in common with our present world. It must operate according to general and dependable laws; and it must involve real dangers, difficulties, problems, obstacles, and possibilities of pain, failure, sorrow, frustration, and defeat. If it did not contain the particular trials and perils which—subtracting man's own very considerable contribution—our world contains, it would have to contain others instead.

To realize this is not, by any means, to be in possession of a detailed theodicy. It is to understand that this world, with all its "heartaches and the thousand natural shocks that flesh is heir to," an environment so manifestly not designed for the maximization of human pleasure and the minimization of human pain, may be rather well adapted to the quite different purpose of "soul-making."[9]

These considerations are related to theism as such. Specifically, Christian theism goes further in the light of the death of Christ, which is seen paradoxically both (as the murder of the divine Son) as the worst thing that has ever happened and (as the occasion of man's salvation) as the best thing that has ever happened. As the supreme evil turned to supreme good, it provides the paradigm for the distinctively Christian reaction to evil. Viewed from the standpoint of Christian faith, evils do not cease to be evils; and certainly, in view of Christ's healing work, they cannot be said to have been sent by God. Yet, it has been the persistent claim of those seriously and wholeheartedly committed to Christian discipleship that tragedy, though truly tragic, may nevertheless be turned, through a man's reaction to it, from a cause of despair and alienation from God to a stage in the fulfillment of God's loving purpose for that individual. As the greatest of all evils, the crucifixion of Christ, was made the occasion of man's redemption, so good can be won from other evils. As Jesus saw his execution by the Romans as an experience which God desired him to accept, an experience which was to be brought within the sphere of the divine purpose and made to serve the divine ends, so the Christian response to calamity is to accept the adversities, pains, and afflictions which life brings, in order that they can be turned to a positive spiritual use.[10]

At this point, theodicy points forward in two ways to the subject of life after death.

First, although there are many striking instances of good being triumphantly brought out of evil through a man's or a woman's reaction to it, there are many other cases in which the opposite has happened. Sometimes obstacles breed strength of character, dangers evoke courage and unselfishness, and calamities produce patience and moral steadfastness. But sometimes they lead, instead, to resentment, fear, grasping selfishness, and disintegration of character. Therefore, it would seem that any divine purpose of soul-making which is at work in earthly history must continue beyond this life if it is ever to achieve more than a very partial and fragmentary success.

Second, if we ask whether the business of soul-making is worth all the toil and sorrow of human life, the Christian answer must be in terms of a future good which is great enough to justify all that has happened on the way to it.[11]

Notes

[1] Edgar Brightman's *A Philosophy of Religion* (Englewood Cliffs, NJ.: Prentice-Hall, Inc., 1940), Chaps. 8–10, is a classic exposition of one form of this view.

[2] See Augustine's *Confessions*, Book VII, Chap. 12; *City of God*, Book XII, Chap. 3; *Enchiridion*, Chap. 4.

[3] The word "theodicy" from the Greek *theos* (God) and *dike* (righteous) means the justification of God's goodness in face of the fact of evil.

[4] J. L. Mackie, "Evil and Omnipotence," *Mind* (April, 1955), p. 209. A similar point is made by Antony Flew in "Divine Omnipotence and Human Freedom," *New Essays in Philosophical Theology*. An important critical comment on these arguments is offered by Ninian Smart in "Omnipotence, Evil and Supermen," *Philosophy* (April, 1961), with replies by Flew (January, 1962) and Mackie (April, 1962).

[5] Flew, in *New Essays in Philosophical Theology*.

[6] As Aquinas said, ". . . nothing that implies a contradiction falls under the scope of God's omnipotence." *Summa Theologica*, Part I, Question 25, article 4.

[7] This is the nature of David Hume's argument in his discussion of the problem of evil in his *Dialogues*, Part XI.

[8] See Irenaeus' *Against Heresies*, Book IV, Chaps. 37 and 38.

[9] This brief discussion has been confined to the problem of human suffering. The large and intractable problem of animal pain is not taken up here. For a discussion of it, see, for example, Nels Ferre, *Evil and the Christian Faith* (New York: Harper & Row, Publishers, Inc., 1947), Chap. 7; and Austin Farrer, *Love Almighty and Ills Unlimited* (New York: Doubleday & Company, Inc., 1961), Chap. 5.

[10] This conception of providence is stated more fully in John Hick, *Faith and Knowledge* (Ithaca: Cornell University Press, 1957), Chap. 7, from which some sentences are incorporated in this paragraph.

[11] In his later book, *Evil and the God of Love*, Professor Hick discusses in detail how the appeal to a life after death completes his theodicy.

Chapter VIII: Freedom

What does it mean to be free? Sustained consideration of this question continues to open the self to the manifold of possibilities, or possible ways to be, in the world. Reflection about the meaning of freedom leads one to the metaphysical issue of whether freedom is even possible. Are we, as human beings, fated? Is every aspect of our life causally determined? Is it possible that we have been predestined by a higher power? Is human freedom, after all, merely an illusion?

On the other hand, the moral dimension of life presupposes that human beings are free and are therefore accountable for their lives and actions. To what extent are humans capable of self-determination? What makes an action free? Are moral limits essential for freedom or do they restrict freedom? What is the relationship between freedom and goodness? What is the relationship between freedom and truth? Is there such a thing as absolute freedom? Is freedom the ability to do whatever one pleases? How should the freedom of the individual be related to the stability of the social order? What is the relationship of freedom to human happiness?

This section covers the range of philosophical positions on freedom beginning with essays on fate and hard determinism and ending with essays dealing with choice, human dignity, freedom and inner strength.

Most of us have, at one time or another, entertained the notion that somehow things were meant to be. Many believe that critical events in life did not just happen but were inevitable. According to Richard Taylor, "a fatalist . . . is someone who believes that whatever happens is and always was unavoidable." Taylor's story of Osmo illustrates the dilemma of fate and free choice. The protagonist, Osmo, attempts to alter his fate by means of a number of rationally calculated choices. Ironically, it was precisely Osmo's choices that brought about his tragic fate. Was Osmo free or was he fated?

Freedom versus determinism is a classic philosophical problem. If human beings are free, then determinism is false, but if human beings are determined, then they are not free. Baron d'Holbach claimed, "The actions of a man are never free." In his essay "Determinism," d'Holbach makes a strong case for causal determinism. He compares the course of human life on the earth to the course of the planets in the heavens. As the planets, of necessity, follow a line through the heavens so too, "man's life is a line that nature commands him to describe upon the surface of the earth, without his ever being able to swerve from it, even for an instant."

Sarvepalli Radhakrishnan was India's most distinguished twentieth-century philosopher. He held posts as professor of philosophy at Calcutta and Oxford and rose to become president of India. In "Karma and Freedom" he argues that although the law of Karma governs the orderedness of human life, human beings are nevertheless free. In other words, the law of Karma entails neither fatalism nor a negation of freedom. Karma, he contends, is a principle of continuity. He puts it this way, "every single thought, word and deed enters into the living chain of causes which make us what we are." He continues, "Freedom is not caprice, nor is Karma necessity." Using an analogy of a card game Radhakishnan reasons that the hand dealt to the player is determined by the law of Karma, but he is free to play the game as he wishes.

Jean Paul Sartre was France's most eminent twentieth-century philosopher. Sartre was a philosopher, novelist, essayist, playwright and political activist. Freedom is a central theme in his many writings. In "Absolute Freedom," Sartre states that, "freedom is identical with my existence." In this selection Sartre tells us that human beings are "condemned to be free." That is, the only limitation on human freedom is that one is not free to not be free. The implication of Sartre's position for the individual is the disclosure that "I am condemned to be wholly responsible for myself." "To be," says Sartre *"is to choose oneself."* Human existence, in Sartre's characterization of existentialism, precedes essence.

Feodor Dostoyevsky's chapter, "The Legend of the Grand Inquisitor," and B. F. Skinner's article, "Freedom and the Control of Men," both deal with the philosophical problem of freedom versus happiness. Both selections set up the problem in a way that suggests that human freedom is incompatible with human happiness. Therefore, human beings must choose whether to be free or happy. To be happy, what is needed is control, not freedom. Is there a way to reconcile freedom and human happiness?

In Dostoyevsky's "Legend" the external controls are institutionalized. During the time of the Spanish Inquisition (the historical setting of the story), the power of the Roman Catholic Church was all-pervasive. In the narrative the cardinal, the Grand Inquisitor, boasts "they have vanquished freedom and have done so to make men happy." Dostoyevsky contrasts the external control that institutionalized religion imposes on individuals with the liberating freedom of the truth as manifest in Christ. Skinner is a product of the twentieth century and his controls come not from the waning power of institutionalized religion but from the enframing power of technology. Skinner's view has clear implications for human and social engineering. His controls stand in opposition to ideas of human freedom and dignity.

In "Choice and Human Dignity," Viktor Frankl shares insights from his experience in a concentration camp. He tells us that "everything can be taken from a man but one thing: the last of the human freedoms—to choose one's attitude in any given set of circumstances, to choose one's own way." By making authentically human choices, Frankl teaches us, we can find meaning in suffering.

In the final selection in this chapter, "Freedom and Inner Strength," Rollo May declares, "Freedom is man's capacity to take a hand in his own development. It is our capacity to mold ourselves." According to May, the key to inward freedom is "choosing one's self." In the process of choosing one's self, freedom is achieved in time. Choosing one's self involves living with an attitude of "aliveness and decisiveness" and accepting the responsibility for fulfilling one's own destiny.

Fate

Richard Taylor

We all, at certain moments of pain, threat, or bereavement, are apt to entertain the idea of fatalism, the thought that what is happening at a particular moment is unavoidable, that we are powerless to prevent it. Sometimes we find ourselves in circumstances not of our own making, in which our very being and destinies are so thoroughly anchored that the thought of fatalism can be quite overwhelming, and sometimes consoling. One feels that whatever then happens, however good or ill, will be what those circumstances yield, and we are helpless. Soldiers, it is said, are sometimes possessed by such thoughts. Perhaps all men would feel more inclined to them if they paused once in a while to think of how little they ever had to do with bringing themselves to wherever they have arrived in life, how much of their fortunes and destinies were decided for them by sheer circumstance, and how the entire course of their lives is often set, once and for all, by the most trivial incidents, which they did not produce and could not even have foreseen. If we are free to work out our destinies at all, which is doubtful, we have a freedom that is at best exercised within exceedingly narrow paths. All the important things—when we are born, of what parents, into what culture, whether we are loved or rejected, whether we are male or female, our temperament, our intelligence or stupidity, indeed everything that makes for the bulk of our happiness and misery—all these are decided for us by the most casual and indifferent circumstances, by sheer coincidences, chance encounters, and seemingly insignificant fortuities. One can see this in retrospect if he searches, but few search. The fate that has given us our very being has given us also our pride and conceit, and has thereby formed us so that, being human, we congratulate ourselves on our blessings, which we call our achievements, blame the world for our blunders, which we call our misfortunes, and scarcely give a thought to that impersonal fate which arbitrarily dispenses both. . . .

A fatalist . . . is someone who believes that whatever happens is and always was unavoidable. He thinks it is not up to him what will happen a thousand years hence, next year, tomorrow, or the very next moment. Of course he does not pretend always to *know* what is going to happen. Hence, he might try sometimes to read signs and portents, as meteorologists and astrologers do, or to contemplate the effects upon him of the various things that might, for all he knows, be fated to occur. But he does not suppose that whatever happens could ever have really been avoidable.

A fatalist thus thinks of the future in the way we all think of the past, for all men are fatalists as they look *back* on things. To a large extent we know what has happened—some of it we can even remember—whereas the future is still obscure to us, and we are therefore tempted to invest it, in our imagination, with all sorts of "possibilities." The fatalist resists this temptation, knowing that mere ignorance can hardly give rise to any genuine possibility in things. He thinks of both past and future "under the aspect of eternity," the way God is supposed to view them. We all think of the past this way, as something settled and fixed, to be taken for what it is. We are never in the least tempted to try to modify it. It is not in the least up to us what happened last year, yesterday, or even a moment ago, any more than are the motions of the heavens or the political developments in Tibet. If we are not fatalists, then we might think that past things once were up to us, to bring about or prevent, as long as they were still future—but this expresses our attitude toward the future, not the past.

Such is surely our conception of the whole past, whether near or remote. But the consistent fatalist thinks of the future in the same way. We say of past things that they are no longer within our power. The fatalist says they never were.

A fatalistic way of thinking most often arises from theological ideas, or from what are generally thought to be certain presuppositions of science and logic. Thus, if God is really all-knowing and all-powerful, it is not hard to suppose that He has arranged for everything to happen just as it is going to happen, that He already knows every detail of the whole future course of the world and there is nothing left for you and me to do except watch things unfold, in the here and hereafter. But without bringing God into the picture, it is not hard to suppose, as we have seen, that everything that happens is wholly determined by what went before it, and hence that whatever happens at any future time is the only thing that can then happen, given what precedes it. Or even disregarding that, it seems natural to suppose that there is a body of truth concerning what the future holds, just as there is such truth concerning what is contained in the past, whether or not it is known to any man or even to God, and hence, that everything asserted in that body of truth will assuredly happen, in the fullness of time, precisely as it is described therein.

No one needs to be convinced that fatalism is the only proper way to view the past. That it is also the proper way to view the future is less obvious, due in part, perhaps, to our vastly greater ignorance of what the future holds. The consequences of holding such fatalism are obviously momentous. To say nothing of the consolation of fatalism, which enables a person to view all things as they arise with the same undisturbed mind with which he contemplates even the most revolting of history's horrors, the fatalist teaching also relieves one of all tendency toward both blame and approbation of others and of both guilt and conceit in himself. It promises that a perfect understanding is possible, and removes the temptation to view things in terms of human wickedness and moral responsibility. This thought alone, once firmly grasped, yields a sublime acceptance of all that life and nature offer, whether to oneself or one's fellows; and although it thereby reduces one's pride, it simultaneously enhances the feelings, opens the heart, and expands the understanding. . . .

Let us suppose that God has revealed a particular set of facts to a chosen scribe who, believing (correctly) that they came from God, wrote them all down. The facts in question then turned out to be all the more or less significant episodes in the life of some perfectly ordinary man named Osmo. Osmo was entirely unknown to the scribe, and in fact to just about everyone, but there was no doubt concerning whom all these facts were about, for the very first thing received by the scribe from God, was: "He of whom I speak is called Osmo." When the revelations reached a fairly voluminous bulk and appeared to be completed, the scribe arranged them in chronological order and assembled them into a book. He at first gave it the title *The Life of Osmo, as Given by God.* but thinking that people would take this to be some sort of joke, he dropped the reference to God.

The book was published, but attracted no attention whatsoever, because it appeared to be nothing more than a record of the dull life of a very plain man named Osmo. The scribe wondered, in fact, why God had chosen to convey such a mass of seemingly pointless trivia.

The book eventually found its way into various libraries, where it gathered dust until one day a high school teacher in Indiana, who rejoiced under the name of Osmo, saw a copy on the shelf. The title caught his eye. Curiously picking it up and blowing the dust off, he was thunderstruck by the opening sentence: "Osmo is born in Mercy Hospital in Auburn, Indiana, on June 6, 1942, of Finnish parentage, and after nearly losing his life from an attack of pneumonia at the age of five, he is enrolled in the St. James school there." Osmo turned pale. The book nearly fell from his hands. He thumbed back in excitement to discover who had written it. Nothing was given of its authorship nor, for that matter, of its publisher. His questions of the librarian produced no further information, he being as ignorant as Osmo of how the book came to be there.

So Osmo, with the book pressed tightly under his arm, dashed across the street for some coffee, thinking to compose himself and then examine the book with care. Meanwhile he glanced at a few more of its opening remarks, at the things said there about his difficulties with his younger sister, how he was slow in learning to read, of the summer on Mackinac Island, and so on. His emotions now somewhat quieted, Osmo began a close reading. He noticed that everything was expressed in the present tense, the way newspaper headlines are written. For example, the text read, "Osmo is born in Mercy Hospital," instead of saying he was born there, and it recorded that he quarrels with his sister, is a slow student, is fitted with dental braces at age eight, and so on, all in the journalistic present tense. But the text itself made quite clear approximately when all these various things happened, for everything was in chronological order, and in any case each year of its subject's life constituted a separate chapter, and was so titled—"Osmo's Seventh Year," "Osmo's Eighth Year," and so on through the book.

Osmo became absolutely engrossed, to the extent that he forgot his original astonishment, bordering on panic, and for a while even lost his curiosity concerning authorship. He sat drinking coffee and reliving his childhood, much of which he had all but forgotten until the memories were revived by the book now before him. He had almost forgotten the kitten, for example, and had entirely forgotten its name, until he read, in the chapter called "Osmo's Seventh Year," this observation: "Sobbing, Osmo takes Fluffy, now quite dead, to the garden, and buries her next to the rose bush." Ah yes! And then there was Louise, who sat next to him in the eighth grade—it was all right there. And how he got caught smoking one day. And how he felt when his father died. On and on. Osmo became so absorbed that he quite forgot the business of the day, until it occurred to him to turn to Chapter 26, to see what might be said there, he having just recently turned twenty-six. He had no sooner done so than his panic returned, for lo! what the book said was *true*! That it rains on his birthday for example, that his wife fails to give him the binoculars he had hinted he would like, that he receives a raise in salary shortly thereafter, and so on. Now how in God's name, Osmo pondered, could anyone know that, apparently before it had happened? For these were quite recent events, and the book had dust on it. Quickly moving on, Osmo came to this: "Sitting and reading in the coffee shop across from the library, Osmo, perspiring copiously, entirely forgets, until it is too late, that he is supposed to collect his wife at the hairdresser's at four." Oh my god! He had forgotten all about that. Yanking out his watch, Osmo discovered that it was nearly five o'clock—too late. She would be on her way home by now, and in a very sour mood.

Osmo's anguish at this discovery was nothing, though, compared to what the rest of the day held for him. He poured more coffee, and it now occurred to him to check the number of chapters in this amazing book. Only twenty-nine! But surely, he thought, that doesn't mean anything. How anyone could have gotten all this stuff down so far was puzzling enough, to be sure, but no one in God's earth could possibly know in advance how long this or that man is going to live. (Only God could know that sort of thing, Osmo reflected.) So he read along; though not without considerable uneasiness and even depression, for the remaining three chapters were on the whole discouraging. He thought he had gotten that ulcer under control, for example. And he didn't see any reason to suppose his job was going to turn out that badly, or that he was really going to break a leg skiing; after all, he could just give up skiing. But then the book ended on a terribly dismal note. It said: "And Osmo, having taken Northwest flight 569 from O'Hare, perishes when the aircraft crashes on the runway at Fort Wayne, with considerable loss of life, a tragedy rendered the more calamitous by the fact that Osmo had neglected to renew his life insurance before the expiration of the grace period." And that was all. That was the end of the book.

So *that's* why it had only twenty-nine chapters. Some idiot thought he was going to get killed in a plane crash. But, Osmo thought, he just wouldn't get on that plane. And this would also remind him to keep his insurance in force.

(About three years later our hero, having boarded a flight for St. Paul, went berserk when the pilot announced they were going to land at Fort Wayne instead. According to one of the stewardesses, he tried to hijack the aircraft and divert it to another airfield. The Civil Aeronautics Board cited the resulting disruptions as contributing to the crash that followed as the plane tried to land.)

Osmo's extraordinary circumstances led him to embrace the doctrine of fatalism. Not quite completely, perhaps, for there he was, right up to the end, trying vainly to buck his fate—trying, in effect, to make a fool of God, though he did not know this, because he had no idea of the book's source. Still, he had the overwhelming evidence of his whole past life to make him think that everything was going to work out exactly as described in the book. It always had. It was, in fact, precisely this conviction that terrified him so.

But now let us ask these questions, in order to make Osmo's experiences more relevant to our own. First, why did he become, or nearly become, a fatalist? Second, just what did his fatalism amount to? Third, was his belief justified in terms of the evidence he had? And finally, is that belief justified in terms of the evidence we have—or in other words, should we be fatalists too?

This last, of course, is the important metaphysical question, but we have to approach it through the others.

Why did Osmo become a fatalist? Osmo became a fatalist because there existed a set of true statements about the details of his life, both past and future, and he came to know what some of these statements were and to believe them, including many concerning his future. That is the whole of it.

No theological ideas entered into his conviction, nor any presuppositions about causal determinism, the coercion of his actions by causes, or anything of this sort. The foundations of Osmo's fatalism were entirely in logic and epistemology, having only to do with truth and knowledge. Ideas about God did not enter in, for he never suspected that God was the ultimate source of those statements. And at no point did he think God was *making* him do what he did. All he was concerned about was that someone seemed somehow to *know* what he had done and was going to do.

What, then, did Osmo believe? He did not, it should be noted, believe that certain things were going to happen to him, *no matter what*. That does not express a logically coherent belief. He did not think he was in danger of perishing in an airplane crash even in case he did not get into any airplane, for example, or that he was going to break his leg skiing, whether he went skiing or not. No one believes what he considers to be plainly impossible. If anyone believes that a given event is going to happen, he does not doubt that those things necessary for its occurrence are going to happen too. The expression, "no matter what," by means of which some philosophers have sought an easy and even childish refutation of fatalism, is accordingly highly inappropriate in any description of the fatalist conviction.

Osmo's fatalism was simply the realization that the things described in the book were unavoidable.

Of course we are all fatalists in this sense about some things, and the metaphysical question is whether this familiar attitude should not be extended to everything. We know the sun will rise tomorrow, for example, and there is nothing we can do about it. Each of us knows he is sooner or later going to die, too, and there is nothing to be done about that either. We normally do not know just when, of course, but it is mercifully so! For otherwise we would simply sit checking off the days as they passed, with growing despair, like a man condemned to the gallows and knowing the hour set for his execution. The tides ebb and flow, and heavens revolve, the seasons follow in order, generations arise and pass, and no one speaks of taking preventive measures. With respect to those things each of us recognizes as beyond his control, we are of necessity fatalists.

The question of fatalism is simply: Of all the things that happen in the world, which, if any, are avoidable? And the philosophical fatalist replies: None of them. They never were. Some of them only seemed so.

Was Osmo's fatalism justified? Of course it was. When he could sit right there and read a true description of those parts of his life that had not yet been lived, it would be idle to suggest to him that his future might, nonetheless, contain alternative possibilities. The only doubts Osmo had were whether those statements could really be true. But here he had the proof of his own experience, as one by one they were tested. Whenever he tried to prevent what was set forth he of course failed. Such failure, over and over, of even the most herculean efforts, with never a single success, must surely suggest, sooner or later, that he was *destined* to fail. Even to the end, when Osmo tried so desperately to save himself from the destruction described in the book, his effort was totally in vain—as he should have realized it was going to be had he really known that what was said there was true. No power in heaven or earth can render false a statement that is true. It has never been done, and never will be.

Is the doctrine of fatalism, then, true? This amounts to asking whether our circumstances are significantly different from Osmo's. Of course we cannot read our own biographies the way he could. Only men who become famous ever have their lives recorded, and even so, it is always in retrospect. This is unfortunate. It is too bad that someone with sufficient knowledge—God, for example—cannot set down the lives of great men in advance, so that their achievements can be appreciated better by their contemporaries, and indeed, by their predecessors—their parents, for instance. But mortals do not have the requisite knowledge, and if there is any god who does, he seems to keep it to himself.

None of this matters, as far as our own fatalism is concerned. For the important thing to note is that, of the two considerations that explain Osmo's fatalism, only one of them was philosophically relevant, and that one applies to us no less than to him. The two considerations were: (1) there existed a set of true statements about his life, both past and future, and (2) he came to know what those statements were and to believe them. Now the second of these two considerations explains why, as a matter of psychological fact, Osmo became fatalistic, but it has nothing to do with the validity of that point of view. Its validity is assured by (1) alone. It was not the fact that the statements happened to be written down that rendered the things they described unavoidable: that had nothing to do with it at all. Nor was it the fact that, because they had been written, Osmo could read them. His reading them and coming to believe them likewise had nothing to do with the inevitability of what they described. This was ensured simply by there being such a set of statements, whether written or not, whether read by anyone or not, and whether or not known to be true. All that is required is that they should be true.

Each of us has but one possible past, described by that totality of statements about us in the past tense, each of which happens to be true. No one ever thinks of rearranging things there; it is simply accepted as given. But so also, each of us has but one possible future, described by that totality of statements about oneself in the future tense, each of which happens to be true. The sum of these constitutes one's biography. Part of it has been lived. The main outlines of it can still be seen, in retrospect, though most of its details are obscure. The other part has not been lived, though it most assuredly is going to be, in exact accordance with that act of statements just referred to. Some of its outlines can already be seen, in prospect, but it is on the whole more obscure than the part belonging to the past. We have at best only premonitory glimpses of it. It is no doubt for this reason that not all of this part, the part that awaits us, is perceived as given, and men do sometimes speak absurdly of altering it—as though what the future holds, as identified by any true statement in the future tense, might after all *not* hold.

Osmo's biography was all expressed in the present tense because all that mattered was that the things referred to were real events; it did not matter to what part of time they belonged. His past consisted of those things that preceded his reading of the book, and he simply accepted it as given. He was not tempted to revise what was said there, for he was sure it was true. But it took the book to make him realize that his future was also something given. It was equally pointless for him to try to revise what was said there, for it, too, was true. As the past contains what has happened, the future contains what will happen, and neither contains, in addition to these things, various other things that did not and will not happen.

Of course we know relatively little of what the future contains. Some things we know. We know the sun will go on rising and setting, for example, that taxes will be levied and wars rage, that men will continue to be callous and greedy, and that people will be murdered and robbed. It is just the details that remain to be discovered. But the same is true of the past; it is only a matter of degree. When I meet a total stranger I do not know, and will probably never know, what his past has been, beyond certain obvious things—that he had a mother, and things of this sort. I know nothing of the particulars of that vast realm of fact that is unique to his past. And the same for his future, with only this difference—that *all* men are strangers to me as far as their futures are concerned, and here I am even a stranger to myself.

Yet there is one thing I know concerning any stranger's past and the past of everything under the sun; namely, that whatever it might hold, there is nothing anyone can do about it now. What has happened cannot be undone. The mere fact that it has happened guarantees this.

And so it is, by the same token, of the future of everything under the sun. Whatever the future might hold, there is nothing anyone can do about it now. What will happen cannot be altered. The mere fact that it is going to happen guarantees this. . . .

Determinism

Baron d'Holbach

In whatever manner man is considered, he is connected to universal nature, and submitted to the necessary and immutable laws that she imposes on all the beings she contains, according to their peculiar essences or to the respective properties with which, without consulting them, she endows each particular species. **Man's life is a line that nature commands him to describe upon the surface of the earth, without his ever being able to swerve from it, even for an instant.** He is born without his own consent; his organization does in nowise depend upon himself; his ideas come to him involuntarily; his habits are in the power of those who cause him to contract them; he is unceasingly modified by causes, whether visible or concealed, over which he has no control, which necessarily regulate his mode of existence, give the hue to his way of thinking, and determine his manner of acting. He is good or bad, happy or miserable, wise or foolish, reasonable or irrational, without his will being for anything in these various states. Nevertheless, in spite of the shackles by which he is bound, it is pretended he is a free agent, or that independent of the causes by which he is moved, he determines his own will, and regulates his own condition.

However slender the foundation of this opinion, of which everything ought to point out to him the error, it is current at this day and passes for an incontestable truth with a great number of people, otherwise extremely enlightened; it is the basis of religion, which, supposing relations between man and the unknown being she has placed above nature, has been incapable of imagining how man could merit reward or deserve punishment from this being, if he was not a free agent. Society has been believed interested in this system; because an idea has gone abroad, that if all the actions of man were to be contemplated as necessary, the right of punishing those who injure their associates would no longer exist. At length human vanity accommodated itself to a hypothesis which, unquestionably, appears to distinguish man from all other physical beings, by assigning to him the special privilege of a total independence of all other causes, but of which a very little reflection would have shown him the impossibility. . . .

The will, as we have elsewhere said, is a modification of the brain, by which it is disposed to action, or prepared to give play to the organs. This will is necessarily determined by the qualities, good or bad, agreeable or painful, of the object or the motive that acts upon his senses, or of which the idea remains with him, and is resuscitated by his memory. In consequence, he acts necessarily, his action is the result of the impulse he receives either from the motive, from the object, or from the idea which has modified his brain, or disposed his will. When he does not act according to this impulse, it is because there comes some new cause, some new motive, some new idea, which modifies his brain in a different manner, gives him a new impulse, determines his will in another way, by which the action of the former impulse is suspended: thus, the sight of an agreeable object, or its idea, determines his will to set him in action to procure it; but if a new object or a new idea more powerfully attracts him, it gives a new direction to his will, annihilates the effect of the former, and prevents the action by which it was to be procured. This is the mode in which reflection, experience, reason, necessarily arrests or suspends the action of man's will: without this he would of necessity have followed the anterior impulse which carried him toward a then desirable object. **In all this he always acts according to necessary laws from which he has no means of emancipating himself.**

If when tormented with violent thirst, he figures to himself in idea, or really perceives a fountain, whose limpid streams might cool his feverish want, is he sufficient master of himself to desire or not to desire the object competent to satisfy so lively a want? It will no doubt be conceded, that it is impossible he should not be desirous to satisfy it; but it will be said— if at this moment it is announced to him that the water he so ardently desires is poisoned, he will, notwithstanding his vehement thirst, abstain from drinking it: and it has, therefore, been falsely concluded that he is a free agent. The fact, however, is, that the motive in either case is exactly the same: his own conservation. The same necessity that determined him to drink before he knew the water was deleterious upon this new discovery equally determined him not to drink; the desire of conserving himself either annihilates or suspends the former impulse; the second motive becomes stronger than the preceding, that is, the fear of death, or the desire of preserving himself, necessarily prevails over the painful sensation caused by his eagerness to drink: but, it will be said, if the thirst is very parching, an inconsiderate man without regarding the danger will risk swallowing the water. Nothing is gained by this remark: in this case, the anterior impulse only regains the ascendancy; he is persuaded that life may possibly be longer preserved, or that he shall derive a greater good by drinking the poisoned water than by enduring the torment, which, to his mind, threatens instant dissolution; thus the first becomes the strongest and necessarily urges him on to action. Nevertheless, in either case, whether he partakes of the water, or whether he does not, the two actions will be equally necessary; they will be the effect of that motive which finds itself most puissant; which consequently acts in the most coercive manner upon his will.

This example will serve to explain the whole phenomenon of the human will. This will, or rather the brain, finds itself in the same situation as a bowl, which, although it has received an impulse that drives it forward in a straight line, is deranged in its course whenever a force superior to the first obliges it to change its direction. The man who drinks the poisoned water appears a madman; but the actions of fools are as necessary as those of the most prudent individuals. The motives that determine the voluptuary and the debauchee to risk their health, are as powerful, and their actions are as necessary, as those which decide the wise man to manage his. But, it will be insisted, the debauchee may be prevailed on to change his conduct: this does not imply that he is a free agent; but that motives may be found sufficiently powerful to annihilate the effect of those that previously acted upon him; then these new motives determine his will to the new mode of conduct he may adopt as necessarily as the former did to the old mode. . . .

The errors of philosophers on the free agency of man, have arisen from their regarding his will as the *primum mobile,* the original motive of his actions; for want of recurring back, they have not perceived the multiplied, the complicated causes which, independently of him, give motion to the will itself; or which dispose and modify his brain, whilst he himself is purely passive in the motion he receives. Is he the master of desiring or not desiring an object that appears desirable to him? Without doubt it will be answered, no: but he is the master of resisting his desire, if he reflects on the consequences. But, I ask, is he capable of reflecting on these consequences, when his soul is hurried along by a very lively passion, which entirely depends upon his natural organization, and the causes by which he is modified? Is it in his power to add to these consequences all the weight necessary to counterbalance his desire? Is he the master of preventing the qualities which render an object desirable from residing in it? I shall be told: he ought to have learned to resist his passions; to contract a habit of putting a curb on his desires. I agree to it without any difficulty. But in reply, I again ask, is his nature susceptible of this modification? Does his boiling blood, his unruly imagination, the igneous fluid that circulates in his veins, permit him to make, enable him to apply true experience in the moment when it is wanted? And even when his temperament has capacitated him, has his education, the examples set before him, the ideas with which he has been inspired in early life, been suitable to make him contract this habit of repressing his desires? Have not all these things rather contributed to induce him to seek with avidity, to make him actually desire those objects which you say he ought to resist?

The ambitious man cries out: you will have me resist my passion; but have they not unceasingly repeated to me that rank, honors, power, are the most desirable advantages in life? Have I not seen my fellow citizens envy them, the nobles of my country sacrifice every thing to obtain them? In the society in which I live, am I not obliged to feel, that if I am deprived of these advantages, I must expect to languish in contempt; to cringe under the rod of oppression?

The *miser* says: you forbid me to love money, to seek after the means of acquiring it: alas! does not every thing tell me that, in this world, money is the greatest blessing; that it is amply sufficient to render me happy? In the country I inhabit, do I not see all my fellow citizens covetous of riches? but do I not also witness that they are little scrupulous in the means of obtaining wealth? As soon as they are enriched by the means which you censure, are they not cherished, considered and respected? By what authority, then, do you defend me from amassing treasure? What right have you to prevent my using means, which, although you call them sordid and criminal, I see approved by the sovereign? Will you have me renounce my happiness?

The *voluptuary* argues: you pretend that I should resist my desires; but was I the maker of my own temperament, which unceasingly invites me to pleasure? You call my pleasures disgraceful; but in the country in which I live, do I not witness the most dissipated men enjoying the most distinguished rank? Do I not behold that no one is ashamed of adultery but the husband it has outraged? Do not I see men making trophies of their debaucheries, boasting of their libertinism, rewarded with applause?

The *choleric man* vociferates: you advise me to put a curb on my passions, and to resist the desire of avenging myself: but can I conquer my nature?

Can I alter the received opinions of the world? Shall I not be forever disgraced, infallibly dishonored in society, if I do not wash out in the blood of my fellow creatures the injuries I have received?

The *zealous enthusiast* exclaims: you recommend me mildness; you advise me to be tolerant; to be indulgent to the opinions of my fellow men; but is not my temperament violent? Do I not ardently love my God? Do they not assure me, that zeal is pleasing to him; that sanguinary inhuman persecutors have been his friends? As I wish to render myself acceptable in his sight, I therefore adopt the same means.

In short, **the actions of man are never free**; they are always the necessary consequence of his temperament, of the received ideas, and of the notions, either true or false, which he has formed to himself of happiness; of his opinions, strengthened by example, by education, and by daily experience. So many crimes are witnessed on the earth only because every thing conspires to render man vicious and criminal; the religion he has adopted, his government, his education, the examples set before him, irresistibly drive him on to evil: under these circumstances, morality preaches virtue to him in vain. In those societies where vice is esteemed, where crime is crowned, where venality is constantly recompensed, where the most dreadful disorders are punished only in those who are too weak to enjoy the privilege of committing them with impunity, the practice of virtue is considered nothing more than a painful sacrifice of happiness. Such societies chastise, in the lower orders, those excesses which they respect in the higher ranks; and frequently have the injustice to condemn those in the penalty of death, whom public prejudices, maintained by constant example, have rendered criminal.

Karma and Freedom

Sarvepalli Radhakrishnan

The two pervasive features of all nature, connection with the past and creation of the future, are present in the human level. The connection with the past at the human stage is denoted by the word "Karma" in the Hindu systems. The human individual is a self-conscious, efficient portion of universal nature with his own uniqueness. His history stretching back to an indefinite period of time binds him with the physical and vital conditions of the world. Human life is an organic whole where each successive phase grows out of what has gone before. We are what we are on account of our affinity with the past. Human growth is an ordered one and its orderedness is indicated by saying that it is governed by the law of Karma.

Karma literally means action, deed. **All acts produce their effects which are recorded both in the organism and the environment.** Their physical effects may be short-lived but their moral effects (samskara) are worked into the character of the self. **Every single thought, word and deed enters into the living chain of causes which makes us what we are.** Our life is not at the mercy of blind chance or capricious fate. The conception is not peculiar to the Oriental creeds. The Christian Scriptures refer to it. "Be not deceived; God is not mocked: for whatsoever a man soweth, that shall he also reap." Jesus is reported to have said on the Mount, "Judge not that ye be not judged, for with what judgment ye judge, ye shall be judged, and with what measure ye mete, it shall be measured to you again."

Karma is not so much a principle of retribution as one of continuity. Good produces good, evil evil. Love increases our power of love, hatred our power of hatred. It emphasises the great importance of right action. Man is continuously shaping his own self. The law of Karma is not to be confused with either a hedonistic or a juridical theory of rewards and punishments. The reward for virtue is not a life of pleasure nor is the punishment for sin pain. Pleasure and pain may govern the animal nature of man but not his human. Love which is a joy in itself suffers; hatred too often means a perverse kind of satisfaction. Good and evil are not to be confused with material well-being and physical suffering.

Karma and Freedom

All things in the world are at once causes and effects. They embody the energy of the past and exert energy on the future. Karma or connection with the past is not inconsistent with creative freedom. On the other hand it is implied by it. The law that links us with the past also asserts that it can be subjugated by our free action. Though the past may present obstacles, they must all yield to the creative power in man in proportion to its sincerity and insistence. The law of Karma says that each individual will get the return according to the energy he puts forth. The universe will respond to and implement the demands of the self. Nature will reply to the insistent call of spirit. "As is his desire, such is his purpose; as is his purpose, such is the action he performs; what action he performs, that he procures for himself." "Verily I say unto you that whoever shall say to this mountain, 'Be lifted up and cast into the sea,' and shall not doubt in his heart but believe fully that what he says shall be, it shall be done for him." When Jesus said, "Destroy this temple and I will raise it again in three days" he is asserting the truth that the spirit within us is mightier than the world of things. There is nothing we cannot achieve if we want it enough. Subjection to spirit is the law of universal nature. The principle of Karma has thus two aspects, a retrospective and a prospective, continuity with the past and creative freedom of the self.

The urge in nature which seeks not only to maintain itself at a particular level but advance to a higher becomes conscious in man who deliberately seeks after rules of life and principles of progress. "My father worketh hitherto, and I work." Human beings are the first among nature's children who can say "I" and consciously collaborate with the "father" the power that controls and directs nature, in the fashioning of the world. They can substitute rational direction for the slow, dark, blundering growth of the subhuman world. We cannot deny the free action of human beings however much their origin may be veiled in darkness. The self has conative tendencies, impulses to change by its efforts the given conditions, inner and outer, and shape them to its own purpose.

The problem of human freedom is confused somewhat by the distinction between the self and the will. The will is only the self in its active side and freedom of the will really means the freedom of the self. It is determination by the self.

It is argued that self-determination is not really freedom. It makes little difference whether the self is moved from without or from within. A spinning top moved from within by a spring is as mechanical as one whipped into motion from without. The self may well be an animated automaton. A drunkard who takes to his glass habitually does so in obedience to an element in his nature. The habit has become a part of his self. If we analyse the contents of the self, many of them are traceable to the influence of the environment and the inheritance from the past. If the individual's view and character are the product of a long evolution, his actions which are the outcome of these cannot be free. The feeling of freedom may be an illusion of the self which lives in each moment of the present, ignoring the determining past. In answer to these difficulties, it may be said that the self represents a form of relatedness or organisation, closer and more intimate than that which is found in animal, plant or atom. Self-determination means not determination by any fragment of the self's nature but by the whole of it. Unless the individual employs his whole nature, searches the different possibilities and selects one which commends itself to his whole self, the act is not really free.

Sheer necessity is not to be found in any aspect of nature; complete freedom is divine and possible only when the self becomes co-extensive with the whole. Human freedom is a matter of degree. We are most free when our whole self is active and not merely a fragment of it. We generally act according to our conventional or habitual self and sometimes we sink to the level of our subnormal self.

Freedom is not caprice, nor is Karma necessity. Human choice is not unmotived or uncaused. If our acts were irrelevant to our past, then there would be no moral responsibility or scope for improvement. Undetermined beginnings, upstart events are impossible either in the physical or the human world. Free acts cannot negate continuity. They arise within the order of nature. Freedom is not caprice since we carry our past with us. The character, at any given point, is the condensation of our previous history. What we have been enters into the "me" which is now active and choosing. The range of one's natural freedom of action is limited. No man has the universal field of possibilities for himself. The varied possibilities of our nature do not all get a chance and the cosmic has its influence in permitting the development of certain possibilities and closing down others. Again, freedom is dogged by automatism. When we make up our mind to do a thing, our mind is different from what it was before. When a possibility becomes an actuality, it assumes the character of necessity. The past can never be cancelled, though it may be utilised. Mere defiance of the given may mean disaster, though we can make a new life spring up from the past. Only the possible is the sphere of freedom. We have a good deal of present constraint and previous necessity in human life. But necessity is not to be mistaken for destiny which we can neither defy nor delude. Though the self is not free from the bonds of determination, it can subjugate the past to a certain extent and turn it into a new course. Choice is the assertion of freedom over necessity by which it converts necessity to its own use and thus frees itself from it. "The human agent is free." He is not the plaything of fate or driftwood on the tide of uncontrolled events. He can actively mould the future instead of passively suffering the past. The past may become either an opportunity or an obstacle. Everything depends on what we make of it and not what it makes of us. Life is not bound to move in a specific direction. Life is a growth and a growth is undetermined in a measure. Though the future is the sequel of the past, we cannot say what it will be. If there is no indetermination, then human consciousness is an unnecessary luxury.

Our demand for freedom must reckon with a universe that is marked by order and regularity. Life is like a game of bridge. The cards in the game are given to us. We do not select them. They are traced to past Karma but we are free to make any call as we think fit and lead any suit. Only we are limited by the rules of the game. We are more free when we start the game than later on when the game has developed and our choices become restricted. But till the very end there is always a choice. A good player will see possibilities which a bad one does not. The more skilled a player the more alternatives does he perceive. A good hand may be cut to pieces by unskilfull play and the bad play need not be attributed to the frowns of fortune. Even though we may not like the way in which the cards are shuffled, we like the game and we want to play. Sometimes wind and tide may prove too strong for us and even the most noble may come down. The great souls find profound peace in the consciousness that the stately order of the world, now lovely and luminous, now dark and terrible, in which man finds his duty and destiny, cannot be subdued to known aims. It seems to have a purpose of its own of which we are ignorant. Misfortune is not fate but providence.

The law of Karma does not support the doctrine of predestination. There are some who believe that only the predestination of certain souls to destruction is consistent with divine sovereignty. God has a perfect right to deal with his creatures even as a potter does with his clay. St. Paul speaks of "vessels of wrath fitted to destruction." Life eternal is a gracious gift of God. Such a view of divine sovereignty is unethical. God's love is manifested in and through law.

In our relations with human failures, belief in Karma inclines us to take a sympathetic attitude and develop reverence before the mystery of misfortune. The more understanding we are, the less do we pride ourselves on our superiority. Faith in Karma induces in us the mood of true justice or charity which is the essence of spirituality. We realise how infinitely helpless and frail human beings are. When we look at the warped lives of the poor, we see how much the law of Karma is true. If they are lazy and criminal, let us ask what chance they had of choosing to be different. They are more unfortunate than wicked. Again, failures are due not so much to "sin" as to errors which lead us to our doom. In Greek tragedy man is held individually less responsible and circumstances or the decisions of Moira more so. The tale of Oedipus Rex tells us how he could not avoid his fate to kill his father and marry his mother, in spite of his best efforts. The parting of Hector and Andromache in Homer is another illustration. In Shakespeare again, we see the artist leading on his characters to their destined ends by what seems a very natural development of their foibles, criminal folly in Lear or personal ambition in Macbeth. The artist shows us these souls in pain. Hamlet's reason is puzzled, his will confounded. He looks at life and at death and wonders which is worse. Goaded by personal ambition, Macbeth makes a mess of it all. Othello kills his wife and kills himself because a jealous villain shows him a handkerchief. When these noble souls crash battling with adverse forces we feel with them and for them; for it might happen to any of us. We are not free from the weaknesses that broke them, whatever we call them, stupidity, disorder, vacillation or, if you please, insane ambition and self-seeking. To-day the evil stars of the Greek tragedians are replaced by the almighty laws of economics. Thousands of young men the world over are breaking their heads in vain against the iron walls of society like trapped birds in cages. We see in them the essence of all tragedy, something noble breaking down, something sublime falling with a crash. We can only bow our heads in the presence of those broken beneath the burden of their destiny. The capacity of the human soul for suffering and isolation is immense. Take the poor creatures whom the world passes by as the lowly and the lost. If only we had known what they passed through, we would have been glad of their company. It is utterly wrong to think that misfortune comes only to those who deserve it. The world is a whole and we are members one of another, and we must suffer one for another. In Christianity, it needed a divine soul to reveal how much grace there is in suffering. To bear pain, to endure suffering, is the quality of the strong in spirit. It adds to the spiritual resources of humanity.

Absolute Freedom

Jean Paul Sartre

It is strange that philosophers have been able to argue endlessly about determinism and free-will, to cite examples in favor of one or the other thesis without ever attempting first to make explicit the structures contained in the very idea of *action*. The concept of an act contains, in fact, numerous subordinate notions which we shall have to organize and arrange in a hierarchy: to act is to modify the *shape* of the world; it is to arrange means in view of an end; it is to produce an organized instrumental complex such that by a series of concatenations and connections the modification effected on one of the links causes modifications throughout the whole series and finally produces an anticipated result. But this is not what is important for us here. We should observe first that an action is on principle *intentional*. The careless smoker who has through negligence caused the explosion of a powder magazine has not *acted*. On the other hand the worker who is charged with dynamiting a quarry and who obeys the given orders has acted when he has produced the expected explosion; he knew what he was doing or, if you prefer, he intentionally realized a conscious project.

This does not mean, of course, that one must foresee all the consequences of his act. The emperor Constantine when he established himself at Byzantium, did not foresee that he would create a center of Greek culture and language, the appearance of which would ultimately provoke a schism in the Christian Church and which would contribute to weakening the Roman Empire. Yet he performed an act just in so far as he realized his project of creating a new residence for emperors in the Orient. Equating the result with the intention is here sufficient for us to be able to speak of action. But if this is the case, we establish that the action necessarily implies as its condition the recognition of a "desideratum"; that is, of an objective lack or again of a *négatité* the action necessarily implies as its condition the recognition of a [negativity]. The intention of providing a rival for Rome can come to Constantine only through the apprehension of an objective lack: Rome lacks a counterweight; to this still profoundly pagan city ought to be opposed a Christian city which at the moment *is missing*. Creating Constantinople is understood as an act only if first the conception of a new city has preceded the action itself or at least if this conception serves as an organizing theme for all later steps. But this conception cannot be the pure representation of the city as *possible*. It apprehends the city in its essential characteristic, which is to be a *desirable* and not yet realized possible.

This means that from the moment of the first conception of the act, consciousness has been able to withdraw itself from the full world of which it is consciousness and to leave the level of being in order frankly to approach that of non-being. Consciousness in so far as it is considered exclusively in its being, is perpetually referred from being to being and can not find in being any motive for revealing non-being. The imperial system with Rome as its capital functions positively and in a certain real way which can be easily discovered. Will someone say that the taxes are collected badly, that Rome is not secure from invasions, that it does not have the geographical location which is suitable for the capital of a Mediterranean empire which is threatened by barbarians, that its corrupt morals make the spread of the Christian religion difficult? How can anyone fail to see that all these considerations are *negative*; that is, that they aim at what is not, not at what is. To say that sixty percent of the anticipated taxes have been collected can pass, if need be for a positive appreciation of the situation *such at it is*. To say that they are *badly* collected is to consider the situation across a situation which is posited as an absolute end but which precisely *is not*. To say that the corrupt morals at Rome hinder the spread of Christianity is not to consider this diffusion for what it is; that is, for a propagation at a rate which the reports of the clergy can enable us to determine. It is to posit the diffusion in itself as insufficient; that is, as suffering from a secret nothingness. But it appears as such only if it is surpassed toward a limiting-situation posited *a priori* as a value (for example, toward a certain rate of religious conversions, toward a certain mass morality). This limiting-situation can not be conceived in terms of the simple consideration of the real state of things; for the most beautiful girl in the world can offer only what she *has*, and in the same way the most miserable situation can by itself be designated only as it *is* without any reference to an ideal nothingness.

In so far as man is immersed in the historical situation, he does not even succeed in conceiving of the failures and lacks in a political organization or determined economy; this is not, as is stupidly said, because he "is accustomed to it," but because he apprehends it in its plenitude of being and because he can not even imagine that he can exist in it otherwise. For it is necessary here to reverse common opinion and on the basis of what it is not, to acknowledge the harshness of a situation or the sufferings which it imposes, both of which are motives for conceiving of another state of affairs in which things would be better for everybody. It is on the day that we can conceive of a different state of affairs that a new light falls on our troubles and our suffering and that we *decide* that these are unbearable. A worker in 1830 is capable of revolting if his salary is lowered, for he easily conceives of a situation in which his wretched standard of living would be not as low as the one which is about to be imposed on him. But he does not represent his sufferings to himself as unbearable; he adapts himself to them not through resignation but because he lacks the education and reflection necessary for him to conceive of a social state in which these sufferings would not exist. Consequently *he* does not act. Masters of Lyon following a riot, the workers at Croix-Rousse do not know what to do with their victory; they return home bewildered, and the regular army has no trouble in overcoming them. Their misfortunes do not appear to them "habitual" but rather *natural;* they *are,* that is all, and they constitute the worker's condition. They are not detached; they are not seen in the clear light of day, and consequently they are integrated by the worker with his being. He suffers without considering his suffering and without conferring value upon it. To suffer and to *be* are one and the same for him. His suffering is the pure affective tenor of his nonpositional consciousness, but he does not contemplate it. Therefore this suffering can not be in itself a *motive* for his acts. Quite the contrary, it is after he has formed the project of changing the situation that it will appear intolerable to him. This means that he will have had to give himself room, to withdraw in relation to it, and will have to have effected a double nihilation: on the one hand, he must posit an ideal state of affairs as a pure *present* nothingness; on the other hand, he must posit the actual situation as nothingness in relation to this state of affairs. He will have to conceive of a happiness attached to his class as a pure possible—that is, presently as a certain nothingness—and on the other hand, he will return to the present situation in order to illuminate it in the light of this nothingness and in order to nihilate it in turn by declaring: "I *am not* happy."

Two important consequences result. (1) No factual state whatever it may be (the political and economic structure of society, the psychological "state," *etc.*) is capable by itself of motivating any act whatsoever. For an act is a projection of the for-itself toward what is not, and what is can in no way determine by itself what is not. (2) No factual state can determine consciousness to apprehend it as a *négatité* or as a lack. Better yet no factual state can determine consciousness to define it and to circumscribe it since, as we have seen, Spinoza's statement, "Omnis determinatio est negatio" [All determination is a negation], remains profoundly true. Now every action has for its express condition not only the discovery of a state of affairs as "lacking in—," *i.e.*, as a *négatité*—but also, and before all else, the constitution of the state of things under consideration into an isolated system. There is a factual state—satisfying or not—only by means of the nihilating power of the for-itself. But this power of nihilation can not be-limited to realizing a simple *withdrawal* in relation to the world. In fact in so far as consciousness is "invested" by being, in so far as it simply suffers what is, it must be included in being. It is the organized form—worker-finding-his-suffering-natural—which must be surmounted and denied in order for it to be able to form the object of a revealing contemplation. This means evidently that it is by a pure wrenching away from himself and the world that the worker can posit his suffering as unbearable suffering and consequently can *make of it the motive* for his revolutionary action. This implies for consciousness the permanent possibility of effecting a rupture with its own past, of wrenching itself away from its past so as to be able to consider it in the light of a non-being and so as to be able to confer on it the meaning which *it has* in terms of the project of a meaning which it *does not have*. Under no circumstances can the past in any way by itself produce *an act;* that is, the positing of an end which turns back upon itself so as to illuminate it. This is what Hegel caught sight of when he wrote that "the mind is the negative," although he seems not to have remembered this when he came to presenting his own theory of action and of freedom. In fact as soon as one attributes to consciousness this negative power with respect to the world and itself, as soon as the nihilation forms an integral part of the *positing* of an end, we must recognize that the indispensable and fundamental condition of all action is the freedom of the acting being.

Thus at the outset we can see what is lacking in those tedious discussions between determinists and the proponents of free will. The latter are concerned to find cases of decision for which there exists no prior cause, or deliberations concerning two opposed acts which are equally possible and possess causes (and motives) of exactly the same weight. To which the determinists may easily reply that there is no action without a *cause* and that the most insignificant gesture (raising the right hand rather than the left hand, *etc.*) refers to causes and motives which confer its meaning upon it. Indeed the case could not be otherwise since every action must be *intentional;* each action must, in fact, have an end, and the end in turn is referred to a cause. Such indeed is the unity of the three temporal ekstases; the end or temporalization of my future implies a cause (or motive); that is, it points toward my past, and the present is the upsurge of the act. To speak of an act without a cause is to speak of an act which would lack the intentional structure of every act; and the proponents of free will by searching for it on the level of the act which is in the process of being performed can only end up by rendering the act absurd. But the determinists in turn are weighing the scale by stopping their investigation with the mere designation of the cause and motive. The essential question in fact lies beyond the complex organization "cause-intention-act-end"; indeed we ought to ask how a cause (or motive) can be constituted as such.

Now we have just seen that if there is not act without a cause, this is not in the sense that we can say that there is no phenomenon without a cause. In order to be a *cause;* the *cause* must be *experienced* as such. Of course this does not mean that it is to be thematically conceived and made explicit as in the case of deliberation. But at the very least it means that the for-itself must confer on it its value as cause or motive. And, as we have seen, this constitution of the cause as such can not refer to another real and positive existence; that is, to a prior cause. For otherwise the very nature of the act as engaged intentionally in non-being would disappear. The motive is understood only by the end; that is, by the non-existent. It is therefore in itself a *négatité*. If I accept a niggardly salary it is doubtless because of fear; and fear is a motive. But it is *fear of dying from starvation;* that is, this fear has meaning only outside itself in an end ideally posited, which is the preservation of a life which I apprehend as "in danger." And this fear is understood in turn only in relation to the *value which* I implicitly give to this life; that is, it is referred to that hierarchal system of ideal objects which are values. Thus the motive makes itself understood as what it is by means of the ensemble of beings which "are not," by ideal existences, and by the future. Just as the future turns back upon the present and the past in order to elucidate them, so it is the ensemble of my projects which turns back in order to confer upon the *motive* its structure as a motive. It is only because I escape the in-itself by nihilating myself toward my possibilities that this in-itself can take on value as cause or motive. Causes and motives have meaning only inside a projected ensemble which is precisely an ensemble of non-existents. And this ensemble is ultimately myself as transcendence; it is Me in so far as I have to be myself outside of myself.

If we recall the principle which we established earlier—namely that it is the apprehension of a revolution as possible which gives to the workman's suffering its value as a motive—we must thereby conclude that it is by fleeing a situation toward our possibility of changing it that we organize this situation into complexes of causes and motives. The nihilation by which we achieve a withdrawal in relation to the situation is the same as the ekstasis by which we project ourselves toward a modification of this situation. The result is that it is in fact impossible to find an act without a motive but that this does not mean that we must conclude that the motive causes the act; the motive is an integral part of the act. For as the resolute project toward a change is not distinct from the act, the motive, the act, and the end are all constituted in a single upsurge. Each of these three structures claims the two others as its meaning. But the organized totality of the three is no longer explained by any particular structure, and its upsurge as the pure temporalizing nihilation of the in-itself is one with freedom. It is the act which decides its ends and its motives, and the act is the expression of freedom. . . .

In our attempt to reach to the heart of freedom we may be helped by the few observations which we have made on the subject in the course of this work and which we must summarize here. . . . We established the fact that if negation comes into the world through human-reality, the latter must be a being who can realize a nihilating rupture with the world and with himself; and we established that the permanent possibility of this rupture is the same as freedom. But on the other hand, we stated that this permanent possibility of nihilating what I am in the form of "having-been" implies for man a particular type of existence. We were able then to determine by means of analyses like that of bad faith that human reality is its own nothingness. For the for-itself, to be is to nihilate the in-itself which it is. Under these conditions freedom can be nothing other than this nihilation. It is through this that the for-itself escapes its being as its essence; it is through this that the for-itself is always something other than what can be said of it. For in the final analysis the for-itself is the one which escapes this very denomination, the one which is already beyond the name which is given to it, beyond the property which is recognized in it. To say that the for-itself has to be what it is, to say that it is what it is not while not being what it is, to say that in it existence precedes and conditions essence or inversely according to Hegel, that for it "Wesen ist was gewesen ist" [Essence is what was]—all this is to say one and the same thing: to be aware that man is free. Indeed by the sole fact that I am conscious of the causes which inspire my action, these causes are already transcendent objects for my consciousness; they are outside. In vain shall I seek to catch hold of them; I escape them by my very existence: I am condemned to exist forever beyond my essence, beyond the causes and motives of my act. I am condemned to be free. This means that no limits to my freedom can be found except freedom itself or, if you prefer, that we are not free to cease being free. To the extent that the for-itself wishes to hide its own nothingness from itself and to incorporate the in-itself as its true mode of being, it is trying also to hide its freedom from itself.

The ultimate meaning of determinism is to establish within us an unbroken continuity of existence in itself. The motive conceived as a psychic fact—*i.e.*, as a full and given reality—is, in the deterministic view, articulated without any break with the decision and the act, both of which are equally conceived as psychic givens. The in-itself has got hold of all these "data"; the motive provokes the act as the physical cause its effect; everything is real, everything is full. Thus the refusal of freedom can be conceived only as an attempt to apprehend oneself as being-in-itself; it amounts to the same thing. Human reality may be defined as a being such that in its being its freedom is at stake because human reality perpetually tries to refuse to recognize its freedom. Psychologically in each one of us this amounts to trying to take the causes and motives as *things*. We try to confer permanence upon them. We attempt to hide from ourselves that their nature and their weight depend each moment on the meaning which I give to them; we take them for constants. This amounts to considering the meaning which I gave to them just now or yesterday—which is irremediable because it is *past*—and extrapolating from it a character fixed still in the present. I attempt to persuade myself that the cause *is* as it was. Thus it would pass whole and untouched from my past consciousness to my present consciousness. It would inhabit my consciousness. This amounts to trying to give an essence to the for-itself. In the same way people will posit ends as transcendences, which is not an error. But instead of seeing that the transcendences there posited are maintained in their being by my own transcendence, people will assume that I encounter them upon my surging up in the world; they come from God, from nature, from "my" nature, from society. These ends ready made and pre-human will therefore define the meaning of my act even before I conceive it, just as causes as pure psychic givens will produce it without my even being aware of them.

Cause, act, and end constitute a *continuum*, a *plenum*. These abortive attempts to stifle freedom under the weight of being (they collapse with the sudden upsurge of anguish before freedom) show sufficiently that freedom in its foundation coincides with the nothingness which is at the heart of man. Human-reality is free because it *is not enough*. It is free because it is perpetually wrenched away from itself and because it has been separated by a nothingness from what it is and from what it will be. It is free, finally, because its present being is itself a nothingness in the form of the "reflection-reflecting." Man is free because he is not himself but presence to himself. The being which is what it is can not be free. Freedom is precisely the nothingness which *is made-to-be* at the heart of man and which forces human-reality *to make itself* instead of to be. As we have seen, for human reality, **to be is to *choose oneself*;** nothing comes to it either from the outside or from within which it can *receive or accept.* Without any help whatsoever, it is entirely abandoned to the intolerable necessity of making itself be—down to the slightest detail. Thus freedom is not *a* being; it is *the being* of man—i.e., his nothingness of being. If we start by conceiving of man as a plenum, it is absurd to try to find in him afterwards moments or psychic regions in which he would be free. As well look for emptiness in a container which one has filled beforehand up to the brim! Man can not be sometimes slave and sometimes free; he is wholly and forever free or he is not free at all.

These observations can lead us, if we know how to use them, to new discoveries. They will enable us first to bring to light the relations between freedom and what we call the "will." There is a fairly common tendency to seek to identify free acts with voluntary acts and to restrict the deterministic explanation to the world of the passions. In short the point of view of Descartes. The Cartesian will is free, but there are "passions of the soul." Again Descartes will attempt a physiological interpretation of these passions. Later there will be an attempt to instate a purely psychological determinism. Intellectualistic analyses such as Proust, for example, attempts with respect to jealousy or snobbery can serve as illustration for this concept of the passional "mechanism." In this case it would be necessary to conceive of man as simultaneously free and determined, and the essential problem would be that of the relations between this unconditioned freedom and the determined processes of the psychic life: how will it master the passions, how will it utilize them for its own benefit? A wisdom which comes from ancient times—the wisdom of the Stoics—will teach us to come to terms with these passions so as to master them;

in short it will counsel us how to conduct ourselves with regard to affectivity as man does with respect to nature in general when he obeys it in order better to control it. Human reality therefore appears as a free power besieged by an ensemble of determined processes. One will distinguish wholly free acts, determined processes over which the free will has power, and processes which on principle escape the human-will.

It is clear that we shall not be able to accept such a conception. But let us try better to understand the reasons for our refusal. There is one objection which is obvious and which we shall not waste time in developing; this is that such a trenchant duality is inconceivable at the heart of the psychic unity. How in fact could we conceive of a being which could be *one* and which nevertheless on the one hand would be constituted as a series of facts determined by one another—hence existents in exteriority—and which on the other hand would be constituted as a spontaneity determining itself to be and revealing only itself? *A priori* this spontaneity would be capable of no action on a determinism already *constituted*. On what could it act? On the object itself (the present psychic fact)? But how could it modify an in-itself which by definition is and can be only what it is? On the actual law of the process? This is self-contradictory. On the antecedents of the process? But it amounts to the same thing whether we act on the present psychic fact in order to modify it in itself or act upon it in order to modify its consequences. And in each case we encounter the same impossibility which we pointed out earlier. Moreover, what instrument would this spontaneity have at its disposal? If the hand can clasp, it is because it can be clasped. Spontaneity, since by definition it is *beyond reach* can not in turn *reach;* it can produce only itself. And if it could dispose of a special instrument, it would then be necessary to conceive of this as of an intermediary nature between free will and determined passions—which is not admissible. For different reasons the passions could get no hold upon the will. Indeed it is impossible for a determined process to act upon a spontaneity, exactly as it is impossible for objects to act upon consciousness. Thus any synthesis of two types of existents is impossible; they are not homogeneous; they will remain each one in its incommunicable solitude. The only bond which a nihilating spontaneity could maintain with mechanical process would be the fact that it *produces itself by an internal negation directed toward these existents.* But then the spontaneity will exist precisely only in so far as it denies concerning itself that it is these passions. Henceforth the ensemble of the determined pathos will of necessity be apprehended by spontaneity as a pure transcendent; that is, as what is necessarily *outside*, as what *is* not it. This internal negation would therefore have for its effect only the dissolution of the pathos in the world, and the pathos would exist as some sort of object in the midst of the world for a free spontaneity which would be simultaneously will and consciousness. This discussion shows that two solutions and only two are possible: either man is wholly determined (which is inadmissible, especially because a determined consciousness—*i.e.*, a consciousness externally motivated—becomes itself pure exteriority and ceases to be consciousness) or else man is wholly free....

But this is not all: the will, far from being the unique or at least the privileged manifestation of freedom, actually—like every event of the for-itself—must presuppose the foundation of an original freedom in order to be able to constitute itself as will. The will in fact is posited as a reflective decision in relation to certain ends. But it does not create these ends. It is rather a mode of being in relation to them: it decrees that the pursuit of these ends will be reflective and deliberative. Passion can posit the same ends. For example, if I am threatened, I can run away at top speed because of my fear of dying. This passional fact nevertheless posits implicitly as a supreme end the value of life. Another person in the same situation will, on the contrary, understand that he must remain at his post even if resistance at first appears more dangerous than flight; he "will stand firm." But his goal, although better understood and explictly posited, remains the same as in the case of the emotional reaction. It is simply that the methods of attaining it are more clearly conceived; certain of them are rejected as dubious or inefficacious, others are more solidly organized. The difference here depends on the choice of means and on the degree of reflection and of making explicit, not on the end. Yet the one who flees is said to be "passionate," and we reserve the term "voluntary" for the man who resists. Therefore the question is of a difference of subjective attitude in relation to a transcendent end. But if we wish to avoid the error which we denounced earlier and not consider these transcendent ends as pre-human and as an *a priori* limit to our transcendence then we are indeed compelled to recognize that they are the temporalizing projection of our freedom. Human reality can not receive its ends, as we have seen, either from outside or from a so-called inner "nature." It chooses them and by this very choice confers upon them a transcendent existence as the external limit of its projects. From this point of view—and if it is understood that **the existence of the *Dasein* [person] precedes and**

commands its essence—human reality in and through its very upsurge decides to define its own being by its ends. It is therefore the positing of my ultimate ends which characterizes my being and which is identical with the sudden thrust of the freedom which is mine. And this thrust is an *existence*; it has nothing to do with an essence or with a property of a being which would be engendered conjointly with an idea.

Thus since **freedom is identical with my existence**, it is the foundation of ends which I shall attempt to attain either by the will or by passionate efforts. Therefore it can not be limited to voluntary acts. Volitions, on the contrary, like passions are certain subjective attitudes by which we attempt to attain the ends posited by original freedom. By original freedom, of course, we should not understand a freedom which would be *prior* to the voluntary or passionate act but rather a foundation which is strictly contemporary with the will or the passion and which these *manifest*, each in its own way. Neither should we oppose freedom to the will or to passion as the "profound self" of Bergson is opposed to the superficial self; the for-itself is wholly selfness and can not have a "profound self," unless by this we mean certain transcendent structures of the psyche. Freedom is nothing but the *existence* of our will or of our passions in so far as this existence is the nihilation of facticity; that is, the existence of being which is its being in the mode of having to be it. We shall return to this point. In any case let us remember that the will is determined within the compass of motives and ends already posited by the for-itself in a transcendent projection of itself toward its possibles. If this were not so, how could we understand deliberation, which is an evaluation of means in relation to already existing ends?

If these ends are already posited, then what remains to be decided at each moment is the way in which I shall conduct myself with respect to them; in other words, the attitude which I shall assume. Shall I act by volition or by passion? Who can decide except me? In fact, if we admit that circumstances decide for me (for example, I can act by volition when faced with a minor danger but if the peril increases, I shall fall into passion), we thereby suppress all freedom. It would indeed be absurd to declare that the will is autonomous when it appears but that external circumstances strictly determine the moment of its appearance. But, on the other hand, how can it be maintained that a will which does not yet exist can suddenly decide to shatter the chain of the passions and suddenly stand forth on the fragments of these chains? Such a conception would lead us to consider the will as a *power* which sometimes would manifest itself to consciousness and at other times would remain hidden, but which would in any case possess the permanence and the existence "in-itself" of a property. This is precisely what is inadmissible. It is, however, certain that common opinion conceives of the moral life as a struggle between a will-thing and passion-substances. There is here a sort of psychological Manichaeism which is absolutely insupportable.

Actually it is not enough to will; it is necessary to will to will. Take, for example, a given situation: I can react to it emotionally. We have shown elsewhere that emotion is not a physiological tempest; it is a reply adapted to the situation; it is a type of conduct, the meaning and form of which are the object of an intention of consciousness which aims at attaining a particular end by particular means. In fear, fainting and cataplexie aim at suppressing the danger by suppressing the consciousness of the danger. There is an *intention* of losing consciousness in order to do away with the formidable world in which consciousness is engaged and which comes into being through consciousness. Therefore we have to do with magical behavior provoking the symbolic satisfactions of our desires and revealing by the same stroke a magical stratum of the world. In contrast to this conduct voluntary and rational conduct will consider the situation scientifically, will reject the magical, and will apply itself to realizing determined series and instrumental complexes which will enable us to resolve the problems. It will organize a system of means by taking its stand on instrumental determinism. Suddenly it will reveal a technical world; that is, a world in which each instrumental-complex refers to another larger complex and so on. But what will make me decide to choose the magical aspect or the technical aspect of the world? It can not be the world itself, for this in order to be manifested waits to be discovered. Therefore it is necessary that the for-itself in its project must choose being the one by whom the world is revealed as magical or rational; that is, the for-itself must as a free project of itself give to itself magical or rational existence. It is responsible for either one, for the for-itself can *be* only if it has chosen itself. Therefore the for-itself appears as the free foundation of its emotions as of its volitions. My fear *is* free and manifests my freedom; I have put all my freedom into my fear, and I have chosen myself as fearful in this or that circumstance. Under other circumstances I shall exist as deliberate and courageous, and I shall have put all my freedom into my courage. In relation to freedom there is no privileged psychic phenomenon. All my "modes of being" manifest freedom equally since they are all ways of being my own nothingness. . . .

Yet if the motive is transcendent, if it is only the irremediable being which we have to be in the mode of the "was," if like all our past it is separated from us by a breadth of nothingness, then it can act only if it is *recovered;* in itself it is without force. It is therefore by the very thrust of the engaged consciousness that a value and a weight will be conferred on motives and on prior causes. What they have been does not depend on consciousness, but consciousness has the duty of maintaining them in their existence in the past. I have willed this or that: here is what remains irremediable and which even constitutes my essence, since my essence is what I have been. But the meaning held for me by this desire, this fear, these objective considerations of the world when presently I project myself toward my futures—this must be decided by me alone. I determine them precisely and only by the very act by which I project myself toward my ends. The recovery of former motives—or the rejection or new appreciation of them—is not distinct from the project by which I assign new ends to myself and by which in the light of these ends I apprehend myself as discovering a supporting cause in the world. Past motives, past causes, present motives and causes, future ends, all are organized in an indissoluble unity by the very upsurge of a freedom which is beyond causes, motives, and ends.

The result is that a voluntary deliberation is always a deception. How can I evaluate causes and motives on which I myself confer their value before all deliberation and by the very choice which I make of myself? The illusion here stems from the fact that we endeavor to take causes and motives for entirely transcendent things which I balance in my hands like weights and which possess a weight as a permanent property. Yet on the other hand we try to view them as contents of consciousness, and this is self-contradictory. Actually causes and motives have only the weight which my project—*i.e.,* the free production of the end and of the known act to be realized—confers upon them. When I deliberate, the chips are down. And if I am brought to the point of deliberating, this is simply because it is a part of my original project to realize motives by means of *deliberation* rather than by some other form of discovery (by passion, for example, or simply by action, which reveals to me the organized ensemble of causes and of ends as my language informs me of my thought).

There is therefore a choice of deliberation as a procedure which will make known to me what I project and consequently what I am. And *the choice of deliberation is organized with the ensemble motives-causes and end by free spontaneity.* When the will intervenes, the decision is taken, and it has no other value than that of making the announcement...

The essential consequence of our earlier remarks is that **man being condemned to be free carries the weight of the whole world on his shoulders**; he is responsible for the world and for himself as a way of being. We are taking the word "responsibility" in its ordinary sense as "consciousness (of) being the incontestable author of an event or of an object." In this sense the responsibility of the for-itself is overwhelming since he is the one by whom it happens that there is a world; since he is also the one who makes himself be, then whatever may be the situation in which he finds himself, the for-itself must wholly assume this situation with its peculiar coefficient of adversity, even though it be insupportable. He must assume the situation with the proud consciousness of being the author of it, for the very worst disadvantages or the worst threats which can endanger my person have meaning only in and through my project; and it is on the ground of the engagement which I am that they appear. It is therefore senseless to think of complaining since nothing foreign has decided what we feel, what we live, or what we are.

Furthermore this absolute responsibility is not resignation; it is simply the logical requirement of the consequences of our freedom. What happens to me happens through me, and I can neither affect myself with it nor revolt against it nor resign myself to it. Moreover everything which happens to me is *mine*. By this we must understand first of all that I am always equal to what happens to me *qua* man, for what happens to a man through other men and through himself can be only human. The most terrible situations of war, the worst tortures do not create a non-human state of things; there is no non-human situation. It is only through fear, flight, and recourse to magical types of conduct that I shall decide on the non-human, but this decision is human, and I shall carry the entire responsibility for it. But in addition the situation is *mine* because it is the image of my free choice of myself, and everything which it presents to me is *mine* in that this represents me and symbolizes me. Is it not I who decide the coefficient of adversity in things and even their unpredictability by deciding myself?

Thus there are no *accidents* in a life; a community event which suddenly bursts forth and involves me in it does not come from the outside. If I am mobilized in a war, this war is *my* war; it is in my image and I deserve it. I deserve it first because I could always get out of it by suicide or by desertion; these ultimate possibles are those which must always be present for us when there is a question of envisaging a situation. For lack of getting out of it, I have *chosen* it. This can be due to inertia, to cowardice in the face of public opinion, or because I prefer certain other values to the value of the refusal to join in the war (the good opinion of my relatives, the honor of my family, etc.). Anyway you look at it, it is a matter of a choice. This choice will be repeated later on again and again without a break until the end of the war. Therefore we must agree with the statement by J. Romains, "In war there are no innocent victims." If therefore I have preferred war to death or to dishonor, everything takes place as if I bore the entire responsibility for this war. Of course others have declared it, and one might be tempted perhaps to consider me as a simple accomplice. But this notion of complicity has only a juridical sense, and it does not hold here. For it depended on me that for me and by me this war should not exist, and I have decided that it does exist. There was no compulsion here, for the compulsion could have got no hold on a freedom. I did not have any excuse; for as we have said repeatedly in this book, the peculiar character of human-reality is that it is without excuse. Therefore it remains for me only to lay claim to this war.

But in addition the war is *mine* because by the sole fact that it arises in a situation which I cause to be and that I can discover it there only by engaging myself for or against it, I can no longer distinguish at present the choice which I make of myself from the choice which I make of the war. To live this war is to choose myself through it and to choose it through my choice of myself. There can be no question of considering it as "four years of vacation" or as a "reprieve," as a "recess," the essential part of my responsibilities being elsewhere in my married, family, or professional life. In this war which I have chosen I choose myself from day to day, and I make it mine by making myself. If it is going to be four empty years, then it is I who bear the responsibility for this.

Finally, as we pointed out earlier, each person is an absolute choice of self from the standpoint of a world of knowledges and of techniques which this choice both assumes and illumines; each person is an absolute upsurge at an absolute date and is perfectly unthinkable at another date. It is therefore a waste of time to ask what I should have been if this war had not broken out, for I have chosen myself as one of the possible meanings of the epoch which imperceptibly led to war. I am not distinct from this same epoch; I could not be transported to another epoch without contradiction. Thus *I am* this war which restricts and limits and makes comprehensible the period which preceded it. In this sense we may define more precisely the responsibility of the for-itself if to the earlier quoted statement, "There are no innocent victims," we add the words, "We have the war we deserve." Thus, totally free, undistinguishable from the period for which I have chosen to be the meaning, as profoundly responsible for the war as if I had myself declared it, unable to live without integrating it in *my* situation, engaging myself in it wholly and stamping it with my seal, I must be without remorse or regrets as **I am without excuse;** for from the instant of my upsurge into being, **I carry the weight of the world by myself alone without anything or any person being able to lighten it.**

Yet this responsibility is of a very particular type. Someone will say, "I did not ask to be born." This is a naive way of throwing greater emphasis on our facticity. I am responsible for everything, in fact, except for my very responsibility, for I am not the foundation of my being. Therefore everything takes place as if I were compelled to be responsible. I am *abandoned* in the world, not in the sense that I might remain abandoned and passive in a hostile universe like a board floating on the water, but rather in the sense that I find myself alone and without help, engaged in a world for which I bear the whole responsibility without being able, whatever I do, to tear myself away from this responsibility for an instant. For I am responsible for my very desire of fleeing responsibilities. To make myself passive in the world, to refuse to act upon things and upon others is still to choose myself, and suicide is one mode among others of being-in-the-world. Yet I find an absolute responsibility for the fact that my facticity (here the fact of my birth) is directly inapprehensible and even inconceivable, for this fact of my birth never appears as a brute fact but always across a projective reconstruction of my for-itself. I am ashamed of being born or I am astonished at it or I rejoice over it, or in attempting to get rid of my life I affirm that I live and I assume this life as bad. Thus in a certain sense I *choose* being born. This choice itself is integrally affected with facticity since I am not able not to choose, but this facticity in turn will appear only in so far as I surpass it toward my ends. Thus facticity is everywhere but inapprehensible; I never encounter anything except my responsibility. That is why I can not ask, "*Why* was I born?" or curse the day of my birth or declare that I did not ask to be born, for these various attitudes toward my birth—*i.e.,* toward the *fact* that I realize a presence in the world—are absolutely nothing else but ways of assuming this birth in full responsibility and of making it *mine.* Here again I encounter only myself and my projects so that finally my abandonment—*i.e.,* my facticity—consists simply in the fact that **I am condemned to be wholly responsible for myself.** I am the being which is in such a way that in its being its being is in question. And this "is" of my being *is* as present and inapprehensible.

Under these conditions since every event in the world can be revealed to me only as an *opportunity* (an opportunity made use of, lacked, neglected, *etc.*), or better yet since everything which happens to us can be considered as a *chance* (*i.e.,* can appear to us only as a way of realizing this being which is in question in our being) and since others as transcendences-transcended are themselves only *opportunities* and *chances,* the responsibility of the for-itself extends to the entire world as a peopled-world. It is precisely thus that the for-itself apprehends itself in anguish; that is, as a being which is neither the foundation of its own being nor of the Other's being nor of the in-itselfs which form the world, but a being which is compelled to decide the meaning of being—within it and everywhere outside of it. The one who realizes in anguish his condition as *being* thrown into a responsibility which extends to his very abandonment has no longer either remorse or regret or excuse; he is no longer anything but a freedom which perfectly reveals itself and whose being resides in this very revelation. But as we pointed out at the beginning of this work, most of the time we flee anguish in bad faith.

The Legend of the Grand Inquisitor

Feodor Dostoyevsky

"My story is laid in Spain, in Seville, in the most terrible time of the Inquisition, when fires were lighted every day to the glory of God, and 'in the splendid *auto da fé* the wicked heretics were burnt.' Oh, of course, this was not the coming in which He will appear according to His promise at the end of time in all His heavenly glory, and which will be sudden 'as lightning flashing from east to west.' No, He visited His children only for a moment, and there where the flames were crackling round the heretics. In His infinite mercy He came once more among men in that human shape in which He walked among men for three years fifteen centuries ago. He came down to the 'hot pavement' of the southern town in which on the day before almost a hundred heretics had, *ad majorem gloriam Dei*, been burnt by the cardinal, the Grand Inquisitor, in a magnificent *auto da fé*, in the presence of the king, the court, the knights, the cardinals, the most charming ladies of the court, and the whole population of Seville.

"He came softly, unobserved, and yet, strange to say, everyone recognized Him. That might be one of the best passages in the poem. I mean, why they recognized Him. The people are irresistibly drawn to Him, they surround Him, they flock about Him, follow him. He moves silently in their midst with a gentle smile of infinite compassion. The sun of love burns in His heart, light and power shine from His eyes, and their radiance, shed on the people, stirs their hearts with responsive love. He holds out His hands to them, blesses them, and a healing virtue comes from contact with Him, even with His garments. An old man in the crowd, blind from childhood, cries out, 'O Lord, heal me and I shall see thee!' and, as it were, scales fall from his eyes and the blind man sees Him. The crowd weeps and kisses the earth under His feet. Children throw flowers before Him, sing, and cry hosannah. 'It is He—it is He!' all repeat. 'It must be He, it can be no one but Him!' He stops at the steps of the Seville cathedral at the moment when the weeping mourners are bringing in a little open white coffin. In it lies a child of seven, the only daughter of a prominent citizen. The dead child lies hidden in flowers. 'He will raise your child,' the crowd shouts to the weeping mother. The priest, coming to meet the coffin, looks perplexed, and frowns, but the mother of the dead child throws herself at His feet with a wail. 'If it is Thou, raise my child!'

she cries, holding out her hands to Him. The procession halts, the coffin is laid on the steps at His feet. He looks with compassion, and His lips once more softly pronounce, 'Maiden, arise!' and the maiden arises. The little girl sits up in the coffin and looks around, smiling with wide-open wondering eyes, holding a bunch of white roses they had put in her hand.

"There are cries, sobs, confusion among the people, and at that moment the cardinal himself, the Grand Inquisitor, passes by the cathedral. He is an old man, almost ninety, tall and erect, with a withered face and sunken eyes, in which there is still a gleam of light. He is not dressed in his gorgeous cardinal's robes, as he was the day before, when he was burning the enemies of the Roman Church—at that moment he was wearing his coarse, old, monk's cassock. At a distance behind him come his gloomy assistants and slaves and the 'holy guard.' He stops at the sight of the crowd and watches it from a distance. He sees everything; he sees them set the coffin down at His feet, sees the child rise up, and his face darkens. He knits his thick grey brows and his eyes gleam with a sinister fire. He holds out his finger and bids the guards take Him. And such is his power, so completely are the people cowed into submission and trembling obedience to him, that the crowd immediately makes way for the guards, and in the midst of deathlike silence they lay hands on Him and lead Him away. The crowd instantly bows down to the earth, like one man, before the old inquisitor. He blesses the people in silence and passes on. The guards lead their prisoner to the close, gloomy vaulted prison in the ancient palace of the Holy Inquisition and shut Him in it. The day passes and is followed by the dark, burning 'breathless' night of Seville. The air is 'fragrant with laurel and lemon.' In the pitch darkness the iron door of the prison is suddenly opened and the Grand Inquisitor himself comes in with a light in his hand. He is alone; the door is closed at once behind him. He stands in the doorway and for a minute or two gazes into His face. At last he goes up slowly, sets the light on the table and speaks.

"'Is it Thou? Thou?' but receiving no answer, he adds at once, 'Don't answer, be silent. What canst Thou say, indeed? I know too well what Thou wouldst say. And Thou hast no right to add anything to what Thou hadst said of old. Why, then, art Thou come to hinder us? For Thou hast come to hinder us, and Thou knowest that. But dost Thou know what will be tomorrow? I know not who Thou art and care not to know whether it is Thou or only a semblance of Him, but tomorrow I shall condemn Thee and burn Thee at the stake as the worst of heretics. And the very people who have today kissed Thy feet, tomorrow at the faintest sign from me will rush to heap up the embers of Thy fire. Knowest Thou that? Yes, maybe Thou knowest it,' he added with thoughtful penetration, never for a moment taking his eyes off the Prisoner."

"I don't quite understand, Ivan. What does it mean?" Alyosha, who had been listening in silence, said with a smile. "Is it simply a wild fantasy, or a mistake on the part of the old man—some impossible *quid pro quo*?"

"Take it as the last," said Ivan, laughing, "if you are so corrupted by modern realism and can't stand anything fantastic. If you like it to be a case of mistaken identity, let it be so. It is true," he went on, laughing, "the old man was ninety, and he might well be crazy over his set idea. He might have been struck by the appearance of the Prisoner. It might, in fact, be simply his ravings, the delusion of an old man of ninety, over-excited by the *auto da fé* of a hundred heretics the day before. But does it matter to us after all whether it was a mistake of identity or a wild fantasy? All that matters is that the old man should speak out, should speak openly of what he had thought in silence for ninety years."

"And the Prisoner too is silent? Does He look at him and not say a word?"

"That's inevitable in any case," Ivan laughed again. "The old man has told Him He hasn't the right to add anything to what He has said of old. One may say it is the most fundamental feature of Roman Catholicism, in my opinion at least. 'All has been given by Thee to the Pope,' they say, 'and all, therefore, is still in the Pope's hands, and there is no need for Thee to come now at all. Thou must not meddle for the time, at least.' That's how they speak and write too—the Jesuits, at any rate. I have read it myself in the works of their theologians. 'Hast Thou the right to reveal to us one of the mysteries of that world from which Thou has come?' my old man asks Him, and answers the question for Him. 'No, Thou hast not; that Thou mayest not add to what has been said of old, and mayest not take from men the freedom which Thou didst exalt when Thou wast on earth. Whatsoever Thou revealest anew will encroach on men's freedom of faith; for it will be manifest as a miracle, and the freedom of their faith was clearer to Thee than anything in those days fifteen hundred years ago. Didst Thou not often say then, "I will make you free"? But now Thou hast seen these "free" men,' the old man adds suddenly with a pensive smile. 'Yes, we've paid dearly for it,' he goes on, looking sternly at Him, 'but now it is ended and over for good. Dost Thou not believe that it's over for good? Thou lookest meekly at me and deignest not even to be wroth with me. But let me tell Thee that now, today, people are more persuaded than ever that they have perfect freedom, yet they have brought their freedom to us and laid it humbly at our feet. But that has been our doing. Was this what Thou didst? Was this Thy freedom?'"

"I don't understand again," Alyosha broke in. "Is he ironical, is he jesting?"

"Not a bit of it! He claims it as a merit for himself and his Church that at last **they have vanquished freedom and have done so to make men happy**. 'For now' (he is speaking of the Inquisition, of course) 'for the first time it has become possible to think of the happiness of men. Man was created a rebel; and how can rebels be happy? Thou was warned,' he says to Him. 'Thou hast had no lack of admonitions and warnings, but Thou didst not listen to those warnings; Thou didst reject the only way by which men might be made happy. But, fortunately, departing Thou didst hand on the work to us. Thou hast promised, Thou hast established by Thy word, Thou hast given to us the right to bind and to unbind, and now, of course, Thou canst not think of taking it away. Why, then, hast Thou come to hinder us?"

"And what's the meaning of 'no lack of admonitions and warnings'?" asked Alyosha.

"Why, that's the chief part of what the old man must say."

"'The wise and dread spirit, the spirit of self-destruction and non-existence,' the old man goes on, 'the great spirit talked with Thee in the wilderness, and we are told in the books that he "tempted" Thee. Is that so? And could anything truer be said than what he revealed to Thee in three questions and what Thou didst reject, and what in the books is called "the temptation"? And yet if there has ever been on earth a real stupendous miracle, it took place on that day, on the day of the three temptations. The statement of those three questions was itself the miracle. If it were possible to imagine simply for the sake of argument that those three questions of the dread spirit had perished utterly from the books, and that we had to restore them and to invent them anew, and to do so had gathered together all the wise men of the earth—rulers, chief priests, learned men, philosophers, poets—and had set them the task to invent three questions, such as would not only fit the occasion, but express in three words, three human phrases, the whole future history of the world and of humanity—dost Thou believe that all the wisdom of the earth united could have invented anything in depth and force equal to the three questions which were actually put to Thee then by the wise and mighty spirit in the wilderness? From those questions alone, from the miracle of their statement, we can see that we have here to do not with the fleeting human intelligence, but with the absolute and eternal. For in those three questions the whole subsequent history of mankind is, as it were, brought together into one whole, and foretold, and in them are united all the unsolved historical contradictions of human nature. At the time it could not be so clear, since the future was unknown; but now that fifteen hundred years have passed, we see that everything in those three questions was so justly divined and foretold, and has been so truly fulfilled, that nothing can be added to them or taken from them.

"'Judge Thyself who was right—Thou or he who questioned Thee then? Remember the first question; its meaning, in other words, was this: "Thou wouldst go into the world, and art going with empty hands, with some promise of freedom which men in their simplicity and their natural unruliness cannot even understand, which they fear and dread—for nothing has ever been more insupportable for a man and a human society than freedom. But seest Thou these stones in this parched and barren wilderness? Turn them into bread, and mankind will run after Thee like a flock of sheep, grateful and obedient, though for ever trembling, lest Thou withdraw Thy hand and deny them Thy bread." But Thou wouldst not deprive man of freedom and didst reject the offer, thinking, what is that freedom worth, if obedience is bought with bread? Thou didst reply that man lives not by bread alone. But does Thou know that for the sake of that earthly bread the spirit of the earth will rise up against Thee and will strive with Thee and overcome Thee, and all will follow him, crying, "Who can compare with this beast? He has given us fire from heaven!" Dost Thou know that the ages will pass, and humanity will proclaim by the lips of their sages that there is no crime, and therefore no sin; there is only hunger? "Feed men, and then ask of them virtue!" that's what they'll write on the banner, which they will raise against Thee, and with which they will destroy Thy temple. Where Thy temple stood will rise a new building; the terrible tower of Babel will be built again, and though, like the one of old, it will not be finished, yet Thou mightest have prevented that new tower and have cut short the sufferings of men for a thousand years; for they will come back to us after a thousand years of agony with their tower. They will seek us again, hidden underground in the catacombs, for we shall be again persecuted and tortured. They will find us and cry to us, "Feed us, for those who have promised us fire from heaven haven't given it!" And then we shall finish building their tower, for he finishes the building who feeds them. And we alone shall feed them in Thy name, declaring falsely that it is in Thy name. Oh, never, never can they feed themselves without us! No science will give them bread so long as they remain free. In the end they will lay their freedom at our feet, and say to us, "Make us your slaves, but feed us." They will understand themselves, at last, that freedom and bread enough for all are inconceivable together, for never, never will they be able to share between them! They will be convinced, too, that they can never be free, for they are weak, vicious, worthless and rebellious. Thou didst promise them the bread of Heaven, but, I repeat again, can it compare with earthly bread in the eyes of the weak, ever sinful and ignoble race of man? And if for the sake of the bread of Heaven thousands and tens of thousands shall follow Thee, what is to become of the millions and tens of thousands of millions of creatures who will not have the strength to forego the earthly bread for the sake of the heavenly? Or dost Thou care only for the tens of thousands of the great and strong, while the millions, numerous as the sands of the sea, who are weak but love Thee, must exist only for the sake of the great and strong? No, we care for the weak too. They are sinful and rebellious, but in the end they too will become obedient. They will marvel at us and look on us as gods, because we are ready to endure the freedom which they have found so dreadful and to rule over them—so awful it will seem to them to be free. But we shall tell them that we are Thy servants and rule them in Thy name. We shall deceive them again, for we will not let Thee come to us again. That deception will be our suffering, for we shall be forced to lie.

"'This is the significance of the first question in the wilderness, and this is what Thou hast rejected for the sake of that freedom which Thou hast exalted above everything. Yet in this question lies hid the great secret of this world. Choosing "bread," Thou wouldst have satisfied the universal and everlasting craving of humanity—to find some one to worship. **So long as man remains free he strives for nothing so incessantly and so painfully as to find some one to worship.** But man seeks to worship what is established beyond dispute, so that all men would agree at once to worship it. For these pitiful creatures are concerned not only to find what one or the other can worship, but to find something that all would believe in and worship; what is essential is that all may be *together* in it. This craving for *community* of worship is the chief misery of every man individually and of all humanity from the beginning of time. For the sake of common worship they've slain each other with the sword. They have set up gods and challenged one another, "Put away your gods and come and worship ours, or we will kill you and your gods!" And so it will be to the end of the world, even when gods disappear from the earth; they will fall down before idols just the same. Thou didst know, Thou couldst not but have known, this fundamental secret of human nature, but Thou didst reject the one infallible banner which was offered Thee to make all men bow down to Thee alone—the banner of earthly bread; and Thou hast rejected it for the sake of freedom and the bread of Heaven. Behold what Thou didst further. And all again in the name of freedom! I tell Thee that man is tormented by no greater anxiety than to find some one quickly to whom he can hand over that gift of freedom with which the ill-fated creature is born. But only one who can appease their conscience can take over their freedom. In bread there was offered Thee an invincible banner; give bread, and man will worship Thee, for nothing is more certain than bread. But if some one else gains possession of his conscience—oh! then he will cast away Thy bread and follow after him who has ensnared his conscience. In that Thou wast right. For the secret of man's being is not only to live but to have something to live for. Without a stable conception of the object of life, man would not consent to go on living, and would rather destroy himself than remain on earth, though he had bread in abundance. That is true. But what happened? Instead of taking men's freedom from them, Thou didst make it greater than ever! Didst Thou forget that man prefers peace, and even death, to freedom of choice in the knowledge of good and evil? Nothing is more seductive for man than his freedom of conscience, but nothing is a greater cause of suffering. And behold, instead of giving a firm foundation for setting the conscience of man at rest for ever, Thou didst choose all that is exceptional, vague and enigmatic; Thou didst choose what was utterly beyond the strength of men, acting as though Thou didst not love them at all—Thou who didst come to give Thy life for them! Instead of taking possession of men's freedom, Thou didst increase it, and burdened the spiritual kingdom of mankind with its sufferings forever. Thou didst desire man's free love, that he should follow Thee freely, enticed and taken captive by Thee. In place of the rigid ancient law, man must hereafter with free heart decide for himself what is good and what is evil, having only Thy image before him as his guide. But didst Thou not know he would at last reject even Thy image and Thy truth, if he is weighed down with the fearful burden of free choice? They will cry aloud at last that the truth is not in Thee, for they could not have been left in greater confusion and suffering than Thou hast caused, laying upon them so many cares and unanswerable problems.

"'So that, in truth, Thou didst Thyself lay the foundation for the destruction of Thy kingdom, and no one is more to blame for it. Yet what was offered Thee? There are three powers, three powers alone, able to conquer and to hold captive for ever the conscience of these impotent rebels for their happiness—those forces are miracle, mystery and authority. Thou hast rejected all three and hast set the example for doing so. When the wise and dread spirit set Thee on the pinnacle of the temple and said to Thee, "If Thou wouldst know whether Thou art the Son of God then cast Thyself down, for it is written: the angels shall hold him up lest he fall and bruise himself, and Thou shalt know then whether Thou art the Son of God and shall prove then how great is Thy faith in Thy Father." But Thou didst refuse and wouldst not cast Thyself down. Oh! of course, Thou didst proudly and well, like God; but the weak, unruly race of men, are they gods? Oh, Thou didst know then that in taking one step, in making one movement to cast Thyself down, Thou wouldst be tempting God and have lost all Thy faith in Him, and wouldst have been dashed to pieces against that earth which Thou didst come to save. And the wise spirit that tempted Thee would have rejoiced. But I ask again, are there many like Thee? And couldst Thou believe for one moment that men, too, could face such a temptation? Is the nature of men such, that they can reject miracle, and at the great moments of their life, the moments of their deepest, most agonising spiritual difficulties, cling only to the free verdict of the heart? Oh, Thou didst know that Thy deed would be recorded in books, could be handed down to remote times and the utmost ends of the earth, and Thou didst hope that man, following Thee, would cling to God and not ask for a miracle. But Thou didst not know that when man rejects miracle he rejects God too; for man seeks not so much God as the miraculous. And as man cannot bear to be without the miraculous, he will create new miracles of his own for himself, and will worship deeds of sorcery and witchcraft, though he might be a hundred times over a rebel, heretic and infidel. Thou didst not come down from the Cross when they shouted to Thee, mocking and reviling Thee, "Come down from the cross and we will believe that Thou art He." Thou didst not come down, for again Thou wouldst not enslave man by a miracle, and didst crave faith given freely, not based on miracle. Thou didst crave for free love and not the base raptures of the slave before the might that has overawed him for ever. But Thou didst think too highly of men therein, for they are slaves, of course, though rebellious by nature. Look round and judge; fifteen centuries have passed, look upon them. Whom hast Thou raised up to Thyself? I swear, man is weaker and baser by nature than Thou hast believed him! Can he, can he do what Thou didst? By showing him so much respect, Thou didst, as it were, cease to feel for him, for Thou didst ask far too much from him—Thou who hast loved him more than Thyself! Respecting him less, Thou wouldst have asked less of him. That would have been more like love, for his burden would have been lighter. He is weak and vile. What though he is everywhere now rebelling against our power, and proud of his rebellion? It is the pride of a child and a schoolboy. There are little children rioting and barring out the teacher at school. But their childish delight will end; it will cost them dear. They will cast down temples and drench the earth with blood. But they will see at last, the foolish children, that, though they are rebels, they are impotent rebels, unable to keep up their own rebellion. Bathed in their foolish tears, they will recognise at last that He who created them rebels must have meant to mock at them. They will say this in despair, and their utterance will be a blasphemy which will make them more unhappy still, for man's nature cannot bear blasphemy, and in the end always avenges it on itself. And so unrest, confusion and unhappiness—that is the present lot of man after Thou didst bear so much for their freedom! Thy great prophet tells in vision and in image, that he saw all those who took part in the first resurrection and that they were of each tribe twelve thousand. But if there were so many of them, they must have been not men but gods. They had borne Thy cross, they had endured scores of years in the barren, hungry wilderness, living upon locusts and roots—and Thou mayest indeed point with pride at those children of freedom, of free love, of free and splendid sacrifice for Thy name. But remember that they were only some thousands; and what of the rest? And how are the other weak ones to blame, because they could not endure what the strong have endured? How is the weak soul to blame that it is unable to receive such terrible gifts? Canst Thou have simply come to the elect and for the elect? But if so, it is a mystery and we cannot understand it. And if it is a mystery, we too have a right to preach a mystery, and to teach them that it's not the free judgment of their hearts, not love that matters, but a mystery which they must follow blindly, even against their conscience. So we have done. We have corrected Thy work and have founded it upon *miracle, mystery* and *authority*. And men rejoiced that they were again led like sheep, and that the terrible gift that had brought them such suffering, was, at last, lifted from their hearts. Were we right teaching them this? Speak. Did we not love mankind, so meekly acknowledging their feebleness, lovingly lightening their burden, and permitting their weak nature even sin with our sanction? Why hast Thou come now to hinder us? And why dost

Thou look silently and searchingly at me with Thy mild eyes? Be angry. I don't want Thy love, for I love Thee not. And what use is it for me to hide anything from Thee? Don't I know to Whom I am speaking? All that I can say is known to Thee already. And is it for me to conceal from Thee our mystery? Perhaps it is Thy will to hear it from my lips. Listen, then. We are not working with Thee, but with *him*—that is our mystery. It's long—eight centuries—since we have been on *his* side and not on Thine. Just eight centuries ago, we took from him what Thou didst reject with scorn, that last gift he offered Thee, showing Thee all the kingdoms of the earth. We took from him Rome and the sword of Caesar, and proclaimed ourselves sole rulers of the earth, though hitherto we have not been able to complete our work. But whose fault is that? Oh, the work is only beginning, but it has much to suffer, but we shall triumph and shall be Caesars, and then we shall plan the universal happiness of man. But Thou mightest have taken even then the sword of Caesar. Why didst Thou reject that last gift? Hadst Thou accepted that last counsel of the mighty spirit, Thou wouldst have accomplished all that man seeks on earth—that is, some one to worship, some one to keep his conscience, and some means of uniting all in one unanimous and harmonious antheap, for the craving for universal unity is the third and last anguish of men. Mankind as a whole has always striven to organise a universal state. There have been many great nations with great histories, but the more highly they were developed the more unhappy they were, for they felt more acutely than other people the craving for worldwide union. The great conquerors, Timours and Ghenghis-Khan, whirled like hurricanes over the face of the earth striving to subdue its people, and they too were but the unconscious expression of the same craving for universal unity. Hadst Thou taken the world and Caesar's purple, Thou wouldst have founded the universal state and have given universal peace. For who can rule men if not he who holds their conscience and their bread in his hands? We have taken the sword of Caesar, and in taking it, of course, have rejected Thee and followed *him*. Oh, ages are yet to come of the confusion of free thought, of their science and cannibalism. For having begun to build their tower of Babel without us, they will end, of course, with cannibalism. But then the beast will crawl to us and lick our feet and spatter them with tears of blood. And we shall sit upon the beast and raise the cup, and on it will be written, "Mystery." But then, and only then, the reign of peace and happiness will come for men. Thou art proud of Thine elect, but Thou hast only the elect, while we give rest to all. And besides, how many of those elect, those mighty ones who could become elect, have grown weary waiting for Thee, and have transferred and will transfer the powers of their spirit and the warmth of their heart to the other camp, and end by raising their *free* banner against Thee. Thou didst Thyself lift up that banner. But with us all will be happy and will no more rebel nor destroy one another as under Thy freedom. Oh, we shall persuade them that they will only become free when they renounce their freedom to us and submit to us. And shall we be right or shall we be lying? They will be convinced that we are right, for they will remember the horrors of slavery and confusion to which Thy freedom brought them. Freedom, free thought and science, will lead them into such straits and will bring them face to face with such marvels and insoluble mysteries, that some of them, the fierce and rebellious, will destroy themselves, others, rebellious but weak, will destroy one another, while the rest, weak and unhappy, will crawl fawning to our feet and whine to us: "Yes, you were right, you alone possess His mystery, and we come back to you, save us from ourselves!"

"'Receiving bread from us, they will see clearly that we take the bread made by their hands from them, to give it to them, without any miracle. They will see that we do not change the stones to bread, but in truth they will be more thankful for taking it from our hands than for the bread itself! For they will remember only too well that in old days, without our help, even the bread they made turned to stones in their hands, while since they have come back to us, the very stones have turned to bread in their hands. Too, too well they know the value of complete submission! And until men know that, they will be unhappy. Who is most to blame for their not knowing it, speak? Who scattered the flock and sent it astray on unknown paths? But the flock will come together again and will submit once more, and then it will be once for all. Then we shall give them the quiet humble happiness of weak creatures such as they are by nature. Oh, we shall persuade them at last not to be proud, for Thou didst lift them up and thereby taught them to be proud. We shall show them that they are weak, that they are only pitiful children, but that childlike happiness is the sweetest of all. They will become timid and will look to us and huddle close to us in fear, as chicks to the hen. They will marvel at us and will be awestricken before us, and will be proud at our being so powerful and clever, that we have been able to subdue such a turbulent flock of thousands of millions. They will tremble impotently before our wrath, their minds will grow fearful, they will be just as ready at a sign from us to pass to laughter and rejoicing, to happy mirth and childish song. Yes, we shall set them to work, but in their leisure hours we shall make their life like a child's game, with children's songs and innocent dance. Oh, we shall allow them even sin, they are weak and helpless, and they will love us like children because we allow them to sin. We shall tell them that every sin will be expiated, if it is done with our permission, that we allow them to sin because we love them, and the punishment for these sins we take upon ourselves. And we shall take it upon ourselves, and they will adore us as their saviours, who have taken on themselves their sins before God. And they will have no secrets from us. We shall allow or forbid them to live with their wives and mistresses, to have or not to have children—according to whether they have been obedient or disobedient—and they will submit to us gladly and cheerfully. The most painful secrets of their conscience, all, all they will bring to us, and we shall have an answer for all. And they will be glad to believe our answer, for it will save them from the great anxiety and terrible agony they endure at present in making a free decision for themselves. And all will be happy, all the millions of creatures except the hundred thousand who rule over them. For only we, we who guard the mystery, shall be unhappy. There will be thousands of millions of happy babes, and a hundred thousand sufferers who have taken upon themselves the curse of the knowledge of good and evil. Peacefully they will die, peacefully they will expire in Thy name, and beyond the grave they will find nothing but death. But we shall keep the secret, and for their happiness we shall allure them with the reward of heaven and eternity. Though if there were anything in the other world, it certainly would not be for such as they. It is prophesied that Thou wilt come again in victory, Thou wilt come with Thy chosen, the proud and strong, but we will say that they have only saved themselves, but we have saved all. We are told that the harlot who sits upon the beast, and holds in her hands the *mystery*, shall be put to shame, that the weak will rise up again, and will rend her royal purple and will strip naked her loathsome body. But then I will stand up and point out to Thee the thousand millions of happy children who have known no sin. And we who have taken their sins upon us for their happiness will stand up before Thee and say: "Judge us if Thou canst and darest." Know that I too have been in the wilderness, I too have lived on roots and locusts, I too prized the freedom with which Thou hast blessed men, and I too was striving to stand among Thy elect, among the strong and powerful, thirsting "to make up the number." But I awakened and would not serve madness. I turned back and joined the ranks of those *who have corrected Thy work*. I left the proud and went back to the humble, for the happiness of the humble. What I say to Thee will come to pass, and our dominion will be built up. I repeat, tomorrow Thou shalt see that obedient flock who at a sign from me will hasten to heap up the hot cinders about the pile on which I shall burn Thee for coming to hinder us. For if any one has ever deserved our fires, it is Thou. Tomorrow I shall burn Thee. Dixi.' "

Ivan stopped. He was carried away as he talked and spoke with excitement; when he had finished, he suddenly smiled.

Alyosha had listened in silence; towards the end he was greatly moved and seemed several times on the point of interrupting, but restrained himself. Now his words came with a rush.

"But . . . that's absurd!" he cried, flushing. "Your poem is in praise of Jesus, not in blame of Him—as you meant it to be. And who will believe you about freedom? Is that the way to understand it? That's not the idea of it in the Orthodox Church . . . That's Rome, and not even the whole of Rome, it's false—those are the worst of the Catholics, the Inquisitors, the Jesuits. . . . And there could not be such a fantastic creature as your Inquisitor. What are these sins of mankind they take on themselves? Who are these keepers of the mystery who have taken some curse upon themselves for the happiness of mankind? When have they been seen? We know the Jesuits, they are spoken ill of, but surely they are not what you describe? They are not that at all, not at all. . . . They are simply the Romish army for the earthly sovereignty of the world in the future, with the Pontiff of Rome for Emperor . . . that's their ideal, but there's no sort of mystery or lofty melancholy about it. . . . It's simple lust of power, of filthy earthly gain, of domination—something like a universal serfdom with them as masters—that's all they stand for. They don't even believe in God perhaps. Your suffering inquisitor is a mere fantasy."

"Stay, stay," laughed Ivan, "how hot you are! A fantasy you say, let it be so! Of course it's a fantasy. But allow me to say: do you really think that the Roman Catholic movement of the last centuries is actually nothing but the lust of power, of filthy earthly gain? Is that Father Païssy's teaching?"

"No, no, on the contrary, Father Païssy did once say something rather the same as you . . . but of course it's not the same, not a bit the same, Alyosha hastily corrected himself.

"A precious admission, in spite of your 'not a bit the same.' I ask you why your Jesuits and Inquisitors have united simply for vile material gain? Why can there not be among them one martyr oppressed by great sorrow and loving humanity? You see, only suppose that there was one such man among all those who desire nothing but filthy material gain—if there's only one like my old inquisitor, who had himself eaten roots in the desert and made frenzied efforts to subdue his flesh to make himself free and perfect. But yet all his life he loved humanity, and suddenly his eyes were opened, and he saw that it is no great moral blessedness to attain perfection and freedom, if at the same time one gains the conviction that millions of God's creatures have been created as a mockery, that they will never be capable of using their freedom, that these poor rebels can never turn into giants to complete the tower, that it was not for such geese that the great idealist dreamt his dream of harmony. Seeing all that he turned back and joined—the clever people. Surely that could have happened?"

"Joined whom, what clever people?" cried Alyosha completely carried away. "They have no such great cleverness and no mysteries, and secrets. . . . Perhaps nothing but Atheism, that's all their secret. Your inquisitor does not believe in God, that's his secret!"

"What if it is so! At last you have guessed it. It's perfectly true that that's the whole secret, but isn't that suffering, at least for a man like that, who has wasted his whole life in the desert and yet could not shake off his incurable love of humanity? In his old age he reached the clear conviction that nothing but the advice of the great dread spirit could build up any tolerable sort of life for the feeble, unruly, 'incomplete, empirical creatures created in jest.' And so, convinced of this, he sees that he must follow the counsel of the wise spirit, the dread spirit of death and destruction, and therefore accept lying and deception, and lead men consciously to death and destruction, and yet deceive them all the way so that they may not notice where they are being led, that the poor blind creatures may at least on the way think themselves happy. And note, the deception is in the name of Him in Whose ideal the old man had so fervently believed all his life long. Is not that tragic? And if only one such stood at the head of the whole army 'filled with the lust of power only for the sake of filthy gain'—would not one such be enough to make a tragedy? More than that, one such standing at the head is enough to create the actual leading idea of the Roman Church with all its armies and Jesuits, its highest idea. I tell you frankly that I firmly believe that there has always been such a man among those who stood at the head of the movement. Who knows, there may have been some such even among the Roman Popes. Who knows, perhaps the spirit of that accursed old man who loves mankind so obstinately in his own way, is to be found even now in a whole multitude of such old men, existing not by chance but by agreement, as a secret league formed long ago for the guarding of the mystery, to guard it from the weak and the unhappy, so as to make them happy. No doubt it is so, and so it must be indeed. I fancy that even among the Masons there's something of the same mystery at the bottom, and that that's why the Catholics so detest the Masons as their rivals breaking up the unity of the idea, while it is so essential that there should be one flock and one shepherd. . . . But from the way I defend my idea I might be an author impatient of your criticism. Enough of it."

"You are perhaps a Mason yourself!" broke suddenly from Alyosha. "You don't believe in God," he added, speaking this time very sorrowfully. He fancied besides that his brother was looking at him ironically. "How does your poem end?" he asked, suddenly looking down. "Or was it the end"

"I meant it to end like this. When the Inquisitor ceased speaking he waited some time for his Prisoner to answer him. His silence weighed down upon him. He saw that the Prisoner had listened intently all the time, looking gently in his face and evidently not wishing to reply. The old man longed for Him to say something, however bitter and terrible. But He suddenly approached the old man in silence and softly kissed him on his bloodless aged lips. That was all his answer. The old man shuddered. His lips moved. He went to the door, opened it, and said to Him: 'Go, and come no more. . . . come not at all, never, never!' And he let Him out into the dark alleys of the town. The Prisoner went away."

"And the old man?"

"The kiss glows in his heart, but the old man adheres to his idea."

"And you with him, you too?" cried Alyosha, mournfully.

Ivan laughed.

"Why, it's all nonsense, Alyosha. It's only a senseless poem of a senseless student, who could never write two lines of verse. Why do you take it so seriously? Surely you don't suppose I am going straight off to the Jesuits, to join the men who are correcting His work? Good Lord, it's no business of mine. I told you, all I want is to live on to thirty, and then . . . dash the cup to the ground!"

"But the little sticky leaves, and the precious tombs, and the blue sky, and the woman you love! How will you live, how will you love them?" Alyosha cried sorrowfully. "With such a hell in your heart and your head, how can you? No, that's just what you are going away for, to join them . . . if not, you will kill yourself, you can't endure it."

"There is a strength to endure everything," Ivan said with a cold smile.

"What strength?"

"The strength of the Karamazov—the strength of the Karamazov baseness."

"To sink into debauchery, to stifle your soul with corruption, yes?"

"Possibly even that . . . only perhaps till I am, thirty I shall escape it, and then."

"How will you escape it? By what will you escape it? That's impossible with your ideas."

"In the Karamazov way, again."

"'Everything is lawful,' you mean? Everything is lawful, is that it?"

Ivan scowled, and all at once turned strangely pale.

"Ah, you've caught up yesterday's phrase, which so offended Miusov—and which Dmitri pounced upon so naively and paraphrased!" he smiled queerly.

"Yes, if you like, 'everything is lawful' since the word has been said. I won't deny it. And Mitya's version isn't bad."

Alyosha looked at him in silence.

"I thought that going away from here I have you at least," Ivan said suddenly, with unexpected feeling; "but now I see that there is no place for me even in your heart, my dear hermit. The formula, 'all is lawful,' I won't renounce—will you renounce me for that, yes?"

Alyosha got up, went to him and softly kissed him on the lips.

"That's plagiarism," cried Ivan, highly delighted. "You stole that from my poem. Thank you though. Get up, Alyosha, it's time we were going, both of us." . . .

Freedom and the Control of Men

B. F. Skinner

The second half of the twentieth century may be remembered for its solution of a curious problem. Although Western democracy created the conditions responsible for the rise of modern science, it is now evident that it may never fully profit from that achievement. The so-called "democratic philosophy" of human behavior to which it also gave rise is increasingly in conflict with the applications of the methods of science to human affairs. Unless this conflict is somehow resolved, the ultimate goals of democracy may be long deferred.

Just as biographers and critics look for external influences to account for the traits and achievements of the men they study, so science ultimately explains behavior in terms of "causes" or conditions which lie beyond the individual himself. As more and more causal relations are demonstrated, a practical corollary becomes difficult to resist: it should be possible to *produce* behavior according to plan simply by arranging the proper conditions. Now, among the specifications which might reasonably be submitted to a behavioral technology are these: Let men be happy, informed, skillful, well behaved, and productive.

This immediate practical implication of a science of behavior has a familiar ring, for it recalls the doctrine of human perfectibility of eighteenth- and nineteenth-century humanism. A science of man shares the optimism of that philosophy and supplies striking support for the working faith that men can build a better world and, through it, better men. The support comes just in time, for there has been little optimism of late among those who speak from the traditional point of view. Democracy has become "realistic," and it is only with some embarrassment that one admits today to perfectionistic or utopian thinking.

The earlier temper is worth considering, however. History records many foolish and unworkable schemes for human betterment, but almost all the great changes in our culture which we now regard as worthwhile can be traced to perfectionistic philosophies. Governmental, religious, educational, economic, and social reforms follow a common pattern. Someone believes that a change in a cultural practice—for example, in the rules of evidence in a court of law, in the characterization of man's relation to

God, in the way children are taught to read and write, in permitted rates of interest, or in minimal housing standards—will improve the condition of men: by promoting justice, permitting men to seek salvation more effectively, increasing the literacy of a people, checking an inflationary trend, or improving public health and family relations, respectively. The underlying hypothesis is always the same: that a different physical or cultural environment will make a different and better man.

The scientific study of behavior not only justifies the general pattern of such proposals; it promises new and better hypotheses. The earliest cultural practices must have originated in sheer accidents. Those which strengthened the group survived with the group in a sort of natural selection. As soon as men began to propose and carry out changes in practice for the sake of possible consequences, the evolutionary process must have accelerated. The simple practice of making changes must have had survival value. A further acceleration is now to be expected. As laws of behavior are more precisely stated, the changes in the environment required to bring about a given effect may be more clearly specified. Conditions which have been neglected because their effects were slight or unlooked for may be shown to be relevant. New conditions may actually be created, as in the discovery and synthesis of drugs which affect behavior.

This is no time, then, to abandon notions of progress, improvement, or, indeed, human perfectibility. **The simple fact is that man is able, and now as never before, to lift himself by his own bootstraps.** In achieving control of the world of which he is a part, he may learn at last to control himself.

Timeworn objections to the planned improvement of cultural practices are already losing much of their force. Marcus Aurelius was probably right in advising his readers to be content with a haphazard amelioration of mankind. "Never hope to realize Plato's republic," he sighed, ". . . for who can change the opinions of men? And without a change of sentiments what can you make but reluctant slaves and hypocrites?" He was thinking, no doubt, of contemporary patterns of control based upon punishment or the threat of punishment which, as he correctly observed, breed only reluctant slaves of those who submit and hypocrites of those who discover modes of evasion. But we need not share his pessimism, for the opinions of men can be changed. The techniques of indoctrination which were being devised by the early Christian Church at the very time Marcus Aurelius was writing are relevant, as are some of the techniques of psychotherapy and of advertising and public relations. Other methods suggested by recent scientific analyses leave little doubt of the matter.

The study of human behavior also answers the cynical complaint that there is a plain "cussedness" in man which will always thwart efforts to improve him. We are often told that men do not want to be changed, even for the better. Try to help them, and they will outwit you and remain happily wretched. Dostoevsky claimed to see some plan in it. "Out of sheer ingratitude," he complained, or possibly boasted, "man will play you a dirty trick, just to prove that men are still men and not the keys of a piano. . . . And even if you could prove that a man is only a piano key, he would still do something out of sheer perversity—he would create destruction and chaos—just to gain his point. . . . And if all this could in turn be analyzed and prevented by predicting that it would occur, then man would deliberately go mad to prove his point." This is a conceivable neurotic reaction to inept control. A few men may have shown it, and many have enjoyed Dostoevsky's statement because they tend to show it. But that such perversity is a fundamental reaction of the human organism to controlling conditions is sheer nonsense.

So is the objection that we have no way of knowing what changes to make even though we have the necessary techniques. That is one of the great hoaxes of the century—a sort of booby trap left behind in the retreat before the advancing front of science. Scientists themselves have unsuspectingly agreed that there are two kinds of useful propositions about nature—facts and value judgments—and that science must confine itself to "what is," leaving "what ought to be" to others. But with what special sort of wisdom is the nonscientist endowed? Science is only effective knowing, no matter who engages in it. Verbal behavior proves upon analysis to be composed of many different types of utterances, from poetry and exhortation to logic and factual description, but these are not all equally useful in talking about cultural practices. We may classify useful propositions according to the degrees of confidence with which they may be asserted. Sentences about nature range from highly probable "facts" to sheer guesses. In general, future events are less likely to be correctly described than past. When a scientist talks about a projected experiment, for example, he must often resort to statements having only a moderate likelihood of being correct; he calls them hypotheses.

Designing a new cultural pattern is in many ways like designing an experiment. In drawing up a new constitution, outlining a new educational program, modifying a religious doctrine, or setting up a new fiscal policy, many statements must be quite tentative. We cannot be sure that the practices we specify will have the consequences we predict, or that the consequences will reward our efforts. This is in the nature of such proposals. They are not value judgments—they are guesses. To confuse and delay the improvement of cultural practices by quibbling about the word *improve* is itself not a useful practice. Let us agree, to start with, that health is better than illness, wisdom better than ignorance, love better than hate, and productive energy better than neurotic sloth.

Perhaps the most crucial part of our democratic philosophy to be reconsidered is our attitude toward freedom—or its reciprocal, the control of human behavior. We do not oppose all forms of control because it is . . . "human nature" to do so. The reaction is not characteristic of all men under all conditions of life. It is an attitude which has been carefully engineered, in large part by what we call the "literature" of democracy. With respect to some methods of control (for example, the threat of force), very little engineering is needed, for the techniques or their immediate consequences are objectionable. Society has suppressed these methods by branding them "wrong," "illegal," or "sinful." But to encourage these attitudes toward objectionable forms of control, it has been necessary to disguise the real nature of certain indispensable techniques, the commonest examples of which are education, moral discourse, and persuasion. The actual procedures appear harmless enough. They consist of supplying information, presenting opportunities for action, pointing out logical relationships, appealing to reason or "enlightened understanding," and so on. Through a masterful piece of misrepresentation, the illusion is fostered that these procedures do not involve the control of behavior; at most, they are simply ways of "getting someone to change his mind." But analysis not only reveals the presence of well-defined behavioral processes, it demonstrates a kind of control no less inexorable, though in some ways more acceptable, than the bully's threat of force.

Let us suppose that someone in whom we are interested is acting unwisely—he is careless in the way he deals with his friends, he drives too fast, or he holds his golf club the wrong way. We could probably help him by issuing a series of commands: don't nag, don't drive over sixty, don't hold your club that way. Much less objectionable would be "an appeal to reason." We could show him how people are affected by his treatment of them, how accident rates rise sharply at higher speeds, how a particular grip on the club alters the way the ball is struck and corrects a slice. In doing so we resort to verbal mediating devices which emphasize and support certain "contingencies of reinforcement"—that is, certain relations between behavior and its consequences—which strengthen the behavior we wish to set up. The same consequences would possibly set up the behavior without our help, and they eventually take control no matter which form of help we give. The appeal to reason has certain advantages over the authoritative command. A threat of punishment, no matter how subtle, generates emotional reactions and tendencies to escape or revolt. Perhaps the controllee merely "feels resentment" at being made to act in a given way, but even that is to be avoided. When we "appeal to reason," he "feels freer to do as he pleases." The fact is that we have exerted *less* control than in using a threat; since other conditions may contribute to the result, the effect may be delayed or, possibly in a given instance, lacking. But if we have worked a change in his behavior at all, it is because we have altered relevant environmental conditions, and the processes we have set in motion are just as real and just as inexorable, if not as comprehensive, as in the most authoritative coercion.

"Arranging an opportunity for action" is another example of disguised control. The power of the negative form has already been exposed in the analysis of censorship. Restriction of opportunity is recognized as far from harmless. As Ralph Barton Perry said in an article which appeared in the Spring, 1953, *Pacific Spectator*, "Whoever determines what alternatives shall be made known to man controls what that man shall choose *from*. He is deprived of freedom in proportion as he is denied access to any ideas, or is confined to any range of ideas short of the totality of relevant possibilities." But there is a positive side as well. When we present a relevant state of affairs, we increase the likelihood that a given form of behavior will be emitted. To the extent that the probability of action has changed, we have made a definite contribution. The teacher of history controls a student's behavior (or, if the reader prefers, "deprives him of freedom") just as much in *presenting* historical facts as in suppressing them. Other conditions will no doubt affect the student, but the contribution made to his behavior by the presentation of material is fixed and, within its range, irresistible.

The methods of education, moral discourse, and persuasion are acceptable not because they recognize the freedom of the individual or his right to dissent, but because they make only *partial* contributions to the control of his behavior. The freedom they recognize is freedom from a more coercive form of control. The dissent which they tolerate is the possible effect of other determiners of action. Since these sanctioned methods are frequently ineffective, we have been able to convince ourselves that they do not represent control at all. When they show too much strength to permit disguise, we give them other names and suppress them as energetically as we suppress the use of force. Education grown too powerful is rejected as propaganda or "brainwashing," while really effective persuasion is described as "undue influence," "demagoguery," "seduction," and so on.

If we are not to rely solely upon accident for the innovations which give rise to cultural evolution, we must accept the fact that some kind of control of human behavior is inevitable. We cannot use good sense in human affairs unless someone engages in the design and construction of environmental conditions which affect the behavior of men. Environmental changes have always been the condition for the improvement of cultural patterns, and we can hardly use the more effective methods of science without making changes on a grander scale. We are all controlled by the world in which we live, and part of that world has been and will be constructed by men. The question is this: Are we to be controlled by accident, by tyrants, or by ourselves in effective cultural design?

The danger of the misuse of power is possibly greater than ever. It is not allayed by disguising the facts. We cannot make wise decisions if we continue to pretend that human behavior is not controlled, or if we refuse to engage in control when valuable results might be forthcoming. Such measures weaken only ourselves, leaving the strength of science to others. The first step in a defense against tyranny is the fullest possible exposure of controlling techniques. A second step has already been taken successfully in restricting the use of physical force. Slowly, and as yet imperfectly, we have worked out an ethical and governmental design in which the strong man is not allowed to use the power deriving from his strength to control his fellow men. He is restrained by a superior force created for this purpose—the ethical pressure of the group, or more explicit religious and governmental measures. We tend to distrust superior forces, as we currently hesitate to relinquish sovereignty in order to set up an international police force. But it is only through such counter-control that we have achieved what we call peace—a condition in which men are not permitted to control each other through force. In other words, control itself must be controlled.

Science has turned up dangerous processes and materials before. To use the facts and techniques of a science of man to the fullest extent without making some monstrous mistake will be difficult and obviously perilous. It is no time for self-deception, emotional indulgence, or the assumption of attitudes which are no longer useful. Man is facing a difficult test. He must keep his head now, or he must start again—a long way back.

Choice and Human Dignity

Viktor Frankl

This [narrative] . . . does not claim to be an account of facts and events but of personal experiences, experiences which millions of prisoners have suffered time and again. It is the inside story of a concentration camp, told by one of its survivors. This tale is not concerned with the great horrors, which have already been described often enough (though less often believed), but with the multitude of small torments. In other words, it will try to answer this question: How was everyday life in, a concentration camp reflected in the mind of the average prisoner?

Most of the events described here did not take place in the large and famous camps, but in the small ones where most of the real extermination took place. This story is not about the suffering and death of great heroes and martyrs, nor is it about the prominent Capos—prisoners who acted as trustees, having special privileges—or well-known prisoners. Thus it is not so much concerned with the sufferings of the mighty, but with the sacrifices, the crucifixion and the deaths of the great army of unknown and unrecorded victims. It was these common prisoners, who bore no distinguishing marks on their sleeves, whom the Capos really despised. While these ordinary prisoners had little or nothing to eat, the Capos were never hungry; in fact many of the Capos fared better in the camp than they had in their entire lives. Often they were harder on the prisoners than were the guards, and beat them more cruelly than the SS men did. These Capos, of course, were chosen only from those prisoners whose characters promised to make them suitable for such procedures, and if they did not comply with what was expected of them, they were immediately demoted. They soon became much like the SS men and the camp wardens and may be judged on a similar psychological basis.

It is easy for the outsider to get the wrong conception of camp life, a conception mingled with sentiment and pity. Little does he know of the hard fight for existence which raged among the prisoners. This was an unrelenting struggle for daily bread and for life itself, for one's own sake or for that of a good friend.

In attempting this psychological presentation and a psychopathological explanation of the typical characteristics of a concentration camp inmate, I may give the impression that the human being is completely and unavoidably influenced by his surroundings. (In this case the surroundings being the unique structure of camp life, which forced the prisoner to conform his conduct to a certain set pattern.) But what about human liberty? Is there no spiritual freedom in regard to behavior and reaction to any given surroundings? Is that theory true which would have us believe that man is no more than a product of many conditional and environmental factors—be they of a biological, psychological or sociological nature? Is man but an accidental product of these? Most important, do the prisoners' reactions to the singular world of the concentration camp prove that man cannot escape the influences of his surroundings? Does man have no choice of action in the face of such circumstances?

We can answer these questions from experience as well as on principle. The experiences of camp life show that man does have a choice of action. There were enough examples, often of a heroic nature, which proved that apathy could be overcome, irritability suppressed. Man *can* preserve a vestige of spiritual freedom, of independence of mind, even in such terrible conditions of psychic and physical stress.

We who lived in concentration camps can remember the men who walked through the huts comforting others, giving away their last piece of bread. They may have been few in number, but they offer sufficient proof that **everything can be taken from a man but one thing: the last of the human freedoms—to choose one's attitude in any given set of circumstances, to choose one's own way.**

And there were always choices to make. Every day, every hour, offered the opportunity to make a decision, a decision which determined whether you would or would not submit to those powers which threatened to rob you of your very self, your inner freedom; which determined whether or not you would become the plaything of circumstance, renouncing freedom and dignity to become molded into the form of the typical inmate.

Seen from this point of view, the mental reactions of the inmates of a concentration camp must seem more to us than the mere expression of certain physical and sociological conditions. Even though conditions such as lack of sleep, insufficient food and various mental stresses may suggest that the inmates were bound to react in certain ways, in the final analysis it becomes clear that the sort of person the prisoner became was the result of an inner decision, and not the result of camp influences alone. Fundamentally, therefore, any man can, even under such circumstances, decide what shall become of him—mentally and spiritually. He may retain his human dignity even in a concentration camp. Dostoevski said once, "There is only one thing that I dread: not to be worthy of my sufferings." These words frequently came to my mind after I became acquainted with those martyrs whose behavior in camp, whose suffering and death, bore witness to the fact that the last inner freedom cannot be lost. It can be said that they were worthy of their sufferings; the way they bore their suffering was a genuine inner achievement. It is this spiritual freedom—which cannot be taken away—that makes life meaningful and purposeful.

An active life serves the purpose of giving man the opportunity to realize values in creative work, while a passive life of enjoyment affords him the opportunity to obtain fulfillment in experiencing beauty, art, or nature. But there is also purpose in that life which is almost barren of both creation and enjoyment and which admits of but one possibility of high moral behavior: namely, in man's attitude to his existence, an existence restricted by external forces. A creative life and a life of enjoyment are banned to him. But not only creativeness and enjoyment are meaningful. If there is a meaning in life at all, then there must be a meaning in suffering. Suffering is an ineradicable part of life, even as fate and death. Without suffering and death human life cannot be complete.

The way in which a man accepts his fate and all the suffering it entails, the way in which he takes up his cross, gives him ample opportunity even under the most difficult circumstances—to add a deeper meaning to his life. It may remain brave, dignified and unselfish. Or in the bitter fight for self-preservation he may forget his human dignity and become no more than an animal. Here lies the chance for a man either to make use of or to forego the opportunities of attaining the moral values that a difficult situation may afford him. And this decides whether he is worthy of his sufferings or not.

Do not think that these considerations are unworldly and too far removed from real life. It is true that only a few people are capable of reaching such high moral standards. Of the prisoners only a few kept their full inner liberty and obtained those values which their suffering afforded, but even one such example is sufficient proof that man's inner strength may raise him above his outward fate. Such men are not only in concentration camps. Everywhere man is confronted with fate, with the chance of achieving something through his own suffering.

Take the fate of the sick—especially those who are incurable. I once read a letter written by a young invalid, in which he told a friend that he had just found out he would not live for long, that even an operation would be of no help. He wrote further that he remembered a film he had seen in which a man was portrayed who waited for death in a courageous and dignified way. The boy had thought it a great accomplishment to meet death so well. Now—he wrote—fate was offering him a similar chance.

Those of us who saw the film called *Resurrection* taken from a book by Tolstoy—years ago, may have had similar thoughts. Here were great destinies and great men. For us, at that time, there was no great fate; there was no chance to achieve such greatness. After the picture we went to the nearest cafe, and over a cup of coffee and a sandwich we forgot the strange metaphysical thoughts which for one moment had crossed our minds. But when we ourselves were confronted with a great destiny and faced with the decision of meeting it with equal spiritual greatness, by then we had forgotten our youthful resolutions of long ago, and we failed.

Perhaps there came a day for some of us when we saw the same film again, or a similar one. But by then other pictures may have simultaneously unrolled before one's inner eye; pictures of people who attained much more in their lives than a sentimental film could show. Some details of a particular man's inner greatness may have come to one's mind, like the story of the young woman whose death I witnessed in a concentration camp. It is a simple story. There is little to tell and it may sound as if I had invented it; but to me it seems like a poem.

This young woman knew that she would die in the next few days. But when I talked to her she was cheerful in spite of this knowledge. "I am grateful that fate has hit me so hard," she told me. "In my former life I was spoiled and did not take spiritual accomplishments seriously." Pointing through the window of the hut, she said, "This tree here is the only friend I have in my loneliness." Through that window she could see just one branch of a chestnut tree, and on the branch were two blossoms. "I often talk to this tree," she said to me. I was startled and didn't quite know how to take her words. Was she delirious? Did she have occasional hallucinations? Anxiously I asked her if the tree replied. "Yes." What did it say to her? She answered, "It said to me, 'I am here—I am here—I am life, eternal life.'"

We have stated that that which was ultimately responsible for the state of the prisoner's inner self was not so much the enumerated psychophysical causes as it was the result of a free decision. Psychological observations of the prisoners have shown that only the men who allowed their inner hold on their moral and spiritual selves to subside eventually fell victim to the camp's degenerating influences. . . .

Any attempt at fighting the camp's psychopathological influence on the prisoner by psychotherapeutic or psychohygienic methods had to aim at giving him inner strength by pointing out to him a future goal to which he could look forward. Instinctively some of the prisoners attempted to find one on their own. It is a peculiarity of man that he can only live by looking to the future—sub specie aeternitatis. And this is his salvation in the most difficult moments of his existence, although he sometimes has to force his mind to the task. . . .

. . . Nietzsche's words, **"He who has a *why* to live for can bear with almost any *how*,"** could be the guiding motto for all psychotherapeutic and psychohygienic efforts regarding prisoners. Whenever there was an opportunity for it, one had to give them a why—an aim—for their lives, in order to strengthen them to bear the terrible *how* of their existence. Woe to him who saw no more sense in his life, no aim, no purpose, and therefore no point in carrying on. He was soon lost. The typical reply with which such a man rejected all encouraging arguments was, "I have nothing to expect from life any more." What sort of answer can one give to that? . . .

The tender beginnings of a psychotherapy or psychohygiene were, when they were possible at all in the camp, either individual or collective in nature. The individual psychotherapeutic attempts were often a kind of "life-saving procedure." These efforts were usually concerned with the prevention of suicides. A very strict camp ruling forbade any efforts to save a man who attempted suicide. It was forbidden, for example, to cut down a man who was trying to hang himself. Therefore, it was all important to prevent these attempts from occurring.

I remember two cases of would-be suicide, which bore a striking similarity to each other. Both men had talked of their intentions to commit suicide. Both used the typical argument—they had nothing more to expect from life. In both cases it was a question of getting them to realize that life was still expecting something from them; something in the future was expected of them. We found, in fact, that for the one it was his child whom he adored and who was waiting for him in a foreign country. For the other it was a thing, not a person. This man was a scientist and had written a series of books which still needed to be finished. His work could not be done by anyone else, any more than another person could ever take the place of the father in his child's affections.

This uniqueness and singleness which distinguishes each individual and gives a meaning to his existence has a bearing on creative work as much as it does on human love. When the impossibility of replacing a person is realized, it allows the responsibility which a man has for his existence and its continuance to appear in all its magnitude. A man who becomes conscious of the responsibility he bears toward a human being who affectionately waits for him, or to an unfinished work, will never be able to throw away his life. He knows the "why" for his existence, and will be able to bear almost any "how."

The opportunities for collective psychotherapy were naturally limited in camp. The right example was more effective than words could ever be; A senior block warden who did not side with the authorities had, by his just and encouraging behavior, a thousand opportunities to exert a far-reaching moral influence on those under his jurisdiction. The immediate influence of behavior is always more effective than that of words. But at times a word was effective too, when mental receptiveness had been intensified by some outer circumstances: I remember an incident when there was occasion for psychotherapeutic work on the inmates of a whole hut, due to an intensification of their receptiveness because of a certain external situation.

It had been a bad day. On parade, an announcement had been made about the many actions that would, from then on, be regarded as sabotage and therefore punishable by immediate death by hanging. Among these were crimes such as cutting small strips from our old blankets (in order to improvise ankle supports) and very minor "thefts." A few days previously a semi-starved prisoner had broken into the potato store to steal a few pounds of potatoes. The theft had been discovered and some prisoners had recognized the "burglar." When the camp authorities heard about it they ordered that the guilty man be given up to them or the whole camp would starve for a day. Naturally the 2,500 men preferred to fast.

On the evening of this day of fasting we lay in our earthen huts—in a very low mood. Very little was said and every word sounded irritable. Then, to make matters even worse, the light went out. Tempers reached their lowest ebb. But our senior block warden was a wise man. He improvised a little talk about all that was on our minds at that moment. He talked about the many comrades who had died in the last few days, either of sickness or of suicide. But he also mentioned what may have been the real reason for their deaths: giving up hope. He maintained that there should be some way of preventing possible future victims from reaching this extreme state. And it was to me that the warden pointed to give this advice.

God knows, I was not in the mood to give psychological explanations or to preach any sermons—to offer my comrades a kind of medical care of their souls. I was cold and hungry, irritable and tired, but I had to make the effort and use this unique opportunity. Encouragement was now more necessary than ever.

So I began by mentioning the most trivial of comforts first. I said that even in this Europe in the sixth winter of the Second World War, our situation was not the most terrible we could think of. I said that each of us had to ask himself what irreplaceable losses he had suffered up to then. I speculated that for most of them these losses had really been few. Whoever was still alive had reason for hope. Health, family, happiness, professional abilities, fortune, position in society—all these were things that could be achieved again or restored. After all, we still had all our bones intact. Whatever we had gone through could still be an asset to us in the future. And I quoted from Nietzsche: "*Was mich nicht umbringt, macht mich stärker.*" (That which does not kill me, makes me stronger.)

Then I spoke about the future. I said that to the impartial the future must seem hopeless. I agreed that each of us could guess for himself how small were his chances of survival. I told them that although there was still no typhus epidemic in the camp, I estimated my own chances at about one in twenty. But I also told them that, in spite of this, I had no intention of losing hope and giving up. For no man knew what the future would bring, much less the next hour. Even if we could not expect any sensational military events in the next few days, who knew better than we, with our experience of camps, how great chances sometimes opened up, quite suddenly, at least for the individual; For instance, one might be attached unexpectedly to a special group with exceptionally good working conditions—for this was the kind of thing which constituted the "luck" of the prisoner.

But I did not only talk of the future and the veil which was drawn over it. I also mentioned the past; all its joys, and how its light shown even in the present darkness. Again I quoted a poet—to avoid sounding like a preacher myself—who had written, *"Was Du erlebst, kann keine Macht der Welt Dir rauben."* (What you have experienced, no power on earth can take from you.) Not only our experiences, but all we have done, whatever great thoughts we may have had, and all we have suffered, all this is not lost, though it is past; we have brought it into being. Having been is also a kind of being, and perhaps the surest kind.

Then I spoke of the many opportunities of giving life a meaning. I told my comrades (who lay motionless, although occasionally a sigh could be heard) that human life, under any circumstances, never ceases to have a meaning, and that this infinite meaning of life includes suffering and dying, privation and death. I asked the poor creatures who listened to me attentively in the darkness of the hut to face up to the seriousness of our position. They must not lose hope but should keep their courage in the certainty that the hopelessness of our struggle did not detract from its dignity and its meaning. I said that someone looks down on each of us in difficult hours—a friend, a wife, somebody alive or dead, or a God—and he would not expect us to disappoint him. He would hope to find us suffering proudly—not miserably—knowing how to die.

And finally I spoke of our sacrifice, which had meaning in every case. It was in the nature of this sacrifice that it should appear to be pointless in the normal world, the world of material success. But in reality our sacrifice did have a meaning. Those of us who had any religious faith, I said frankly, could understand without difficulty. I told them of a comrade who on his arrival in camp had tried to make a pact with Heaven that his suffering and death should save the human being he loved from a painful end. For this man, suffering and death were meaningful; his was a sacrifice of the deepest significance. He did not want to die for nothing. None of us wanted that.

Chapter VIII: Freedom

The purpose of my words was to find a full meaning in our life, then and there, in that hut and in that practically hopeless situation. I saw that my efforts had been successful. When the electric bulb flared up again, I saw the miserable figures of my friends limping toward me to thank me with tears in their eyes. But I have to confess here that only too rarely had I the inner strength to make contact with my companions in suffering and that I must have missed many opportunities for doing so.

Freedom and Inner Strength

Rollo May

I. What Freedom Is

Freedom is man's capacity to take a hand in his own development. It is our capacity to mold ourselves. Freedom is the other side of consciousness of self: if we were not able to be aware of ourselves, we would be pushed along by instinct or the automatic march of history, like bees or mastodons. But by our power to be conscious of ourselves, we can call to mind how we acted yesterday or last month, and by learning from these actions we can influence, even if ever so little, how we act today. And we can picture in imagination some situation tomorrow—say a dinner date, or an appointment for a job, or a Board of Directors meeting and by turning over in fantasy different alternatives for acting, we can pick the one which will do best for us. . . .

As the person gains more consciousness of self, his range of choice and his freedom proportionately increase. Freedom is cumulative; one choice made with an element of freedom makes greater freedom possible for the next choice. Each exercise of freedom enlarges the circumference of the circle of one's self.

We do not mean to imply that there are not an infinite number of deterministic influences in anyone's life. If you wished to argue that we are determined by our bodies, by our economic situation, by the fact that we happened to be born into the twentieth-century in America, and so on, I would agree with you; and I would add many more ways in which we are psychologically determined, particularly by tendencies of which we are unconscious. But no matter how much one argues for the deterministic viewpoint, he still must grant that there is a *margin in which the alive human being can be aware of what is determining him*. And even if only in a very minute way to begin with, he can have some say in how he will react to the deterministic factors.

Freedom is thus shown in how we relate to the deterministic realities of life. If you set out to write a sonnet, you run up against all kinds of recalcitrant realities in the laws of rhyme and scanning, and in the necessity of fitting words together; or if you build a house, you confront all kinds of determining elements in bricks and mortar and lumber. It is essential that you know your material and accept its limits. But *what* you say in the sonnet, as Alfred Adler used to emphasize, is uniquely yours. The pattern and the style in which you build your house are products of how you, with an element of freedom, use the reality of the given materials.

The arguments of "freedom *versus* determinism" are on a false basis, just as it is false to think of freedom as a kind of isolated electric button called "free will." Freedom is shown in according one's life with realities—realities as simple as the needs for rest and food, or as ultimate as death. Meister Eckhart expressed this approach to freedom in one of his astute psychological counsels, "When you are thwarted, it is your own attitude that is out of order." Freedom is involved when we accept the realities not by blind necessity but by choice. This means that the acceptance of limitations need not at all be a "giving up," but can and should be a constructive act of freedom; and it may well be that such a choice will have more creative results for the person than if he had not had to struggle against any limitation whatever. The man who is devoted to freedom does not waste time fighting reality; instead, as Kierkegaard remarked, he "extols reality."

Let us take as an illustration a situation in which people are very much controlled, namely when they are sick with a disease like tuberculosis. In almost every action they are rigidly conditioned by the facts that they are in a sanatorium under a strict regime, have to rest such and such time, can walk only fifteen minutes a day, and so on. But there is all the difference in the world in how persons relate to the reality of the disease. Some give up, and literally invite their own deaths. Others do what they are supposed to do, but they continually resent the fact that "nature" or "God" has given them such a disease and though they outwardly obey they inwardly rebel against the rules. These patients generally won't die, but neither do they get well. Like rebels in any area in life, they remain on a plateau perpetually marking time.

Other patients, however, frankly confront the fact that they are very seriously ill; they let this tragic fact sink into consciousness through plentiful hours of contemplation as they lie in beds on the sanatorium porch. They seek in their consciousness of self to understand what was wrong in their lives beforehand that they should have succumbed to the illness. They use the cruelly deterministic fact of being sick as an avenue to new self-knowledge. These are the patients who can best choose and affirm the methods and the self-discipline—which never can be put into rules, but vary from day to day—which will bring them victoriously through the disease. They are the ones who not only achieve physical health, but who also are ultimately enlarged, enriched and strengthened by the experience of having had the disease. They affirm their elemental freedom to know and to mold deterministic events; they meet a severely deterministic fact with freedom. It is doubtful whether anyone really achieves health who does not responsibly choose to be healthy, and whoever does so choose becomes more integrated as a person by virtue of having had a disease.

Through his power to survey his life, man can transcend the immediate events which determine him. Whether he has tuberculosis or is a slave like the Roman philosopher Epictetus or a prisoner condemned to death, he can still in his freedom choose how he will relate to these facts. And how he relates to a merciless realistic fact like death can be more important for him than the fact of death itself. Freedom is most dramatically illustrated in the "heroic" actions, like Socrates' decision to drink the hemlock rather than compromise; but even more significant is the undramatic, steady day-to-day exercise of freedom on the part of any person developing toward psychological and spiritual integration in a distraught society like our own.

Thus freedom is not just the matter of saying "Yes" or "No" to a specific decision: it is the power to mold and create ourselves. Freedom is the capacity, to use Nietzsche's phrase, "to become what we truly are."

II. What Freedom Is Not

We can understand more clearly what freedom is if we first look at what it is not. Freedom is not rebellion. Rebellion is a normal *interim* move toward freedom: it occurs to some extent when the little child is trying to exercise his muscles of independence through the power to say "No"; it occurs more clearly when the adolescent is trying to become independent of parents. In adolescence (as possibly in other stages too) the strength of the rebelliousness against what the parents stand for is often excessive because the young person is fighting his own anxiety at stepping out into the world. When parents say "Don't" he often must scream defiance at them, because that "don't" is exactly what he feels the craven side of himself is saying, the side of himself which is tempted to take refuge behind the walls of parental protection.

But rebellion is often confused with freedom itself. It becomes a false port in the storm because it gives the rebel a delusive sense of being really independent. The rebel forgets that rebellion always presupposes an outside structure—of rules, laws, expectations—against which one is rebelling; and one's security, sense of freedom and strength are dependent actually on this external structure. They are "borrowed," and can be taken away like a bank loan which can be called in at any moment. Psychologically many persons stop at this stage of rebellion. Their sense of inner moral strength comes only from knowing what moral conventions they do not live up to. . . .

Since the rebel gets his sense of direction and vitality from attacking the existing standards and mores, he does not have to develop standards of his own. Rebellion acts as a substitute for the more difficult process of struggling through to one's own autonomy, to new beliefs, to the state where one can lay new foundations on which to build. The negative forms of freedom confused freedom with license, and overlooked the fact that freedom is never the opposite to responsibility.

Another common error is to confuse freedom with *planlessness*. Some writers these days argue that if the system of economic laissez-faire—"letting everyone do as he wishes"—were altered as history marches on, our freedom would vanish with it. The argument of these authors often goes something like this: "Freedom is like a living thing. It is indivisible. And if the individual's right to own the means of production is taken away, he no longer has the freedom to earn his living in his own way. Then he can have no freedom at all."

Well, if these writers were right it would indeed be unfortunate—for who then could be free? Not you nor I nor anyone else except a very small group of persons—for in this day of giant industries, only the minutest fraction of citizens can own the means of production anyway. Laissez-faire was a great idea, as we have seen, in earlier centuries: but times change, and almost everyone nowadays earns his living by virtue of belonging to a large group, be it an industry, or a university, or a labor union. It is a vastly more interdependent world, this "one world" of our twentieth century, than the world of the entrepreneurs of earlier centuries or of our own pioneer days; and freedom must be found in the context of economic community and the social value of work, not in everyone's setting up his own factory or university. . . .

I have often wondered why there is such anxiety and such an outcry that freedom will be lost unless we preserve the old laissez-faire practices. Is not one of the reasons the fact that modern man has so thoroughly surrendered *inward* psychological and spiritual freedom to the routine of his work and to the mass patterns of social conventions that he feels the only vestige of freedom left to him is the opportunity for economic aggrandizement? Has he made the freedom to compete with his neighbor economically a last remnant of individuality, which therefore must stand for the whole meaning of freedom? That is to say, if the citizen of the suburbs could not buy a new car each year, build a bigger house, and paint it a slightly different color from his neighbor's, might he feel that his life would have no purpose, and that he would not exist as a person? The great weight placed on competitive, laissez-faire freedom seems to me to show how much we have lost a real understanding of freedom. . . .

This [essay] . . . is on psychology rather than economics or sociology; and we touch on the larger picture only because man always lives in a social world, and that world conditions his psychological health. We simply propose that our social and economic ideal be *that society which gives the maximum opportunity for each person in it to realize himself, to develop and use his potentialities and to labor as a human being of dignity giving to and receiving from his fellow men*. The good society is, thus, the one which gives the greatest freedom to its people—freedom defined not negatively and defensively, but positively, as the opportunity to realize ever greater human values. It follows that collectivism, as in fascism and communism, is the denial of these values, and must be opposed at all costs. But we shall successfully overcome them only as we are devoted to positive ideals which are better, chiefly the building of a society based on a genuine respect for persons and their freedom.

III. "Choosing One's Self"

Freedom does not come automatically; it is achieved. And it is not gained at a single bound; it must be achieved each day. As Goethe forcefully expresses the ultimate lesson learned by Faust:

> "Yes! to this thought I hold with firm persistence;
> The last result of wisdom stamps it true:
> *He only earns his freedom and existence*
> *Who daily conquers them anew.*"

The basic step in achieving inward freedom is "choosing one's self." This strange-sounding phrase of Kierkegaard's means to affirm one's responsibility for one's self and one's existence. It is the attitude which is opposite to blind momentum or routine existence: it is an attitude of aliveness and decisiveness; it means that one recognizes that he exists in his particular spot in the universe, and he accepts the responsibility for this existence. This is what Nietzsche meant by the "will to live"—not simply the instinct for self-preservation, but the will to accept the fact that one is one's self, and to accept responsibility for fulfilling one's own destiny, which in turn implies accepting the fact that one must make his basic choices himself.

We can see more clearly what choosing one's self and one's existence means by looking at the opposite—choosing not to exist, that is to commit suicide. The significance of suicide lies not in the fact that people actually kill themselves in any large numbers. It is indeed a very rare occurrence except among psychotics. But psychologically and spiritually the thought of suicide has a much wider meaning. There is such a thing as psychological suicide in which one does not take his own life by a given act, but dies because he has chosen—perhaps without being entirely aware of it—not to live. Not infrequently one hears of incidents like that in the disaster not long ago of a sinking fishing boat. A young man in his twenties clung in the choppy waters to a floating timber with an older man for an hour or so, and talked to the older man about how he felt too young to die. Finally, with the words, "I'm finished; good-bye, Pop," he let go of the timber and sank. Of course we do not know the inner psychological processes in the fact that a person, apparently with some strength left, seems to give up and die; but it is a fair guess that some inner tendency not to choose to live is in operation.

Another illustration is in the lives of persons who have dedicated themselves to certain tasks, such as taking care of a sick loved one or finishing an important work. They keep going under difficult circumstances as though they had determined they "had" to live; and then when the task is completed, when "success" is attained, they proceed to die as though by some inner decision. Kierkegaard wrote twenty books in fourteen years, completed them at the early age of forty-two, and then—we almost say "in conclusion"—he took to his bed and died.

These ways of choosing not to live show how crucial it can be to choose to live. It is doubtful whether anyone really begins to live, that is, to affirm and choose his own existence, until he has frankly confronted the terrifying fact that he could wipe out his existence but *chooses* not to. Since one is free to die, he is free also to live. The mass patterns of routine are broken: he no longer exists as an accidental result of his parents having conceived him, of his growing up and living as an infinitesimal item on the treadmill of cause-and-effect, marrying, begetting new children, growing old and dying. Since he could have chosen to die but chose not to, every act thereafter has to some extent been made possible because of that choice. Every act then has its special element of freedom.

People often actually go through the experience of committing psychological suicide in some sector of their lives. We shall present two illustrations which we hope will make the basic point clear. A woman believes she cannot live unless a certain man loves her. When he marries someone else, she contemplates suicide. In the course of her meditating on the idea for some days, she fantasies, "Well, assume I did do it." But then she suddenly thinks, "After I've done it, it would still be good to be alive in other ways—the sun still shines, water is still cool to the body, one can still make things," and the suggestion creeps in that there may still be other people to love. So she decides to live. Assuming the decision is made for positive reasons rather than just the fear of dying or inertia, the conflict may actually have given her some new freedom. It is as though the part of her which clung to the man did commit suicide, and as a result she can begin life anew. This is the increased aliveness Edna St. Vincent Millay describes in "Renascence":

> Ah, up from the ground sprang I
> And hailed the earth with such a cry
> As is not heard save from a man
> Who has been dead, and lives again.[*]

Or a young man feels he can never be happy unless he gains some fame. He begins to realize that he is competent and valuable, let us say as an assistant professor; but the higher he gets on the ladder the clearer he sees that there are always persons above him, that "many are called but few are chosen," that very few people gain fame anyway, and that he may end up just a good and competent teacher. He might then feel that he would be as insignificant as a grain of sand, his life meaningless, and he might as well not be alive. The idea of suicide creeps into his mind in his more

---

[*] Lines from "Renascence" in *Renascence and Other Poems*. Published by Harper & Brothers. Copyright 1912, 1940 by Edna St. Vincent Millay.

despondent moods. Sooner or later he, too, thinks, "All right, assume I've done it—what then?" And it suddenly dawns on him that, if he came back after the suicide, there would be a lot left in life even if one were not famous. He then chooses to go on living, as it were, without the demand for fame. It is as though the part of him which could not live without fame does commit suicide. And in killing the demand for fame, he may also realize as a by-product that the things which yield lasting joy and inner security have very little to do with the external and fickle standards of public opinion anyway. He may then appreciate the more than flippant wisdom in Ernest Hemingway's remark, "Who the hell wants fame over the week-end? I want to write well." And finally, as a result of the partial suicide, he may clarify his own goals and arrive at more of a feeling for the joy which comes from fulfilling his own potentialities, from finding and teaching the truth as he sees it and adding his own unique contribution arising from his own integrity rather than the servitude to fame.

We would emphasize again that the actual process of these partial psychological suicides is much more complex than these illustrations imply: Actually some people—perhaps most people—move in the opposite direction when they have to renounce a demand: they retreat, constrict their lives and become less free. But we wish only to make clear that there is a positive aspect to partial suicide, and that the dying of one attitude or need may be the other side of the birth of something new (which is a law of growth in nature not at all limited to human beings). One can choose to kill a neurotic strategy, a dependency, a clinging, and then find that he can choose to live as a freer self. The woman in our example would no doubt find with clearer insight that her so-called love for the man for whom she would have committed suicide was really not love at all, but clinging parasitism balanced by desire to have power over the man. A "dying" to part of one's self is often followed by a heightened awareness of life, a heightened sense of possibility.

When one has consciously chosen to live, two other things happen. First, his responsibility for himself takes on a new meaning. He accepts responsibility for his own life not as something with which he has been saddled, a burden forced upon him: but as a something he has chosen himself. For this person, himself, now exists as a result of a decision he himself has made. To be sure, any thinking person realizes in theory that freedom and responsibility go together; if one is not free, one is an automaton and there is obviously no such thing as responsibility, and if one cannot be responsible for himself, he can't be trusted with freedom.

But when one has "chosen himself," this partnership of freedom and responsibility becomes more than a nice idea: he experiences it on his own pulse; in his choosing himself, he becomes aware that he has chosen personal freedom and responsibility for himself in the same breath.

The other thing which happens is that discipline from the outside is changed into *self-discipline*. He accepts discipline not because it is commanded—for who can command someone who has been free to take his own life?—but because he has chosen with greater freedom what he wants to do with his own life, and discipline is necessary for the sake of the values he wishes to achieve. This self-discipline can be given fancy names—Nietzsche called it "loving one's fate" and Spinoza spoke of obedience to the laws of life. But whether, bedecked by fancy terms or not, it is, I believe, a lesson everyone progressively learns in his struggle toward maturity.

Chapter IX: Immortality

The topic of this section calls upon us to consider the following question: "What does it mean to be mortal?" A reflective examination of this question gives us insight into the human condition—about the way we are in this world. To be human means to be time-bound and death-bound. Human mortality is a condition of limitation. Is it possible to be freed from limitation? Can I escape my mortality? Can I triumph over death?

Many find Daniel Kolak's story, "The Wine Is in the Glass," disturbing because people don't just die unexpectedly in "safe" situations. In the narrative a man dies in a restaurant waiting for his dinner—his wine was still in the glass. The man's death is sudden. Even as others inquire whether the man needs help, Kolak (as narrator) brings the finality of the man's death home to the reader with the blunt statement, "He can't answer, he is dead."

Recently, I learned that an undergraduate philosophy student died instantly in an automobile accident. The tragedy occurred when an oncoming car swerved into the young coed's lane because the driver sneezed and lost control of the vehicle. The young woman's life was snuffed out in the space of a sneeze. Life is fragile and the above stories, one fiction and one fact, disclose the hard truth that tomorrow is promised to no one. Only while we are alive can we answer and our lives ultimately give an answer to the deep questions for the soul.

In "The Law of the Spirits," Valerie Hansen presents a Chinese view about the dead that has its roots in a long tradition of belief. According to Hansen,

> The majority of the dead, it was thought, went to an underworld. There they retained the power to influence events on earth. If they wanted to hurt the living, they could play tricks, cause illness, provoke misfortune, or even bring death. Some of the deceased performed miracles and came to be worshipped as gods.

This selection goes on to explain how the living used the law of the spirits to protect themselves from the dead.

Wang Chong's essay, "A Treatise on Death," attempts to refute the deeply embedded Chinese views about the dead that we examined in the preceding selection. "Let us try to prove," he says, "by means of the species of creatures that the dead do not become spiritual beings, do not possess consciousness, and cannot hurt people." By way of a series of arguments Wang Chong argues that the body decays and returns to dust and that the vital forces carried by the blood become exhausted. At the moment of death, the vital forces (i.e., soul) are extinct. He leaves the reader with the rhetorical question, "What is there to become a spiritual being?"

John Hospers argues that the notion of disembodied existence makes no sense. All attempts to speak about, or even imagine, a disembodied existence involves the language of bodies. Hospers puts it this way, "There is a whole web of meaning-connections between perceiving and having a body; when we try to break all the connections we appear to be reduced to unintelligibility."

Plato's "Phaedo" is a companion dialogue to the "Apology." In the closing pages of the "Apology" the philosopher Socrates reflects that death is one of two things—"either death is a state of nothingness and utter unconsciousness, or, as men say, there is a change and migration of the soul from this world to another." From this initial disjunctive position, Socrates gives us a framework in which to think about the problems of death and immortality. The conversations in "Phaedo" take place in Socrates' prison cell on the day of his execution. His students come to visit their teacher one last time and the philosophical discussions revolve around proofs for the soul's immortality. Since death is the final separation of the soul from the body, "Phaedo" presents a series of arguments to show that "the soul resembles the divine and, the body the mortal." Plato's "Knowledge Is Recollection," which appears in Chapter III of this volume, presents an additional argument for immortality based on the soul's pre-existence.

Epicurus' philosophy is primarily concerned with living a good life; a happy life. He equates happiness with pleasure. However, pleasure for Epicurus is not the immediate pleasure of the senses, but the lasting pleasures of the mind. The goal in Epicurus' thought is to attain freedom from pain in both the body and the mind (a tranquil state that the Greeks called *ataraxia*). A rational understanding of reality, according to Epicurus' teachings, would free the mind from fear of the gods and fear of death. Epicurus adopts the materialistic metaphysics of Democritus and attempts to show that life and death are mutually exclusive. Epicurus explains his position this way, "so long as we exist death is not with us; but when death comes, then we do not exist." Since the individual and death never meet, the exhortation is clear—do not fear death!

Through faithful devotion to Amitabha, the Buddha, and through recitation of his name, one can be reborn in the western paradise—the pure land. "This world Sukhavati, which is the world system of the lord Amitabha, is rich and prosperous, comfortable, fertile, delightful and crowded with many Gods and men." The Sandskrit term, "Sukhavati," literally means "the blissful." It is called the "Happy Land." Pure Land Buddhism is part of the Mahayana tradition and its devotees live blissfully in the western paradise until entering final nirvana.

The passages from *I Corinthians 15* and *I Thessalonians 4* contain the fullest exposition of death, resurrection and immortality in the New Testament. These accounts provide ways to overcome the objections voiced by Wang Chong and John Hospers. Contrary to much Christian teaching the New Testament does not teach that the soul is immortal nor does it talk about a disembodied existence. The Christian view teaches the resurrection of the dead. The various resurrections of the dead are all future events and will occur with the coming of Christ. (After all, why would there be a need for resurrections *if* the dead go immediately to heaven?) Until the time of the resurrection, the dead remain dead—the physical body decomposes and the soul is exhausted. The New Testament teaches that the dead will be resurrected with spiritual bodies at some time in the future. The life of that new body will be spirit, not soul. Soul is the life of the physical body and as the Hebrew scripture in the book of Leviticus teaches, this life is in the blood. Eternal life, biblically, is the life of God whose nature is spirit. The hope for humankind resides in Christ who was made unto men and women a life quickening spirit. A careful reading of the text makes it clear that eternal life is a spiritual reality. "Flesh and blood," in verse 50, is a figure of speech, *synecdoche*, for the mortal human being of body and soul. The teaching is clear: "flesh and blood cannot inherit the kingdom of heaven."

The Wine Is in the Glass

Daniel Kolak

In this short story a man sits alone in a restaurant. While waiting for his food to arrive, he ruminates.

The wine is in the glass.

There is a man looking at the wine, thinking: there is wine in the glass and it is true that there is wine in the glass. I am the man looking at the glass, thinking: what is in the man, in me?

The man picks up the glass, raises the rim to his lips, purses his lips and, slowly, takes a sip. He swallows. He puts the glass back down onto the table.

There is now a little less wine in the glass. But now there is a little wine in the man, who thinks: the wine is still wine, it is in me. Soon it will change from wine to blood. It will become me. The wine becomes my blood. He smiles, and thinks: I don't know how to turn blood into wine but I know how to turn wine into blood. Actually, I don't. I couldn't do it outside me. Inside me, I just do it. Automatically. Without effort or thought. This is not a miracle. This is digestion. He burps (quietly, under his breath, to himself).

There are creases in the white tablecloth. He straightens them and wonders why, what the significance of it is. He concludes there is no significance. To the act of removing creases from a tablecloth, that is. Why, then, did he do it? He doesn't know. But he cares that he doesn't know. And, it bothers him that he cares. It also bothers him, now that he has reflected upon it, that he can't quite remove the creases. They have been ironed in. It wouldn't take much to do the ironing right. Whoever was ironing the tablecloth was in a hurry, or perhaps careless. If whoever ironed the tablecloth had been more attentive to the tablecloth now he, an ordinary man in a rather expensive restaurant passing time with ordinary thoughts while waiting to order his hopefully extraordinary dinner, would not be trying to straighten out the creases and thinking about it and also at the same time wondering why he was thinking about an inconsequential crease in an inconsequential tablecloth. He would be doing something else, thinking about something else or maybe not thinking about anything.

The man smiles to himself. To acknowledge that it is only to himself that he smiled he lowers his eyes to the crease on the tablecloth and shakes his head a little just in case anyone else is looking. Why did he do that? He does not know anybody in this restaurant. Nobody knows him. What does he care? But he does. How strange, he thinks, that he should be so self-conscious. He glances around the restaurant. No one is looking at him. Back to the crease in the tablecloth. Then to the wine in the glass. His image is in the wine.

The waiter, who noticed the man looking, rushes over.

"Ready to order, sir?"

"I'll have the blackened grouper."

"Baked potato or cottage fries?"

"What are cottage fries? Never mind. Baked potato."

"Like chips. Sliced."

"I'll have the baked."

"Salad or cole slaw?"

"Cole slaw. No. Make that salad."

"What kind of dressing would you like, sir?"

"What have you got?"

"We've got—"

"Italian?"

"Is creamy all right?"

"You don't have, ah, regular?"

"Our house is vinaigrette."

"Oh."

"Would you like that?"

"Fine."

The man stares at his image staring back at him from the wine in the glass while the waiter rushes off toward the kitchen. The man picks up the glass and then, changing his mind, puts it back down. His image stares back at him. He forgot to ask about bread. He would like some bread with his wine before the salad comes. He looks up but the waiter is gone.

The man thinks: what should I think about? I am by myself in a restaurant waiting for my food and I have time to think. But there is nothing in particular he wants to think about. Yet he feels anxious—only slightly—feeling as if he wants something only he doesn't quite know what. The food, ordered, would be coming. He would eat it and enjoy it and then walk to his car and drive home. Laughing (to himself) he shakes his head again. Why is he anticipating going home after the restaurant? Where else but home would he go? Translucent and dim little pictures flash through his consciousness, superimposed over his field of vision but so very dimly that he knows it is too much to think of them as actual pictures. They are like shadows of pictures. A bit like interference from another channel on a television set, only dimmer. The future, perhaps, inter-fearing with the present? He laughs at the pun. Inter-fearing. A possible future, perhaps. How strange, he thinks, that such thoughts run through his head. Thoughts paying attention to thoughts (inter-fearing with themselves) and thinking about why this is happening and then remarking—to whom, themselves?—that they are aware of what they (the thoughts) are doing—

The waiter comes with the salad and, the man is glad to see, a basket with fresh-baked bread. He remembers the time his girlfriend brought a basket, similar to this one, from Mexico as a present for his parents and there had been, hidden in it, some tiny eggs that had hatched into bugs. They discovered the bugs because the freshly hatched bugs made strange noises inside the wicker and so they put it out on the balcony in the snow. The bugs died. They threw the basket away anyway, just in case there were some eggs left in the basket.

"Here you go, sir."

"Is that baked here?"

"No, sir." The waiter takes the wine from the cooler and fills the glass. "We get it. Enjoy."

"Thank you."

The crust is nice and thick, dark, and the bread is still warm. The butter is whipped. The man breaks off a piece of bread, butters it, takes several bites. While still chewing he lifts the glass to his lips and soaks the bread and butter in his mouth with the wine.

"Mmmmm," he says aloud, but softly, only to himself.

The wine is very white and very dry and the tartness of it is delicious with the sweetness of the butter and the saltiness of the rich, whole-wheat bread.

His thoughts are just running now, he is not paying attention to them—so that if someone interrupted him right now and asked, "What are you thinking about?" the man would more than likely look up, surprised, and say, with a full mouth, "Hm?" then quickly swallow and add, "Oh, I don't know. I was daydreaming," and he probably couldn't say what he was daydreaming about. But he was daydreaming about his girlfriend.

The salad is a bit soggy, he thinks, but very good. Very green. He thinks: I am turning food into thought, and then, thinks: why am I thinking about turning food into thought (into myself)? Is that what is happening? Is that what digestion is—turning food into thought and, among other things, into things like fingernails, liver cells, and blood? How do you get thoughts out of wine and bread?

Now, if something else were happening—say, a beautiful woman had walked into the restaurant, alone, and had sat within eyesight—he would be involved in this something else, whatever it would have happened to be. He would not be thinking about his own thoughts and the puzzling question of why he is thinking about his own thoughts. Rather, he would be looking, admiring her, undressing her in his mind, wondering what it would be like to do something sexual and preferably obscene with her— What a thought, he thought, while chewing on your salad! There is not even a suitable woman around who fits appropriately into his (only remotely realized) fantasy. An elderly couple sits several tables away and anyway the old woman has her back to him. Not very suitable. But perhaps they have a daughter. He begins laughing, until suddenly a piece of salad goes down the wrong way and he chokes. It is a big piece, too big, he knows (even though this is the one thing his mother had never particularly nagged him about) he didn't chew it properly, and he thinks: I just inhaled salad! What if I die?

Unable to breathe, he takes several gulps of wine to try and wash the green leaf down but it doesn't go down either, he can't even get the wine into his throat. It dribbles, rejected, down his chin. The salad gets lodged even deeper. Gasping loudly now, he tries hitting himself on the back but this only makes him panic more. Nothing is working. He sees the elderly couple looking.

The old man asks, "You all right?"

Like a fool (he thinks this to himself—"What a fool I am for nodding"), he nods. But he is not all right, he can't talk or breathe and his heart is pounding. He will pass out (he thinks, and his thinking is correct) if he doesn't get some oxygen soon.

The old man stands up, his napkin in his wrinkled hands held over his lap like a loin cloth. "Help? Some help? Do you need help?"

The old woman brings her scrunched napkin to her mouth, covering the lower part of her face like a veil. "What's the matter? Are you choking?"

Veils? Loin cloths? Why am I thinking like this, in analogies, he wonders? I might be dying!

The waiter does not hear the noise, he is in the kitchen on the telephone, taking a reservation.

"I say, are you all right?" shouts the old man.

He can't answer, he is dead. (You think this is too sudden. People don't just die like that. But maybe a piece of plaque got loose in the arteries around his heart. Or maybe you just don't like it when the hero of the story dies. But this guy was not a hero. He was just an ordinary guy in a restaurant thinking about his thoughts when the salad did him in. You don't even know his name or what he does [used to do] for a living or anything.)

The wine, undrunk, is in the glass. It is made from fermented grapes which (before they are crushed) grow in vineyards where seeds feed on water and sunlight and earth and whatever else seeds can use to turn earth into fruit—for instance corpses like the one the man has just become. (Look, even if it would have taken a little longer, what's the difference?) Soon, waiters (who are not called "waiters") dressed in black (just like the waiter in the kitchen who has just gotten off the phone but will be back on the phone shortly, only blacker) will deliver the man—with a pompous ceremony even more formal than the one that would have delivered the blackened grouper (and which now the cook will himself gladly eat)—to the seeds and animals none of whom has ever paid a bill. The bill for this future ceremony (with music, there will be very sad ethnic music from the Mediterranean region, the man himself specified it), gratuities included, has been paid, well in advance, by the man who will soon be (if he isn't already) in the coffin. To be served, like the white wine in the glass, well chilled.

At home on the man's desk lies a letter the man had composed but not yet sent to his girlfriend:

> I want to make love to you. I want to touch you so that I can feel the texture of what you are. I want my feeling you to make you feel. The feeling of feeling you is the feeling of ecstasy. I want to make you stop, then go. Then stop, then go. To get so close that the dizzyness of the distance between us becomes a whirlpool of madness, danger, desire. When I look without looking I see my seeing and there you are: a mystery that moves. Into you I ascend into myself and forget that I too am no one. The veil of the world is the veil between us. Soft and transparent and warm like gauze. To love you is to be wounded. Sorrow is the joy of knowing the unknown. I don't want a looking-back but a looking-at: I want to know you now or not at all. Now is the place for knowing, touching, feeling, seeing. Now is now. My now is yours, forever.

Nice letter. Really, he was quite an extraordinary man. Oh, well. I could go on. But what would be the point? The man is dead.

The Law of the Spirits

Valerie Hansen

In traditional China, as in most cultures, there was some uncertainty about what happened after death. Some Buddhist sects promised rebirth in a paradise, and Daoism, immortality to a chosen few. **Still, the majority of the dead, it was thought, went to an underworld. There they retained the power to influence events on earth. If they wanted to hurt the living, they could play tricks, cause illness, provoke misfortune, or even bring death.** Some of the deceased performed miracles and came to be worshiped as gods. The Chinese feared the dead, but they believed that they adhered to their own laws. The three readings below from the eleventh and twelfth centuries show how the living used the law of the spirits to protect themselves from the dangers that the dead posed.

The first document is a model tomb contract from *The New Book of Earth Patterns* (*Dili xinshu*), a government manual for siting graves initially published in 1071. Starting in the first century C.E., if not earlier, and continuing through to the twentieth century, some Chinese buried tomb contracts with the dead. Mimicking this-worldly contracts for the purchase of land, these contracts recorded the purchase of a grave plot from the earth gods. Tomb contracts were intended to ward off the dangers that resulted from penetrating deep into the earth to dig a grave. The practice seems to have peaked in the Song dynasty (960–1279), when the government paid for such contracts to be drawn up on behalf of dead officials. Just after the Song had fallen, Zhou Mi (1232–1298) said: "Today when people make tombs they always use a certificate to buy land, made out of catalpa wood, on which they write in red, saying: 'Using 99,999 strings of cash, we buy a certain plot, and so forth'" (Zhou Mi, *Guixin zashi* [Xuejin taoyuan edition], bieji xia 7a–b). Nine was an auspicious number, hence the figure 99,999. The money in these contracts was not real money, but spirit money (facsimiles of real money) that could be burnt. Not all contracts were written on catalpa wood. Hundreds of lead and stone tomb contracts have been excavated, and presumably more were written on cheaper materials, like paper or wood, that have since decayed.

The New Book of Earth Patterns was written at imperial order by a team of scholars, headed by Wang Zhu, who examined preexisting ritual manuals and then compiled this book. This manual was intended for official use, but commoners also consulted it, Wang Zhu tells us. In the section about tomb contracts, this book cites *The Spirit Code* (*Guilū*) to say that burial without using a tomb contract is tantamount to wrongful burial and very unlucky. The idea of a law code for spirits raises interesting issues: Why should spirits have a law code? Is it written down? What is its relation to human law? These questions are not easily answered, but the widespread use of tomb contracts reveals that many people believed (or hoped) that the spirits of the dead could be bound by contracts. The similarity of the contracts to this-worldly contracts also suggests that people thought the law of the spirits resembled earthly law.

Because *The New Book of Earth Patterns* spells out the many steps of an official funeral ritual, it describes the ritual context in which tomb contracts were used. The manual specifies that any official with the posthumous rank of lord or marquis and below (or any commoners paying for their own funerals) should have two iron contracts: one was to be placed in the temporary aboveground funeral structure and the other, buried in front of the coffin. Then a prayer was said. Once prayer was completed, the two copies of the contract were held together and the characters for agreement (*hetong*) were written on the seam where the two join. Borrowed from real life, this practice ensured that either the buyer or seller could check the authenticity of a contract by matching it with their copy to see if the characters met exactly. If they did, then the contract was authentic and the signatories were bound to honor it. If they did not, it was a forgery. At the end of the funeral, the participants took the iron contract in the temporary funeral structure and buried it in the ground. That was the gods' copy. The one at the foot of the coffin was for the master of the tomb, the dead official. He needed to have his copy with him in case he had a dispute in the underworld with the spirits of the dead about his ownership of his funeral plot.

The text of the model contract follows contemporary land contracts very closely. It gives the date of the transaction, here the date of the funeral, and the name of the buyer, the dead person, without naming the seller, the lord of the earth. As was true of land contracts, the dimensions of the plot are given in two ways: on a grid with the north-south and east-west axes, and by naming the neighbors, who were the animals who watched over the four directions. The price was the usual 99,999 strings of cash as well as five-colored paper offerings. The contract then specifies the consequences if the contract is violated: any spirits who return from the dead (read: to bother the deceased or his living kin) will be tied up and handed over to earl of the rivers. Like a land contract, the contract contains a clause saying it will take effect once the money and land have been exchanged, which in this case must mean when the paper money is burned at the funeral and the body interred. The contract ends with the names of the witnesses, who can serve as intermediaries should any disputes occur, and the names of the guarantors, who will make good the buyer's price should he or she fail to come up with the money. The mystical identities of the neighbors, witnesses, and guarantor mark this as a tomb contract. After the end of the contract comes an amendment specifically prohibiting the former occupants of the grave plot from approaching the dead. Only if they stay 10,000 *li* (a great distance) away can the deceased and his or her kin enjoy peace and good fortune. The contract ends by invoking the statutes and edicts of Nūqing, the emissary of the Five Emperors of the directions (north, south, east, west, and middle). These statutes and edicts are part of the spirit law code.

Of fifteen excavated contracts I have found that follow the model given in *The New Book of Earth Patterns*, eleven date to the Song. They show a surprising geographic range, which testifies to the wide circulation the manual enjoyed: to the west, from Xinjiang and Sichuan; to the north, from Shanxi and Shaanxi; in Central China, from Hebei, Henan, Hubei, and Anhui; and to the southeast, from Jiangsu, Zhejiang, Jiangxi, and Fujian. Most of these tombs contain lavish grave goods, suggesting the people who used this text were well-off.

The New Book of Earth Patterns does not explicitly mention the dangers the spirits of the dead pose to the newly dead or their living kin, but another text found in a tomb in Southeast China, in Jiangxi, does. The text is written on the eight-sided body of a cypress figure, which had a carved human head with ears, eyes, mouth, and nose. Dated 1090, the figure was found in the tomb of the eighth daughter of the Yi family, a woman from an important local family (according to her biography, which is only partially quoted in the excavation report). She was interred in a wood coffin enclosed in a stone coffin. With her were buried two pottery vases, a pottery figure, her biography carved on a stone plaque, porcelain plates, wooden combs, iron scissors, an iron knife, an iron stick, a copper mirror, a large ax, and some items of relatively high quality: a silver comb, two silver bracelets, and a pair of gold earrings. Clearly, this was an expensive burial.

This text presumes a different relationship with the spirits of the dead from that presumed in *The New Book of Earth Patterns*. Here there is no contract with the lord of the earth for the purchase of the grave. Instead a cedar figure is deputed by those who preside over the world of the dead to prevent any lawsuits against the dead woman's family. The text repeats the same phrases over and over in its list of who cannot be summoned or sued by those in the middle of the earth, that is, the spirits of the dead. It does not say what such a summons would result in, but presumably the people mentioned in the text—the dead woman's children, husband, siblings, family, and in-laws—would suffer some kind of misfortune or even death. Those in the middle of the earth also have the power to bring epidemics. And they can summon fields, silkworms, farm animals, and trees, and so cause havoc on people's farms. Because this text is designed to protect the dead and their descendants, its repetitious phrasing takes on the quality of an incantation. The cypress figure is the subterranean equivalent of a henchman whose job it is to prevent anyone from serving his mistress with a court summons.

The final text shows what happens when the underworld court issues a summons. It is an anecdote from a collection called *The Record of the Listener* (*Yijianzhi*). From 1157 to 1202 an official named Hong Mai transcribed thousands of strange and unusual tales. Many of these tales, like the one translated here, are about people who visit the netherworld and come back. The Chinese word for death, *si*, means both to faint and to lose consciousness; many people had unusual visions when they fainted, which they recounted on awakening. The events and miracles Hong Mai describes may defy belief, but these were the kind of stories circulating in twelfth-century China, and Hong Mai often, as here, gives the name of the person who told him the anecdote. This source, then, can provide insight into the beliefs of common people in the Song dynasty, people who could not afford elaborate burials like those specified in *The New Book of Earth Patterns* or like that of eighth woman in the Yi family.

The anecdote begins with the facts of the case: how the debtor Mr. Lin bribed the clerks in the local court to frame the lender, Registrar Xia. The one person willing to speak out on Registrar Xia's behalf is Liu Yuan Balang. In his eloquent refusal to be bought off by Mr. Lin's underlings, he raises the possibility of a court in the underworld where wrongs can be righted. Registrar Xia then dies, after instructing his sons to bury all the relevant documents concerning Mr. Lin's unpaid debt, because he plans to sue in the underworld court. A month later Mr. Lin's eight underlings die. And Liu Yuan Balang has a premonition that he is going to be summoned to testify. Because he is convinced of his innocence, he does not fear that he personally has to stand trial, so he assures his wife that he will return after two or three days. And he loses consciousness.

The narrative resumes when he wakes up. He has indeed been summoned to the netherworld court to serve as a witness. When Liu Yuan Balang arrives, he sees that Registrar Xia has succeeded in his suit against Mr. Lin's eight underlings, whose necks are encased in a wooden frame called a cangue. Liu's account reveals much about the workings of the netherworld court, which are similar but not identical to those of a human court; in this vision, the presiding official is the king of the netherworld, not an underworld district magistrate. As on earth, he is served by clerks, who keep records and guide the prisoners from place to place. On hearing Liu's account, he awards him an extra ten years of life.

The king sits in judgment on the dead, who await their appearances before him in a kind of purgatory that Liu visits on his way out. There Liu sees people who have committed various offenses. They tell him they "borrowed" money, rent, and possessions, but in fact they stole them with no intent to return the goods. Now that they are awaiting trial, they claim to have borrowed the items. Some ask for money. Others ask their family members for merits; this reflects the Buddhist belief that merits accrued by one person for doing good deeds can be transferred to another. The king urges Liu to tell the living about his court, and then the runner who has accompanied Liu asks for a bribe. The always righteous Liu refuses, and he wakes up in this world when the clerk in the netherworld pushes him to the ground. The proof that he did indeed journey to the netherworld is twofold: his false topknot lies dislodged on his pillow, and he lives for an extra decade past eighty. The story concludes with Hong Mai's explanation of how he heard it.

The central theme in this story is justice. Registrar Xia is unable to obtain justice in human courts, but, as Liu Yuan Balang suspects, the underworld does have a court where wrongs can be righted. Many accounts of visits to the netherworld survive, and many tell of bureaucratic incompetence, of clerks who summon someone with an identical or a similar name by mistake. These people are then allowed to return to life. Strikingly, no one is ever punished in the subterranean court for a crime he or she did not commit. What about the real villain, Mr. Lin? The account does not reveal his fate, and the reader knows only that Registrar Xia is able to sue the eight underlings. Mr. Lin may be punished after he dies when he is tried before the king. Or perhaps he has already been punished, but Liu simply does not see him because he was not party to the bribery attempt.

The story about Registrar Xia and Mr. Lin illustrates exactly what the people who used tomb contracts and the cedar figure feared. Registrar Xia may be dead, but he is still able to bring charges against the living in the underworld court. He causes not only the deaths of the eight underlings but also their continued suffering in the afterlife. Other spirits had the same power to sue in underworld courts. Digging a grave is dangerous: one could unwittingly antagonize the previous owners, who could claim title to the plot. That was why people used tomb contracts. That was not the only danger. Once someone went before the underworld court, a host of charges could be brought against the deceased and their descendants based on their previous conduct. It was in order to block those charges that the eighth woman of the Yi family buried the cypress figure in her tomb.

The legalistic vision of the afterlife so evident in these three readings is striking and suggests that they are products of people thoroughly familiar with the earthly legal system. The model tomb contract in *The New Book of Earth Patterns* is like a contract to purchase land. The cedar person is like a henchman hired to prevent the issuing of summonses. And Registrar Xia encounters a court in the netherworld very much like the one in the human world—except that justice is done there.

The model tomb contract is from Wang Zhu, *Dili xinshu* (Beijing library Jin edition), 14:13a. The text written on a cedar figure is from Peng Shifan and Tang Changpu, "Jiangxi faxian jizuo BeiSong jinian mu," *Wenwu* 5 (1980): 29. The tale from *The Record of the Listener* is from Hong Mai, *Yijian zhi* (Beijing: Zhonghua shuju, 1981), *zhiwu* 5:1086.

Further Reading

Valerie Hansen, *Changing Gods in Medieval China* (Princeton: Princeton University Press, 1990); Valerie Hansen, *Negotiating Daily Life in Traditional China: How Ordinary People Used Contracts, 600–1400* (New Haven: Yale University Press, 1995), where an earlier version of the translation below appears. I would like to thank Victor Mair, Liu Xinru, and Bao Weimin for their help with these translations, and the late Anna Seidel for her many insights into the netherworld system of justice.

A Model Tomb Contract from *The New Book of Earth Patterns*

Blank year, month, and day. An official of blank title, named blank, died on blank year, month, and day. We have prognosticated and found this auspicious site, which is suitable for the grave, in this plain, in this district, in this county, and in this prefecture. We use 99,999 strings of cash as well as five-colored offerings of good faith to buy this plot of land. To the east and west, it measures so many steps, to the south and north, it measures so many steps. To the east is the green dragon's land, to the west the white tiger's, to the south the vermillion sparrow's, and to the north the dark warrior's.

The four borders are controlled by the imperial guard. The deputy of the grave mound and the earl of the tomb sealed it off by pacing the borders and the thoroughfares; the generals made orderly the paths through the fields so that for one thousand autumns and ten thousand years no spirit will return from the dead. If any dare to contravene, then the generals and neighborhood heads are ordered to tie them up and hand them to the earl of the rivers.

We have prepared meat, wine, preserved fruits, and a hundred types of sacrificial food. All these things constitute a contract of our sincerity.

When the money and land have been exchanged, the order will be given to the workers and carpenters to construct the tomb. After the deceased is peacefully buried, this will forever guarantee eternal good fortune.

The witness represents the years and months. The guarantor is the direct emissary of this day.

Bad ethers and heterodox spirits are not allowed to trespass. Those formerly living in the residence of the deceased must forever stay 10,000 *li* away. If any violate this contract, the main clerks of the earth government will be personally responsible for punishing them. The master of the tomb, and all his own kin and in-laws, whether living or dead, will enjoy peace and good fortune. Hastily, hastily, in accordance with the statutes and edicts of the emissary of the Five Directional Emperors, Nüqing.

A Text Written on a Cypress Figure

On the twenty-second day of the sixth month of the fifth year of the Yuanyou reign (1090), Teacher Qiao Dongbao of the western region association of the Five-Willow District, Pengze County, Jiang Prefecture, died and the grave of his late wife, the eighth woman of the Yi family, was relocated. The elders of the Haoli death precinct by Mount Tai, the envoy of the Celestial Emperor, and the emissary of the First Emperor's True Law, aware that the spirits disturbed by the relocation of the grave might call the living, issued an enlightened decree that one cedar person should cut off all summons and suits from the middle of the Earth.

If the eighth woman's sons and daughters are summoned, the cypress person should block the summons. If Teacher is summoned by name, the cypress person should block the summons. If her family is summoned, the cypress person should block the summons. If the siblings are summoned, the cypress person should block the summons. If the in-laws are summoned to testify, the cypress person should block the summons. If pestilence and plague are summoned, the cypress person should block the summons. If the fields or silkworms or the six domestic animals—horses, cattle, sheep, chickens, dogs, and pigs—are summoned, the cypress person should block the summons. If the first and second trees are summoned, the cypress person should block the summons. If the summoning does not end, the cypress person should block the summons. Quickly, quickly in accordance with the statutes and edicts.

A Tale from *The Record of the Listener*

Registrar Xia of Ningbo and the wealthy Mr. Lin together bought a concession to sell wine in a government store. They sold the wine wholesale to other stores, who paid their share depending on how much wine they sold. After many years, Mr. Lin owed Register Xia two thousand strings of cash. Registrar Xia realized he would not get the money back so he sued Mr. Lin in the prefectural court. The clerks took a bribe and twisted his words to reverse the story so that Registrar Xia became the debtor. Prior to this Mr. Lin ordered eight of his underlings to change the accounts to show that he was in the right. Registrar Xia refused to change his story and was put in jail and beaten. Accordingly he fell ill.

In the prefecture lived a man named Liu Yuan Balang, who was generous and did not trouble himself over details, and who was upset by Registrar Xia's treatment. He proclaimed to the crowd, "My district has this type of wrongful injustice. Registrar Xia is telling the truth about the money from the wine but is miserable in jail. What is the point of prefectural and county officials? I wish they would call me as a witness, as I myself could tell the truth, which would definitely cause someone else to be beaten."

Lin's eight underlings secretly heard what he said and were afraid it would leak out and harm their case, so they sent two eloquent men who extended their arms to invite Liu to drink with them at a flagged pavilion, where they talked about the case and said: "Why are you concerning yourself with other people's affairs? Have some more wine." When the wine was done, they pulled out paper money with a face value of two hundred strings and gave it to Liu saying, "We know that your household is poor, so this is a little to help you."

Liu furiously replied, "The likes of you start with unrighteous intent and then bring an unrighteous case. Now you again use unrighteous wealth to try to corrupt me. I would prefer to die of hunger. I refuse even one cash of your money. This twisting of the straight and distortion of truth is definitely not going to be resolved in this world. If there is no court in the netherworld, then let the matter rest. If there is such a court, it must have a place where wrongs can be righted." Then he called the bar owner, "How much was today's bill?"

He said, "1,800 cash."

Liu said, "Three people drank together, so I owe six hundred." He suddenly took off his coat and pawned it to pay the bill.

After a while, Registrar Xia's illness worsened, and he was released from jail to die. As he was about to die, he warned his sons: "I die a wronged man. Place in my coffin all the previous leases for the wine concessions and contracts specifying each person's share so that I can vigorously sue in the underworld."

After just one month Mr. Lin's eight underlings abruptly died one by one.

After another month, Liu was at home when he suddenly felt shaky, and everything went dark. He said to his wife, "What I see is not good. It must be that Registrar Xia's case is being heard, and I'm wanted as a witness, so I must die. But since I have led a peaceful life with no other bad deeds, I probably will return to life, so don't bury my corpse for a period of three days. After that you can decide what to do." Late that night he lost consciousness.

After two nights he sat up with a start and said, "Recently, two government clerks chased me. We went about thirty miles and reached the government office. We encountered an official wearing a green robe who came out from a room in the hall. When I looked at him, I realized it was

Registrar Xia. He repeatedly apologized and said, 'I am sorry to trouble you to come. All the documents are in good order, we just want you to serve as a witness briefly. It shouldn't be too taxing.' Then I saw Lin's eight underlings, all wearing one cangue that was five meters long and had eight holes for their heads.

"Suddenly we heard that the king was in his palace, and the clerks led us to the court. The king said, 'The matter of Xia's family needn't be discussed. Only tell me everything that happened when you drank wine upstairs.'

"I testified, 'These two men sent an invitation. Then we drank five cups of wine and bought three types of soup. They wanted to give me paper money with a face value of two hundred strings of cash, but I didn't dare accept it.'

"The king looked left and right, sighed, and said, 'The world still has good people like this. They really are important. We should discuss how to reward him, so let's take a look at his allotted lifespan.'

"A clerk went out and after a moment came back and said, 'A total of seventy-nine years.'

"The king said, 'A poor man doesn't accept money, how can we not reward him? Add another decade to his lifespan.'

"He then ordered the clerk who had brought me to take me to see the jail in the earth. Then I saw many types of people and prisoners in fetters. They were all from the city or the counties of my prefecture. Some bore cangues and some were tied up; some were sentenced to be beaten. When they saw me coming, one by one they cried out and sobbed. They then told me their names and addresses and asked me to return to the world to tell their families. Some said they had borrowed somebody's money, some said they had borrowed somebody's rent, some said they had borrowed somebody's possessions, and some said they had stolen people's land and harvest. They all asked their families to return their goods so as to lessen the sentences they had to serve in the underworld. Others asked for money and others for merit to be transferred by their relatives. I couldn't bear to look at them and turned away, and I still heard ceaseless sighs.

"As I went again to the palace, the king said, 'Since you have completed your tour, when you return to life, please tell each detail to the living, and teach them about the underworld court.' I bowed and took my leave.

"As I went out the gate, the clerk seeing me off wanted money, and I steadfastly refused. He berated me, 'For two or three days I have served you. How is it that you don't even say thank you? Moreover, give me 10,000 strings.' I again refused him saying, 'I myself have nothing to eat, so where am I going to get extra money for you?' The clerk then grasped and knocked off my topknot. He pushed me on the ground, and then I regained consciousness."

He rubbed his head, which was already bald, and his topknot lay between the pillows. Sheriff Wang Yi from Jinan, Shandong, lived in Ningbo at the time and himself saw that it was as told here.

Around 1180, Liu had his eightieth birthday, and he fell ill. Sheriff Wang went to see him and was very concerned. Liu said, "Sheriff, you needn't worry. I haven't died." Afterward he turned out not to be ill. He was probably counting the additional years the king of the netherworld had given him.

When he reached ninety-one, he died. Sheriff Wang is now the administrator of public order in Raozhou, Jiangxi. This story was told by Administrator Wang.

A Treatise on Death

Wang Chong

People today say that when men die they become spiritual beings (*kuei*, ghosts), are conscious, and can hurt people. **Let us try to prove by means of the species of creatures that the dead do not become spiritual beings, do not possess consciousness, and cannot hurt people.** How shall we prove this? We do so by means of other creatures. Man and other creatures are all creatures. When other creatures die, they do not become spiritual beings. Why should man alone become a spiritual being when he dies? If people can make a distinction between man and other creatures as to which cannot become a spiritual being, they will still find it difficult to make clear why [man] becomes a spiritual being but [other creatures] do not. If they cannot make a distinction, then how do they know that men become spiritual beings [inasmuch as other creatures do not]?

Man can live because of his vital forces. At death his vital forces are extinct. What makes the vital forces possible is the blood. When a person dies, his blood becomes exhausted. With this his vital forces are extinct, and his body decays and becomes ashes and dust. What is there to become a spiritual being?

If a man has neither ears nor eyes (senses), he will have no consciousness. Hence men who are dumb and blind are like plants and trees. When the vital forces have left man, is it simply like a man without ears or eyes? [The whole body] decays and disappears. It becomes diffused and invisible, and is therefore called a spiritual being (*kuei-shen*, earthly and heavenly spirits). When people see the shape of spiritual beings, they of course do not see the vital forces of the dead. Why? Because the very name "spiritual being" means what is diffused and invisible. When a man dies, his spirit ascends to heaven and his flesh and bones return (*kuei*) to earth, and that is why an earthly spiritual being (*kuei*) [and a heavenly spiritual being (*shen*)] are so-called. To be an earthly spiritual being (*kuei*) means to return (*kuei*). . . . To be a heavenly spiritual being (*shen*) means to expand (*shen*). When the expansion reaches its limit, it ends and begins again. Man is born of spiritual forces. At death he returns to them. Yin and yang are called *kuei-shen*. After people die, they are also called *kuei-shen*.

The vital forces produce man just as water becomes ice. As water freezes into ice, so the vital forces coagulate to form a man. When ice melts, it becomes water. When a man dies, he becomes spirit again. He is called spirit just as melted ice changes its name to water. As people see that its name has changed, they say that it has consciousness, can assume physical form, and can hurt people. But they have no basis for saying so.

People see ghosts with the form of living men. From the fact that they appear in the form of living men, we know that they are not spirits of the dead. How can we show that to be true? When a sack is filled with rice or a bag with millet the rice will stay in the sack or the millet in the bag. It will be full and firm, standing up and visible. When people look at it, they know that it is a sack of rice or a bag of millet. How? Because the contents of the sack or bag can be clearly discerned from the shape. If the sack has a hole and the rice runs out, or if the bag is torn and the millet is lost, the sack or bag will either be thrown away or folded up. When people look at it, it can no longer be seen. The spirit of man is stored up inside the body in the same way as the millet is in the bag or rice in the sack. At death the body decays and the vital forces disintegrate like the sack having a hole or the bag having been torn and the rice running out or the millet being lost. When the rice has run out or the millet is lost, the sack or bag no longer keeps its shape. How can the vital forces of man still possess a body and be seen by men when they have disintegrated and become extinct? . . .

Since the beginning of the universe and rulers of high antiquity, people who died according to their allotted time or died at middle age or prematurely have numbered in the hundreds of millions. The number of men living today is not as great as that of the dead. If everyone who dies becomes an earthly spirit, there should be an earthly spirit at every place on the road. If men see spirits when they are about to die, they should see millions and millions filling the hall and crowding the road instead of only one or two. . . .

Now, people say that a spiritual being is the spirit of a dead man. If the earthly spirit is really the spirit of a dead man, then when people see it, they ought to see the form of a nude, for there is no reason why they should see any garments. Why? Because garments have no spirit. When a man dies, they decay along with his body. How can they be worn by a spirit?

Man is intelligent and wise because he possesses the forces of the Five Constant Virtues (of humanity, righteousness, propriety, wisdom, and faithfulness). The five forces are in him because there are the five internal organs in his body (namely, heart, liver, stomach, lungs, and kidneys, which correspond to the five virtues). If the five organs are unimpaired, he is wise. If they become diseased, he becomes hazy and confused. Being hazy and confused, he becomes stupid and foolish. When a man dies, the five organs rot and decay. As they rot and decay, the Five Constant Virtues will have nothing to attach to. What embodies wisdom will be destroyed, and what exercises wisdom will be gone. The body needs the vital forces in order to be complete, and the vital forces need the body in order to have consciousness. There is in the world no fire burning from itself. **How can there be a spirit in the world that has consciousness from itself but is without a body?** . . .

Is the Notion of Disembodied Existence Intelligible?

John Hospers

Hume alleged that if two things, or qualities, A and B, always occur together, they can be imagined to occur separately (the one without the other), and it is a matter of empirical inquiry whether they do. As a general principle one could question this; can color occur without extension? can color occur without shape? But let us ask, in the present context, whether consciousness can occur without a body, even though all the instances of consciousness we are familiar with are related (causally or otherwise) to bodies.

Try to imagine yourself without a body. Imagine thinking thoughts, having feelings and memories, and even having experiences of seeing, hearing, and so on *without* the sense organs that in this life are the empirically necessary conditions of having these experiences. Having eyes is one thing; seeing colors is another. Isn't it conceivable—whether or not it occurs in fact—to see colors even though you lack the sense organs which in your present life are the *means* by which you see colors?

You go to bed one night and go to sleep, then awaken some hours later and see the sunlight streaming in the window, the clock pointing to eight, the mirror at the other side of the room; and you wonder what you will do today. Still in the bed, you look down where your body should be, but you do not see your body—the bedsheets and blankets are there, but there is no body under them. Startled, you look in the mirror, and see the reflection of the bed, the pillows, and blankets, and so on—but no *you;* at least there is no reflection of your face or body in the mirror. "Have I become invisible?" you ask yourself. Thinking of H. G. Wells' invisible man, who could be touched but not seen, you try to touch yourself; but there is nothing there to be touched. A person coming into the room would be unable to see or touch you, or to hear you either; a person could run his hands over the entire bed without ever coming in contact with a body. You are now thoroughly alarmed at the idea that no one will know you exist. You try to walk forward to the mirror, but you have no feet. You might find the objects near the mirror increasing in apparent size, just *as if* you were

Is the Notion of Disembodied Existence Intelligible? 613

walking toward the mirror. These experiences might occur as before, the only difference being that there is no body that can move or be seen or touched.

Now, have we succeeded in at least imagining existence without a body? Not quite. There are implicit references to body even in the above description. You see—with eyes?—*no,* you have no eyes, since you have no body. But let that pass for the moment; you have experiences similar to what you *would* have if you had eyes to see with. But how can you *look* toward the foot of the bed or toward the mirror? Isn't looking an activity that requires having a body? How can you look in one direction or another if you have no head to turn? And this isn't all; we said that you can't touch your body because there is no body there; how did you discover this? Did you reach out with your fingers to touch the bed? But you have no fingers, since you have no body. What would you touch (or try to touch) *with?* You move, or seem to move, toward the mirror—but what is it that moves or seems to move? Not your body, for again you have none. All the same, things seem to get larger in front of you and smaller behind you, just as if you were moving. In front of and behind what? Your body? Your body seems to be involved in every activity we try to describe even though we have tried to imagine existing without it.

Every step along the way is riddled with difficulties. It is not just that we are accustomed to think of people as having bodies and can't get out of the habit. This makes things more difficult, but it is only part of the problem. The fact is that you can't imagine doing things like looking in a different direction without turning your head, which is usually the result of a decision to do this—and of course you can't turn your head if you have no head to turn. If you *decide* to turn your head, you can't carry out this decision in the absence of a head, and so on. There seems to be a whole nest of difficulties—not merely technical but logical—constantly embedded in the attempted description.

> There is no necessary, conceptual, connection between the experience we call "seeing" and the processes that physiologists tell us happen in the eye and brain; the statement "James can still see, although his optic centers are destroyed," is very unlikely in inductive grounds but perfectly intelligible—after all, people used the word "see" long before they had any idea of things happening in the optic centers of the brain. It therefore appears to be clearly conceivable that seeing and other "sensuous" experiences might go on continuously even after death of the organism with which they are now

associated, and that the inductive reasons for doubting whether this ever happens might be outweighed by the evidence of Psychical Research.

I think it is an important conceptual inquiry to consider whether *really* disembodied seeing, hearing, pain, hunger, emotion, etc., are so clearly intelligible as is supposed in this common philosophical point of view. . . .

"The verb, 'to see' has its meaning for me because I *do* see—I have that experience!" Nonsense. As well suppose that I can come to know what a minus quantity is by setting out to lose weight. What shows a man to have the concept *seeing* is not merely that he sees, but that he can take an intelligent part in our everyday use of the word "seeing." Our concept of sight has its life only in connection with a whole set of other concepts, some of them relating to the behavior of people who see things. (I express exercise of this concept in such utterances as, "I can't see, it's too far off—now it's coming into view!" "He couldn't see me, he didn't look round," "I caught his eye," etc.

. . . [T]he exercise of one concept is intertwined with the exercise of others; as with a spider's web, some connections may be broken with impunity; but if you break enough the whole web collapses—the concept becomes unusable. Just such a collapse happens, I believe when we try to think of seeing, hearing, pain, emotion, etc., going on independently of a body.[1]

There is a whole web of meaning-connections between perceiving and having a body; when we try to break all the connections we appear to be reduced to unintelligibility. But perhaps we used a bad example; perhaps we can imagine thinking, wondering, doubting, and so on (mental operations) taking place without a body. *Where* do these operations occur? They occur, one might say, in a mind; and a mind, unlike a brain, does not exist at any physical *place*. But what do you think about? Surely about a world that is not your mind. And what causes you to have the thoughts you do? Not a brain process, because you have no brain. And once again the description begins to be suspect. What is the *you*?

Note

[1] P. T. Geach, *Mental Acts: Their Content and Their Objects* (London: Routledge, 1965), pp. 112–113. See also selection 23, pp. 227 ff.

Phaedo

Plato

And were we not saying long ago that the soul when using the body as an instrument of perception, that is to say, when using the sense of sight or hearing or some other sense (for the meaning of perceiving through the body is perceiving through the senses)—were we not saying that the soul too is then dragged by the body into the region of the changeable, and wanders and is confused; the world spins round her, and she is like a drunkard, when she touches change?

Very true.

But when returning into herself she reflects, then she passes into the other world, the region of purity, and eternity, and immortality, and unchangeableness, which are her kindred, and with them she ever lives, when she is by herself and is not let or hindered, then she ceases from her erring ways, and being in communion with the unchanging is unchanging. And this state of the soul is called wisdom?

That is well and truly said, Socrates, he replied.

And to which class is the soul more nearly alike and akin, as far as may be inferred from this argument, as well as from the preceding one?

I think, Socrates, that, in the opinion of everyone who follows the argument, the soul will be infinitely more like the unchangeable—even the most stupid person will not deny that.

And the body is more like the changing?

Yes.

Yet once more consider the matter in another light: When the soul and the body are united, then nature orders the soul to rule and govern, and the body to obey and serve. Now which of these two functions is akin to the divine? and which to the mortal? Does not the divine appear to you to be that which naturally orders and rules, and the mortal to be that which is subject and servant?

True.

And which does the soul resemble?

The soul resembles the divine, and the body the mortal—there can be no doubt of that, Socrates.

Then reflect, Cebes: of all which has been said is not this the conclusion?—that the soul is in the very likeness of the divine, and immortal, and intellectual, and uniform, and indissoluble, and unchangeable; and that the body is in the very likeness of the human, and mortal, and unintellectual, and multiform, and dissoluble, and changeable. Can this, my dear Cebes, be denied?

It cannot.

But if it be true, then is not the body liable to speedy dissolution? and is not the soul almost or altogether indissoluble?

Certainly.

Must we not, said Socrates, ask ourselves what that is which, as we imagine, is liable to be scattered, and about which we fear? and what again is that about which we have no fear? And then we may proceed further to inquire whether that which suffers dispersion is or is not of the nature of soul—our hopes and fears as to our own souls will turn upon the answers to these questions.

Very true, he said.

Now the compound or composite may be supposed to be naturally capable, as of being compounded, so also of being dissolved; but that which is uncompounded, and that only, must be, if anything is, indissoluble.

Yes; I should imagine so, said Cebes.

And the uncompounded may be assumed to be the same and unchanging, whereas the compound is always changing and never the same.

I agree, he said.

Then now let us return to the previous discussion. Is that idea or essence, which in the dialectical process we define as essence or true existence—whether essence of equality, beauty, or anything else—are these essences, I say, liable at times to some degree of change? or are they each of them always what they are, having the same simple self-existent and unchanging forms, not admitting of variation at all, or in any way, or at any time?

They must be always the same, Socrates, replied Cebes.

And what would you say of the many beautiful—whether men or horses or garments or any other things which are named by the same names and may be called equal or beautiful,—are they all unchanging and the same always, or quite the reverse? May they not rather be described as almost always changing and hardly ever the same, either with themselves or with one another?

The latter, replied Cebes; they are always in a state of change.

And these you can touch and see and perceive with the senses, but the unchanging things you can only perceive with the mind—they are invisible and are not seen?

That is very true, he said.

Well then, added Socrates, let us suppose that there are two sorts of existences—one seen, the other unseen.

Let us suppose them.

The seen is the changing, and the unseen is the unchanging?

That may be also supposed.

And, further, is not one part of us body, another part soul?

To be sure.

And to which class is the body more alike and akin?

Clearly to the seen—no one can doubt that.

And is the soul seen or not seen?

Not by man, Socrates.

And what we mean by 'seen' and 'not seen' is that which is or is not visible to the eye of man?

Yes, to the eye of man.

And is the soul seen or not seen?

Not seen.

Unseen then?

Yes.

Then the soul is more like to the unseen, and the body to the seen?

That follows necessarily, Socrates.

Letter to Menoeceus

Epicurus

Let no one when young delay to study philosophy, nor when he is old grow weary of his study. For no one can come too early or too late to secure the health of his soul. And the man who says that the age for philosophy has either not yet come or has gone by is like the man who says that the age for happiness is not yet come to him, or has passed away. Wherefore both when young and old a man must study philosophy, that as he grows old he may be young in blessings through the grateful recollection of what has been, and that in youth he may be old as well, since he will know no fear of what is to come. We must then meditate on the things that make our happiness, seeing that when that is with us we have all, but when it is absent we do all to win it.

The things which I used unceasingly to commend to you, these do and practice, considering them to be the first principles of the good life. First of all believe that god is a being immortal and blessed, even as the common idea of a god is engraved on men's minds, and do not assign to him anything alien to his immortality or ill-suited to his blessedness: but believe about him everything that can uphold his blessedness and immortality. For gods there are, since the knowledge of them is by clear vision. But they are not such as the many believe them to be: for indeed they do not consistently represent them as they believe them to be. And the impious man is not he who denies the gods of the many, but he who attaches to the gods the beliefs of the many. For the statements of the many about the gods are not conceptions derived from sensation, but false suppositions, according to which the greatest misfortunes befall the wicked and the greatest blessings the good by the gift of the gods. For men being accustomed always to their own virtues welcome those like themselves, but regard all that is not of their nature as alien.

Become accustomed to the belief that death is nothing to us. For all good and evil consists in sensation, but death is deprivation of sensation. And therefore a right understanding that death is nothing to us makes the mortality of life enjoyable, not because it adds to it an infinite span of time, but because it takes away the craving for immortality. For there is nothing terrible in life for the man who has truly comprehended that there is nothing terrible in not living. So that the man speaks but idly who says that he fears death not because it will be painful when it comes, but because it is painful in anticipation. For that which gives no trouble when it comes, is but an empty pain in anticipation. So death, the most terrifying of ills, is nothing to us, since **so long as we exist death is not with us; but when death comes, then we do not exist.** It does not then concern either the living or the dead, since for the former it is not, and the latter are no more.

But the many at one moment shun death as the greatest of evils, at another yearn for it as a respite from the evils in life. But the wise man neither seeks to escape life nor fears the cessation of life, for neither does life offend him nor does the absence of life seem to be any evil. And just as with food he does not seek simply the larger share and nothing else, but rather the most pleasant, so he seeks to enjoy not the longest period of time, but the most pleasant.

And he who counsels the young man to live well, but the old man to make a good end, is foolish, not merely because of the desirability of life, but also because it is the same training which teaches to live well and to die well. Yet much worse still is the man who says it is good not to be born, but

> once born make haste to pass the gates of Death.
>
> [Theognis, 427]

For if he says this from conviction why does he not pass away out of life? For it is open to him to do so, if he had firmly made up his mind to this. But if he speaks in jest, his words are idle among men who cannot receive them.

We must then bear in mind that the future is neither ours, nor yet wholly not ours, so that we may not altogether expect it as sure to come, nor abandon hope of it, as if it will certainly not come.

We must consider that of desires some are natural, others vain, and of the natural some are necessary and others merely natural; and of the necessary some are necessary for happiness, others for the repose of the body, and others for very life. The right understanding of these facts enables us to refer all choice and avoidance to the health of the body and the soul's freedom from disturbance, since this is the aim of the life of blessedness. For it is to obtain this end that we always act, namely, to avoid pain and fear. And when this is once secured for us, all the tempest of the soul is dispersed, since the living creature has not to wander as though in search of something that is missing, and to look for some other thing by which he can fulfill the good of the soul and the good of the body. For it is then that we have need of pleasure, when we feel pain owing to the absence of pleasure; but when we do not feel pain, we no longer need pleasure. And for this cause we call pleasure the beginning and end of the blessed life. For we recognize pleasure as the first good innate in us, and from pleasure we begin every act of choice and avoidance, and to pleasure we return again, using the feeling as the standard by which we judge every good.

And since pleasure is the first good and natural to us, for this very reason we do not choose every pleasure, but sometimes we pass over many pleasures, when greater discomfort accrues to us as the result of them: and similarly we think many pains better than pleasures, since a greater pleasure comes to us when we have endured pains for a long time. Every pleasure then because of its natural kinship to us is good, yet not every pleasure is to be chosen: even as every pain also is an evil, yet not all are always of a nature to be avoided. Yet by a scale of comparison and by the consideration of advantages and disadvantages we must form our judgment on all these matters. For the good on certain occasions we treat as bad, and conversely the bad as good.

And again independence of desire we think a great good—not that we may at all times enjoy but a few things, but that, if we do not possess many, we may enjoy the few in the genuine persuasion that those have the sweetest pleasure in luxury who least need it, and that all that is natural is easy to be obtained, but that which is superfluous is hard. And so plain savours bring us a pleasure equal to a luxurious diet, when all the pain due to want is removed; and bread and water produce the highest pleasure, when one who needs them puts them to his lips. To grow accustomed therefore to simple and not luxurious diet gives us health to the full, and makes a man alert for the needful employments of life, and when after long intervals we approach luxuries, disposes us better towards them, and fits us to be fearless of fortune.

When, therefore, we maintain that pleasure is the end, we do not mean the pleasures of profligates and those that consist in sensuality, as is supposed by some who are either ignorant or disagree with us or do not understand, but freedom from pain in the body and from trouble in the mind. For it is not continuous drinkings and revellings, nor the satisfaction of lusts, nor the enjoyment of fish and other luxuries of the wealthy table, which produce a pleasant life, but sober reasoning, searching out the motives for all choice and avoidance, and banishing mere opinions, to which are due the greatest disturbance of the spirit.

Of all this the beginning and the greatest good is prudence. Wherefore prudence is a more precious thing even than philosophy: for from prudence are sprung all the other virtues, and it teaches us that it is not possible to live pleasantly without living prudently and honourably and justly, nor, again, to live a life of prudence, honour, and justice without living pleasantly. For the virtues are by nature bound up with the pleasant life, and the pleasant life is inseparable from them. For indeed who, think you, is a better man than he who holds reverent opinions concerning the gods, and is at all times free from fear of death, and has reasoned out the end ordained by nature? He understands that the limit of good things is easy to fulfill and easy to attain, whereas the course of ills is either short in time or slight in pain: he laughs at destiny, whom some have introduced as the mistress of all things. He thinks that with us lies the chief power in determining events, some of which happen by necessity and some by chance, and some are within our control; for while necessity cannot be called to account, he sees that chance is inconstant, but that which is in our control is subject to no master, and to it are naturally attached praise and blame. For, indeed, it were better to follow the myths about the gods than to become a slave to the destiny of the natural philosophers: for the former suggests a hope of placating the gods by worship, whereas the latter involves a necessity which knows no placation. As to chance, he does not regard it as a god as most men do (for in a god's acts there is no disorder), nor as an uncertain cause of all things: for he does not believe that good and evil are given by chance to man for the framing of a blessed life, but that opportunities for great good and great evil are afforded by it. He therefore thinks it better to be unfortunate in reasonable action than to prosper in unreason. For it is better in a man's actions that what is well chosen should fail, rather than that what is ill chosen should be successful owing to chance.

Meditate therefore on these things and things akin to them night and day by yourself, and with a companion like to yourself, and never shall you be disturbed waking or asleep, but you shall live like a god among men. For a man who lives among immortal blessings is not like to a mortal being.

from Scripture of the Pure Land

This world Sukhavati, Ananda, which is the world system of the Lord Amitabha, is rich and prosperous, comfortable, fertile, delightful and crowded with many Gods and men. And in this world system, Ananda, there are no hells, no animals, no ghosts, no Asuras and none of the inauspicious places of rebirth. And in this our world no jewels make their appearance like those which exist in the world system Sukhavati.

And that world system Sukhavati, Ananda, emits many fragrant odours, it is rich in a great variety of flowers and fruits, adorned with jewel trees, which are frequented by flocks of various birds with sweet voices, which the Tathagata's miraculous power has conjured up. And these jewel trees, Ananda, have various colours, many colours, many hundreds of thousands of colours. They are variously composed of the seven precious things, in varying combinations, i.e. of gold, silver, beryl, crystal, coral, red pearls, or emerald. Such jewel trees, and clusters of banana trees and rows of palm trees, all made of precious things, grow everywhere in this Buddha-field. On all sides it is surrounded with golden nets, and all round covered with lotus flowers made of all the precious things. Some of the lotus flowers are half a mile in circumference, others up to ten miles. And from each jewel lotus issue thirty-six hundred thousand kotis of rays. And at the end of each ray there issue thirty-six hundred thousand kotis of Buddhas, with golden-coloured bodies, who bear the thirty-two marks of the superman, and who, in all the ten directions, go into countless world systems, and there demonstrate Dharma.

And further, Ananda, in this Buddha-field there are nowhere any mountains—black mountains, jewel mountains, Sumerus, kings of mountains, circular mountains and great circular mountains. But the Buddha-field is everywhere even, delightful like the palm of the hand, and in all its parts the ground contains a great variety of jewels and gems.

And many kinds of rivers flow along in this world system Sukhavati. There are great rivers there, one mile broad, and up to fifty miles broad and twelve miles deep. And all these rivers flow along calmly, their water is fragrant with manifold agreeable odours, in them there are bunches of flowers to which various jewels adhere, and they resound with various sweet sounds. And the sound which issues from these great rivers is as pleasant as that of a musical instrument, which consists of hundreds of thousands of kotis of parts, and which, skilfully played, emits a heavenly music. It is deep, commanding, distinct, clear, pleasant, and one never tires of hearing it, it always agrees with one and one likes to hear it, like the words "Impermanent, peaceful, calm, and not-self." Such is the sound that reaches the ears of those beings.

And, Ananda, both the banks of those great rivers are lined with variously scented jewel trees, and from them bunches of flowers, leaves, and branches of all kinds hang down. And if those beings wish to indulge in sports full of heavenly delights on those river-banks, then, after they have stepped into the water, the water in each case rises as high as they wish it to—up to the ankles, or the knees, or the hips, or their sides, or their ears. And heavenly delights arise. Again, if beings wish the water to be cold, for them it becomes cold; if they wish it to be hot, for them it becomes hot; if they wish it to be hot and cold, for them it becomes hot and cold, to suit their pleasure. And those rivers flow along, full of water scented with the finest odours, and covered with beautiful flowers, resounding with the sounds of many birds, easy to ford, free from mud, and with golden sand at the bottom. And all the wishes those beings may think of, they all will be fulfilled, as long as they are rightful.

And as to the pleasant sound which issues from the water (of these rivers), that reaches all the parts of this Buddha-field. And everyone hears the pleasant sound he wishes to hear, i.e. he hears of the Buddha, the Dharma, the Samgha, of the (six) perfections, the (ten) stages, the powers, the grounds of self-confidence, of the special dharmas of a Buddha, of the analytical knowledges, of emptiness, the signless, and the wishless, of the uneffected, the unborn, of non-production, non-existence, non-cessation, of calm, quietude, and peace, of the great friendliness, the great compassion, the great sympathetic joy, the great evenmindedness, of the patient acceptance of things which fail to be produced, and of the acquisition of the stage where one is consecrated (as a Tathagata). And, hearing this, one gains the exalted zest and joyfulness, which is associated with detachment, dispassion, calm, cessation, Dharma, and brings about the state of mind which leads to the accomplishment of enlightenment. And nowhere in this world-system Sukhavati does one hear of anything unwholesome, nowhere of the hindrances, nowhere of the states of punishment, the states of woe and the bad destinies, nowhere of suffering. Even of feelings which are neither pleasant nor unpleasant one does not hear there, how much less of suffering! And that, Ananda, is the reason why **this world-system is called the "Happy Land" (Sukhavati).** But all this describes it only in brief, not in detail. One aeon might well reach its end while one proclaims the reasons for happiness in the world-system Sukhavati, and still one could not come to the end of (the enumeration of) the reasons for happiness.

Moreover, Ananda, all the beings who have been reborn in this world-system Sukhavati, who are reborn in it, or who will be reborn in it, they will be exactly like the Paranirmitavasavartin Gods; of the same colour, strength, vigour, height and breadth, dominion, store of merit, and keenness of superknowledges; they enjoy the same dresses, ornaments, parks, palaces, and pointed towers, the same kind of forms, sounds, smells, tastes, and touchables, just the same kinds of enjoyments. And the beings in the world-system Sukhavati do not eat gross food, like soup or raw sugar; but whatever food they may wish for, that they perceive as eaten, and they become gratified in body and mind, without there being any further need to throw the food into the body. And if, after their bodies are gratified, they wish for certain perfumes, then the whole of that Buddha-field becomes scented with just that kind of heavenly perfumes. But if someone does not wish to smell that perfume, then the perception of it does not reach him. In the same way, whatever they may wish for comes to them, be it musical instruments, banners, flags, etc.; or cloaks of different colours, or ornaments of various kinds. If they wish for a palace of a certain colour, distinguishing marks, construction, height, and width, made of various precious things, adorned with hundreds of thousands of pinnacles, while inside it various heavenly woven materials are spread out, and it is full of couches strewn with beautiful cushions—then just such a palace appears before them. In those delightful palaces, surrounded and honoured by seven times seven thousand Apsarases, they dwell, play, enjoy, and disport themselves.

And the beings who are touched by the winds, which are pervaded with various perfumes, are filled with a happiness as great as that of a monk who has achieved the cessation of suffering.

And in this Buddha-field one has no conception at all of fire, sun, moon, planets, constellations, stars, or blinding darkness, and no conception even of day and night, except (where they are mentioned) in the sayings of the Tathagata. There is nowhere a notion of monks possessing private parks for retreats.

And all the beings who have been born, who are born, who will be born in this Buddha-field, they all are fixed on the right method of salvation, until they have won Nirvana. And why? Because there is here no place for and no conception of the two other groups, i.e. of those who are not fixed at all, and those who are fixed on wrong ways. For this reason also that world-system is called the "Happy Land."

And further again, Ananda, in the ten directions, in each single direction, in Buddha-fields countless like the sands of the river Ganges, Buddhas and Lords countless like the sands of the river Ganges glorify the name of the Lord Amitabha, the Tathagata, praise him, proclaim his fame, extol his virtue. And why? Because all beings are irreversible from the supreme enlightenment if they hear the name of the Lord Amitabha, and, on hearing it, with one single thought only raise their hearts to him with a resolve connected with serene faith.

And if any beings, Ananda, again and again reverently attend to this Tathagata, if they will plant a large and immeasurable root of good, having raised their hearts to enlightenment, and if they vow to be reborn in that world system, then, when the hour of their death approaches, that Tathagata Amitabha, the Arhat, the fully Enlightened One, will stand before them, surrounded by hosts of monks. Then, having seen that Lord, and having died with hearts serene, they will be reborn in just that world-system Sukhavati. And if there are sons or daughters of good family, who may desire to see that Tathagata Amitabha in this very life, they should raise their hearts to the supreme enlightenment, they should direct their thought with extreme resoluteness and perseverance unto this Buddha-field and they should dedicate their store of merit to being reborn therein.

Death Is Swallowed Up in Victory

I Corinthians 15

12 Now if Christ be preached that he rose from the dead, how say some among you that there is no resurrection of the dead?
13 But if there be no resurrection of the dead, then is Christ not risen:
14 And if Christ be not risen, then *is* our preaching vain, and your faith *is* also vain.
15 Yea, and we are found false witnesses of God: because we have testified of God that he raised up Christ: whom he raised not up, if so be that the dead rise not.
16 For if the dead rise not, then is not Christ raised:
17 And if Christ be not raised, your faith *is* vain: ye are yet in your sins.
18 Then they also which are fallen asleep in Christ are perished.
19 If in this life only we have hope in Christ, we are of all men most miserable.
20 But now is Christ risen from the dead, *and* become the firstfruits of them that slept.
21 For since by man *came* death, by man *came* also the resurrection of the dead.
22 For as in Adam all die, even so in Christ shall all be made alive.
23 But every man in his own order: Christ the firstfruits; afterward they that are Christ's at his coming.
24 Then *cometh* the end, when he shall have delivered up the kingdom to God, even the Father; when he shall have put down all rule and all authority and power.
25 For he must reign, till he hath put all enemies under his feet.
26 **The last enemy *that* shall be destroyed *is* death.**

27 For he hath put all things under his feet. But when he saith all things are put under *him, it is* manifest that he is excepted, which did put all things under him.

28 And when all things shall be subdued unto him, then shall the Son also himself be subject unto him that put all things under him, that God may be all.

29 Else what shall they do which are baptized for the dead, if the dead rise not at all? why are they then baptized for the dead?

30 And why stand we in jeopardy every hour?

31 I protest by your rejoicing which I have in Christ Jesus our Lord, I die daily.

32 If after the manner of men I have fought with beasts at Ephesus, what advantageth it me, if the dead rise not? let us eat and drink; for tomorrow we die.

33 Be not deceived: evil communications corrupt good manners.

34 Awake to righteousness, and sin not; for some have not the knowledge of God: I speak *this* to your shame.

35 But some *man* will say, How are the dead raised up? and with what body do they come?

36 *Thou* fool, that which thou sowest is not quickened, except it die:

37 And that which thou sowest, thou sowest not that body that shall be, but bare grain, it may chance of wheat, or of some other *grain:*

38 But God giveth it a body as it hath pleased him, and to every seed his own body.

39 All flesh *is* not the same flesh: but *there* is one *kind of* flesh of men, another flesh of beasts, another of fishes, *and* another of birds.

40 *There are* also celestial bodies, and bodies terrestrial: but the glory of the celestial *is* one, and the *glory* of the terrestrial *is* another.

41 *There is* one glory of the sun, and another glory of the moon, and another glory of the stars: for *one* star differeth from *another* star in glory.

42 So also *is* the resurrection of the dead. It is sown in corruption; it is raised in incorruption:

43 It is sown in dishonour; it is raised in glory: it is sown in weakness; it is raised in power:

44 It is sown a natural body; it is raised a spiritual body. There is a natural body, and there is a spiritual body.

45 And so it is written, The first man Adam was made a living soul; the last Adam *was made* a quickening spirit.

46 Howbeit that *was* not first which is spiritual, but that which is natural; and afterward that which is spiritual.

47 The first man *is* of the earth, earthy: the second man *is* the Lord from heaven.

48 As *is* the earthy, such *are* they also that are earthy: and as *is* the heavenly, such *are* they also that are heavenly.

49 And as we have borne the image of the earthy, we shall also bear the image of the heavenly.

50 Now this I say, brethren, that flesh and blood cannot inherit the kingdom of God; neither doth corruption inherit incorruption.

51 Behold, I shew you a mystery; We shall not all sleep, but we shall all be changed.

52 In a moment, in the twinkling of an eye, at the last trump: for the trumpet shall sound, and the dead shall be raised incorruptible, and we shall be changed.

53 For this corruptible must put on incorruption, and this mortal *must* put on immortality.

54 **So when this corruptible shall have put on incorruption, and this mortal shall have put on immortality, then shall be brought to pass the saying that is written, Death is swallowed up in victory.**

The Dead in Christ Shall Rise First

I Thessalonians 4

13 But I would not have you to be ignorant, brethren, concerning them which are asleep, that ye sorrow not, even as others which have no hope.

14 For if we believe that Jesus died and rose again, even so them also which sleep in Jesus will God bring with him.

15 For this we say unto you by the word of the Lord, that we which are alive *and* remain unto the coming of the Lord shall not prevent them which are asleep.

16 For the Lord himself shall descend from heaven with a shout, with the voice of the archangel, and with the trumpet of God: and the dead in Christ shall rise first:

17 Then we which are alive *and* remain shall be caught up together with them in the clouds, to meet the Lord in the air: and so shall we ever be with the Lord.

18 Wherefore comfort one another with these words.

Chapter X: Meaning

Concerning the meaning of life, no general or abstract question will adequately serve as a point of departure for our search into the essence of meaning. Rather, the first and guiding question must be particular and must issue from the depths of one's own subjectivity. The question that each individual must ask of himself or herself is this: "What is the meaning of *my* existence?" In other words, confronted with the fact of our own concrete existence in a world, (i.e., finding yourself in a world that you neither created nor made and in a life you never asked for) how can I, a unique individual, make sense of my life?

John Barth uses the journey as a metaphor for human life. His "Night-Sea Journey," a marvelous creative fiction, addresses philosophical questions about meaning that arise in the process of trying to "reach the Shore." Barth tells us, "One way or another, no matter which theory of our journey is correct, it's myself I address; to whom I rehearse as to a stranger our history and condition, and will disclose my secret hope though I sink for it."

Tao Chien's poem "Substance, Shadow, and Spirit" shows attitudes toward life held by one person. Substance looks at human morality and the finality of life: "When wine is offered, don't refuse." Shadow represents the Confucian point of view that effort and good works will result in a reputation that will live on. The reader may recall that in Chapter V of this volume, Confucius states, "The superior man dislikes the thought of his name not being mentioned after his death." Spirit reflects the Taoist attitude: "Give yourself to the waves of Great Change neither happy nor yet afraid, and when it's time to go, then simply go without any unnecessary fuss."

The philosopher Tolstoy was haunted by two questions: "Why?" and "What after?" The first question asks for meaning and purpose. Why am I here? What do I live for? And, perhaps, what am I willing to die for? The second question raises the possibilities of immortality that we discussed in the previous section of this text. However, in this context it raises the question of whether the locus of meaning can be found in this life. What, in fact, is worth living for? Pleasure? Self? Others? Goodness? Beauty? God? Freedom? These are questions that only the individual alone can settle. Tolstoy finds his answer in faith. "Faith," Tolstoy tells us, "is the power of life. If a man lives he believes in something."

Albert Camus was an existentialist writer. Existentialism is a philosophical orientation that emphasizes the existence of the individual in the world as a free and responsible agent determining his or her development. According to Camus, "There is but one truly serious philosophical problem, and that is suicide." Whether life is worth living is the fundamental question of philosophy. Camus' "absurd hero" revolts against the futility of life and through freedom authentically appropriates both life and meaning.

Martin Buber was a Jewish existentialist philosopher and theologian. In "Response," Buber tells us, "This fragile life between birth and death can nevertheless be a fulfillment—if it is a dialogue." Life is both a trust and a response. Each of us is addressed by life's great questions and each of us is called to respond authentically. "We practice responsibility for that realm of life allotted and entrusted to us for which we are able to respond, that is, for which we have a relation of deeds that may count—in all our inadequacy—as a proper response."

Questions for the Soul concludes with Bertrand Russell's "Three Passions." Reflecting on his long, active and influential life Russell writes, "Three passions, simple but overwhelmingly strong, have governed my life: the longing for love, the search for knowledge, and unbearable pity for the suffering of mankind." He concludes his essay as follows: "This has been my life. I have found it worth living, and would gladly live it again if the chance were offered to me."

Philosophy should help us all lead better lives. It is hoped that *Questions for the Soul* will help individuals lead lives worth living.

Night-Sea Journey

John Barth

"One way or another, no matter which theory of our journey is correct, it's myself I address; to whom I rehearse as to a stranger our history and condition, and will disclose my secret hope though I sink for it.

"Is the journey my invention? Do the night, the sea, exist at all, I ask myself, apart from my experience of them? Do I myself exist, or is this a dream? Sometimes I wonder. And if I am, who am I? The Heritage I supposedly transport? But how can I be both vessel and contents? Such are the questions that beset my intervals of rest.

"My trouble is, I lack conviction. Many accounts of our situation seem plausible to me—where and what we are, why we swim and whither. But implausible ones as well, perhaps especially those, I must admit as possibly correct. Even likely. If at times, in certain humors—stroking in unison, say, with my neighbors and chanting with them 'Onward! Upward!'—I have supposed that we have after all a common Maker, Whose nature and motives we may not know, but Who engendered us in some mysterious wise and launched us forth toward some end known but to Him—if (for a moodslength only) I have been able to entertain such notions, very popular in certain quarters, it is because our night-sea journey partakes of their absurdity. One might even say: I can believe them *because* they are absurd.

"Has that been said before?

"Another paradox: it appears to be these recesses from swimming that sustain me in the swim. Two measures onward and upward, flailing with the rest, then I float exhausted and dispirited, brood upon the night, the sea, the journey, while the flood bears me a measure back and down: slow progress, but I live, I live, and make my way, aye, past many a drowned comrade in the end, stronger, worthier than I, victims of their unremitting *joie de nager*. I have seen the best swimmers of my generation go under. Numberless the number of the dead! Thousands drown as I think this thought, millions as I rest before returning to the swim. And scores, hundreds of millions have expired since we surged forth, brave in our innocence, upon our dreadful way. 'Love! Love!' we sang then, a quarter-billion strong, and churned the warm sea white with joy of swimming! Now all are gone down—the buoyant, the sodden, leaders and followers, all gone under, while wretched I swim on. Yet these same reflective intervals that keep me afloat have led me into wonder, doubt, despair—strange emotions for a swimmer!—have led me, even, to suspect . . . that our night-sea journey is without meaning.

"Indeed, if I have yet to join the hosts of the suicides, it is because (fatigue apart) I find it no meaningfuller to drown myself than to go on swimming.

"I know that there are those who seem actually to enjoy the night-sea; who claim to love swimming for its own sake, or sincerely believe that 'reaching the Shore,' 'transmitting the Heritage' (*Whose* Heritage, I'd like to know? And to whom?) is worth the staggering cost. I do not. Swimming itself I find at best not actively unpleasant, more often tiresome, not infrequently a torment. Arguments from function and design don't impress me: granted that we can and do swim, that in a manner of speaking our long tails and streamlined heads are 'meant for' swimming; it by no means follows—for me, at least—that we *should* swim, or otherwise endeavor to 'fulfill our destiny.' Which is to say, Someone Else's destiny, since ours, so far as I can see, is merely to perish, one way or another, soon or late. The heartless zeal of our (departed) leaders, like the blind ambition and good cheer of my own youth, appalls me now; for the death of my comrades I am inconsolable. If the night-sea journey has justification, it is not for us swimmers ever to discover it.

"Oh, to be sure, 'Love!' one heard on every side: 'Love it is that drives and sustains us!' I translate: we don't know *what* drives and sustains us, only that we are most miserably driven and, imperfectly, sustained. *Love* is how we call our ignorance of what whips us. 'To reach the Shore,' then: but what if the Shore exists in the fancies of us swimmers merely, who dream it to account for the dreadful fact that we swim, have always and only swum, and continue swimming without respite (myself excepted) until we die? Supposing even that there *were* a Shore—that, as a cynical companion of mine once imagined, we rise from the drowned to discover all those vulgar superstitions and exalted metaphors to be literal truth: the giant Maker of us all, the Shores of Light beyond our night-sea journey!—whatever would a swimmer do there? The fact is, when we imagine the Shore, what comes to mind is just the opposite of our condition: no more night, no more sea, no more journeying. In short, the blissful estate of the drowned.

"'Ours not to stop and think; ours but to swim and sink. . . .' Because a moment's thought reveals the pointlessness of swimming. 'No matter,' I've heard some say, even as they gulped their last: 'The night-sea journey may be absurd, but here we swim, will-we nill-we, against the flood, onward and upward, toward a Shore that may not exist and couldn't be reached if it did.' The thoughtful swimmer's choices, then, they say, are two: give over thrashing and go under for good, or embrace the absurdity; affirm in and for itself the night-sea journey; swim on with neither motive nor destination, for the sake of swimming, and compassionate moreover with your fellow swimmer, we being all at sea and equally in the dark. I find neither course acceptable. If not even the hypothetical Shore can justify a sea-full of drowned comrades, to speak of the swim-in-itself as somehow doing so strikes me as obscene. I continue to swim—but only because blind habit, blind instinct, blind fear of drowning are still more strong than the horror of our journey. And if on occasion I have assisted a fellow-thrasher, joined in the cheers and songs, even passed along to others strokes of genius from the drowned great, it's that I shrink by temperament from making myself conspicuous. To paddle off in one's own direction, assert one's independent right-of-way, overrun one's fellows without compunction, or dedicate oneself entirely to pleasures and diversions without regard for conscience—I can't finally condemn those who journey in this wise; in half my moods I envy them and despise the weak vitality that keeps me from following their example. But in reasonabler moments I remind myself that it's their very freedom and self-responsibility I reject, as more dramatically absurd, in our senseless circumstances, than tailing along in conventional fashion. Suicides, rebels, affirmers of the paradox—nay-sayers and yea-sayers alike to our fatal journey—I finally shake my head at them. And splash sighing past their corpses, one by one, as past a hundred sorts of others: friends, enemies, brothers; fools, sages, brutes—and nobodies, million upon million. I envy them all.

"A poor irony: that I, who find abhorrent and tautological the doctrine of survival of the fittest (*fitness* meaning, in my experience, nothing more than survival-ability, a talent whose only demonstration is the fact of survival, but whose chief ingredients seem to be strength, guile, callousness), may be the sole remaining swimmer! But the doctrine is false as well as repellent: Chance drowns the worthy with the unworthy, bears up the unfit with the fit by whatever definition, and makes the night-sea journey essentially *haphazard* as well as murderous and unjustified.

"'You only swim once.' Why bother, then?

"'Except ye drown, ye shall not reach the Shore of Life.' Poppycock.

"One of my late companions—that same cynic with the curious fancy, among the first to drown—entertained us with odd conjectures while we waited to begin our journey. A favorite theory of his was that the Father does exist, and did indeed make us and the sea we swim—but not a-purpose or even consciously; He made us, as it were, despite Himself, as we make waves with every tail-thrash, and may be unaware of our existence. Another was that He knows we're here but doesn't care what happens to us, inasmuch as He creates (voluntarily or not) other seas and swimmers at more or less regular intervals. In bitterer moments, such as just before he drowned, my friend even supposed that our Maker wished us unmade; there was indeed a Shore, he'd argue, which could save at least some of us from drowning and toward which it was our function to struggle—but for reasons unknowable to us He wanted desperately to prevent our reaching that happy place and fulfilling our destiny. Our 'Father,' in short, was our adversary and would-be killer! No less outrageous, and offensive to traditional opinion, were the fellow's speculations on the nature of our Maker: that He might well be no swimmer Himself at all, but some sort of monstrosity, perhaps even tailless; that He might be stupid, malicious, insensible, perverse, or asleep and dreaming; that the end for which He created and launched us forth, and which we flagellate ourselves to fathom, was perhaps immoral, even obscene. Et cetera, et cetera: there was no end to the chap's conjectures, or the impoliteness of his fancy; I have reason to suspect that his early demise, whether planned by 'our Maker' or not, was expedited by certain fellow-swimmers indignant at his blasphemies.

"In other moods, however (he was as given to moods as I), his theorizing would become half-serious, so it seemed to me, especially upon the subjects of Fate and Immortality, to which our youthful conversations often turned. Then his harangues, if no less fantastical, grew solemn and obscure, and if he was still baiting us, his passion undid the joke. His objection to popular opinions of the hereafter, he would declare, was their claim to general validity. Why need believers hold that *all* the drownèd rise to be judged at journey's end, and non-believers that drowning is final without exception? In *his* opinion (so he'd vow at least), nearly everyone's fate was permanent death; indeed he took a sour pleasure in supposing that every 'Maker' made thousands of separate seas in His creative lifetime, each populated like ours with millions of swimmers, and that in almost every instance both sea and swimmers were utterly annihilated, whether accidentally or by malevolent design. (Nothing if not pluralistical, he imagined there might be millions and billions of 'Fathers,' perhaps in some 'night-sea' of their own!) However—and here he turned infidels against him with the faithful—he professed to believe that in possibly a single night-sea per thousand, say, one of its quarter-billion swimmers (that is, one swimmer in two hundred fifty billions) achieved a qualified immortality. In some cases the rate might be slightly higher; in others it was vastly lower, for just as there are swimmers of every degree of proficiency, including some who drown before the journey starts, unable to swim at all, and others created drownèd, as it were, so he imagined what can only be termed impotent Creators, Makers unable to Make, as well as uncommonly fertile ones and all grades between. And it pleased him to deny any necessary relation between a Maker's productivity and His other virtues—including, even, the quality of His creatures.

"I could go on (*he* surely did) with his elaboration of these mad notions—such as that swimmers in other night-seas needn't be of our kind; that Makers themselves might belong to different *species*, so to speak; that our particular Maker mightn't Himself be immortal, or that we might be not only His emissaries but His 'immortality,' continuing His life and our own, transmogrified, beyond our individual deaths. Even this modified immortality (meaningless to me) he conceived as relative and contingent, subject to accidental or deliberate termination: his pet hypothesis was that Makers and swimmers *each generate the other*—against all odds, their number being so great—and that any given 'immortality-chain' could terminate after any number of cycles, so that what was 'immortal' (still speaking relatively) was only the cyclic process of incarnation, which itself might have a beginning and an end. Alternatively he liked to imagine cycles within cycles, either finite or infinite: for example, the 'night-sea,' as it were, in which Makers 'swam' and created night-seas and swimmers like ourselves, might be the creation of a larger Maker, Himself one of many, Who in turn et cetera. Time itself he regarded as relative to our experience, like magnitude: who knew but what, with each thrash of our tails, minuscule seas and swimmers, whole eternities, came to pass—as ours, perhaps, and our Maker's Maker's, was elapsing between the strokes of some supertail, in a slower order of time?

"Naturally I hooted with the others at this nonsense. We were young then, and had only the dimmest notion of what lay ahead; in our ignorance we imagined night-sea journeying to be a positively heroic enterprise. Its meaning and value we never questioned; to be sure, some must go down by the way, a pity no doubt, but to win a race requires that others lose, and like all my fellows I took for granted that I would be the winner. We milled and swarmed, impatient to be off, never mind where or why, only to try our youth against the realities of night and sea; if we indulged the skeptic at all, it was as a droll, half-contemptible mascot. When he died in the initial slaughter, no one cared.

"And even now I don't subscribe to all his views—but I no longer scoff. The horror of our history has purged me of opinions, as of vanity, confidence, spirit, charity, hope, vitality, everything—except dull dread and a kind of melancholy, stunned persistence. What leads me to recall his fancies is my growing suspicion that I, of all swimmers, may be the sole survivor of this fell journey, tale-bearer of a generation. This suspicion, together with the recent sea-change, suggests to me now that nothing is impossible, not even my late companion's wildest visions, and brings me to a certain desperate resolve, the point of my chronicling.

"Very likely I have lost my senses. The carnage at our setting out; our decimation by whirlpool, poisoned cataract, sea-convulsion; the panic stampedes, mutinies, slaughters, mass suicides; the mounting evidence that none will survive the journey—add to these anguish and fatigue; it were a miracle if sanity stayed afloat. Thus I admit, with the other possibilities, that the present sweetening and calming of the sea, and what seems to be a kind of vasty presence, song, or summons from the near upstream, may be hallucinations of disordered sensibility. . . .

"Perhaps, even, I am drowned already. Surely I was never meant for the rough-and-tumble of the swim; not impossibly I perished at the outset and have only imaged the night-sea journey from some final deep. In any case, I'm no longer young, and it is we spent old swimmers, disabused of every illusion, who are most vulnerable to dreams.

"Sometimes I think I am my drownèd friend.

"Out with it: I've begun to believe, not only that *She* exists, but that She lies not far ahead, and stills the sea, and draws me Herward! Aghast, I recollect his maddest notion: that our destination (which existed, mind, in but one night-sea out of hundreds and thousands) was no Shore, as commonly conceived, but a mysterious being, indescribable except by paradox and vaguest figure: wholly different from us swimmers, yet our complement; the death of us, yet our salvation and resurrection; simultaneously our journey's end, mid-point, and commencement; not membered and thrashing like us, but a motionless or hugely gliding sphere of unimaginable dimension; self-contained, yet dependent absolutely, in some wise, upon the chance (always monstrously improbable) that one of us will survive the night-sea journey and reach . . . Her! *Her*, he called it, or *She*, which is to say, Other-than-a-he. I shake my head; the thing is too preposterous; it is myself I talk to, to keep my reason in this awful darkness. There is no She! There is no You! I rave to myself; it's Death alone that hears and summons. To the drowned, all seas are calm. . . .

"Listen: my friend maintained that in every order of creation there are two sorts of creators, contrary yet complementary, one of which gives rise to seas and swimmers, the other to the Night-which-contains-the-sea and to What-waits-at-the-journey's-end: the former, in short, to destiny, the latter to destination (and both profligately, involuntarily, perhaps indifferently or unwittingly). The 'purpose' of the night-sea journey—but not necessarily of the journeyer or of either Maker!—my friend could describe only in abstractions: *consummation, transfiguration, union of contraries, transcension of categories*. When we laughed, he would shrug and admit that he understood the business no better than we, and thought it ridiculous, dreary, possibly obscene. 'But one of you,' he'd add with his wry smile, 'may be the Hero destined to complete the night-sea journey and be one with Her. Chances are, of course, you won't make it.' He himself, he declared, was not even going to try; the whole idea repelled him; if we chose to dismiss it as an ugly fiction, so much the better for us; thrash, splash, and be merry, we were soon enough drownèd. But there it was, he could not say how he knew or why he bothered to tell us, any more than he could say what would happen after She and Hero, Shore and Swimmer, 'merged identities' to become something both and neither. He quite agreed with me that if the issue of that magical union had no memory of the night-sea journey, for example, it enjoyed a poor sort of immortality; even poorer if, as he rather imagined, a swimmer-hero plus a She equaled or became merely another Maker of future night-seas and the rest, at such incredible expense of life. This being the case—he was persuaded it was—the merciful thing to do was refuse to participate; the genuine heroes, in his opinion, were the suicides, and the hero of heroes would be the swimmer who, in the very presence of the Other, refused Her proffered 'immortality' and thus put an end to at least one cycle of catastrophes.

"How we mocked him! Our moment came, we hurtled forth, pretending to glory in the adventure, thrashing, singing, cursing, strangling, rationalizing, rescuing, killing, inventing rules and stories and relationships, giving up, struggling on, but dying all, and still in darkness, until only a battered remnant was left to croak 'Onward, upward,' like a bitter echo. Then they too fell silent—victims, I can only presume, of the last frightful wave—and the moment came when I also, utterly desolate and spent, thrashed my last and gave myself over to the current, to sink or float as might be, but swim no more. Whereupon, marvelous to tell, in an instant the sea grew still! Then warmly, gently, the great tide turned, began to bear me, as it does now, onward and upward will-I nill-I, like a flood of joy—and I recalled with dismay my dead friend's teaching.

"I am not deceived. This new emotion is Her doing; the desire that possesses me is Her bewitchment. Lucidity passes from me; in a moment I'll cry 'Love!' bury myself in Her side, and be 'transfigured.' Which is to say, I die already; this fellow transported by passion is not I; *I am he who abjures and rejects the night-sea journey!* I. . . .

"I am all love. 'Come!' She whispers, and I have no will.

"You who I may be about to become, whatever You are: with the last twitch of my real self I beg You to listen. It is *not* love that sustains me! No; though Her magic makes me burn to sing the contrary, and though I drown even now for the blasphemy, I will say truth. What has fetched me across this dreadful sea is a single hope, gift of my poor dead comrade: that You may be stronger-willed than I, and that by sheer force of concentration I may transmit to You, along with Your official Heritage, a private legacy of awful recollection and negative resolve. Mad as it may be, my dream is that some unimaginable embodiment of myself (or myself plus Her if that's how it must be) will come to find itself expressing, in however garbled or radical a translation, some reflection of these reflections. If against all odds this comes to pass, may You to whom, through whom I speak, do what I cannot: terminate this aimless, brutal business! Stop Your hearing against Her song! Hate love!

"Still alive, afloat, afire. Farewell then my penultimate hope: that one may be sunk for direst blasphemy on the very shore of the Shore. Can it be (my old friend would smile) that only utterest nay-sayers survive the night? But even that were Sense, and there is no sense, only senseless love, senseless death. Whoever echoes these reflections: be more courageous than their author! An end to night-sea journeys! Make no more! And forswear me when I shall forswear myself, deny myself, plunge into Her who summons, singing . . .

"'Love! Love! Love!'"

Substance, Shadow, and Spirit[1]

T'ao Ch'ien

I. Substance to Shadow

Earth and heaven endure forever,
Streams and mountains never change.
Plants observe a constant rhythm,
Withered by frost, by dew restored.
But man, most sentient being of all,
In this is not their equal.
He is present here in the world today,
Then leaves abruptly, to return no more.
No one marks there's one man less—
Not even friends and family think of him;
The things that he once used are all that's left
To catch their eye and move them to grief.
I have no way to transcend change,
That it must be, I no longer doubt.
I hope you will take my advice:
When wine is offered, don't refuse.

II. Shadow to Substance

No use discussing immortality
When just to keep alive is hard enough.
Of course I want to roam in paradise
But it's a long way there and the road is lost.
In all the time since I met up with you
We never differed in our grief and joy.
In shade we may have parted for a time,
But sunshine always brings us close again.
Still this union cannot last forever—
Together we will vanish into darkness.
The body goes; that fame should also end
Is a thought that makes me burn inside.[2]
Do good, and your love will outlive you;

Surely this is worth your every effort.
While it is true, wine may dissolve care
That is not so good a way as this.

III. Spirit's Solution

The Great Potter cannot intervene—
All creation thrives of itself.
That Man ranks with Earth and Heaven
Is it not because of me?
Though we belong to different orders,
Being alive, I am joined to you,
Bound together for good or ill
I cannot refuse to tell you what I know:
The Three August Ones were great saints[3]
But where are they living today?
Though P'eng-tsu lasted a long time[4]
He still had to go before he was ready.
Die old or die young, the death is the same.[5]
Wise or stupid, there is no difference.
Drunk every day you may forget,
But won't it shorten your life span?
Doing good is always a joyous thing
But no one has to praise you for it.
Too much thinking harms my life;
Just surrender to the cycle of things,
Give yourself to the waves of the Great Change
Neither happy nor yet afraid.
And when it is time to go, then simply go
Without any unnecessary fuss.

Notes

[1] This is a Buddhist poem. Substance focuses on the fact of human mortality—life can be made acceptable only by recourse to the wine bottle. Perhaps he believes in Taoist practices which tried alchemy, diet, and breath-control in a search for long life. Shadow is clearly Confucian in desiring a reputation for good deeds that will live after him. Spirit comes out for a stoical acceptance of life and death that has affinities with Taoism. Though the bias is for Spirit's position, all of the attitudes are held by one person—an internal conflict. The

Preface states the point of departure for the poem: everyone is attached to life and this attachment is irreconcilable with the inevitability of death.

2. *burn inside:* Confucius has a similar statement in the *Analects*, XV, 19.
3. *Three August Ones:* These cannot be identified with certainty. Various suggestions have been made by Chinese commentators.
4. *a long time:* Traditionally, he lived eight-hundred years, a record even in Chinese, and he died regretting that he had not lived out his span.
5. *Die old. . . .* These lines reflect still a passage in the *Lish Tsu* (7.2a): "Among the living there are wise and foolish, noble and mean: this is how they differ. Dead there is corruption and extinction: it is in this that they are the same. . . . Ten-year-olds die and centenarians die, the good and the saintly die and the wicked and the stupid die."

My Confession

Leo Tolstoy

Although I regarded authorship as a waste of time, I continued to write during those fifteen years. I had tasted of the seduction of authorship, of the seduction of enormous monetary remunerations and applauses for my insignificant labour, and so I submitted to it, as being a means for improving my material condition and for stifling in my soul all questions about the meaning of my life and life in general.

In my writings I advocated, what to me was the only truth, that it was necessary to live in such a way as to derive the greatest comfort for oneself and one's family.

Thus I proceeded to live, but five years ago something very strange began to happen with me: I was overcome by minutes at first of perplexity and then of an arrest of life, as though I did not know how to live or what to do, and I lost myself and was dejected. But that passed, and I continued to live as before. Then those minutes of perplexity were repeated oftener and oftener, and always in one and the same form. These arrests of life found their expression in ever the same questions: "Why? Well, and then?"

At first I thought that those were simply aimless, inappropriate questions. It seemed to me that that was all well known and that if I ever wanted to busy myself with their solution, it would not cost me much labour,—that now I had no time to attend to them, but that if I wanted to I should find the proper answers. But the questions began to repeat themselves oftener and oftener, answers were demanded more and more persistently, and, like dots that fall on the same spot, these questions, without any answers, thickened into one black blotch.

There happened what happens with any person who falls ill with a mortal internal disease. At first there appear insignificant symptoms of indisposition, to which the patient pays no attention; then these symptoms are repeated more and more frequently and blend into one temporally indivisible suffering. The suffering keeps growing, and before the patient has had time to look around, he becomes conscious that what he took for an indisposition is the most significant thing in the world to him,—is death.

The same happened with me. I understood that it was not a passing indisposition, but something very important, and that, if the questions were going to repeat themselves, it would be necessary to find an answer for them. And I tried to answer them. The questions seemed to be so foolish, simple, and childish. But the moment I touched them and tried to solve them, I became convinced, in the first place, that they were not childish and foolish, but very important and profound questions in life, and, in the second, that, no matter how much I might try, I should not be able to answer them. Before attending to my Samára estate, to my son's education, or to the writing of a book, I ought to know why I should do that. So long as I did not know why, I could not do anything. I could not live. Amidst my thoughts of farming, which interested me very much during that time, there would suddenly pass through my head a question like this: "All right, you are going to have six thousand desyatínas of land in the Government of Samára, and three hundred horses,—and then?" And I completely lost my senses and did not know what to think farther. Or, when I thought of the education of my children, I said to myself: "Why?" Or, reflecting on the manner in which the masses might obtain their welfare, I suddenly said to myself: "What is that to me?" Or, thinking of the fame which my works would get me, I said to myself: "All right, you will be more famous than Gógol, Púshkin, Shakespeare, Molière, and all the writers in the world,—what of it?" And I was absolutely unable to make any reply. The questions were not waiting, and I had to answer them at once; if I did not answer them, I could not live. . . .

All that happened with me when I was on every side surrounded by what is considered to be complete happiness. I had a good, loving, and beloved wife, good children, and a large estate, which grew and increased without any labour on my part. I was respected by my neighbours and friends, more than ever before, was praised by strangers, and, without any self-deception, could consider my name famous. With all that, I was not deranged or mentally unsound,—on the contrary, I was in full command of my mental and physical powers, such as I had rarely met with in people of my age: physically I could work in a field, mowing, without falling behind a peasant; mentally I could work from eight to ten hours in succession, without experiencing any consequences from the strain. And while in such condition I arrived at the conclusion that I could not live, and, fearing death, I had to use cunning against myself, in order that I might not take my life.

This mental condition expressed itself to me in this form: my life is a stupid, mean trick played on me by somebody. Although I did not recognize that "somebody" as having created me, the form of the conception that some one had played a mean, stupid trick on me by bringing me into the world was the most natural one that presented itself to me.

Involuntarily I imagined that there, somewhere, there was somebody who was now having fun as he looked down upon me and saw me, who had lived for thirty or forty years, learning, developing, growing in body and mind, now that I had become strengthened in mind and had reached that summit of life from which it lay all before me, standing as a complete fool on that summit and seeing clearly that there was nothing in life and never would be. And that was fun to him—

But whether there was or was not that somebody who made fun of me, did not make it easier for me. I could not ascribe any sensible meaning to a single act, or to my whole life. I was only surprised that I had not understood that from the start. All that had long ago been known to everybody. Sooner or later there would come disease and death (they had come already) to my dear ones and to me, and there would be nothing left but stench and worms. All my affairs, no matter what they might be, would sooner or later be forgotten, and I myself should not exist. So why should I worry about all these things? How could a man fail to see that and live,—that was surprising! A person could live only so long as he was drunk; but the moment he sobered up, he could not help seeing that all that was only a deception and a stupid deception at that! Really, there was nothing funny and ingenious about it, but only something cruel and stupid.

Long ago has been told the Eastern story about the traveller who in the steppe is overtaken by an infuriated beast. Trying to save himself from the animal, the traveller jumps into a waterless well, but at its bottom he sees a dragon who opens his jaws in order to swallow him. And the unfortunate man does not dare climb out, lest he perish from the infuriated beast, and does not dare jump down to the bottom of the well, lest he be devoured by the dragon, and so clutches the twig of a wild bush growing in a cleft of the well and holds on to it. His hands grow weak and he feels that soon he shall have to surrender to the peril which awaits him at either side; but he still holds on and sees two mice, one white, the other black, in even measure making a circle around the main trunk of the bush to which he is clinging and nibbling at it on all sides. Now, at any moment, the bush will break and tear off, and he will fall into the dragon's jaws. The traveller sees this and knows that he will inevitably perish; but while he is still clinging, he sees some drops of honey hanging on the leaves of the bush, and he reaches out for them with his tongue and licks the leaves. Just so I hold on to the branch of life knowing that the dragon of death is waiting inevitably for me, ready to tear me to pieces, and I cannot understand why I have fallen on such suffering. And I try to lick that honey which used to give me pleasure; but now it no longer gives me joy, and the white and the black mouse day and night nibble at the branch to which I am holding on. I clearly see the dragon, and the honey is no longer sweet to me. I see only the inevitable dragon and the mice, and am unable to turn my glance away from them. That is not a fable, but a veritable, indisputable, comprehensible truth.

The former deception of the pleasures of life, which stifled the terror of the dragon, no longer deceives me. No matter how much one should say to me, "You cannot understand the meaning of life, do not think, live!" I am unable to do so, because I have been doing it too long before. Now I cannot help seeing day and night, which run and lead me up to death. I see that alone, because that alone is the truth. Everything else is a lie.

The two drops of honey that have longest turned my eyes away from the cruel truth, the love of family and of authorship, which I have called an art, are no longer sweet to me.

"My family—" I said to myself, "but my family, my wife and children, they are also human beings. They are in precisely the same condition that I am in: they must either live in the lie or see the terrible truth. Why should they live? Why should I love them, why guard, raise, and watch them? Is it for the same despair which is in me, or for dulness of perception? Since I love them, I cannot conceal the truth from them,—every step in cognition leads them up to this truth. And the truth is death."

"Art, poetry?" For a long time, under the influence of the success of human praise, I tried to persuade myself that that was a thing which could be done, even though death should come and destroy everything, my deeds, as well as my memory of them; but soon I came to see that that, too, was a deception. It was clear to me that art was an adornment of life, a decoy of life. But life lost all its attractiveness for me. How, then, could I entrap others ? So long as I did not live my own life, and a strange life bore me on its waves; so long as I believed that life had some sense, although I was not able to express it,—the reflections of life of every description in poetry and in the arts afforded me pleasure, and I was delighted to look at life through this little mirror of art;

but when I began to look for the meaning of life, when I experienced the necessity of living myself, that little mirror became either useless, superfluous, and ridiculous, or painful to me. I could no longer console myself with what I saw in the mirror, namely, that my situation was stupid and desperate. . . .

By abandoning myself to the bright side of knowledge I saw that I only turned my eyes away from the question. No matter how enticing and clear the horizons were that were disclosed to me, no matter how enticing it was to bury myself in the infinitude of this knowledge, I comprehended that these sciences were the more clear, the less I needed them, the less they answered my question.

"Well, I know," I said to myself, "all which science wants so persistently to know, but there is no answer to the question about the meaning of my life." But in the speculative sphere I saw that, in spite of the fact that the aim of the knowledge was directed straight to the answer of my question, or because of that fact, there could be no other answer than what I was giving to myself: "What is the meaning of my life?"—"None." Or, "What will come of my life?"—"Nothing." Or, "Why does everything which exists exist, and why do I exist?"—"Because it exists."

Putting the question to the one side of human knowledge, I received an endless quantity of exact answers about what I did not ask: about the chemical composition of the stars, about the movement of the sun toward the constellation of Hercules, about the origin of species and of man, about the forms of infinitely small, imponderable particles of ether; but the answer in this sphere of knowledge to my question what the meaning of my life was, was always: "You are what you call your life; you are a temporal, accidental conglomeration of particles. The interrelation, the change of these particles, produces in you that which you call life. This congeries will last for some time; then the interaction of these particles will cease, and that which you call life and all your questions will come to an end. You are an accidentally cohering globule of something. The globule is fermenting. This fermentation the globule calls its life. The globule falls to pieces, and all fermentation and all questions will come to an end." Thus the clear side of knowledge answers, and it cannot say anything else, if only it strictly follows its principles.

With such an answer it appears that the answer is not a reply to the question. I want to know the meaning of my life, but the fact that it is a particle of the infinite not only gives it no meaning, but even destroys every possible meaning. . . .

I lived for a long time in this madness, which, not in words, but in deeds, is particularly characteristic of us, the most liberal and learned of men. But, thanks either to my strange, physical love for the real working class, which made me understand it and see that it is not so stupid as we suppose, or to the sincerity of my conviction, which was that I could know nothing and that the best that I could do was to hang myself,—I felt that if I wanted to live and understand the meaning of life, I ought naturally to look for it, not among those who had lost the meaning of life and wanted to kill themselves, but among those billions departed and living men who had been carrying their own lives and ours upon their shoulders. And I looked around at the enormous masses of deceased and living men,—not learned and wealthy, but simple men,—and I saw something quite different. I saw that all these billions of men that lived or had lived, all, with rare exceptions, did not fit into my subdivisions, and that I could not recognize them as not understanding the question, because they themselves put it and answered it with surprising clearness. Nor could I recognize them as Epicureans, because their lives were composed rather of privations and suffering than of enjoyment. Still less could I recognize them as senselessly living out their meaningless lives, because every act of theirs and death itself was explained by them. They regarded it as the greatest evil to kill themselves. It appeared, then, that all humanity was in possession of a knowledge of the meaning of life, which I did not recognize and which I condemned. It turned out that rational knowledge did not give any meaning to life, excluded life, while the meaning which by billions of people, by all humanity, was ascribed to life was based on some despised, false knowledge.

The rational knowledge in the person of the learned and the wise denied the meaning of life but the enormous masses of men, all humanity recognized this meaning in an irrational knowledge. This irrational knowledge was faith, the same that I could not help but reject. That was God as one and three, the creation in six days, devils and angels, and all that which I could not accept so long as I had not lost my senses.

My situation was a terrible one. I knew that I should not find anything on the path of rational knowledge but the negation of life, and there, in faith, nothing but the negation of reason, which was still more impossible than the negation of life. From the rational knowledge it followed that life was an evil and men knew it,—it depended on men whether they should cease living, and yet they lived and continued to live, and I myself lived, though I had known long ago that life was meaningless and an evil. From faith it followed that, in order to understand life, I must renounce reason, for which alone a meaning was needed.

There resulted a contradiction, from which there were two ways out: either what I called rational was not so rational as I had thought; or that which to me appeared irrational was not so irrational as I had thought. And I began to verify the train of thoughts of my rational knowledge.

In verifying the train of thoughts of my rational knowledge, I found that it was quite correct. The deduction that life was nothing was inevitable; but I saw a mistake. The mistake was that I had not reasoned in conformity with the question put by me. The question was, "Why should I live?" that is, "What real, indestructible essence will come from my phantasmal, destructible life? What meaning has my finite existence in this infinite world?" And in order to answer this question, I studied life.

The solutions of all possible questions of life apparently could not satisfy me, because my question, no matter how simple it appeared in the beginning, included the necessity of explaining the finite through the infinite, and vice versa.

I asked, "What is the extra-temporal, extra-causal, extra-spatial meaning of life?" But I gave an answer to the question, "What is the temporal, causal, spatial meaning of my life?" The result was that after a long labour of mind I answered, "None." . . .

When I saw that [. . . for philosophy the solution remains insoluble] I understood that it was not right for me to look for an answer to my question in rational knowledge, and that the answer given by rational knowledge was only an indication that the answer might be got if the question were differently put, but only when into the discussion of the question should be introduced the question of the relation of the finite to the infinite. I also understood that, no matter how irrational and monstrous the answers might be that faith gave, they had this advantage that they introduced into each answer the relation of the finite to the infinite, without which there could be no answer.

No matter how I may put the question, "How must I live?" the answer is, "According to God's law." "What real result will there be from my life?"—"Eternal torment or eternal bliss." "What is the meaning which is not destroyed by death?"—"The union with infinite God, paradise."

Thus, outside the rational knowledge, which had to me appeared as the only one, I was inevitably led to recognize that all living humanity had a certain other irrational knowledge, faith, which made it possible to live.

All the irrationality of faith remained the same for me, but I could not help recognizing that it alone gave to humanity answers to the questions of life, and, in consequence of them, the possibility of living.

The rational knowledge brought me to the recognition that life was meaningless,—my life stopped, and I wanted to destroy myself. When I looked around at people, at all humanity, I saw that people lived and asserted that they knew the meaning of life. I looked back at myself: I lived so long as I knew the meaning of life. As to other people, so even to me, did faith give the meaning of life and the possibility of living.

Looking again at the people of other countries, contemporaries of mine and those passed away, I saw again the same. Where life had been, there faith, ever since humanity had existed, had given the possibility of living, and the chief features of faith were everywhere one and the same.

No matter what answers faith may give, its every answer gives to the finite existence of man the sense of the infinite,—a sense which is not destroyed by suffering, privation, and death. Consequently in faith alone could we find the meaning and possibility of life. What, then, was faith? I understood that faith was not merely an evidence of things not seen, and so forth, not revelation (that is only the description of one of the symptoms of faith), not the relation of man to man (faith has to be defined, and then God, and not first God, and faith through him), not merely an agreement with what a man was told, as faith was generally understood,—that faith was the knowledge of the meaning of human life, in consequence of which man did not destroy himself, but lived. **Faith is the power of life. If a man lives he believes in something.** If he did not believe that he ought to live for some purpose, he would not live. If he does not see and understand the phantasm of the finite, he believes in that finite; if he understands the phantasm of the finite, he must believe in the infinite. Without faith one cannot live. . . .

In order that all humanity may be able to live, in order that they may continue living, giving a meaning to life, they, those billions, must have another, a real knowledge of faith, for not the fact that I, with Solomon and Schopenhauer, did not kill myself convinced me of the existence of faith, but that these billions had lived and had borne us, me and Solomon, on the waves of life.

Then I began to cultivate the acquaintance of the believers from among the poor, the simple and unlettered folk, of pilgrims, monks, dissenters, peasants. The doctrine of these people from among the masses was also the Christian doctrine that the quasi-believers of our circle professed. With the Christian truths were also mixed in very many superstitions, but there was this difference: the superstitions of our circle were quite unnecessary to them, had no connection with their lives, were only a kind of an Epicurean amusement, while the superstitions of the believers from among the labouring classes were to such an extent blended with their life that it would have been impossible to imagine it without these superstitions,—it was a necessary condition of that life. I began to examine closely the lives and beliefs of these people, and the more I examined them, the more did I become convinced that they had the real faith, that their faith was necessary for them, and that it alone gave them a meaning and possibility of life. In contradistinction to what I saw in our circle, where life without faith was possible, and where hardly one in a thousand professed to be a believer, among them there was hardly one in a thousand who was not a believer. In contradistinction to what I saw in our circle, where all life passed in idleness, amusements, and tedium of life, I saw that the whole life of these people was passed in hard work, and that they were satisfied with life. In contradistinction to the people of our circle, who struggled and murmured against fate because of their privations and their suffering, these people accepted diseases and sorrows without any perplexity or opposition, but with the calm and firm conviction that it was all for good. In contradistinction to the fact that the more intelligent we are, the less do we understand the meaning of life and the more do we see a kind of a bad joke in our suffering and death, these people live, suffer, and approach death, and suffer in peace and more often in joy. In contradistinction to the fact that a calm death, a death without terror or despair, is the greatest exception in our circle, a restless, insubmissive, joyless death is one of the greatest exceptions among the masses. And of such people who are deprived of everything which for Solomon and for me constitutes the only good of life, and who withal experience the greatest happiness, there is an enormous number. I cast a broader glance about me. I examined the life of past and present vast masses of men, and I saw people who in like manner had understood the meaning of life, who had known how to live and die, not two, not three, not ten, but hundreds, thousands, millions. All of them, infinitely diversified as to habits, intellect, culture, situation, all equally and quite contrary to my ignorance knew the meaning of life and of death, worked calmly, bore privations and suffering, lived and died, seeing in that not vanity, but good.

I began to love those people. The more I penetrated into their life, the life of the men now living, and the life of men departed, of whom I had read and heard, the more did I love them, and the easier it became for me to live. Thus I lived for about two years, and within me took place a transformation, which had long been working within me, and the germ of which had always been in me. What happened with me was that the life of our circle,—of the rich and the learned,—not only disgusted me, but even lost all its meaning. All our acts, reflections, sciences, arts,—all that appeared to me in a new light. I saw that all that was mere pampering of the appetites, and that no meaning could be found in it; but the life of all the working masses, of all humanity, which created life, presented itself to me in its real significance. I saw that that was life itself and that the meaning given to this life was truth, and I accepted it.

The Death of Ivan Ilych

Leo Tolstoy

Ivan Ilych saw that he was dying, and he was in continual despair.

In the depth of his heart he knew he was dying, but not only was he not accustomed to the thought, he simply did not and could not grasp it.

The syllogism he had learnt from Kiezewetter's Logic: "Caius is a man, men are mortal, therefore Caius is mortal," had always seemed to him correct as applied to Caius, but certainly not as applied to himself. That Caius—man in the abstract—was mortal, was perfectly correct, but he was not Caius, not an abstract man, but a creature quite, quite separate from all others. He had been little Vanya, with a mamma and a papa, with Mitya and Volodya, with the toys, a coachman and a nurse, afterwards with Katenka and with all the joys, griefs, and delights of childhood, boyhood, and youth. What did Caius know of the smell of that striped leather ball Vanya had been so fond of? Had Caius kissed his mother's hand like that, and did the silk of her dress rustle so for Caius? Had he rioted like that at school when the pastry was bad? Had Caius been in love like that? Could Caius preside at a session as he did? "Caius really was mortal, and it was right for him to die; but for me, little Vanya, Ivan Ilych, with all my thoughts and emotions, it's altogether a different matter. It cannot be that I ought to die. That would be too terrible."

Such was his feeling.

"If I had to die like Caius I should have known it was so. An inner voice would have told me so, but there was nothing of the sort in me and I and all my friends felt that our case was quite different from that of Caius. And now here it is!" he said to himself, "It can't be. It's impossible! But here it is. How is this? How is one to understand it?"

He could not understand it, and tried to drive this false, incorrect, morbid thought away and to replace it by other proper and healthy thoughts. But that thought, and not the thought only but the reality itself, seemed to come and confront him.

And to replace that thought he called up a succession of others, hoping to find in them some support. He tried to get back into the former current of thoughts that had once screened the thought of death from him. But strange to say, all that had formerly shut off, hidden, and destroyed, his consciousness of death, no longer had that effect. Ivan Ilych now spent most of his time in attempting to re-establish that old current. He would say to himself: "I will take up my duties again—after all I used to live by them." And banishing all doubts he would go to the law courts, enter into conversation with his colleagues, and sit carelessly as was his wont, scanning the crowd with a thoughtful look and leaning both his emaciated arms on the arms of his oak chair; bending over as usual to a colleague and drawing his papers nearer he would interchange whispers with him, and then suddenly raising his eyes and sitting erect would pronounce certain words and open the proceedings. But suddenly in the midst of those proceedings the pain in his side, regardless of the stage the proceedings had reached, would begin its own gnawing work. Ivan Ilych would turn his attention to it and try to drive the thought of it away, but without success. *It* would come and stand before him and look at him, and he would be petrified and the light would die out of his eyes, and he would again begin asking himself whether *It* alone was true. And his colleagues and subordinates would see with surprise and distress that he, the brilliant and subtle judge, was becoming confused and making mistakes. He would shake himself, try to pull himself together, manage somehow to bring the sitting to a close, and return home with the sorrowful consciousness that his judicial labours could not as formerly hide from him what he wanted them to hide, and could not deliver him from *It*. And what was worst of all was that *It* drew his attention to itself not in order to make him take some action but only that he should look at *It*, look it straight in the face: look at it and with out doing anything, suffer inexpressibly.

And to save himself from this condition Ivan Ilych looked for consolations—new screens—and new screens were found and for a while seemed to save him, but then they immediately fell to pieces or rather became transparent, as if *It* penetrated them and nothing could veil *It*. . . .

His wife returned late at night. She came in on tiptoe, but he heard her, opened his eyes, and made haste to close them again. She wished to send Gerasim away and to sit with him herself, but he opened his eyes and said: "No, go away."

"Are you in great pain?"

"Always the same."

"Take some opium."

He agreed and took some. She went away.

Till about three in the morning he was in a state of stupefied misery. It seemed to him that he and his pain were being thrust into a narrow, deep black sack, but though they were pushed further and further in they could not be pushed to the bottom. And this, terrible enough in itself, was accompanied by suffering. He was frightened yet wanted to fall through the sack, he struggled but yet co-operated. And suddenly he broke through, fell, and regained consciousness. Gerasim was sitting at the foot of the bed dozing quietly and patiently, while he himself lay with his emaciated stockinged legs resting on Gerasim's shoulders; the same shaded candle was there and the same unceasing pain.

"Go away, Gerasim," he whispered.

"It's all right, sir. I'll stay a while."

"No. Go away."

He removed his legs from Gerasim's shoulders, turned sideways onto his arm, and felt sorry for himself. He only waited till Gerasim had gone into the next room and then restrained himself no longer but wept like a child. He wept on account of his helplessness, his terrible loneliness, the cruelty of man, the cruelty of God, and the absence of God.

"Why hast Thou done all this? Why hast Thou brought me here? Why, why dost Thou torment me so terribly?"

He did not expect an answer and yet wept because there was no answer and could be none. The pain again grew more acute, but he did not stir and did not call. He said to himself: "Go on! Strike me! But what is it for? What have I done to Thee? What is it for?"

Then he grew quiet and not only ceased weeping but even held his breath and became all attention. It was as though he were listening not to an audible voice but to the voice of his soul, to the current of thoughts arising within him.

"What is it you want?" was the first clear conception capable of expression in words, that he heard.

"What do you want? What do you want?" he repeated to himself.

"What do I want? To live and not to suffer," he answered.

And again he listened with such concentrated attention that even his pain did not distract him.

"To live? How?" asked his inner voice.

"Why, to live as I used to—well and pleasantly."

"As you lived before, well and pleasantly?" the voice repeated.

And in imagination he began to recall the best moments of his pleasant life. But strange to say none of those best moments of his pleasant life now seemed at all what they had then seemed—none of them except the first recollections of childhood. There, in childhood, there had been something really pleasant with which it would be possible to live if it could return. But the child who had experienced that happiness existed no longer, it was like a reminiscence of somebody else.

As soon as the period began which had produced the present Ivan Ilych, all that had then seemed joys now melted before his sight and turned into something trivial and often nasty.

And the further he departed from childhood and the nearer he came to the present the more worthless and doubtful were the joys. This began with the School of Law. A little that was really good was still found there—there was light-heartedness, friendship, and hope. But in the upper classes there had already been fewer of such good moments. Then during the first years of his official career, when he was in the service of the Governor, some pleasant moments again occurred: they were the memories of love for a woman. Then all became confused and there was still less of what was good; later on again there was still less that was good, and the further he went the less there was. His marriage, a mere accident, then the disenchantment that followed it, his wife's bad breath and the sensuality and hypocrisy: then that deadly official life and those preoccupations about money, a year of it, and two, and ten, and twenty, and always the same thing. And the longer it lasted the more deadly it became. "It is as if I had been going downhill while I imagined I was going up. And that is really what it was. I was going up in public opinion, but to the same extent life was ebbing away from me. And now it is all done and there is only death."

"Then what does it mean? Why? It can't be that life is so senseless and horrible. But if it really has been so horrible and senseless, why must I die and die in agony? There is something wrong!"

"**Maybe I did not live as I ought to have done,**" it suddenly occurred to him. "**But how could that be, when I did everything properly?**" he replied, and immediately dismissed from his mind this, the sole solution of all the riddles of life and death, as something quite impossible.

"Then what do you want now? To live? Live how? Live as you lived in the law courts when the usher proclaimed "The judge is coming!" The judge is coming, the judge!" he repeated to himself. "Here he is, the judge. But I am not guilty!" he exclaimed angrily. "What is it for?" And he ceased crying, but turning his face to the wall continued to ponder on the same question: Why, and for what purpose, is there all this horror? But however much he pondered he found no answer. And whenever the thought occurred to him, as it often did, that it all resulted from his not having lived as he ought to have done, he at once recalled the correctness of his whole life and dismissed so strange an idea.

Another fortnight passed. Ivan Ilych now no longer left his sofa. He would not lie in bed but lay on the sofa, facing the wall nearly all the time. He suffered ever the same unceasing agonies and in his loneliness pondered always on the same insoluble question: "What is this? Can it be that it is Death?" And the inner voice answered: "Yes, it is Death."

"Why these sufferings?" And the voice answered, "For no reason—they just are so." Beyond and besides this there was nothing.

From the very beginning of his illness, ever since he had first been to see the doctor, Ivan Ilych's life had been divided between two contrary and alternating moods: now it was despair and the expectation of this uncomprehended and terrible death, and now hope and an intently interested observation of the functioning of his organs. Now before his eyes there was only a kidney or an intestine that temporarily evaded its duty, and now only that incomprehensible and dreadful death from which it was impossible to escape.

These two states of mind had alternated from the very beginning of his illness, but the further it progressed the more doubtful and fantastic became the conception of the kidney, and the more real the sense of impending death.

He had but to call to mind what he had been three months before and what he was now, to call to mind with what regularity he had been going downhill, for every possibility of hope to be shattered.

Latterly during that loneliness in which he found himself as he lay facing the back of the sofa, a loneliness in the midst of a populous town and surrounded by numerous acquaintances and relations but that yet could not have been more complete anywhere—either at the bottom of the sea or under the earth—during that terrible loneliness Ivan Ilych had lived only in memories of the past. Pictures of his past rose before him one after another. They always began with what was nearest in time and then went back to what was most remote—to his childhood—and rested there. If he thought of the stewed prunes that had been offered him that day, his mind went back to the raw shrivelled French plums of his childhood, their peculiar flavour and the flow of saliva when he sucked their stones, and along with the memory of that taste came a whole series of memories of those days: his nurse, his brother, and their toys. "No, I musn't think of that. . . . It is too painful," Ivan Ilych said to himself, and brought himself back to the present—to the button on the back of the sofa and the creases in its morocco. "Morocco is expensive, but it does not wear well: there had been a quarrel about it. It was a different kind of quarrel and a different kind of morocco that time when we tore father's portfolio and were punished, and mamma brought us some tarts. . . ." And again his thoughts dwelt on his childhood, and again it was painful and he tried to banish them and fix his mind on something else.

Then again together with that chain of memories another series passed through his mind—of how his illness had progressed and grown worse. There also the further back he looked the more life there had been. There had been more of what was good in life and more of life itself. The two merged together. "Just as the pain went on getting worse and worse, so my life grew worse and worse," he thought. "There is one bright spot there at the back, at the beginning of life, and afterwards all becomes blacker and blacker and proceeds more and more rapidly—in inverse ratio to the square of the distance from death," thought Ivan Ilych. And the example of a stone falling downwards with increasing velocity entered his mind. Life, a series of increasing sufferings, flies further and further towards its end—the most terrible suffering. "I am flying. . . ." He shuddered, shifted himself, and tried to resist, but was already aware that resistance was impossible, and again with eyes weary of gazing but unable to cease seeing what was before them, he stared at the back of the sofa and waited—awaiting that dreadful fall and shock and destruction.

"Resistance is impossible!" he said to himself. "If I could only understand what it is all for! But that too is impossible. An explanation would be possible if it could be said that I have not lived as I ought to. But it is impossible to say that," and he remembered all the legality, correctitude, and propriety of his life. "That at any rate can certainly not be admitted," he thought, and his lips smiled ironically as if someone could see that smile and be taken in by it. "There is no explanation! Agony, death . . . What for?"

Another two weeks went by in this way and during that fortnight an event occurred that Ivan Ilych and his wife had desired. Petrishchev formally proposed. It happened in the evening. The next day Praskovya Fëdorovna came into her husband's room considering how best to inform him of it, but that very night there had been a fresh change for the worse in his condition. She found him still lying on the sofa but in a different position. He lay on his back, groaning and staring fixedly straight in front of him.

She began to remind him of his medicines, but he turned his eyes towards her with such a look that she did not finish what she was saying; so great an animosity, to her in particular, did that look express.

"For Christ's sake let me die in peace!" he said.

She would have gone away, but just then their daughter came in and went up to say good morning. He looked at her as he had done at his wife, and in reply to her inquiry about his health said dryly that he would soon free them all of himself. They were both silent and after sitting with him for a while went away.

"Is it our fault?" Lisa said to her mother. "It's as if we were to blame! I am sorry for papa, but why should we be tortured?"

The doctor came at his usual time. Ivan Ilych answered "Yes" and "No," never taking his angry eyes from him, and at last said: "You know you can do nothing for me, so leave me alone."

"We can ease your sufferings."

"You can't even do that. Let me be."

The doctor went into the drawing-room and told Praskovya Fëdorovna that the case was very serious and that the only resource left was opium to allay her husband's sufferings, which must be terrible.

It was true, as the doctor said, that Ivan Ilych's physical sufferings were terrible, but worse than the physical sufferings were his mental sufferings, which were his chief torture.

His mental sufferings were due to the fact that that night, as he looked at Gerasim's sleepy, good-natured face with his prominent cheekbones, the question suddenly occurred to him: "What if my whole life has really been wrong?"

It occurred to him that what had appeared perfectly impossible before, namely that he had not spent his life as he should have done, might after all be true. **It occurred to him that his scarcely perceptible attempts to struggle against what was considered good by the most highly placed people, those scarcely noticeable impulses which he had immediately suppressed, might have been the real thing, and all the rest false.** And his professional duties and the whole arrangement of his life and of his family, and all his social and official interests, might all have been false. He tried to defend all those things to himself and suddenly felt the weakness of what he was defending. There was nothing to defend.

"But if that is so," he said to himself, "and I am leaving this life with the consciousness that I have lost all that was given me and it is impossible to rectify it—what then?"

He lay on his back and began to pass his life in review in quite a new way. In the morning when he saw first his footman, then his wife, then his daughter, and then the doctor, their every word and movement confirmed to him the awful truth that had been revealed to him during the night. In them he saw himself—all that for which he had lived—and saw clearly that it was not real at all, but a terrible and huge deception which had hidden both life and death. This consciousness intensified his physical suffering tenfold. He groaned and tossed about, and pulled at his clothing which choked and stifled him. And he hated them on that account.

He was given a large dose of opium and became unconscious, but at noon his sufferings began again. He drove everybody away and tossed from side to side.

His wife came to him and said:

"Jean, my dear, do this for me. It can't do any harm and often helps. Healthy people often do it."

He opened his eyes wide.

"What? Take communion? Why? It's unnecessary! However . . ."

She began to cry.

"Yes, do, my dear. I'll send for our priest. He is such a nice man."

"All right. Very well," he muttered.

When the priest came and heard his confession, Ivan Ilych was softened and seemed to feel a relief from his doubts and consequently from his sufferings, and for a moment there came a ray of hope. He again began to think of the vermiform appendix and the possibility of correcting it. He received the sacrament with tears in his eyes.

When they laid him down again afterwards he felt a moment's ease, and the hope that he might live awoke in him again. He began to think of the operation that had been suggested to him. "To live! I want to live!" he said to himself.

His wife came in to congratulate him after his communion, and when uttering the usual conventional words she added:

"You feel better, don't you?"

Without looking at her he said "Yes."

Her dress, her figure, the expression of her face, the tone of her voice, all revealed the same thing. "This is wrong, it is not as it should be. All you have lived for and still live for is falsehood and deception, hiding life and death from you." And as soon as he admitted that thought, his hatred and his agonizing physical suffering again sprang up, and with that suffering a consciousness of the unavoidable, approaching end. And to this was added a new sensation of grinding shooting pain and a feeling of suffocation.

The expression of his face when he uttered that "yes" was dreadful. Having uttered it, he looked her straight in the eyes, turned on his face with a rapidity extraordinary in his weak state and shouted:

"Go away! Go away and leave me alone!"

From that moment the screaming began that continued for three days, and was so terrible that one could not hear it through two closed doors without horror. At the moment he answered his wife he realized that he was lost, that there was no return, that the end had come, the very end, and his doubts were still unsolved and remained doubts.

"Oh! Oh! Oh!" he cried in various intonations. He had begun by screaming "I won't!" and continued screaming on the letter O.

For three whole days, during which time did not exist for him, he struggled in that black sack into which he was being thrust by an invisible, resistless force. He struggled as a man condemned to death struggles in the hands of the executioner, knowing that he cannot save himself. And every moment he felt that despite all his efforts he was drawing nearer and nearer to what terrified him. He felt that his agony was due to his being thrust into that black hole and still more to his not being able to get right into it. He was hindered from getting into it by his conviction that his life had been a good one. That very justification of his life held him fast and prevented his moving forward, and it caused him most torment of all.

Suddenly some force struck him in the chest and side, making it still harder to breathe, and he fell through the hole and there at the bottom was a light. What had happened to him was like the sensation one sometimes experiences in a railway carriage when one thinks one is going backwards while one is really going forwards and suddenly becomes aware of the real direction.

"Yes, it was all not the right thing," he said to himself, "but that's no matter. It can be done. But what is the right thing?" he asked himself, and suddenly grew quiet.

This occurred at the end of the third day, two hours before his death. Just then his schoolboy son had crept softly in and gone up to the bedside. The dying man was still screaming desperately and waving his arms. His hand fell on the boy's head, and the boy caught it, pressed it to his lips, and began to cry.

At that very moment Ivan Ilych fell through and caught sight of the light, and it was revealed to him that though his life had not been what it should have been, this could still be rectified. He asked himself, "What is the right thing?" and grew still, listening. Then he felt that someone was kissing his hand. He opened his eyes, looked at his son, and felt sorry for him. His wife came up to him and he glanced at her. She was gazing at him open-mouthed, with undried tears on her nose and cheek and a despairing look on her face. He felt sorry for her too.

"Yes, I am making them wretched," he thought. "They are sorry, but it will be better for them when I die." He wished to say this but had not the strength to utter it. "Besides, why speak? I must act," he thought. With a look at his wife he indicated his son and said: "Take him away . . . sorry for him . . . sorry for you too. . . ." He tried to add, "forgive me," but said "forgo" and waved his hand, knowing that He whose understanding mattered would understand.

And suddenly it grew clear to him that what had been oppressing him and would not leave him was all dropping away at once from two sides, from ten sides, and from all sides. He was sorry for them, he must act so as not to hurt them: release them and free himself from these sufferings. "How good and how simple!" he thought. "And the pain?" he asked himself. "What has become of it? Where are you, pain?"

He turned his attention to it.

"Yes, here it is. Well, what of it? Let the pain be."

"And death . . . where is it?

He sought his former accustomed fear of death and did not find it. "Where is it? What death?" There was no fear because there was no death.

In place of death there was light.

"So that's what it is!" he suddenly exclaimed aloud. "What joy!"

To him all this happened in a single instant, and the meaning of that instant did not change. For those present his agony continued for another two hours. Something rattled in his throat, his emaciated body twitched, then the gasping and rattle became less and less frequent.

"It is finished!" said someone near him.

He heard these words and repeated them in his soul.

"Death is finished," he said to himself. "It is no more!"

He drew in a breath, stopped in the midst of a sigh, stretched out, and died.

The Myth of Sisyphus

Albert Camus

An Absurd Reasoning

Absurdity and Suicide

There is but one truly serious philosophical problem, and that is suicide. Judging whether life is or is not worth living amounts to answering the fundamental question of philosophy. All the rest—whether or not the world has three dimensions, whether the mind has nine or twelve categories—comes afterwards. These are games; one must first answer. And if it is true, as Nietzsche claims, that a philosopher, to deserve our respect, must preach by example, you can appreciate the importance of that reply, for it will precede the definitive act. These are facts the heart can feel; yet they call for careful study before they become clear to the intellect.

If I ask myself how to judge that this question is more urgent than that, I reply that one judges by the actions it entails. I have never seen anyone die for the ontological argument. Galileo, who held a scientific truth of great importance, abjured it with the greatest ease as soon as it endangered his life. In a certain sense, he did right. That truth was not worth the stake. Whether the earth or the sun revolves around the other is a matter of profound indifference. To tell the truth, it is a futile question. On the other hand, I see many people die because they judge that life is not worth living. I see others paradoxically getting killed for the ideas or illusions that give them a reason for living (what is called a reason for living is also an excellent reason for dying). I therefore conclude that the meaning of life is the most urgent of questions. How to answer it? On all essential problems (I mean thereby those that run the risk of leading to death or those that intensify the passion of living) there are probably but two methods of thought: the method of La Palisse and the method of Don Quixote. Solely the balance between evidence and lyricism can allow us to achieve simultaneously emotion and lucidity. In a subject at once so humble and so heavy with emotion, the learned and classical dialectic must yield, one can see, to a more modern attitude of mind deriving at one and the same time from common sense and understanding. . . .

Chapter X: Meaning

All great deeds and all great thoughts have a ridiculous beginning. Great works are often both on a streetcorner or in a restaurant's revolving door. So it is with absurdity. The absurd word more than others derives its nobility from this abject birth. In certain situations, replying "nothing" when asked what one is thinking about may be pretense in a man. Those who are loved are well aware of this. But if that reply is sincere, if it symbolizes that odd state of soul in which the void becomes eloquent, in which the chain of daily gestures is broken, in which the heart vainly seeks the link that will connect it again, then it is as it were the first sign of absurdity.

It happens that the stage sets collapse. Rising streetcar, four hours in the office or the factory meal, streetcar, four hours of work, meal, sleep and Monday Tuesday Wednesday Thursday Friday and Saturday according to the same rhythm—this path is easily followed most of the time. But one day the "why" arises and everything begins in that weariness tinged with amazement. "Begins"—this is important. Weariness comes at the end of the acts of a mechanical life, but at the same time it inaugurates the impulse of consciousness. It awakens consciousness and provokes what follows. What follows is the gradual return into the chain or it is the definitive awakening. At the end of the awakening comes in time, the consequence: suicide or recovery. In itself weariness has something sickening about it. Here, I must conclude that it is good. For everything begins with consciousness and nothing is worth anything except through it. There is nothing original about these remarks. But they are obvious; that is enough for a while, during a sketchy reconnaissance in the origins of the absurd. Mere "anxiety," as Heidegger says, is at the source of everything.

Likewise and during every day of an unillustrious life, time carries us. But a moment always comes when we have to carry it. We live on the future: "tomorrow," "later on," "when you have made your way," "you will understand when you are old enough" Such irrelevancies are wonderful, for, after all, it's a matter of dying. Yet a day comes when a man notices or says that he is thirty. Thus he asserts his youth. But simultaneously he situates himself in relation to time. He takes his place in it. He admits that he stands at a certain point on a curve that he acknowledges having to travel to its end. He belongs to time, and by the horror that seizes him, he recognizes his worst enemy. Tomorrow, he was longing for tomorrow, whereas everything in him ought to reject it. That revolt of the flesh is the absurd.

A step lower and strangeness creeps in: perceiving that the world is "dense," sensing to what a degree a stone is foreign and irreducible to us, with what intensity nature or a landscape can negate us. At the heart of all beauty lies something inhuman, and these hills, the softness of the sky, the outline of these trees at this very minute lose the illusory meaning with which we had clothed them, henceforth more remote than a lost paradise. The primitive hostility of the world rises up to face us across millennia. For a second we cease to understand it because for centuries we have understood in it solely the images and designs that we had attributed to it beforehand, because henceforth we lack the power to make use of that artifice. The world evades us because it becomes itself again. That stage scenery masked by habit becomes again what it is. It withdraws at a distance from us. Just as there are days when under the familiar face of a woman, we see as a stranger her we had loved months or years ago, perhaps we shall come even to desire what suddenly leaves us so alone. But the time has not yet come. Just one thing: that denseness and that strangeness of the world is the absurd.

Men, too, secrete the inhuman. At certain moments of lucidity, the mechanical aspect of their gestures, their meaningless pantomime makes silly everything that surrounds them. A man is talking on the telephone behind a glass partition; you cannot hear him, but you see his incomprehensible dumb show: you wonder why he is alive. This discomfort in the face of man's own inhumanity, this incalculable tumble before the image of what we are, this "nausea," as a writer of today calls it, is also the absurd. Likewise the stranger who at certain seconds comes to meet us in a mirror, the familiar and yet alarming brother we encounter in our own photographs is also the absurd.

I come at last to death and to the attitude we have toward it. On this point everything has been said and it is only proper to avoid pathos. Yet one will never be suffficiently surprised that everyone lives as if no one "knew." This is because in reality there is no experience of death. Properly speaking, nothing has been experienced but what has been lived and made conscious. Here, it is barely possible to speak of the experience of others' deaths. It is a substitute, an illusion, and it never quite convinces us. That melancholy convention cannot be persuasive. The horror comes in reality from the mathematical aspect of the event. If time frightens us, this is because it works out the problem and the solution comes afterward. All the pretty speeches about the soul will have their contrary convincingly proved, at least for a time. From this inert body on which a slap makes no mark the soul has disappeared. This elementary and definitive aspect of the adventure constitutes the absurd feeling. Under the fatal lighting of that destiny, its uselessness becomes evident. No code of ethics and no effort are justifiable *a priori* in the face of the cruel mathematics that command our condition.

Let me repeat: all this has been said over and over. I am limiting myself here to making a rapid classification and to pointing out these obvious themes. They run through all literatures and all philosophies. Everyday conversation feeds on them. There is no question of reinventing them. But it is essential to be sure of these facts in order to be able to question oneself subsequently on the primordial question. I am interested—let me repeat again—not so much in absurd discoveries as in their consequences. If one is assured of these facts, what is one to conclude, how far is one to go to elude nothing? Is one to die voluntarily or to hope in spite of everything? . . .

Of whom and of what indeed can I say: "I know that!" This heart within me I can feel, and I judge that it exists. This world I can touch, and I likewise judge that it exists. There ends all my knowledge, and the rest is construction. For if I try to seize this self of which I feel sure, if I try to define and to summarize it, it is nothing but water slipping through my fingers. I can sketch one by one all the aspects it is able to assume, all those likewise that have been attributed to it, this upbringing, this origin, this ardor or these silences, this nobility or this vileness. But aspects cannot be added up. This very heart which is mine will forever remain indefinable to me. Between the certainty I have of my existence and the content I try to give to that assurance, the gap will never be filled. Forever I shall be a stranger to myself. In psychology as in logic, there are truths but no truth. Socrates' "Know thyself" has as much value as the "Be virtuous" of our confessionals. They reveal a nostalgia at the same time as an ignorance. They are sterile exercises on great subjects. They are legitimate only in precisely so far as they are approximate.

And here are trees and I know their gnarled surface, water and I feel its taste. These scents of grass and stars at night, certain evenings when the heart relaxes—how shall I negate this world whose power and strength I feel? Yet all the knowledge on earth will give me nothing to assure me that this world is mine. You describe it to me and you teach me to classify it. You enumerate its laws and in my thirst for knowledge I admit that they are true. You take apart its mechanism and my hope increases. As the final stage you teach me that this wonderous and multicolored universe can be reduced to the atom and that the atom itself can be reduced to the electron. All this is good and I wait for you to continue. But you tell me of an invisible planetary system in which electrons gravitate around a nucleus. You explain this world to me with an image. I realize then that you have been reduced to poetry: I shall never know. Have I the time to become indignant? You have already changed theories. So that science that was to teach me everything ends up in a hypothesis, that lucidity founders in metaphor, that uncertainty is resolved in a work of art. What need had I of so many efforts? The soft lines of these hills and the hand of evening on this troubled heart teach me much more. I have returned to my beginning. I realize that if through science I can see phenomena and enumerate them, I cannot, for all that, apprehend the world. Were I to trace its entire relief with my finger, I should not know any more. And you give me the choice between a description that is sure but that teaches me nothing and hypotheses that claim to teach me but that are not sure. A stranger to myself and to the world, armed solely with a thought that negates itself as soon as it asserts, what is this condition in which I can have peace only by refusing to know and to live, in which the appetite for conquest bumps into walls that defy its assaults? To will is to stir up paradoxes. Everything is ordered in such a way as to bring into being that poisoned peace produced by thoughtlessness, lack of heart, or fatal renunciations.

Hence the intelligence, too, tells me in its way that this world is absurd. Its contrary, blind reason, may well claim that all is clear; I was waiting for proof and longing for it to be right. But despite so many pretentious centuries and over the heads of so many eloquent and persuasive men, I know that is false. On this plane, at least, there is no happiness if I cannot know. That universal reason, practical or ethical, that determinism, those categories that explain everything are enough to make a decent man laugh. They have nothing to do with the mind. They negate its profound truth, which is to be enchained. In this unintelligible and limited universe, man's fate henceforth assumes its meaning. A horde of irrationals has sprung up and surrounds him until his ultimate end. In his recovered and now studied lucidity, the feeling of the absurd becomes clear and definite. I said that the world is absurd, but I was too hasty. This world in itself is not reasonable, that is all that can be said. But what is absurd is the confrontation of this irrational and the wild longing for clarity whose call echoes in the human heart. The absurd depends as much on man as on the world. For the moment it is all that links them together. It binds them one to the other as only hatred can weld two creatures together....

Absurd Freedom

Now the main thing is done, I hold certain facts from which I cannot separate. What I know, what is certain, what I cannot deny, what I cannot reject—this is what counts. I can negate everything of that part of me that lives on vague nostalgias, except this desire for unity, this longing to solve, this need for clarity and cohesion. I can refute everything in this world surrounding me that offends or enraptures me, except this chaos, this sovereign chance and this divine equivalence which springs from anarchy. I don't know whether this world has a meaning that transcends it. But I know that I do not know that meaning and that it is impossible for me just now to know it. What can a meaning outside my condition mean to me? I can understand only in human terms. What I touch, what resists me—that is what I understand. And these two certainties—my appetite for the absolute and for unity and the impossibility of reducing this world to a rational and reasonable principle—I also know that I cannot reconcile them. What other truth can I admit without lying, without bringing in a hope I lack and which means nothing within the limits of my condition?

If I were a tree among trees, a cat among animals, this life would have a meaning, or rather this problem would not arise, for I should belong to this world. I should *be* this world to which I am now opposed by my whole consciousness and my whole insistence upon familiarity. This ridiculous reason is what sets me in opposition to all creation. I cannot cross it out with a stroke of the pen. What I believe to be true I must therefore preserve. What seems to me so obvious, even against me, I must support. And what constitutes the basis of that conflict, of that break between the world and my mind, but the awareness of it? If therefore I want to preserve it, I can through a constant awareness, ever revived, ever alert. This is what, for the moment, I must remember. At this moment the absurd, so obvious and yet so hard to win, returns to a man's life and finds its home there. At this moment too, the mind can leave the arid, dried-up path of lucid effort. That path now emerges in daily life. It encounters the world of the anonymous impersonal pronoun "one," but henceforth man enters in with his revolt and his lucidity. He has forgotten how to hope. This hell of the present is his Kingdom at last. All problems recover their sharp edge. Abstract evidence retreats before the poetry of forms and colors. Spiritual conflicts become embodied and return to the abject and magnificent shelter of man's heart. None of them is settled. But all are transfigured. Is one going to die, escape by the leap, rebuild a mansion of ideas and forms to one's own scale? Is one, on the contrary, going to take up the heart-rending and marvelous wager of the absurd? Let's make a final effort in this regard and draw all our conclusions. The body, affection, creation, action, human nobility will then resume their places in this mad world. At last man will again find there the wine of the absurd and the bread of indifference on which he feeds his greatness.

Let us insist again on the method: it is a matter of persisting. At a certain point on his path the absurd man is tempted. History is not lacking in either religions or prophets, even without gods. He is asked to leap. All he can reply is that he doesn't fully understand, that it is not obvious. Indeed, he does not want to do anything but what he fully understands. He is assured that this is the sin of pride, but he does not understand the notion of sin; that perhaps hell is in store, but he has not enough imagination to visualize that strange future; that he is losing immortal life, but that seems to him an idle consideration. An attempt is made to get him to admit his guilt. He feels innocent. To tell the truth, that is all he feels—his irreparable innocence. This is what allows him everything. Hence, what he demands of himself is to live *solely* with what he knows, to accommodate himself to what is, and to bring in nothing that is not certain. He is told that nothing is. But this at least is a certainty. And it is with this that he is concerned: he wants to find out if it is possible to live *without appeal*. . . .

Now I can broach the notion of suicide. It has already been felt what solution might be given. At this point the problem is reversed. It was previously a question of finding out whether or not life had to have a meaning to be lived. It now becomes clear, on the contrary, that it will be lived all the better if it has no meaning. Living an experience, a particular fate, is accepting it fully. Now, no one will live this fate, knowing it to be absurd, unless he does everything to keep before him that absurd brought to light by consciousness. Negating one of the terms of the opposition on which he lives amounts to escaping it. To abolish conscious revolt is to elude the problem. The theme of permanent revolution is thus carried into individual experience. Living is keeping the absurd alive. Keeping it alive is, above all, contemplating it. Unlike Eurydice, the absurd dies only when we turn away from it. One of the only coherent philosophical positions is thus revolt. It is a constant confrontation between man and his own obscurity. It is an insistence upon an impossible transparency. It challenges the world anew every second. Just as danger provided man the unique opportunity of seizing awareness, so metaphysical revolt extends awareness to the whole of experience. It is that constant presence of man in his own eyes. It is not aspiration, for it is devoid of hope. That revolt is the certainty of a crushing fate, without the resignation that ought to accompany it.

This is where it is seen to what a degree absurd experience is remote from suicide. It may be thought that suicide follows revolt—but wrongly. For it does not represent the logical outcome of revolt. It is just the contrary by the consent it presupposes. Suicide, like the leap, is acceptance at its extreme. Everything is over and man returns to his essential history. His future, his unique and dreadful future—he sees and rushes toward it. In its way, suicide settles the absurd. It engulfs the absurd in the same death. But I know that in order to keep alive, the absurd cannot be settled. It escapes suicide to the extent that it is simultaneously awareness and rejection of death. It is, at the extreme limit of the condemned man's last thought, that shoelace that despite everything he sees a few yards away, on the very brink of his dizzying fall. The contrary of suicide, in fact, is the man condemned to death.

That revolt gives life its value. Spread out over the whole length of a life, it restores its majesty to that life. To a man devoid of blinders, there is a finer sight than that of the intelligence at grip with a reality that transcends it. The sight of human pride is unequaled. No disparagement is of any use. That discipline that the mind imposes on itself, that will conjured up out of nothing that face-to-face struggle have something exceptional about them. To impoverish that reality whose inhumanity constitutes man's majesty is tantamount to impoverishing him himself. I understand then why the doctrines that explain everything to me also debilitate me at the same time. They relieve me of the weight of my own life, and yet I must carry it alone. At this juncture I cannot conceive that a skeptical metaphysics can be joined to an ethics of renunciation.

Consciousness and revolt, these rejections are the contrary of renunciation. Everything that is indomitable and passionate in a human heart quickens them, on the contrary, with its own life. It is essential to die unreconciled and not of one's own free will. Suicide is a repudiation. The absurd man can only drain everything to the bitter end, and deplete himself. The absurd is his extreme tension, which he maintains constantly in solitary effort, for he knows that in that consciousness and in that day-to-day revolt he gives proof of his only truth, which is defiance. This is a first consequence. . . .

The Myth of Sisyphus

The gods had condemned Sisyphus to ceaselessly rolling a rock to the top of a mountain, whence the stone would fall back of its own weight. They had thought with some reason that there is no more dreadful punishment than futile and hopeless labor.

If one believes Homer, Sisyphus was the wisest and most prudent of mortals. According to another tradition, however, he was disposed to practice the profession of highwayman. I see no contradiction in this. Opinions differ as to the reasons why he became the futile laborer of the underworld. To begin with, he is accused of a certain levity in regard to the gods. He stole their secrets. Ægina, the daughter of Æsopus, was carried off by Jupiter. The father was shocked by that disappearance and complained to Sisyphus. He, who knew of the abduction, offered to tell about it on condition that Æsopus would give water to the citadel of Corinth. To the celestial thunderbolts he preferred the benediction of water. He was punished for this in the underworld. Homer tells us also that Sisyphus had put Death in chains. Pluto could not endure the sight of his deserted, silent empire. He dispatched the god of war, who liberated Death from the hands of her conqueror.

It is said also that Sisyphus, being near to death, rashly wanted to test his wife's love. He ordered her to cast his unburied body into the middle of the public square. Sisyphus woke up in the underworld. And there, annoyed by an obedience so contrary to human love, he obtained from Pluto permission to return to earth in order to chastise his wife. But when he had seen again the face of this world, enjoyed water and sun, warm stones and the sea, he no longer wanted to go back to the infernal darkness. Recalls, signs of anger, warnings were of no avail. Many years more he lived facing the curve of the gulf, the sparkling sea, and the smiles of earth. A decree of the gods was necessary. Mercury came and seized the impudent man by the collar and, snatching him from his joys, led him forcibly back to the underworld, where his rock was ready for him.

You have already grasped that Sisyphus is the absurd hero. He *is*, as much through his passions as through his torture. His scorn of the gods, his hatred of death, and his passion for life won him that unspeakable penalty in which the whole being is exerted toward accomplishing nothing. This is the price that must be paid for the passions of this earth. Nothing is told us about Sisyphus in the underworld. Myths are made for the imagination to breathe life into them. As for this myth, one sees merely the whole effort of a body straining to raise the huge stone, to roll it and push it up a slope a hundred times over; one sees the face screwed up, the cheek tight against the stone, the shoulder bracing the clay-covered mass, the foot wedging it, the fresh start with arms outstretched, the wholly human security of two earth-clotted hands. At the very end of his long effort measured by skyless space and time without depth, the purpose is achieved. Then Sisyphus watches the stone rush down in a few moments toward that lower world whence he will have to push it up again toward the summit. He goes back down to the plain.

It is during that return, that pause, that Sisyphus interests me. A face that toils so close to stones is already stone itself! I see that man going back down with a heavy yet measured step toward the torment of which he will never know the end. That hour like a breathing-space which returns as surely as his suffering, that is the hour of consciousness. At each of those moments when he leaves the heights and gradually sinks toward the lairs of the gods, he is superior to his fate. He is stronger than his rock.

If this myth is tragic, that is because its hero is conscious. Where would his torture be, indeed, if at every step the hope of succeeding upheld him? The workman of today works every day in his life at the same tasks, and this fate is no less absurd. But it is tragic only at the rare moments when it becomes conscious. Sisyphus, proletarian of the gods, powerless and rebellious, knows the whole extent of his wretched condition: it is what he thinks of during his descent. The lucidity that was to constitute his torture at the same time crowns his victory. There is no fate that cannot be surmounted by scorn. . . .

If the descent is thus sometimes performed in sorrow, it can also take place in joy. This word is not too much. Again I fancy Sisyphus returning toward his rock, and the sorrow was in the beginning. When the images of earth cling too tightly to memory, when the call of happiness becomes too insistent, it happens that melancholy rises in man's heart: this is the rock's victory, this is the rock itself. The boundless grief is too heavy to bear. These are our nights of Gethsemane. But crushing truths perish from being acknowledged. Thus, Œdipus at the outset obeys fate without knowing it. But from the moment he knows, his tragedy begins. Yet at the same moment, blind and desperate, he realizes that the only bond linking him to the world is the cool hand of a girl. Then a tremendous remark rings out: "Despite so many ordeals, my advanced age and the nobility of my soul make me conclude that all is well." Sophocles' Œdipus, like Dostoevsky's Kirilov, thus gives the recipe for the absurd victory. Ancient wisdom confirms modern heroism.

One does not discover the absurd without being tempted to write a manual of happiness. "What! by such narrow ways—?" There is but one world, however. Happiness and the absurd are two sons of the same earth. They are inseparable. It would be a mistake to say that happiness necessarily springs from the absurd discovery. It happens as well that the feeling of the absurd springs from happiness. "I conclude that all is well," says Œdipus, and that remark is sacred. It echoes in the wild and limited universe of man. It teaches that all is not, has not been, exhausted. It drives out of this world a god who had come into it with dissatisfaction and a preference for futile sufferings. It makes of fate a human matter, which must be settled among men.

All Sisyphus' silent joy is contained therein. His fate belongs to him. His rock is his thing. Likewise, the absurd man, when he contemplates his torment, silences all the idols. In the universe suddenly restored to its silence, the myriad wondering little voices of the earth rise up. Unconscious, secret calls, invitations from all the facts they are the necessary reverse and price of victory. There is no sun without shadow, and it is essential to know the night. The absurd man says yes and his effort will henceforth be unceasing. If there is a personal fate, there is no higher destiny or at least there is but one which he concludes inevitable and despicable. For the rest, he knows himself to be the master of his days. At that submoment when man glances backward over a life, Sisyphus returning toward his rock, in the slight pivoting he contemplates that series of the related actions which becomes his fate, created in him, combined under his memory's eye and so sealed by his death. Thus, convinced of the wholly human origin of all that is human, a blind man eager to see who knows that the night has no end, he is still on the go. The rock is so rolling.

I leave Sisyphus at the foot of the mountain. One always finds one's burden again. But Sisyphus teaches the higher fidelity that negates the gods and raises rocks. He too concludes that all is well. This universe henceforth without a mass seems to him neither sterile nor futile. Each atom of that stone, each mineral flake of that night filled mountain, in itself forms a world. The struggle itself toward the heights is enough to be a man's heart. One must imagine Sisyphus happy.

Response

Martin Buber

Response

This fragile life between birth and death can nevertheless be a fulfillment—if it is a dialogue. In our life and experience we are addressed; by thought and speech and action, by producing and by influencing we are able to answer. For the most part we do not listen to the address, or we break into it with chatter. But if the word comes to us and the answer proceeds from us then human life exists, though brokenly, in the world. The kindling of the response in that "spark" of the soul, the blazing up of the response, which occurs time and again, to the unexpectedly approaching speech, we term responsibility. **We practice responsibility for that realm of life allotted and entrusted to us for which we are able to respond, that is, for which we have a relation of deeds which may count—in all our inadequacy—as a proper response.**

Responsibility

The idea of responsibility is to be brought back from the province of specialized ethics into that of lived life. Genuine responsibility exists only where there is real responding.

Responding to what?

To what happens to one, to what is to be seen and heard and felt. Each concrete hour allotted to the person, with its content drawn from the world and from destiny, is speech for the man who is attentive. Attentive, for no more than that is needed in order to make a beginning with the reading of the signs that are given to you.

Ethics

Ethical life has entered into religious life, and cannot be extracted from it. There is no responsibility unless there is One to whom one is responsible, for there is no response where there is no address. In the last resort, religious life means concreteness itself, the whole concreteness of life without reduction, grasped dialogically, included in the dialogue.

Reality

With all deference to the world continuum of space and time I know as a living truth only concrete world reality which is constantly, in every moment, reached out to me. I can separate it into its component parts, I can compare them and distribute them into groups of similar phenomena, I can derive them from earlier and reduce them to simpler phenomena; and when I have done all this I have not touched my concrete world reality. Inseparable, incomparable, irreducible, now, happening once only, it gazes upon me with an awesome look.

Symbols

Dogmas and rules are merely the result, subject to change, of the human mind's attempt to make comprehensible, by a symbolic order of the knowable and doable, the working of the unconditional it experiences within itself. Primary reality is constituted by the effect of the unconditional upon the human mind which, sustained by the force of its own vision, unflinchingly faces the supreme power. Man's mind thus experiences the unconditional as that great something which is set over against it, as the Thou as such. By creating symbols, the mind comprehends what is in itself incomprehensible: thus, in symbol and adage, the illimitable God reveals Himself to the human mind, which gathers the flowing universal currents into the receptacle of an affirmation that declares the Lord reigns in this and in no other way. Or man's mind captures a flash of the original source of light in the mirror of some rule which declares that the Lord must be served in this and in no other way. But neither symbol nor adage makes man unworthy or untrue; they are rather forms the unconditional itself creates within man's mind which, at this particular time, has not yet developed into a more effective tool. "For the divine wishes to evolve within mankind." In mankind's great ages, the divine, in invisible becoming, outgrows old symbolisms and blossoms forth in new ones. The symbol becomes ever more internalized, moves ever closer to the heart, and is ever more deeply submerged in life itself; and the man who five thousand years ago saw it in the stars, sees it today in the eyes of a friend. It is not God who changes, only theophany—the manifestation of the divine in man's symbol-creating mind: until no symbol is adequate any longer, and none is needed, and life itself, in the miracle of man's being with man, becomes a symbol—until God is actually present when one man clasps the hand of another.

Dualism

We shall accomplish nothing at all if we divide our world and our life into two domains, one in which God's command is paramount, the other governed exclusively by the laws of economics, politics, and the "simple self-assertion" of the group. Such dualism is far more ominous than the naturalism I spoke of before. Stopping one's ears so as not to hear the voice from above is breaking the connection between existence and the meaning of existence. But he who hears the voice and sets a limit to the area beyond which its rule shall not extend is not merely moving away from God, like the person who refuses to listen; he is standing up directly against Him.

Imitatio

Man cannot "be like unto God," but with all the inadequacy of each of his days, he can follow God at all times, using the capacity he has on that particular day—and if he has used the capacity of that day to the full, he has done enough. This is not a mere act of faith; it is an entering into the life that has to be lived on that day with all the active fullness of a created person.

Limits

Human life and humanity come into being in genuine meetings. There man learns not merely that he is limited by man, cast upon his own finitude, partialness, need of completion, but his own relation to truth is heightened by the other's different relation to the same truth—different in accordance with his individuation, and destined to take seed and grow differently. Men need, and it is granted to them, to confirm one another in their individual being by means of genuine meetings. But beyond this they need, and it is granted to them, to see that the truth, which the soul gains by its struggle, is flashing up for the others, the brothers, in a different way, and equally confirmed.

The Primary Word

The primary word I-Thou can be spoken only with the whole being. Concentration and fusion into the whole being can never take place through my agency, nor can it ever take place without me. I become through my relation to the Thou; as I become I, I say Thou.

All real living is meeting.

Obstacles

The relation to the Thou is direct. No system of concepts, no foreknowledge, and no fancy intervene between I and Thou. The memory itself is transformed as it plunges out of its isolation into the unity of the whole. No set purpose, no greed, and no anticipation intervene between I and Thou. Desire itself is transformed as it plunges out of its dream into the appearance. Every means is an obstacle. Only when every means has collapsed does the meeting come about.

It-Thou

In all the seriousness of truth, hear this: without It man cannot live. But he who lives with It alone is not a man.

How powerful is the unbroken world of It, and how delicate are the appearances of the Thou!

Truth

Is there a truth we can possess? Can we appropriate it? There certainly is none we can pick up and put in our pocket. But the individual can have an honest and uncompromising attitude toward the truth; he can have a legitimate relationship to truth and hold and uphold it all his life. A man may serve Truth for seven years and yet another seven and still not win her, but his relationship has become more genuine and true, more and more truth itself. He cannot achieve this relationship to truth without breaking through his conditionality. He cannot shed it altogether; that is never within his power. But he can, at least, sense something of unconditionality—he can breathe its air. From that time on, this "something of" will quicken his relationship to the truth. Human truth becomes real when one tries to translate one's relationship to truth into the reality of one's life. And human truth can be communicated only if one throws one's self into the process and answers for it with one's self.

The Eternal Thou

The extended lines of relations meet in the eternal Thou.

Every particular Thou is a glimpse through to the eternal Thou; by means of every particular Thou the primary word addresses the eternal Thou.

Thinking

If we are serious about thinking between I and Thou, then it is not enough to cast our thoughts toward the other subject of thought framed by thought. We should also, with the thinking, precisely with the thinking, live toward the other man, who is not framed by thought but bodily present before us; we should live toward his concrete life. We should live not toward another thinker of whom we wish to know nothing beyond his thinking but, even if the other is a thinker, toward his bodily life over and above his thinking—rather, toward his person, to which, to be sure, the activity of thinking also belongs.

Hope

The hope for this hour depends upon the renewal of dialogical immediacy between men. But let us look beyond the pressing need, the anxiety and care of this hour. Let us see this need in connection with the great human way. Then we shall recognize that immediacy is injured not only between man and man, but also between the being called man and the source of his existence. At its core the conflict between the mistrust and trust of man conceals the conflict between the mistrust and trust of eternity. If our mouths succeed in genuinely saying "thou," then, after long silence and stammering, we shall have addressed our eternal "Thou" anew. Reconciliation leads toward reconciliation.

Reciprocity

Philosophy errs in thinking of religion as founded in a noetic act, even if an inadequate one, and in therefore regarding the essence of religion as the knowledge of an object which is indifferent to being known. As a result, philosophy understands faith as an affirmation of truth lying somewhere between clear knowledge and confused opinion. Religion, on the other hand, insofar as it speaks of knowledge at all, does not understand it as a noetic relation of a thinking subject to a neutral object of thought, but rather as mutual contact, as the genuinely reciprocal meeting in the fullness of life between one active existence and another. Similarly, it understands faith as the entrance into this reciprocity, as binding oneself in relationship with an undemonstrable and unprovable, yet even so, in relationship, knowable Being, from whom all meaning comes.

Courage and Love

The relation of the spirit to the elemental forces and urges must not be interpreted from the point of view of pure thought. An attempt at interpretation must consider the influence of the spirit upon life. But—regardless of what it may call itself or be called at any given moment—the spirit which is not content in the area of thought and expresses itself in all of life becomes manifest as the power of faith. In the domain of the human soul, it appears as faithful courage and faithful love. Based on the power of faith, the spirit exerts its influence upon the world through its agents, courage and love. These constitute its power which may well govern the elemental forces because it has known them from the earliest times, and knows what is their due. Though in one historical era after another the spirit may seem dethroned and exiled, it does not lose its power. Again and again, unexpectedly and unpredictably, it causes what is intrinsic in the course of history through its agents, faithful courage and faithful love.

Education

The education I mean is a guiding toward reality and realization. That man alone is qualified to teach who knows how to distinguish between appearance and reality, between seeming realization and genuine realization, who rejects appearance and chooses and grasps reality, no matter what world-view he chooses. This education educates the adherents of all world-views to genuineness and to truth. It educates each of them to take his world-view seriously: to start from the genuineness of its ground and to move toward the truth of its goal.

Three Passions

Bertrand Russell

Three passions, simple but overwhelmingly strong, have governed my life: the longing for love, the search for knowledge, and unbearable pity for the suffering of mankind. These passions, like great winds, have blown me hither and thither, in a wayward course, over a deep ocean of anguish, reaching to the very verge of despair.

I have sought love, first, because it brings ecstasy—ecstasy so great that I would often have sacrificed all the rest of life for a few hours of this joy. I have sought it, next, because it relieves loneliness—that terrible loneliness in which one shivering consciousness looks over the rim of the world into the cold unfathomable lifeless abyss. I have sought it, finally, because in the union of love I have seen, in a mystic miniature, the prefiguring vision of the heaven that saints and poets have imagined. This is what I sought, and though it might seem too good for human life, this is what—at last—I have found.

With equal passion I have sought knowledge. I have wished to understand the hearts of men. I have wished to know why the stars shine. And I have tried to apprehend the Pythagorean power by which number holds sway above the flux. A little of this, but not much, I have achieved.

Love and knowledge, so far as they were possible, led upward toward the heavens. But always pity brought me back to earth. Echoes of cries of pain reverberate in my heart. Children in famine, victims tortured by oppressors, helpless old people a hated burden to their sons, and the whole world of loneliness, poverty, and pain make a mockery of what human life should be. I long to alleviate the evil, but I cannot, and I too suffer.

This has been my life. I have found it worth living, and would gladly live it again if the chance were offered me.

Appendix

Truth and Validity

Irving M. Copi

An argument ... is any group of propositions of which one is claimed to follow from the others, which are regarded as providing evidence for the truth of that one.... An argument is not a mere collection of propositions, but has a structure. In describing this structure, the terms "premiss" and "conclusion" are usually employed. The *conclusion* of an argument is that proposition which is affirmed on the basis of the other propositions of the argument, and these other propositions which are affirmed as providing evidence or reasons for accepting the conclusion are the *premisses* of that argument.

It should be noted that "premiss" and "conclusion" are relative terms: one and the same proposition can be a premise of one argument and a conclusion in another. Consider, for example, the following argument:

> No act performed involuntarily should be punished.
> Some criminal acts are performed involuntarily.
> Therefore some criminal acts should not be punished.

Here the proposition *some criminal acts should not be punished* is the conclusion, and the other two propositions are the premisses. But the first premiss in this argument, *no acts performed involuntarily should be punished*, is the conclusion in the following (different) argument:

> No act beyond the control of the agent should be punished.
> All involuntary acts are beyond the control of the agent.
> Therefore no act performed involuntarily should be punished.

No proposition, taken all by itself, in isolation, is either a premiss or a conclusion. It is a premiss only when it occurs in an argument which assumes it for the sake of showing that some other proposition is thereby justified. And it is a conclusion only when it occurs in an argument which attempts to establish or prove it on the basis of other propositions which are assumed. This notion is common enough: it is like the fact that a man, taken by himself, is neither an employer nor an employee, but may be either in different contexts, employer to his gardener, employee of the firm for which he works.

Arguments are traditionally divided into two different types, *deductive* and *inductive*. While every argument involves the claim that its premisses provide evidence for the truth of its conclusion, only a *deductive* argument claims that its premises provide *conclusive* evidence. In the case of deductive arguments the technical terms "valid" and "invalid" are used in place of "correct" and "incorrect." A deductive argument is *valid* when its premises do provide conclusive evidence for its conclusion, that is, when premises and conclusion are so related that it is absolutely impossible for the premises to be true unless the conclusion is true also. Every deductive argument is either valid or invalid, and the task of deductive logic is to clarify the nature of the relationship which holds between premises and conclusion in a valid argument, and thus to allow us to discriminate between valid and invalid arguments. . . .

An inductive argument, on the other hand, does not claim that its premises give conclusive evidence for the truth of its conclusion, but only that they provide *some* evidence for it. Inductive arguments are neither *valid* nor *invalid* in the sense in which those terms are applied to deductive arguments. Inductive arguments may, of course, be evaluated as better or worse, according to the degree of likelihood or probability which their premises confer upon their conclusions. . . .

Truth and falsehood may be predicated of propositions, but never of arguments. And the properties of validity and invalidity can belong only to deductive arguments, never to propositions. There is a connection between the validity or invalidity of an argument and the truth or falsehood of its premises and conclusion, but this connection is by no means a simple one. Some valid arguments contain only true propositions, as, for example:

> All whales are mammals.
> All mammals have lungs.
> Therefore all whales have lungs.

But an argument may contain false propositions exclusively, and be valid nevertheless, as, for example:

> All spiders have six legs.
> All six legged creatures have wings.
> Therefore all spiders have wings.

This argument is valid because *if* its premises were true its conclusion would have to be true also, even though in fact they are all false. On the other hand, if we reflect upon the argument:

> If I owned all the gold in Fort Knox, then I would be very wealthy.
> I do not own all the gold in Fort Knox.
> Therefore I am not very wealthy.

we see that although its premisses and conclusion are true, the argument is invalid. That the premisses *could* be true and the conclusion false, if not immediately apparent, may be made clear by considering that if I were to inherit a million dollars, the premisses would remain true while the conclusion would become false. This point is further illustrated by the following argument, which is of the same form as the preceding one:

> If Rockefeller owned all the gold in Fort Knox, then Rockefeller would be very wealthy.
> Rockefeller does not own all the gold in Fort Knox.
> Therefore Rockefeller is not very wealthy.

The premisses of this argument are true, and its conclusion is false. Such an argument cannot be valid, because it is impossible for the premisses of a valid argument to be true while its conclusion is false.

The preceding examples show that there are valid arguments with false conclusions, as well as invalid arguments with true conclusions. Hence the truth or falsehood of its conclusion does not determine the validity or invalidity of an argument. Nor does the validity of an argument guarantee the truth of its conclusion. There are perfectly valid arguments which have false conclusions—but any such argument must have at least one false premise. The term "sound" is introduced to characterize a valid argument all of whose premisses are true. Clearly the conclusion of a *sound* argument is true. A deductive argument fails to establish the truth of its conclusion if it is *unsound*, which means either that it is not *valid*, or that not all of its premisses are *true*. To test the truth or falsehood of premisses is the task of science in general, since premisses may deal with any subject matter at all. The logician is not so much interested in the truth or falsehood of propositions as in the logical relations between them, where by the "logical" relations between propositions we mean those which determine the correctness or incorrectness of arguments in which they may occur. Determining the correctness or incorrectness of arguments falls squarely within the province of logic. The logician is interested in the correctness even of arguments whose premisses might be false. . . .

Common Fallacies and Errors of Reasoning

Peter A. Facoine

Question: How can I resist being deceived by someone's faulty reasoning?

Fact: Some deceptions are so common they have made names for themselves.

A Few Famous Fallacies

A *fallacy* is a mistaken argument, one that should not be accepted as a demonstration of the truth of its conclusion. Fallacies can result from a variety of causes. Some are simply mistakes, for example, errors in the application of sophisticated research methods. Some result from relying on false assumptions. Some occur because of formal (structural) errors in the way the argument's statements are put together. Here are some classic types of fallacies:

Appeal to ignorance. Claiming that the mere absence of a reason for rejecting an opinion counts as a good reason to accept it.

Appeal to the mob. Claiming that because "everyone" believes something it must be true.

Ad hominem attacks. Claiming that supposed deficiencies in a person's character, heritage, sex, nationality, or some other aspect of personality are grounds for rejecting the truth of what the person says.

Equivocation. Relying on the vagueness or ambiguity of words or phrases in order to demonstrate a point.

False cause. Any of a group of fallacies based on false assumptions regarding causality. For example, assuming that because event A happened after event B that B must be a cause of A.

Misuse of authority: Claiming that whatever an authoritative person says about anything (particularly anything outside his or her field of expertise) must be true.

Irrelevant appeal. Any of a group of fallacies, such as misuse of authority, which give as the reason for accepting a conclusion a rationale that is not demonstrably relevant to the truth or falsity of that conclusion. For example, appeal to celebrity status, appeal to what "everyone thinks," appeal to occult forces, appeal to astrological conditions, appeal to novelty or tradition.

The gambler's fallacy. Any of a group of fallacies that rely on errors regarding probability, such as that random events are causally connected.

Composition. Claiming that a characteristic of each part of a thing is necessarily a characteristic of the whole thing.

Division. Claiming that a characteristic of the whole thing is necessarily a characteristic of each of its parts.

Straw man fallacy. Claiming that by refuting the weakest of a series of arguments for a given claim, one has successfully refuted the claim.

Affirming the consequent. Fallaciously reasoning that if P, then Q. Q. Therefore, P. For example, the occurrence of A is sufficient to bring about an occurrence of B. B happened. So, A must have happened. Wrong; something else, C, might also be a sufficient condition for B, and this time it was C, not A, that caused B.

Denying the antecedent. Fallaciously reasoning that if P, then Q. Not P. Therefore, not Q. For example, the occurrence of X is sufficient to bring about an occurrence of Y. But X did not happen. So, Y will not happen." Wrong; something else, W, might also be a sufficient condition for Y, and W could lead to Y this time.

Playing with numbers. Any of a group of fallacies that misuses numbers, especially percentages and raw numbers, to exaggerate or diminish the apparent significance of the conclusion.

False dilemma. Claiming that there are no more options to consider, that a choice must be made between the options at hand, or that all of the options at hand are undesirable.

Begging the question. Relying on the truth of the intended conclusion as a basis to support one or more of an argument's premises. (This error is also sometimes called *reasoning in a circle*.)

Emotional appeal. Not strictly speaking an argument, this tactic plays on a person's emotions (fear, affection, anxiety, etc.) in order to get the person to do something, such as to buy an object or to agree with a given opinion or point of view.

Index of Philosophers' Quotations

Anaxagoras
    Mind is unlimited, autonomous, and pure.   116
    Mind set in order all that was, is, and will be.   117

Anaximander
    The apeiron (that is, the "infinite unbounded") is the primary principle of all things.   108

Anaximenes
    Our souls, which are pneuma (that is, air) keep us together as the pneuma binds together the cosmos.   108

Anselm, Saint
    Hence, something greater than which nothing can be conceived so truly exists that it cannot be conceived not to be.   462

Aquinas, Saint Thomas
    The existence of God can be proved in five ways.   471

Aristotle
    Every art and every scientific inquiry, and similarly every action and purpose, may be said to aim at some good.   356
    . . . happiness is an activity of soul in accordance with complete or perfect virtue.   362
    . . . friendship is a kind of virtue or implies virtue. It is also indispensable to life. For nobody would choose to live without friends, although he were in possession of every other good.   367

Barth, John
    One way or another, no matter which theory of our journey is correct, it's myself I address; to whom I rehearse as to a stranger our history and condition, and will disclose my secret hope though I sink for it.   633

Benedict, Ruth
    . . . morality differs in every society, and is a convenient term for socially approved habits.   410

Index of Philosophers' Quotations

Benjamin, Walter
    Even the most perfect reproduction of a work of art is lacking in one element: its presence in time and space, its unique existence at the place where it happens to be.   440

    The presence of the original is the prerequisite to the concept of authenticity.   440

Berkeley, George
    For as to what is said of the absolute existence of unthinking things without any relation to their being perceived, that is to me perfectly unintelligible. Their *esse* is *percipi*, nor is it possible they should have any existence out of the minds or thinking things which perceive them.   125

    ... certainly no idea, whether faint or strong, can exist otherwise than in a mind perceiving it.   130

Bhagavad Gita
    To action alone hast thou a right and never at all to its fruit; let not the fruits of action be thy motive; neither let there be in thee any attachment to inaction.   328

Bradley, Francis H.
    Truth is an ideal expression of the Universe, at once coherent and comprehensive.   268

Brannigan, Michael C.
    Philosophy in India is essentially concerned with self-deliverance.   67

    The key idea in Chinese philosophical thought, however, is harmony.   71

    [Japanese] philosophy is typified by its concern for immediacy, sensitivity, and relationship.   76

Buber, Martin
    This fragile life between birth and death can nevertheless be a fulfillment—if it is a dialogue.   676

    We practice responsibility for that realm of life allotted and entrusted to us for which we are able to respond, that is, for which we have a relation of deeds which may count—in all our inadequacy—as a proper response.   676

Camus, Albert
    There is but one truly serious philosophical problem, and that is suicide.   665

Chong, Wang
    Let us try to prove by means of the species of creatures that the dead do not become spiritual beings, do not possess consciousness, and cannot hurt people.   609

Index of Philosophers' Quotations

How can there be a spirit in the world that has consciousness from itself but is without a body? — 611

Code, Lorraine
... the sex of the knower is epistemologically significant. — 237

Confucius
"Is there one word which may serve as a rule of practice for all one's life?" The Master said, "Is not Reciprocity such a word? What you do not want done to yourself, do not do to others." — 341

I Corinthians 15
The last enemy *that* shall be destroyed *is* death. — 626

So when this corruptible shall have put on incorruption, and this mortal shall have put on immortality, then shall be brought to pass the saying that is written, Death is swallowed up in victory. — 628

Democritus
In truth, nothing exists but atoms and the void. — 117

Descartes, René
It is now some years since I detected how many were the false beliefs that I had from my earliest youth admitted as true, and how doubtful was everything I had since constructed on this basis; and from that time I was convinced that I must once for all seriously undertake to rid myself of all the opinions which I had formerly accepted, and commence to build anew from the foundation. — 181

I shall nevertheless make an effort and follow anew the same path as that on which I yesterday entered, i.e. I shall proceed by setting aside all that in which the least doubt could be supposed to exist, just as if I had discovered that it was absolutely false; and I shall ever follow in this road until I have met with something which is certain, or at least, if I can do nothing else, until I have learned for certain that there is nothing in the world that is certain. — 185

And noticing that this truth—*I think, therefore I am*—was so firm and so certain that the most extravagant suppositions of the sceptics were unable to shake it, I judged that I could accept it without scruple as the first principle of the philosophy I was seeking. — 194

d'Holbach, Baron
Man's life is a line that nature commands him to describe upon the surface of the earth, without his ever being able to swerve from it, even for an instant. — 521

In all this he always acts according to necessary laws from which he has no means of emancipating himself. — 522

The actions of man are never free. — 525

Dostoyevsky, Fedor

... they have vanquished freedom and have done so to make men happy. — 551

So long as man remains free he strives for nothing so incessantly and so painfully as to find some one to worship. — 553

Eddington, Sir Arthur

The whole trend of modern scientific views is to break down the separate categories of "things," "influences," "forms," etc., and to substitute a common background of all experience. — 121

I need not tell you that modern physics has by delicate test and remorseless logic assured me that my second scientific table is the only one which is really there—wherever "there" may be. On the other hand I need not tell you that modern physics will never succeed in exorcising that first table—strange compound of external nature, mental imagery, and inherited prejudice—which lies visible to my eyes and tangible to my grasp. — 122

Empedocles

The sources from which all has come are earth, water, air, and fire. — 115

Love brings scattered things together. At another time Strife rends them apart. — 115

Epicurus

... so long as we exist death is not with us; but when death comes, then we do not exist. — 619

Frankl, Viktor

... everything can be taken from a man but one thing: the last of the human freedoms—to choose one's attitude in any given set of circumstances, to choose one's own way — 571

The way in which a man accepts his fate and all the suffering it entails, the way in which he takes up his cross, gives him ample opportunity even under the most difficult circumstances—to add a deeper meaning to his life. It may remain brave, dignified and unselfish. Or in the bitter fight for self-preservation he may forget his human dignity and become no more than an animal. — 572

Griffiths, Morwenna

Feminist writing questions and challenges the assumption that emotion, feeling, nature, and bodies are in opposition to rationality, mind, and freedom. — 58

... truth and knowledge become distorted when feelings are not acknowledged. — 59

Index of Philosophers' Quotations

Grimshaw, Jean
 ... the idea that virtue is in some way *gendered*, that the standards and criteria of morality are different for women and men, is one that has been central to the ethical thinking of a great many philosophers.   390

Hansen, Valerie
 Still, the majority of the dead, it was thought, went to an underworld. There they retained the power to influence events on earth. If they wanted to hurt the living, they could play tricks, cause illness, provoke misfortune, or even bring death.   598

Heidegger, Martin
 The essence of truth reveals itself as freedom.   302
 As letting beings be, freedom is intrinsically the resolutely open bearing that does not close up in itself. All comportment is grounded in this bearing and receives from it directedness toward beings and disclosure of them.   304

Heraclitus
 Everything flows and nothing remains fixed.   109
 No one steps twice into the same river since the waters flow on and on.   109
 Change alone does not change.   109

Hesse, Hermann
 Seeking means: to have a goal; but finding means: to be free, to be receptive, to have no goal.   95
 Knowledge can be communicated, but not wisdom. One can find it, live it, be fortified by it, do wonders through it, but one cannot communicate and teach it.   97
 Time is not real.   97

Hick, John
 To many, the most powerful positive objection to belief in God is the fact of evil.   500
 ... if God is perfectly loving, he must wish to abolish evil; and if he is all-powerful, he must be able to abolish evil. But evil exists; therefore God cannot be both omnipotent and perfectly loving.   500

Hospers, John
 There is a whole web of meaning-connections between perceiving and having a body; when we try to break all the connections we appear to be reduced to unintelligibility.   614

Hume, David

To begin with clear and self-evident principles, to advance by timorous and sure steps, to review frequently our conclusions, and examine accurately all their consequences; though by these means we shall make both a slow and a short progress in our systems; are the only methods, by which we can ever hope to reach truth, and attain a proper stability and certainty in our determinations.	200
All the objects of human reason or inquiry may naturally be divided into two kinds, to wit, "Relations of Ideas," and "Matters of Fact."	220
All inferences from experience, therefore, are effects of custom, not of reasoning.	233

Huxley, T. H.

This principle may be stated in various ways, but they all amount to this: that it is wrong for a man to say that he is certain of the objective truth of any proposition unless he can produce evidence which logically justifies that certainty.	497

James, William

What, in short, is the truth's cash-value in experiential terms?	270
Truth *happens* to an idea.	270
In truths dependent on our personal action, then, faith based on desire is certainly a lawful and possibly an indispensable thing.	493
In concreto, the freedom to believe can only cover living options which the intellect of the individual cannot by itself resolve; and living options never seem absurdities to him who has them to consider.	496

Kant, Immanuel

Enlightenment is man's release from his self-incurred tutelage.	19
An age cannot bind itself and ordain to put the succeeding one into such a condition that it cannot extend its (at best very occasional) knowledge, purify itself of errors, and progress in general enlightenment. That would be a crime against human nature.	22
Nothing can possibly be conceived in the world, or even out of it, which can be called good without qualification, except a *good will*.	373
I am never to act otherwise than so *that I could also will that my maxim should become a universal law*.	376

Kierkegaard, Søren

Subjectivity is the truth.	288
. . . but when I let the proof go, the existence is there. But this act of letting go is surely also something; . . . it is a *leap*.	483
Existence emerges from the demonstration by a leap.	484

Index of Philosophers' Quotations

Kolak, Daniel
    He can't answer, he is dead.   596

Krishnamurti, J.
    The ambitious man has never found his true vocation; if he had, he would not be ambitious.   403

Kuang-Ming Wu
    ... beauty is less of a subject to be independently discussed than a pervasive attitude and atmosphere in which one moves and has one's being.   454

Lao Tzu
    The Tao that can be told of is not the eternal Tao;
    The name that can be named is not the eternal name.   103

Locke, John
    This, therefore, being my purpose—to inquire into the original, certainty, and extent of *human knowledge*, together with the grounds and degrees of *belief, opinion,* and *assent*.   206

    Let us then suppose the mind to be, as we say, white paper, void of all characters, without any ideas:—How comes it to be furnished?   210

    To this I answer, in one word, from EXPERIENCE. In that all our knowledge is founded; and from that it ultimately derives itself.   210

Mao Tse-Tung
    If you want to know a certain thing or a certain class of things directly, you must personally participate in the practical struggle to change reality, to change that thing or class of things, for only thus can you come into contact with them as phenomena; only through personal participation in the practical struggle to change reality can you uncover the essence of that thing or class of things and comprehend them.   244

    There can be no knowledge apart from practice.   245

May, Rollo
    Freedom is man's capacity to take a hand in his own development. It is our capacity to mold ourselves.   579

Meno
    ... you seem to me both in your appearance and in your power over others to be very like the flat torpedo fish, who torpifies those who come near him and touch him, as you have now torpified me, I think. [spoken about Socrates]   148

Index of Philosophers' Quotations

Mill, John Stuart
    The creed which accepts as the foundation of morals "utility" or the "greatest happiness principle" holds that actions are right in proportion as they tend to promote happiness; wrong as they tend to produce the reverse of happiness.   380

    It is better to be a human being dissatisfied than a pig satisfied; better to be Socrates dissatisfied than a fool satisfied.   382

Nagami, Isamu
    We cannot escape the "taken-for-grantedness" of our world.   318

    We are living in a constant transformative process within the horizon of encounters between different people. If we are open and responsive to other people in dialogue, then Mystery can lead humans to learn to trust and find a way of reconciling the differences of culture and existence.   318

Nietzsche, Friedrich
    Nothing is beautiful, except man alone: all aesthetics rests upon this naïvete, which is its *first* truth.   427

    The continuous development of art is bound up with the *Apollinian* and *Dionysian* duality.   431

    He who has a *why* to live for can bear with almost any *how*.   574

Onyewuenyi, Innocent
    Philosophizing is a universal experience. Every culture has its own worldview.   78

Paley, William
    ... the inference, we think, is inevitable, that the watch must have had a maker.   468

Parmenides
    You cannot know or say that which is Not.   112
    Thought and Being are one and the same.   113

Pascal, Blaise
    ... you must wager.   475
    The heart has its reasons of which reason knows nothing.   479
    It is the heart which perceives God and not the reason.   479

Plato
    ... all learning is but recollection.   149
    [Who then are the true philosophers?] Those who are lovers of the vision of truth.   161

Index of Philosophers' Quotations

Would you not admit that both the sections of this division have different degrees of truth, and that the copy is to the original as the sphere of opinion is to the sphere of knowledge?	172
And now, let me show in a figure how far our nature is enlightened or unenlightened.	175
. . . you will not misapprehend me if you interpret the journey upwards to be the ascent of the soul into the intellectual world . . .	178
. . . the idea of good appears last of all, and is seen only with an effort; and, when seen, is also inferred to be the universal author of all things beautiful and right, parent of light and of the lord of light in this visible world, and the immediate source of reason and truth in the intellectual; and that this is the power upon which he who would act rationally either in public or private life must have his eye fixed.	176
Whereas, our argument shows that the power and capacity of learning exists in the soul already.	179
And if . . . man's life is ever worth the living, it is when he has attained this vision of the very soul of beauty.	426
The soul resembles the divine, and the body the mortal . . .	616

Pythagoras
Number is the ruling principle that maintains the eternal stability, of things in the universe. — 119

Radhakrishnan, Sarvepalli
All acts produce their effects which are recorded both in the organism and the environment. — 526

Every single thought, word and deed enters into the living chain of causes which makes us what we are. — 526

Freedom is not caprice, nor is Karma necessity — 528

Rilke, Rainer Maria
Go into yourself. — 416

What is necessary, after all, is only this: solitude, vast inner solitude. To walk inside yourself and meet no one for hours—that is what you must be able to attain. — 416

Russell, Bertrand
The value of philosophy is, in fact, to be sought largely in its very uncertainty. — 88

Thus, while diminishing our feeling of certainty as to what things are, it greatly increases our knowledge as to what they may be; it removes the somewhat arrogant dogmatism of those who have never travelled into the region of liberating doubt, and it keeps alive our sense of wonder by showing familiar things in an unfamiliar aspect. — 88

Index of Philosophers' Quotations

Thus a belief is true when there is a corresponding fact, and is false when there is no corresponding fact. — 261

Three passions, simple but overwhelmingly strong, have governed my life: the longing for love, the search for knowledge, and unbearable pity for the suffering of mankind. — 682

Sandrisser, Barbara

The secret of infinity, then, can be said to be the moment in time when we perceive an elegant truth. — 451

Sartre, Jean Paul

... to be is to *choose oneself*... — 538

... the existence of the *Dasein* [person] precedes and commands its essence... — 540

... freedom is identical with my existence... — 541

... man being condemned to be free carries the weight of the whole world on his shoulders... — 544

... I am without excuse;... I carry the weight of the world by myself alone without anything or any person being able to lighten it. — 546

... I am condemned to be wholly responsible for myself. — 547

Scripture of the Pure Land

This world Sukhavati, Ananda, which is the world system of the Lord Amitabha, is rich and prosperous, comfortable, fertile, delightful and crowded with many Gods and men. — 622

This world-system is called the "Happy Land" (Sukhavati). — 624

Shankara

The Atman is its own witness, since it is conscious of itself. The Atman is no other than Brahman. — 140

Simic, Charles

Whoever reads philosophy reads himself as much as he reads the philosopher. I am in a dialogue with certain decisive events in my life as much as I am with the ideas on the page. — 4

And it all comes together: poetry, philosophy, history. I see—in the sense of being able to picture and feel the human weight of another's solitude. — 9

Skinner, B. F.

The simple fact is that man is able, and now as never before, to lift himself by his own bootstraps. — 565

Index of Philosophers' Quotations

Socrates
    For if you kill me you will not easily find a successor to me, who,   39
    if I may use such a ludicrous figure of speech, am a sort of gadfly,
    given to the State by God; and the State is a great and noble steed who
    is tardy in his motions owing to his very size, and requires to be stirred
    into life.

    . . . the unexamined life is not worth living.   45

    . . . know of a certainty, that no evil can happen to a good man, either in   48
    life or after death.

    . . . I perplex others, not because I am clear, but because I am utterly   148
    perplexed myself.

    . . . all learning is but recollection.   149

T'ao Ch'ien
    Give yourself to the waves of the Great Change   642
    Neither happy nor yet afraid.
    And when it is time to go, then simply go
    Without any unnecessary fuss.

Taylor, Richard
    A fatalist . . . is someone who believes that whatever happens is and   512
    always was unavoidable.

Thales
    Water is the basis for all things.   108

    Gods are in all things.   108

I Thessalonians 4
    For the Lord himself shall descend from heaven with a shout, with   629
    the voice of the archangel, and with the trumpet of God: and the dead
    in Christ shall rise first: Then we which are alive *and* remain shall be
    caught up together with them in the clouds, to meet the Lord in the
    air: and so shall we ever be with the Lord.

Thoreau, Henry David
    The mass of men lead lives of quiet desperation.   50

    I went to the woods because I wished to live deliberately, to front   53
    only the essential facts of life, and see if I could not learn what it had
    to teach, and not, when I came to die, discover that I had not lived.

Tolstoy, Leo
    The activity of art is based on the fact that a man, receiving through   435
    his sense of hearing or sight another man's expression of feeling, is
    capable of experiencing the emotion which moved the man who
    expressed it.

My situation was a terrible one. I knew that I should not find anything on the path of rational knowledge but the negation of life, and there, in faith, nothing but the negation of reason, which was still more impossible than the negation of life.	649
Faith is the power of life. If a man lives he believes in something.	651
"Maybe I did not live as I ought to have done," it suddenly occurred to him. "But how could that be, when I did everything properly?"	658
It occurred to him that his scarcely perceptible attempts to struggle against what was considered good by the most highly placed people, those scarcely noticeable impulses which he had immediately suppressed, might have been the real thing, and all the rest false.	661

Voltaire

The state of this good man caused me real pain; no one was either more reasonable or more honest than he. I perceived that the greater the lights of his understanding and the sensibility of his heart, the more unhappy he was.	326
. . . it appears that to prefer reason to felicity is to be very mad.	327

Waley, Arthur

Hui Tzu said to Chuang Tzu, "Your teachings are of no practical use." Chuang Tzu said, "Only those who already know the value of the useless can be talked to about the useful."	12

Whitehead, Alfred North

The importance of knowledge lies in its use, in our active mastery of it—that is to say, it lies in wisdom.	11
It should be the chief aim of a university professor to exhibit himself in his own true character—that is, as an ignorant man thinking, actively utilising this small share of knowledge.	11

Xunzi

The nature of man is evil; his goodness is the result of his activity.	351

Yahya ibn ʿAdi

Character is a state of the soul by which man performs his acts without either forethought or choice.	349

Zeno

Achilles, thus, can never catch the tortoise.	114